TUN

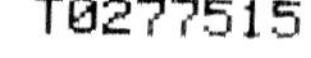

OSCAR SCAFIDI

www.bradtguides.com

Bradt Guides Ltd, UK
The Globe Pequot Press Inc, USA

Bradt GUIDES
TRAVEL TAKEN SERIOUSLY

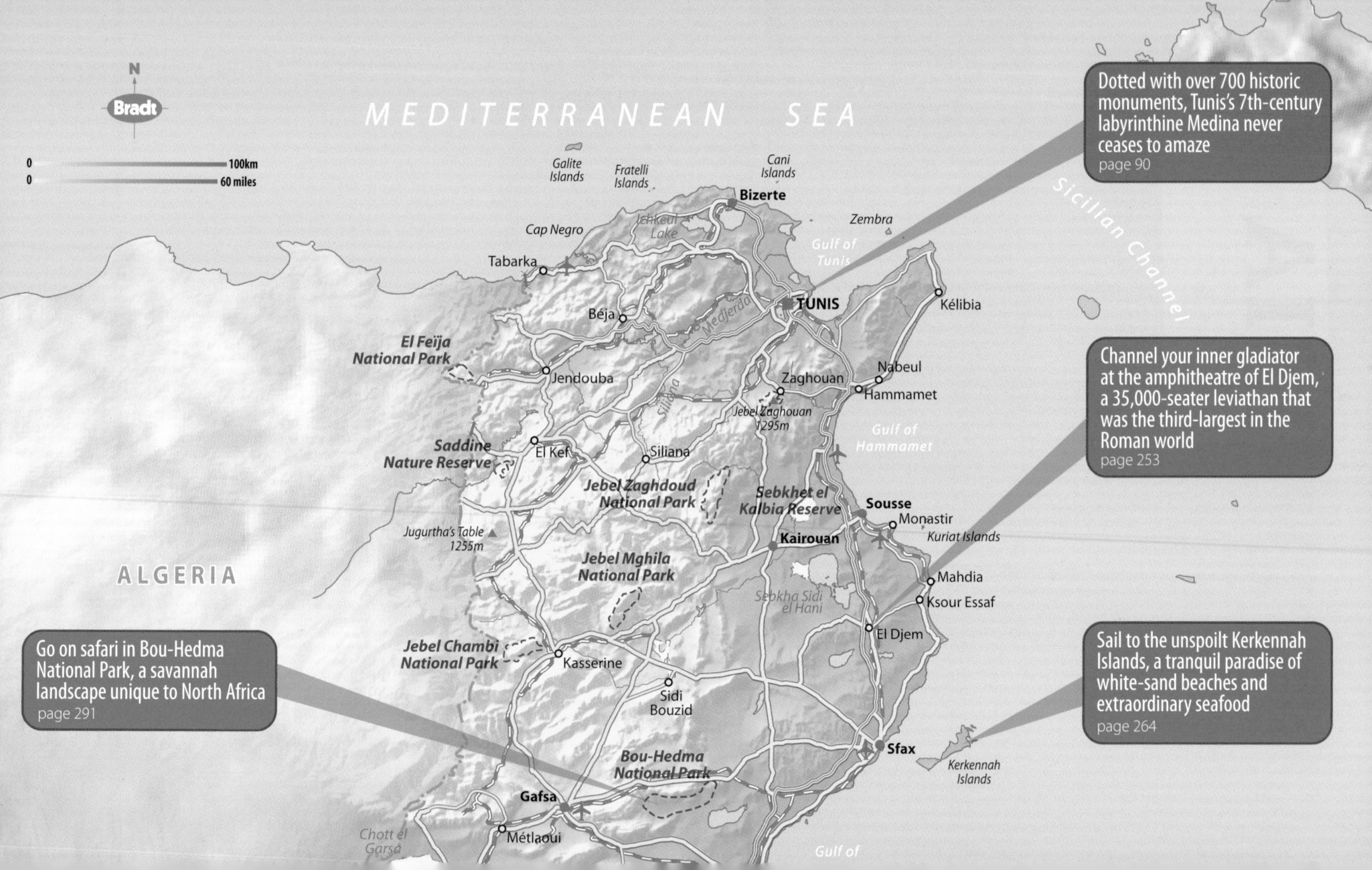
N
Bradt
0 100km
0 60 miles
MEDITERRANEAN SEA
Dotted with over 700 historic monuments, Tunis's 7th-century labyrinthine Medina never ceases to amaze
page 90
Sicilian Channel
Channel your inner gladiator at the amphitheatre of El Djem, a 35,000-seater leviathan that was the third-largest in the Roman world
page 253
Sail to the unspoilt Kerkennah Islands, a tranquil paradise of white-sand beaches and extraordinary seafood
page 264
Go on safari in Bou-Hedma National Park, a savannah landscape unique to North Africa
page 291
Galite Islands
Fratelli Islands
Cani Islands
Bizerte
Zembra
Cap Negro
Ichkeul Lake
Gulf of Tunis
Tabarka
TUNIS
Kélibia
Béja
Medjerda
El Feïja National Park
Jendouba
Zaghouan
Nabeul
Hammamet
Siliana
Jebel Zaghouan 1295m
Gulf of Hammamet
Saddine Nature Reserve
El Kef
Siliana
Jebel Zaghdoud National Park
Sebkhet el Kalbia Reserve
Sousse
Monastir
Kuriat Islands
Jugurtha's Table 1255m
Kairouan
ALGERIA
Jebel Mghila National Park
Mahdia
Sebkha Sidi el Hani
Ksour Essaf
El Djem
Jebel Chambi National Park
Kasserine
Sidi Bouzid
Bou-Hedma National Park
Sfax
Kerkennah Islands
Gafsa
Chott el Garsa
Métlaoui
Gulf of

Head to Djerba for some of the country's finest beaches, world-class kitesurfing and the oldest synagogue in Africa
page 312
Embrace your inner Star Wars nerd at the barren Chott el Djerid salt flats, home of the Lars Homestead
page 354
Watch a mountain sunset from a traditional troglodyte cave dwelling in Chenini
page 333
Explore the rolling Saharan sand dunes of the Grand Erg Oriental by camel
page 364
Hazoua
Chott el Djerid
Kebili
Douz
Gabès
Houmt Souk
Djerba
Zarzis
Medenine
Chenini
Tataouine
Ra's Ajdir
GRAND ERG ORIENTAL
Jebil National Park
Sidi Toui National Park
Bir Zar
Borj el Khadra
ALGERIA
LIBYA
KEY
Capital
Major town
Other town
Village
Airport
Mountain peak
Border crossing
Motorway
Main road
Other road

TUNISIA
DON'T MISS...

COASTLINE

With over 1,000km of Mediterranean coastline, you are never far from the sea in Tunisia; pictured here, the rocky, forested cliffs of the RafRaf Peninsula PAGE 191
(OS)

STAR WARS FILM SETS

Southern Tunisia is home to a dozen Star Wars filming locations, the most famous being the Lars Homestead on the barren Chott el Djerid salt flats PAGE 354
(Le/S)

LANDSCAPES

It's not all desert – the dense pine forests surrounding Aïn Draham are just one of the surprisingly diverse landscapes found in Tunisia's interior PAGE 160
(sP/A)

ARCHAEOLOGICAL TREASURES

Tunisia offers a wealth of archaeological sites, ranging from Neolithic dolmens and Punic burial sites to Roman cities and Byzantine forts; pictured here, the Capitol at Dougga PAGE 124
(LJ/S)

WORLD WAR II SITES

The scene of decisive fighting during the Allied invasion of North Africa during World War II, Tunisia's landscapes still bear the scars of war; pictured here, the North Africa American Cemetery near Tunis PAGE 103
(sd/S)

TUNISIA
IN COLOUR

above (MH/S) The UNESCO-listed Baths of Antoninus are the star attraction at Carthage PAGE 102

below left (A/S) Hilltop Sidi Bou Saïd is a jumble of whitewashed houses with blue-painted doors PAGE 104

below right (SS) The souks of Tunis Medina are a joy to explore PAGE 90

bottom right (AW/S) Shiny new Place du Gouvernement offers a fabulous view of the Tunis skyline PAGE 93

Home to one of Tunis's best beaches, La Marsa retains the air of an old-fashioned summer resort PAGE 106

above (IP/A)

Housing the world's largest collection of Roman mosaics, the Bardo is North Africa's most spectacular archaeological museum PAGE 108

right (BTWI/S)

The 43m-high minaret of Zitouna Mosque is one of the capital's most impressive sights PAGE 92

below (BTWI/S)

AUTHOR

Oscar Scafidi is an African political risk and security consultant, travel writer and international educator. Originally from the UK and Italy, he has travelled across 30 African countries and lived in Sudan, Angola, Madagascar and Tunisia, currently residing in Mozambique. In 2016, he wrote the first ever English-language guidebook to Equatorial Guinea, and in 2012 and 2018 he updated the *Bradt Guide to Angola*. In 2016, Oscar and his friend, Alfy Weston, set a new Guinness World Record as the first people to kayak, hike and wade 1,300km from source to sea along Angola's longest river, the Rio Kwanza. His book about the expedition, *Kayak The Kwanza*, was released in March 2019. In 2022, Oscar and a different friend, Ben Ziehm Stephen, did the same along Madagascar's longest river, the Mangoky; a book and documentary about this expedition will be released in 2023.

AUTHOR'S STORY

I moved to Tunisia in August 2019. My original plan had been to use it as a base from which to research and write a Bradt Guide to Guinea-Bissau in West Africa. However, I was shocked to discover upon my arrival that no major English-language publisher had released a guidebook to Tunisia since the beginning of the Arab Spring in early 2011. I quickly put together a proposal for a Bradt guidebook and set to work in early 2020.

My research lasted all of a month before the Covid-19 pandemic struck. I spent months under lockdown, and was faced with local travel restrictions and curfews well into 2022. A project that should have taken 14 months sprawled out across three years. Many tourism sites mothballed throughout the pandemic and, sadly, many operators went out of business altogether.

Despite these issues, I was able to get out and explore all 24 governorates of this incredible, surprising country. Not only that, but I was able to film all my adventures for publication on my YouTube channel, Scafidi Travels, as well as photographing numerous sites of interest for my Instagram account oscarscafidi and my Twitter accounts ScafidiTravels & BradtTunisia.

What you hold in your hands represents the culmination of the most difficult professional endeavour of my life, and one of which I am immensely proud. I am also very thankful to Bradt for their patience and continued support throughout the countless delays and stumbling blocks this project has faced. Whether you are a local or foreign visitor, I hope this guidebook gives you the tools and confidence required to explore some of the wonderful sights, landscapes and experiences that this country has to offer.

COVID-19

Please note that research for this guide was carried out during the Covid-19 pandemic. Because of the impact of the crisis on tourism, some businesses or services listed in the text may no longer operate. We will post any information we have about these on **w** bradtguides.com/updates. And we'd of course be grateful for any updates you can send us during your own travels, which we will add to that page for the benefit of future travellers.

First edition published June 2023
Bradt Guides Ltd
31a High Street, Chesham, Buckinghamshire, HP5 1BW, England
www.bradtguides.com
Print edition published in the USA by The Globe Pequot Press Inc,
PO Box 480, Guilford, Connecticut 06437-0480

Cover research: Pepi Bluck, Perfect Picture

ISBN: 9781784777517

British Library Cataloguing in Publication Data
A catalogue record for this book is available from the British Library

Photographs Alamy.com: Danita Delimont (DD/A), Hemis (H/A), Idealink Photography (IP/A), Nature Picture Library (NPL/A), skazarPhoto (sP/A); Bilel Haouet (BH); Oscar Scafidi (OS); Shuttestock.com: Agarianna76 (Ag/S), Alexeye30 (A/S), Leonid Andronov (LA/S), Adisa Ad/S), Authentic travel (At/S), Allen Brown (AB/A), BTWImages (BTWI/S), Gonzalo Buzonni (GB/S), Christophe Cappelli (CC/S), rolando criniti (rc/S), Podolnaya Elena (PE/S), Fotystory (F/S), Georgegid (G/S), Diego Giacalone (DG/S), Michal Hlavica (MH/S), jjmillan (j/S), Jess Kraft (JK/S), Lev Levin (LL/S), leshiy985 (Le/S), Lizavetta (L/S), Lukasz Janyst (LJ/S), Ivan Mateev (IM/S), piotreknik (p/S), skazarphoto (s/S), stu.dio (sd/S), WitR (W/S), Andreas Wolochow (AW/S); Superstock.com: (SS)

Cover Ksar Ouled Soltane (HA)
Back cover Top: Traditional boats along the Tunisian coast (p/S); Below left: El Djem Amphitheatre (G/S); Below right: Ceramics for sale (Ad/S)
Title page Clockwise from left: Chott el Djerid (LJ/S); Sidi Bou Saïd (L/S); Thuburbo Majus (LJ/S)

Maps David McCutcheon FBCart.S

Typeset by Ian Spick, Bradt Guides and Chris Reed, BBR Design
Production managed by Jellyfish Print Solutions; printed in India
Digital conversion by www.dataworks.co.in

Acknowledgements

This guidebook was not an individual effort. It could not have been completed without the guidance and support of countless people, ranging from Redditors to diplomats (and of course, the very patient team over at Bradt Guides!). One thing that struck me on my travels around the country was the enthusiasm of the Tunisian public for a new guidebook, and their willingness to give their time to help me share more of the country's vast sustainable tourism potential. I cannot possibly name everyone that contributed individually, but please be assured that, whether you are the Garde Nationale officers who helped me with directions or the random farmer I hitched a lift from in Mareth, I am very grateful!

My thanks go to the following people, without whom this book could not have been completed: Omar at Tunisia Expat Assistance, I will be forever grateful for your friendship and logistics assistance with everything from fixing The Beast to getting around Kasserine safely; Mohamed Ghadiri, your extensive local knowledge and generosity with your time had a huge positive impact on the Tataouine section of this guidebook; all the lads at Big Truck Garage, especially Amir and Safouène, my research involved over 30,000km of driving around Tunisia and your excellent mechanical work helped keep my 4x4 out of trouble, both on- and off-road; Davin Anderson at Galaxy Tours, Star Wars fans will certainly be able to pick up on your passion, dedication and knowledge when it comes to this unique aspect of Tunisia's film history; Trevor Sheehan, your contributions to the World War II battlefield sections of this guide were invaluable; the team at the British Embassy in Tunisia, especially Deputy Head of Mission, Matthew Forman, and Joanne Richardson, for the numerous opportunities to share this project with a wider audience; the team at the British-Tunisian Society, especially Amira Ben-Gacem, for their unwavering support in developing Tunisia's tourism potential; the team at the USAID-funded Visit Tunisia Project, especially Luis Zapater and Michele McKenzie, for all the opportunities to collaborate on this project with our shared goals; and Steve Hamilton, thanks for ensuring we did not step on a landmine while hunting for Rommel's bunker along the Mareth Line! Finally, many thanks to Alaeddine, Tenast _Imazighen and the editorial team at Amazigh World News, for the assistance with the language guides.

I would also like to thank the following people for their contributions, both big and small, to the final text: Rafram Chaddad, Rob Edmunds, Zakher Bouragaoui, Slim Ben Mamou, Jan Bakker, JoAnna Haugen, Roman Podkolzine, Houda Bakir, Chaim Motzen, Patrick Bourseaux, Tarek Chaabouni, Elizia Volkmann, Manal Berrached, Frerik Kampman, Karim Benabdallah, James Wasilenko, José Froehling, Monaem Bejaoui, Haithem Ounaies, Kevin Dyck, Philip Assis, Ross 'Rovers Return' Gill, Manolo, Salem Ettaieb, Pauline at SOUKRA, Emilie Hagedoorn, Erin Brown, Nick at Multiply Tunisia, Shabeena Sultana, Mohamed Temimi, Maryam Fgaier, Gabriella Incisa Di Camerana, Amir Ben-Gacem, Hajer Hmila, Monica, Sofia Terragni and Allison Bryan.

Thanks go out to my friends and family for being so supportive during this difficult project, and to Dr Taverna for sharing her wisdom on successful expedition leadership. Finally, I would like to thank Tunisia's Ministry of Tourism for providing me with the support and accreditation necessary to complete this project successfully.

HOW TO USE THIS GUIDE

AUTHORS' FAVOURITES Finding genuinely characterful accommodation or that unmissable off -the-beaten-track cafe can be difficult, so these authors' favourites will point you in the right direction. They are marked with a ✷.

PRICE CODES Throughout this guide we have used price codes to indicate the cost of those places to stay and eat listed in the guide. For a key to these price codes, see page 56 for accommodation and page 57 for restaurants.

MAPS

Keys and symbols Maps include alphabetical keys covering the locations of those places to stay, eat or drink that are featured in the book. Note that regional maps may not show all hotels and restaurants in the area: other establishments may be located in towns shown on the map.

Grids and grid references Several maps use gridlines to allow easy location of sites. Map grid references are listed in square brackets after the name of the place or site of interest, with page number first, eg: [57 C3].

A NOTE ON YOUTUBE VIDEO QR CODES

In Appendix 3, there is a list of QR codes linking to over 140 relevant videos on my YouTube channel (You Tube Scafidi Travels), designed to offer you a more immersive feel of what Tunisia has to offer. My aim while writing and filming has been to step off the beaten tourist track and shine a light on sustainable tourism opportunities in Tunisia's lesser-visited governorates (especially the 'interior'). Look out for the ⚑ symbol alongside sights and hotels to see if there is a corresponding video. Videos on the channel are also organised into playlists, divided both thematically (such as 'Tunisia's Star Wars Filming Sites' or 'Tunisia's Archaeological Sites') and by governorate. This means that new videos can continue to be added to these playlists even after publication. It also means that you can browse the channel simultaneously with the book to find inspiration for what to do while on your Tunisian holiday.

OTHER ICONS IN THIS GUIDE

- Star Wars filming location
- World War II site

Contents

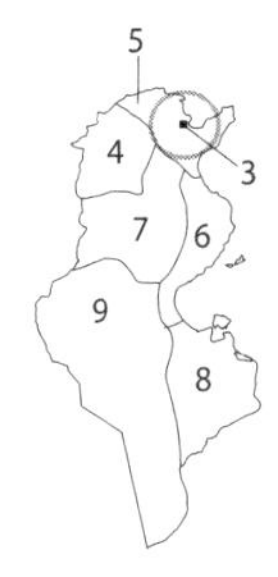

LIST OF MAPS

KEY TO SYMBOLS

International boundary
Airport
Car park
Bus station etc
Car hire/taxis
Ferry
Small ferry
Cycle hire
TGM station
Tourist information
Museum/art gallery
Theatre/cinema
Important/historic building
Fort
City gate
Post office
Internet
Toilets
Shopping mall
Hospital
Pharmacy
Bank
Embassy/consulate
Statue/monument
Historic (archaeological) site
Star Wars location
Hotel/guesthouse
Restaurant
Nightclub
Café
Bar
Mosque
Church
Synagogue
Tomb/mausoleum
Cemetery
Battlefield
Cave
Viewpoint
Vineyard
Kitesurfing
Scuba diving
Golf course
Lighthouse
Funfair/theme park
Beach
Border post
Summit (height in metres)
Stairs
Medina/souk
Pedestrian
Urban market
Urban park
Shopping centre/mall
National park/reserve
Marsh/wetlands

Introduction

If you type 'Tunisia' into Google, you will no doubt find images of package beach resorts along the Mediterranean coastline, or Orientalist images of camels on sand dunes. But this diverse country has much more to offer than that. A recurring comment on my YouTube channel – from both Tunisians and foreigners alike – is: 'I had no idea there were things like this in Tunisia.' So what is it that surprises people?

First, the breadth of landscapes on offer. People come expecting to find rolling sand dunes and pristine white-sand beaches, and in this respect they will not be disappointed. But there are also snow-capped, pine-forested mountains in the northwest near the Algerian border, where lies the ancient settlement of Aïn Draham, deliberately developed in the 1930s by the French to resemble a Swiss mountain retreat. In the centre of the country, Bou-Hedma National Park is home to relicts of pre-Saharan savannah, where you'll spot acacia trees, ostriches and herds of grazing oryx that would not look out of place in a safari park in southern Africa. Off the east coast, the low-lying Kerkennah Islands boast palm trees and shallow, Caribbean-like waters teeming with fish life, while the hills around Tataouine are reminiscent of the USA's Badlands, with the palaeontology to match. The further off the beaten track you head, the more Tunisia will surprise you.

The country is also home to eight UNESCO World Heritage Sites, one of the highest tallies of any African country. These encompass a broad array of cultural and natural sites, including vast networks of pre-Roman and Roman ruins, excellent examples of historic Islamic architecture and a unique waterfowl habitat with a lake that is both freshwater and saltwater. Archaeology enthusiasts will be amazed at the lack of crowds at sites like Dougga or El Djem, which compare very favourably with their counterparts on the Italian mainland. The country has an even longer Tentative List, made up of equally breath-taking sites that, with a little more investment and promotion, could one day join the UNESCO ranks. All are easy to reach, thanks to the country's excellent road network, and cheap to visit.

Tunisia's tourism industry had a difficult first decade after the 2011 revolution, marred by high-profile terrorist attacks and then, just as things were starting to recover, the Covid-19 pandemic. Despite these difficulties, a new model for tourism is emerging in the post-pandemic period. Tunisia is home to an exciting ecosystem of young entrepreneurs and digital developers who are helping to build a sustainable tourism sector. Whether you want a virtual-reality tour of the Punic Ports in Carthage, a fully catered kayaking and camping trip along the Bizerte coastline or a foodie tour of Tunis Medina, these experiences are now only a few clicks away on your smartphone. It is time to forget the bad old days of the Ben Ali dictatorship and the Club 18–30 model for Tunisian tourism. Those exploring Tunisia today will find a welcoming, outward-looking society that is keen to share its vibrant culture, rich history and beautiful landscapes with a wider audience, in an increasingly sustainable way.

Part One

GENERAL INFORMATION

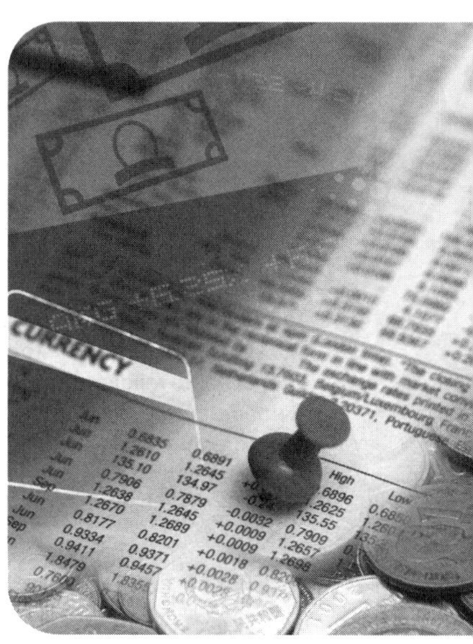

TUNISIA AT A GLANCE

Location On the north coast of Africa, south of the Mediterranean
Neighbouring countries Libya and Algeria
Size 163,610km^2
Climate Varies widely based on latitude and altitude. There are vast differences between the deserts of the Sahara in the south, the Khroumirie Mountains on the northwestern border with Algeria and the more Mediterranean climate of the northern coastal zones.
Status Republic
Population 12.26 million (2021 estimate)
Life expectancy 74.9 (male), 79.2 (female) (2021 estimate)
Capital Tunis
Economy The services sector dominates, with tourism playing a significant role
GDP US$46.8 billion (2021 estimate)
Language Modern Standard Arabic is the official language, as defined in the new 2022 constitution, though Tunisian Arabic (Tounsi) is the spoken language, and not intelligible to many other Arabic speakers outside North Africa. French is widely spoken, with English also growing in significance as it is now a compulsory subject in state schools. Amazigh languages are also spoken by some communities in Tunisia's south.
Religion Islam is the state religion. There are also small populations of Catholic Christians and Jews.
Currency Tunisian dinar (DT)
Exchange rate £1 = 3.81DT, US$1 = 3.09DT, €1 = 3.35DT (March 2023)
National airline and airport Tunisair; Tunis-Carthage International Airport (IATA code: TUN)
International telephone code +216
Time GMT+1
Electrical voltage 230V, 50Hz
Weights and measures Metric
Flag Red background centred by a white disk containing a five-pointed star surrounded by a red crescent
National sport Football
Public holidays Fixed holidays are 1 January, 20 March, 9 April, 1 May, 25 July, 13 August, 15 October and 17 December. There are also a number of moveable religious public holidays, based on the lunar calendar, such as Ramadan, Eïd es Seghir, Eïd el Kebir, Muharram and Mouled (see page 61 for more).

1

Background Information

GEOGRAPHY

Covering an area of 163,610km^2, the Republic of Tunisia measures 750km north–south and averages 150km west–east. The Gulf of Tunis is included in the northern coastal (330km) zone while to the south, forming part of the east-facing coast (1,270km), are the gulfs of Hammamet and Gabès, the latter lying between the islands of Djerba in the south and Kerkennah in the north. Tunisia is far from a mountainous land: less than 1% is over 1,000m and more than 65% is under 350m; the highest land is in the north and west, home to Jebel Chambi, its highest peak (1,544m). Nor is this a land of rivers: the only major river is the Oued Medjerda in the north.

Tunisia can be split into three main regions. **Northern Tunisia** has a rugged north-facing coastline – an extension of the mainly sandstone Algerian Atlas, which rises into a distinctive range known as the Northern Tell. In places these uplands, with altitudes exceeding 1,000m, are covered with cork oak and pine. The southern flanks of the Tell in the Béja region are lower, more open and more fertile. To the east are the rich alluvial plains around Bizerte. The Oued Medjerda cuts a wide fertile valley to the south of these ranges, flowing northeast to enter the Gulf of Tunis. This is Tunisia's major agricultural region, noted particularly for cereals. Further south, aligned southwest–northeast, is an extension of the higher, broader and mainly limestone Saharan Atlas, which forms the distinctive Dorsal/High Tell region with its harsher climate and sparser vegetation. The Dorsal range, including Tunisia's highest point, ends in the northeast at the Cap Bon Peninsula, Tunisia's wealthiest region, with a mild climate, fertile soil and a dense population.

Central Tunisia is a lower central plateau of semi-arid steppe. Its harsh environment renders the area bleak and barren, especially in the west. Only the lower, eastern steppe offers opportunities for stock raising and cereal cultivation. The **Sahel**, a low-lying and flat westward extension of the coastal plain, has seasonal salt lakes (*chotts*) and sandy soils with a widespread, dense cover of olive groves, which are supported by light rainfall, heavy dews and the tempering influence of the Mediterranean Sea.

Lying south of the steppes and stretching from the Algerian border to the sea, **southern Tunisia** is an area of low-lying *chotts* which are flooded during the winter and which dry to give extensive seasonal salt flats. Other depressions, where the water table is exposed or very close to the surface, produce the spectacular green oases of date palms. The depressions in the north and the level summits of the Jebel Dahar to the east give way to the sand dunes of the Great Eastern Erg and rocky wastes.

Tunisians tend to be deeply attached to their home regions and, even if they move away for work, return home frequently. The most populated area is the economically dominant eastern seaboard.

CLIMATE

Northern Tunisia has an archetypically Mediterranean climate, with hot dry summers and warm, wet, westerly winds in winter. As you move southwards, Saharan influence increases and the landscape becomes progressively more arid. Rainfall is irregular across the country, with annual averages ranging from 1,000mm in northern regions to just 200–400mm on the central plateau and less than 200mm in the south. Humidity is generally low nationwide, especially away from the coast and towards the south. However, in July and August, high temperatures and humidity combined can prove a trying combination in the coastal areas.

The prevailing wind is from the west, though in summer northeast winds also occur. A fierce, hot sirocco-type wind from the Sahara, the *shihili*, takes temperatures into the mid 40°C range in the summer and relative humidity to 10%, and has serious effects on human and plant life. Temperatures are influenced by proximity to the coast, but are generally warmer in the south; summers can be hot by day and over warm at night. Gabès, on the southern coast, averages around 29°C in August with 33.1°C in Tozeur (on a similar longitude but inland). It can get unbearably hot (45°C) by day and surprisingly cool (10°C) by night inland in southern Tunisia. In August 2021, a heatwave set new temperature records across the country, including a sweltering 49°C in Tunis!

NATURAL HISTORY AND CONSERVATION

Tunisia has a diverse landscape and a wide variety of natural habitats. The Mediterranean coastline is varied, with rugged inaccessible cliffs and smooth sandy bays. Coastal wetlands include deltas, salt marshes and estuaries, while inland lakes and reservoirs provide fresh water. The *maquis* and *garrigue* (dense scrub) contrast with agricultural areas across the north and centre of the country, while mountain ranges such as the Atlas provide their own climate, delaying flowering and shortening seasons. Even the southern desert areas provide contrasts with a mixture of sands (*erg*), gravels (*reg*) and rock (*hammada*) set with the occasional oasis.

Many habitats are under threat, either from pollution, urbanisation, desertification or the use of pesticides and chemicals for farming. Conservation issues, championed by home-grown NGOs, are beginning to attract public interest and there are currently 17 national parks and 27 nature reserves dotted around the country. Note, however, that just because somewhere is marked as a park or reserve on a map, this does not guarantee tourist infrastructure (or even a signpost for the entrance).

In both the Mediterranean and desert regions, wildlife faces the problem of adapting to drought and the accompanying heat. Periods without rain can vary from four months on the shores of the Mediterranean to several years in some parts of the Sahara. Plants and animals have, therefore, evolved numerous coping methods: some plants have extensive root systems; others have hard, shiny leaves or an oily surface to reduce water loss through transpiration. Shrubs such as the thorny broom have small, sparse leaves, relying on stems and thorns to attract sunlight and produce food. Animals like the critically endangered Addax antelope (*Addax nasomaculatus*) obtain all their moisture requirements from vegetation and rarely need to drink. Where rain is a rare occurrence, plants and animals have developed a short life cycle combined with years of dormancy. When rain does arrive, the desert can burst into life: plants seed, flower and disperse within a few weeks or even days.

FLORA Most of northern Tunisia lies in the Mediterranean region, and only a few thousand years ago was covered by evergreen forest. Humans have intervened extensively since then and there is a variety of plant life for the visitor to discover – many of the larger species having been imported from elsewhere in the world. The spring flowers which cover the fields, hillsides and ancient ruins of the north are a particular attraction for people from areas where farming relies more heavily on pesticides. That great and colourful climber, the **bougainvillea**, smothering walls with its sprays of purple, red, yellow and white 'paper flowers', will inevitably make an appearance, as will **hibiscus**, an import from China particularly popular for hedges.

Jasmine is another common species. Two pinkish-white flowering varieties are popular, *Jasminum officinale* and *Jasminum grandiflorum*, which – as its name indicates – has big flowers and larger, more rounded leaves. Both are used to make the *machmoum*, a jasmine bouquet that is an indispensable fashion accessory for a Tunisian summer evening, worn jauntily behind the ear or in a corsage. Making a machmoun involves carefully inserting jasmine buds into fine stems of alfa grass, bound together with a cotton thread. An orange or fig leaf provides a cradle for the unopened buds, which are held together with another thread which, once removed, allows the flowers to open during the evening.

Palm trees are popular on urban avenues, where both the ordinary date palm and elegant *Washingtonia*, which grows to great heights, are seen. Also common are **plane trees**, which provide leafy shade in summer but let in the light through winter, and purple-flowering **jacaranda** with delicate foliage and great sprays of pale mauve flowers.

In the interior, the **prickly pear cactus** and the **agave** are used to hedge in olive and almond groves. Both are naturalised imports from the Americas. With its wide, flat and thorny 'leaves', the prickly pear forms great barriers which dissuade foraging goats and sheep. You may see new plantations where chunks of the plant have been pushed into the earth to take root. The pear-shaped fruit, an attractive yellow-orange colour, is collected by small children with long canes. Ripe at summer's end, it is known as *sultan el ghilla*, the 'sultan of fruit', and is both delicious and constipating.

Evergreen forest is found in the Khroumirie Mountains south of Tabarka. **Holm oak** and **cork oak** are the characteristic trees, and there is a dense undergrowth of various thorn trees and juniper, where wild boar are found. Further south, in the Dorsal range, the climate is drier and forests are mainly composed of **Aleppo pines**. This tree thrives on dry hillsides, regenerating after fire. It has long needles, which give the landscape great splashes of bright green in spring. The La Kessera region south of Makthar has particularly fine pine forests.

FAUNA

Mammals Mammals have a difficult existence throughout Tunisia, owing to human disturbance and habitat fragmentation. Consequently, many (such as Tunisia's foxes and some deer) have become nocturnal and their presence may only be indicated by droppings and tracks. Nevertheless, some mammals common in northern Europe can be seen in Tunisia's Mediterranean environments, including fox, rabbit, hare, red deer, Barbary stag and at least two species of hedgehog. Otters and lesser weasels are less frequently seen. Despite widespread hunting (some of which is organised in Hammamet and Aïn Draham), wild boar is common wherever there is enough cover in deciduous woodlands. Striped hyenas and African golden wolves are still present in some remote areas of central and southern Tunisia, although populations are likely under a lot of pressure from farmers and few studies into population numbers have been completed. The attractive fennec fox, native to the deserts of North Africa and known for its oversized ears, is frequently illegally trapped and sold into the pet trade.

Once widespread, big cats are now rare – leopard, Atlas lion and serval cat are no longer present. The lynx, sand cat and caracal might hang on in some remote steppe and desert areas, but have not been observed in the wild for many years. There are at least three species of gazelle in North Africa: Dorcas gazelle prefer steppe; mountain gazelle inhabit vast forests, especially where juniper is present; and desert gazelle are found in the northern Sahara. The latter is under high poaching pressure, often hunted by vehicle, its only defence being its speed. A number of Tunisian and European NGOs are doing excellent work reintroducing large mammals that had previously gone extinct in the wild in Tunisia, such as the Scimitar-horned oryx in Bou-Hedma (page 291) and the Cuvier's gazelle in Jebel Serj (page 138).

Tunisia is also home to at least 18 species of bat, all of them insectivorous. One of the best places to see them is at the country's smallest nature reserve in Cap Bon (page 209). Recent ringing has shown that bats will migrate according to the season to exploit changing food sources. Other rodents include the large-eyed sand rat, the gerbil, the rare fat-tailed gerbil and the jerboa, native to desert areas but difficult to spot.

Reptiles and amphibians **Tortoises** are widespread in North Africa. The best distributed is the Greek tortoise, which can reach a maximum size of 20cm and is often found wandering in gardens in the Tunis suburbs. Small, freshwater pond terrapins are found in all Mediterranean habitats, with the Spanish pond turtle more common in Tunisia.

Tunisia's waters also contain three species of marine **turtle**: the leatherback, the loggerhead and the green, although the latter is rarely spotted. The loggerhead nests on the Kuriat islands (off Monastir) and along the coastline at Chebba (page 251).

Some 30 species of **lizard** are present, common species being the Algerian sand racer and the ocellated skink – not to be confused with the wall gecko, a species of plump, soft-skinned, nocturnal lizards with adhesive pads on their toes that are also common wall climbers. Sand racers are frequently seen on coastal dunes, while sand fish and sand swimmers take advantage of deep sand to avoid predators and find cooler temperatures in the desert. The ocellated skink is impressive in size, growing to 20cm, and can be spotted basking in urban environments.

There are over 30 **snake** species in Tunisia's Mediterranean areas alone, but only viperine and cobra types are venomous. The Egyptian cobra exists in southern Tunisia (its upper limit being Kairouan), as do vipers, which can be identified by their triangular heads, short plump bodies and zigzag markings. The horned viper lies just below the surface of sand, with its horns projecting, waiting for prey. The rare Javelin sand boa stays underground most of the time. Most snakes will instinctively avoid contact with human beings and will only strike if disturbed or threatened.

Marine life As a landlocked sea, the only area of the Mediterranean with any significant tidal range is in the extreme west. Without strong tides and currents bringing nutrients, it is somewhat impoverished in terms of marine life. Fish and shellfish, nevertheless, have figured prominently in the diet of coastal people for centuries, with sardines, anchovies, mullet, sole, squid and prawns being particularly popular. Tuna and swordfish are also widely caught. Overfishing, leading to the depletion of stocks, has become increasingly problematic, especially with incursions by well-equipped Italian fishing fleets into Tunisian waters.

Of the sea mammals, Tunisia had a small colony of Mediterranean monk seals on the outlying northern archipelago of La Galite, although sadly the last observation was back in 1986. Bottlenose and common dolphins are also seen off the coast, even while sailing in the Bay of Tunis (page 77). The Gulf of Gabès is also a popular spot for rays and sharks, and the fishermen off Sfax have been known to accidentally catch a great white in their drag nets, as these sharks come into the Gulf of Gabès to breed. The authorities are not so keen on publicising these catches, given their proximity to popular beach resorts on the east coast!

Butterflies and moths Owing to the lack of vegetation on which to lay eggs, **butterflies** are scarce in the steppe and desert areas. In contrast, the Mediterranean fringe is often rich in species, some quite exotic. The life cycle – mating, egg production, caterpillar, pupa, butterfly – can be swift, with some species having three cycles in one year. The most common in the early spring is the painted lady, which migrates northwards from North Africa, often reaching as far as the UK. Other familiar species include the Moroccan orange tip, festoon, Cleopatra, swallowtail, two-tailed pasha and clouded yellow.

Moths are also widely represented but are largely nocturnal and rarely seen. Day-flying moths include the red-spotted burnet and hummingbird hawk moth, which feeds on tube-shaped flowers. The largest moth of the area is the giant peacock moth, with a wingspan of up to 15cm.

Birds Neither the Mediterranean nor the desert areas are particularly rich in resident bird species, but both can become temporarily swollen by birds on passage, who fly northwards in spring and then return southwards in increased numbers after breeding in the autumn. Small birds, such as whitethroat, nightjar and wryneck, tend to migrate on a broad front, often crossing the desert and Mediterranean Sea without stopping. Larger birds, including eagles, storks and vultures, adopt a different strategy, as they depend on soaring rather than sustained flight. As they rely on thermals created over land, they opt for short sea crossings such as the route running via Tunisia, Malta and Sicily. Summer visitors include the swift and swallow, which spend the winter months south of the Equator, while winter visitors like wader and wildfowl breed in northern Europe and come south to escape the colder temperatures in winter.

The Mediterranean itself has a poor selection of seabirds, although gannets and shearwaters do crop up during the winter. Wetland areas are home to night and squacco heron, while spoonbill, ibis and both little and cattle egrets are also common. Greater flamingos breed in a number of locations when conditions are right, such as Sahline in Monastir Governorate, and are a regular feature of Tunis's coastal areas. Waders such as avocet and black-winged stilt are also typical wetland birds. Resident ducks, however, are confined to specialities such as the white-headed duck, marbled teal and ferruginous duck.

The desert and steppe have their own specialist resident birds, which have developed survival strategies. Raptors include the long-legged buzzard and the lanner falcon, which prefer mountain areas, while ground birds include the Houbara bustard and the cream-coloured courser. Dupont's lark is also reluctant to fly, except during its spectacular courtship display. The orange-beaked trumpeter finch is frequently seen at oases, while the insectivorous desert wheatear is typical of the erg and reg regions.

Elsewhere, the crested lark and Sardinian warbler are frequently seen on the roadside, while overhead wires often contain corn buntings, with their jangling song, and European and blue-cheeked bee-eaters. Numerous varieties of eagle include Bonelli's, booted, short-toed and golden. Of the vultures, the griffon is the most widely encountered. The black kite is more catholic in its choice of habitat, but the Montagu's harrier prefers open farmland.

HISTORY

Tunisia has been inhabited for tens of thousands of years, with Stone Age flint tools found near Tozeur dated at over 92,000 years old. A succession of Palaeolithic cultures, including the Mousterian and Aterian peoples, occupied the south and centre of the country. More recently, a distinct Capsian civilisation existed around Gafsa from 7000BC to 4500BC, which then transitioned to Amazigh after 3000BC, although this is poorly understood by anthropologists (page 337).

THE RISE OF CARTHAGE Like other parts of the Mediterranean, the North African coastal regions became an area for competition between the Greeks and the Phoenicians, who needed to trade in Africa's commodities. They vied for control of the coastal areas in Libya and eventually created an uneasy division of the region between themselves. The Greeks took over Egypt after the creation of the Ptolemaic Kingdom on the death of Alexander the Great in 323BC and incorporated Cyrenaica (eastern Libya) into the new kingdom. The Phoenicians, however, harried in their original Lebanese home of Tyre by the Assyrians and Persians, created a commercial empire based in Carthage, on the coast of northern Tunisia close to the modern capital of Tunis. Founded in 814BC, Carthage was to become the leading maritime power in the western Mediterranean.

Carthage had trading posts in the Balearic Islands, Sardinia and the western end of Sicily, and by the 6th century had also achieved footholds in Corsica, with Etruscan aid. In 480BC, the Carthaginians organised a great expedition to extend their influence in Sicily – but with disastrous results. At the Battle of Himera, the Carthaginian forces were crushed by the rulers of Agrigentum and Syracuse – a huge disaster for the ruling Magonid family. Henceforth, Carthage restricted its efforts to maintaining its valuable network of trading posts.

Trade flourished from the 5th to 3rd centuries BC, with Punic merchants providing the link between Africa and the Mediterranean. They traded in gold, ivory (highly prized for statues of the gods) and slaves from Africa, silver from Spain, copper from Sardinia and olive oil from Sicily, exchanging them against manufactured products from the eastern Mediterranean such as Greek pottery and textiles. Explorers were sent to prospect distant coasts: Himilcon reached Finistère in Brittany, while Hannon sailed along the western coast of Africa, possibly as far as the Gulf of Guinea. Commerce with people from foreign lands was based on barter – the Carthaginians first struck coins in the late 4th century.

ROMAN CONQUEST Conflict between Carthage and the expanding Roman state was inevitable. Both had interests in Sicily which, for Rome, was of vital strategic importance. Three conflicts between the two powers ensued, known as the Punic Wars (264–146BC). These wars are famous today for the incredible but ultimately unsuccessful exploits of the Carthaginian statesman and general, Hannibal, who marched an army containing elephants over the Alps to invade Italy in 218BC during the Second Punic War. Less than two years later, at the Battle of Cannae, he inflicted a defeat so crushing on the Romans that it is still taught in military academies to this day, with debate continuing to rage as to exactly how many tens of thousands of Roman soldiers his army slaughtered that day.

As a result of the Second Punic War, Carthage was expelled from Sicily in 201BC. Rome continued to view Carthage as a strategic threat, to the point that the city was eventually razed to the ground in 146BC, after three years of warfare. A century after the fall of Punic Carthage, North Africa was organised into five Roman provinces: Africa Vetus, Africa Nova, Numidia, Mauretania Caesariensis and Mauretania Tingitana, although some of these were, in practice, Roman vassal states ruled by friendly local leaders. In the coastal and agricultural regions, the sedentary Amazigh populations were largely Romanised and North Africa, in cultural terms, was now part of the Mediterranean world, its gods and goddesses assimilated to imported Roman deities. Emperor Augustus reconstituted the area as a unified Roman colony, and it became headquarters of the *proconsul* (a Roman provincial governor) and capital of the Roman province of Africa Proconsularis. The boundaries of this coastal Roman province stretched from western Libya all the way to northeastern Algeria.

Under Roman rule, Carthage quickly became one of the most important cities of the empire. In the 1st century AD, the twin provinces of Africa Proconsularis and Aegyptus (Roman Egypt) were a major source of wheat for Rome. Other farming activities developed, notably the cultivation of olives and vines, thanks to the establishment of irrigation programmes. Indigenous villages and Roman settlements (*colonia*) became prosperous towns. The most fortunate towns, such as Dougga, became fully fledged *municipia*, managed by Roman magistrates and embellished with fine temples, baths and market squares.

Nevertheless, administrators in Africa Proconsularis faced a problem of border security, with nomad tribes and local dynasties constantly threatening stability. The problem was solved by creating the *limes* (page 365), a border region along the desert edge in which former legionaries settled. This meant that although the area was permeable to trade, resistance to tribal incursion could be rapidly mobilised from the resident population.

In addition to the commercial and cultural interpenetration of North Africa and Rome, this cultural interaction was intensified by two other factors. First, the region had long been in contact with Greek culture and, indeed, through the Phoenicians, with Levantine culture. Secondly, as a result of the destruction of the Kingdom of Judea in AD70, large numbers of Jews migrated into North Africa and Judaism intermixed with Amazigh culture to a significant extent, as the surviving contemporary Jewish traditions in Tunisia show.

EARLY CHRISTIANITY, THE VANDALS AND BYZANTINE RECONQUEST The eastern part of North Africa, and in particular the provinces of Africa Vetus and Africa Nova (Byzacena in the late Roman period), was the site of major developments in the early history of the Christian church. Initially, the church was much persecuted by the Roman emperors, who tended to blame Christians for the various problems facing their vast empire. In 249, Carthage became the seat of an important bishopric: the forceful Cyprian, one of the great figures of the early church who led the African church at a time when Emperor Trajan had increased the level of persecution. He eventually died a martyr in 258, but the church continued to attract numerous new adepts and divided into warring factions supporting different theological positions. By 313, Emperor Constantine came to believe that the only hope for the survival of the empire was for Christianity to become the official religion – and so became the first emperor to embrace it, with his Edict of Milan proclaiming religious tolerance throughout the empire.

One of the great figures of the early church, St Augustine, rose to prominence in Africa. Son of a pagan father and a Christian mother, he misspent his youth at Carthage, where he studied and taught, before leaving for Milan. In his *Confessions*, he wrote of his life as a young man in the cosmopolitan capital of Africa, describing it as 'a hotbed of sinful desires'. He had a mistress and a thoroughly hedonistic time – but once converted to Christianity, he criticised the licentiousness of Carthage's student population.

The early 5th century proved the high point of the Christian presence in Africa. The Roman Empire was crumbling under external threats, and North Africa was invaded by a Teutonic tribe based in Spain: the Vandals, who by 429 had conquered as far as eastern Cyrenaica, and ten years later took Carthage. The aim of Vandal ruler Gaiseric was clear: a rich homeland for his people and independence from the Roman Empire. Their capture of Africa deprived Rome of corn supplies and created a dangerous precedent: the Vandal Kingdom was the first independent state within the borders of the empire. Feeble attempts at liberating the North African provinces were launched from Constantinople in the 440s, but to little avail.

The Vandals were able to use the captured Byzantine fleet for raids on Italy and Sicily, and in 455 King Gaiseric, benefiting from the chaos left behind in northern Italy and Gaul by Attila and his Huns, succeeded in looting Rome itself. The eastern emperors feared the Vandals would expand into the vital corn-growing lands of Egypt and in 468 launched an expeditionary force against them, but it was a total disaster. As a result, Gaiseric was able to take Sicily, Rome's oldest province. The end of the Roman Empire in western Europe was nigh (in 476 to be exact): central power collapsed, and Roman populations came to co-exist with Visigoth and other Germanic settler populations.

Despite their victory, the Vandals were not efficient managers in their new North African homeland. Although they have gone down in history as the most destructive people of the ancient Mediterranean world, certain contemporary writers left a rather different image. Byzantine historian Procopius wrote: 'They spend all their days in the baths and in consuming sumptuous repasts...they pass their time in spectacles, circus games and amusements.' All of which gave the Byzantines time to get organised.

In 533, the Byzantines reasserted their control under Emperor Justinian and his general, Belisarius. However, this was to prove unpopular, not least because of the onerous taxation system necessary to cover Byzantium's heavy military expenditure as it tried to confront the Sassanids in Asia as well as maintain its position in the Mediterranean. A little more than a century later, when Byzantine rule in Africa was threatened once more, this time by the expansion of Islam, local populations showed little enthusiasm for supporting Constantinople's continued hegemony in the region.

ISLAMIC CONQUEST In the first half of the 7th century, under the sway of a new revealed religion, Islam, Semitic tribes of the western Arabian desert made considerable conquests in the Fertile Crescent – a crescent-shaped stretch of land encompassing modern-day Syria, Lebanon, Iraq, Jordan, Israel and Palestine. The tribes' sudden unity under the charismatic leadership of the Prophet Muhammad came at a time when the two great powers of the region, the Sassanian Empire (centring on what is now Iran and Iraq), and the Byzantines in Syro-Palestine, were weak after years of fighting. The Muslim Arabs were not to stop at the Middle East, however, and continued their conquests westwards into Byzantine North Africa.

In 642, ten years after the death of the Prophet Muhammad, Arab armies, acting as the vanguard of Islam, conquered Egypt. To secure his conquest, Arab commander Amr Ibn al-As immediately decided to move westwards into Cyrenaica where the local Amazigh population submitted to the new invaders. However, no real attempt was made to complete the conquest until 665, largely because of internal problems within the new Islamic Empire. Then, after two feints southwestwards towards the Fezzan, an army under Okba ibn Nafi conquered what is now Tunisia and set up the first Islamic centre here at Kairouan in 670. Four years later, the Arabs in Kairouan were able to persuade Kusayla – an Amazigh ruler whose authority spread right across Tunisia and modern Algeria as far as the Oued Muluwiya in Morocco – to convert to Islam (although this is disputed in some sources). Shortly afterwards, in a famous expeditionary raid to scout the unvanquished areas to the west, Okba ibn Nafi swept across North Africa along the northern edge of the Sahara as far as the Atlantic coast in Morocco, into the land of the Sanhadja Amazigh who dominated the major western trans-Saharan trade routes.

EARLY ISLAMIC RULE Following the conquest of Morocco in 682, the Umayyad territories extended right across to the Atlantic, and their capital was Kairouan. In 704, the eastern Maghreb was constituted as a separate province by the Umayyads following the conquests of Okba ibn Nafi. It became the *wilaya* (province) of Ifrikiya, which covered what is now western Libya, Tunisia and eastern Algeria. The emirs of Ifrikiya thus represented the person of the caliph, the leading authority in Islam, across a vast expanse of territory. Unfortunately, authority was not easily imposed and, by levying extensive taxes on the Amazigh beyond what Islam allowed, the Arabs created much resentment. The inferior status given to Amazigh warriors in the Arab armies which conquered Spain in 711–18 was another factor in fuelling resentment.

Consequently, major Amazigh rebellions broke out. Another challenge arose in the form of the Kharijites, a sect that rejected the hereditary succession of the caliphate, insisting that an imam should be chosen by the community on the basis of learning and religiosity. These theological disagreements led to full-scale civil warfare within the Islamic community, known as the First Fitna (656–61). In 741, a Kharijite-Amazigh army defeated an Arab army in the major Battle of Bagdoura (near modern-day Fès), though the position was reversed the following year when the Umayyad governor of Egypt was victorious in two battles near Kairouan. Over the next 20 years, Ifrikiya receded to just the eastern Maghreb, ruled from Kairouan by a series of able governors with the co-operation of the Arab warrior caste.

THE AGHLABIDS The clan rule which typified North Africa in the late 8th century ended in 800 when Ibrahim ibn al-Aghlab was made ruler of Ifrikiya, based in Tunis. His brief was to manage Abbasid possessions in North Africa without relying on Baghdad for financial support. In practice, granting Ifrikiya to al-Aghlab was to lead to the establishment of a local dynasty. He began his reign by imposing peace on the turbulent Amazigh and Arab tribes of Tunisia. There was a great deal of opposition, not least from the vested interests of the Islamic jurists in Tunis and Kairouan and the Arab garrisons in the main towns, who had grown slack and oppressive. In a short time, regional groups were put down and order restored.

Al-Aghlab's successors kept up the peace and there began a period of artistic and architectural development. Under Abou Ibrahim Ahmed (856–63), the Great Mosque in Tunis was restored. The Aghlabids were particularly active in water storage and irrigation, most famously creating the large storage basins at Kairouan that are still there today (page 280). The royal city of Rakkada near Kairouan was constructed (page 281), built in the tradition of Islamic dynasties, as a strongly fortified palace complex complete with water pools, mosques and housing.

Local dynasties like the Aghlabids were able to dominate the Maghreb from a few small cities, and much of the population was converted to Islam. Nevertheless, Christian and Jewish communities survived; the former until the 11th century, the latter until the present day. Arabic took hold very slowly, with 10th-century writers in the Maghreb observing that the bulk of the population spoke no Arabic.

THE FATIMIDS AND ZIRIDS The beginning of the 10th century saw the arrival in the Maghreb of 'Abd Allāh (known as Ubayd Allah in some non-Shi'ite sources), arch-enemy of the Abbasid caliphs in Baghdad who saw him as leader of a dissident branch of Islam: the Shi'ite sect. Aghlabid rule in the eastern Maghreb collapsed, and in 909 'Abd Allāh made a triumphant entry into the royal capital of Rakkada. He immediately proclaimed himself the *mahdi* and founded the Fatimid Dynasty, after the Prophet's daughter, Fatima, from whom all Shi'ite religious leaders claim descent. In 915, 'Abd Allāh moved to the coast and began work on a new royal capital at Mahdia, indicating the start of a new political leadership.

Relations between the Shi'ite Fatimids in their Mahdia stronghold and the Sunni Muslim majority in cities such as Tunis and Kairouan were strained, not only for theological reasons. Taxation and money from the sale of government posts was spent on numerous campaigns against the Sunnite caliphate. Eventually, in 969, the Fatimids successfully conquered Egypt, leaving behind a tribal chief named Buluggin ibn Ziri as viceroy. He was to create a dynasty of viceroys, referred to as the Zirids, who came to view themselves as the rightful rulers of Ifrikiya. They took up residence in yet another palace-city, Sabra al Mansouriya, just outside Kairouan. Sunni influence was growing all the time, however, and in 1016 there were major anti-Shi'ite riots. Eventually, in 1044, Zirid ruler Al Mu'izz broke with the Fatimids – with disastrous results.

As punishment, the Fatimids directed two great tribal groups, the Beni Hilal and the Beni Sulayman, against the Maghreb; Fatimid caliph Al Mustansir actually 'granted' towns and provinces to these tribal groups. Over 50,000 tribal warriors headed northwest into Ifrikiya, pillaging the countryside. The Zirid state collapsed, and many local emirates – the Khorassanids in Tunis, for example – emerged to fill the power vacuum. Malikite Islam, centring on the Kairouan school of legal theology, emerged as a strong force, underpinned by the belief that the life of the Muslim community should be governed according to the principles of Islamic law. Such a concept was to be crucial to the success of the great Amazigh tribal-based dynasties which emerged in the late 11th and 12th centuries.

THE ALMORAVID, ALMOHADS AND HAFSIDS During the 11th century, the Saharan gold trade was dominated by a nomad Amazigh group based in the High Atlas mountains, known as the Almoravid, who founded a capital at Marrakech in 1062 but had territory stretching from Spain to Algeria. In the 12th century, they were overthrown by the Almohads, also composed of the Amazigh tribes of the High Atlas. United by their common religious cause, the Almohads expanded to conquer the whole of present-day Morocco, Algeria and Tunisia, along with Andalusia.

This political unity, lasting from 1160 to 1260, brought cultural and economic development, including the construction of distinctive mosques such as Bab Jazira in Tunis.

With the disintegration of the Almohad Dynasty, its empire split into three separate kingdoms – roughly corresponding to the independent states of today's central Maghreb (Tunisia, Algeria and Morocco). Ifrikiya (now down to just Tunisia) was ruled by the Hafsids, who saw themselves as the legitimate successors to the Almohads. The claim was widely accepted, even in the Middle East, because the strength of the Hafsids coincided with the Mongol invasions which destroyed Baghdad and the last vestiges of the Abbasid caliphate in 1250.

The Hafsids had to deal with an ever-greater Christian threat. This came in two forms: direct aggression, such as the eighth crusade led by the French King Louis IX, which besieged Tunis unsuccessfully in 1270, and commercial penetration. In the early part of the 13th century, the great Italian trading cities of Pisa, Genoa and Venice, together with Provence in France, obtained trading and residence rights in Ifrikiya. However, the most important dynamic trading state was Aragón which, after 1246, had an ambassador in Tunis, the Hafsid capital.

By 1318, Aragonese influence was on the wane and Hafsid fortunes revived. The Hafsid state was, nonetheless, a Mediterranean state rather than one with its attention directed towards Africa or the Middle East – in part, its finances increasingly depended on piracy, and by the end of the 15th century Hafsid influence had declined once again. Spain, the new threat to the Mediterranean Muslim world, annexed Tripoli in Libya and Béjaïa in modern Algeria in 1510, as the first move in a widening penetration into the Maghreb.

Hafsid rule left an important socio-religious legacy, however. In conjunction with native Tunisian scholars, the Hafsids oversaw the integration of Malikite law as the foundation for the social life of Tunis. Malikite law is one of the four major schools of Islamic law within Sunni Islam, developed by Arab theologian Malik ibn Anas from the 8th century onwards. This trend of Malikite integration became particularly marked under three strong rulers (Abu Al Abbas, Abu Faris and Abu 'Amr Othman) from the late 14th to the late 15th century. Malikite scholars in official posts legitimised Hafsid authority in the eyes of the city populations. The developing Malikite religious awareness also counterbalanced the influence of Sufi saints which, while it led to stability in rural areas, could also create centres of dissidence. The Hafsid rulers thus founded numerous *madrasas* (colleges) which, although at first intended for the study of Almohad doctrine, later came to give instruction in Malikite law. This strong interest in the law, and the idea that *'urf*, local customary law, could have legal validity as long as it did not contradict the shari'a, was to prove a distinctive and long-lasting trait in Tunisian Islam.

OTTOMAN RULE The Hafsid Dynasty came to an end in the mid 16th century. A succession of weak rulers proved no match for the ambitious Habsburgs and Ottomans, for whom the Mediterranean was to be the setting for an imperial struggle for most of the 16th century. Tunis was captured by a Turkish-Algerian pirate, Kherredine Barbarossa (Red Beard), in 1534, but the following year the city fell to Charles V of Spain, who was to reinstate the Habsburgs via puppet rulers. Then, in 1574, the Ottomans finally retook La Goulette and Tunis.

Once the Spaniards had been driven out of Tunisia and the remnants of the Hafsid Dynasty eliminated, the Ottoman commander, Sinan Pasha, was given a mandate to organise the administration of Tunis and its region. From the conquest until the 1620s, the Ottoman military controlled the government and army. A corps of often rowdy janissary troops was stationed in the city, while leadership frequently came from the renegades, dynamic Christians who converted to Islam so they could rise to positions of importance. The task of bringing nomad tribes to heel and collecting taxes from the countryside was entrusted to the bey, a post which was to rival the power of the military leader, the dey, by the late 17th century. The political subordination of Tunis and other cities to the Ottoman Empire took the form of payment of annual tribute to Istanbul and the important place given to the Hanefite school of Sunni Islam (the dominant form of Islam at court in Istanbul).

The early 1600s in Tunis were marked by two soldiers of fortune: Othman Dey and Youssef Dey. The turbulent Ottoman soldiery was disciplined and Djerba, run by Tripoli, was brought under Tunis's authority. Mosques, fortifications and barracks were constructed. Under Youssef Dey in particular, piracy became an important source of revenue, with Mediterranean shipping plundered for valuable goods and captives of all kinds (including European Christians) sold into slavery. The Tunisian fleet had around 20 ships.

Othman Dey gave favourable treatment to the large numbers of Andalusians fleeing Catholic persecution on the Iberian Peninsula, allowing them to settle in Tunisia. Unlike earlier Andalusian immigrants, many were poor. They were given tax exemption for three years, and land grants in the Oued Medjerda Valley and Cap Bon, where they established their own villages. They contributed greatly to the development of agriculture, as well as to the *chechia* (felt cap) industry. The export of this characteristic headgear, so useful for winding a turban on, was to become an important source of revenue for Tunis. A further source of dynamism came from European Jewish immigrants; the first wave, who were originally pushed out of Spain to settle in Livorno and Ancona, migrated to Tunis in 1675.

In the mid 17th century, a renegade of Corsican origin, Murad Bey, rose to prominence, building a power base by using local troops to collect taxes in rural areas. His son, Hammouda, ruled in 1631–66; both received the title of pasha from Istanbul in recognition for their capacity to maintain order in the countryside. Their ability to mobilise tax revenue enabled them to reduce the power of the deys and, from 1665, they controlled customs revenues from European trade as well. The situation deteriorated in the late 17th century, however, with often bloody struggles for influence between the deys and beys.

THE HUSSEINIDS The early 18th century saw complex rounds of political infighting. The last Muradite bey, Murad Ben Ali, was assassinated in 1702. In 1705, the exasperated notables of Tunis requested Hussein Ben Ali, a local member of the Ottoman military caste of Greek origins, take control. He had been deputy bey and understood the weakness of the situation. Through the creation of a local military force, part Tunis citizens, part tribal warriors, he was able to stabilise things, and eventually founded a hereditary dynasty, the Husseinids, around whom some semblance of a nation state began to take shape in the late 18th century.

After defeating an attempt by the Regency of Algiers to conquer Tunisia in 1705, Ben Ali acquired considerable prestige and was able to reorganise the administration and army to suit him. The Turkish military group or *jund* ceased to have any governmental authority, becoming an army corps providing ultimate protection for the bey. The dey became just another official post, and leading Tunisian families and Malikite religious leaders were brought into the spheres of government. The rural areas were administered by local notables or *qaids* – a sort of mix between governor and tax farmer.

Tunisia was now effectively independent and came to be referred to as the Iyalet Tunis, generally translated as the Regency of Tunis to denote the fact that allegiance was still owed to the Sultan-Caliph in Istanbul. The Ottoman Empire, covering vast territories with often poor communications, was a loosely organised affair and could easily tolerate such arrangements.

Despite a certain amount of strife, the Husseinids appeared as hereditary rulers of a nascent Tunisian state over the course of the 18th century. Djerba marked the southeastern limit of their domains, while the northwestern limit was up in the Khroumirie Mountains. This region of the eastern Maghreb had a number of advantages for an emerging dynasty: fertile agricultural lands and a series of well-fortified coastal towns, within a couple of days' horse ride of each other; the population was relatively homogeneous, comprising a settled Malekite Muslim population and nomad tribes; and minorities were small and unlikely to threaten the dynasty. Thus, the Husseinids were able to carve out a role for themselves as intermediaries between the rural and urban subsistence economies and the expanding trade of the Mediterranean. The only people who could have really opposed the Husseinids, the urban populations, benefited from the prosperity brought by this trade, especially in the latter half of the 18th century.

Under Ali II (1759–82) and more prominently his son, Hammouda Bey (1782–1814), the Regency of Tunis emerged as something of a Mediterranean power, albeit only a minor one. Hammouda Bey inherited a prosperous state, and fully intended things to stay that way. He encouraged subordinates to express opinions and came to rule with the assistance of a super-minister, the vizir and lord of the seal, Youssef Sahib al-Tabi'a. Hammouda also spent considerable time and energy in reinforcing his Turkish and Zouawa army corps.

However, his reign was the last during which the Regency of Tunis was treated as an equal of the European powers. No-one in Tunis seems to have foreseen the coming change. At the time, the Europeans were too embroiled in the Napoleonic Wars to pay much attention to North Africa. However, when France was finally defeated in 1815 (the year after Hammouda Bey died), they eventually turned their colonising gaze southwards, partly as a way of rebuilding smashed prestige.

RISING EUROPEAN INFLUENCE A series of factors weakened the Regency of Tunis's position in the Mediterranean and strengthened the European powers of the northern shore. In 1816, British naval officer Lord Exmouth and his fleet successfully put pressure on the beys of Algiers to end Christian slavery. A similar concession was exacted from Tunis. In 1827, when the Greek War of Independence was at its height, the Ottoman fleet, with Tunisian ships, was destroyed at the Battle of Navarino. In 1830, the French took Algiers; Constantine fell in 1837. To the southeast, the Ottomans reconquered Tripoli from the Karamanlis. Tunis now had strong and potentially dangerous neighbours.

Internally, things were little better. The Turkish army corps revolted twice, in 1811 and 1816; the second revolt left the Husseinids with reduced military support. A terrible plague swept the country in 1829. France was strengthening its presence and, in 1829, Hussein Bey signed a capitulation treaty giving the French consul the right to try cases involving French nationals in Tunisia. The government was increasingly forced to borrow from foreign banks, and manufactured goods were beginning to appear, sold far more cheaply than the handmade goods produced in Tunisia. In short, by the 1830s, the writing was on the wall.

In 1837, an energetic ruler, Ahmed I, came to the throne. Son of a Sardinian mother, he was determined to reform his country and sought to reduce European domination in trade. Institutional reforms aimed at increasing taxation on agricultural produce were introduced, monopolies were established, and soap and tobacco factories were built in Tunis. Unfortunately for Ahmed I, these reforms were mainly unsuccessful. Reacting to the increased military strength of the European nations, Ahmed Bey founded the modern Tunisian army based on the Ottoman model and, in 1840, the Bardo military academy opened. By the end of the first decade of Ahmed's reign, a 27,000-strong army had been created.

In 1859, Bey Muhammad III as-Sadiq came to power. One of his first moves, in April 1861, was to implement the first written constitution (*destour*) in the Arab world, a highly progressive document at the time. Despite his best efforts, however, the 1860s were difficult for Tunisia: the doubling of the poll tax in 1864 led to a rebellion, which was fiercely suppressed. There followed drought, a cholera epidemic in 1865 and typhus in 1868. Burdened with debts, the country was reduced to a state of misery, which reforming minister Kheireddine found difficult to overcome. The general depression was reflected in the situation of the country's armed forces, too: the Bardo military academy was disbanded, the supply factories closed, and the number of soldiers (and their salaries) reduced. Increasing debts and a default in August 1867 brought Tunisia's finances under the control of a nine-member international financial commission (Commission Financière Internationale), with representatives from Tunisia, France, the UK and Italy.

A FRENCH PROTECTORATE The events of the 1870s that eventually brought the Regency of Tunis under French 'protection' in 1881 involved corrupt super-ministers, scheming European consuls jockeying for influence, and unscrupulous banking houses. French national prestige took a serious hit after the disastrous Franco-Prussian War (1870–71), which resulted in the German annexation of the French territory of Alsace-Lorraine. Meanwhile, the French were concerned at growing British and Italian influence in Tunisia, neighbouring their valuable colony of Algeria, which since 1848 had been designated a fully fledged *département* of France. Ultimately, they managed to lay the diplomatic groundwork for control of this new Tunisian colony at the Congress of Berlin in 1878, subsequently invading Tunisia on 28 April 1881 under security pretences involving the Algerian border. They imposed the Treaty of Bardo on Muhammed as-Sadiq on 12 May, thereby setting up their new colony and seeing off any foreign threats. Italy's journalists called this episode the 'Schiaffo di Tunisi' (the 'Slap of Tunis').

In the immediate aftermath of the installation of the French Protectorate, Tunisian resistance was confined to tribal groups in the south. A European (predominantly Italian) settler colony began to grow, totalling around 100,000 people and controlling some 800,000ha of the country's best agricultural land. While as-Sadiq remained nominally in charge, he was stripped of any significant political power, with a French Resident-General exercising control on behalf of Paris. The first such colonial administrator with true influence was Pierre Paul Cambon, who ruled from early 1882 to late 1886.

While the loss of life had been relatively low during the initial French conquest, especially when compared with the 'pacification' of neighbouring Algeria, this all changed with the outbreak of World War I. A total of 62,461 Tunisians were called up for active military service on behalf of the French, many of them joining the 4th Tunisian Tirailleurs Regiment, which saw extensive action in French trenches at locations such as Verdun in 1916. The French Ministry of Armed Forces war deaths database (**w** memoiredeshommes.sga.defense.gouv.fr) lists 10,462 Tunisian servicemen who lost their lives during the war.

In 1920, the Constitutional Liberal Party, commonly referred to as the Destour (Constitution) Party, was founded by Tunisian nationalists following the basic idea that Tunisia should become a constitutional monarchy based on the 1861 *destour*: the fact that there was a French Protectorate was no reason for not applying a valid local code of law. In 1921 the party proposed a reform package, including the creation of a Franco-Tunisian assembly, but it made little progress in terms of affecting change. French commercial interests had become too important, and the poorer members of the French and Italian communities, minor officials and government employees had too much to lose.

A more radical current in the Destour Party started to take shape under a bright, charismatic French-trained lawyer: one Habib Bourguiba. The party split at a conference in 1934, with Habib Bourguiba becoming a senior member of the more radical wing, renamed the Neo-Destour, with its power base in the small towns of the Sahel and the growing urban proletariat of Tunis. The remaining Destour Party, with its leader Abdelaziz Thâalbi in exile, quickly lost relevance within the Tunisian nationalist political landscape.

Many of Neo-Destour's senior leaders and founders had risen thanks to the Franco-Arab schools and university education in France, where they had studied law and medicine. The old urban elite of Tunis, the *beldia*, were little represented. For the first time, a political movement was taking shape independently of both the beylical establishment and the leading city families.

The French authorities did their best to stamp out the Neo-Destour, but to no avail: history was on the nationalists' side. The early 1930s was a time of poor harvests and the Great Depression, which led to a huge fall in the price of olive oil, Tunisia's staple agricultural export. Much marginal land was abandoned; drought had terrible effects on nomads, who had lost their ancestral grazing rights as land was enclosed for modern agriculture. The mechanisation of farms also put many out of work. There was a drift towards the towns, which the colonial authorities tried to halt through severe police repression. This all served to increase support for Neo-Destour's nationalist message.

A package of reforms was put forward by the French in early 1938, but that was too late. In April, widespread general protests against colonial rule were met with further repression from French forces, and Neo-Destour's leaders were imprisoned.

When World War II arrived, Germany's *Blitzkrieg* conquest of France meant that the French lost considerable face, and the monarchy under Moncef Bey was not slow to exploit this weakness. Tunisia was under Axis occupation from November 1942 to May 1943 (page 18). Moncef Bey's official position was one of neutrality; however, he oversaw a government in early 1943 that included senior members of Neo-Destour such as Mahmoud El Materi. When the French returned with Allied support, ejecting the Axis troops in May 1943, the nationalist-leaning Moncef Bey was immediately exiled and replaced by Amine Bey, an elderly bespectacled monarch unlikely to provide a figurehead for the nationalist cause. But in the wake of the war and growing domestic agitation, it became clear that some concessions to nationalist sentiment would have to be made.

In 1950, France tried to enforce its position in Tunisia by requiring Amine Bey to accept the idea of 'co-sovereignty', whereby France would gain permanent rights to Tunisian territory – a deeply unpopular act that saw the nationalist following of Habib Bourguiba become a mass movement. As a result, Habib Bourguiba was able to negotiate autonomy for Tunisia in 1955 and, when Morocco was granted independence on 2 March 1956, Tunisia followed suit 18 days later. The situation

TUNISIA DURING WORLD WAR II

The war in North Africa began in neighbouring Libya, then an Italian colony. The Italians decided to invade British-held Egypt in the closing weeks of 1940, thinking that they could quickly destroy British lines of communication to the Middle East, India and the Far East, as well as winning access to the rich oil fields of Iran and the Arabian Peninsula. In reality, the war raged, with many changes of fortune for the combatants, until May 1943.

Although the Italian armies made some progress in Egypt in 1940, they were soon expelled. Faced with what appeared to be an Italian collapse, German troops and armour were moved into Tripolitania (northwest Libya) in February 1941. The Axis army was led by General Rommel with skill and audacity, supported by a strong air force. The balance in the desert war changed in mid 1942. The Allies gradually won superiority in the air and gained freedom of movement at sea. The Germans and Italians increasingly lacked adequate armour, reinforcements and strategy as Rommel's personal health also deteriorated. On the Allied side, General Montgomery took over leadership and began a build-up of the Eighth Army sufficient to overwhelm the well-trained and experienced Afrika Korps. Montgomery opened his attack at El Alamein in Egypt on 23 October 1942 and, after 11 days of hard fighting, the Axis army was beaten back and retreated by rapid stages to the west to make a last stand in Tunisia.

The German attempt to hold on in this last section of North Africa was made difficult by sea and airborne landings by Allied (including US) troops in Morocco and Algeria in November 1942. These two countries were liberated with comparative ease when French Vichy units, formerly collaborating with the Germans, were brought round to support the invasion. German and Italian reinforcements were rushed to Tunis, and a battle began to stop the advance of Allied units from the west as they fought their way in from Algeria and from the south through Libya. German attacks in the Battle of Kasserine in the hills north of Gafsa during January and February 1943 almost succeeded in halting the Allied progress, but Rommel's final assault against Montgomery's advancing Eighth Army arriving from Libya failed in early March. Axis troops retreated northwards behind the Mareth Line on the Gulf of Gabès, before being outflanked and being forced to withdraw by Montgomery's troops. A concluding series of battles in northern Tunisia saw the Allies push through the Medjerda Valley to Tunis and Bizerte in May 1943, effectively ending Axis resistance in North Africa.

In 2006, an excellent film was released that dealt with the experiences of North African troops fighting for the Free French Army (mainly Algerians). Titled *Indigènes* in French and the somewhat less controversial *Days of Glory* in English, it won multiple awards at the 2006 Cannes Film Festival and was nominated for an Academy Award for Best Foreign Language Film.

elsewhere in the French Empire was favourable to such a development. France had been defeated in Indochina and was facing simmering disturbances in Algeria, then considered as an integral part of France. The mid 1950s were clearly the wrong time to become bogged down in some sort of guerrilla warfare in a minor possession like Tunisia. In any case, France's rulers felt that their economic interests and influence could be protected by other means.

INDEPENDENT TUNISIA The kingdom of independent Tunisia was very different from the Beylicate of the 1861 *destour* – it was a firmly modern state of the French centralising tradition. A republic was proclaimed in 1957.

Unlike neighbouring Algeria (independent in 1962), Tunisia had the advantage of having a strong, single-minded leadership with a clear vision of the future. For Habib Bourguiba, Tunisia had fallen under French domination thanks to the decadence and corruption of the beys. Radical changes, including removing the country's traditional institutions if necessary, would be needed to bring about progress to the benefit of all. Bourguiba made use of both his immense personal prestige and the fact that the constitution was being revised to push forward major reforms.

First, in 1956, a Personal Status Code became law, replacing Tunisia's Malekite-influenced Islamic law and the Rabbinic courts in all matters of personal status. The new unified code abolished polygamy and introduced equality between the sexes regarding divorce. Minimum marriage ages were introduced, and the marriage of non-Muslim men to Muslim women was legalised.

Education was vastly expanded in the 1960s, which in hindsight was a key element behind Tunisia's later economic success. The principle of free and universal primary education was accepted and the Sadiki College model, with sciences taught in French and humanities in Arabic, was extended to the rest of the educational system. The University of Tunis was set up in 1960. Women's education was expanded rapidly, and by 1961 there were over 200,000 girls in school.

Land reform was another key area. The country had large amounts of property, notably agricultural land, held under the traditional Islamic mortmain system or *habous*. (The use and product of land could be left for future generations by the founder of the *habous*.) The system was abolished, and 175,000ha of land was sold off between 1956 and 1961. Choice property went to reward loyal party followers.

Nevertheless, Bourguiba faced considerable pressure to achieve results for poorer members of Tunisian society, and it was this pressure that may have led him to introduce a rather limited version of socialist development in the 1960s. The concept of socialism entered Bourguiba's speeches, and the Neo-Destour was renamed the Parti Socialiste Destourien (PSD) in 1964. Agricultural co-operatives were set up to manage 150,000ha of the former *habous* lands, and the farms confiscated from French and Italian farmers in 1964. The socialist experiment was managed by Ahmed Ben Salah, one-time secretary-general of the UGTT, the main labour union, who gradually became a sort of super-minister, and for a time seemed to be being groomed to succeed Bourguiba.

But Ben Salah ran up against well-established interests. When it began to look as though privately owned estates (some belonging to members of old Tunisois families close to the presidency) might be nationalised, opposition began to grow. Sahel landholders were unhappy about risking the loss of their profitable olive groves, while other families in trade had suffered from import restrictions. The final straw was a World Bank report in 1969 criticising Ben Salah's management of the economy. Bourguiba decided that the co-operative movement had had its day, and dismissed Ben Salah. He was charged with treason and condemned to ten years' imprisonment, though he escaped three years later and fled into exile.

The end of the socialist experiment coincided with a notable improvement in Tunisia's economic situation. Older Tunisians look back on the 1970s with nostalgia – a time of technocratic rule, when business became legitimate. While Bourguiba was suffering from ill health, the party's new prime minister, Hédi Nouira, presided over the liberalisation of the Tunisian economy in his cold, efficient way. Fortunes were made – not all of them honestly – and consumer goods returned to the market. Education continued to expand, and there were plenty of jobs in the civil service and new import substitution industries. Incentives were set up to bring investment into Tunisia, including the famous Loi 72, which offered a range of tax breaks to foreign investors willing to put money into export-oriented businesses. A new constitution was promulgated in 1976, reflecting Bourguiba's increasing inability to control all areas of policy, despite remaining President of Tunisia. The new constitution entrusted executive authority to the cabinet headed by prime minister Hédi Nouira, although the President retained the ultimate veto on policy.

Nouira and his cabinet governed effectively and, in the public's mind, came to replace Bourguiba, who spent increasing periods of time abroad for medical treatment. This situation was not to last, however, as Nouira was forced to retire from public life in 1980 after a heart attack. His successor, former Arabic teacher, Mohammad Mzali, proved to be a demagogue and was nicknamed 'Bozo le clown' on account of his haircut. The government gained a reputation for corruption and nepotism (the premier's wife, Fathia Mzali, became Tunisia's first Minister for Women). Left-wing groups, which during the 1970s had been under considerable repression, were replaced by a growing radical Islamic movement as the main source of opposition to the regime.

The crisis was at its most acute by August 1986, when a carefully worked-out, World Bank-sponsored structural adjustment plan was adopted. The aim was twofold: the reduction of macroeconomic imbalances and the creation of a stable basis for growth. The plan put forward several fast-working remedies and long-term strategies to help the Tunisian economy on its way to achieving faster growth.

Shortly after the reforms had been launched, Habib Bourguiba, increasingly out of touch with the mood in the country, demanded the retrial of a number of Islamic revivalist dissidents, in an attempt to ensure their conviction (and potentially the death penalty). It was clear that the president had lost his grip. On 7 November 1987, President Bourguiba was controversially declared medically unfit to govern, owing to being senile, and the prime minister at the time, one Zine el Abidine Ben Ali, took over as president until elections could be organised. Bourguiba was quickly whisked away to his hometown of Monastir for medical treatment.

TUNISIA UNDER BEN ALI The early Ben Ali years, broadly speaking 1987 to 1994, were devoted to ensuring stability, implementing the structural adjustment programme and making major institutional reforms, notably in education and investment legislation. The challenge from the revivalist Islamic movement was removed, and several major political reforms implemented. Life presidency was abolished, parties with a regional or religious basis were outlawed and political exiles were allowed to return. National reconciliation was the order of the day to ensure favourable ground for '*et taghyir*' or 'le Changement', as the shift in social, economic and political life is referred to in Tunisian newspeak.

By the mid 1990s Tunisia had come through the period of structural investment successfully. There was no longer any risk of violent internal political upheaval and the process of building an investment-oriented economy was well under way, based on closer links with Europe. A more business-friendly environment and improved legislation was attracting investors, and compared with its North African neighbours, Tunisia was easily the most stable in the region.

Unfortunately, Ben Ali had strong authoritarian tendencies. He ran unopposed in the 1989 and 1994 presidential elections and, although he faced two other presidential candidates in 1999, still managed to secure 99.45% of the vote. The question of Ben Ali's successor gained prominence in the early 2000s, with technocrat Mohammad Jegham, a former minister, and Hédi Jilani, a leading industrialist close to the government, often mentioned. With Ben Ali due to step down in 2004 after 15 years in power, he organised a referendum in 2002 to abolish the constitutional three-term limit for incumbent presidents and raise the maximum age limit of a sitting president from 70 to 75. Unsurprisingly, it passed with 99.52% of the vote, with a barely believable 95.59% turnout. This paved the way for him to secure a fourth term in 2003, winning 94.48% of the vote.

The last years of the Ben Ali presidency were characterised by increasing political repression, widespread state-sanctioned corruption and a worsening human rights record. A Human Rights Watch report written in 2008 noted:

> The government uses the threat of terrorism and religious extremism as a pretext to crack down on peaceful dissent. There are continuous and credible reports of torture and ill-treatment being used to obtain statements from suspects in custody…Human rights defenders and dissidents face surveillance, arbitrary travel bans, dismissal from work, interruptions in phone service, and physical assaults…None of the domestic print and broadcast media offers critical coverage of government policies, apart from a few low-circulation magazines.

That same year, a secret cable from the US Embassy in Tunis to Washington (released by WikiLeaks) detailed the various corrupt schemes in which the president's extended family was allegedly involved, including his nephew stealing the yacht of a well-connected French businessman, his late brother being convicted *in absentia* for drugs trafficking and his wife expropriating state land to build an international school – which she then sold to international investors for massive profits. These injustices and the nepotism behind them were key drivers of discontent among the public. The economic disparity between those connected to Ben Ali's regime and the rest of society became even more visible thanks to the global financial crisis of 2008, which meant stagnant growth and higher unemployment. These issues were magnified by the long-term neglect of Tunisia's interior regions in favour of the coastal ones.

THE TUNISIAN REVOLUTION AND THE ARAB SPRING In October 2009, Ben Ali was elected to his fifth term with 89.62% of the vote. A year later, on 17 December 2010, a fruit and vegetable street trader named Mohamed Bouazizi ran into some difficulties with corrupt police and municipal officials in his hometown of Sidi Bouzid. As had happened to him numerous times in the past, Bouazizi's wares were confiscated by the police because he did not have a street-vending permit, and he did not have the money to pay the bribe required to get them back. To make matters worse, his family members allege that he was beaten and humiliated by police and municipal officials during the confiscation. Having been refused an audience at the governor's office where he had gone to complain, at 11.30 Bouazizi stood on the road outside, doused himself in fuel, and set himself on fire. All this happened less than an hour after the initial confrontation. He died in hospital on 4 January 2011.

There had been many hints at discontent with Ben Ali's rule before this incident, such as the violently repressed 2008 miners' strikes in Gafsa over poor pay and dangerous working conditions. However, it was Bouazizi's tragic act of desperation that catalysed nationwide protests. Angry crowds gathered on the streets of Sidi Bouzid within hours of Bouazizi's self-immolation. A few weeks later and protests had spread to the capital, further fuelled by the WikiLeaks revelations of the Ben

Ali family's corruption-fuelled lavish lifestyles. Despite violent police crackdowns, Ben Ali could not suppress the protests as he had done in 2008 in Gafsa. In public addresses, he suggested a few concessions aimed at placating the angry crowds, but by 14 January 2011 things had become so bad that Ben Ali declared a state of emergency and fled to Saudi Arabia, where he would die in exile eight years later.

Events in Tunisia presaged a series of anti-government uprisings across the Middle East and North Africa (MENA) region. On 11 February, less than a month after Ben Ali's departure, Egyptian President Hosni Mubarak resigned following mass protests against his 30-year rule. Colonel Gaddafi was overthrown in Libya that August, then killed in October, while Yemeni President Ali Abdullah Saleh was replaced the following February. Having toppled a 23-year dictatorship and ignited the Arab Spring, the people of Tunisia wanted a very different political arrangement for their country.

TUNISIA'S NASCENT DEMOCRACY An interim government filled the void left by Ben Ali's departure, setting the framework for subsequent reforms, such as recognising new political parties. Ennahda, a so-called Islamist party, narrowly won the first post-revolution national election in October 2011, forming a coalition with two secular, centre-left parties: the Democratic Forum for Labour and Liberties (Ettakatol) and the Congress for the Republic. However, it should be noted that the policy divisions between 'secular' and 'Islamist' parties in Tunisia are not as clear cut as Western observers might expect. A constitutional drafting process began, with a progressive new constitution passed with parliament's near-unanimous support on 26 January 2014.

The security and economic situation in the country started to deteriorate in 2013, with the assassination of two left-leaning politicians (Mohamed Brahmi and Chokri Belaid) and the growth of influence of terrorist groups such as al-Qaeda and ISIS. Proportional to its population, Tunisia became one of the largest sources of foreign fighters in the conflicts in Iraq, Libya and Syria, and this soon had an impact in the country itself. On 18 March 2015, two gunmen marched into the Bardo National Museum in Tunis, killing 20 foreign tourists and two Tunisians before being shot by security forces. The gunmen, both Tunisians, were suspected of receiving weapons training from al-Qaeda in Libya. A few months later, on 26 June, a lone gunman opened fire on a beach in Port El Kantaoui in Sousse Governorate, killing 38 foreign tourists (including 30 Brits) before being killed by security forces; ISIS claimed responsibility for the attack.

The attacks decimated Tunisia's tourism industry, which at the time provided employment for more Tunisians than any other sector except agriculture. UK package-holiday providers abandoned the country until July 2017, and high-spending West European arrivals were substituted for Algerian and Russian visitors, who spend proportionally far less per capita while on holiday. Tourism numbers were only just recovering when the Covid-19 pandemic hit in early 2020, lurching the sector into another crisis.

TUNISIA TODAY In October 2019, Tunisians went to the polls and elected former constitutional law professor Kais Saied as their president. He was known to many Tunisians as a commentator on the post-revolution 2014 constitution, appearing on news programmes as a talking head to explain the constitutional writing process to the public (although he was ultimately quite critical of the final draft). While debates over religious identity provoked heated discussion during Tunisia's 2012–14 constitutional drafting process, the final draft – voted on with 97% of support by so-called Islamist and secularist parties alike – appeared to resolve those disputes in a framework hailed by constitutional scholars as democratic and even progressive.

Growing frustrated with parliamentary deadlock and the stalling of his economic and anti-corruption reform plans, in July 2021 President Saied invoked emergency powers to dismiss Prime Minister Hichem Mechichi, suspend the elected parliament and assume executive control of the government. At the time the move was widely popular, but since then dissenting voices have grown amid concerns of a slide back to authoritarianism. Eventually President Saied released a road map back to parliamentary democracy, with a referendum on the new constitution he had a significant role in authoring held in July 2022. It passed with 94.6% of voters in favour, although turnout was low and many opponents chose to boycott the vote rather than vote no.

GOVERNMENT AND POLITICS

Tunisia was the only country from the Arab Spring to successfully transition to peaceful, democratic rule. Under the 2014 constitution, it was a unitary, hybrid parliamentary-presidential democratic republic with the president as head of state, an appointed prime minister and 217 MPs in the unicameral Assembly of the Representatives of the People. The president was directly elected for a five-year term, while MPs were elected via proportional representation (with highly progressive quotas to ensure gender, youth and disabled representation) for five-year terms. Such a system has produced the highest proportion of female MPs in the Arab world.

Under the new 2022 constitution, however, the size of parliament will be reduced to 161 seats and called the Assembly of Representatives of the People. Parliament will also become bicameral, with a new chamber called the Council of Regions and Districts elected by members of local councils across Tunisia's 24 governorates. The first elections for this body were held on 17 December 2022. Political parties (as opposed to individuals) were prohibited from competing. The new constitution marks a return to a centralised, powerful presidential system. Supporters believe it will help break the deadlock of ten years of weak coalitions in parliament, while critics argue it is regressive and removes many checks and balances present in the 2014 constitution.

The country is divided into 24 governorates of widely varying sizes and populations. At 38,889km^2, Tataouine is the largest in terms of area but also one of the most sparsely populated; by contrast, the smallest governorate, Tunis, is the most densely populated. Governorates are administered by a governor, who is usually appointed by the prime minister. However, since President Saied's suspension of parliament, governors have been directly appointed by the president.

ECONOMY

Tunisia has seen steady economic development and reconstruction since the damage created during the country's brief period as a setting for Allied–Axis conflicts during World War II (page 18). Since independence, development strategy has, broadly speaking, been constant, despite a flirtation with a form of state socialism in the 1960s.

Compared with other North African countries, Tunisia has a more diversified economy. Its modest oil resources have been an advantage in providing funding for non-oil development but have never been sufficient to encourage reliance on petroleum. There is, nevertheless, a certain vulnerability to external economic pressures including the vagaries of international trade, foreign aid flows, variations in tourist numbers and access to the EU for Tunisia's trade and labour. A youthful and fairly fast-growing population creates an added need for economic growth.

AGRICULTURE Until recently, farming was the basis of the economy, although its dominance has reduced significantly since the early 2000s. In 2019 it employed 13.8% of the labour force and produced about 9.64% by value of all national output. Chief crops are cereals, citrus, olives, dates and grapes. Olive oil is an important export; during the 2019–20 season, Tunisia exported more than 330,000 tonnes of it, generating 4.25% of the total 2020 budget. However, ask any Tunisian and they will tell you that they suffer from heavy competition from the Spanish and Italians, whom they accuse of rebottling Tunisian olive oil and selling it as European. Around 100,000 Tunisians make their living from fishing or aquaculture, producing a total catch of over 150,000 tonnes per annum.

ENERGY Tunisia's oil industry by no means compares with that of Libya or Algeria. As of late 2021 it was producing around 40,000 barrels per day, compared with Libya which produced 1.1 million barrels. Production comes from the El Borma field in the south, the Sbeïtla field in the centre and the Itayem fields close to Sfax, all of which feed to a refinery and export complex at Skhira. The Ashtart field offshore in the Gulf of Gabès (near the Kerkennah islands) is also productive and more recent discoveries have been made both offshore and in the Cap Bon areas.

Gas has also become important to the Tunisian economy. Miskar gas field in the Gulf of Gabès was brought on stream by British Gas in 1995, enabling Tunisia to export more oil and to use less Algerian gas. Elf Aquitaine has made considerable investments in developing the Ashtart field. However, growing frustrations with the country's political instability and unstable regulatory environment mean that international oil and gas companies such as Royal Dutch Shell, Eni and OMV have been keen to sell their Tunisian assets in recent years.

PHOSPHATES Phosphates were discovered in southwestern Tunisia in 1885. A mining concession was granted in 1896, and the Gafsa Phosphates and Railway Company set up in 1897. Today, it remains a large producer and exporter of phosphates with annual production running at 3.8 million tonnes in 2021, putting Tunisia in the top ten global exporters. Plans were announced in early 2022 to try to double production levels to 8 million tonnes by 2024, to take advantage of high global phosphate prices. Phosphate production in Tunisia has always been a politically sensitive affair, with workers down in Gafsa staging regular protests because of low pay and alleged unsafe working conditions. The waste from extraction is both toxic and mildly radioactive, with local communities and NGOs complaining about the environmental impacts of the industry in the areas where it operates (which tend to be the more deprived areas).

MANUFACTURING Tunisia has made remarkable steps in effective industrialisation, most of it small scale and private sector. Manufacturing accounted for 18% of the workforce in 2019 and 14.8% of national production. Industry is located principally along the northern part of the east coast, with the main products being cement, flour, steel, cables, textiles and beverages. Tunisia has one of the most expensive secondhand vehicle markets in the world, thanks to a very frustrating quota system that caps the number of vehicle imports annually, and imposes heavy taxes on those that do get brought in. As a result, there is a small but growing vehicle manufacturing industry, such as the iconic Wallyscar brand, which since 2006 has been producing small, relatively cheap vehicles that look a bit like a shrunken Jeep Wrangler.

The cement industry has undergone extensive privatisation, and there are numerous companies working exclusively for the export market. The textile industry is very significant, with 9.2 billion dinars' worth of exports in 2021. Piece-goods are made up in Tunisia for re-export back to manufacturers in western Europe. Levis, for example, subcontracts extensively in the Monastir region, exporting finished goods back to its main European headquarters in Belgium. However, as in many parts of the world, low-wage Tunisian textile workers have complained about conditions and insecure employment contracts. Five-year tax-break incentives offered in 2016 encouraged many manufacturers to set up shop in Tunisia; however, the Tunisian Forum for Economic and Social Rights estimated that only 50% of these clothing companies remained in business once their tax breaks expired, leaving many Tunisians in the sector suddenly unemployed.

TOURISM The tourist industry is a major employer and foreign exchange earner, but has been on a roller-coaster ride over the past decade. Compared with 7.83 million in 2010, Tunisia saw a year-on-year drop of over 2 million tourists because of the revolution the following year, and suffered a similar decline in the wake of the terrorist attacks in 2015. Things were looking positive again in 2019, with a record 9.43 million arrivals, but then the Covid-19 pandemic shot numbers back down to just above 2 million in 2020.

The industry is developing from its traditional east-coast strongholds (Hammamet and the Sahel) to the south, where Djerba is proving a popular destination. Desert tourism has been encouraged with considerable subsidies to spread the benefits of the industry wider, although there are still areas of the country blessed by considerable public investments in tourism (mainly the east coast) and others that receive very little funding (mainly the interior). Travelling around the country's package tourism hubs, such as in Sousse or Hammamet, the devastation wrought by the 2015 terrorist attacks is easy to see in the lines of abandoned waterfront hotels. The pandemic put the nail in the coffin for many more of these businesses that were reliant on short-term visitors from Europe.

However, many involved in the sector (this author included) view the pandemic as an opportunity to reset Tunisia's tourism industry to a more sustainable and equitable model. In February 2022, the United States Agency for International Development (USAID) announced a five-year, US$50 million project called Visit Tunisia, designed to help the vital tourism sector rebound through public–private sector partnerships and digital innovations that capitalise on the country's rich natural, cultural and historical heritage. The hope is that this project will generate up to 15,000 sustainable tourism-related jobs in communities that have not previously benefited from tourism, with a particular focus on the northwest subregion.

There is also great opportunity in growing the domestic tourism market. Many affluent Tunisians, locked out of their usual holiday destinations of France and Italy during the pandemic, were forced to holiday in their own country in 2020–21. As a desert camp operator in Djerba said to me in the summer of 2020: 'I never realised there were so many wealthy Tunisians!' Encouraging locals to explore their own incredible country will hopefully be at the forefront of any future initiatives by the Ministry of Tourism, and is a key aim of my YouTube Channel, Scafidi Travels.

TECH Tunisia has a young, well-educated workforce that is struggling to find jobs. More than a third of university graduates are unemployed. Following a series of language reform policies (1997–2007), English has been taught as a compulsory subject in Tunisian state primary and secondary schools. This means that many young Tunisians now speak English, French and Arabic, a huge advantage for those entrepreneurs who wish to move into the tech space. Tunisian start-ups abound, in spaces as diverse as robotics and AI, to ride hailing and expense reports management. One of the apps recommended in this guide, Historiar, a mobile application for cultural tours (page 102), was only founded in August 2019. The extremely low cost of living in Tunisia compared with western Europe should make Tunis a tech hub; however, innovators complain about the stifling influences of Tunisian bureaucracy, in particular that the financial regulatory environment does not allow cryptocurrencies or use of payment platforms such as PayPal to accept funds from international clients. The de facto ban on drone use (page 388) is also a considerable hindrance to some in the tech space.

PEOPLE

The Tunisian population is a true melting pot of influences. The contemporary population is the result of a long history, during which various settlers passed through. While the earliest populations of northwestern Africa were probably Hamitic, the ancestors of today's Amazigh, there have been numerous other inputs (including the Phoenicians and Romans and, in particular, Arabs, who first began

A BRIEF HISTORY OF TUNISIA'S JEWISH POPULATION

Rafram Chaddad (@rafram_x)

The history of Jews in Tunisia is complex and has many layers. The first Jews are documented in mosaics and history books within the historical kingdom of Carthage. They lived in a city called Shalombo ('peace inside' in Hebrew), today known as Salammbô, a district close to the historic Punic port in Tunis.

According to local legends, five families of high priests (Cohen Gadol) fled from Jerusalem after the destruction of the first temple in 587–586BC. They were not welcomed in Shalombo and settled instead on Djerba, making the island's living community the oldest continuously inhabited Jewish settlement in the world. They built El Ghriba Synagogue, the oldest documented synagogue in the world, which has been renovated multiple times since then. In the 7th century, further Jews arrived with the Arab tribes and settled mostly in Kairouan, founding one of the world's most important Jewish centres, together with Cairo. Today a holy Muslim city, Kairouan was home of the Geonim ('geniuses' in Hebrew), a group of rabbis who ruled the Jewish world writing *Halakha*, the collective body of Jewish canonical behaviour and rules.

The next big wave of Jewish immigration happened in the 15th century, with Sephardic Jews arriving from Andalusia following their deportation by King Ferdinand II and Queen Isabella I. They settled all over Tunisia and brought with them Andalusian styles of architecture and cuisine. They also went to Djerba, where they interacted with the old community of priests but formed a new Jewish community. They settled around 6km to the north, in Hara Kebira, in the southeastern section of the modern settlement of Houmt Souk. Today, this forms the largest Jewish community in Tunisia.

to arrive in the 7th century). The mid-11th-century Hilalian invasions strengthened the Arab component, arabising the Amazigh-speaking countryside and removing the Arab–Amazigh divide which has remained much more significant in Algeria and Morocco. Until the 1950s, there was a significant Jewish community (see below), based mainly in Tunis, Kairouan and Djerba. As of the late 18th century, a European population of mainly French, Italian, Sicilian and Maltese, with a few Greeks and even the odd migrant from the Baltic states, settled in the coastal towns, and was particularly numerous in the mid 20th century. Finally, there is a sub-Saharan African component to Tunisia's population, originally the result of the slave trade, which was finally abolished on Tunisian territory in 1846 by Bey Ahmed I.

European travellers writing about Tunisia in the mid 19th century liked to make sweeping generalisations about the local people they encountered, and distinguished between three main indigenous groups: the Turks, the Moors and the Arabs. (Notably absent was any mention of the Amazigh population, or Berbers as they used to be known.) The Turks were the Tunisian ruling and military elite, and Ottoman Turkish was their prestige language. Travellers wrote of the Moorish population of the cities, who were described as 'refined' and 'polite'. Seventeenth-century immigrants from Andalusia were a component of this. The third designation, Arab, seems to have been reserved for the less cosmopolitan members of Tunisia's population at the time (ie: the vast majority). This urban–rural divide was also highlighted by the Ottoman rulers, designating townspeople the *beldia* (meaning 'people from the *balad* or town'), whereas

Another wave of Jews came in the 17th century from the Tuscan city of Livorno, where they were persecuted by the local priest. They settled mostly in Tunis and were called the Grana Jews. They had a rich commercial network with the Mediterranean ports and founded the Suq el Grana, the Grana market in the old medina of Tunis, which is still present today. In Tunis they remained separate from the earlier Twensa Jewish community, with their own kosher and court systems and even their own chief rabbi. The two communities were only merged under one chief rabbi in 1899. Later, at the end of the 19th century, Tunis became a haven for Jews from Greece, Poland and other places wishing to escape persecution.

During the 20th century, Tunis's Jewish community made up almost a third of the city's population and reached a peak of more than 100,000 before the outbreak of World War II. Theatres, newspapers and publishing houses translated world literature and original texts into Judeo Tunisian, a Tunisian language written in the Hebrew alphabet. In the 1940s, during World War II, the Germans arrived in Tunisia, the only Arab country to suffer direct Nazi rule. Many Jews were sent to concentration camps in Europe, while others worked for the Germans, building the defence lines against the Allies. Victor Perez, the boxing world flyweight champion in 1931, died in Auschwitz.

After the war, Jews from the south left and moved to newly established Israel. Following the Six-Day War in 1967, tensions grew between Jews and Muslims in Tunis and the Jews emigrated, mainly to France, leaving a hole in the cultural life of Tunis. Today the country is home to around 1,500 Jews, mostly on Djerba, where there are still 11 active synagogues. The small community in Tunis is not as religious and has two active synagogues: one in Tunis and one in La Goulette.

sedentary country folk and the nomads were *el arab*. Mannerisms, speech and dress were highly different.

When the French protectorate of Tunisia was declared in 1881, the country's cities were already quite cosmopolitan, having sizeable Italian, Sicilian and Maltese populations. These swelled with an influx of civil servants from France. In the early 20th century, there were further arrivals fleeing the wars of Europe. After the Russian Revolution, a small White Russian community arrived at Bizerte aboard Admiral Wrengel's fleet, escaping the Bolsheviks. There were Greeks involved in sponge fishing. Later came Italians and Spaniards fleeing fascism in their homelands.

In numerical terms, the Italian community was initially the most significant, calculated at 80,000 in 1903. As the largest European group, they had to be handled carefully by the French administration, especially as Italy considered Tunisia as *terra perduta*, the colony which should have been. In the 1930s, to counteract the growing influence of fascism, French nationality was granted extensively to Italians resident in Tunisia. The Tunisian Jewish community also became increasingly gallicised during the 75 years of the French protectorate. Education spread rapidly, and the growing wealth of both Twensa and Grana Jews was reflected in a move from the medinas to new, well-planned neighbourhoods. Today, the cosmopolitan nature of urban colonial Tunisia is romanticised, recalled with nostalgia in films such as Férid Boughedir's *Un été à La Goulette*, a memorial to a Mediterranean mix of peoples.

Upon independence, many of the socio-ethnic divisions within Tunisian society faded, thanks to factors such as the abolition of the monarchy, the mass exodus of the country's Jewish population, the slower departure of European settlers and rapid urbanisation. The population has risen from 4 million in 1961 to just under 12 million at the time of writing. The growth rate has slowed dramatically, however, from 2.75% per annum in 1961 to around 1% today, the result of sustained family-planning programmes. In 1965, the World Bank recorded GDP per capita as US$218, compared with US$3,924 in 2021.

Just under 70% of the population is urban and the main cities have expanded enormously since the turn of the millennium. Affluence is growing, albeit very unevenly; education, health care and consumer goods are available in a way unthinkable a couple of generations ago but, unfortunately, employment far less so. This is especially true for the younger generation, who are leaving Tunisia at an alarming pace and heading for the likes of France, the USA, Italy and Germany. Many Tunisians have either lived and worked abroad or have a family member who is currently part of the 1.3 million strong diaspora of 'chez nous', as they are jokingly referred to by those still resident in Tunisia.

LANGUAGE

According to the 2022 constitution, Modern Standard Arabic is the only official language in Tunisia, though in practice French is very widely used. For day-to-day conversation, Tunisian Arabic (Tounsi) is used – this is very different from Modern Standard Arabic and not intelligible to the majority of Arabic speakers from other countries. Tounsi features a lot of loan words, especially from French, Spanish, Italian and Turkish, and you will find many Tounsi speakers code-switch between Tounsi and French mid-sentence. To complicate matters further, Tunisians also use Franco-Arabic while talking online, which is a mixture of Arabic, French and English using the Latin script. An excellent Tounsi–English online dictionary, with 17,000 entries including example sentences and audio pronunciations, can be found at **w** derja.ninja.

Street signs and official notices are generally in Modern Standard Arabic, which is also used in the context of legal and official government activities, plus political speeches. Classical Arabic, which is the standardised literary form of Arabic used in the Koran, is reserved for religious activities, although President Saied tends to give his political speeches in this ultra-formal style. French is the language of business, science and higher education.

Many younger Tunisians also speak English, given that it is now a compulsory subject in the state educational system. You may find that if you start a conversation with a question in French, they respond in English. Italian – in part thanks to the availability of Italian television and radio (page 376) – is often understood in the north and the deep south, which sees its fair share of Italian overlanders. Judeo-Tunisian Arabic is spoken by some members of the older generations of Tunisia's remaining Jewish population, as well as by a larger group of Tunisian Jews in the diaspora (now mainly in Israel).

Today the Tunisian language situation is complex – and changing. Behind the multilingual screen lies a range of personal attitudes and aspirations. How you get on in life is linked to your language ability, and few Tunisians have any doubt that mastery of at least one European language is essential for access to science and technology. French is certainly very useful for achieving a decent university degree and almost indispensable for a well-paid job. At the same time, there is a lot of anti-French language sentiment; among the generation which passed through the university system in the 1970s and early 1980s, there is an oft-expressed desire to 'Arabise'. Among the younger generation, meanwhile, is a desire to switch from French to English, both because this is (to a certain extent) economically savvy, and as a protest against perceived French cultural imperialism in Tunisia, both before and after independence.

Arabisation has become bogged down in the process of creating terminology, and several competing national language academies, notably in Cairo and Damascus, are involved in trying to keep up with the flood of new words in the main world languages. The truth is that Arabic has lacked the effective language policy that updated Hebrew, for example, and transformed it into the language of the State of Israel in a generation. In any case, Tunisians are a pragmatic lot, and a Gaddafi-style Arabic-only stance is unlikely: it would interfere with the making of money far too much. For the moment, basic literacy in Modern Standard Arabic looks set to maintain its position in the education system, especially at primary level, alongside French for technical and commercial purposes and English for access to the wider business and educational worlds.

AMAZIGH *With thanks to Amazigh World News (w amazighworldnews.com)*
The Amazigh language is spoken in tiny rural communities in the Matmata region (Tamezret), near Tataouine (Douiret) and in some villages on Djerba. In Arabic, the blanket term 'Shilha' is used to refer to all Amazigh languages across the Maghreb; however, there are several closely related languages present in Tunisia, known by linguists as the East Zenati languages. These include Tamazight (spoken in Djerba), Chenini (spoken in Chenini), Matmata Berber (spoken in Matmata) and Douri (spoken in Douiret). Amazigh speakers are present throughout the country, but tend to be concentrated in the south. Although it is estimated that up to 1 million Tunisians have some working knowledge of the languages, few people speak Tunisia's Amazigh languages as their mother tongue; they are consequently classified by UNESCO as being in danger of extinction. See page 375 for a list of handy Amazigh phrases.

RELIGION AND DAILY LIFE

The overwhelming majority of Tunisians identify as Muslims, mainly Sunni, and Article 1 of the 2014 constitution identified Islam as the state religion, whereas the 2022 constitution notes that Tunisia belongs to the Islamic Ummah (worldwide community). Articles 27 and 28 of the 2022 constitution guarantee freedom of conscience and belief as well as religious freedoms, provided they do not compromise public security. Tunisia has small communities of Christians (mainly Catholic; in the low tens of thousands) and Jews (in the low thousands). As Islam is a religion similar to Christianity and Judaism in certain aspects of its philosophical content, Muslims recognise that these three religions have a common basis, and Jews and Christians are referred to as *ahl al-kitab*, 'people of the book' (both Moses and Jesus are prophets for Muslims). Nevertheless, there are considerable differences between the revealed religions in ritual, public observance of religious customs and the role of religion in daily life, and when travelling in Tunisia it is important to be aware of this. There are also considerable regional differences in observances and practices between the (generally) more cosmopolitan coastal regions and the (generally) more conservative interior and south.

Eating pork, gambling and drinking alcohol are not permitted under most interpretations of Islam, although none of these things are illegal in Tunisia. Alcohol is relatively easy to purchase in the 'caves' of large supermarkets, although these close during public holidays and for the whole of Ramadan, and are often either closed on Fridays or restricted to foreigners only. Bars and nightclubs across the country are awash with alcohol, including locally produced beers and spirits. Pork products, beyond cured pork in some supermarkets, are very hard to find (although, again, not illegal).

In the matter of dress, habits have changed hugely in only a few generations. The veil disappeared after independence and young women no longer automatically cover their heads as their grandmothers might have done. Even the 'headscarf and long dress', the modern version of Islamic dress, widespread in Egypt, for example, is rarely seen unless you are in a very conservative, rural community. Tunisian Islam, and indeed North African Islam as a whole, is a long way from more conservative forms practised elsewhere. While in traditional families the women's domain is most definitely the home, the overwhelming trend is for Tunisian women to have an education and career. Yet there remains much progress to be made in terms of gender equality: in 2022, the Global Gender Gap Report ranked Tunisia as 120th out of 146 countries surveyed.

EDUCATION

Since independence in 1956, successive Tunisian governments have placed an emphasis on the development of the educational sector, spending heavily by regional standards.

The basic education system in Tunisia consists of nine years of compulsory schooling: six in primary and three in lower-secondary. Students must pass exams to move from the primary to lower-secondary tier. They then have more exams (the *examen national de fin d'Études de l'enseignement de base*) at the end of their nine years of education, which result in a Diplôme de Fin d'Études de l'Enseignement. In the 2021 academic year (which runs from September to June), 62% of pupils passed their year nine exams. Once you have a Diplôme, you can access four years of upper-secondary education, which leads to another exam: the Tunisian Baccalaureate or Examen National du Baccalauréat, which you need to pass in order to get into university. Tunis el Manar, Sousse, Sfax and the University of Carthage are some of the more prestigious higher education institutions in the country, although many Tunisians choose to head abroad to study, especially in France, Canada and the USA.

Since the 1970s, classes have been taught in Modern Standard Arabic apart from some technical and science subjects, which are taught in French. English was introduced as a compulsory subject in both primary and lower-secondary between 1997 and 2007. School attendance is compulsory up until age 16 (the end of year nine) and free for all children.

The last major survey on literacy in Tunisia was carried out by UNESCO in 2014, which showed that the literacy rate was 79%, increasing to 96% for those aged 15–24. Female students have a lower drop-out rate than male students, and by the time students reach university the difference is stark: in 2019 only 22.6% of eligible males enrolled in tertiary education, compared with 41.7% of eligible females.

CULTURE

ARTS AND ARCHITECTURE Owing to its rich history and continuous habitation for at least the past 100,000 years, Tunisia has a wealth of diverse archaeological sites, architecture and craft forms. The **Romans** (often building on **Punic** foundations) left Tunisia with a wealth of wonderful sites – especially at Dougga, Chemtou and Sbeïtla – and the finest collection of Roman mosaics in the world, housed in the Bardo Museum. Elsewhere, there are dolmens (megalithic tombs) at Ellès and also Neolithic rock paintings in the caves of Ghomrassen in Tataouine Governorate.

Tunisia is also rich in **Islamic architecture**. Though mosques cannot generally be visited by non-Muslims there are some notable exceptions, including (occasionally)

THE ART OF THE MOSAIC

The oldest figurative mosaics in Tunisia date from the beginning of the 2nd century AD, composed by artists who came over from the Hellenistic regions of the eastern Mediterranean. These mosaics have a number of Hellenistic traits: they rival wall paintings in their subtle tones and detail; the themes – Nile landscapes, rural idylls, and the post-banquet 'unswept floor' motif – were popular in the East. Later, towards the end of the 2nd century AD, strong regional schools of mosaic work emerged. New themes became popular, generally inspired by daily life in Roman Africa: hunting, the sea, amphitheatre games and farm life. In the late 3rd century, technique become cruder and mosaics more abstract – some, executed for early Christian buildings, had a strong symbolic charge, only obvious to the initiated observer given that the Christian communities were initially persecuted. In the mid 4th century, Christian mosaic work emerged – a good example from this period is a fine portrait of a female saint (today in the Museum of Carthage; page 104) and more naïve work such as that from certain Tabarka Christian tombs.

It was generally thought that the art of the mosaic largely disappeared in the 6th century under the Vandals, though finds at Thuburbo Majus (page 218) and Moknine (page 245) contradict this view. After the Arab invasions of the 7th century, mosaic work disappeared from Africa entirely, although the Fatimid caliph of Mahdia called in mosaicists to decorate his palace in the 10th century.

the colonnade of the Zitouna Mosque in Tunis and the UNESCO-listed Great Mosque in Kairouan. On the coast at Monastir and Sousse, there are some well-preserved *ribats*, early medieval fortresses built to defend the Muslim communities of the Sahel. This Islamic architectural heritage was used as inspiration in the French colonial period, with the development of the **neo-Moorish style** seen in many public buildings, such as national railway stations, Dar Sebastian in Hammamet (page 203) and the municipal government building in Sfax, which houses the archaeological museum (page 261). In the late 1990s, new official buildings and hotels across Tunisia often incorporated features of traditional architecture in a throwback to this early-20th-century style.

Tunisia's northern coastal cities boast an interesting mix of architecture beyond the neo-Moorish style. In the 1930s, most official commissions for buildings tended to go to French architects, which meant that architects from Tunisia's large Italian community had to look to the private sector. The result was some very fine **Art Deco** and **modernist** apartment buildings in the Lafayette and Passage districts of Tunis. One of the most surprising buildings of this period is the Villa du Zodiaque (page 204) by Italian architect Ugo Chiarini, a modernist country house built to a perfectly radiocentric plan and situated in the countryside south of Grombalia near Hammamet. The (inaccurate) local legend goes that the villa was built as a present from a leading member of the Italian community to Mussolini.

The post-war period in Tunisia produced some visually striking buildings. Construction materials were in short supply and, from 1943 to 1947, a strong team of architects, many of whom had started their careers in Morocco, were in charge of seeing that the country got new public buildings. The **Sahel-style** vernacular building, with its whitewashed courtyard houses and vaulted rooms, was the model adopted for schools, training centres and administrative buildings across the country, many of which can still be seen today. One of the post-war team's leading architects, Frenchman **Jacques Marmey**, was to stay in Tunisia until 1975, contributing to the construction of many iconic buildings. The former presidential palace at Rakkada, Kairouan, is a Marmey building, which he worked on in 1956–60.

In the 1960s, Tunisia was proving to itself and the world that it was a modern nation. **Olivier Clément Cacoub** emerged as the leading architect, favoured by President Bourguiba (and a number of other African presidents too) for the design of official buildings and hotels. The Hotel Aïn Oktor, located on the thermal springs in Korbous (page 206), is a Cacoub building, as are many buildings in Monastir, President Bourguiba's hometown, which was also redesigned by Cacoub.

PAINTING AND PHOTOGRAPHY Easel painting took root in Tunisia soon after the arrival of the French protectorate. A number of European artists passed through, the most important being **Paul Klee** and **Auguste Macke**, both immortalised on the walls of La Badira Hotel in Hammamet (page 201). Struck by the intense light and the forms and colours of St Germain (today the Tunis suburb of Ezzahra) and Kairouan, Klee drew on his experience in Tunisia for the rest of his career. In the 1940s and 1950s, a number of Tunisian painters emerged, the so-called **École de Tunis**. Some were self-taught and others trained at the Tunis École des Beaux Arts or abroad; many imitated European styles, while others opted to illustrate the rich heritage of oral literature and the street life of their home towns.

After independence, a generation of Tunisian painters came to the fore, working in a number of registers such as calligraphic, abstract and naïve. **Nja Mahdaoui** produces vast expanses of calligraphic signs, and his work can be seen in the National Museum of Modern and Contemporary Art (MACAM) in Tunis while

Rachid Koraïchi, an Algerian based in France and Tunisia, works with a repertoire of talismanic symbols and Arabic script in a variety of materials. Koraïchi is also responsible for the Jardin d'Afrique migrant cemetery in Zarzis (page 311).

Similarly, a number of artists emerged in the wake of the 2011 revolution. Foremost among them is **Mohamed Ben Soltane**, an artist and gallery curator hailed as one of the most promising artists on Tunisia's contemporary arts scene, producing highly political pieces in photographs and cartoons. Also prominent is **Nadia Khiari**, famous for her collections about the Arab Spring featuring the revolutionary cartoon cat Willis from Tunis. Announcements on her exhibitions can be found on her Twitter (@willisfromtunis) and Facebook (@willis.fromtunis) pages.

This next generation of young Tunisian artists, many of whom now work outside the country, also includes **Faten Gaddes** (NYC-based photographer), **Ismaïl Bahri** (visual artist and filmmaker), **Mouna Karray** (photographer), **Héla Ammar** (visual artist), **Nicène Kossentini** (photographer and filmmaker) and **Bchira Triki Bouazizi** (both an artist and curator/patron). And who could forget **Rafram Chaddad**, whose multidisciplinary work mixes art and cuisine (page 82).

CINEMA Back in the 1950s, the ingredients for a good Arabic-language film were a dose of kitsch, lots of sentimentality and plenty of singing under the stars on the banks of the Nile. Things changed after independence, however, with the return to Tunisia of young European-trained directors brimming with ideas. The Carthage Film Festival was created in 1966, and continues to provide a biannual meeting point for the African and Arab film industries, while independent Tunisia set up its first film laboratory, the SATPEC, in 1967. In the mid 1970s, a few Tunisian films were taken on by international distribution companies, including Naceur Ktari's *Les Ambassadeurs* (1976), a sharp critique of the conditions of migrant workers in Europe, and Rida Behi's sardonic look at the side effects of tourism, *Le Soleil des Hyènes* (1977). However, the most famous films shot in Tunisia in the 1970s were undoubtedly the original Star Wars movies, with George Lucas kicking off principal photography for the franchise in southern Tunisia in early 1976 (page 39).

However, it was President Bourguiba's wife's nephew, the flamboyant Tarak Ben Ammar, who put Tunisia on the international directors' circuit. In the ex-president's hometown of Monastir, he set up a studio complex where acclaimed director Roman Polanski filmed part of *Pirates* (1986) and (curiously) a number of films featuring Christ were made, including *Monty Python's Life of Brian* (1979) and Zeffirelli's *Jesus of Nazareth* (1977).

At the end of the 1980s, producer Ahmed Attia's Cinétéléfilm came up with three highly successful art house films: *L'Homme de cendres* (*Man of Ashes*; 1986) and *Les Sabots en or* (*Golden Horseshoes*; 1989), both by Nouri Bouzid, and Férid Boughedir's *Halfaouine – Child of the Terraces* (1990). For its bold treatment of prostitution, the effects of child abuse and the relations between the Muslim and Jewish communities, *L'Homme de cendres* was condemned by critics, while *Les Sabots en or* grew out of Bouzid's experience as a political prisoner in the 1970s. *Halfaouine*, however, beat all records for a film in Tunisia. A loving and sometimes whimsical portrayal of growing up in Tunis in the 1960s, its sensitive treatment of sexuality and the separation of the sexes in the still-codified world of an old part of the city ensured the film's success.

In the early 1990s, a clutch of Tunisian films won international prizes, with Moufida Tlatli's 1994 *Les Silences du Palais* (*The Silences of the Palace*), a maid's-eye view of a mid-1950s Tunis aristocratic home, really putting Tunisian cinema on the map. However, the late 1990s and early 2000s is generally characterised as a period of stagnation in Tunisian cinema, as large production companies monopolised state film-making grants and helped Ben Ali's government decide who did and did not get to have their stories heard.

Change did gradually come after Ben Ali was overthrown. The 2012 documentary *Babylon*, by Youssef Chebbi, Ismaël Chebbi and Eddine Ala Slim, followed the construction and eventual dismantling of a massive refugee camp near the Ras Jdir border between Libya and Tunisia. Despite receiving no government support, it won a series of international film prizes including at the Marseille Film Festival. Likewise, Jilani Saadi's *Bidoun 2* (2014) was an ultra-low-budget road-trip tale set against the backdrop of the drafting of the post-revolution constitution. Its success helped show that the state and its favoured production houses would no longer have the same level of influence over cinematic output as they once had done.

The 2020 film *The Man Who Sold His Skin*, by Tunisian director Kaouther Ben Hania, was internationally produced with collaboration from French, Tunisian, German, Belgian, Swedish, Turkish and Cypriot production companies. It went on to be nominated for Best International Feature Film at the 93rd Academy awards and won prizes at both the Venice and Stockholm international film festivals.

SPORT **Football** (soccer) is the number one spectator sport and, as in the other North African countries, is a great unifying factor. If local politics is dull, then football gives people something to debate. At age six or seven, little lads are out in the street or on a piece of rough ground, kicking a football about. Their heroes are teams such as Tunis rivals Espérance (known as Taraji in Arabic) and Club Africain, and international stars like Ronaldo and Messi. Having failed to qualify for the 2010 and 2014 World Cups, the Tunisian national squad (nicknamed 'The Eagles of Carthage') managed to qualify for the 2018 World Cup in Russia, registering their first victory in the finals for 40 years by beating Panama (before being eliminated at the group stage). In the 2022 World Cup, they were eliminated at the group stage – despite a historic 1–0 victory over holders France.

Basketball and **handball** are also very popular in Tunisia. Both the ten-team Championnat National A and Tunisian Handball League were founded in 1956, of which the most successful teams are ES Radès and Espérance de Tunis respectively. Games tend to happen on Wednesdays for handball and over the weekend for basketball, and tickets can be bought from the relevant stadium or sometimes on the club websites.

A rising star in Tunisian **tennis** is Ons Jabeur, who made both the Wimbledon and US Open singles finals in 2022. She is currently ranked number two in the world by the WTA. Jabeur became the first Arab and African woman to take a WTA 1000 title in May 2022 when she won the Madrid Open. Jabeur is very popular and the whole country goes crazy every time she plays!

2

Practical Information

WHEN TO VISIT

Generally, spring, early summer or autumn are the best times to visit Tunisia, though the country sees wild climatic variations throughout the year, ranging from snowstorms to sandstorms. Perched on the edge of the Sahara, it gets very hot in summer, which is the most popular time for Tunisians resident abroad to return home for a visit (or a wedding). There is almost constant sunshine, the Mediterranean makes swimming comfortable and businesses tend to keep longer opening hours. It is also a great time of year for outdoor activities, including camping, in Tunisia's higher and cooler northwestern governorates such as Jendouba. However, it gets extremely hot in the south, and any form of urban tourism can quickly turn into an overly sweaty affair.

If you are not a fan of high temperatures, visit in either spring (Apr–May) or autumn (Sep–Oct). This is especially true if you would like to explore the desert in comfort or are keen to encounter the best winds for kitesurfing down in Djerba. Those visiting popular coastal areas will still find plenty of sunshine in these months, but with fewer crowds and lower hotel rates. Spring is also the best time to see many of Tunisia's wonderful archaeological sites, when the likes of Dougga and Bulla Reggia are blooming with wild flowers.

Visitors should not be put off considering a winter visit either. Average high temperatures in popular desert sites such as Douz or Tozeur rarely dip below 17°C during the festive period (although the temperature drops significantly at night), and who wouldn't want to experience the magic of seeing snowfall in North Africa up in Aïn Draham? This is also the best time of year for catching Tunisia's limited surf season over in Tabarka.

If planning a trip, do note when Ramadan falls (page 61), as many businesses, hotels and restaurants shut down during this period.

HIGHLIGHTS

With eight UNESCO World Heritage Sites (the third-highest number of any African country, denoted in this section by an asterisk), and a 1,148km-long Mediterranean coastline, Tunisia is not short on highlights, regardless of where you choose to base yourself and where you decide to explore. Visitors to the capital can check out the world-famous **Bardo Museum**, home to the world's most significant collection of Roman mosaics, while the 7th-century labyrinthine **Medina*** is dotted with over 700 historic monuments and never ceases to throw up something new upon repeated visits. Also in Tunis, **Carthage***, with its mixture of Punic, Roman, Vandal, Byzantine and Arab elements, is one of Africa's – if not the world's – premier archaeological sites.

The northeast features the birders' paradise of **Ichkeul National Park*** as well as the ruins of **Kerkouane*** – the only site in the country where you can see Phoenician-Punic structures that have not been demolished by the Romans. Heading west, more Roman remains are found at **Bulla Regia** (where villas were built underground to avoid the heat) and **Dougga***, formerly the capital city of an important Libyco-Punic state and boasting a 3,500-seat theatre that is still used today. Just south is 600m-high **Jugurtha's Table**, a unique natural monument with a bloody history.

The interior is home to the **Great Mosque of Kairouan***, the fourth-holiest site in Islam, situated in the most ancient Arabo-Muslim base in the Maghreb, dating to the 7th century, as well as another of Tunisia's impressive archaeological sites at **Sbeïtla**. Hidden away in a valley is **Bou-Hedma National Park**, unique to both Tunisia and North Africa as it houses relicts of the region's pre-Saharan savannah, complete with acacia trees, oryx, gazelle and ostriches that would not look out of place on a safari in South Africa.

Heading east, the coastal Sahel features the **amphitheatre of El Djem***, a 35,000-seater leviathan that was the third-largest in the Roman world. **Sousse**, generally known for its pristine beaches and holiday resorts, also has a wonderful 8th-century **medina***, with the best-preserved *ribat* (fort) in the country. Off the coast of nearby Sfax are the tranquil and unspoilt **Kerkennah Islands**, a true paradise of white-sand beaches and extraordinary seafood.

Continuing southeast, the island of **Djerba** offers both relaxation and culture, with some of the country's finest beaches and the oldest synagogue in Africa. World War II buffs can also retrace the steps of Generals George S Patton or Bernard Montgomery as they chased German general Erwin Rommel ('The Desert Fox') across southern Tunisia in 1942–43, by hiking along the preserved fortifications of the **Mareth Line**. There are some unusual accommodation options here too: sleep in a **troglodyte cave hotel** in Chenini, camp at the summit of the **abandoned ancient city** of Guermessa, or even stay in one of the fortified granaries (*ksar*, plural *ksour*) converted into hotels in Tataouine Governorate.

Finally, in the far southwest is the **Grand Erg Oriental**, the rolling sand dunes of the Sahara, where you can camp, trek with camels and get a glimpse of nomadic desert life. This area was also used as a backdrop by George Lucas in the 1970s and 1990s for his **Star Wars** movies, and it is still possible to visit many of the filming locations, including the iconic Lars Homestead on the Chott el Djerid salt flats. Just to the north of here, you can also ride the bey of Tunis's former **royal train**, the Lézard Rouge, through the sweeping landscapes of the Selja Gorge.

SUGGESTED ITINERARIES

Tunisia is a small country with an excellent road network. The drive from Tunis to Remada, which is as far south into the Sahara as you can get before the Tunisian military start asking to see permits, takes only 7½ hours (and is less than 650km). It is therefore possible to see a lot during a one- or two-week visit, as long as you plan sensibly. The main issue tends to be visitors and tour group organisers being overly ambitious and dedicating too much time to driving, in order to cram in the maximum number of sites. A couple of tips for planning:

- **Drive, don't fly:** Whether you rent a vehicle or zip around in a *louage* (local taxi minibus), it is usually faster than flying when you factor in the almost inevitable delays on Tunisair Express.

- **Don't spend all day in the car:** I have seen itineraries that take visitors straight from Tunis-Carthage International Airport down to Djerba for lunch (a 6-hour 30-minute drive), then over to Chenini to spend the night (a further 2-hour drive). While this is certainly doable, it is not ideal, and you will end up zooming past many amazing sites that warrant a visit in their own right. One way of avoiding this is to select only one part of the country to focus on during your visit. Alternatively, fly into one airport but out of another (such as into Djerba-Zarzis but out of Tunis-Carthage), thereby reducing the need for a circular itinerary.
- **Use Tunisia's dars**: Tunisia has a fantastic network of *maisons d'hôtes* – smaller accommodation options, like B&Bs, that sprung up after the revolution in all sorts of weird places. They give much more flexibility to your itinerary than relying on arriving at a hotel every night, which will usually involve getting to an urban centre. And, in many cases, they are both more appealing and better value for money.

DAY TRIPS FROM TUNIS A large number of sights are within a 2-hour drive of Tunis, making for excellent day trips. **Hiking** is possible at RafRaf, Ras Jebel, Boukornine and even slightly further afield at Zaghouan, while for **beaches** you are spoiled for choice, assuming you do not wish to remain in the capital, which has good beaches at Gammarth. There are excellent options on the nearer points of the Cap Bon Peninsula, such as Hammamet and Nabeul, as well as over in RafRaf, the private beaches of Ghar el-Melh (which need booking in advance) and the more remote sands west of Bizerte. You could even charter a **sailboat** from Sidi Bou Saïd harbour to take you over to the beaches of Korbous, or over to Zembra Island, both of which hold the promise of seeing dolphins at certain times of year.

For **archaeological sites** try Thuburbo Majus, Uthina or the Water Temple at Zaghouan, and for **military history** head to the German military cemetery at Borj Cedria, the Commonwealth cemetery at Medjez El Bab or the Commonwealth, Italian and French military cemeteries at Enfidha; there are also some very unusual Serbian World War I graves at Bizerte. For **gastronomy**, try Borj Lella cheese farm in Béja or Cap Bon's wine estates around Grombalia, which offer combined wine tastings and lunches. Villa Ma-Amoura near Nabeul is a good stop for vegetarians and vegans.

WEEKENDS FROM TUNIS Both **Tabarka** and **Aïn Draham** are less than 3 hours from Tunis and offer a wealth of good accommodation options. This is a great part of the country to hike, surf, mountain bike and camp and, if you nip to nearby Beni M'Tir, you can also kayak. En route, there are a lot of potential stopping points to eat in places like Béja or Bizerte.

The A1 motorway allows for ready access to much of Tunisia's coastline, and weekends on the **Cap Bon Peninsula** are popular. **Hammamet** and **Nabeul** are the traditional choices, offering top-quality waterfront hotels, but do not be afraid to explore: **El Haouaria**, for example, is also an excellent base. Depending on how long you wish to drive for, you could also check out the dars, restaurants and historic sites of **Sousse**, **Monastir**, **Mahdia** or even **Sfax** (which has the added bonus of taking you past the UNESCO-listed **El Djem amphitheatre**).

Heading inland, you could base yourself in Tunisia's highest governorate capital, **El Kef**, and explore the **Jugurtha's Table** massif, the archaeological museum and marble quarry at **Chemtou** or the 4,500-year-old megalithic dolmens at **Ellès**.

GETTING OFF THE BEATEN TRACK IN TUNISIA

If you would like an itinerary incorporating Tunisia's more off-the-beaten-track highlights, the following 14 attractions can be covered in an extremely rushed week or a leisurely two-week trip. Starting in Tunis, organise a dinner with Jewish-Tunisian artist Rafram Chaddad. Then, head to the German military cemetery at Borj Cedria, less than an hour from the capital. The following day, go hiking around the ancient Roman lead mines of Jebel Ressas. On day three, head to the Roman archaeological site of Thuburbo Majus, before stopping at Borj Lella cheese farm for an all-you-can-eat cheese lunch extravaganza, and then spending the night in Tabarka. On day four, head south to the incredible Chemtou Archaeological Museum, then on to the Kasserine Pass. On day five, hitch a lift on the Lézard Rouge tourist train through Seldja Gorge, before heading east and spending the night in Bou-Hedma National Park. The following day is spent hiking along the Mareth Line, including a visit to Rommel's command bunker from World War II, and the Mareth Military Museum. On day seven, hike up to the ancient, abandoned mountaintop settlement of Guermessa, before moving on to Tataouine where you can visit the palaeontology museum and explore the various dinosaur footprints and remains in the area. Your last day will be spent in the far west around Tozeur, visiting the various Star Wars and Indiana Jones filming sites in the desert.

CLASSIC DESERT EXPERIENCE Though this can be done over six nights, this itinerary is probably best split across ten days or a fortnight, especially if you want to spend more time in the dunes. After a whistle-stop tour of Tunis, head to Sfax, stopping at the amphitheatre of El Djem en route. The next day, drive to Djerba and spend two nights exploring the island, before heading on to either Guermessa, Chenini, Matmata or Tamezret, depending on whether you want to camp, sleep in a troglodyte cave or overnight in a Star Wars film set. On day five, drive south to the desert encampments of Ksar Ghilane for a night – although a more expensive and remote alternative (involving more driving) is to stay at Camp Mars in Jebil National Park. For your final night, wash away all the sand in the oasis town of Tozeur, being sure to stop in at Douz on the way, as well as taking in the scenery as you cross the iconic Chott el Djerid salt lake. Alternatively, you could visit the slightly quieter nearby oasis town of Nefta, home to one of the country's best dars (Dar Hi Life).

NORTH AND CENTRAL TUNISIA Sticking to north and central Tunisia, you could spend two nights in Tabarka, using this as a base from which to explore Aïn Draham, Bulla Regia, Dougga and the beautiful, forested coastline along to Cap Serrat. From there, head down to El Kef for one night, a good base to explore Jugurtha's Table and the still-functional Roman baths of Hammam Mellegue. Next, head east to Kairouan for one night, stopping at the archaeological site of Makthar or taking a detour to Sbeïtla en route. Your last two nights can be spent on the coast: perhaps dedicating a night to either Mahdia, Monastir or Sousse, before heading northwards to somewhere on Cap Bon (top choices would include Hammamet, Nabeul, Korba or El Haouaria). On the way north, you have the option of stopping in at Enfidha to visit the World War II graves or taking a slight detour to visit the ancient Water Temple at Zaghouan.

WORLD WAR II SITES *With Trevor Sheehan (w africanstalingrad.com)*
Tunisia is littered with significant battlefields, mainly in the centre and south. Starting at Wadi Akarit, an excellent 300km route explores the battlefields of El Hamma, Ksar Ghilane and Medenine, finishing in Mareth, home to the Mareth Line and a very comprehensive military museum. If you are in Kairouan, you could tag 100km on to your journey and visit the battlefields of El Haouareb and the Kasserine Pass, while in the north don't miss Hill 609, Longstop Hill and Takrouna. For specialist tour operators, see page 40, and look out for the symbol across the guide for more information on World War II sites.

BIRDING Tunisia has 46 Important Bird Areas, so you are spoiled for choice when it comes to where to go. Where you base yourself will be largely dependent on the time of year and what types of bird you wish to see, but you should probably dedicate a fair amount of time to Bizerte and Nabeul governorates. If you can find a birding guide that can get you permits to visit Zembra or the Galite islands, even better! (For birding guide recommendations, see page 41.) BirdLife International has identified a number of areas across the country as having significant numbers of a globally threatened species, or other species of global conservation concern, including the Galite Islands, Ichkeul National Park, Zembra Island, Korba Lagoon and Chott el Djerid.

You could also try visiting a few other out-of-the-way birding sites that are known to local guides, such as Kneiss Island in the south of Sfax Governorate, the Thyna Saltpans immediately to the south of Sfax, Bou-Hedma National Park or even Sidi Toui National Park in the southeast by the Libyan border (though be sure to check travel advisory notices before visiting).

STAR WARS SITES *With Davin Anderson (w galaxytours.com)*
Star Wars tourism in Tunisia can be divided into three geographically distinct circuits spread across the southern part of the country: a one-day tour around Djerba; a two-day trip in Tataouine and Medenine; and a three-day tour around Tozeur, which takes in the iconic Lars Homestead. While all three could be completed in a week, it makes more sense to take your time and spread the driving over ten days to a fortnight. See page 40 for more details on organised tours and look out for the symbol across the guide for more information on Star Wars sites.

VIA AUGUSTINA (w via-augustina.org) This Italian NGO runs hikes that retrace the steps of the early Christian theologian, St Augustine, who walked across Africa Proconsularis in the 4th century AD (page 10). There are two main hikes, both of which start in Annaba, Algeria and head eastwards into Tunisia, finishing near Tunis. The Medjerda hike (350–400km), named after the valley it follows through Tunisia, heads south from Annaba to St Augustine's birthplace, Souk Ahras (ancient Thagaste), before swinging westwards across the border, following the Medjerda Valley through the Roman sites of Chemtou, Bulla Regia and Membressa (modern Medjez El Bab), before arriving in Carthage. The second, much longer route (500–600km), known as the Southern Circuit, heads south to Souk Ahras but then continues southwards to M'Daourouch (ancient Madauros), where St Augustine studied, and Tébessa, joining the Roman imperial road that heads eastwards all the way to Carthage, passing through Haïdra, Althiburos, El Kef and Dougga en route. The hikes are usually done in multi-day sections, although there is nothing stopping you from using the GPS tracks to retrace St Augustine's steps independently.

TOUR OPERATORS

UK

Andante Travels w andantetravels.co.uk. Offer tours of Tunisia's archaeological sites with a dedicated guest lecturer.

Jules Verne Travel w vjv.com. Luxury tours of Tunisia's cultural sites, taking in up to 2 of the country's UNESCO World Heritage Sites.

Responsible Travel w responsibletravel.com. Offers carefully screened, sustainable, cultural & culinary tours of Tunisia.

Travel Local w travellocal.com. A UK-based website where you can book direct with selected travel companies, allowing you to communicate with an expert ground operator without having to go through a 3rd-party travel operator or agent. Your booking with the local company has full financial protection, but note that travel to the destination is not included. Member of ABTA, ASTA.

Western Desert Battlefield Tours w western-desert.de. Guided tours to the battlefields of North Africa led by Steve Hamilton, who has completed over 100 tours in the region.

NORTH AMERICA

✷ **Galaxy Tours** w galaxytours.com. The leader in Tunisia-specific Star Wars tourism, connecting the global Star Wars community to Tunisia, the real-world home of fictional Tatooine. Creates immersive experiences at the Star Wars film & recce sites in Tunisia via exclusive luxury tours, interactive travel apps, fan-focused events & memorabilia merchandise.

Iconic Journeys Worldwide w iconicjourneysworldwide.com. Specialists in cultural & historical travel, offering luxury 10- & 18-day tours.

Marriott Bonvoy Experiences Tunisia w activities.marriott.com/tunisia-bt2/things-to-do. The hotel chain offers over 120 instantly bookable experiences across the country, from cultural tours to outdoor adventures. You can also book them using Bonvoy loyalty points.

✷ **Mosaic North Africa** w mosaicnorthafrica.com. Specialises in tours to Morocco, Algeria, Tunisia & Egypt, with Tunisia-specific itineraries.

PromoTunisia w promotunisia.com. Specialises in cultural & historical discovery of Tunisia, specifically small-group itineraries led by Tunisian historians.

GERMANY

On The Front Tours w onthefront.com. Specialises in World War II tours, helping visitors uncover the Battle of Tunisia during the infamous North Africa campaign against the 'Desert Fox'.

TUNISIA

Association de Spéléologie et d'Escalade de Zaghouan w speleo-tunisie.com; f groups/Tunisian.caving.lovers. Offers organised hiking, caving, canyoning and & biking trips in and around Parc National Jebel Zaghouan.

Association GreenWay m 27 159 195; f randonneepedestre. Tunis-based hiking & camping organisation offering trips across the north. At the time of writing, they were setting up a new campsite in Beni M'Tir.

Association Tunisienne Des Randonneurs w randotunisie.tn. Tunis-based NGO promoting the development of the hiking community in Tunisia, which organises hikes throughout the country, including in national parks such as El Feïja.

Compass Travel w compasstravel.tn. Offers flight & hotel booking, ferry tickets, visa assistance, vehicle hire & tours around Tunisia.

Comptoir des Déserts Tunisie w deserts-tunisie.com. Over 20 years of experience offering tours of Tunisia's Dahar & desert regions.

Dar to Dar w dartodar.travel. Specialises in high-end, tailor-made trips incorporating some of Tunisia's most beautiful dars.

Logistique Organisation Voyage m 98 351 175; w lov-tunisie.com. Specialises in 4x4 excursions & rallies in the desert.

Open Tunisia Luxury Travel & Tourism t 70 247 890/9; w opentunisia.com. Tunisian agency established in 2010 offering custom tours around the country.

RideNXplore Tunisia m 27 479 947; w ridenxplore.com; ride_n_xplore_tunisia. Organised cycle tours around Tunisia on Royal Enfield Himalayan motorbikes. Amazing concept!

Saharansky w saharansky.com. Multi-award-winning outfit, originally focusing on desert tours in the south of the country, with offices in Tunis, Douz & Djerba. Has now added countrywide tours and outdoor experience packages to its website.

Siroko Travel w en.sirokotravel.com. Whether on foot, horseback or on a camel, owner

Mr Houssem Ben Azouz offers some amazing tours specialising in trekking & ecotourism.

Tacapes Tours w tacapes-tours.com. Offers a full range of tours including archaeological sites, hiking, camel trekking & yoga retreats.

Tunisia Ecotourism w tunisiaecotourism.com. Sustainable tour packages built around cycling, birdwatching, cultural & archaeological themes.

✷ **Tunisian Campers** f Tunisiancampers.official. This community of outdoor enthusiasts hosts camping trips, outdoor activities (including kayaking), eco-friendly sporting events & more, in some of Tunisia's most remote & rarely explored corners.

What To Do Tunisia w whattodointunisia.com. Offers nationwide experiences ranging from horseriding to birdwatching & paragliding, searchable by location, price & distance.

Birdwatching

Association Les Amis des Oiseaux e secretariat@aao-birdlife.tn or aao.bird@planet.tn; f AAO.tn. Conservation organisation dedicated to Tunisia's birdlife which organises various birding tours across the country, including around El Haouaria in Cap Bon.

Bécasse Écologie w becasse-ecologie.com. Based in Tunis but with an office in Belgium, this outfit offers specialised birdwatching tours.

✷ **Mohamed El Golli** e prof.elgolli@gmail.com. A highly recommended birding guide, specialising in trips to Cap Bon. Extremely knowledgeable, enthusiastic & multilingual, speaking English, French, Arabic, Greek & Russian.

TUNISIAN BOOKING PLATFORMS

Association Touristique de l'Autre Sud (ATAS) w autresud.com. Platform covering accommodation, guides, restaurants & museums in Medenine, Tataouine & Gabès governorates. Provides contact information for members, but does not take bookings through its website.

✷ **Destination Dahar** w destinationdahar.com. Innovative ecotourism outfit & booking platform for the Dahar region, offering accommodation, camping, hiking & organised culinary, cultural, artisanal & adventure activities. Also helped set up the 194km La Grande Traversée du Dahar regional hiking route, which runs from Tamezret to Douiret.

Teskerti.tn w teskerti.tn. Tunisian ticketing website for concerts, sports and live events.

Tunrooms w tunrooms.com. Essentially a Tunisian version of Airbnb. Great selection of dars nationwide.

✷ **WildyNess** w wildyness.com. Great platform that lets you choose nationwide experiences around various themes. Also run Star Wars hikes in the south of the country.

RED TAPE

VISAS Tunisia is a relatively simple place to visit for many nationalities. Citizens from just under 100 countries – including the USA, Canada, UK, Australia, New Zealand, India, China and those in the EU, much of North Africa and the Middle East – can visit visa-free for up to 90 days. For longer stays, or if you intend to visit for non-tourism purposes (for example to work), then you will require a visa, obtained from a Tunisian consulate in your country of residence. Prices vary but can be high; a multiple-entry business visa for a US citizen is currently US$180, while single entry is US$90. It is possible to enter Tunisia on a tourism visa and then convert this into a Carte de Séjour (residency permit) while in-country, which enables you to work.

Overstaying your tourist visa is not seen as a big issue. At the time of writing, you were simply charged 20DT per week of overstay, payable at the immigration counter as you leave the airport. Note that this is not paid in cash but in *timbres fiscaux* (fiscal stamps, which look like actual stamps) – these are not available at the desk, but you can get them from most banks (including those in the departures hall of Tunis-Carthage Airport), usually in denominations of 60DT.

EMBASSIES AND CONSULATES A full list of embassies in Tunisia (and Tunisian diplomatic missions abroad) can be found at w embassypages.com/tunisia. Note that consular hours for some embassies tend to be shorter than official opening hours, so call to check before going to drop off or pick up visa documentation. Also note that consular services are sometimes carried out at different locations from the actual embassy, and that many of the busier consulates outsource their visa processing to private-sector companies.

WORKING IN TUNISIA Tunisia is a dream destination for many expatriates: extremely cheap rent, good quality of living, a highly educated workforce (often speaking French and English) and with excellent, quick transport links to the EU. However, it is a nightmare for self-employed people to secure a work visa and residency permit (Carte de Séjour). Without a Tunisian employer to sponsor your application, things get very complicated very quickly. For more information, scan the QR code to watch my 20-minute video guide on how to secure yourself a work visa and Carte de Séjour by setting up your own Tunisian company. For assistance with this process, contact **Hmila Law Firm** ✷ (1 Rue du Lac Léman, Lac 1, Tunis; m 24 717 005; e hajer.hmila@gmail.com).

For help with other red tape associated with life in Tunisia, such as navigating bureaucracy, paying bills, long-term car rentals or organising vehicle or home repairs, contact Omar at **Tunisia Expat Assistance** ✷ (m 22 402 204; e tunexpatassist@gmail.com; f tunexpatassist), who really does make life in Tunisia easier!

It is sometimes possible to convert a tourist visa into a work visa while in-country, but this is a highly bureaucratic process if you do not have a Tunisia-based employer to support your application.

GETTING THERE AND AWAY

BY AIR Tunisia has good regional air connections, and an especially good network of flights to and from Europe. Between them, its three busiest airports (Tunis-Carthage, Monastir Habib Bourguiba and Enfidha-Hammamet) have direct flights to cities in more than 20 European countries (including the likes of London and Paris), and a few other destinations, mainly across the MENA region, such as Casablanca, Istanbul, Dubai and Doha. Note, however, that the national carrier, Tunisair, has a very poor punctuality record and processes refunds at a snail's pace. Be sure to do your research before booking with them.

BY LAND It is possible to drive or take public transport into Tunisia from both Algeria and Libya. Opening hours are generally 07.00–19.00 daily, although restrictions can be imposed on Fridays, Sundays and national holidays. Note, however, that it is not possible to obtain a visa at either border, so be sure to arrange one in advance and arrive at the border with it already affixed in your passport. Customs on the Tunisian side allow you to drive your vehicle into the country for 90 days, and it will be stamped into your passport. Note that you will be required to show the vehicle registration certificate and insurance details.

To/from Algeria There are six official border control posts, listed from north to south below. Note that the furthest southern border crossing between Tunisia and Algeria is in Tozeur Governorate, and it is not possible to cross over from Kebili or Tataouine governorates (ie: the final 400km of the border) without special arrangements in place first. These would likely need to be made in Tataouine or Remada (page 368). Do also check your embassy's security recommendations before attempting such an overland journey; currently, the UK

Foreign, Commonwealth and Development Office (FCDO) advises against travel to within 30km of the Tunisian border that adjoins the Algerian provinces of Illizi and Ouargla, as well as in the Jebel Chambi mountainous area.

- Oum Tboul, between Tabarka and Souarekh (a busy crossing)
- Babouche (known as PCT El Aïoun), between Aïn Draham and El Aïoun (a busy crossing)
- Between Sakiet Sidi Youssef and El Haddada
- Bou Chebka, between Darnayah and El Alaouinia
- Between Sidi Boubaker and Bir El-Ater
- Between Hazoua and Taleb Larbi

To/from Libya Despite sharing a 416km-long border, there are only two official border control posts between Tunisia and Libya. The Ras Ajdir-Ben Guerdane crossing is the busiest, and queues are sometimes very long. As with Algeria, the southernmost border crossing is still a good 225km from the southern tip of Tunisia, and it is not possible to cross the border at Borj el Khadra (even though the ancient oasis town of Gadamis is only 12km to the south). Do also check your embassy's security recommendations before attempting such an overland journey; currently, the UK FCDO advises against all travel to Libya.

- Ras Jedir, between Ben Gardane and Abu Kammash (a very busy crossing)
- Dehiba-Wazin, between Dehiba and Wazin

BY FERRY Tunisia's main international ferry port is in La Goulette, 12km east of Tunis's city centre. There are regular connections between the capital and France, mainland Italy and Sicily, operated by four companies. Check-in offices are located at the port, and most companies also have sales points in Tunis. Arrival from Europe involves being processed by immigration, customs and having your vehicle x-rayed, which can be a time-consuming process. There are a lot of taxis around once you disembark, but it is possible to get into Tunis via public transport. The closest train station to the ferry terminal is Gare Port La Goulette–Sud, and the closest TGM station is Le Bac. Note that the customs officers at La Goulette can be quite fastidious, and the immigration authorities can sometimes demand proof of accommodation, which is generally not asked for from those arriving at Tunisia's airports. Tunisia also has a southern ferry port at Zarzis in Médenine Governorate, which has summer connections to Marseilles and (as of February 2023) a ferry to Tripoli.

Compagnie Tunisienne de Navigation
122 Rue Radhia Haddad; w ctn.com.tn. Twice-weekly services to Marseille (22hrs; €125/170 passenger/vehicle) & Genoa (22hrs; €106/150 passenger/vehicle), as well as a once-weekly summer ferry between Zarzis Port in Medenine Governorate & Marseille (31–40hrs; €148/470 passenger/vehicle).
Corsica Linea Marsa Mall, Rte de la Marsa; w corsicalinea.com. Thrice-weekly service to Marseille (21½hrs; €115/160 passenger/vehicle).
Grandi Navi Veloci w gnv.it. Thrice-weekly service to Genoa (24–25½hrs; €78/230 passenger/vehicle), plus once-weekly services to Palermo (12hrs; €42/60 passenger/vehicle) & Civitavecchia (28hrs; €54/109 passenger/vehicle). Booking office in Tunis is D'Alessandro Travel (45 Av Habib Bourguiba; w dalessandrotravel.com).
Grimaldi Lines La Goulette; w grimaldi-lines.com. Twice-weekly ferries to Palermo (11½–15½hrs; €34/47 passenger/vehicle) & Salerno (25hrs; €43/75 passenger/vehicle), plus a once-weekly service to Civitavecchia (18hrs; €56/85 passenger/vehicle).

Malaria was thankfully eradicated from Tunisia in 1979, removing one of the main medical concerns when it comes to travel on the African continent. With adequate preparation, the chances of serious medical mishap are small. Within Tunisia, a range of good-quality clinics, hospitals and pharmacies can be found in the capital and the major urban centres along the eastern coast; most of the larger beach hotels also have their own clinic or a doctor on call. In the poorer interior governorates, however, facilities are far more limited and basic.

If you need emergency medical assistance during your trip, dial 190 and ask for an ambulance. You should contact your insurance or medical assistance provider promptly if you are referred to a medical facility for treatment. Doctors and pharmacists often speak decent English, and consultation and laboratory fees (in particular blood tests) are inexpensive by international standards – so if in doubt, seek medical help. Note that ambulances in Tunisia are often run by private providers, so you may need to arrange payment for your trip to the hospital separately. Similarly, hospital care will generally need to be paid for at the time. The US embassy in Tunis has a list of health-care providers, including dentists and medical specialists: w tn.usembassy.gov/u-s-citizen-services/local-resources-of-u-s-citizens/doctors.

PREPARATIONS Sensible preparation will go a long way to ensuring your trip goes smoothly. Particularly for first-time visitors to Africa, this includes a visit to a travel clinic to discuss matters such as vaccinations. A list of travel clinic websites worldwide is available at w itsm.org, and other useful websites for prospective travellers include w travelhealthpro.org.uk/countries and w fitfortravel.nhs.uk.

The following points are worth noting:

- Don't travel without comprehensive **medical travel insurance** that will fly you home in an emergency.
- Make sure all your **immunisations** are up to date. A yellow fever vaccination is not compulsory, although you may be asked to show proof if travelling from a country on the WHO list of countries with risk of yellow fever transmission. It's also unwise to travel to Tunisia without being up to date on tetanus, polio and diphtheria (usually given as a three-in-one vaccine), hepatitis A and typhoid. Immunisation against hepatitis B and possibly tuberculosis (TB) may also be recommended.
- Though advised for most travellers, a pre-exposure course of **rabies** vaccination, involving three doses taken over a minimum of 21 days, is particularly important if you intend to have contact with animals, or are likely to be 24 hours away from medical help. It is possible to get post-exposure prophylaxis in many urban centres in Tunisia, often free of charge.
- Anybody travelling away from major centres should carry a personal **first-aid kit**. Contents might include a quick-drying antiseptic (eg: iodine or potassium permanganate), band-aids, high-factor sunscreen, insect repellent, paracetamol, antifungal cream (eg: clotrimazole or Canesten), antibiotics such as azithromycin (if recommended by a doctor for severe diarrhoea in high-risk travellers), antibiotic eye drops, tweezers, a digital thermometer and a needle-and-syringe kit with accompanying letter from a health-care professional.
- Bring any drugs or devices relating to **known medical conditions** with you. That applies both to those who are on medication prior to departure, and those who are, for instance, allergic to bee stings, or are prone to attacks of asthma. Always

check with the country's embassy to identify any restricted medications. Carry a copy of your prescription and a letter from your primary care physician or GP explaining why you need the medication.

- Prolonged immobility on long-haul flights can result in **deep-vein thrombosis (DVT)**, which can be dangerous if the clot travels to the lungs to cause a pulmonary embolism. The risk increases with age, and is higher in obese or pregnant travellers, heavy smokers, those taller than 6ft/1.8m or shorter than 5ft/1.5m. Anybody with a history of clots, recent major operation or varicose veins surgery, cancer, a stroke or heart disease is also at higher risk. If any of these criteria apply, consult a doctor before you travel.

POSSIBLE MEDICAL PROBLEMS IN TUNISIA

Travellers' diarrhoea Many visitors to unfamiliar destinations suffer a dose of travellers' diarrhoea, usually as result of consuming contaminated food or water. Rule one in avoiding diarrhoea and other sanitation-related diseases is to wash your hands regularly, particularly before snacks and meals. As for what food you can safely eat, a useful maxim is: 'peel it, boil it, cook it, or forget it'. This means that fruit you have washed and peeled yourself should be safe, as should hot cooked foods. However, raw foods, cold cooked foods, salads, fruit salads prepared by others, ice cream and ice are all risky. It is rarer to get sick from drinking contaminated water, but it can happen. Bottled water is safe and widely available, although if you want to limit plastic use, buying your own filter bottle or a water purifier (such as Aquapure) is an eco-friendly alternative.

If you suffer a bout of diarrhoea, it is dehydration that makes you feel awful, so drink lots of water and other clear fluids. These can be infused with sachets of oral rehydration salts. If diarrhoea persists beyond a couple of days, it is possible it is a symptom of a more serious sanitation-related illness (typhoid, cholera, dysentery, worms, etc), so get to a doctor. You should also seek medical advice immediately if you develop a fever, notice blood or mucus in the stool or experience symptoms such as confusion, severe abdominal pain, jaundice or rash. Have a lower threshold for seeking help with young children, the elderly and other vulnerable travellers. If the diarrhoea is greasy and bulky, and is accompanied by sulphurous (eggy) burps, one likely cause is the parasite *Giardia*. Seek medical advice if you suspect this.

Schistosomiasis Also known as bilharzia, schistosomiasis is an unpleasant parasitic disease transmitted by freshwater snails most often associated with reedy shores. It has been reported in the past in Tunisia, although the WHO estimates that transmission was probably interrupted in 2012, so the risk for most travellers is likely to be very low. It cannot be caught in hotel swimming pools or the ocean, but travellers may be exposed during wading, swimming, bathing or washing clothes in freshwater streams, rivers or lakes. Ideally you should avoid swimming in any fresh water other than an artificial pool. Schistosomiasis is often asymptomatic in its early stages, but some people experience an intense immune reaction, including fever, cough, abdominal pain and an itchy rash, around four to six weeks after infection. Later symptoms vary but often include a general feeling of tiredness and lethargy. If you have been exposed, you can be tested for bilharzia at a specialist travel or tropical medicine clinic, ideally at least six weeks after likely exposure. Fortunately, it is easy to treat at present.

Hepatitis B This viral infection is transmitted by exposure to infected blood or body fluids. This may occur during sexual contact or as a result of blood-to-blood contact (eg: from contaminated equipment during medical and dental treatment, tattooing or piercing, and intravenous drug use). Over 2% of the population of Tunisia may be persistently infected with hepatitis B. High-risk or longer-term travellers should consider vaccination before travel.

Rabies At least five people died of rabies in Tunisia in 2021. This deadly disease can be carried by any mammal and is usually transmitted to humans via a bite or a scratch that breaks the skin. In particular, beware of village dogs habituated to people, but assume that any mammal that bites or scratches you (or even licks an open wound) might be rabid even if it looks healthy. First, scrub the wound with soap under a running tap for 10–15 minutes, or while pouring water from a jug, then pour on a strong iodine or alcohol solution, which will guard against infections and might reduce the risk of the virus entering the body.

Whether or not you underwent pre-exposure vaccination, it is vital to obtain post-exposure prophylaxis as soon as possible after the incident. Post-exposure treatment is available in Tunisia in many public hospitals and private clinics. Those who have not been immunised will need a full course of injections as well as rabies immunoglobulin (RIG), but this product is expensive and may be hard to come by – another reason why pre-exposure vaccination should be encouraged. If you have had the full three doses of pre-exposure vaccine, then you will not need the RIG, but just two further doses of vaccine three days apart. It is important to tell the doctor if you have had pre-exposure vaccine – carry your vaccine record with you. If you have had a partial course of vaccines (one or two doses) before exposure, you may not need RIG, but be guided by your medical assistance or insurance provider. Treatment may differ if your immune system is weakened, eg: if you take immunosuppressant medication. Death from rabies is probably one of the worst ways to go, and once you show symptoms it is too late to do anything – the mortality rate is almost 100%.

Tetanus Tetanus is caught through deep dirty wounds, including animal bites, so ensure that such wounds are thoroughly cleaned. Immunisation protects for ten years, provided you don't have an overwhelming number of tetanus bacteria on board. If you are wounded and haven't had a tetanus vaccine in the last ten years, or you are unsure, get a booster immediately.

HIV Rates of HIV infection are low in Tunisia: in 2020, its prevalence among people aged 15–49 was less than 0.1%. Barrier contraception (eg: condoms or femidoms) greatly reduces the risk of transmission.

Tick bites Ticks in Africa may spread tick-bite fever along with a few dangerous rarities. They should ideally be removed complete as soon as possible to reduce the chance of infection. The best way to do this is to grasp the tick with your fingernails as close to your body as possible, and pull it away steadily and firmly at right angles to your skin (do not jerk or twist it). If possible, douse the wound with alcohol (any spirit will do) or iodine. If you are travelling with small children, remember to check their heads, and particularly behind the ears, for ticks. Spreading redness around the bite, a fever or aching joints after a tick bite imply that you have an infection that requires antibiotic treatment, so seek medical advice.

Skin infections Any mosquito bite or small nick is an opportunity for a skin infection in warm humid climates, so clean and cover the slightest wound in a good drying antiseptic such as dilute iodine, potassium permanganate or crystal (or gentian) violet. Prickly heat, most likely to be contracted at the humid coast, is a fine pimply rash that can be alleviated by cool showers, dabbing (not rubbing) dry and talc, and sleeping naked under a fan or in an air-conditioned room. Fungal infections also get a hold easily in hot moist climates so wear 100% cotton socks and underwear and shower frequently.

Eye problems Bacterial conjunctivitis (pink eye) is a common infection in Africa, particularly for contact-lens wearers. Symptoms are sore, gritty eyelids that often stick closed in the morning. They will need treatment with antibiotic drops or ointment. Lesser eye irritation should settle with bathing in salt water and keeping the eyes shaded. If an insect flies into your eye, extract it with great care, ensuring you do not crush or damage it, otherwise you may get a nastily inflamed eye from secreted toxins.

Sunstroke and dehydration Overexposure to the sun can lead to short-term sunburn or sunstroke, and increases the long-term risk of skin cancer. Wear a T-shirt and waterproof sunscreen when swimming. On safari or walking in the direct sun, cover up with long, loose clothes, wear a hat, and use high-factor sunscreen. The glare and the dust can be hard on the eyes, so bring UV-protecting sunglasses. A less direct effect of the tropical heat is dehydration, so drink more fluids than you would at home.

OTHER SAFETY CONCERNS

Snake and other bites Snakes are very secretive and bites are a genuine rarity; however, Tunisia is home to a variety of venomous species including the Moorish viper (*Daboia mauritanica*), the Saharan horned viper (*Cerastes cerastes*), the Sahara sand viper (*C. vipera*) and the Egyptian cobra (*Naja haje*). As the names suggest, many of these snakes tend to be found in the desert south. Certain spiders and scorpions can also deliver venomous bites and stings. In all cases, the risk is minimised by wearing closed shoes and trousers when walking in the bush, and watching where you put your hands and feet, especially in rocky areas or when gathering firewood. If bitten, then, you are unlikely to have received venom; keeping this fact in mind may help you to stay calm. Many 'traditional' first-aid techniques do more harm than good: tourniquets are dangerous; suction and electrical inactivation devices do not work. The only treatment is antivenom. In case of a bite that you fear may have been from a venomous snake:

- Try to keep calm – it is likely that no venom has been dispensed
- Prevent movement of the bitten limb by applying a splint
- Keep the bitten limb *below* heart height to slow the spread of any venom
- If you have a crêpe bandage, wrap it around the whole limb (eg: all the way from the toes to the thigh), as tight as you would for a sprained ankle or a muscle pull
- Evacuate to a hospital

And remember:

- Never give aspirin which may exacerbate bleeding (paracetamol is safe)
- Never cut or suck the wound
- Do not apply ice packs or electric current
- Do not apply a tourniquet
- Do not try to capture or kill the snake, as this may result in further bites

Car accidents Dangerous driving is probably the biggest threat to life and limb in most parts of Africa, and Tunisia is no exception. Between 2016 and 2020, a total of 11,113 people died on Tunisia's roads. On a self-drive visit, drive defensively, being especially wary of stray livestock, random debris on the road, and aggressive overtaking manoeuvres. Many vehicles will not use their headlights or their indicators appropriately, so avoid driving at night and pull over in heavy storms. On a chauffeured tour, don't be afraid to tell the driver to slow or calm down if you think they are driving too fast or recklessly.

SAFETY

Travellers in Tunisia are unlikely to experience threats to their personal security, though you should apply the same precautionary measures as when travelling elsewhere (using hotel safes, carrying valuables as close to the body as possible, etc). Tunisia has a wealth of ATMs and money-changing offices in urban centres, so you should not need to carry large amounts of cash – though do be careful when withdrawing large sums, as bag snatching and pickpocketing is more common in crowded tourist areas and in high season. Be aware of your surroundings and note that many snatching incidents occur with perpetrators approaching the victim on a moped, grabbing their phone or bag and then speeding away. It is wise to keep photocopies of important documents (including your passport, driving licence and airline ticket) somewhere separate from the actual items.

Report any incident which involves you or your possessions. An insurance claim for theft of any size will require the backing of a police report – which will be laboriously typed out for you (in Arabic) at the police station in whichever area the incident took place. If involvement with the police is more serious, for instance a driving accident, remain calm, and contact the nearest consular office without delay.

POLICE The Tunisian police come in many different types: the city police (grey-blue uniforms), who do traffic duty and urban checkpoints; the Garde Nationale (Arabic: El Haras; green and khaki uniforms), who you will most likely bump into in rural areas; the *unités d'intervention* (black 'ninja' uniforms), a rapid intervention force dealing with terrorism and who will often be seen at events with large crowds (like sporting events); and, of course, plain-clothes police. There is also a separate environmental police but, judging by the state of some of Tunisia's beaches, it remains unclear exactly what they get up to.

When passing through the numerous checkpoints you will encounter on Tunisia's road network, police will generally wave you through as soon as they realise you are foreign (unless you are Libyan), perhaps with a cursory check of your vehicle registration (*carte grise*) or passport. While corruption is certainly a problem in some areas, tourists do not tend to be targeted for bribe requests by the side of the road, and the vast majority of police will behave professionally in their interactions with tourists. In rural areas, the Garde Nationale has checkpoints on main routes and as you arrive in certain small towns; they are almost always polite and professional and can be helpful on the state of roads and with directions, particularly after heavy rain. They sometimes get a little sensitive about you vanishing off into remote rural areas (for camping or 4x4 trips, for example), and might ask for details of your itinerary, or even come and check on you if you are camping, to make sure you are OK. There are certain restricted military sites around the country (page 289) that they will prevent you from accessing via their checkpoints.

At some archaeological sites, such as Dougga or Sbeïtla, plain-clothes police will sometimes appear and ask to see your documentation. Again, in the vast majority of cases they are polite and professional, although you may need to nudge them to show some ID before handing over any of your documentation.

TERRORISM Tunisia has suffered some very high-profile terrorist attacks since the revolution in 2011 (page 22), but the situation has stabilised in recent years, and the probability of being caught up in a terrorism incident today is very low. However, that does not mean that you should be complacent, so do check embassy travel advice before moving around the country.

Visitors should note that the vast majority of terrorist incidents in Tunisia target Tunisian security forces and occur in remote, rural areas of the Kasserine or Kef governorates in the west of the country, near the Algerian border, where the Tunisian government is fighting an ongoing insurgency against two terrorist groups: the Islamic State-linked Jund al-Khilafah-Tunisia (JAK-T) and the al-Qaeda in the Islamic Maghreb (AQIM)-linked Katiba Okba ibn Nafi (KUIN). At the time of writing, Jebel Chambi (including the entire surrounding national park) was also closed because of counter-insurgency operations, and the military was operating around Jebel Salloum and Jebel Sammamma (both in Kasserine Governorate), around Mount Mghila (on the border between Kasserine and Sidi Bouzid governorates) and around Jebel Orbata (Gafsa Governorate). You are unlikely to be allowed anywhere near these places owing to Garde Nationale checkpoints, but do check local travel advice before venturing into rural areas.

WOMEN TRAVELLERS

Tunisia is viewed as one of the most progressive countries in the Arab world in terms of women's rights, especially in education and political participation. According to the World Economic Forum's Global Gender Gap Report 2022, it was ranked fourth in the region after the UAE, Israel and Lebanon – though, for context, it still only ranked 120th out of the 146 countries surveyed.

Since 2004, sexual harassment has been legally punishable in Tunisia, with a fine of up to 3,000DT and a potential one-year prison sentence. In 2017 these provisions were further strengthened, and the Tunisian police take complaints of sexual harassment or sexual assault made by women travellers seriously. Survey data suggests that sexual harassment (especially cat-calling) can be a problem, especially by groups of young men, although not on the same scale as in nearby Egypt or Morocco. While noting that the country is overall low-risk in terms of criminal threats to foreigners, the US Overseas Security Advisory Council (OSAC) reports that sexual assaults occur throughout Tunisia, more often in rural areas and impoverished neighbourhoods. It also notes that sexual harassment of women is common aboard the metro system in Tunis.

The twin concepts of *hishma* (shame) and *ihtiram* (respect) may be useful, as you may get rid of a consistent pesterer by saying *haram alayk* ('shame on you') or *ma tehshemsh* ('have you no shame'). Other precautionary measures you can take include:

- Avoiding the metro system, especially at night
- Downloading a ride-hailing app such as Bolt instead of hailing taxis by the side of the road
- Avoiding travelling alone in contexts with large groups of young men (such as cafés showing live football or live music events)

- Seeking local advice before travelling through unfamiliar areas

If you are the victim of sexual assault, it is advisable to contact your embassy or consulate for assistance as soon as you are able (page 41). Most university hospitals in Tunisia have specialist facilities for helping victims of sexual assault. If you wish to report the crime to the Tunisian authorities, then each police or Garde Nationale department has a specialised unit to investigate crimes of violence against women. It must include women among its members and will be able to organise an interpreter if you are unable to speak French or Arabic.

Founded in 2011, gender equality NGO **Aswat Nissa** (meaning 'Women's Voices' in Arabic) has been at the forefront of the anti-harassment movement for the past decade. It advocates for the integration of the gender approach in all public policy areas, supporting women to voice their opinions and to become active members in the public and political spheres of the Tunisian society. See its website for more information: w aswatnissa.org/en/home.

TRAVELLERS WITH DISABILITIES

Despite a growing public awareness, Tunisia is not a very easy country to get around for those with physical disabilities. All airports are wheelchair accessible, and airlines should be able to make accommodations to assist you airside and landside should your mobility be reduced. It is generally a good idea to give your airline plenty of notice to make special arrangements (Tunisair requests at least 48 hours before arrival). All four companies offering ferry connections from Europe to Tunis (page 43) should also be able to make accommodations for travellers with disabilities.

Public transport across Tunisia, however, is generally not wheelchair accessible. Trains, inter-governorate buses and louages all have steps, do not have ramps and do not have dedicated wheelchair-parking spaces on board. Travel by road is possible via specialist taxi or minibus services dedicated to travellers with disabilities, which can be organised by your hotel, or via privately renting an appropriately equipped vehicle.

Newer chain hotels in the higher price brackets are generally more wheelchair accessible, especially in tourist hubs such as Tunis, Hammamet and Sousse. It is very rare to find an older building or traditional dar that is wheelchair accessible, though surprising exceptions include Dar el Kobba in Tozeur (page 348) and Dar Benti in Monastir (page 242).

The UK's **gov.uk** website (w gov.uk/government/publications/disabled-travellers/disability-and-travel-abroad) has a downloadable guide giving general advice and practical information for travellers with a disability (and their companions) preparing for overseas travel. The **Society for Accessible Travel and Hospitality** (w sath.org) also provides some general information. **Disabled Holidays** (w disabledholidays.com) also has over 20 listings for accessible hotels across Tunisia. For more information you can also contact the **Association Tunisienne d'Accessibilité aux Personnes Handicapées** (f ATAPH.TN).

LGBTQIA+ TRAVELLERS *With Mawjoudin (w mawjoudin.org)*

Though slightly better than some of its peers in the region, Tunisia is not very LGBTQIA+ friendly. Same-sex sexual activity has been criminalised under Article 230 of Tunisia's criminal code since 1913, with penalties of up to three years in prison – which have been known to be implemented. In June 2020, a court in Kef Governorate sentenced two men accused of sodomy to two years in prison each, three days after they had been arrested. In December 2021, this case went all the way to Tunisia's highest court, with human rights groups hoping that an overturned conviction would set a precedent to decriminalise same-sex sexual activity in Tunisia. At the time of writing, the court had yet to issue a judgment.

Gay visitors have long been a feature of the Tunisian tourist scene, especially in tourist hubs like Tunis, Sousse and Hammamet, although at a discrete level. Public displays of affection between same-sex couples are probably not a good idea, especially in more conservative, rural areas, though nobody will bat an eyelid if same-sex foreigners book a hotel room together. There is no open, commercialised gay scene; however, there are a few LGBTQIA+-friendly bars and nightclubs in Tunis. None advertise themselves openly as such (with good reason), but people have learnt to read between the lines on social media when venues mention 'open-minded crowds'. Discretion is always advised, given the presence of tourism police in some areas, as well as the potential for plain-clothes police presence in some bars and clubs. Tunisia has a number of home-grown NGOs advocating for LGBTQIA+ rights, such as Mawjoudin (**w** mawjoudin.org), which runs an annual Queer Film Festival, and Damj (f damj.tunisie).

TRAVELLING WITH CHILDREN *With Allison Bryan*

Tunisians love children, especially babies. Society revolves around kids and, if you travel around with infants, people are likely to come up to you and compliment them, start a conversation about your children and perhaps even give them a hug or kiss.

Most venues are child friendly, and you will see young children in restaurants with their families late into the night. However, the high chairs provided can sometimes be unsafe, even in the nicest of venues, so be sure to check before using. Most upper-end hotels have kids' clubs, and often babysitters for hire for a small fee. Children under two stay free at most places, but there are not always cots available, so check before booking.

Most medicines are easy to find in Tunisia's good network of pharmacies, but some common prescription ones, such as nystatin (an antifungal medication), are not available. Nappies, baby formula and wipes are readily available as long as you do not have a preference for specific brands. Jars of baby food can be hard to find, as well as rice cereal without honey or sugar, so bring your own or bring a steamer and masher to make your own.

Many hire cars in Tunisia do not safely take child car seats or have locking seat belts, though you can request this while booking – just note that some rental agencies will not understand what you are asking for, so be as specific as possible.

Pushchairs are not a great choice for little ones given the accessibility issues in some venues and uneven walking surfaces in many urban locations (although they are handy in resorts), so it's better to bring a child carrier (like a backpack or baby carrier).

WHAT TO TAKE

If you are backpacking, it is possible to travel very light in Tunisia. Many hotels and dars will have a laundry service of some kind, and clothing can be obtained very cheaply in the city *fripes* (page 89), so less is more in terms of packing. Finding good-quality footwear is a pain, however, so bring any specialist shoes you might need (such as running shoes or hiking boots). Ensure that your rucksack is built to survive the holds of rural buses and sitting on the roof-rack of a louage. If you do acquire a carpet or other bulky souvenir, there is plenty of cheap luggage on sale for a checked bag on the way home.

Regarding clothing, outside of summer you will need woollens or a fleece for evenings. Regardless of your gender, you will not be allowed into certain government buildings, embassies or consulates while wearing shorts or flip-flops, so bring appropriate clothing and footwear for such occasions. Tunisians like to dress well, and smartness is appreciated.

If you are hoping to travel into the desert, you will need a warm sleeping bag and, to be safe, a tent that is comfortable in temperatures of 0–5°C. The penetrating cold of the desert at night is a well-known phenomenon, so bring your warm undergarments. The coastal towns have higher humidity, with a particularly damp cold in winter, so bring layers and a lightweight, weatherproof raincoat.

Tunisian pharmacies are very cheap for commonly used items such as anti-diarrhoea tablets, antiseptic creams, antibiotics and rehydration salts, though things like suncream are surprisingly expensive, and other items (like water-sterilisation or motion-sickness tablets) are difficult to find. Be sure to bring any charging cables you might need, especially for laptops, as these are a pain to find.

MONEY AND BUDGETING

The major unit of currency in Tunisia is the dinar (listed as DT in this guidebook, but sometimes seen as TND); 1 dinar = 1,000 millimes. Coins as low as 5 millimes are in circulation, though the only ones you will see day to day are the 50, 100 and 200 millimes coins (yellow metal), plus the cupronickel (ie: silver-looking) 500 millimes, 1DT and 2DT coins (of which the latter two look confusingly similar). There is also a bi-metal 5DT coin that looks like a British £2 coin. Notes in circulation are 5, 10, 20 and 50DT (with most ATMs now dispensing new, pink 20DT notes). All coins and notes have international figures on them, although it can be hard to see the values on old 500 millimes, 1DT and 2DT coins.

Rates fluctuate, and in March 2023, US $1 = 3.09DT, UK £1 = 3.81DT and Euro 1 = 3.35DT. At the time of writing, an impending deal with the IMF meant that the rates might soon be subject to significant variation. The dinar is a closed currency, so dinars may not be taken out of Tunisia and you cannot buy them at bureaux de change outside Tunisia. If you have bought too many dinars in-country, you can exchange them back into dollars, sterling or euros at a bank on production of exchange receipts; note that ATM receipts are not accepted for this transaction, only receipts from a bureau de change or bank, so be careful how much you withdraw. When you arrive in Tunisia, if you wish to import a quantity of foreign currency equal to or greater than the equivalent of 25,000DT, you must declare it to Customs upon arrival. Then, upon departure, if you as a non-resident are trying to re-export foreign currencies equal to or greater than the equivalent of 5,000DT, you also need to declare it. Foreign residents in Tunisia have an even smaller allowance at 3,000DT equivalent per calendar year.

BANKS AND ATMS Arriving at any of the major international airports (Tunis-Carthage, Monastir Habib Bourguiba, Enfidha-Hammamet or Djerba-Zarzis), there are exchange facilities and several ATMs landside. Foreign Mastercard and Visa cards do work in Tunisian ATMs (best to bring both with you just in case), so it is usually easier to withdraw from a cashpoint as and when you need it than to change foreign currency. Note that ATMs in Tunisia will charge anything up to 12DT per withdrawal, and sometimes you will not be told about this charge until after you have withdrawn your money, so keep an eye on your receipts to work out which banks' ATMs work best with your particular card. Many ATMs limit individual withdrawals to 300DT, although some go as high as 1,000DT per transaction. How much total cash you can withdraw from a Tunisian ATM in a 24-hour period is decided by your card provider back home.

Banks are generally open at some stage between 08.30 and 17.00 Monday to Friday, although they tend to take extravagant lunch breaks, shorten their working hours during winter and Ramadan, and are almost never open on weekends. With many processes requiring lots of stamping and manual data entry into antiquated computer systems, banking in Tunisia can be a slow process involving a lot of queuing. Access to foreign-exchange facilities is tightly controlled in Tunisia, owing to the closed currency, although foreigners can purchase euros and US dollars in banks and forex shops by showing a passport. There is a black market for both currencies, although the rates are not usually worth the hassle (or illegality).

CREDIT CARDS Credit cards are widely accepted at banks, higher-end hotels, restaurants and shops, but it is wise to check first. Card terminal errors and internet connection problems can sometimes lead to card rejections, making for some very awkward situations at supermarket checkout counters if you are not also carrying cash. Acceptance rates tend to be higher with Visa than Mastercard around the country. American Express is very rarely accepted outside the five-star hotels. Before inputting your pin on the card terminal, be sure to check where the decimal marker (a comma in Tunisia, as in Europe, rather than a dot) has been placed and that there isn't a zero too many. You don't want to accidentally be paying thousands rather than tens of dinars!

BUDGETING In 2022, Mercer's Cost of Living Survey ranked Tunis in the top ten cheapest cities in the world for expatriates to live and work in (of 227 surveyed), thanks to low costs of transport (including heavily subsidised fuel), food, alcohol, tobacco and entertainment.

Some basic food products are subsidised in Tunisia, so flour-based goods (such as bread and pasta), cooking oil, sugar, rice and semolina (used for couscous) are very cheap. A baguette will set you back around 250 millimes (about 7p), while seasonal fruit and vegetables will be around 0.5–2DT per kilo, with imported items such as avocados costing significantly more. In ordinary cafés, you'll likely pay 800 millimes for bottled water or 1–2DT for a coffee, though popular tourist-zone cafés will charge considerably more. A 250ml bottle of Celtia beer in the supermarket will cost less than 3DT but can be up to 12DT in a fancy restaurant.

As a guideline, louages tend to charge about 4.5DT per hour of drive time, inter-governorate SNTRI buses about 4DT per hour, and trains about 5DT per hour (but you can reduce this by travelling second class). Museum and archaeological site entry varies by location (with many archaeological sites being free), but more famous places charge anywhere from 5DT to 12DT for non-resident entry.

As a **shoestring/budget traveller**, it is possible to get by in Tunisia for 40DT per day. There is much atmosphere to soak up for free in many urban centres, and almost all of Tunisia's national parks and natural reserves are free to enter. For 20DT, you can get a room with a bed and maybe a sink and access to communal showers, but not much else (note that if you are travelling as a pair, you can get double rooms that work out cheaper than 20DT per person). Anything less will be pretty rough, and probably inadvisable for single female travellers. Out of season, there may be some latitude to negotiate in smaller hotels. Another 10DT will cover either around a 9km taxi ride in a city, or about 2 hours of travel in a louage if you are moving between locations, and your final 10DT should get you two hot meals out of three and some good local fresh produce, but prepare to get very sick of baguettes.

For a **mid-range** budget, plan on spending about 90–100DT per day. For this price you can get yourself a decent(ish) private hotel room with en suite and air conditioning (maybe even access to a pool) for about 50–60DT, then have the rest to spend on travel, food and entertainment. While in Tunis or Sousse, you could even splash out and start using ride-hailing apps rather than flagging down cheaper taxis.

A **luxury** travel experience in Tunisia can be incredibly affordable. Plan on spending about 500DT per day if you want to stay in only four- or five-star hotels, eat in expensive restaurants and zip around in your own private vehicle. Award-winning five-star hotels such as La Badira in Hammamet (page 201) have rooms for as cheap as 255DT per night during low season, although this increases significantly in high season. You can have a slap-up meal in a very good restaurant for 50DT, although the price is likely to shoot up if you start ordering expensive wine. You can also pick up a decent rental car from an airport from an international rental agency that includes collision damage waiver, free breakdown assistance and unlimited mileage for about 115DT per day. You could, of course, go cheaper by hiring directly from a Tunisian rental agency upon arrival, or looking for a vehicle with a driver.

GETTING AROUND

BY AIR Flights around Tunisia are handled by Tunisair Express (w tunisairexpress.net), the domestic wing of national carrier Tunisair. It offers a limited set of routes, mainly connecting Tunis to various governorate capitals, plus a 40-minute flight connecting Monastir and Djerba. You can buy tickets online via the somewhat dysfunctional Tunisair Express website, or by using an online travel agent. Those wishing to purchase in person can do so in any Tunisair outlet (or the Tunisair Express outlet at 10 Rue de l'Artisanat in Tunis), at their airport counters or at one of Tunisia's many high-street travel agencies. Like its parent company, Tunisair Express has serious problems with running punctual services and communicating with customers. The general pattern is that early-morning flights are more likely to leave on time, with delays and cancellations cascading throughout the day. My approach while writing this guidebook was that there was nowhere in the country far enough away to be worth risking a delayed Tunisair Express flight rather than driving, but those on a more limited timetable may disagree.

BY ROAD

Louages Louages are minibuses that act as shared taxis across Tunisia. They tend to be white, identifiable by a red, blue or yellow stripe down the side. They leave when full, and prices are fixed by the Tunisian government (see w transport.tn and search 'Tarif du transport non régulier des personnes par les voitures "louage"'). Expect to pay around 4.5DT per hour of drive time on any route. Everyone gets an allocated seat and they are generally in good working order, although the driving is a bit hit and miss. Larger urban centres have more than one louage station depending on the destination, so be sure to check which station you will end up in as some are quite far from the centre.

Inter-governorate buses The Société Nationale du Transport Rural et Interurbain (SNTRI; w sntri.com.tn) operates cheap, air-conditioned buses between governorates. See its website for timetables and fares, but expect to pay around 4DT per hour of drive time on any route. As with louages, larger urban centres can have more than one SNTRI station depending on the destination, so do check where you are going.

Driving The large international rental agencies are present at many of Tunisia's international airports, though these are relatively expensive. It is usually cheaper to have a Tunisian tour agency organise your vehicle rental and meet you with the car upon arrival. Some will even send all the paperwork and a card terminal for the drop-off and collect the car by arrangement at the end of the rental, so you don't need to set foot in a rental office. When collecting a hire car, ensure the vehicle's documentation is all up to date, including the insurance and road tax (which is indicated by a coloured sticker with a date on it on the right-hand side of the windshield) and the registration card (*carte grise*).

People drive on the right in Tunisia. Note that the police like to set up speed traps and are especially hot on speeding offences: do not break the speed limit or you risk being fined which is a painfully slow process that involves the confiscation of your vehicle documentation while you head to the nearest bank to pay the fine and return with the receipt. Speed limits vary between 50km/h in most urban areas up to 90km/h on multi-lane urban express roads and 110km/h on the motorway. Driving is probably most chaotic on the urban express roads, where vehicles will weave in and out of lanes, frequently undertaking, so be sure to check your mirrors before changing lanes. The road surfaces can also get very slippery after rain, although they are generally in a good state of repair. Pot-holes are not generally a concern. Police checkpoints are common, especially when entering or leaving an urban area (page 48).

There is a large community of 4x4 enthusiasts in Tunisia, and many overlanders drive down from Europe to the Sahara. If you need spare parts or repairs, visit the Tunis-based Big Truck Garage Shop ✷ (f BigTruckGarageShop) – the best 4x4 repair centre in the country.

Taxis Official taxis (yellow with a red number on top) can be found in all Tunisia's urban centres, and are an extremely cheap and convenient way of getting from A to B while exploring. Confusingly, a red light beaming out from the dashboard means they are available, and a green light means they are occupied! Prices are fixed, so you should always request that drivers use the meter (*compteur, s'il vous plaît*). The price is 900 millimes for the pick-up then an additional 582 millimes per kilometre. The meter will also tick up 153 millimes per minute of waiting (such as in traffic). Between 21.00 and 05.00, prices increase by 50%, and there is a 10% charge for a taxi with air conditioning on. Drivers are also entitled to charge 1DT per suitcase they put in the back, and an additional 3DT per airport pick-up. Note yellow taxis are not allowed to leave their registered city, so you cannot take one from Tunis to Hammamet, for example.

In Tunis and Sousse, you can also use ride-hailing apps such as Bolt or Oto. Prices are always higher than just flagging a taxi down (usually double a metered taxi with Bolt), but you have the added convenience of knowing the price up front and being able to hail a ride at any time of day or night. You also have the added safety of being able to share your journey details with others. Surge-pricing is also a feature of these apps at busy times.

As in many countries, the dedicated airport taxis (often white in colour) are extortionately priced, have a bad reputation and should always be avoided.

BY RAIL Tunisia's train lines are run by the Société Nationale des Chemins de Fer Tunisiens (SNCFT; **w** sncft.com.tn). Tickets can be bought online between 11 days and 10 minutes before departure, or at the train station. There are three classes of travel available (Première, Deuxième and Confort), but no sleeper cars (though first class does have allocated seating). Third-class tickets sometimes need to be booked in person rather than online. Those looking to travel extensively across Tunisia's rail network can also purchase a railcard (Abonnement Ordinaire – grandes lignes), which gives up to a 60% discount on long-distance tickets, valid for between one and 12 months. You will need to fill out an application form and provide two recent passport photos at your nearest railway station ticket office.

Note that trains tend to be more expensive than louages and buses, are not always very comfortable and sometimes suffer serious delays and cancellations on longer routes. It might be convenient for some tourists to catch the train from Tunis to Hammamet, but otherwise you will likely be better off using another form of transport. That is unless you are a train aficionado, in which case the journey from Tunis down to Tozeur or Gabès might sound appealing.

ACCOMMODATION

HOTELS Tunisia is awash with hotels of varying quality, from international chains with spas and private beaches to cheaper options offering not much more than a bed and four walls. This is especially the case on the coast between Hammamet and Mahdia, where many of the hotels built during the boom years of package-holiday tourism in the 1990s have since seen better days, given the troubles the tourism sector has faced over the last decade or so. Beware that in some of the older budget options, the only thing keeping the business afloat is its alcohol licence, so check to see whether your hotel lobby has filled up with local lads drinking Celtia before checking in.

DARS Also known as *maisons d'hôtes*, dars are Tunisia's answer to B&Bs. Although only made legal after the revolution, they have since proliferated and can be found in most urban centres, as well as some very remote rural locations. They tend to be more appealing and better value for money than similarly priced hotels (especially in the mid-range bracket), with a more personalised service. Breakfast is usually included, although other meals may need to be arranged in advance. Dars can generally be divided into two categories: those in lovingly restored medina homes and those acting as boutique hotel-resorts outside city centres, offering everything from tree-house accommodation to farm stays.

ACCOMMODATION PRICE CODES

Prices are based on the cost of a double room per night.

Luxury	**$$$$$**	270+DT
Upmarket	**$$$$**	110–270DT
Mid-range	**$$$**	30–110DT
Budget	**$$**	10–30DT
Shoestring	**$**	<10DT

HOSTELS AND OTHER BUDGET ACCOMMODATION You will often find ultra-cheap sleeping options in the medinas or near transport hubs such as louage or inter-governorate bus stops. In less urban locations, youth hostels tend to fall into this category, which have the added benefit of sometimes also offering camping. Breakfast will cost you extra, as will the use of air conditioning or heating, if those facilities are offered at all.

CAMPING Camping is an increasingly popular pastime in Tunisia, with dedicated campsites springing up, especially in the north of the country. Pitches go for as low as 5DT, although a more usual range is 10–20DT, with some glamping and ecotourism campsites charging considerably more. Campsites attached to youth hostels tend to have better shared facilities and can offer breakfast for an additional fee, but also get very busy during school holidays and festivals. At the higher-price end of this category, glamping and ecotourism campsites can offer local dining experiences as well as organised hiking, kayaking, mountain biking and other outdoor activities.

EATING AND DRINKING

FRUIT AND VEGETABLES Tunisian cooks have a wonderful selection of field-fresh ingredients to choose from. Fruit and vegetables are of a quality rarely equalled in northern Europe and North America, and all are seasonal. The most common fruit are dates (Arabic: *tmer*), and the season runs from October to December (though you can buy them year-round). There are over 100 types, but the best, the *deglet nour*, come from desert oases, particularly Tozeur and Nefta. *Pastèque* (watermelon; Arabic: *della'*) is particularly refreshing in summer, while in early autumn restaurants add bowls of ruby-red pomegranate seeds (Arabic: *rumène*) to their dessert menus, served with sugary, rose-flavoured water.

In markets, look out for the soft, apricot-coloured *bousa'a* (as the medlar is known in Arabic), ready in May, while in late June a special variety of peach can be found: the flat, mole-skinned *boutabguia*, called *pêche de vigne* in French. When ripe, the boutabguia has wonderfully juicy white flesh. In July, crunchy little pears appear, known as *inzas bouguidma* (literally 'bite-sized'). There are numerous varieties of grapes, the most evocatively named being the long, translucent green *bazoula* (breast-shaped) grapes. Autumn finds the markets full of citrus fruit: look out for lemon-like bergamotes or lime (the taste approximates to soapy Earl Grey) and tiny green *lime beldi* (sweet lime).

On the vegetable front, Tunisian markets are full of greens much used in the preparation of stews and salads. Broad-leaved parsley or *ma'adnous*, essential for flavouring many dishes, is always available, and no decent couscous sauce will be made without *klefs*, a sort of celery. In summer, the small fleshy leaves of *badalika* are used to make cooling salads. And if you want something to take home, try cheap and aromatic dried bay leaves (*rand*), a sachet of dried mint (*na'na'*) or even a bushel of lemon verbena (*trunjiya*), ideal for making a soothing, sleep-inducing infusion when you return home.

RESTAURANT PRICE CODES

Prices are based on the average cost of a main course.

Expensive	$$$$$	50+DT
Above average	$$$$	30–50DT
Mid-range	$$$	10–30DT
Cheap & cheerful	$$	3–10DT
Rock bottom	$	<3DT

SPICES AND PICKLES No Tunisian meal would be complete without *harissa* – a thick piquant paste used to give flavour to all sorts of dishes, and given as a dip at restaurants before the starters arrive (the finest *harissa 'arbi*, 'homemade harissa', comes from Nabeul); too much is best countered by eating bread rather than drinking water.

Tunisian cuisine uses a number of typical pickles, either served as starters or snacks in their own right or as additions to main dishes and sandwiches. Look out for: *akhchef*, preserved quince slices; *filfil barr l'abid*, tiny red peppers used to decorate food and eaten to stimulate the appetite; *filfil m'sayer*, large green peppers, pickled whole; *imalah*, crinkle-cut carrots, cauliflower and turnips preserved in brine; and *turshi*, thin slices of pickled turnip. *Limoun* (preserved lemon) is often used in fish dishes and occasionally salads.

STARTERS *Chorba* is a delicious soup with a tomato and oil base. It usually contains a grain base such as *frik* (green durum wheat) or *freekeh* (bulgur wheat), and sometimes whatever meat is at hand. Two working-class soups found in working men's eateries or souk areas are *hergma*, a strong soup made from sheep or goats' feet, chopped and boiled at great length, and *lablabi*, a hearty soup of chickpeas, served at any time of the day and especially popular in winter.

Brik is popular countrywide: a deep-fried pastry containing egg and generally tuna, possibly potato and parsley, or even cheese. Often served as a starter, it is also eaten at the end of every *iftar* during Ramadan. Tunisian salads are particularly varied and fresh, the most popular including *salade d'aubergines* (grilled aubergines, finely chopped to a near paste-like consistency, served chilled with olive oil, lemon juice and capers), *salade méchouia* (finely chopped, mixed grilled vegetables served cold, decorated with tuna and egg – sometimes quite spicy) and *salade tunisienne* (a variant of *salade niçoise* with tomatoes, onions, green peppers, sometimes cucumber, and the usual tuna and egg garnish). You may also be offered *ummek houriya*, carrots boiled with peeled garlic, mashed to a paste and seasoned with olive oil, a little vinegar, harissa and black pepper, served chilled and garnished with capers.

MAINS Couscous is found on almost every menu, and the Tunisian version has a tomato sauce, unlike the Algerian and Moroccan versions, where the sauce is served separately. The buttermilk that accompanies a good couscous is called *leben*, and is sold in cartons in Tunisian supermarkets. Other popular staples include *kamounia* (a slowly cooked meat, octopus or squid stew, strongly flavoured with cumin), *koucha* (roast lamb with potatoes and peppers cooked in the oven) and *loubiya* (stewed mutton with white beans). *Marcassin* (meat of the wild boar piglet, the only pork you are likely to find in this Muslim country) has a strong flavour and is served with a rich gravy. (Pork is called *hallouf*, which is also slang for a 'tricky' person.) At roadside restaurants you will find *mechoui*, grilled meat (usually lamb) served with a small dish of harissa and olive oil. Look out too for *merguez*, small spicy mutton or beef sausages, generally grilled – the red colour gives an indication of the amount of chilli used in their preparation and is a guide to how fiery they will be.

Other popular Tunisian dishes include *shakshuka* – ratatouille with eggs, tomatoes, peppers, garlic and onions – and *keftaji* – fried onions, pumpkin, tomatoes, peppers and eggs, chopped up and served with either meatballs (*ka'abir*) or fried liver. *Tajine* in Tunisia is not a stew but a form of quiche, with meat and vegetables, cooked in the oven. Varieties include *tajine ma'kouda*, which contains broad-leaved parsley, potato and peas and is sometimes flavoured with smoked herring (*renga*), and *tajine malsouka*, with egg and chicken between layers of filo pastry.

In terms of fish, the best are the *rouget* (red mullet), *mulet* (mullet), *merou* (cod), *loup de mer* (perch) and sole. You can have your fish *grillé/mechoui* (barbecued) or *frit/mukli* (fried). *Kabkabou* is oven-baked fish with saffron, preserved lemons and vegetables. *Crevettes royales* (king prawns), *cigale de mer* (slipper lobster) and *homard* (lobster) are best eaten in places like Tabarka on the rocky northern coast and at El Haouaria, although La Goulette has some excellent seafood restaurants too. Seafood pasta, often with a spicy tomato sauce, is a very popular dish in seaside locations, and tends to feature mussels, squid or cuttlefish and prawns.

DESSERTS Like all Mediterranean countries, Tunisia has many varieties of dessert, all very sweet and sticky. The Ottoman influence is clear. If you go to a Tunisian wedding or a traditional patisserie, you will almost certainly get the chance to try some of the many varieties of *helw* (small sweet cakes) such as *baklawa* (puff pastry with lots of honey and nuts), *bjaouia* (a sort of cake combining almonds, pistachio nuts and puffed pastry), *loukoum* (Turkish delight), *makroud* (semolina cake with crushed dates, baked in oil and dipped in honey) and *m'lebbes* or *calissons de Sfax* (round sweets made of sweetened ground almonds covered in white icing sugar). *Masfouf*, a dessert made from fine semolina flour served with dates, raisins, pistachio nuts and pine nuts, is a meal in itself and particularly eaten for the *suhour*, the early-morning Ramadan meal taken before fasting begins. Tunisians also eat a sort of pine nut custard called *assida bi-zgougou* made especially for the Mouled (the annual celebration of the Prophet Muhammad's birthday).

FAST FOOD Sandwiches and wraps across Tunisia share several common ingredients such as harissa, egg, tuna and salade méchouia. *Kaskrout kafteji* is an open baguette stuffed with harissa, potato, cucumber, onion, olive oil, tuna and eggs (boiled or fried), while *mlawi* uses similar ingredients (but can add meat) in an open flatbread. *Makloub* is a thicker, heartier open sandwich that uses pizza dough and often adds cheese. *Baguette farcie* incorporates meat and cheese in the dough before baking, resulting in a very dense, filling sandwich! *Fricassé* is a

TUNISIAN JEWISH CUISINE

Rafram Chaddad (@rafram_x)

Unlike other Jewish cuisines around the world, Tunisian Jewish cuisine is deeply ingrained in everyday life. While Jews in most parts of the world often suffered as a minority, which led to isolation from the local population, Jews in Tunisia had a relatively easy life, and in the 1950s they owned many of the restaurants across the capital, which made Jewish food both desired by and accessible to most Tunisians.

Two of the most famous Tunisian Jewish dishes are *pkaila*, a Persian-like, dark-coloured main based on a confit of spinach and butter beans, and *banataj*, a croquette stuffed with fish or meat that came with Jewish immigrants from Andalusia. Other specialities that arrived in Tunisia with Jews from abroad are *hraimi*, a spicy red fish dish brought over by Libyan Jews visiting the synagogue in Djerba 150 years ago, and *tortellini in brodo* (tortellini in broth), which came with Livornese Jews to Tunis. The Tunisian sandwich (*cascroute tounsi* aka *kaskrout kafteji*) and its plated equivalent (*Shan tounsi*), both involving tuna, vegetables and eggs, are said to have been invented by a poor Tunisian Jew who was collecting ingredients from merchants in the market and later compiled these dishes.

smaller sandwich made with fried dough and filled with the usual egg, tuna, salad and harissa mix. Lastly, *sandwich chapatie* are dense discs of bread filled with all the usual ingredients plus cheese (often of the Kraft slice variety), looking a little like a McDonald's breakfast muffin.

VEGETARIANS AND VEGANS Vegetarian and vegan options on the average Tunisian restaurant menu tend to be quite limited, unless you are in a higher-end establishment or one that specifically caters to these dietary needs. Note that tuna and eggs are put in almost everything, so you will need to be very clear about not wanting them in your salads. Outside urban centres, telling a waiter that you are vegan is likely to elicit confusion, so it is best to be very explicit about the things you do not want in your meal. To ask for something without meat is *sans viande/bilesh leham*.

DRINK The national drink is **tea**, which comes as *tay akhdhar/thé vert* (green tea) and *tay ahmar/thé rouge*, a dark, sugar-saturated brew. In tourist-oriented places, it is often served with tiny, white flavoursome pine nuts floating in it, which makes it both more delicious and more expensive. **Coffee** is also widely drunk, generally served as very strong espresso.

The most common and cheapest **beer** is Celtia (a Tunisian lager that everyone is very proud of), but Tunisian-made Stella, as well as imported beers such as Heineken and Amstel, can also be found.

The Tunisians have been making **wine** for over 2,000 years. Given the massive price difference between imported and Tunisian wines, you might consider trying some of the local produce while visiting. Red or rosé is generally a safer bet than white, although this is changing. Note, however, that the reds are probably more acidic than most palates are used to and vary in quality. Domaine Neferis in Nabeul Governorate is a good place to try some of the country's finest wines, and it offers tours and tasting experiences (page 205).

Tunisia also produces three types of **spirits**. *Boukha* is made from distilled figs, while *thibarine* is a strong, sweet liqueur dreamed up by the White Fathers at their model farm at Thibar, near Dougga (page 119). Finally, *laghmi* is palm-tree sap left to ferment immediately after it is collected – and it tastes like sweet rocket fuel.

PUBLIC HOLIDAYS AND FESTIVALS

1 January	New Year's Day (in the Gregorian calendar)
20 March	Independence Day (anniversary of independence from France in 1956)
9 April	Martyrs' Day (anniversary of the 1938 Tunis riots, during which a number of demonstrators died when French troops fired on the crowd)
1 May	International Labour Day (Fête du Travail)
25 July	Republic Day (anniversary of the declaration of the Tunisian Republic in 1957)
13 August	Women's Day (Fête de la Femme)
15 October	Evacuation Day (anniversary of the departure of French troops from Bizerte in 1963)
17 December	National Revolution and Youth Day (anniversary of the Tunisian Revolution that ousted President Ben Ali, celebrated on 14 January until 2021)

RELIGIOUS HOLIDAYS Religious holidays are scheduled according to the lunar-based Hejira calendar. The lunar year is shorter than the solar year, so the Muslim year moves forward by 11 days every Christian year (thus, every five years, Ramadan completely switches seasons). The year 2023 corresponds to the Muslim year 1444–45.

The main holiday is **Ramadan**, a month of fasting and sexual abstinence during daylight hours. Note that the start of Ramadan can vary by a day, depending on the *ru'ya*, whether the crescent moon has been observed or not by the religious authorities whose job it is to declare Ramadan. During Ramadan, the whole country switches to a different rhythm. Public offices and many private businesses shift to shorter hours, and the general pace slows down during the daytime. Tunisians in general do not eat in public during the day, and the vast majority of cafés and restaurants, except those frequented by resident Europeans and tourists, are closed during daylight hours. The cities are quite lively at night, as everyone gathers for a meal to break their fast (*iftar*); you might receive an invitation to go for iftar with a Tunisian friend or acquaintance. Ramadan can be an interesting time to visit Tunisia as a tourist (depending on the types of activities you wish to take part in), but to be avoided if possible when you need to do business.

Ramadan ends with **Eïd es Seghir** (or Eïd al-Fitr: the Lesser Eïd), a two-day holiday, and 70 days later follows **Eïd el Kebir** (or Eïd al-Adhâ: the Great Eïd), which commemorates how God rewarded Ibrahim's faith by sending down a lamb for him to sacrifice instead of his son. Where possible, every family sacrifices a sheep on this day.

Other celebrations include **Muharram**, the first day of the Muslim year, and **Mouled**, the celebration of the Prophet Muhammad's birthday.

FESTIVALS Since independence the Tunisian authorities have developed a number of festivals, from live music events to more regional affairs that have grown out of local products and traditions. The main concentration of festivals is over the summer period, but you should be able to find something going on regardless of when you visit.

March

Festival de la Médina (Tunis) Annual 2-week festival held during Ramadan in the Medina. Restored historic buildings host live music & singers performing a classical Arabic & Tunisian repertoire.

Festival International des Ksour Sahariens (Tataouine) A week-long tourist-office effort to put the far south on the map. Parades, concerts & sporting events, but none too exciting.

Festival de Poulpes (Kerkennah Islands) Celebrating the end of the octopus harvest on the islands, this week-long festival culminates with a cookery competition to crown the best octopus couscous.

June

Festival de l'Épervier (El Haouaria) Running for over 50 years, this 4-day festival celebrates the local falcon-hunting tradition that dates to Carthaginian times. Also features live music.

Jazz à Carthage (Tunis) Large 5-day jazz festival attracting talent from across the globe.

Tabarka Jazz Festival The streets of this quiet northwestern port come alive with jazz for a week.

July

Festival International de Musique Symphonique d'El Djem International symphony orchestras play in the splendid surroundings of the Roman amphitheatre in El Djem for a whole month (usually until mid-Aug).

Festival International du Cheval Arabe de Meknassy This town has a long tradition of animal husbandry, so expect dressage, racing & all things horse-related at this 3-day event that has been running since 1975. Dates alternate between July & November.

Carnival of Awussu (Sousse) An annual street parade on 24 July, whose origins may go back to ancient Phoenician or Amazigh traditions.
Ulysse Music Festival (Djerba) Large 2-week music festival with mythological themes.
Festival du Malouf (Testour) A time for this provincial town in northern Tunisia to remember its unique Andalusian musical heritage, set across two weeks.

July/August

Hammamet International Festival Established in 1964, this month-long music festival is held in the grounds of the former party villa of millionaire Romanian aesthete, Georges Sebastian.
Festival International de Carthage (Tunis) Established in 1964, this month-long series of concerts is held in the Roman theatre.
Festival International de Sousse Running for over 60 years, this large, month-long music festival attracts talent from across the region. Also includes film screenings & other artistic exhibitions.
Festival International de Dougga A week-long festival of live music in the incredibly preserved, UNESCO-listed Roman theatre. A unique experience.

August

Kharja de Sidi Bou Saïd Religious brotherhoods of Tunis gather to process up to the shrine of Sidi Bou Saïd. Festivities last until dawn.

November

Les Dunes Électroniques (Nefta) Running since 2014, this large w/end techno music festival takes place out in the desert.

December

Festival des Oasis (Tozeur) A popular 2-week festival in the main southwestern oasis town. Parades, camel fights & concerts all pull in the tourists & celebrate the date harvest.
Festival du Sahara (Douz) Another big w/end desert festival, & the oldest festival in Tunisia, dating to 1910. Displays of horsemanship, *sloughi* (desert greyhound) & camel races, parades & the like. A jolly occasion.

SHOPPING

Tunisia has some interesting craftwork, though unfortunately many of the more interesting, good-value items are difficult to transport (ie: rush mats, wrought iron) or are very expensive (ie: silk garments). If you are looking for cheap gifts, then there is a wealth of things to choose from – though the tourist souks often feature items imported from Egypt, India, Pakistan and West Africa.

Haggling is expected in the tourist bazaars, but less so in non-touristy areas. Start lower than you would expect to pay, be polite and good humoured, enjoy the experience and, if the final price doesn't suit, walk away. The experience can be highly entertaining. In the end, the price you pay must be the price the item is worth to you. Salesmen (and you will generally be dealing with men) will want to find out your country of origin and job to get an idea of your purchasing power. You may be quite impressed by the linguistic skills of some traders, as they effortlessly flick between French, Italian, German and English in an attempt to sell. All in all, the souk experience requires you to be assertive without being rude. If this does not sound appealing, there are plenty of concept stores offering artisanal wares for fixed prices (page 88).

Export permits should not be necessary for any of the items listed here, though see **w** aeroportdetunis.com (click 'Customs') for more information.

CARPETS In Tunisia, there are three main types of handmade carpet. The classic **knotted carpets**, usually made of wool on a cotton base, come from the vertical looms of homes and workshops in Kairouan. The patterns are geometric, usually based on a central medallion in the form of single and double diamond shapes.

Their weave is of hand knots of the *ghordes* type, with long tufts looped around the warp. **Mergoum**, the other popular weave, is different, having short tufts emerging on the underside of the warps. Of the two, the mergoum is cheaper and made for the tourist trade, while the classic knotted carpet tends to appeal more to locals. Finally, bold and colourful **kilims** are made in Djerba and Sbeïtla. When shopping, don't be pushed into buying a carpet. It is common to be invited into the carpet shop and be offered tea, but you are under no obligation to buy.

Some southern towns, including Gabès, produce **flat-weave tapestries** with stylised camels and the like. Perhaps the easiest piece to take home is a *bakhnoug*: a tightly woven woollen shawl with cotton embroidery. Unfortunately, high-quality *bakhnoug* are a rarity now.

OTHER CRAFTS Finding something really original to take home will take time. Basketwork is a good, cheap find, and you might see some fine rush mats in Nabeul (page 197) or *nattes*, mats made from plaited alfa grass, in Hergla (page 236). Some of the finer nattes with geometric designs make good wall hangings. Old-fashioned hammered metal kitchen articles in copper or silvery zinc-plating (*maillechort/mqezder*) are also a good buy – try Souk En Nhas in Tunis or the main street in Kairouan (page 278). Then there is simple, rural hand-shaped pottery from the north, sometimes painted up with geometric designs. In the Tunis medina, look for the rather fine traditional men's tunics (*jebba*) in silk and linen. Given that Tunisia is a major centre for garment manufacture, another option is to pick up a nice pair of jeans or a shirt in a modern shopping mall.

If you do not fancy hunting around souks and shops for a perfect gift, try browsing the Artisans d'Art website (w artisansdart.tn), which collates all sorts of artisanal creations thematically or by geographic location. You will still have to go and fetch the item from whichever vendor or concept store it is in, but at least you can peruse from the comfort of your device first! You could also try w soukra.co, which offers a doorway into Tunisia's burgeoning designer community by offering access to goods by Tunisian entrepreneurs.

FOOD On the whole, the best things to buy in Tunisia are foodstuffs. The markets are full of spices, dried herbs and various condiments which cost a small fortune in European supermarkets. Try for locally produced olive oil, olives, capers, real harissa, bay leaves, dried mint and various spices. Dates are also a splendid present and can be bought on the branch in kilo-size boxes. There are also various flower waters, especially orange and geranium, much used in traditional patisserie, as well as almond syrup (*sirop d'orgeat*), which makes a refreshing summer drink.

Tunisia has a wide variety of supermarkets stocking most of the items available back home, even if you have to hunt around or pay a premium. The larger branches tend to keep longer hours, often 08.00–22.00 daily. Note that not all stores have a *cave* (a separate section selling alcohol) and, even if they do, it will not always be open. Caves usually close on public holidays, during Ramadan and sometimes on Fridays, though in some stores they simply allow entry on Fridays to foreigners only.

ARTS AND ENTERTAINMENT

Tunisia has an extensive, diverse arts scene, and does an excellent job of promoting it. Barely a month goes by without a **music festival** taking place somewhere in the country (page 61), with the summer being a particular highlight of the calendar.

You will have your pick of live music venues, from edgy metal clubs in La Goulette to watching symphonic orchestras in El Djem's amphitheatre or enjoying jazz with views of the 16th-century Genoese fort in Tabarka. With so many well-established music festivals, so easily accessible from Europe, Tunisia's largest cities also often attract an impressive array of international acts, from American cellist Yo-Yo Ma to German techno DJ Innellea.

Theatres and theatrical groups operate across the country, with performances taking place in everything from modern constructions (such as the network of Tunisian and foreign cultural centres) to French colonial spaces (such as the theatres in Bizerte or the Théâtre municipal de Tunis). Likewise, you could spend weeks touring the **art galleries and exhibition spaces** the country has to offer, especially given the flourishing post-revolution arts scene (page 32). Outside the major urban centres there are all sorts of weird and wonderful artistic creations to be found, such as the underground gallery in Dahmani (Althiburos; page 149) or artist Rachid Koraïchi's touching Jardin d'Afrique monument in Zarzis (page 311).

Visiting the **cinema** is a popular pastime, and most urban centres will have at least one. Tunisia also has a very well-established film industry of its own, which recently received its first Oscar nomination (page 34).

In popular tourist destinations such as Tunis, Sousse or Djerba, you will find **nightlife** on offer like in any Western city, with a variety of bars, live music venues, nightclubs and even the odd casino. Tunis in particular has a bustling variety of nightlife centred around Gammarth, where bars and clubs (many on the beach) are open well into the early hours.

MEDIA AND COMMUNICATIONS

NEWSPAPERS It used to be the case that French-language press dominated the circulation figures for Tunisian newspapers. However, over the past 20 years or so Arabic-language press has really made a comeback, and today the printed news tends to be read in Arabic, although most newspapers often have a translated French-language edition. Some of the most significant newspapers in Tunisia, based on circulation, are *Al Chourouk* (Arabic), *La Presse de Tunisie* (French), *Assarih* (Arabic) and *Assabah* (Arabic) with its translation *Le Temps* (French).

TV AND RADIO Tunisia's state-owned public broadcaster, Établissement de la Télévision Tunisienne (or TT for short), has two terrestrial channels: El Watania 1 (featuring a mixture of news, entertainment and sports) and El Watania 2 (mainly documentaries, dramas and children's programming). Italian national broadcaster RAI was available on Tunisian terrestrial screens from 1960, when the Rome Olympics was beamed into Tunisian homes, right the way through to 2010, which helps to explain why so many older Tunisians can speak or understand at least rudimentary Italian.

There are also a selection of privately run channels, such as the very popular El Hiwar El Tounsi (which started life as an anti-Ben Ali channel, located abroad), Nessma El Jadida (formerly linked to both Silvio Berlusconi and Tunisian 2019 presidential candidate, Nabil Karoui) and Hannibal TV (which seems to have been intermittently on and off the air since mid 2019). The pattern among many of these channels, dating to the Ben Ali era, is one of political activism and friction with the ruling authorities, sometimes leading to shutdowns.

The public broadcaster Établissement de la Radio Tunisienne (RT) manages four national stations and a selection of regional ones. One of these national stations,

Radio Tunis Chaîne Internationale (RTCI), carries programming in French, Italian, English, Spanish and German. Radio broadcasting was tightly controlled under President Ben Ali, and it was not until 2003 that the sector began to liberalise and allow private players into the market, starting with Mosaïque FM, which has gone on to become one of the largest stations in the country, and a key source of news for many Tunisians. Other channels include Shems FM (formerly part-owned by Ben Ali's daughter), Express FM, Radio IFM and the awesome Misk FM. Many radio stations had part of their shares confiscated by the Tunisian state following the revolution, including Shems FM and Mosaïque FM. Italian radio stations are also receivable in the north of the country, especially on the Cap Bon Peninsula.

TELEPHONE All Tunisian landline numbers have eight digits, the first two digits being the sub-regional prefix (covering a group of three to four geographically linked governorates); always dial all eight digits. To dial Tunisia from abroad, +216 is the international access code followed by the eight-digit number.

There are three phone networks in Tunisia: the local Tunisie Telecom (numbers beginning with 7/9), Qatari provider Ooredoo (numbers beginning with 2) and the French Orange Tunisie (numbers beginning with 3/5), all of which provide landlines, mobile numbers and home internet services. There are also two mobile virtual network operators (MVNO): Elissa and Nessma (numbers beginning with 4), piggybacking off the Tunisie Telecom and Ooredoo mobile networks respectively.

Inter-network call costs are much higher than intra-network call costs so, as in many parts of Africa, users arbitrage the system using dual or tri-SIM mobiles or by having more than one mobile phone. SIM cards are only a few dinars, but you will need to show your passport to get registered. You can then top up using scratch cards. Mobile data works out at about 1DT per GB. Theoretically, it should be possible to buy further credit online via the Tunisie network websites, but this service only accepts Tunisian-registered cards, and even then it does not always work. If you do not wish to queue for credit, use an online service like w mobilerecharge.com or w sobflous.tn to top-up using an international card.

Numbers beginning with 1 are government service numbers, such as 190 (ambulance), 193 (Garde Nationale), 197 (police) and 198 (fire). Dispatchers will not always speak English, but if you repeat the location and the service you require, they will usually get the message.

INTERNET Internet cafés (usually labelled as publinet) are widely available across Tunisia and very cheap, although you may find yourself accessing the internet through an ancient desktop PC. An easier solution is to find a regular café, restaurant or shisha bar that offers free Wi-Fi, or to buy a local SIM at the airport. All three providers operating in Tunisia offer these; I used Ooredoo during my time in Tunisia and found its coverage to be good across the country, but if venturing into the desert it pays to also have a Tunisie Telecom SIM to hand.

While there was widespread internet monitoring and censorship during the Ben Ali era, there seems to be less evidence of this today. In 2021 US human rights and democracy non-profit Freedom House noted that Tunisia's internet freedom score remained the highest in the MENA region, with no instances of politically motivated blocking during the reporting period. Onion Router and VPN services work fine in Tunisia.

POST La Poste Tunisienne (PTT) handles postage and affordable banking services in Tunisia and has locations all over the country (see w poste.tn for a list). It also has

GOVERNORATE DIALLING CODES

GOVERNORATE	AREA CODE
Ariana	70, 71 and 79
Béja	78
Ben Arous	70, 71 and 79
Bizerte	72
Gabès	75
Gafsa	76
Jendouba	78
Kairouan	77
Kasserine	77
Kebili	75
Kef	78
Mahdia	73
Manouba	70, 71 and 79
Medenine	75
Monastir	73
Nabeul	72
Sfax	74
Sidi Bouzid	76
Siliana	78
Sousse	73
Tataouine	75
Tozeur	76
Tunis	70, 71 and 79
Zaghouan	72

a separate parcel delivery service, Rapid-Poste (**w** rapidposte.poste.tn), which is ironic given its slow speed. Both keep complicated opening hours, varying between winter, summer (July and August) and Ramadan.

Owing to Tunisia's Byzantine import and export regulations, posting a parcel is a tricky affair that may involve quite a lot of time explaining to a Rapid-Poste agent exactly what you are sending out of the country. It is better not to seal the parcel before you arrive at the postal location, so that you can show the agent what is inside.

Receiving a parcel is even more difficult, and if you fall foul of the regulations your parcel will either be held at the post office until you go and negotiate/pay the import taxes, or held at one of the country's customs warehouses (such as next to Tunis-Carthage International Airport), forcing you to head down there and collect it. Note that while the processes here might seem a little arbitrary, there is unlikely to be outright corruption involved, and you should be able to pay the relevant fees and leave with your parcel eventually. Be sure to check with Tunisia's Customs Agency before posting anything to check the potential import tax implications (**w** douane.gov.tn).

Courier services such as DHL and FedEx are available, but much more expensive. If couriering a parcel into the country, be sure to note whether the courier will provide a door-to-door service, or whether it will hand your parcel over to a local partner for final delivery. Your parcel will have a much better chance of arriving at your front door promptly if it is not handed over to Rapid-Poste.

CULTURAL ETIQUETTE

APPEARANCE In Tunisia, cleanliness and neatness matter, especially in formal contexts. People are as smart as they can afford to be, and if you have to go to the police station or any other official building, shorts and flip-flops will not be acceptable. Outside of this context, or when visiting a mosque, you are unlikely to be told how to dress. Tunisians are used to foreigners in most parts of the country, and to foreigners walking around wearing all manner of clothing. How appropriate your outfit will be really depends on context: something you would wear at a beach resort in Sousse is probably going to be regarded somewhat more quizzically in Matmata or Tataouine.

COURTESY A certain amount of formality makes life run smoothly in Tunisia. You will see that there is much handshaking and kissing on the cheek. Entering an office or a meeting, or joining a group of friends, you should be sure to shake everyone's hand. With people you have come to know well, you kiss once on each cheek on meeting them, and probably on leaving them too. Even if there are ten people or more in a room, greet everyone with a handshake – though it may not be appropriate for men to shake hands with older, headscarf-wearing women, so use your common sense.

Going into a shop or at a bank or PTT counter, say *bonjour* or *sabah el khir*. To say thank you, you have a barrage of terms at your disposal in Tunisian, including *merci alayk*, *inshallah merci*, *barakallaw fik*, and the more formal *shokran*. To a young person serving in a shop or restaurant, you might say *inshallah farhatik* ('may you have a joyful wedding') to get a smile.

One final point: when it comes to getting on to public transport or in the immigration queues at most Tunisian airports, politeness often goes out of the window – so be ready to be assertive.

BEGGING Tunisia does not have the intense poverty of, say, Egypt, and there are few beggars visible in most of the areas frequented by tourists. You may come across people walking down traffic queues, selling packets of tissues or other small items. It is unlikely that they will be too persistent, but have a few small coins ready. Some polite Arabic phrases to refuse making a donation include *rebbi yenoub* ('may God act for you'), or *rebbi/Allah yusahel* ('may God make things easier').

MOSQUES Visitors to mosques (where permitted) and other religious buildings will normally be expected to remove their shoes, and cover-all garments will be available for hire to enable the required standard of dress to be met. Only a few mosques are visitable by non-Muslims in Tunisia, including the Great Mosque and Barber's Mosque in Kairouan (pages 279 and 280), and sometimes the colonnade of the Zitouna Mosque in Tunis (page 92). On no account go into a mosque uninvited; if you do happen to wander in accidentally (which can happen, as the purpose of some buildings is not always clear from the outside), you will be politely asked to leave by the caretaker or imam.

PROHIBITIONS Ignore all offers of drugs. Possession of narcotics is a very serious offence in Tunisia and there is a mandatory minimum jail sentence of one year for anyone caught in possession of any quantity of an illegal drug, including cannabis.

TIMEKEEPING Tunisian society, both in the private and public spheres, has a somewhat more relaxed attitude to timekeeping than in the West. However, it is still a good idea to turn up on time for your appointments, especially if you are meeting someone senior to you. Meetings are best held Monday to Thursday. During Ramadan, especially the last two weeks, timekeeping tends to become even more relaxed as people strive to combine work, fasting, large family meals and late-night socialising.

TIPPING Tipping in Tunisia is important for waiters and others in low-wage service sector jobs. In a restaurant, 10–15% is pretty standard. Taxi drivers generally do not expect to be tipped. With the growth of delivery apps such as Kool and Jumia, tipping culture is slowly spreading to food-delivery drivers, although again, it is not an expectation.

TRAVELLING POSITIVELY *JoAnna Haugen, founder of Rooted (w rootedstorytelling.com; RootedStorytelling)*

At the heart of responsible tourism is respect. Just as you'd expect people to be respectful if they visited your home, it's important to be mindful of how your actions impact the people and environment around you while you travel throughout Tunisia. As a responsible traveller, a good question to fall back as you journey through Tunisia (or any destination) is: If this was my home, how would I expect someone to behave?

Remain aware of your environmental footprint. Waste infrastructure isn't well developed in much of the country, so avoid creating excess rubbish. When possible, use reusable products like a water bottle or coffee cup and tote bag for shopping. Be mindful of water usage by keeping showers short and turn off lights and air conditioning when you leave your accommodation.

Take extra care to preserve Tunisia's historic landmarks and cultural heritage. Respect areas that have been roped off to visitors, don't walk on or touch fragile sites, and leave artefacts undisturbed. To protect natural landscapes, stay on marked or well-trodden trails. If you encounter wildlife while enjoying outdoor activities – leave it alone.

The people you interact with throughout Tunisia will undoubtedly leave a memorable impression on you, but keep in mind that you are a guest. Be aware of local customs and respond accordingly. This includes, for example, dressing modestly in appropriate situations and avoiding eating and drinking openly during Ramadan. Don't take photos of anyone without asking for permission first (importantly, get explicit permission from parents before taking photos of kids), and make sure you let people know if you plan to post those photos to social media.

LOCAL CHARITIES AND NGOS

Association Amal Pour la Famille et l'Enfant 71 286 372; e amalpourlafamille@hotmail.fr; amalpourlafamille. Works to support single mothers & their children & prevent the abandonment of children born out of wedlock.

Association Beyti e beity.tunisie@gmail.com; w beity-tunisie.org. An NGO helping victims of gender-based violence, including by providing emergency accommodation for women.

Centre Hippique Mahdia m 24 751 464; e gabi_incisa@yahoo.com; w mahdiahorses.com; centrehippiquemahdia. Italian founder Gabriella has been in Tunisia for over 30 years & runs this horseriding centre with a difference. Not only does it offer lessons for those wishing to learn to ride, but it also breeds rare Barb & Arabian horses, as well as Mogod ponies. The centre also offers animal-based therapy sessions for children. A worthy cause & well worth a visit!

C'est à Vous De Changer Bizerte e cvcbizerte@hotmail.com; changer.bizerte. Environmental youth organisation fighting to protect Tunisia's coastal spaces. Visitors can contact it to get involved with its work.

Didon m 52 878 878; e tunisie.didon@gmail.com; DIDONTN1. A youth-focused Tunisian NGO doing great work in cultural & socio-economic development & tackling youth unemployment.

Gaïa 70 527 440; e contact@fth-gaia.org; FTHSIDITHABET. A therapy farm for young people with disabilities, about 15km northwest of Tunis. It also offers education & vocational training for children with disabilities from low-income families, & produces organic products which you can purchase in its online shop: w fth-gaia.shop.

Mission Pawssible Animal Rescue e info@mission-pawssible.org; missionpaws. A project dedicated to helping animals in crisis situations, with a focus on North Africa & the Balkans. It does great work helping Tunisia's many street cats & street dogs & is always looking for volunteers.

Part Two

THE GUIDE

3

Grand Tunis

Tunisia's capital and seat of political power, Tunis exerts an outsized influence on the country's economy and culture. The greater metropolitan area, known as Grand Tunis, incorporates the governorates of Tunis, Ariana, Ben Arous and Manouba, and is home to more than 2.7 million Tunisians – almost a quarter of the country's population. The capital's complex history is visible all around: the area is home to two of Tunisia's eight UNESCO World Heritage attractions – the ancient Medina, its narrow alleyways packed with fountains, mosques, mausoleums, dars and street vendors of every stripe, and the vast archaeological site of Carthage – as well as a number of world-class museums and other attractions. You are also never far from the sea, with Grand Tunis offering a wide assortment of excellent beaches and waterfront restaurants. Though the city is sometimes treated as a transit point for those heading to the beach resorts and desert further south, it has much to offer prospective tourists, especially given the distinct vibe of its different neighbourhoods.

HISTORY

AN ANCIENT BATTLEGROUND As a natural harbour on the southern shores of the busy Mediterranean Sea, Tunis has been a site of invasion and occupation for thousands of years. The coastlines to the north and south, around Bizerte and Cap Bon, are littered with Aterian and Iberomaurusian sites from the Middle and Upper Palaeolithic. It therefore seems likely that these civilisations were present in the harbour around Tunis while moving along Tunisia's northeastern coast, even if detailed archaeological evidence is lacking. Given the city's useful coastal location, it is also likely that there was an Amazigh settlement in the Grand Tunis area well before the Phoenicians sailed over from Tyre and founded Carthage in 814BC. The etymology of the name Tunis, originally Tunes, indicates a Numidian Amazigh origin as many of their settlement names began with a 'T'.

Throughout its ancient history, Tunis had the misfortune of being next door to the bellicose city-state of Carthage, meaning that invaders wishing to attack Carthage would often attack Tunis first. This happened in 395BC, when Diodorus of Sicily tells us that following a Carthaginian defeat in Sicily, the local populations around Tynes (Tunis) took the opportunity to briefly seize the settlement. The tyrant Agathocles of Syracuse also managed to wrest control of the city from the Carthaginians in 310BC. In 256BC during the First Punic War, Tunis was captured by Roman Consul Marcus Atilius Regulus, although they were booted out the following year by Spartan mercenary Xanthippus of Carthage. The city was then besieged by Carthaginian general Hamilcar Barca in 238BC during the Mercenary War, which had erupted three years earlier when Carthage decided it was a good idea to not pay the agreed wages owed to tens of thousands of mercenaries who had fought for them during the First Punic War. In 204BC, during the Second Punic

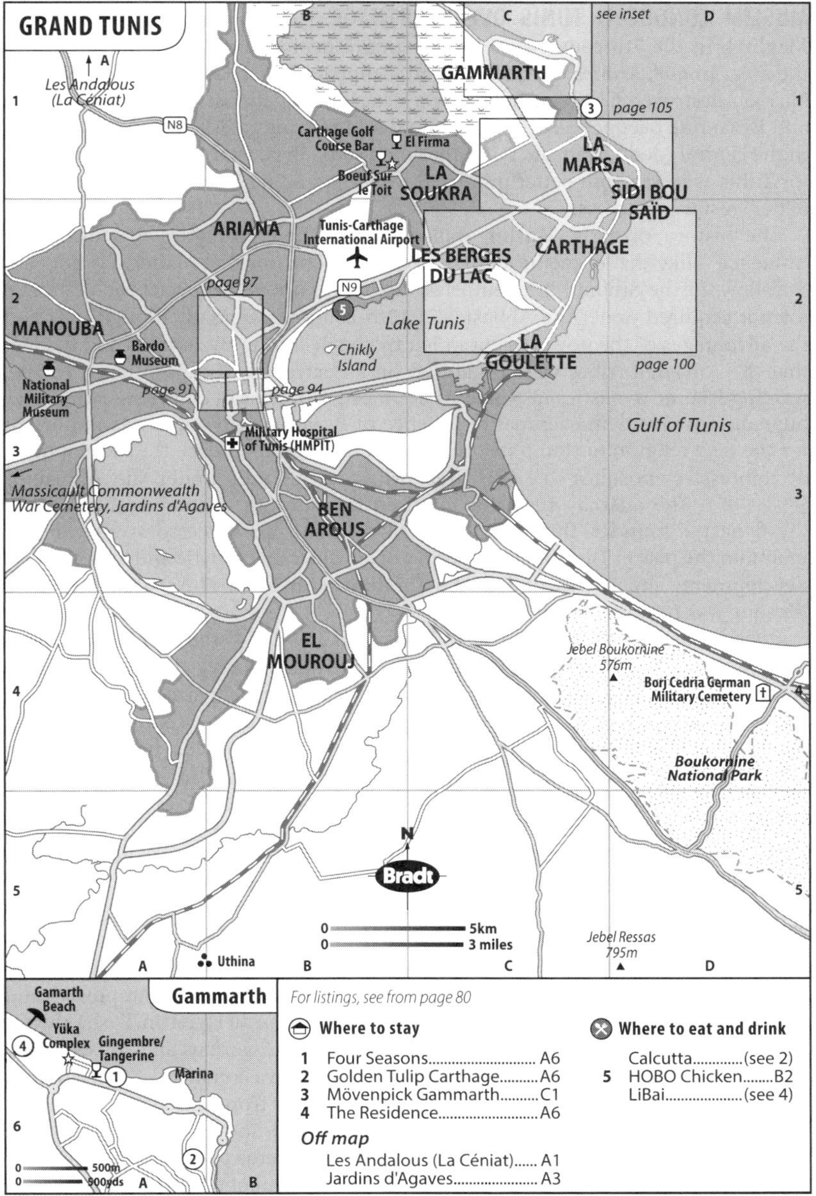

War, the Roman commander Scipio Africanus and King Masinissa of Numidia occupied Tunis as part of a wider campaign of conquest in Carthaginian territory. The whole area was attacked again and finally destroyed by the Romans under Scipio Africanus at the conclusion of the Third Punic War in 146BC. Despite all this destruction, the area was prosperous throughout Roman imperial and later Byzantine rule.

MUSLIM CONQUEST: TUNIS OVER CARTHAGE The Muslim conquest of the Maghreb in the 7th century AD brought more misfortune for the inhabitants of the area. In 698, armies of the Umayyad Caliphate under General Hassan ibn al-Nu'man destroyed Carthage following a siege, ending almost 750 years of Roman and Byzantine occupation. They were no doubt seeking to establish a strong point in the central Mediterranean, but rather than settle in coastal Carthage, they opted for Tunis as it was both better protected from marauding Byzantine fleets and had better freshwater access.

The history of early Muslim dynasties and their struggles for power and influence – like that of medieval dynasties in Europe, for that matter – is not easy to follow. In the 8th and 9th centuries, Islam had not yet assumed the definitive form it acquired under the Abbasids in 10th-century Baghdad. Though they had the advantages of the power vacuum left by the declining Byzantines and the fact that the Amazigh tribes were organised on an extremely localised basis, fragile, warring Islamic dynasties in North Africa faced problems of communicating over huge distances and an eventual resurgence of Byzantine power. It was important for the new religion to stamp its presence on the region – hence the development of impressive mosques like the Great Mosque in Tunis under the Aghlabids (794–905). The anarchy that characterised the late 8th century was ended by the dynasty's founder, Ibrahim Ibn Al-Aghlab, and his successors were able to maintain the peace. There began a period of considerable artistic and architectural development, and it was under Abu Ibrahim Ahmad (856–63) that the Great Mosque was restored.

It was under the rule of the Hafsid Dynasty (1230–1574) that Tunis blossomed, with more than 100,000 inhabitants within its walls. During the 13th and 14th centuries, the central part of the old city reached its present size. The town grew in importance through trade with southern Europe, and as a centre of Malekite learning. The Hafsid sultans, originally vassals of the Almohads, had to establish their legitimacy to rule, and one way to do this was through the strengthening of Islamic orthodoxy. They founded a number of *madrasas* or colleges where students of religion and law at the Zitouna Mosque were housed. By building a power base among a scholar class, the Hafsids thus hoped to counter the potentially dangerous leadership of Sufi saints based in the countryside.

THE 16TH CENTURY: OTTOMAN AND HABSBURG CONFLICT Between 1534 and 1574 the city went through a period of turbulence. At the time, the Mediterranean was the theatre of fierce conflicts between the expansionist European powers and the Ottoman Turks. The city was first attacked by Hızır Hayrettin Pasha, better known as the pirate Barbarossa, then captured by the Algerians and subsequently by Don Juan of Austria. It was only with the Turkish invasion in 1574 that a period of calm returned. The influx of 80,000 Muslim refugees from Andalusia at the start of the 17th century gave a renewed vitality to the city and its surroundings. The Andalusians were skilled farmers and gave a new impetus to the *chechia* industry (the manufacture of the felt hats that were exported throughout the Mediterranean for over three centuries).

Tunis was thus the capital of a minor Ottoman province. Links with Istanbul were always weak, however, and over the course of the 17th century a local dynasty emerged in the form of the descendants of a corsair adventurer. By the early 18th century, the citizens of Tunis had had enough of dynastic infighting, and they called upon one Hussein Ben Ali to restore peace and order. By the end of the 18th century, his descendants had themselves established dynastic rule.

COSMOPOLITAN TUNIS: 1800–1950 In the early 19th century, the beys did their best to keep up with the changes taking place on the northern side of the Mediterranean. The dangers facing the country became more apparent after the occupation of Algiers by France in 1830 and the increasing competition between the colonial powers. Despite the reforms initiated by Ahmed Bey (1837–55), and the efforts of reforming prime minister Kheireddine Pasha in the second half of the 19th century, pressure from the newly industrialising powers to the north grew. The city was to grow out of all recognition.

Epidemics in the early 19th century took a heavy toll among the local Muslim and Jewish populations. Even before the French declared their protectorate over Tunisia in 1881, there was an influx of Europeans, especially Italians and Sicilians. The Tunisian government granted concessions to Europeans in exchange for loans, and professional people moved in to manage the modern businesses. Poor Sicilian and Maltese immigrants provided the semi-skilled labour. A new neighbourhood began to take shape on reclaimed land to the east of the Medina, the future Ville Nouvelle. France built a fine new consulate (1860), and the foundations of the Cathédrale St-Vincent-de-Paul were laid. A British company financed the construction of a railway to La Marsa between 1874 and 1876.

In the 1880s, the French hesitated as to whether they should continue to extend their Ville Nouvelle to the east of the Medina. After all, it had a reputation as an insalubrious place, despite the sewage lines which had been put in by the municipality founded in 1857. A new coastal location was felt to be suitable. Carthage was out of the question, given the proximity of a beylical palace. Radès, on the coast south of Tunis, would have been ideal; however, the strength of the Italian community made such a move impossible. The Italians had interests in the British-funded railway line linking Tunis to La Marsa and the La Goulette port. Italian interests, namely one Mme Fasciotti, also held the concession for rubble removal and dumping, an important operation given the number of crumbling ramparts to be demolished and the value of the new infill land. Above all, the French had to placate Italian interests wherever possible, given the fact that the newly unified Kingdom of Italy had colonial designs too.

Thus, the city centre of Tunis as we know it today was built on reclaimed land to the east of the old Medina. Growth was rapid – one source mentions more than 800 new buildings going up between 1881 and 1894. As of 1860, the French had asserted economic authority in Tunisia, and between 1881 and 1900 they made their presence felt in physical terms. The old world of the Medina, its people's lives codified by Muslim and Jewish law, was marginalised. The Europeans who had lived in the old town in the 1880s gradually moved out, eventually followed by the wealthier Muslim notables and the increasingly Europeanised Jews.

The main symbols of the new French protectorate were in place by the end of the 1890s: a new barracks at the Kasbah (completed in 1898 but today demolished), the cathedral (completely rebuilt by 1897) and, most importantly, the modern port (completed in 1892).

In the first half of the 20th century, Tunis became a dual city. At its centre was the old town with its mosques and narrow streets, around which spread the new town. Business was concentrated in the Ville Nouvelle, and new residential areas were created – leafy Montfleury, southwest of the Medina, Lafayette, second home to the Jewish community with the large Art Deco Synagogue Daniel Osiris, the Cité Jardin and Mutuelleville.

WORLD WAR II AND THE GROWTH OF NATIONALISM Tunis was occupied by the Germans for six months during World War II. For both Axis and Allies, the city functioned as a staging post for supplies and troops. The port and parts of the city, notably Petite Sicile and the Kherba in the eastern Medina, were bombarded. After the war, which wrought considerable damage in the Tunisian countryside, immigration from the rural areas increased dramatically. The population of the Medina rose from 120,000 in 1936 to 230,000 in 1946. The Muslim bourgeoisie, increasingly westernised, sought homes in the new residential areas.

It was in the early 1950s that Tunis became a focus for an increasingly vocal nationalist movement. Happily, however, there was never much widespread violence, especially when compared with neighbouring Algeria. The independence movement was led by educated, urban Tunisians, many of them from the Sahel. Independence was quickly conceded by France in 1956.

RAPID CHANGES AFTER INDEPENDENCE: DEMOLITION AND EXPANSION The population of Greater Tunis rose rapidly in the 1950s, resulting in vast expansion into the surrounding countryside, often at the expense of good farming land. After independence, the Italian, Tunisian Jewish and French populations mainly departed, sometimes owing to official government policy, but often because of growing hostilities caused by geopolitical events (such as the Arab-Israeli Wars and the Bizerte Crisis). The city's Muslim population acquired the property left behind at knock-down prices or by squatting. The movement of the old Tunisoise families out of the Medina accelerated, and an influx of poor rural migrants brought about a huge change in the make-up of the oldest neighbourhoods. The great city residences were divided up as rooming houses or *oukalas*, in local parlance.

In the eyes of President Bourguiba, and indeed of many of the leading figures of the newly independent Tunisian Republic, the Medina was a symbol of past oppressions, and as such was to be swept away. In the early 1960s, there were great schemes for opening up an avenue to extend the main Avenue Bourguiba as far as the Zitouna Mosque. In the event, nothing was done – the Medina had far too many poor and potentially rebellious inhabitants that were too costly to rehouse in one go. Numerous demolitions took place on the southern and western sides of the Medina, however. The Kasbah barracks, most of the Sidi Abdallah gate and the walls from Bab el Assal at the northern end to the southern Bab el Fella were demolished and the modernist Maison du Parti was constructed on the new Kasbah esplanade, while excavations of the site revealed traces of the original Hafsid fortress. (The remains were later subsumed by a vast underground car park.) The city centre also saw its share of new buildings – the imposing Ministry of the Interior on the main avenue and three large new hotels: the blue tower of the Hotel Africa, the distinctive inverted pyramid of the (now sadly abandoned) Hotel du Lac, and the bulky Hotel International, at the junction of the Avenue de Paris and the Avenue Bourguiba.

21ST-CENTURY TUNIS: THE EVER-EXPANDING SUBURBS Tunis has continued to grow over the past decades. New residential areas appeared almost overnight, the most spectacular being the Berges du Lac, a set of modern business districts built on land reclaimed from the lagoon which separates Tunis from its coastal suburbs. Gammarth, Raoued and Les Jardins de Carthage have also seen significant expansion in recent years, although the downturn in tourism revenue caused by the Tunisian Revolution, the terror attacks of 2015 and the Covid-19 pandemic have left many hotels abandoned, and many construction projects half-finished.

Like any other Mediterranean town, Tunis is increasingly segregated in socio-economic terms. The poorest social groups tend to opt for self-built housing west of the city centre. It should be stressed, however, that Tunis does not have housing problems on anything like the scale of Casablanca's bidonvilles or the multi-occupancy of old cities like Fès.

GETTING THERE AND AWAY

BY AIR Tunis is a hub for domestic and international transport, although many holidaymakers prefer to fly directly into airports nearer the beach resorts (such as Djerba-Zarzis, Enfidha-Hammamet or Monastir Habib Bourguiba). Tunis-Carthage International Airport [71 B2] is on the N9 just north of Lake Tunis, less than 7km northeast of the Medina and around 11km from the coastal suburbs of La Marsa, Sidi Bou Saïd and Carthage. There are licensed taxis available outside arrivals; however, they have a bad reputation for trying to rip off newly arrived passengers, often quoting inflated prices in euros and trying to charge large fees for transporting your bags. You are better off having your hotel organise transport or downloading a ride-hailing app such as Bolt or Oto and using this to get into town, which should cost less than 15DT. It is also possible to take the number 635 and 35 buses, which leave from outside arrivals every half-hour between 06.00 and 18.00 (1DT) and terminate at Tunis Marine railway station [94 D2], from where you can take the TGM (page 76) to other parts of the city. Tickets can be bought on the bus in cash.

BY ROAD Tunis sits at the centre of Tunisia's motorway network, with the A1 highway running southwards as far as Gabès, the A3 heading westwards as far as Bou Salem and the A4 heading northwards to Bizerte. Note that the A1 is a toll road, payable in cash, although fees for each section are rarely above 2DT for a car. There are also fixed and mobile speed cameras along sections of all three highways. Parking in central Tunis is a nightmare, so try to arrange with your hotel to have a space ready for your arrival. Paid street parking is somewhat more plentiful in La Marsa, Sidi Bou Saïd, Gammarth and Carthage, usually costing 1–2DT per hour with a 2-hour maximum stay. Make sure you have plenty of coins handy!

Louages can drop you at the main stops of Moncef Bey (if coming from the south) or Gare Routière Nord (if coming from the north or west). You can also take an SNTRI inter-governorate bus (page 55); the main hubs in Tunis are at Gare Routière Nord (Bab Saâdoun) and Gare Routière Sud (Bab Alioua).

BY RAIL The main SNCFT train station is Gare de Tunis [94 B4], 500m south of the Théâtre Municipal. Cheap but infrequent services run from as far south as Tozeur and Gabès, as far west as El Kef and Ghardimaou and as far north as Bizerte. Getting a train into Tunis puts you in the very heart of the action, with the Medina less than 500m to the west.

BY FERRY The main port for passenger ferries is in La Goulette [100 D4], 12km east of the city centre; Corsica Linea, Compagnie Tunisienne de Navigation, Grandi Navi Veloci and Grimaldi Lines run services to Italy and France, specifically Genoa, Palermo, Salerno, Civitavecchia and Marseille. They have ticket offices in Tunis and the port. For more details on arriving by ferry, see page 43.

ORIENTATION

Tunisia's capital lies on the western shores of **Lake Tunis**. A useful point of reference for the centre is tree-lined **Avenue Habib Bourguiba**, which has a large clock tower at its eastern end nearest the lake and stretches westwards to the Medina's entrance. It is home to important government buildings, embassies, the Cathédrale St-Vincent-de-Paul and numerous historic Art Nouveau buildings. **Belvedere Park**, 2km north of Avenue Habib Bourguiba, and the **Jellaz Cemetery**, 1.4km south, mark the extremities of the central area you will likely wish to explore on foot. The far older **Medina** sits just to the west; with its narrow alleyways, it is a much easier place to get lost. Here, the busy **Bab el Bhar**, with its fountain and street vendors, marks the eastern entrance most visitors use, which eventually leads you to the Zitouna Mosque in the heart of the Medina. The world-famous **Bardo Museum** sits behind the Medina, a full 4km to the west of Avenue Habib Bourguiba.

Venturing eastwards from the centre towards Tunis-Carthage Airport, you will first encounter the modern developments of **Lac 1** and **Lac 2** (officially Les Berges du Lac), named because of their lakefront location. To the north of Lac 2 is the residential area of **La Soukra**, from where it is another 5km east to the Gulf of Tunis, with the affluent neighbourhoods of **Gammarth**, **La Marsa**, **Sidi Bou Saïd**, **Carthage** and the port of **La Goulette** dotted along the coast from north to south.

GETTING AROUND

BY RAIL The 25km, SNCFT-run line heads southeast along the coast from Tunis as far as Erriadh, just over the border in Nabeul Governorate. Travellers might find this line useful for reaching Boukornine National Park (nearest station Hammam-Lif – page 109) or the Borj Cedria Cemetery (nearest station Borj Cedria – page 109).

BY METRO Tunis's light-rail system (*metro léger*) is run by the Société des Transports de Tunis (Transtu; w transtu.tn). There are six lines radiating out from the Ville Nouvelle: Line 1 heads southeast to Ben Arous; Line 2 northwards to Ariana; Lines 3 and 5 northwest to Ibn Khaldoun and Intilaka respectively; Line 4 westwards to Kheireddine in Manouba; and Line 6 southwards to El Mourouj. For La Goulette, Carthage, Sidi Bou Saïd or La Marsa, you will need the Tunis–Goulette–Marsa (TGM) light rail, which was the first railway in Tunisia, inaugurated in 1872.

Metro and TGM tickets must be purchased before travel at either the main stations or a post office. Journeys are priced by stops travelled, with short journeys costing less than 1DT.

BY BUS The public bus network in Grand Tunis is also run by Transtu. Some of its longest lines even venture into the northern sections of Zaghouan, the far east of Béja and the southeast of Bizerte Governorate, although for most inter-governorate travel you will want an SNTRI bus (page 55). The buses are cheap and often overloaded during rush hour. Some lines begin service before 05.00 and run until after 23.00. A map of all lines is available at w opengeodata-ageos-tunisie.hub.arcgis.com/datasets/bus-stations-lignes-transtu-tunis/explore. The main bus station downtown is Gare Barcelone [94 B3], next to the train station. There is also a useful bus station at Tunis Marine, where the TGM light rail terminates, if you wish to head east to Carthage, La Marsa and La Goulette.

BY TAXI Official taxis (page 55) can be found all over Tunis. Their condition varies, but the majority are roadworthy with seat belts. Ride-hailing apps such as Bolt and Oto also operate in the city.

BY BICYCLE Central Tunis does not have a cycling culture and, given the standards of driving, this is unsurprising. However, it is not uncommon to see people heading out of the city for weekend rides in the countryside, and cycling in the suburbs around the Gulf of Tunis is a much more relaxing experience. Buying spare parts is not a problem from any of the large sports stores dotted around Tunis (such as Decathlon). Bike-hire companies include:

Jhonny Bikes [107 B3] Av de la Mosquée, La Marsa; e contact@jhonnybikes.tn; f JhonnyBikes; ⌚ 10.00–22.00 Tue–Sun, 10.00–19.00 Mon. Bike rental & organised tours from 15DT.
Le Lemon Tour [100 E2] 6 Rue Mathos, Carthage; w lelemontour.com; ⌚ 09.00–18.00 daily. A well-established outfit offering half-/full-day rentals for 15/25DT.
Nomadic Bike 2 Rue Senegal; ☎ 21 584 447; f selsemnomadicbike; ⌚ 07.00–late daily. This wood-fronted café just north of the Bardo Museum offers rental & organises cycling trips around the country via its Facebook page.
Vélorution Tunisie 16 Av Tahar Ben Achour; w velorutiontunisie.com; ⌚ 10.00–19.00 daily. A well-established association promoting bicycle use in Tunisia, organising cycling events throughout the country (including bike tours of the Medina!).

TOURIST INFORMATION AND TOUR OPERATORS

The **Office National du Tourisme Tunisien (ONTT)** has three offices in Tunis, the most useful of which is near the clock tower at the top of Habib Bourguiba Avenue [94 C2] (⌚ 08.00–13.00 & 14.00–17.00 Mon–Fri). They are able to provide a limited selection of maps and site recommendations.

Most of the tour operators listed on page 40 can organise Tunis-specific itineraries for visitors, as can the following:

✷ **Let's Go Sailing Tunisia** m 23 304 023; f letsgosailingtunisia; e sofboud@yahoo.fr. The affable Captain Sofiane charters his 12m yacht from Sidi Bou Said harbour for up to 7 passengers, offering day trips over to Korbous, as well as more adventurous sails over to La Galite, Zembra and even Pantelleria! Highly recommended.
Central Tunis e contact@centraltunis.com; f centraltunis. This art collective organises great thematic tours via its Facebook page, including very popular street-food walking tours.
Doolesha w doolesha.net. 'Doolesha' is an old Tunisian word meaning to 'stroll at a slow pace for pleasure'. This small collective project, consisting mainly of architects, offers walking tours of the Medina which blend stories old & new with architecture, artisanal crafts & modern Medina life to give a deep understanding of this UNESCO World Heritage Site & the people who live here.
✷ **Mohamed Nabli** m 23 332 308; e mohamednabli.med78@gmail.com, nabli.med78@gmail.com. If there is a more knowledgeable guide when it comes to the Medina, I have yet to meet them! Through his network of contacts, he is able to showcase parts of the Medina that would be off-limits to other visitors. Speaks perfect English as well as numerous other languages.

WHERE TO STAY

Grand Tunis offers a wealth of accommodation options, both in terms of style and location. The Medina itself is a microcosm of this, with everything from luxuriously restored traditional dars to bargain backpacker hostels. If you do not fancy navigating its winding streets, then two good options are downtown or Ville Nouvelle, where there are also a number of international chain hotels. Those with bigger budgets may want to consider the luxurious dars in Carthage, La Marsa and Sidi Bou Saïd, while Lac 2 and Gammarth also offer plenty of good business-style hotels.

MEDINA

Luxury

Dar 24 [91 B2] (3 rooms) 24 Rue Sidi Ibrahim; m 99 799 617; e iadhoum@yahoo.fr. This renovated, 18th-century 3-bedroom home is available for exclusive booking through Airbnb, though individual B&B rooms are also available. 1 room has a private terrace offering beautiful views of the Sidi Mehrez Mosque & Zaouia Sidi Brahim Riahi. **$$$$$**

Dar El Jeld [91 B3] (16 rooms) 5–10 Rue Jeld; 70 016 190; w dareljeld.com. A luxurious boutique hotel located next to the covered bazaar. Offers spacious & modern suites as well as a spa & 1 of the medina's most popular restaurants (page 81). **$$$$$**

Palais Bayram [91 C4] (15 rooms) 6 Rue des Andalous; 31 393 393; m 58 514 415; w palaisbayram.com. Originally the residence of the Ottoman Hanafi Grand Muftis in the 17th century, this luxurious palace barely 100m from the Zitouna Mosque was intricately restored between 2005 & 2014, now offering a unique stay with a hammam & spa. **$$$$$**

Upmarket

✷ **Dar Ben-Gacem Kahia** [91 A2] (8 rooms) 16 Rue Kahia; 71 573 086; w darbengacem.com. A new addition to the Dar Ben-Gacem offering & providing similarly excellent levels of service. It has a spectacular rooftop & hosts monthly culinary & cultural events. **$$$$**

✷ **Dar Ben-Gacem Pasha** [91 B3] (7 rooms) 38 Rue du Pacha; 71 563 742; w darbengacem.com. Located in a renovated 17th-century building, originally the home of artisanal perfumers, with traditionally furnished rooms & local crafts on display. **$$$$**

Dar El Medina [91 B3] (12 rooms) 64 Rue Sidi Ben Arous; 71 563 022; w darelmedina.tn. Traditionally decorated en-suite rooms with a panoramic rooftop terrace. **$$$$**

Hotel Royal Victoria [91 D3] (39 rooms) 5 Pl de la Victoire; 71 320 066; w hotel-royalvictoria.com. Formerly the British Consulate in Tunis (1662–2004), this historic hotel is conveniently located at the eastern Bab el Bhar gate, meaning you are walking distance from both the ancient Medina & the more modern amenities on Av Habib Bourguiba. As you would expect, it is all very opulent with plenty of gold leaf everywhere. Some of the rooms have small balconies overlooking Bab el Bhar. **$$$$**

La Chambre Bleu Tunis [91 B3] (3 rooms) 24 Rue du Diwan; m 22 579 602; w lachambrebleue.net. Former home of the bey of Tunis's war minister in the mid 19th century, this boutique hotel with Italian influences & vintage furniture offers 3 very different rooms, 1 of which used to be the stables of the traditional home. **$$$$**

Mid-range

Dar Ya [91 B3] (13 rooms) 6 Impasse de la Carrière; m 22 880 044; e contact@dar-ya.net; f DarYaTunis. Cosy rooms (both private & dorms) with AC & shared bathrooms in a very central location. Friendly service & great rooftop views of the surrounding Medina. **$$$**

Budget and shoestring

Hotel el Qods [94 A2] (8 rooms) Rue des Tanneurs; 71 340 404; f Elqoods. Rooms have AC & TV, with communal bathrooms. It's basic but good value & a stone's throw from the Medina's east gate. **$$**

Auberge de Jeunesse [91 B3] (40 beds) 25 Rue Essaida Ajoula; 71 574 884; m 98 578 638; f AubergeDeLaMedinaDeTunis. Recently renovated dorms sleeping 2–10 in a restored dar. The dome-covered main courtyard is beautiful. B/fast available. **$**

DOWNTOWN AND VILLE NOUVELLE

Upmarket

✷ **DownTown Tunis Hotel** [97 C3] (57 rooms) 13 Rue de Medine; 71 790 216; w tunisdowntown.com. Well situated near Pl Pasteur & Belvedere Park, this smart, modern hotel offers continental b/fast, business centre, free Wi-Fi, airport transfers & very convenient underground parking. **$$$$**

Hôtel Belvédère Fourati [97 C4] (69 rooms) 10 Av des États-Unis; 71 783 133, 71 782 214; w hotelbelvederetunis.com. This perennial traveller favourite is conveniently located within walking distance from most of the city-centre tourist sights & offers great views of Tunis from the 8th-floor terrace. **$$$$**

Villa Les Palmes [97 C4] (4 rooms) 78 Av Mohamed V; m 25 442 349; w villalespalmes.com. Dating from 1907, this guesthouse with a tree-filled garden offers simply & tastefully decorated rooms; 1 with a balcony. **$$$$**

Mid-range

Ambassadeurs Hotel [97 B4] (145 rooms) 75 Av Taïeb Mhiri; ☎ 71 846 000; w ambassadeurs-hotel.tn. On the road opposite the zoo, this is a cheap option given the central location, but some rooms have noise issues. **$$$**

Budget and shoestring

Grand Hôtel de France [94 A3] (12 rooms) 8 Rue Mustapha M'barek; ☎ 71 324 991. This faded colonial-era hotel is a bargain, especially as you can reduce the price further by opting for a room that uses the communal showers or doesn't have AC. **$$**

CARTHAGE

Carthage Hill [105 D4] (5 rooms) 1 Av El Esfizari; m 52 535 453; w carthagehill.com. A unique set-up, with 3 modern suites in a wooden cabin, 1 stone bungalow & 2 bedrooms in the main house. A large property with ample gardens, backed by wheat fields to the south; everything feels very rural, despite being well located for access to the Antonine Baths & the Punic Ports. **$$$$$**

Villa Didon [100 E1] (11 rooms) Rue Mendes France; ☎ 71 733 433; w villadidoncarthage.com. Luxurious suites larger than most apts in London, where you can sit in the bath & overlook the Mediterranean. Also an excellent spa & restaurant/bar (page 87) on the ground floor, popular with the Instagram crowd. **$$$$$**

SIDI BOU SAÏD

Luxury

La Villa Bleue [105 C1] (13 rooms) 68 Rue Kennedy; ☎ 71 742 000; w lavillableuesidibousaid.com. Perched on top of Sidi Bou Saïd hill, this boutique luxury hotel was originally built in 1991 as a residential house by architect Tarek Ben Miled. Rooms, many with sea views, blend the traditional Arab-Andalusian architectural features of the original home with some modern touches. Also has an excellent restaurant (page 83). **$$$$$**

Maison Dedine [105 G4] (5 rooms) 3 Av Kennedy; m 23 645 000; w maisondedine.com. Offering unparalleled views of the Bay of Tunis & Sidi Bou Saïd port, this award-winning hotel is part of the Small Luxury Hotels of the World community – & it is easy to see why. It has a 12m infinity pool, 4 rooftop terraces & a signature dinner prepared by its chef Luc Pasquier. A very short walk from both the port & Sidi Bou Saïd village. **$$$$$**

Upmarket

Hotel Bou Fares [105 B1] (10 rooms) 15 Rue Sidi Boufares; ☎ 71 740 091; w hotelboufares.com. Down a quiet side street, assorted small rooms range from beautifully tiled to whitewashed walls & vaulted roofs, all around a verdant courtyard. **$$$$**

Hotel Dar Said [105 B1] (24 rooms) Rue Toumi; ☎ 71 729 666; w darsaid.com.tn. Rooms are distributed across 4 patios, built in traditional Arab-Andalusian architectural style, with an attractive pool area that is sometimes open to non-residents. Also offers a hammam & an attractive b/fast buffet. **$$$$**

Mid-range

Hotel Sidi Bou Saïd [105 F3] (22 rooms) Av Sidi Dhrif; ☎ 71 746 775; f hotelsidibousaid. Though rooms are a little dated, this is good value for money & in a great location halfway up the hill between Sidi Bou Saïd & La Marsa. Its terrace offers a superb view of Tunis by night. **$$$**

LA MARSA

Luxury

Dar El Marsa [107 D1] (29 rooms) 75 Av Habib Bourguiba; ☎ 71 728 000; w darelmarsa.com. In a prime location overlooking La Marsa beach, with a great rooftop bar (page 87) & pool that hosts live jazz nights. All rooms are modern with sea views. Spa with hammam, sauna & fitness centre. **$$$$$**

Upmarket

Dar Corniche la Marsa [107 G2] (5 rooms) 3 Rue Abou Tammam; m 97 652 561; w darcornichelamarsa.com. An adults-only boutique hotel metres from the beach, offering breath-taking views of the Mediterranean from 3 of the rooms as well as from the terrace & pool. B/fast includes local specialities such as *mlawi* (Tunisian flatbread), *zrir* (a sesame butter & nut dessert) & *assida bidha* (a b/fast sweet made of fine semolina & water). **$$$$**

Dar Ennassim [105 E3] (9 rooms) 4 Rue du Bigaradier; m 50 815 920, 22 313 331; e darelannabi@yahoo.fr. A sumptuously decorated traditional guesthouse with marble floors, huge beds & panoramic terraces. Also has a rooftop pool. **$$$$**

Dar Jaafar [105 E1] (3 rooms) 6 Bis Rue Ali Riahi; m 53 319 931; e ais.lamine@gmail.com, contact@dar-jaafar.com; also available on Airbnb. Very well located in the heart of La Marsa's residential area & pet friendly, this stylishly decorated home with well-equipped kitchen, AC & private terrace can be rented as a whole. Its website also offers other accommodation options in the area owned by the landlord. **$$$$**

Dar Marsa Cubes [105 E1] (5 rooms) Rue Mondher Ben Ammar; m 55 160 000; w dar-marsa-cubes.com. A stone's throw from the beach, this 19th-century house has characterful rooms individually decorated in the Moorish style, plus swimming pool & a terrace with excellent sea views. **$$$$**

Dar Souad [105 D2] (6 rooms) 56 Av Zine Ben Achour; m 22 800 622; e contact@darsouad.net; w darsouad.net. Set in a 19th-century home, with a very green courtyard & excellent b/fasts of homemade breads, jams, granola, fresh fruit, yoghurt & shakshuka. **$$$$**

Mid-range

The 18 Guest House [107 F2] (2 rooms) 18 Rue d'Amérique; m 98 695 667; f. The cheapest decent bed in La Marsa (unless you jump on Airbnb); simple rooms with AC, a nice garden & friendly hosts. Only a 70m walk down some stairs to the beach. **$$$**

GAMMARTH

Luxury

Four Seasons [71 A6] (203 rooms) Zone Touristique; ☎ 31 260 001; w fourseasons.com/tunis. Leading the pack in terms of Gammarth's 5-star hotels, & with a price tag to match, offering 5 restaurants & bars, private beach & a very popular spa. **$$$$$**

Mövenpick Gammarth [71 C1] (119 rooms) Av Taïeb Mhiri; ☎ 71 741 444; e hotel.gammarth.sales@movenpick.com; f movenpickgammarth. A strong offering from Mövenpick at the foot of the Gammarth hills, featuring Kallisti spa, fitness centre, private beach, indoor & outdoor pools as well as sea views from the 3 restaurants & lobby lounge. Rooms of a very high standard. **$$$$$**

✷ ⚑ **The Residence** [71 A6] (170 rooms) Rue de la Côte d'Ivoire; ☎ 71 910 101; w cenizaro.com/theresidence/tunis. Opened in 1996, The Residence represents great value in this category & also offers the cheapest day passes if you wish to use only the pool & beach facilities. Features a 4,000m² Thalasso spa, private beach & an excellent 18-hole golf course, plus high-end Mediterranean, Tunisian & Chinese restaurants (page 82) & pool bar. Rooms are well-appointed, some with balconies overlooking the pool. **$$$$$**

Les Andalous (La Céniat) [71 A1] (6 rooms) ⊕ 36.936942, 10.143176; m 20 202 233; e contact@lesandalous.com; w lesandalous.com; f. Around 10km northwest of Gammarth, over into Ariana Governorate, this lovingly restored colonial-era farm offers a restaurant, pool, horseriding & hiking. Events such as gastronomic experiences & yoga retreats are advertised on its Facebook page. **$$$$–$$$$$**

Upmarket

Golden Tulip Carthage [71 A6] (264 rooms) Av de la Promenade; ☎ 71 913 000; e info@goldencarthage.com; w goldencarthage.com. Situated in a sprawling compound that is still home to numerous foreign diplomats, this was once one of the most popular luxury hotels in Tunis. These days it feels a little jaded, but the faux Roman ruins & gorgeous sea views are still nothing to be sniffed at. Beloved of business travellers, Covid-19 quarantine guests & US military contractors alike, it's certainly an unusual crowd. Also (bizarrely) home to one of the best Indian restaurants in the country: Calcutta (page 83). **$$$$**

WHERE TO EAT AND DRINK

Tunis is undoubtedly the gastronomic capital of Tunisia. The dizzying variety of cuisines and price ranges here, from street food in the Medina to five-star haute cuisine overlooking the Mediterranean, cannot be found anywhere else in the country. Your main options for good food are either going to be in the centre (including the Medina) or in one of the eastern suburbs, each of which has its own style of eatery. Given the cheap and plentiful taxis, distance from your accommodation should be no barrier to trying somewhere new.

For those on a budget, the Medina is filled with small holes in the wall that will sell you a piping hot baguette farcie for a couple of dinars. Likewise, the main Avenue Habib Bourguiba strip between the clock tower and the Medina entrance of Bab el Bhar has several Tunisian fast-food outlets, and also offers kebabs and various Turkish or Lebanese wraps. There are plenty of cheap food vendors dotted in the eastern suburbs, especially in crowded areas such as La Marsa market and the La Goulette waterfront.

MEDINA

Expensive

Dar El Jeld [91 B3] 5–10 Rue Jeld; 70 016 190; e contact@dareljeld.com; w dareljeld.com; 12.30–14.30 & 19.00–22.00 Mon–Sat. Next door to the dar of the same name (page 78) & open for over 30 years, this elegant, traditional restaurant has a stunning candle-lit courtyard & offers great Tunisian cuisine alongside a good assortment of local wines. Booking recommended, especially on w/ends. $$$$–$$$$$

Above average

El Ali Restaurant & Café [91 C4] 45 Rue Jamaâ Ezzitouna; m 23 811 511; f ElAliRestoEtCafeCulturel; 08.00–20.00 Mon–Sat. Very popular eatery in the Medina, set in a 16th-century building & offering varied Mediterranean & Tunisian fare. $$$$

Restaurant Dar Slah [91 C3] 145 Rue de la Kasbah; 71 261 026; m 58 261 026; w darslah.com; noon–15.30 Mon–Sat. Chef Sadri Smoali heads to the market in the Medina to select fresh ingredients for the traditional & ever-changing daily lunch menu that includes the like of couscous *au osban* (with tripe) & *gnawia* (okra ragout). $$$$

Mid-range

Café Mrabet [91 C4] 27 Souk Ettrouk; 93 420 895; f elmrabettunis; 08.00–21.00 Mon–Sat, 08.00–20.00 Sun. This former saint's shrine is now a café with a richly decorated interior & an attractive glass-roof terrace that offers views of the Zitouna Mosque minaret. Good Tunisian fare, & a decent place to stop for a Turkish coffee during a tour of the Medina. $$$

Dar Belhadj [91 C4] 17 Rue des Tamis; 71 200 894; m 98 362 320; f Darbelhadj1; noon–15.30 & 19.00–22.00 Mon–Sat. Fine Tunisian dining in the heart of the Medina, sometimes with live traditional music. $$$

✷ **Fondouk El Attarine** [91 C4] 9 Souk El Attarine; 71 322 244; e contact@fondoukelattarine.com; f; 10.00–18.00 Mon–Sat. Delicious traditional cuisine with great service, set in a former caravanserai for perfume traders. No-nonsense chalkboard menu which features a few great starters (try the *chorba*), & usually a couscous of the day plus a lamb or fish dish. Also has a handicraft shop & very clean toilets, which is a rarity in the Medina. $$$

DOWNTOWN AND VILLE NOUVELLE

Expensive

L'Astragale [97 C2] 17 Av Charles Nicolle; 71 785 080; m 20 328 639; f restaurant.lastragale; noon–14.45 & 20.00–22.00 Mon–Fri, 20.00–22.00 Sat. Mediterranean haute cuisine with some excellent meat & seafood dishes, & a beautiful courtyard seating area. $$$$$

Above average

La Salle à Manger [97 C3] 3 Rue Imam Sahnoun; 71 793 283; f salleamangerpageofficielle; noon–15.00 & 18.30–00.30 Mon–Sat. French & Italian cuisine with an excellent international wine list. Specialities include spaghetti alla bottarga, octopus carpaccio & tournedos rossini. $$$$

Mid-range

Restaurant El-Walima [97 C5] 35 Rue du Liban; 71 840 309; m 96 349 554; f; 10.00–15.30 daily. Fine Tunisian dining, for lunch only, with an interior fit for the Beys of Tunis (which is ironic, given that this restaurant is run by one of their descendants). $$$

RAFRAM'S RESTAURANT RECOMMENDATIONS

Based in La Goulette, Rafram Chaddad (Instagram @rafram_x) is a Jewish-Tunisian artist and food expert with a particular interest in the country's Jewish-Arab cuisine. These are his tips on the best restaurants to visit for an authentic local experience.

DOWNTOWN

Boléro [94 B3] 6 Rue de Greece; m 20 322 747; ⌚ 08.00–18.00 Mon–Sat. Filled wooden furniture & cigarette smoke, this place feels like no more than an old pub. But don't be put off – it serves decent Tunisian food & has a lot of old Tunis charm. $$$

Restaurant Chez Slah [94 C2] 14 Rue Pierre de Coubertin; ☎ 71 258 588; ⌚ 11.00–23.00 daily. Old-school Tunisian restaurant with a great fish selection – it never fails. $$$

Restaurant La Mamma [94 C2] 11 Rue de Marseille; ☎ 36 117 688; ⌚ noon–late Mon–Sat. Despite the slightly seedy façade, this Italian-Tunisian restaurant serves good pizza every other day & a great selection of seafood pasta, all served with spicy Tunisian sauce. $$$

Kafteji Douiri [94 A3] Rue de Suède; m 21 099 993; ⌚ 07.00–14.00 Mon–Sat. This eatery is famed across Tunisia for one thing: its *kafteji* – a street-food dish made of fried vegetables with eggs & served with chips. You pay at the till take a number & wait – sometimes for as long as an hour, but that gives you time to stroll in the Municipal Market nearby before coming back to eat. $$

CARTHAGE, LA GOULETTE AND LA MARSA

Oiseau Bleu [100 E3] Rue El Jahedh, La Goulette; m 23 563 616; ⌚ noon–22.00 Sat–Thu. A tavern by the sea, usually occupied by drunk painters. Every Sun it hosts a live music show & you can grab some grilled seafood between your beers. $$$$

Restaurant L'Orient [94 B2] Rue Ali Bah Hamba; ☎ 71 252 061; e hatemhentati700@gmail.com; f HHATEMLORIENT; ⌚ 11.00–late daily. A bustling downtown seafood restaurant, full of smoke & Celtia beers. $$$

EASTERN SUBURBS

Expensive

Dar Zarrouk [105 B1] Rue Hédi Zarrouk, Sidi Bou Saïd; ☎ 71 740 591; e restaurant@darzarrouk.tn; f restaurantDarZarrouk; ⌚ 12.30–23.00 Tue–Sun. The former home of the former Mayor of Tunis is a good location for (expensive) outdoor dining when it is warm enough, thanks to the sea views. Good Tunisian-Mediterranean fare, hit-&-miss service with a mainly Tunisian wine list. The inner courtyard also hosts live music nights. $$$$$

La Closerie [105 B4] Rue Ibn El Jazzar, La Soukra; ☎ 70 938 537; w lacloserie.tn; f Lacloserietunis; ⌚ midnight–04.00 Tue–Sun. If you've ever fancied dining at the 46th-best restaurant in the Middle East & North Africa, then you're in luck. The award-winning La Closerie serves gourmet Italian-Mediterranean cuisine, has a fancy wine list & a bar/lounge that is very popular with the young, hip Tunisian crowd. Booking highly advised at w/ends. $$$$$

Le Golfe [105 E1] 5 Rue El Arbi Zarrouk, La Marsa; ☎ 71 748 219; w legolfe.net; f legolferestaurant; ⌚ noon–midnight daily. Since 1955, this Mediterranean restaurant right on the beach has served excellent steaks, a good seafood selection & an extensive international wine list. The place to be seen, whether you are a Tunisian celebrity or foreign diplomat, so expect plenty of people Instagramming their octopus carpaccio. $$$$$

LiBai [71 A6] Rue de la Côte d'Ivoire, Gammarth; ☎ 71 910 101; ⌚ 19.00–midnight daily. Inside The Residence luxury hotel (page 80), this is one of the most expensive Chinese restaurants I have

Restaurant Le Punique [100 E2] Rue Hannibal, Carthage; 71 730 786; 10.00–23.00 daily. Popular eatery with a great selection of seafood & *spaghetti aux fruits de mer*. It has a pleasant balcony on which to enjoy a beer. $$$–$$$$

L'Arbre à Couscous [107 A4] 3 Rue Mami, La Marsa; 71 727 190; f arbreacouscous; noon–15.00 Mon–Sat. Great place for homemade couscous with many options, including a daily special which is published on Facebook. $$$

Restaurant Flouka [100 D4] Av Franklin Roosevelt, La Goulette; m 23 932 217; noon–22.30 Wed–Mon. Good choice if you want the classic La Goulette experience of *poisson complet*. Choose between cultured *karus* (sea bass) or *warka* (sea bream), served after a selection of starters including brik, *salade meschwia* (salad of roast peppers) & *tastira* (another roast veggie salad), all for a very reasonable price. $$$

Restaurant La Victoire (Razgalla) [100 D4] Av Franklin Roosevelt, La Goulette; 71 735 398; noon–22.30 daily. One of La Goulette's many good fish restaurants, Razgalla is one of the oldest establishments & has a decent selection of wild fish. Finish off with the *granité au citron*. $$$

Le Saf Saf [107 D2] Pl du Saf Saf, La Marsa; m 29 349 001; f le.safsaf; 07.00–23.00 Mon–Thu, 07.00–01.00 Fri–Sun. Known across the country, this coffee shop cum restaurant is a popular place for older Tunisians to sit under the tree & talk politics. Don't miss the homemade brik. $$

Lotfi El Khal [100 E2] Av Hédi Chaker, in front of the old mosque; 10.00–14.00 daily. If you are looking for a very local experience, head here to enjoy two of the country's most popular staple foods: the Tunisian sandwich (*cascroute tounsi*) & the Tunisian plate (*Shan tounsi*). Both come with tuna, eggs, potatoes, olives, capers, harissa & fresh vegetables. This is one of the best places in Tunisia, so go early! $$

ever eaten at – which is impressive, given the usual low cost of food in Tunisia – but it certainly is delicious, especially the squid salad with Chinese vermicelli & the Cantonese-style sautéed duck breast. $$$$$

La Table du Chef [100 A2] Rue du Lac Huron, Les Berges du Lac; 36 421 000; e hotel.dulactunis@movenpick.com; 12.30–23.00 daily. Inside the opulent Mövenpick in Lac 1, this offers an atelier dining experience where you can watch the chefs at work in their open kitchen, with one of the best grills in Tunis. No alcohol served, but has a list of fancy non-alcoholic cocktails. $$$$

Above average

✷ **Calcutta** [71 A6] Av de la Promenade, inside the Golden Tulip compound; 71 913 000; e info@goldencarthage.com; f Calcuttagoldentulip; 19.00–23.30 daily. Authentic Indian food is very hard to find in Tunis, but Calcutta delivers in spades, with good service to match. $$$$

✷ **La Spigola** [100 D4] 52 Av Franklin Roosevelt, La Goulette; 71 738 345; f Restaurant.La.Spigola; noon–late daily. On a busy street in La Goulette which is filled with great seafood restaurants, La Spigola stands above the rest. A vast variety of delicious, freshly caught fish & shellfish, loads of tasty starters plus a decent wine list to boot. $$$$

La Villa Bleue [105 C1] 68 Rue Kennedy, Sidi Bou Saïd; 71 742 000; w lavillableuesidibousaid.com; 06.00–22.30 daily. This boutique hotel (page 79) on Sidi Bou Saïd hill has a good restaurant serving mainly high-end Tunisian cuisine. Try the *couscous sfaxien* (fish couscous). $$$$

✷ **Monsoon by Hachi** [105 F4] Rue Ibn Rochd/Av de la République, Amilcar; m 23 318 075; f monsooncarthage; noon–16.00 & 17.00–20.30 daily. A small, excellent Asian restaurant from the same team that ran the legendary (& now closed) Hachi in La Marsa. Great sushi & delicious pad thai. $$$$

✷ **Sushiwan** [105 C2] Bd de la Qualité de Vie; m 29 350 000; e sushiwanshop@gmail.com; w sushiwan.net; f sushiwantunisie; ⌚ noon–23.00 daily. Don't let the roadside location fool you – this is hands down the best sushi in Tunis, with a conveyor belt serving a variety of dishes. $$$$

Tchevap [100 E2] 51 La Goulette Rd, Carthage; ☎ 71 277 089. High-end Italian cuisine with a good wine list. Gets busy in the evenings. $$$$

Mid-range

✷ **A Mi Chemins** [107 D1] 3rd Fl, Zephyr Mall, Rue El Manfalouti, La Marsa; f A.Mi.Chemins; ⌚ 08.00–22.00 daily. Accessed via the side street that is home to the synagogue, this popular rooftop brunch spot with panoramic sea views is eclectically decorated with vintage TVs, radios & colonial-era posters. Good service, great juice selection & plenty of healthy options. $$$

Au Bon Vieux Temps [105 B1] 56 Rue Hédi Zarrouk, Sidi Bou Saïd; ☎ 71 744 733; w aubonvieuxtemps.net; ⌚ noon–midnight daily. Great Tunisian seafood specialities (such as stuffed squid) served in a romantic setting, with amazing views of the Mediterranean below. Not to be confused with the other unrelated Au Bon Vieux Temps in La Marsa. $$$

Au Bon Vieux Temps [107 E2] 1 Rue Abou El Kacem Chebbi, La Marsa; ☎ 71 749 060; m 21 797 173; f bonviemarsa; ⌚ noon–late daily. Not to be confused with Au Bon Vieux Temps in Sidi Bou Saïd. Lively Italian bistro with live music at w/ends & a large outdoor seating area. One of few places with draught beer on tap in La Marsa. No longer taking reservations so turn up early to guarantee a table during busy periods. $$$

Bistro Nippon [107 A4] 29 Rue Tahar Ben Achour, La Marsa; m 24 986 077; w bistronippon.ever.jp; ⌚ noon–15.00 & 18.30–22.00 Mon–Sat. Cool little Japanese bistro focusing on udon & ramen-based dishes, rather than sushi, which is unusual for Tunis. If you liked the bowl your delicious broth was served in, you can buy that too, as all the ceramics are for sale. $$$

bleue! [105 A1] 8 Rue Habib Thameur, Sidi Bou Saïd; ◙ bleue_deli; ⌚ 07.30–22.30 daily. Local deli open for coffee, tea, juices, sweets & a delicious selection of sandwiches & salads. Try the Iraqi chicken sandwich. $$$

Chok Güzel [100 A2] Rue de la Bourse, Lac 2; ☎ 71 198 237; m 26 184 009; f CHOKGUZELLAC2; ⌚ 09.00–22.30 daily. No-nonsense Turkish restaurant with tasty grilled meats & good hummus. Try the meat sword – which is exactly what it sounds like! $$$

✷ **El Houche (The House)** [100 D4] 52 Av Franklin Roosevelt, La Goulette; m 28 413 413; e contact@elhouche.tn; f ElHoucheLaGoulette; ⌚ 12.30–22.30 Tue–Sun. Authentic Djerbian cuisine with lots of seafood options & excellent service. Try the *borghol* (bulgur wheat) with octopus. $$$

Japanese Curry Kitano [105 E2] 39 Rue Salem Bouhajeb, La Marsa; m 54 872 429; w currykitano.ever.jp; f currykitano; ⌚ 18.30–22.00 Tue–Sat. Another very small Japanese restaurant serving delicious rice & udon-based curry dishes. $$$

✷ **K-Zip** [100 B2] Rue de la Perle, Lac 2; m 28 695 727, 21 415 215; f/◙; ⌚ noon–19.00 Mon–Sat. Stylish interior, good service & delicious Korean food with fresh ingredients – try the bibimbap. One of the few places in Tunis where you can get an iced coffee. $$$

Lapero [107 A4] 13 Rue Tahar Ben Achour, La Marsa; m 21 966 966; f laperolamarsa; ⌚ noon–15.00 & 18.30–23.00 Tue–Fri, noon–15.00 & 18.30–22.30 Sat–Sun. Spanish & Mexican tapas & pintxos & delicious sangria in a small hole in the wall. Very busy at w/ends. $$$

Smoky Buns [107 D3] 11 Rue des Hafsides, La Marsa; m 52 645 100; f SmokyBuns.tn; ⌚ noon–22.00 Mon–Sat, noon–20.00 Sun. Trendy burger joint that (unusually) can also serve pork in its burgers. $$$

✷ **Tavernetta** [105 E3] Rue du Sapin, La Marsa; m 52 249 323; f LaTavernettaRestaurants; ⌚ 12.15–15.00 Tue–Sun plus 18.30–22.00 Tue–Sat. An excellent, intimate Italian restaurant hidden down a quiet street (& further hidden by being marked in the wrong place on multiple online maps). Some of the best fresh pasta in Tunis. $$$

Via Mercato [100 A2] Rue de la Bourse, Lac 2; m 25 999 444; f via.mercato.officiel; ⌚ noon–23.00 daily. Great Italian restaurant with walls adorned with football memorabilia, serving excellent pizzas. $$$

Cheap and cheerful

HOBO Chicken [71 B2] Flamingo Center, Bd Cheikh Zayed; m 23 800 731; f HoboTunisie; ⌚ 11.00–23.00 daily. Forget KFC – if you need deep-fried chicken, head to Tunisia's own HOBO Chicken, with outlets dotted all over the country, including in the Manar City & Azur City shopping centres on the way south out of Tunis on the A1. $$

ELSEWHERE IN TUNIS

Go! Sushi [97 A1] Av Youssef Rouissi; m 25 701 107; w gosushi.tn; ⌚ noon–22.00 Sun–Thu, noon–22.30 Fri–Sat. Great quality sushi restaurant up north in Manar 2, although not sure how the Japanese would feel about their signature sushi roll being called 'Kamika Ze'! $$$$

Il Ritrovo Degli Artisti [97 A1] Rue Mohamed Triki, Ennasr; 71 813 610; m 22 975 532; f ritrovodegliartisti; ⌚ 12.30–15.00 & 19.00–22.00 Mon–Sat. Excellent Italian restaurant with some great seafood dishes. $$$

✷ **Le Bambou** [97 A1] 85 Av Hédi Nouira; m 23 690 602; e bamboucuisine@gmail.com; f lebamboucuisineasiatique; ⌚ noon–23.00 daily. In Ennasr 2 (a good 7km north of the Medina), this small Asian restaurant is worth the trek. The sushi & poke bowls are good, as are the *kushiyaki* (Japanese beef skewers), but the real attractions are the Korean dishes. $$$

Le Zink [97 C1] 1 Rue Salah Ben Mahmoud, El Menzah 4; m 54 804 408; e contact.lezink@gmail.com; f lezinktunis; ⌚ 11.30–22.00 daily. One of the best burgers in Tunis, so definitely worth the 5km trek north from the city centre. Opening another branch in La Marsa at the time of writing. $$$

La Seine Patisserie [97 A1] 2 Rue Tahar Memmi, Menzah 6; m 52 516 415; e contact.laseine@gmail.com; f laseine.tn; ⌚ 09.00–17.00 daily. Probably the only patisserie in Tunis offering sweets for those with special dietary requirements, such as sugar-free, gluten-free, vegan & for those on keto diets. Also serves an impressive variety of teas. $$

Jardins d'Agaves [71 A3] ⊕ 36.701786, 10.015452; f jardindagaves; ⌚ Sat–Sun noon–18.00. An excellent new Mexican restaurant with vegetarian options, perched on a hill in an olive grove, on the boundary between Manouba & Ben Arous governorates. Booking essential. $$$

ENTERTAINMENT AND NIGHTLIFE

Many visitors to Tunis head straight to Gammarth for a night out. While this is an easier spot to find international DJs or your typical nightclub experience, there

THE ROSS DOWNTOWN BAR CRAWL

Named after the foreign diplomat who inaugurated this bar crawl in late 2021, this tour of drinking establishments in central Tunis has since become very popular. Begin the evening with a swift rum cocktail in Latin-themed tapas bar, **O'Barrio** [97 D6] (4 Rue de Syrie; m 58 463 647; f obarriotunis; ⌚ 16.00–02.00 daily), before heading 700m southwest for a pint in the rooftop bar at the colonial-era **Majestic Hotel** [94 B1] (36 Av de Paris; 71 332 666; f MajesticHotelTunisie; ⌚ noon–22.00 daily). Built in 1919, this place has a fascinating history, including being requisitioned by the Nazis as headquarters during their occupation of Tunisia in 1942–43. Next, walk 500m southwards to **Chez Vous** [94 B2] (Rue de Marseille; m 29 706 469; f chezvouslounge; ⌚ noon–01.00 daily), which often has a DJ playing. Your fourth stop is **Frida** [94 C3] (Rue Mohamed Aziz Taj; m 28 356 950; f; ⌚ 11.00–01.00 Mon–Sat), less than 300m away, a small bar and tapas joint named after the famous Mexican painter. Finally, end the night 300m west at **Marengo Club** [94 B3] (10 Rue Yougoslavie; m 51 317 465; f MarengoTombouctou; ⌚ noon–midnight Mon–Sat) with some dancing in its lively internal courtyard, often to live contemporary Tunisian music.

are plenty of entertaining establishments to explore downtown and in the eastern suburbs for a fun night.

BARS AND CLUBS

Downtown

Le Comptoir de Tunis [97 D6] 8 Rue de Syrie; 71 832 590; m 58 463 636; f; 17.00–02.00 Mon–Sat. A self-described 'restaurant, lounge & cultural space' hosting karaoke, live music including jazz & blues plus rather popular Mediterranean food.

Le Flamant [97 D6] Av Mohamed V; m 56 100 005; f Restaurantleflamant; noon–02.00 daily. Located inside the 5-star Laico Hotel, this bar-restaurant-lounge hosts contemporary Tunisian music & belly-dancing nights that get quite lively.

Lodge [97 C3] 93 Av Mohamed V; m 50 300 340; f lodgetunis; noon–02.00 daily. This lounge bar has regular DJs, karaoke & live music nights, as well as serving mixed Italian & Tunisian cuisine.

Eastern suburbs

Boeuf Sur le Toit [71 B1] 2036 Av de l'UMA, La Soukra; m 29 780 360; f LeBoeufSurLeToit; 18.00–03.00 daily. An eclectic mix of live music, including rock & Tunisian metal.

Carpe Diem [105 D3] Rte de Gammarth, La Marsa; m 27 330 001; f lecarpediemtunis; 18.00–02.00 daily. A massive outdoor nightclub complex off the Gammarth Highway, this popular spot hosts live bands & DJs from around the world.

Carthage Golf Course Bar [71 B1] 19 Av du 13 Août, La Soukra; m 99 882 398; f golfdecarthage; 09.00–02.00 daily. With sweeping views overlooking the oldest golf course in Tunisia, this is a great spot for a sundowner, although the food is a little hit & miss.

The Cliff [105 F2] Rue Sidi Dhrif; m 29 777 529; e contact@thecliff.tn; w thecliff.tn; noon–midnight Mon–Fri, 12.30–01.00 Sat–Sun. The upstairs restaurant serves expensive, avg-quality Mediterranean fare with hit-&-miss service, but the downstairs wine bar has a separate bar menu with great burgers & pizzas, as well as (so they claim) the largest selection of wine, gin, rum & whiskey in the country. $$$

Dar Tej [107 D1] 7 Av Habib Bourguiba, La Marsa; 71 746 958; f dartej; noon–late daily. Recently refurbished after a fire, this old-school pub is hiding in plain sight on La Marsa's main street. Restaurant on the ground floor, but if you go all the way up the stairs to the top of the building there is a smoky bar offering cheap, ice-cold Celtias & live football.

El Firma [71 B1] 58 Rue des Fruits, La Soukra; m 29 345 135; e info@el-firma.com; f ElFirmaSokra; noon–02.00 daily. Restaurant & lively lounge bar with regular DJ nights. A strange lack of separation between the restaurant & the lounge means the poor diners often have to listen to blasting music from the bar while trying to eat.

The Factory [105 A3] 86 Av Fattouma Bourguiba; m 29 537 574; f thefactorysoukra; 16.00–01.00 Mon–Fri, 13.00–01.00 Sat, 13.00–midnight Sun. Large gastropub with an international menu & plenty of flat-screen TVs for sport. Try the onion rings. $$$

✱ **Gingembre/Tangerine** [71 A6] Complexe Le CAP, Rte Express de Gammarth. Which of the 2 bars is open at this venue depends on the season. In winter, it's Gingembre (w clubgingembre.com; 17.00–01.00 Tue–Thu, 17.00–03.00 Fri–Sat, 11.00–17.00 Sun), a bar that transforms into a club at the w/end & offers brunch on Sun. In the summer, the rooftop Tangerine opens (tangerinerooftop; 18.00–midnight Sun–Thu, 18.00–01.00 Fri–Sat), which is very popular with the Instagram crowd. Both have a good menu of snacks (inc tapas at Tangerine), good music that is not overpowering & an excellent assortment of professionally mixed cocktails. No reservations.

✱ **Le Phoenix de Carthage** (formerly ToBe) [100 E1] Rte de la Marsa; m 20 940 094; f ThePhoenixClub.Carthage; 10.00–02.00 daily. A huge, mainly outdoor bar set among the La Malga cisterns (page 103). Live music, live sports, good table service & some very bold resident cats!

Le Pirate [105 G4] Bd de l'Environnement, Sidi Bou Saïd; m 27 158 005; f; noon–late daily. So-so seafood restaurant, but a great spot for a beer by the marina.

✱ **Plaza Corniche** [107 F3] 22 Rue du Maroc, La Marsa; 71 743 577; f plazacorniche; noon–late daily. Not to be confused with Hotel Plaza Corniche about 80m down the hill, this bar has some incredibly strange décor, from eclectic coloured lighting to some decidedly questionable colonial-era African-kitsch statues. With poolside seating & great views of the Mediterranean, it is the perfect spot for a sundowner. At the time of writing, however, it had lost its alcohol licence & the food was pretty mediocre, so best avoided until that is reinstated.

✷ **Rock N' Rolla** [100 D4] 20 Rue Ali Bach, La Goulette; m 20 077 078; f rocknrollalagoulette; ⌚ 18.00–01.00 daily. A smoky, sweaty rock club, through an unmarked door to the side of the Hôtel Lido, hosting a great selection of Tunisian rock & metal bands throughout the week. Cheap drinks, good service & lively atmosphere.

Roof Top 360° [107 D1] 75 Av Habib Bourguiba, La Marsa; 71 728 000; w darelmarsa.com; ⌚ 09.00–23.30 daily. On the roof of Dar El Marsa hotel (page 79), this restaurant & bar offers incredible panoramic views of La Marsa beach. The Mediterranean cuisine is nothing special, but this is a great spot for sundowners or to grab a drink while watching live jazz on a Fri evening.

V-Lounge & Light Bar [100 E1] Rue Mendes France, Carthage; 71 733 433; w villadidoncarthage.com; f VillaDidonHotel; ⌚ noon–23.00 Mon–Thu, noon–02.00 Fri–Sun. The bar at the Villa Didon hotel (page 79) overlooks the infinity pool & the Mediterranean. Popular with dates ignoring each other while using Instagram. Also hosts nights with live DJs. Hit-&-miss service when busy.

✷ **Wet Flamingo** [100 D4] 126 Av de la République, La Goulette; 31 151 657; f wetflamingo; ⌚ 16.00–01.00 Mon–Sat, 16.00–midnight Sun. It might sound like a strip club, but the Wet Flamingo is actually a gem of an indie bar on the La Goulette waterfront with great music, ice-cold draught beers & a tapas menu.

Yüka Complex [71 A6] Hotel Ardjan, Gammarth; m 55 585 057; f yuka.tunis; ⌚ 10.00–04.00 daily. Large entertainment complex on the waterfront in Gammarth. Once you get past security at the main entrance, you have the choice of a variety of bars, restaurants & clubs including **Yüka** (which has its own pool), the trendy **Birdhouse** rooftop bar, Afro-Latino bar **Barrio** & **The Garrison**, which has to be the world's only *Peaky Blinders*-themed Irish pub (clearly nobody told the owners that *Peaky Blinders* is set in Birmingham!).

THEATRES AND THE ARTS

In 2018, the 60,000m² **City of Culture** [97 D5] was established to celebrate Tunisia's 62nd anniversary of independence. It is a hub for theatre & arts in the capital, containing a library, cinema, art galleries & live performance spaces, as well as both the opera house & modern art museum.

Museum of Modern and Contemporary Art (MACAM) City of Culture; 70 028 351; w macam-tunis.tn; ⌚ 10.00–19.00 Tue–Sun; free. This modern space features exhibitions on colonial art (1861–1949) & the School of Tunis (1949–61), a whole gallery of modern art & various other exhibitions including weaving, ceramics & photography.

Théâtre de l'Opéra de Tunis City of Culture; 70 028 300; f Operadetunis; theatreoperatunis. This 1,650-seat opera theatre is located is home to the Tunisian Symphony Orchestra, the Opera Ballet of Tunis, the Tunisian National Orchestra of Arab Music & the National Troupe of Popular Arts. Events are advertised on Instagram.

Théâtre Municipal [94 B3] Av Habib Bourguiba; 71 259 499, 23 444 763. This iconic Art Deco theatre does not have an active web presence, but you see listings & buy tickets for its live performances on the Tunisian booking platform w teskerti.tn.

Cultural centres

The following all have a media library & language centre, & their active Facebook pages offer details about their various cinema evenings, art exhibitions & other cultural collaborations across the capital.

Goethe-Institut Tunis [97 C4] 6 Rue du Sénégal; 71 848 266; e info@tunis.goethe.org; f goetheinstitut.tunis; ⌚ 09.00–13.00 & 14.00–17.00 Mon–Fri, 09.30–12.30 Sat.

Institut Français de Tunisie [94 B2] 20–22 Av de Paris; 31 325 200; w institutfrancais-tunisie.com; f IFTunisie; ⌚ see website for specific opening hours of different sections, although the restaurant is generally open from 09.00, & the library from 10.00.

Italian Cultural Institute of Tunis [97 C3] 80 Av Mohamed V; 71 142 700; e iictunisi@esteri.it; f IICTunis; ⌚ 09.00–13.00 & 14.00–17.00 Mon–Thu, 09.00–14.00 Fri.

SHOPPING

BOOKSHOPS

Faouzi Hedhili's Bookstore [94 A4] 18 Rue d'Angleterre; 09 359 305; 09.00–18.00 daily. Tucked down an alleyway next door to the yellow-fronted Belhadj cloth store. Originally opened by a Jewish Tunisian just after World War II, Faouzi Hedhili's establishment has claim to be the oldest bookshop in the country & is a fascinating jumble of antique manuscripts along with thousands of other titles. Mr Hedhili hit the international headlines during the Covid-19 pandemic when Tunisian readers crowded to make a purchase there & help the shop weather the severe economic downturn. Sadly, the store was for sale in Sep 2022, & it remains to be seen if the new owners continue the tradition of bookselling.

FNAC [105 B4] Parking Carrefour, La Marsa; 71 130 000; w fnac.tn; 09.00–23.00 daily. Large French retail chain that mainly sells electronics, but also has a café & good assortment of French & English-language books in the back, including the excellent, illustrated English- & French-language *History of Tunisia* by Habib Boularès.

GAÏA [100 B2] Tunisia Mall, Lac 2; 71 669 398; 10.00–21.00 daily. A small book & stationery store at the top of Tunisia Mall with a limited & rather eclectic selection of English-language books (mainly non-fiction).

✷ **Librairie Al Kitab** [94 B2] 43 Av Habib Bourguiba; w alkitab.tn; 08.00–20.00 Mon–Sat, 09.00–14.00 Sun. Open since 1967, this large, well-established Tunisian book chain has an excellent selection of English-language books. Hosts book signings & literary events. Also has a branch in La Marsa [105 E3].

Librairie Clairefontaine [94 B2] 4 Rue d'Alger; 71 255 366; f librairiesclairefontaine; 08.00–20.00 daily. Downtown bookstore open since 1949 stocking mainly French titles, although it has a small English-language section.

Librairie 'Culturel' Zéphyr [107 D1] Zephyr Mall, La Marsa; 71 775 793; w culturel.tn; 09.00–21.00 daily. Large Tunisian bookstore chain with multiple locations across the capital.

Librairie Diwan [91 C4] 9 Rue Sidi Ben Arous, Medina; 71 572 398; 10.00–18.00 Mon–Sat. Offers a wealth of literature from Tunisia & the wider region in English, Arabic & French.

Librairie Fahrenheit 451 [100 E2] Centre Culturel de Carthage, Av Habib Bourguiba; 71 733 676; f fahrenheit451tunis; 09.30–13.00 Mon, 09.30–19.00 Tue–Sat, 10.00–18.00 Sun. A selection of mainly French-language books covering a range of genres including local & regional history. Also hosts art exhibitions & talks.Readers Corner [107 C1] Residence Hannibal, La Marsa; 71 746 196; e asouhayma@yahoo.com; f; 09.00–14.00 & 15.30–20.00 Mon–Fri, 09.00–20.00 Sat, 09.00–19.00 Sun. Mainly children's books in French & English.

CONCEPT STORES

Tunis has a wide variety of concept stores dotted about the city, offering everything from clothing to modern art. These are good shops to browse if looking for gifts to take home, as they almost exclusively feature goods by up-&-coming Tunisian designers. The following are a few of the best in the city, but this list is by no means exhaustive. Instagram & Facebook are the best places to find new stores as & when they pop up.

The Label Store [100 A1] Rue du Parfum, El Aouina; m 50 821 941; f thelabelstoretn; 10.00–14.00 & 15.00–19.00 Mon–Fri, 10.00–15.00 & 16.00–19.00 Sat. This concept store brings together handmade crafts from a selection of Tunisian designers, including ceramics, metals, tableware, seating, mirrors & light fixtures.

L'Artisanerie [97 D3] 44 Rue du Niger; m 29 291 545; f lartisanerietunisie; 10.00–18.00 Mon–Fri, 10.00–16.30 Sat. Wares on sale from a broad collective of Tunisian artisans from as far afield as Aïn Draham & Nefta, including rugs made with 100% recycled wool.

Lyoum [107 A4] 29 Rue Tahar Ben Achour, La Marsa; 71 744 851; w lyoum.co; 14.00–19.00 Mon, 10.00–14.00 & 15.30–19.00 Tue–Fri, 10.00–19.00 Sat, 10.00–15.00 Sun. Established in 2011, this concept store has some great clothing lines, including the very popular camel & palm tree Christmas jumpers! Also has a branch in Menzah & an online shop with international shipping.

Mooja [97 B1] 1 Rue Salem Bouhajeb; m 24 471 336; f moojastore; 10.30–19.30 Mon–Fri, noon–19.30 Sat. Open since 2017, this place is known for rock-chic designs & some very creative T-shirts.

Rock the Kasbah [105 A1] 11 Rue Habib Thameur, Sidi Bou Saïd; 71 775 440; w rockthekasbah.net; 10.00–13.00 & 14.00–19.00 Tue–Sun. Gorgeous furniture & homeware from designer Philippe Xerri, who was responsible for the incredible refurbishment at El Fondouk Djerba in Houmt Souk (page 317), & also has a series of stores in France.

SuperSouk [105 A3] 64 Av Fattouma Bourguiba; m 26 572 434; w supersoukshop.com; 10.00–19.00 daily. An exciting mixture of furniture, clothing, jewellery, food, stationery, leather accessories & craft products from contemporary Tunisian designers in one of the most popular concept stores in the city.

XYZ [107 E2] 7 Rue Omar Ibn Abi Rabia, La Marsa; m 31 147 125; f XYZconceptstore; 10.00–13.00 & 15.30–19.00 Tue–Sat. An expat favourite, stocking home goods, clothing, jewellery & art.

MARKETS The **Medina** offers almost limitless shopping options – so long as you know where to look. Goods tend to be organised thematically along centuries-old established categories: more respectable ('clean') items such as spices, books and perfumes are allowed to be sold nearer the mosques, while trades such as butchers are relegated to the less prominent backstreets. Specific locations or types of vendors will be easier to find with a local guide (page 77). But if you wish to brave it alone, the following will be helpful.

Souk El Attarine (by the Great Mosque) [91 C4] is the place to go for perfume, though goods are more mixed these days, with modern perfumes & imitations outdistancing the traditionally made perfume essences. This is where Tunis brides come to buy their wedding paraphernalia: from perfumes, candles & henna to the silky cat baskets that carry their wedding presents. But there are things for tourists too: delicate gilt bottles & felt fishes covered in sequins to ward off the evil eye. Books are sold on Rue

THE FRIPES OF TUNIS

Tunisia is a regional hub for secondhand clothing. There are an estimated 150,000 secondhand clothes sellers spread across the country, distributing the contents of the 8,000 or so containers of used clothes that arrive in Tunisia's ports every year. Clothing tends to come from Europe (especially nearby Italy and France), but some from as far afield and the USA and Canada. The country's secondhand clothing markets (*fripes*) are very popular with locals and visitors alike. People once turned their noses up at the thought of rifling through piles of imported used clothes that originated in 100kg bundles, but fripes have seen a surge in popularity in recent years thanks to their cost effectiveness, low environmental impact and the possibility of finding a unique addition to your wardrobe.

There are also online stores in Tunis run by people who find pieces in a fripe and then resell them; good examples are **Goya** (@goya_thrift) and **Aubaine** (w nature-najen.com/collections/aubaine).

There are fripes all over the city on different days of the week, but here are a few worth checking out:

Fripe Bousalsa [105 D1] La Marsa; 07.00–16.00 Sun. Great selection of used clothes right in La Marsa.

Fripe Ezzahra Av Taïeb Mhiri, Ezzahra; 07.00–17.00 Thu. A massive fripe in the southern suburb of Ezzahra with a lot of imported clothing. Ezzahra Lycée is the nearest train station if coming from Tunis.

Fripe Hafsia [91 C2] Rue Sidi Sridek, El Hafsia; 07.00–20.00 daily. Probably the largest fripe in the country; a large section burned down in a fire in 2020 but has since been restored.

Sidi Ben Arous, just north of the Zitouna Mosque, while jewellery can be found in the **Souk des Orfèvres** [91 B4] and **Souk el Berka** [91 B4]. For carpets and blankets go to **Souk el Leffa** [91 B4], although carpets are generally much cheaper outside the capital in other production centres such as Kairouan (page 278) and Toujane (page 304). If you get a carpet, be sure you have the receipt and that there is a quality stamp on the back. Leather can be found in numerous tourist-orientated shops, including those on **Souk el Trouk**, an extension of Souk El Attarine [91 C4]. On Souk el Belghadjia, also off Souk El Attarine, you can find old-style Tunis footwear among more modern pieces. See page 93 for a walking tour of the Medina souks.

FOOD There are various fresh food markets dotted around the city, but 2 stand out in terms of selection & quality:

Municipal Market [94 A3] 9 Rue d'Allemagne; ⌚ 06.00–16.00 daily. The central covered market just east of the Medina proper, & by far the largest in the city. Worth a visit just for the sensory overload, packed to the rafters with fresh fruit, vegetables, meats & the catch of the day.
La Marsa Central Market [107 C1] Rue Cherif, La Marsa; ⌚ 06.30–13.00 Mon–Fri, 06.30–15.00 Sat–Sun. The Marché Centrale caters to expats & locals alike. Although much smaller than the main market downtown, it has an excellent selection of fresh products, including fruits that are difficult to find elsewhere. Some of the vendors around the outside of the market also sell assorted foreign cheeses & even pork products, which is rare.

OTHER PRACTICALITIES

HOSPITALS Tunis is a hub for medical tourism (especially plastic surgery), given the low prices of medical & dental care. There is a wealth of private clinics, although standards vary so be sure to check out reviews of the facility online or contact your embassy for advice.

Military Hospital of Tunis (HMPIT) [71 B3] Pl de Tunis; ☎ 71 391 133/111; ⌚ 24hrs. This Ministry of Defence-run facility is one of the largest university hospitals in Africa & has a good reputation. Your best bet for medical emergencies downtown.
Polyclinic Amen La Marsa [105 E3] 15 Av de La République, La Marsa; ☎ 71 749 000, 70 011 670; w marsa.amensante.com; ⌚ 24hrs. Recommended by various international embassies based in Tunis.

POST The main post office [94 A3] (30 Rue Charles de Gaulle; ☎ 71 320 610; ⌚ 08.00–17.00 Mon–Fri, 09.00–12.15 Sat) is in a beautiful Neoclassical building from 1893 in the 19th-century beaux arts tradition. If you are sending parcels abroad, you are better off going with DHL (which has locations throughout the city; w mydhl.express.dhl/tn) or its local partner Rapid-Poste (w rapidposte.poste.tn), which 6 six offices across Tunis.

WHAT TO SEE AND DO

THE MEDINA 🏴 There is no better place to start your exploration of the capital than the Medina. Founded in AD698, it is considered an outstanding example of Arab-Muslim urban development by architectural historians and specialists. The dense web of narrow streets surrounding the main mosque is little changed since the Hafsid Dynasty, which can make for a very confusing walk if you head in without a guide (page 77) or detailed map. The following two walking tours should help you get to know the area.

Walk 1: Faith and trade: the souks and Zitouna Mosque (1¾hrs) This walk explores the finest mosques of old Tunis, winding through the covered souks that were the commercial nerve centre of the city for centuries. The starting point

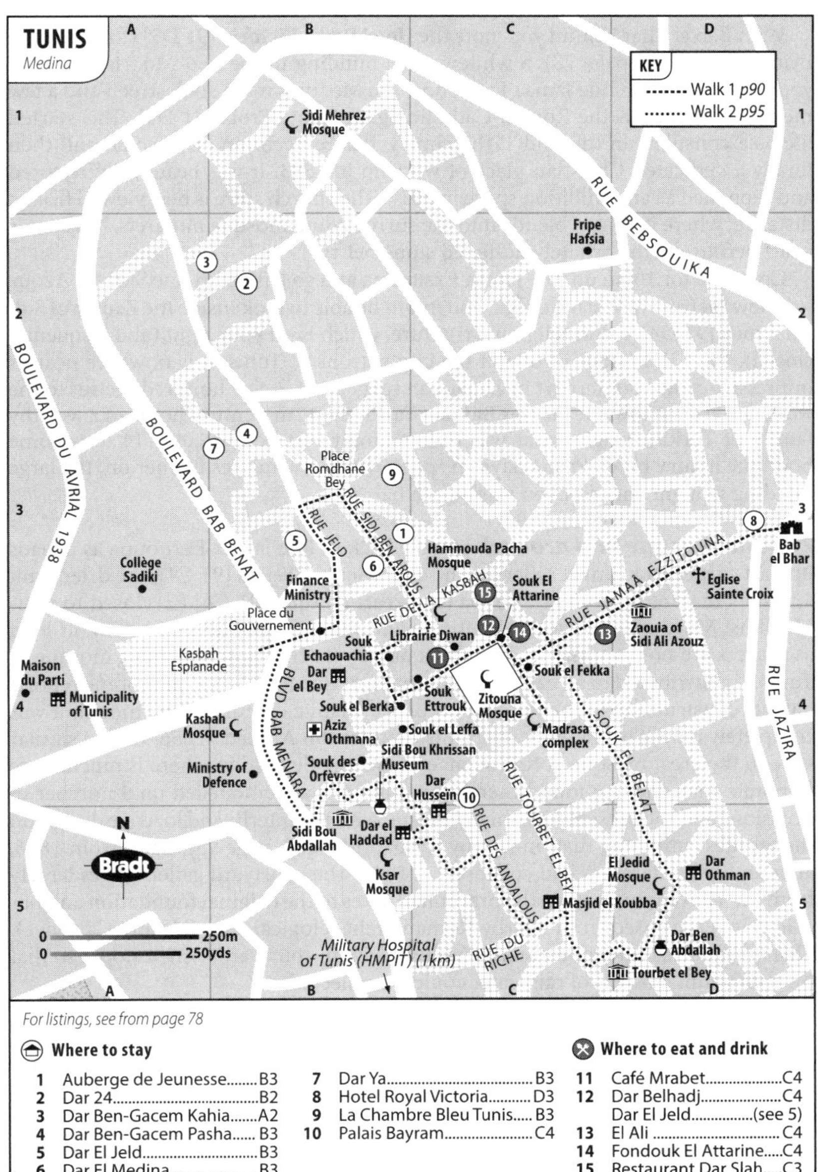

For listings, see from page 78

Where to stay

1 Auberge de Jeunesse........B3
2 Dar 24........B2
3 Dar Ben-Gacem Kahia........A2
4 Dar Ben-Gacem Pasha........B3
5 Dar El Jeld........B3
6 Dar El Medina........B3
7 Dar Ya........B3
8 Hotel Royal Victoria........D3
9 La Chambre Bleu Tunis........B3
10 Palais Bayram........C4

Where to eat and drink

11 Café Mrabet........C4
12 Dar Belhadj........C4
Dar El Jeld........(see 5)
13 El Ali........C4
14 Fondouk El Attarine........C4
15 Restaurant Dar Slah........C3

is **Bab el Bhar** [91 D3] (Sea Gate, sometimes also labelled Porte de France), the old gate on Place de la Victoire on the east side of the Medina. The old city walls are long gone and so the gate, dating from the late 18th century when the walls were rebuilt under the supervision of a Dutch engineer, and restored in the 1980s, stands in isolation. Behind it stand some three-storey former caravanserais of a neighbourhood inhabited mainly by European merchants in the 17th century. Today it is home to a mixture of private residences and businesses.

With Bab el Bhar behind you, note the **Hotel Royal Victoria** [91 D3] (formerly the British Consulate; page 78), a whitewashed building in the neo-Moorish style, to your right. Head up Rue Jamaâ Ezzitouna, the Medina's main souk street, and a few metres on the left is the Roman Catholic **Église Sainte Croix** [91 D3]. This started life as a consulate in the mid 17th century, before becoming a hospital and then finally a dedicated Christian place of worship in 1883. It was beautifully restored and reopened as an exhibition space in 2017. The church spire is best viewed from a distance, where it almost blends into the surrounding mosque minarets, but stands apart because of the ornately designed stone belfry.

Continue for 100m up Rue Jamaâ Ezzitouna and go left down Rue Sidi Ali Azouz for a few metres. With a little luck, you might be able to look inside the **Zaouia of Sidi Ali Azouz** [91 D4], a Sufi religious structure, which is on your right (and frequently closed). Built in honour of one of the city patrons of Tunis, it is nowhere near as impressive as its counterpart in Zaghouan (page 217). A few hundred metres to the west, down a narrow alley is **Dar Bayram Turki**, the 17th-century home of a wealthy family of Turkish origins that was painstakingly restored in 2005–14 to become boutique luxury hotel, Palais Bayram (page 78). A few metres further on, the large building straight ahead of you was once a barracks.

Zitouna Mosque and around Double back to Rue Jamaâ Ezzitouna as it leads up past carpet and trinket sellers to the small **Souk el Fekka** [91 C4], the dried fruit and nuts market in front of **Zitouna (or Great) Mosque** [91 C4] (🕘 closed to non-Muslims; Muslim tourists are sometimes allowed to visit after 14.00 daily, as long as prayers are not in session). The oldest and by far the most venerable mosque in Tunis, it is attributed to an early Arab conqueror, Hassan Ibn Nu'man. Some reports date its construction to the foundation of the Islamic city in AD698, though it was completely rebuilt by the Aghlabid Emir Ibrahim Ibn Ahmed in 856–63 in a similar style to the great mosque at Kairouan; even so, the fluted dome here is much more elaborate than the one found there. The minaret was remodelled on a number of occasions and the present 43m-high version, with the interlinked lozenge design on the façades (imitating that on nearby Kasbah Mosque; page 93), dates from 1896, after an earlier iteration had collapsed in 1892. The courtyard gallery dates largely from the 17th century, while the prayer hall dates to the original foundation and has columns repurposed from nearby Roman archaeological sites (mainly Carthage). This mosque has extensive cisterns under the main courtyard, which slopes so that the maximum amount of rainwater could be collected.

As you view the mosque, note how it is surrounded by souks. There were originally stalls for rent here under the *skifa* (main portico) esplanade. There is a surprising lack of open spaces around the mosque, and no room set aside for fountains nor statuary, which makes it different from similarly aged religious buildings in nearby Italy or Spain.

Go left in front of the mosque and you'll see the three neighbouring madrasas on the right: **Ennakhla**, **el Bachiya** and **Slimaniya** [91 C4] (speak to a guide about organising a tour inside the buildings). There are more than 20 madrasas in the Medina, providing accommodation for students following religious courses in the mosque. Established by beys between 1714 and 1754, these three structures bear witness to the piety of their founders. The Slimaniya, built by Ali Pacha in memory of a favourite son, Suleiman, who died after being poisoned in a dynastic feud, is particularly fine, known for its high porch with green roof tiles (visible from the exterior) and the black-and-white striped arches around its columned interior courtyard.

The souks From the three madrasas, double back to the square in front of the mosque and go left at the other end of Souk el Fekka, up **Souk El Attarine** [91 C4], the perfumers' souk (page 89). At a junction just below the minaret of the mosque, continue straight up **Souk Ettrouk** [91 C4], once the street of the Turkish tailors, and still dedicated to clothing-related trades today. Halfway along is Café Mrabet, an old saint's shrine now functioning as an attractive café (page 81). At the top of the street, turn left into **Souk el Berka** [91 B4], once the main slave market and now the centre of a flourishing jewellery arcade.

Heading back up to Souk Ettrouk, take a right at the west end of the street (also called Souk Ettrouk) and continue straight along a narrow street between the high walls of the **Dar el Bey** [91 B4], today the offices of the Head of Government, on your left, and the outside wall of the *chechia* makers' souk, **Souk Echaouachia** [91 C4], on your right. You should be able to cut through the souk and observe the *chaouachis* hard at work, felting and shaping the red caps or chechias once so characteristic of Tunis. Back in the 19th century, the cap makers were easily the wealthiest and most influential corporation in the city, masters of a pre-industrial manufacturing process. Your coffee stop could be here at one of the cafés in the souk or, if you cut through, at one of the street cafés on Rue Sidi Ben Arous. From here, you have a magnificent view of the Zitouna minaret.

Heading along Rue Sidi Ben Arous away from the minaret, you come to the splendid 17th-century **Hammouda Pacha Mosque** [91 C4] on your right, at the junction with Rue de la Kasbah. The octagonal minaret is characteristic of mosques following the Hanefite rite, one of mainstream Islam's four main rites. Although the Malekite rite dominated North Africa, the Hanefite rite was brought over by the Ottoman Turks from the early 1600s, and the minaret would have been very much a political statement in its day, declaring the supremacy of Tunis's new masters.

Continue straight up Rue Sidi Ben Arous for about 200m to reach **Place Romdhane Bey** [91 B3], a small open area surrounded by workshops. Go up a couple of steps on your left to reach a covered street (or *sabat*) so characteristic of the residential areas of Tunis. There is some magnificent architectural detail here, including a kitsch Tuniso-Rococo double-window feature on one of the houses. From the covered passage, turn left up Rue Jeld, where you will see signs of incipient gentrification, including the upmarket restaurant and hotel **Dar El Jeld** (page 78).

Kasbah Rue Jeld leads to **Place du Gouvernement** [91 B4], with its ficus trees, water feature and shiny granite paving. At the top of the square is an area generally referred to as the Kasbah, after the long-vanished medieval fortifications. Cross the busy road and go up the steps to the main esplanade, which offers a splendid view of some of the key historic buildings of Tunis. Be careful if you take photographs though – don't include men in uniforms.

Straight ahead are key government buildings: the neo-Moorish **Finance Ministry** [91 B4] with its domes and crenellations, and the Dar el Bey, which we passed earlier. Moving clockwise, your gaze hits the **Aziz Othmana** hospital complex [91 B4], named after the medieval princess who was the hospital's original founder in the 17th century. The minaret to the right is that of the **Kasbah Mosque** [91 B4], built in 1231–35. The *darj wa ktef* lozenge motif on the façade recalls that this was a monument to the Almohad brand of Islam, a puritan movement that arose among the Masmouda Amazigh of the High Atlas and spread eastwards across the Maghreb in the 12th century. The same motif, symbolising loyalty to the Almohad cause, can be found on numerous minarets in North Africa, including that of the Zitouna Mosque, which we saw earlier. The galleries on the outside of the mosque are from the late 20th century. Still moving clockwise, there are some remnant walls of the bastion of Sidi Abdallah; a large chunk of the walls and a late-19th-century barracks were demolished after independence (page 74). One final building of note seen from the Kasbah esplanade is the 17th-century, Ottoman-inspired **Sidi Mehrez Mosque** [91 B1]. Unlike the great mosques of Istanbul, it was never to have soaring, pointy topped minarets – instead, it has white egg-shell domes.

The largest building accessible on foot in this area is the **Municipality of Tunis** [91 A4], a vast construction opposite the arcade, behind which is the **Maison du Parti** [91 A4], a modernist building by Olivier Clément-Cacoub, favourite architect of former president Habib Bourguiba. The municipality, refurbished in 1999, again features the *darj wa ktef* lozenge motif, though the Almohad overtones have long since been forgotten. Try to get a look inside the municipality: the over-wrought decoration combines tiles, carved plasterwork and painted wood ceilings, all elements of 18th-century domestic decoration schemes, on a vast scale. The result is somewhat overwhelming.

On the north side of the esplanade is the mid-19th-century **Collège Sadiki** [91 A3]. Founded by Kheireddine Pasha under Sadok Bey (hence the name), it was the first institution in Tunisia to dispense a modern secondary education. Architecturally, it is a typical neo-Moorish building, with traditional features such as a minaret and domes being used to 'dress' what is otherwise a typical school building, in a similar way that Gothic features were used for 19th-century British public schools.

Once you have finished your walking tour, you can either walk 50m west on to Boulevard du 9 Avril 1938 to jump in a taxi or begin the second walking tour from the Kasbah esplanade.

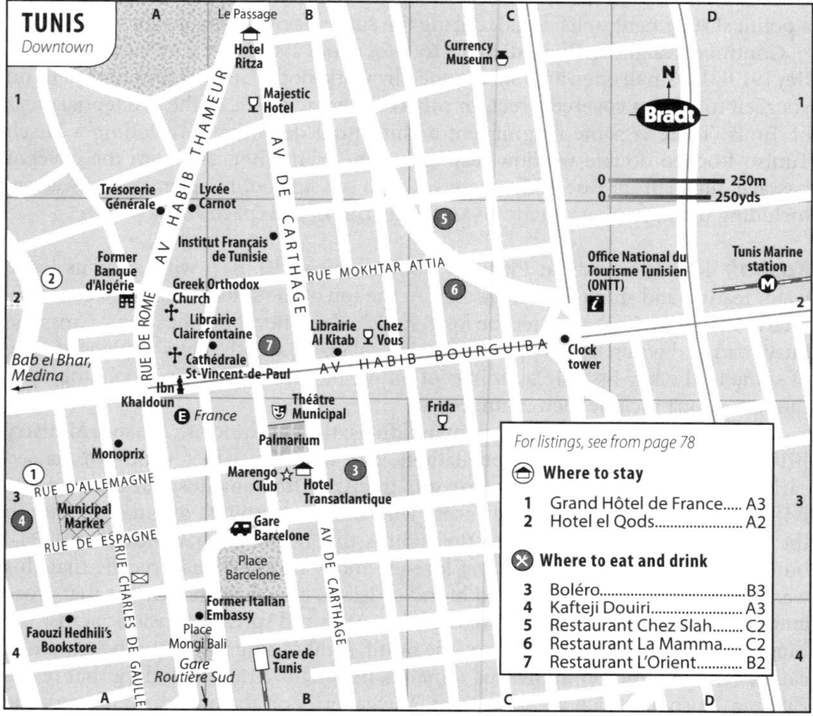

Walk 2: Beldis, beys and a pirate adventurer (1¾hrs) This route through the Medina showcases some of the finest examples of Tunisoise domestic architecture and offers a fascinating insight into life in one of the city's more residential areas. Starting from the **Kasbah** [91 A4], make your way along Boulevard Bab Menara past the Kasbah Mosque (page 93) on your right, followed by the late-19th-century block of the **Ministry of Defence** [91 B4], just off Boulevard Bab Menara down Rue du 2 Mars 1934. Heading southwards, in the middle of the street is a tomb in the form of a red-and-green box, the last resting place of one **Sidi Bou Abdallah** [91 B5] who died here in the 16th century defending Tunis against the Spanish foe. Legend has it that, in true Monty Python style, he continued fighting even after his head had been chopped off.

At the first intersection, turn right into Rue Ben Mahmoud. On your right, the first door is that of the small **Sidi Bou Khrissan Museum** [91 B5], showcasing elaborate carved tombstones – Khorassanid emirs were buried here in the 9th century. With its olive tree and ruined *koubba* (dome), this museum is very much off the tourist circuit. Knock on the door and a member of the family living inside might let you in (no tickets, make a donation), though it was closed at the time of writing.

From here, continue along Rue Ben Mahmoud past the **Restaurant Essaraya**, a somewhat kitsch 'restoration' of an old home (note the plexiglass dome); turning right here, the street widens. On your right, down the narrow Impasse Ettobjiya, is the restored 16th-century **Dar el Haddad** [91 B5], one of the oldest palaces in the Medina. Turn right at the end of this street, where a narrow covered passageway leads out on to Place du Château. The main building here is **Dar Husseïn** [91 C5], originally constructed in the 18th century and much added to in the 19th century, before being taken over by the French military authorities. It is currently home to the INP, the Tunisian National Heritage Institute. In front of it is the **Ksar Mosque** [91 B5], one of Tunis's oldest mosques, dating from 1106, although the huge, irregular stone blocks of the lower walls suggest it was constructed on the site of a much older building. The minaret dates to the 17th century and the prayer hall, as usual closed to visitors, is below street level.

From Place du Château, head down the covered cobbled street to the right of the main door of Dar Husseïn, which leads to a small open space where there is a **hammam** with the characteristic red-and-green door. Turn left down Rue Abri, and then right down one of the finest streets in the Medina – the narrow **Rue des Andalous**, with its studded doors and vaulted sections. At the end, turn left down Rue du Riche where, at the first junction, you come to the Rue Tourbet el Bey. Going left here allows you to have a look at the **Masjid el Koubba** [91 C5], a small domed structure where medieval sociologist Ibn Khaldoun is said to have prayed.

We turn right, however, and after about 75m come to **Tourbet el Bey** [91 D5] (🕘 09.30–16.00 Mon–Sat; 5DT), a mausoleum complex and last resting place of the Husseinid princes and princesses. The term 'tourbet' derives from the Turkish for 'tomb', and most of the great Tunisois families had mausolea near their homes. Built by Ali Pasha II and inaugurated in 1777, this monument is something of a curiosity. Given that the beys lived isolated from their subjects in palaces well outside the city, it is somewhat strange that they subsequently chose to be buried in their midst. The building is an odd stylistic mix: the outside features carved stonework with floral motifs, plus domes covered in the green, scale-shaped tiles which signify a 'burial place' or 'holy person's tomb' in the Tunis streetscape. Inside, the decoration is flamboyant, with characteristic 18th-century tiled panels (though the shiny replacements stand out a mile) and carved stucco work. In the Hall of the Reigning

Princes, the lower walls have elaborate marble marquetry panels, a style imported from nearby Sicily. The princes' tombs are topped with their headgear, turbans and later fezzes of various sizes. Abandoned to its fate after Tunisian independence, it was recently restored during the Covid-19 pandemic.

Leaving the main door of Tourbet el Bey, go right, and right twice more, following the main outside wall of the tourbet. Turn left on to Rue Sidi Kassem and, a few metres down this street, go right under an arch. This brings you to the **Dar Ben Abdallah** [91 D5], an 18th-century palace restored in the early 19th century by an officer of the beylical army. He opted for the Italian touch (galleries, marble fountain with dolphin) very much in favour at the time. The property was later acquired by a wealthy Tunisian silk trader, and today it houses the **Museum of Popular Arts and Traditions** (🕘 winter 10.00–13.00 & 15.00–18.00 Tue–Sun, summer 09.00–noon & 16.00–19.00 Tue–Sun; 5DT). Off the main courtyard are rooms with scenes from Tunisois family life in the fairly recent past. This is the world of the *beldia*, the old Muslim families of Tunis, proud of their traditions. The museum also houses a small display of craft implements in the neighbouring stable area.

From the museum, turn right out on to Rue Sidi Kassem, which leads on to Rue des Teinturiers and the large, early-18th-century **El Jedid Mosque** [91 D5] on your left. Opposite the mosque, go down the covered Rue el Mbazaâ to **Dar Othman** [91 D5], the 17th-century home of corsair leader Othman Dey, where he would have undoubtedly held court. The door has a strikingly modern black-and-white marble surround and the entrance hall (*driba*) has impressive (mainly new) tile panels. The building once housed the Department of Traditional Arts, managed by craft expert Jacques Revault. Trained in Morocco, Revault surely had a traditional Moroccan *riyad* in mind when he planted the courtyard at Dar Othman – if you are allowed inside, you will find a pleasant space planted with hibiscus, pomegranate and cypress trees. Otherwise, Dar Othman follows the usual pattern for a Tunisois house, with narrow sleeping/reception rooms placed around a central courtyard. Today, the building houses the offices of the Conservation de la Médina de Tunis, one of two associations working to preserve the old town and its monuments (the other being the Association de Sauvegarde de la Médina de Tunis).

Double back up Rue el Mbazaâ and turn right into Rue des Teinturiers towards **Souk el Belat** and its numerous herbalist stalls. Continue straight ahead to reach Rue Jamaâ Ezzitouna, the main tourist drag.

A TOUR OF DOWNTOWN AND VILLE NOUVELLE (2hrs) Centred around Avenue Bourguiba, this is one of Tunis's more modern neighbourhoods, dating to the mid 19th century. Back in the 1850s, Avenue Bourguiba started life as the Avenue de la Marine, linking the Medina to the old customs building. Later, under the French, it was renamed Avenue Jules Ferry, after one of the great figures of 19th-century French politics, the instigator of universal free primary education. After independence, the avenue, like so many other main streets in Tunisia's towns, took the name of the new Tunisian republic's first president.

On the avenue, start at the statue of the berobed and turbanned **Ibn Khaldoun** [94 A2]. Around you are a variety of buildings bearing witness to the huge changes that Tunis has seen since the 19th century. Facing the statue, on your left, is the **French Embassy** [94 A3], a simple Neoclassical building and the first significant construction outside the walls of the old city. In its day it must have been very significant, marking the supremacy of the French consuls over their counterparts. Today, it is very easy to spot thanks to the significant security forces presence outside. Opposite the embassy are the twin bell-towers of the 1897 **Cathédrale St-Vincent-**

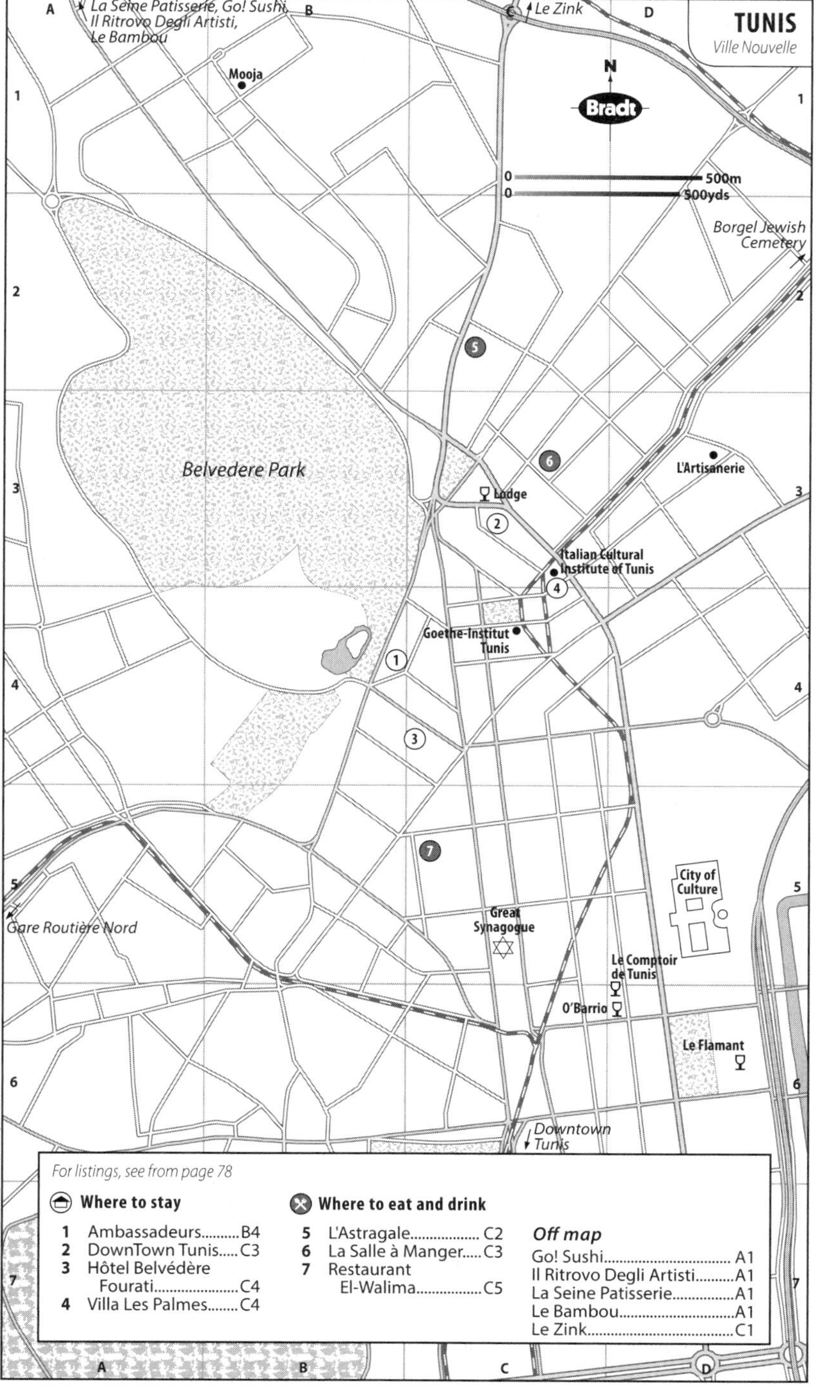
TUNIS
Ville Nouvelle
La Seine Patisserie, Go! Sushi, Il Ritrovo Degli Artisti, Le Bambou
Le Zink
Mooja
Bradt
0 500m
0 500yds
Borgel Jewish Cemetery
Belvedere Park
L'Artisanerie
Lodge
Italian Cultural Institute of Tunis
Goethe-Institut Tunis
Gare Routière Nord
City of Culture
Great Synagogue
Le Comptoir de Tunis
O'Barrio
Le Flamant
Downtown Tunis
For listings, see from page 78
Where to stay
1 Ambassadeurs..........B4
2 DownTown Tunis.....C3
3 Hôtel Belvédère Fourati.....................C4
4 Villa Les Palmes........C4
Where to eat and drink
5 L'Astragale.................C2
6 La Salle à Manger.....C3
7 Restaurant El-Walima................C5
Off map
Go! Sushi...............................A1
Il Ritrovo Degli Artisti..........A1
La Seine Patisserie...............A1
Le Bambou............................A1
Le Zink...................................C1

(w eglisecatholiquetunisie.com; 08.00–noon & 15.00–17.00 Mon–Sat; free); it was a pro-cathedral until 1964, when the Primatial Cathedral of St Louis at Carthage was downgraded. A saintly figure of the 17th century, St Vincent de Paul was once thought to have worked among the Christians held as slaves in Tunis. On the site of the present cathedral there would have been the small 17th-century Chapelle St-Antoine, no doubt built on or next to the ruined remains of the Nova Arx, a Spanish fort built in 1573. The cathedral's cavernous, austere interior can be visited via the side entrance down Rue d'Alger. It runs eight masses a week, mostly in French but also in Arabic and Spanish, with a timetable on its website. Behind Ibn Khaldoun, to the left, built above the arcades at the start of the Avenue de France, is the Art Deco **Immeuble National** built just after World War II and in its day one of the most luxurious apartment buildings in the city.

Leaving Ibn Khaldoun behind, head up the street towards **Bab el Bhar** (page 91). Here, on the eastern edge of the Medina, are the buildings of the **Quartier Franc**, the Frankish or first European quarter, dating to the 1660s. Unlike elsewhere in North Africa, there is no real perceptible separation between the Medina and the buildings on reclaimed land. In Algeria, for example, the French often demolished large areas in old Arab towns, while in Morocco, where the French presence started much later (1912), policy was to build new towns separate from the old cities, partly as a health measure. In Tunisia, however, the French built alongside the Medina, probably in large part because it was impossible to expropriate Muslim-owned farmland and olive groves around the city, and so the only solution was to continue building on land reclaimed from the lagoon by the Italian Fasciotti family.

From Bab el Bhar, head down the **Rue Mustapha M'barek**; the buildings here have some nice neo-Moorish touches in the shape of covered balconies with wooden fretwork, and some Art Nouveau mouldings. Turn left on to Rue d'Allemagne and then right into the fish halls of the **Municipal Market** [94 A3] (1891). The main fruit and vegetable area is housed under a fine wooden structure, which in its day must have represented an absolute revelation in Tunis in terms of the quality of work that went into this public building. Enjoy the colour and smells of the fresh produce. Cutting through the market, and crossing after the butcher's alley, you come out on to **Rue de Espagne** on the far side. Turn left, and on your right, on Rue Charles de Gaulle, is the imposing mass of the central **post office** [94 A3] (1893), a Neoclassical building in the 19th-century beaux arts tradition. It is surprising that such a significant building, symbolising a communications revolution, should be so hemmed in.

Continue down Rue Charles de Gaulle and turn left on to Rue de Russie to reach a small tree-shaded square now called **Place Mongi Bali** [94 A4] after the founder of the Tunisian Scouts. This was once a place of considerable symbolic importance in colonial Tunis. Until independence, the square had a statue of Philippe Thomas, a French army vet and amateur geologist who discovered phosphates in Tunisia in 1896 in the Metlaoui region (page 344). Soon after, Tunisia began exporting phosphates to France via a new railway built from Metlaoui to Sfax. Labour conditions in the phosphate mines were tough, and for obvious reasons the statue was removed after independence. Dominating the square is the **former Italian Embassy**, which is just as impressive as its French counterpart on the main avenue.

On the far side of the square is **Place Barcelone** and the **Gare de Tunis** [94 B4]. The first railway terminus was built in 1878, though the present building dates from 1979. Cross Place Barcelone and on the far side is the main north–south axis of the city, the **Avenue de Carthage**, laid out in 1878.

Head north up Avenue de Carthage to Avenue Habib Bourguiba. At the intersection with the Rue de Yougoslavie is the once elegant **Hotel Transatlantique** [94 B3] (which has some fine Chemla tiles in reception), next door to which is the new **Palmarium mall** [94 B3], a 1998 construction replacing a 1950s complex. Back on the main drag, have a look at the white wedding cake that is the **Théâtre Municipal** (page 87), the work of French architect Jean-Émile Resplandy, inaugurated in November 1902. Plaster sea-nymphs ride across the façade; inside is a world of gilt-and-cream woodwork and red velvet.

Cross Avenue Habib Bourguiba, following the metro line, and turn left up Rue Mokhtar Attia. This brings you out on Rue de Rome, at a junction with an interesting selection of buildings: the beaux arts-style former **Banque d'Algérie** [94 A2], now the home of the Tunis Governorate; the **Greek Orthodox Church** [94 A2], inaugurated in 1901, and an eclectic apartment building with some fine mosaic detailing. Head right, still following the metro line, down the main Avenue Habib Thameur; on your right is the former **Lycée Carnot** [94 B2], a vast 1930s construction, now one of Tunisia's top state lycées, while on your left is the **Trésorerie Générale** [94 B2], a government office again designed by Resplandy, with neo-Moorish decoration.

At this point, you may opt to head back to Avenue Habib Bourguiba for a citronade and a rest. Real architectural enthusiasts, however, will want to continue up Avenue Habib Thameur to **Le Passage**, where there are some nice examples of Tunisian Art Deco, including the angular **Hotel Ritza** [94 B1]. After the Le Passage intersection, Avenue de Paris becomes Avenue de la Liberté, from where it is a 10-minute walk to the amazing Art Deco **Great Synagogue** [97 C5] (also known as the **Synagogue Daniel Osiris**, after the wealthy French benefactor who endowed the construction). Designed by architect Victor Valensi and built between 1933 and 1938, this architectural gem, with its bold shapes and striking interior colour scheme, took its current form after former President Ben Ali paid for restoration works in the 1990s. Security here is tight, and tours must be arranged in advance either through a tour guide (page 77), or by contacting the Assistant to the Chief Rabbi of Tunisia (☎ 71 831 503; e cjt@cjt.org.tn). Those wishing to explore the Jewish cultural heritage in Tunis further might consider heading 1.5km northeast from the synagogue to the **Borgel Jewish Cemetery of Tunis**, which also contains two Commonwealth war graves of World War II. The soldiers belonged to the Pioneer Corps who perished in 1944.

CARTHAGE Just 14km northeast of downtown Tunis, the archaeological complex of Carthage is an exceptional place, the site of an original Phoenician settlement linked to Tyre that eventually evolved into a distinct Carthaginian civilisation. Here you can also see evidence of Roman Carthage, originally developed by Julius Caesar, as well as a former capital of both the Vandals and the Byzantine province of Africa. This unique layering of archaeological elements is one of the reasons why it was recognised in 1979 as a UNESCO World Heritage Site. Modern archaeological excavation began in the 1830s under Danish Consul to the Beylik of Tunis, Christian Tuxen Falbe, and continued via amateur archaeologists such as the Brit Nathan Davis in the 1850s. During French colonial rule there was renewed interest in the site, with significant early contributions from Jean-Baptiste Evariste Charles Pricot de Sainte-Marie.

Visiting Carthage (🕘 winter 08.30–15.00 daily, summer 08.00–18.00 daily; the Carthage Pass (12/9DT non-resident/resident) allows entry to 8 of the ticketed sites

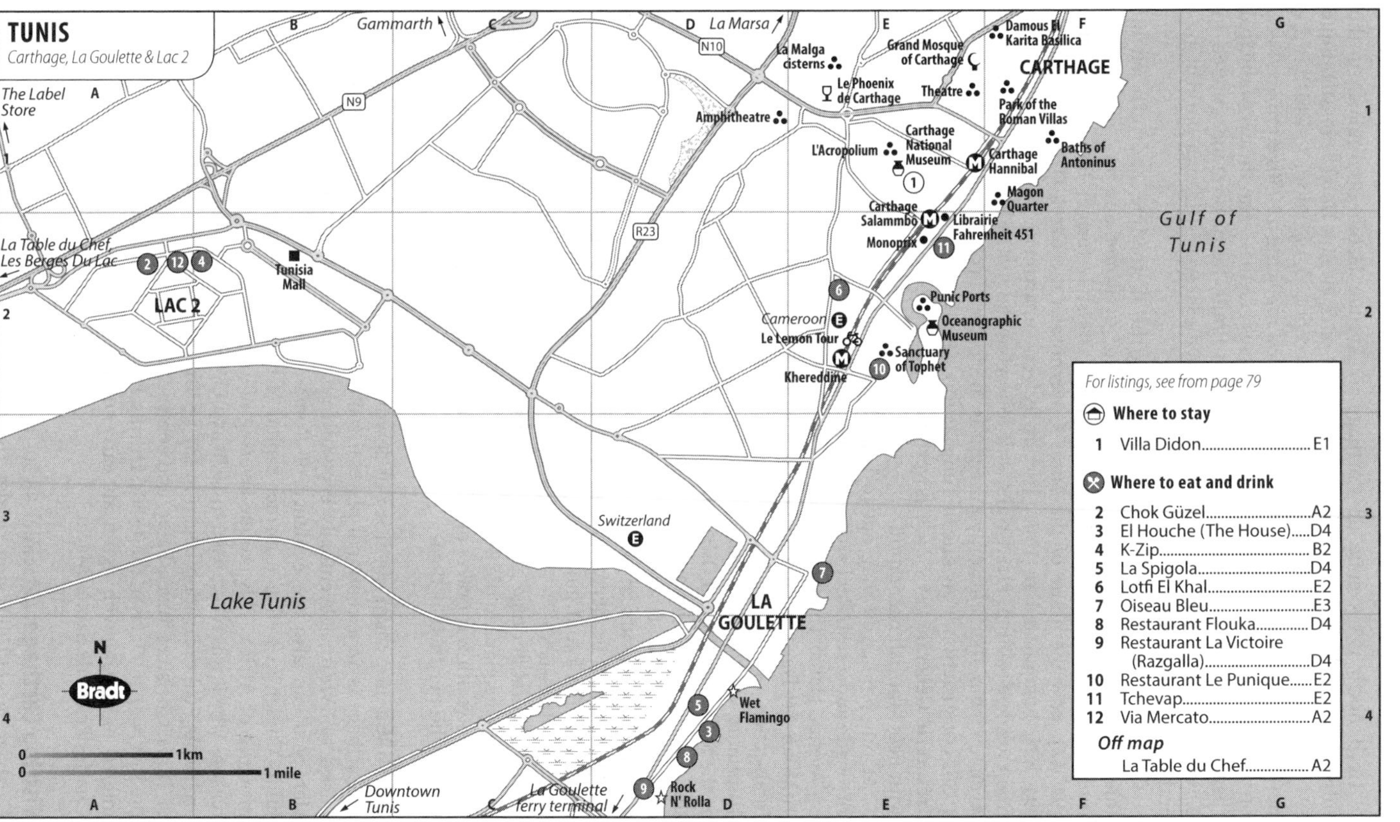
TUNIS
Carthage, La Goulette & Lac 2
The Label Store
Gammarth
La Marsa
N10
N9
R23
La Malga cisterns
Grand Mosque of Carthage
Damous El Karita Basilica
CARTHAGE
Le Phoenix de Carthage
Theatre
Park of the Roman Villas
Amphitheatre
L'Acropolium
Carthage National Museum
Carthage Hannibal
Baths of Antoninus
Magon Quarter
Carthage Salammbo
Librairie Fahrenheit 451
Monoprix
Gulf of Tunis
La Table du Chef, Les Berges Du Lac
Tunisia Mall
LAC 2
Punic Ports
Oceanographic Museum
Cameroon
Le Lemon Tour
Sanctuary of Tophet
Khereddine
Switzerland
Lake Tunis
LA GOULETTE
Wet Flamingo
Rock N' Rolla
Downtown Tunis
La Goulette ferry terminal
Bradt
N
0 1km
0 1 mile
For listings, see from page 79
Where to stay
1 Villa Didon....E1
Where to eat and drink
2 Chok Güzel....A2
3 El Houche (The House)....D4
4 K-Zip....B2
5 La Spigola....D4
6 Lotfi El Khal....E2
7 Oiseau Bleu....E3
8 Restaurant Flouka....D4
9 Restaurant La Victoire (Razgalla)....D4
10 Restaurant Le Punique....E2
11 Tchevap....E2
12 Via Mercato....A2
Off map
La Table du Chef....A2

DIDO, QUEEN OF CARTHAGE

Also known as Elissa, Dido was the mythical founder and first queen of Carthage. She is a key character in the *Aeneid*, a Latin epic poem about the Trojans, written by Virgil between 29 and 19BC. The legend goes that she was forced to flee Tyre, the Phoenician city-state of which she was in charge, after her brother, Pygmalion, murdered her husband, Acerbas.

Dido jumped in a boat and ended up at Utica (page 187) on Tunisia's northeastern coast. She then negotiated with the local Numidian king, Iarbas, for her own land, who said she could have as much land as she was able to cover with an ox hide. Dido cleverly cut the ox hide into long strips, and used it to encircle the entire territory of Carthage. For some reason Iarbas was fine with this, and Dido became the first queen of Carthage.

in the complex; entry is free every 1st Sun of the month plus on bank holidays) A short visit to Carthage gives only an overview. Organised tours are usually only half-day affairs, hardly adequate to get from one end of Carthage to the other (3km) and visit a few remains on some of the 12 main sites. Enthusiasts of all things ancient will want to allow at least a full day if possible. If you are not a ruins enthusiast, try to take in a selection of sites located close to each other. Starting early, you could start in the Salammbô area at the southernmost site, and view the Tophet, the Punic Ports and the main museum on the hill. (You could also do the Oceanographic Museum at the same time.) Real enthusiasts would want to pack in the Baths of Antoninus and a look at the theatre before lunch.

Sanctuary of Tophet [100 E2] (Rue Hannibal) At the southern end of the site, the Tophet houses the remains of the sanctuary of the Carthaginian divinities Tanit and Baal-Hammon, the oldest Punic religious site in Carthage. According to (mainly Roman) legend, for seven centuries the noble Carthaginian families brought their children here to be ritually sacrificed, and urns containing ashes and remains of many children have in fact been found. This site was discovered in 1921 and is considered to be the largest of all known sacrificial compounds. The ashes of the victims, sometimes small children but more often birds and young animals, were placed in a stone-lined trench. Other offerings, such as dishes and lucky charms, were buried too. When the whole area was filled with covered trenches, a layer of earth was placed across and the whole process began again. There is controversy surrounding the nature and extent of child sacrifice within Punic society, given the reliance on Roman sources who were hardly neutral towards the Carthaginians, and the possibility that some remains could be attributable to the naturally high infant mortality at the time. The Sousse Archaeological Museum has an excellent display on this topic (page 231).

Punic Ports [100 E2] Just north of the Tophet is the main harbour, which was the very heart of Carthaginian prosperity. The northern basin, circular in shape and bordered by quays, functioned as a naval base, boasting safe anchorage for 220 vessels. The southern base, originally rectangular in shape, was for merchant ships. The ports, well protected from attack, must have been the keystone of Punic commerce, situated as they were right in the middle of the Mediterranean. The small island in the middle of the northern port was the subject of research by a British archaeological mission in the 1970s, which revealed a fascinating Roman docking system. The island was built up as a circular space, with a spine carrying an upper service gantry, below which ships could be winched up into a covered dry dock. A bridge linked the island to the shore. This sophisticated dock was constructed to handle exports of wheat to Rome. Adjacent was the Commercial Harbour joined to the sea by a dredged channel. This harbour was a large circular basin surrounded by large warehouses.

Today the ports are free to wander around and are a popular spot for weekend fishing. To see them in all their former glory, check out the Historiar app, which allows you to tour 3D virtual-reality reconstructions using your phone (w historiar.io).

At the port you will also find the **Oceanographic Museum** [100 E2] (28 Rue du 2 Mars 1934; 71 730 420; winter 10.00–13.00 & 15.00–18.00 Tue–Sun, summer 09.00–noon & 16.00–19.00 Tue–Sun; 1/0.5DT adult/child). Officially the National Institute of Marine Sciences and Technologies Museum (INSTM), this 11-hall museum has displays on the marine habitats of the region as well as aquariums filled with various species of fish and turtles. There's also a huge whale skeleton outside the front of the museum.

Magon Quarter [100 F1] (Rue Septime Sévère) A fine example of Punic architecture dating from the 5th century BC, the Magon Quarter is approached down Avenue de la République, 700m northeast of the Punic Ports. It was destroyed in 146BC and rebuilt under Caesar Augustus. Following the excavations by the German Archaeological Institute, the site was turned into a garden and it is possible to walk along the restored Roman road by the seafront. A small museum displays household items found during excavations, and models and diagrams illustrate the development of the Punic settlement and the Roman rebuilding a century after its destruction.

Baths of Antoninus ✷ [100 F1] (Impasse des Thermes d'Antonin) This is the site's star attraction, 35m northeast of the Magon Quarter. Developed over a near 20-year period beginning in AD145 under Emperor Antoninus Pius, this was at the time the largest baths complex outside Rome, a testament to the wealth of Africa Proconsularis in the 2nd century AD. One of the best-preserved sites in Carthage, the baths occupy a splendid position between Avenue Habib Bourguiba and the sea. Thanks to the Vandals and various earthquakes, there are only a few pieces of masonry still standing above basement level. However, the remaining 15m-high column gives a good idea of the grandeur that once was.

The baths had a complex array of rooms. The layout is symmetrical around the central axis of the swimming pool, with the frigidarium and caldarium running from the seashore frontage to the second façade, facing west on to the archaeological gardens. The two wings each contained a palaestra or open pillared exercise yard, an indoor gymnasium, hot bath, tepidarium and destrictarium or warmed cleaning room. A laconicum or sweating room was included, while the main frigidarium was shared by both wings. Many of the minor rooms are hexagonal or octagonal in shape. Water for the baths came from the main city aqueduct. Being at sea level, the heating and service areas had to be built above ground, with the boilers immediately below, for efficiency and economy. There is a plan of the site available on the terrace overlooking the caldarium.

Park of the Roman Villas [100 F1] (Rue Aroub) Just west of the baths, on the other side of the railway line, this area gives a sense of what it was like living the high life in Africa Proconsularis during Roman imperial times. With names hinting at the themes of mosaics discovered inside (Lion, Horse, etc), the various restored aristocratic villas are of classical proportions, built around the peristyle or central pillared courtyard giving access to the main living rooms. This form can be seen clearly in the famous and now restored 5th–6th-century AD **House of the Aviary**, named after the subject of its mosaic bearing a well-executed polychrome of a fowl and fruit, today housed in the Bardo Museum (page 108). It has an octagonal garden in the middle of its courtyard. Just to the west of the villas are the poorly preserved remains of the **Odeon**, a former indoor theatre that has been cannibalised for building materials for other structures.

Theatre [100 E1] (Av Didon) Dating to the early 2nd century AD, this was first discovered and excavated by French archaeologist Paul Frédéric Gauckler in 1904, and it took the French colonial authorities less than two years to decide that plastering the whole thing with concrete to create a modern outdoor music venue was the best way to go. Today, thanks to multiple subsequent rounds of 'restoration', there is not much left of the original structure, although a statue of Apollo discovered at the site is now on display at the Bardo Museum. There is also an iconic photograph of Winston Churchill addressing Allied troops here on 1 June 1943, which shows what the theatre once looked like. The modern venue hosts events for the International Festival of Carthage every year.

Grand Mosque of Carthage (Malik ibn Anas Mosque) [100 E1] (Bd de l'Environnement) Inaugurated in 2003 by former President Ben Ali, this huge mosque has a 55m-high minaret and can accommodate up to 1,000 worshippers. Not quite in keeping with its ancient Roman surroundings, it gets very busy during special religious events but is generally closed to visitors.

Damous El Karita Basilica [100 F1] (Bd de l'Environnement) Following Boulevard de l'Environnement as it curves eastwards from the mosque, you come to the ruins of this Byzantine basilica. At over 2,925m² it was an impressive structure in its time, but has proven difficult for archaeologists to definitively identify and date. Today it is very popular with newlyweds, who head down here for photo shoots following their marriage ceremony.

North Africa American Cemetery [105 E4] (553 Rue Roosevelt; 71 747 767; w abmc.gov/north-africa; 09.00–17.00 daily) Dedicated in 1960 by the American Battle Monuments Commission, this 11ha cemetery, 300m north of the basilica, is home to 2,841 American military graves, as well as a memorial to a further 3,724 missing in action. Most of those honoured here are from World War II, from theatres ranging from North Africa to the Persian Gulf.

La Malga cisterns [100 E1] Right next to Le Phoenix de Carthage (page 86), this was Roman Carthage's water-storage system, with supplies pumped all the way from Zaghouan. Free to enter, you can wander inside these almost 100m-long cisterns, which are generally frequented by local shepherds with their goats and sheep.

Amphitheatre [100 D1] Situated at the western entrance to the city, this 19,968m² amphitheatre was once one of the largest and grandest public works in Carthage (along with the Antonine Baths). By the mid 2nd century AD, it was capable of seating 30,000 spectators for displays of gladiatorial combat, wild beast hunts and (eventually) the public execution of criminals and Christians. Sadly, there is very little to see as there has been limited excavation or restoration work here compared with some of the other archaeological sites in the area, and it is not even properly signposted off the N10 road that it connects to.

L'Acropolium [100 E1] (Colline de Byrsa) Also known as the Chapelle St-Louis de Carthage, this religious structure was built in 1884–90 on top of an old Punic temple during the French protectorate, but ceased to be used as a Catholic place of worship in 1993. Until the Covid-19 pandemic, this architectural gem poised on top of Byrsa Hill was used for craft fairs, music events and the odd (very fancy) private function such as weddings. Sadly, however, in January 2021 the building was closed by the Ministry of Cultural Affairs for urgent renovation work. No reopening date had been announced at the time of writing.

Carthage National Museum [100 E1] (Colline de Byrsa) Founded in 1875 in the former seminary of the Catholic White Fathers (Pères Blancs) – whom we have to thank for Thibarine liqueur (page 60) – this museum just behind L'Acropolium houses the single largest collection of Punic artefacts in the country, including many items discovered by renowned French archaeologist Alfred Louis Delattre. Standout items include the extraordinarily well-preserved 4th-century BC sarcophagi of a priest and priestess, as well as the 6th-century AD 'Lady of Carthage' Byzantine mosaic. It was closed at the time of writing, with no reopening date announced; however, it is still worth entering the site on a clear day to access the 3rd-century BC Punic settlement remains in front of the museum, and for the amazing panoramic views over the Punic Ports towards La Goulette.

SIDI BOU SAÏD Sidi Bou Saïd is everyone's favourite Mediterranean village, a jumble of whitewashed houses with blue-painted doors and windows on a hilltop overlooking the sea. Until a couple of decades ago it was quite an isolated place, a fact hard to remember these days when the village car park is full of tourist buses. Yet the back alleys of the village maintain their charm. Cats snooze on doorsteps, canaries trill behind latticework windows, and elaborate studded doors call out to be photographed. And from the heights of the village there are some breath-taking views out across the Mediterranean and the Gulf of Tunis, towards the mountains to the south. The beach down by the marina is also very pleasant, although it gets very crowded at weekends.

Dar Ennejma Ezzahra 🍸 [105 B2] (8 Rue 2 Mars 1934; ☎ 71 746 051; w cmam.nat.tn; ⏲ 08.00–15.00 Mon–Fri (concert times vary); 5DT) A restored palatial residence, formerly home to French painter and musicologist Baron Rodolphe d'Erlanger and his wife, the Italian countess Maria Elisabetta Barbiellini-Amidei. This palace was an interesting location during World War II. It was initially requisitioned as

TUNIS *La Marsa and Sidi Bou Saïd*
For listings, see from page 79

Where to stay

1	Carthage Hill	D4
2	Dar Ennassim	E3
3	Dar Jaafar	E1
4	Dar Marsa Cubes	E1
5	Dar Souad	D2
6	Hotel Bou Fares	B1
7	Hotel Dar Said	B1
8	Hotel Sidi Bou Saïd	F3
9	La Villa Bleue	C1
10	Maison Dedine	G4

Where to eat and drink

11	Au Bon Vieux Temps	B1
12	bleue!	A1
13	Dar Zarrouk	B1
14	Japanese Curry Kitano	E2
15	La Closerie	B4
	La Villa Bleue	(see 9)
16	Le Golfe	E1
17	Monsoon by Hachi	F4
18	Sushiwan	C2
19	Tavernetta	E3

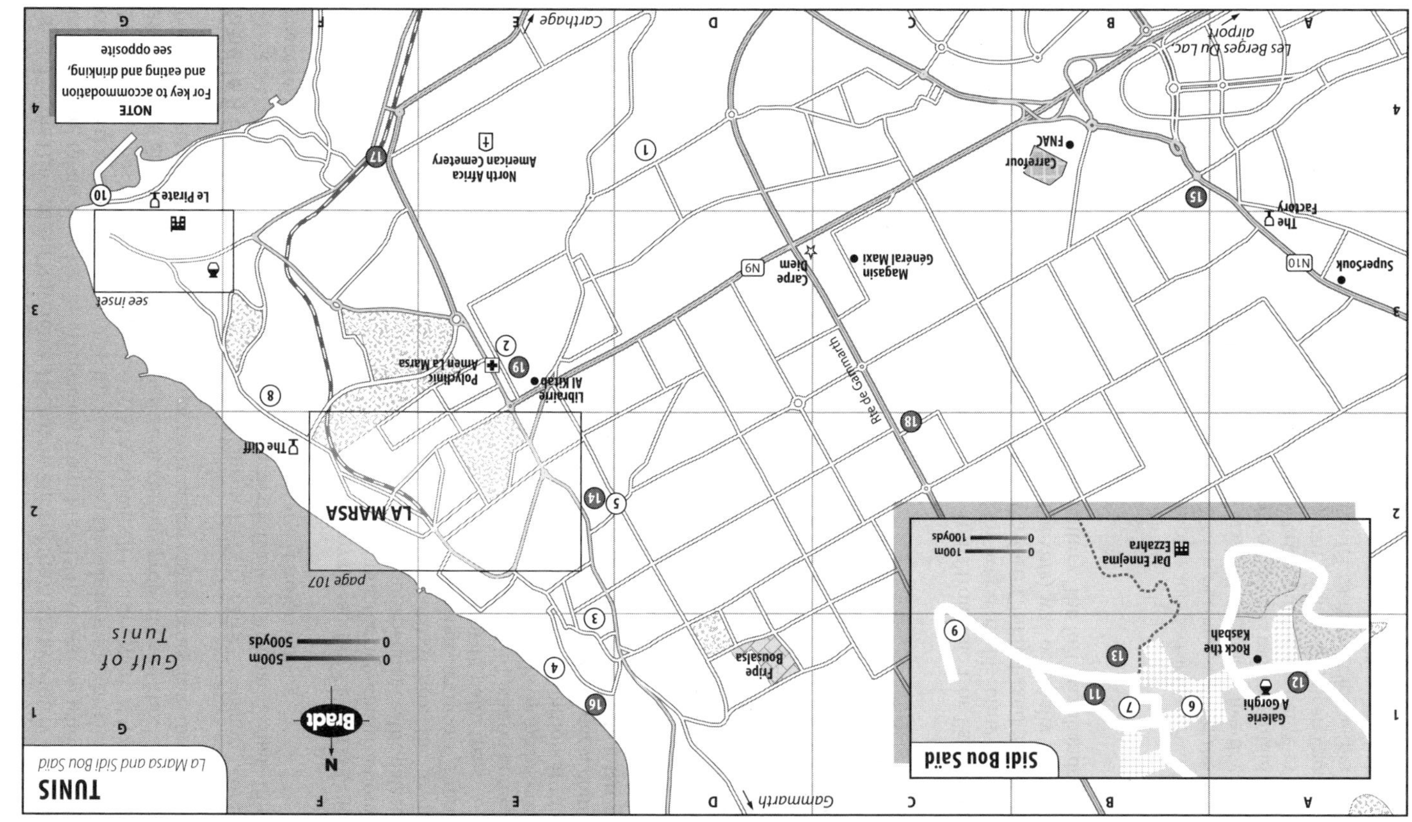
TUNIS
La Marsa and Sidi Bou Saïd
Gulf of Tunis
0 500m
0 500yds
Bradt
N
page 107
LA MARSA
The Cliff
see inset
Le Pirate
NOTE
For key to accommodation and eating and drinking, see opposite
Polyclinic Amen La Marsa
Librairie Al Kitab
North Africa American Cemetery
Carthage
Gammarth
Fripe Bousalsa
Carpe Diem
N9
Rte de Gammarth
Magasin Général Maxi
Carrefour
FNAC
The Factory
N10
SuperSouk
Les Berges Du Lac, airport
Sidi Bou Saïd
0 100m
0 100yds
Dar Ennejma Ezzahra
Rock the Kasbah
Galerie A Gorghi
A B C D E F G
1 2 3 4
1 2 3 4 5 6 7 8 9 10 11 12 13 14 15 16 17 18 19

an HQ by the Luftwaffe in November 1942 at the start of the Axis invasion of Tunisia, before being taken over by the Americans from May 1943 onwards, who used it co-ordinate the Allied invasion of Sicily. Today the palace is home to the Centre des Musiques Arabes et Méditerranéennes (CMAM), which hosts numerous live music events in the grounds. You can also tour the luxurious property and check out the baron's paintings and his incredible collection of musical instruments from the region.

Galerie A Gorghi [105 A1] (3 Rue Sidi El Ghemrini; ☎71 727 927; w agorgi.com; ⌚ 14.30–18.30 daily during exhibitions) Formerly Gallery Ammar Farhat, this space features exhibitions from mainly contemporary Tunisian artists.

LA MARSA At the end of the TGM line is the once royal resort of La Marsa ('the port'). The town grew up around a beylical palace, and among the new constructions a scattering of early-20th-century villas still survives. After independence, the palace was almost completely demolished by vengeful minister Taïeb Mehiri. The town retains traces of the laid-back atmosphere of an old-fashioned summer resort. There is a long, sandy beach (crowded in summer) and a promenade with palm trees.

In the early evening and at weekends, the area around the TGM station comes alive with families out to enjoy the air and an ice cream. Enjoy the atmosphere, smoke a shisha at the Le Saf Saf (page 83), or maybe take in an exhibition at the **Galeri El Marsa** [107 C1] (2 Pl du Saf Saf; ☎71 740 572; w galerielmarsa.com; ⌚ 10.00–18.00 Mon–Sat). Established in 1994 with the mission to generate interest in Arab art, and based in both Tunis and Dubai, this gallery focuses on Tunisian and wider Middle Eastern modern art, especially painting.

Hidden down a backstreet behind Zephyr Mall, you may only notice the **Keren Yéchoua Synagogue** [107 D1] (Rue Slim Haidar) from the 24-hour armed police presence out the front. Built in 1923 thanks to donations from Ariana-based philanthropist, Yéchoua Sauveur Kisraoui, the building is an interesting mix of Jewish and Andalusian architectural influences, all painted in the traditional Sidi Bou Saïd blue and white. You will have to admire it from outside as the building is rarely open these days, except for the odd worship during the summer months. You can get a good view from the roof terrace of A Mi Chemins in the neighbouring mall (page 84).

CHIKLY ISLAND [71 B2] Looking out across Lake Tunis from Lac 1 or Lac 2, you will see a thin strip of land cutting across the water for over 8km, bisecting the lake and ending in a small manmade island topped by a fort: Chikly Island and Fort Santiago. The fort (which gets a mention in *Don Quixote*) was originally Roman, but was expanded by the Spanish in the mid 16th century. The fort was abandoned

KAYAKING FROM LA MARSA TO TABARKA

In July 2021, along with a friend (Dean Mossop), I jumped into a two-person kayak on La Marsa beach and headed 250km northwest along the coastline to Tabarka on the Algerian border. It was a challenging, five-day adventure, during which we wild camped on some of Tunisia's most beautiful Mediterranean beaches, at one stage paddling 11km out to sea between headlands! Our four-video series on the journey can be found by scanning the QR code, and might provide some inspiration for camping trips within easy reach of Tunis.

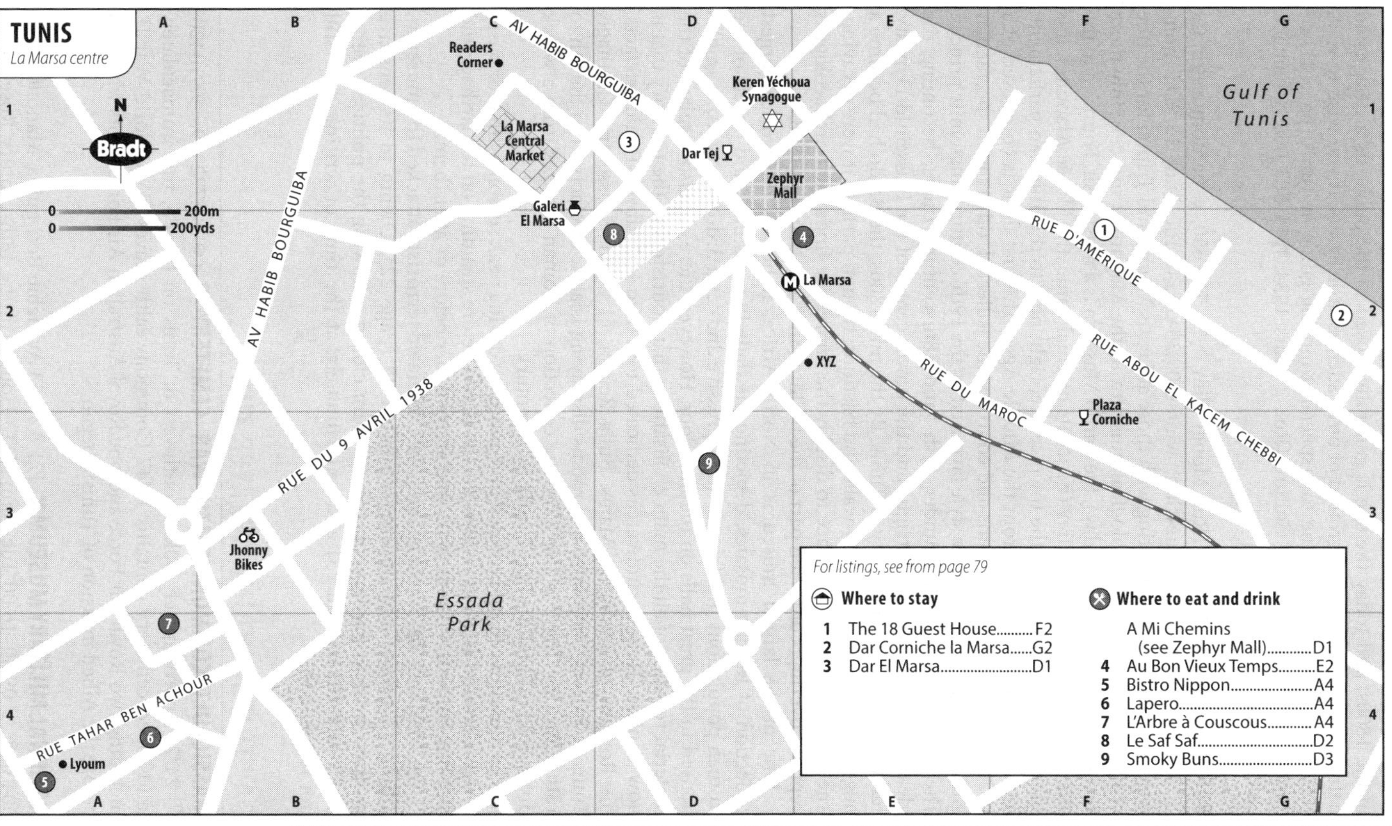
TUNIS
La Marsa centre
Bradt
0 200m
0 200yds
AV HABIB BOURGUIBA
Readers Corner
La Marsa Central Market
Galeri El Marsa
Keren Yéchoua Synagogue
Dar Tej
Zephyr Mall
La Marsa
XYZ
RUE D'AMÉRIQUE
RUE ABOU EL KACEM CHEBBI
RUE DU MAROC
Plaza Corniche
Gulf of Tunis
RUE DU 9 AVRIL 1938
Jhonny Bikes
Essada Park
RUE TAHAR BEN ACHOUR
Lyoum
For listings, see from page 79
Where to stay
1 The 18 Guest House..........F2
2 Dar Corniche la Marsa......G2
3 Dar El Marsa........................D1
Where to eat and drink
A Mi Chemins (see Zephyr Mall)............D1
4 Au Bon Vieux Temps..........E2
5 Bistro Nippon......................A4
6 Lapero...................................A4
7 L'Arbre à Couscous............A4
8 Le Saf Saf..............................D2
9 Smoky Buns.........................D3

in the 1800s, and today the site is generally closed to the public as a designated nature reserve, the nesting ground of birds such as little egrets. If you wish to visit, you could try either speaking to a specialist birding guide in Tunis (page 41) or contacting the Ministry of Culture (Rue 2 Mars 1934; ☎ 71 563 006; e contact.culture@mac.gov.tn).

BARDO MUSEUM [71 A2] (Rue Mongi Slim; ☎ 71 513 650; w bardomuseum.tn; ⏲ summer 09.00–17.00 Tue–Sun, winter 09.30–16.30 Tue–Sun; 13/8DT non-residents/residents) Competing with those at Leptis Magna and Tripoli for the title of most spectacular archaeological museum in the Maghreb (and certainly more accessible than those two today), the Bardo Museum is a must-visit. Founded in the late 19th century under Ali Bey (hence its original name, the Musée Alaouite), it is situated some 5km west of the town centre, right next to the Tunisian parliament, in a former Hafsid palace from the Middle Ages. The first floor is composed of a series of great reception rooms and courts, some galleried, others with spectacular gilding – an indication of the style favoured by the 19th-century Husseinite princes. The palace was extended under 17th- and 18th-century rulers, becoming the ideal setting for dynastic intrigue and the power centre of the Husseinid Dynasty, suitably remote from the city of Tunis. By the mid 1800s, the Bardo had become a huge complex surrounded by walls and bastions, though parts of it were decaying. The French, in need of a place to display the impressive finds their archaeologists kept discovering, converted part of the building into a museum in 1888.

One of the largest museums in North Africa, it houses the world's largest collection of Roman mosaics, depicting the daily life, pastimes and beliefs of the Roman populations in Africa, with impressive 2nd- and 3rd-century AD examples housed in the great halls on the first floor. However, there are also displays of the material remains of all the main civilisations that flourished in the territory that is now Tunisia. These include areas dedicated to: Punic and Libyco-Punic artefacts; the Romans of Thuburbo Majus, Bulla Reggia, El Djem, Sousse and Carthage; Tunisia's Palaeo-Christians; and rooms displaying Islamic artefacts from the 9th to 13th centuries. There is also a unique collection of Roman bronzes from a wreck discovered off Mahdia in the early 20th century.

The museum can get crowded mid-morning during peak season, with tour buses arriving around 10.00 as groups 'do' the Bardo before steaming off to Carthage and Sidi Bou Saïd, so it is best to try and arrive either before or after them.

On 18 March 2015, two Islamic State-affiliated terrorists attacked the museum, killing 22 people and injuring a further 42 (page 22). Owing to its sensitive location next to parliament, the museum closed following the political events of 25 July 2021 (page 23) and unfortunately, at the time of writing, had still not reopened.

DAY TRIPS AROUND GREATER TUNIS

MASSICAULT COMMONWEALTH WAR CEMETERY (⊕ 36.722369, 9.910420; ⏲ 24/7) Approximately 30km southwest of Tunis on the P5, this immaculately landscaped cemetery contains 1,447 Commonwealth graves from World War II, including two Royal Air Force and one Royal Australian Air Force pilots who died before the Allied invasion of Tunisia began.

NATIONAL MILITARY MUSEUM [71 A2] (53 Av Habib Bourguiba, Manouba; ☎ 70 604 018; ⏲ 09.00–16.00 Tue–Sun; 5DT) Housed in the 18th-century Rose Palace of Bey Hammouda Pasha, this museum outlines Tunisia's military history from ancient times to the modern republic. As it is located on a military base, your guide will be a serving member of the Tunisian military. You will also find aircraft and artillery on display in the grounds.

BORJ CEDRIA GERMAN MILITARY CEMETERY [71 D4] (⊕ 36.696778, 10.396895; note the entrance is incorrectly marked on some mapping software; w volksbund.de/en; ⌚ 09.00–18.00 daily; free) Hidden atop a forested hill in Borj Cedria, about 20km southeast of Tunis, this large military cemetery is dedicated to the 8,562 German soldiers who lost their lives during Operation Torch and the subsequent Allied North Africa campaign during World War II. As with other German military grave sites across North Africa, the cemetery is beautifully maintained by Volksbund Deutsche Kriegsgräberfürsorge e.V. and offers panoramic views over the surrounding hills, with graves divided by theatre of operations into six courtyards. Very unusually, the site is the resting place of a Wehrmacht general, General der Panzertruppen Wolfgang Fischer, who died on 1 February 1943 near Mareth when his vehicle accidentally entered an Italian minefield, blowing off his left arm and both legs. Before bleeding to death he wrote a letter to his wife, in which he requested to be buried in Tunisia with his soldiers (normally generals were repatriated to Germany).

This is a very difficult period of history for the modern German government to deal with. The commemoration of members of the Wehrmacht is controversial, especially in countries such as Tunisia where German forces committed war crimes. I am a history teacher by training and have spent over a decade teaching my students about Nazi Germany. As you can tell from my comments in the video tour, I am not sure I agree with the decision of Volksbund not to provide any historical context for visitors – more information about German activities in North Africa between 1939 and 1945 would be useful in helping visitors interpret what they see.

JEBEL BOUKORNINE [71 D4] This 576m-high mountain is in Boukornine National Park, less than an hour's drive from downtown Tunis. The summit, with its large TV mast, is clearly visible across the Bay of Tunis. You can park at the cafés (⊕ 36.726878, 10.328416) and then select a trail to follow (there is even a sign with a map here). Note that the summit of the mountain has an active military presence and is not open to the public, so the 6.5km trail to the top is not currently open, but there are plenty of other hiking routes to choose from.

JEBEL RESSAS [71 D5] Straddling the border between Ben Arous and Nabeul governorates, this 795m-high peak is a satisfying half-day hike, with reasonably well-marked routes and a couple of good spots for camping part way up. This mountain has been mined for lead since Roman times, and part of the standard route to the top actually involves walking through an old mineshaft (but be careful about which ones you enter, as some are hundreds of metres long, pitch black and have some steep drops). Unfortunately, despite the entire area being a nature reserve, there is an active quarry on the south side of the mountain that is slowly encroaching and destroying hiking routes. GPS trails for the various hikes are available on w tunisiatrails.blogspot.com, but be aware you may need to change your route depending on the situation on the ground. The car park for the trail head is at ⊕ 36.618651, 10.335668.

UTHINA (OUDNA) [71 A5] (⊕ 36.609285, 10.170285; ⌚ 09.00–17.00 daily; 8/5DT non-residents/residents) Around 30km south of Tunis and nestling on the

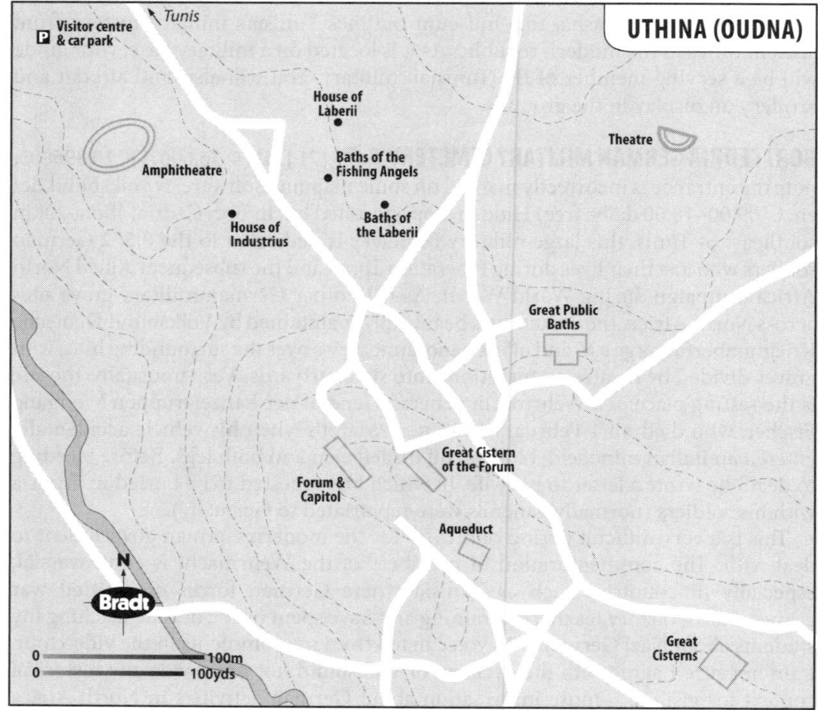

north-facing foothills of the Jebel Mekrima, this archaeological site features one of the oldest and largest preserved amphitheatres of the Roman world, as well as public baths, a forum, capitol and private residences housing mosaics. This was a very wealthy settlement, where Emperor Augustus settled veterans of his 13th Legion following the Final War of the Roman Republic, likely in the vicinity of a pre-existing Punic settlement.

Upon entering the site, you park in front of the main **visitor centre** (home to the ticket office, gift shop, conference hall and toilets). A metal raised walkway feeds from here into the **amphitheatre**. Likely built during the reign of Emperor Hadrian (AD117–38), it was the third-largest theatre in Tunisia after those at Carthage and El Djem, seating up to 16,000 spectators. You can wander underground and see the three lift shafts, used for transporting unfortunate men and beasts up to the arena floor. Today, the amphitheatre has been well restored and is occasionally used for events from live music to CrossFit games.

Walking southeast up the main road through the site, on your right is the **House of Industrius**, built towards the end of the 3rd century AD and covering approximately 700m². Clearly a wealthy man, Mr Industrius would probably not be pleased to hear that his prized mosaic of Venus Anadyomene has been lifted from his living room and transported to the Bardo Museum (page 108).

On the left-hand side of the road are the **Baths of the Fishing Angels**, the **House of Laberii** and the **Baths of the Laberii**, all excavated and restored in 2007–12. The three angels in a boat seem to be having a great time reeling in their nets from a sea overflowing with fish. The Laberii were clearly the wealthiest family in Uthina, with a 30-room residence of over 2,300m². First excavated by French archaeologist Paul

Gauckler in the late 19th century, their home was initially labelled as the House of Ikarios, owing to the mosaic of the Greek mythological character Ikarios handing a vine to the king of Attica. Today it is again housed in the Bardo, alongside the Laberii's fine mosaic of Venus seated on a rock while three cupids play with her veil, and the huge 'oceanic' picture with Neptune, Amphitrite and seahorse-drawn chariots around three boats carrying three ladies and a cluster of cupids. The baths were built in the 3rd century AD, but appear to have been repurposed as a kiln at some stage in the 5th century. If you look east from the baths you will see the **theatre**, though the area remains unexcavated and the above-surface ruins are poorly preserved, so it is probably not worth the trek over there unless you are a real enthusiast.

Continuing southeast, you hit the **Great Public Baths**. Built in the mid 2nd century AD, they were in use for almost 300 years. It is possible to clamber down to the below-ground level of this 12,000m² leviathan of a structure and explore the hallways where the Romans once bathed.

Finally, wander westwards uphill towards the **Capitol** and **Forum** (where it is possible to park your car, if driving yourself). Here you can see the various cisterns and remains of the **aqueduct** that brought in water from springs over 10km away for storage in the various **cisterns**. You will likely drive parallel to more remains of this aqueduct if you head to Uthina from Tunis. Walking up the steps of the Capitol towards the six columns, it is not difficult to imagine the former splendour of this massive public structure. Like the amphitheatre, this was constructed under Emperor Hadrian, and dedicated to the Capitoline Triad of Roman gods (Jupiter, Juno and Minerva). In the rooms below, there is a small display of archaeological remains from the site. One of the most amusing displays is a photo series depicting the post-independence demolition of a French colonial farmhouse that, for some reason, had been built up on top of the Capitol.

4

The Northwest

Telephone code: +78

Encompassing the governorates of Jendouba, Béja, Kef and Siliana, Tunisia's northwest is a diverse region that has seen incredible change throughout its thousands of years of history. Highlights include the coastal town of **Tabarka**, with its imposing 16th-century Genoese fort and vast sandy beaches. Backed by the Khroumirie Mountains, which run across the border into Algeria, this coastline is one of the wettest regions in North Africa, offering some great hiking and camping among the lush cork-oak forests that dot the hills inland from the coast. Every year it hosts a number of ultra-marathons and other outdoor sporting events which take advantage of the wonderful surroundings. Prevailing winds mean that this is also one of the few stretches of coastline in the country where you can surf. Up in the mountains, the settlement of **Aïn Draham** looks as though it has been plucked from a Swiss ski resort – a surprise to all first-time visitors.

Much of the interior is characterised by rolling hills and fertile farmland. This used to be a prolific source of grain for ancient Rome, which explains the wealth of amazing archaeological sites in the area such as **Bulla Regia**, **Maktar** and the UNESCO World Heritage Site of **Dougga**. The farmland has attracted settlers from overseas for hundreds of years, each wave leaving its own mark: Muslim refugees from Andalusia brought their architectural traditions from Spain to **Testour** in the 17th century, while Sicilian and Italian colonial-era migrants helped to develop a unique cheese culture around **Béja**, celebrated every year with a festival. At the southern edge of the region is mighty **Jugurtha's Table**, a flat-topped rocky mesa that offers incredible climbing and hiking opportunities.

CROSSING INTO ALGERIA

There are three border crossing points into Algeria from this region: Oum Tboul, between Tabarka and Souarekh (a busy crossing); Babouche (known as PCT El Aïoun), between Aïn Draham and El Aïoun (a busy crossing); and between Sakiet Sidi Youssef and El Haddada. See page 42 for more on crossing into Algeria.

BÉJA

Béja is the largest of the governorate capitals in the northwest, and the most prosperous. Sitting in the valley of the Oued Medjerda, it is a gateway from Tunis to western areas as far afield as Tabarka, Ghardimaou and Sakiet Sidi Youssef. Its strategic location, combined with the wealth of the surrounding countryside, has seen it targeted by sieges and invasions for thousands of years, though the Husseinid Kasbah is still standing, built on the site of 2nd-century BC Carthaginian fortifications. Today, it is famous for its range of local delicacies, including the *zlabia*

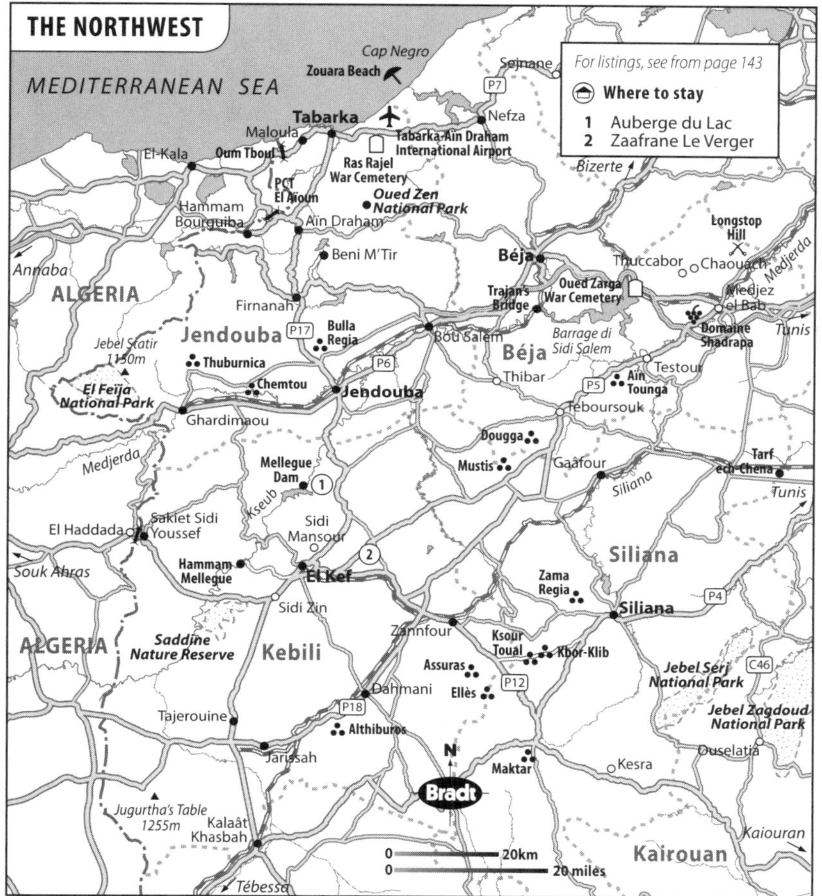

and *mkharek* pastries and the fantastic *rigouta* cheese. If you're here in December, don't miss the month-long, citywide Festival du Fromage (f Festivalfromagebeja), with all sorts of delicious tasting opportunities.

HISTORY The story of Béja (Vaga in Roman times) is one of conquest and reconquest. The first fortifications were built on the site of the current Kasbah over 2,000 years ago, and in that time it has been attacked (and sometimes destroyed) by the Carthaginians, Numidians, Romans, Vandals, Byzantines, Umayyad Caliphate, Fatimids, French colonial forces, Nazis and finally the Allies during World War II.

The 1st-century BC Roman historian, Sallust, hints at the reason for all this fighting, writing in his *Jugurthine War* of 'their rich and populous city…a town of the Numidians called Vaga, the most frequented emporium of the entire kingdom, where many men of Italic race traded and made their homes'. The area was a breadbasket of the Roman Republic and later Roman Empire, making it a key grain-trading town that helped to feed imperial armies as they campaigned across the Mediterranean. Vaga was also a key garrison point on the roads to Cirta and Hippo Regius (in modern Algeria). Emperor Justinian, Byzantine Emperor from AD527 to 565, recognised

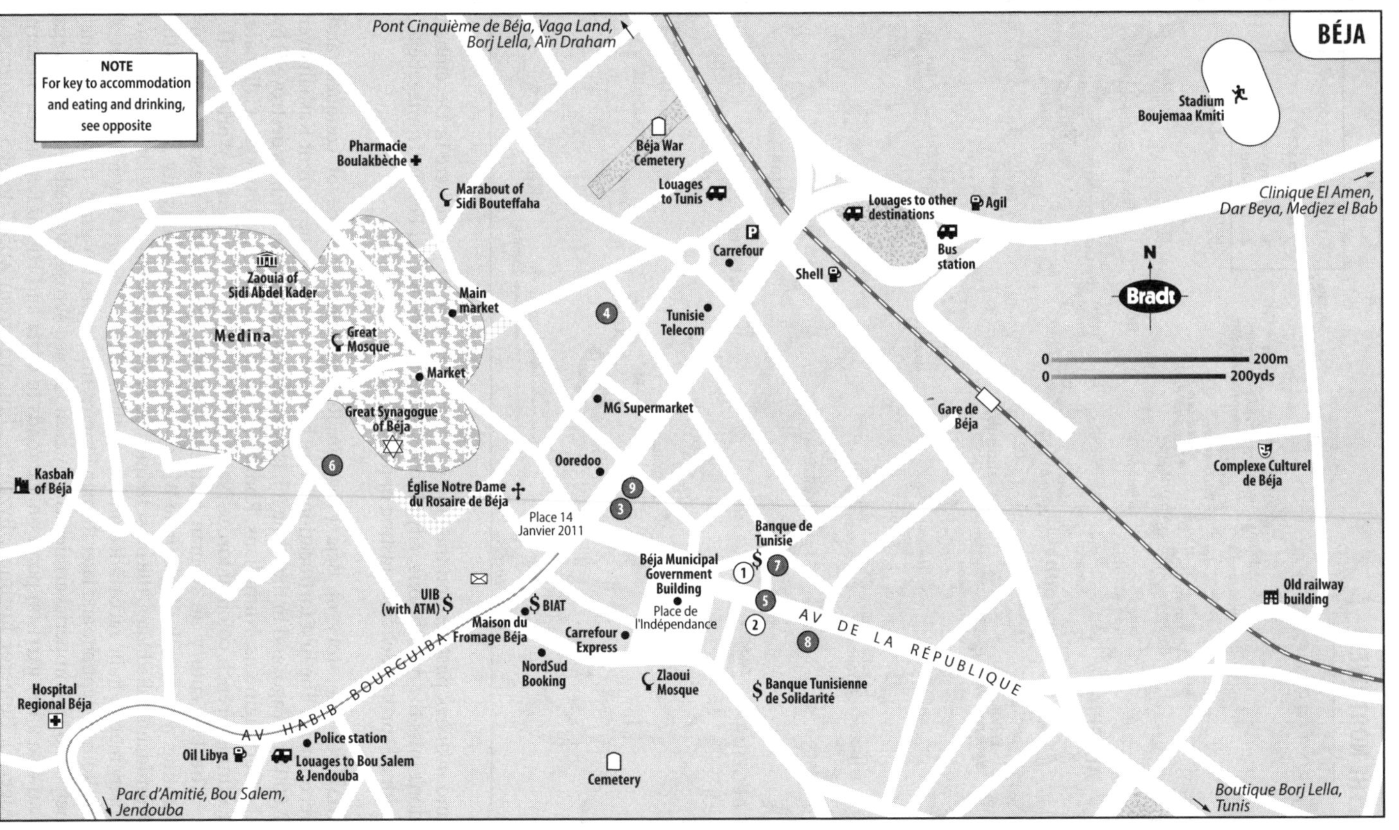
BÉJA
NOTE
For key to accommodation and eating and drinking, see opposite
Pont Cinquième de Béja, Vaga Land, Borj Lella, Aïn Draham
Stadium Boujemaa Kmiti
Pharmacie Boulakbèche
Marabout of Sidi Bouteffaha
Béja War Cemetery
Louages to Tunis
Louages to other destinations
Agil
Clinique El Amen, Dar Beya, Medjez el Bab
Bus station
Carrefour
Shell
N
Bradt
Zaouia of Sidi Abdel Kader
Main market
Medina
Great Mosque
Tunisie Telecom
0 200m
0 200yds
Market
MG Supermarket
Great Synagogue of Béja
Gare de Béja
Ooredoo
Complexe Culturel de Béja
Kasbah of Béja
Église Notre Dame du Rosaire de Béja
Place 14 Janvier 2011
Banque de Tunisie
Béja Municipal Government Building
Place de l'Indépendance
Old railway building
UIB (with ATM)
BIAT
Maison du Fromage Béja
Carrefour Express
AV DE LA RÉPUBLIQUE
NordSud Booking
Zlaoui Mosque
Banque Tunisienne de Solidarité
Hospital Regional Béja
AV HABIB BOURGUIBA
Police station
Oil Libya
Louages to Bou Salem & Jendouba
Cemetery
Parc d'Amitié, Bou Salem, Jendouba
Boutique Borj Lella, Tunis

the strategic importance of the settlement, investing heavily in walled defences for the city. As thanks, the Byzantine historian Procopius of Caesarea tells us that the inhabitants changed the name to Theodorias (after Justinian's wife).

The unification of Italy (Risorgimento) in the late 19th century caused significant political and economic instability in nearby Sicily, encouraging tens of thousands of Sicilians to pack up their belongings and move to Tunisia. Many of them being farmers, they were naturally attracted to the lush farmlands around Béja. The influence of these immigrants can still be seen to this day in Béja's flourishing cheese culture. More recently, Béja saw significant fighting during World War II, today commemorated in the Commonwealth War Cemetery in the northwest of town.

GETTING THERE AND AROUND

By road Béja is 115km west of Tunis (around a 2-hour drive along the A3). For car hire, speak to NordSud Booking (see below) or one of the higher-end hotels (such as Hotel Phenix or Al Kasba). Be warned though: the traffic in Béja can get pretty nail-biting!

The SNTRI **bus** station is on the eastern side of town, near the Hotel Aladino, from where you can catch the bus east to Tunis (2hrs; 8.30DT one-way), or northwards to Aïn Draham (2hrs; 6.90DT one-way). There are three main **louage** stops in Béja: at the south end of Avenue Bourguiba, with services towards Bou Salem and Jendouba; in the northwest of town, with louages towards Tunis; and in the northeast of town around and underneath the motorway flyover, with services to many other destinations.

The town is easily walkable, although the Kasbah is a fair distance from the centre. **Taxis** can be found at Place 14 Janvier 2011 (by the church) in the centre of town. They also tend to loiter by the train, bus and louage stations by the motorway flyover.

By rail The main Gare de Béja is northeast of town, near the motorway flyover. There are usually four SNCFT trains per day to Tunis (2hrs 20mins), with an early departure around 06.00 and the latest one at 16.43. Ghardimaou (which is 90 minutes away) has four daily trains to Béja, starting at 04.25 with a final departure at 15.10.

LOCAL TOUR OPERATORS

NordSud Booking 9 Rue Okba ibn Nafi; t 78 452 200/400; e contact@nordsudbooking.com; w nordsudbooking.com; f Nord.Sud.Booking; ⌚ 08.00–13.00 & 14.00–17.30 Mon–Thu, 08.00–17.00 & 18.00–19.00 Fri, 08.00–13.00 Sat. A good travel agency with a strong online presence & a particular focus on the northwest of Tunisia. Can organise car hire.

WHERE TO STAY

Dar Beya (6 eco domes) ⊕ 36.765948, 9.254514; m 98 319 444; e darbeya.dome@gmail.com; f Dome.Ecologique. 7.5km northeast of Béja on the P11, this ecotourism resort has been inspired by the 'moon cocoon' designs of Iranian architect Nader Khalili. Owner Hamdi Ben Freja has built 6 small eco domes – soil-based

BÉJA
For listings, see left

Where to stay

1 Hotel Phenix
2 Residence Iba

Off map
Dar Beya

Where to eat and drink

3 +216
4 Al Kasba
5 Ben Youssef
6 Boulangerie Sidi Mansour
Brasserie Le Phenix (see 1)
7 Café el Marouani
8 Restaurant Dar Béja
9 Restaurant Mnekbi

Off map
Borj Lella

structures made with 100% natural materials that look as though they have been lifted directly from Tataouine, each accommodating up to 6 people. Set on 2ha of land planted with cherry, olive & almond trees, it is a popular location for weddings, team-building activities & as a base for hiking in the surrounding countryside. B/fast inc; other meals available upon request. **$$$**

Hotel Phenix (24 rooms) Av de la République; 78 450 188; m 23 348 436, 98 154 500; e hotelphenixbeja@yahoo.fr or khelilmnekbi@yahoo.fr. Good-quality rooms with large bathrooms. Some noise from the road but a very good location. The restaurant next door serves excellent Béjaoise specialities. **$$**

Residence Iba (8 rooms) Av de la République. A restaurant, café & budget accommodation complex. **$**

WHERE TO EAT AND DRINK

Béja has a distinctive culinary tradition, influenced by its farming culture and the different communities that have mixed in this part of the country. Many items are steamed, harking back to Amazigh tradition. Some notable Béjaoise specialities include *ftet de Béjà* (slow-cooked lamb with rosemary, served with flatbread), *zlabia* (a honey-dipped, spiral pastry using fermented dough with turmeric, served during Ramadan), *mkharek* (a honey doughnut and another Ramadan favourite) and the fantastic local *rigouta* cheese made from Sicilian-Sardinian sheep's milk.

The best part of town for a cheap meal is the **market** just off Rue Kheireddine Pacha, with plenty of fruit and grilled meat for sale under the shade of a large tree.

✷ **Borj Lella** 36.835134, 9.259039; m 93 203 103, 96 727 272; w borjlella.com; f restaurant.borjlella; 09.00–15.00 Mon–Sun, booking required. Located 15km northeast of Béja, this family farm began 70 years ago & now offers assorted cheeses handcrafted on site from Sicilian-Sardinian sheep's milk. B/fast menu includes locally made items such as *mahkouka* (semolina with dried fruits and nuts) & unlimited cheese. Lunch is also a cheese-lovers' dream, but can also include *ftet de Béjà*. **$$$$**

Al Kasba 11 Rue Habib Haded; 78 454 545; m 94 078 235; 11.30–late daily. The new grey-&-black exterior of this restaurant is hard to miss. It serves good Tunisian cuisine, including local favourite *ftet de Béjà*. **$$$**

Brasserie Le Phenix Av de la République; 78 450 188; m 23 348 436; noon–late daily. Next door to the Hotel Phenix, this offers Mediterranean cuisine as well as specifically Béjaoise recipes. **$$$**

Restaurant Dar Béja 23 Av de la République; 78 443 680; m 99 940 204; e darbeja123@gmail.com; 08.00–23.30 daily. This simple family-style restaurant offers good service & delicious local dishes, such as *couscous Borzguène*, a sweet & savoury dish with couscous, lamb on the bone, dates & nuts from nearby Kef. **$$$**

+216 Av Habib Bourguiba; 08.00–23.00 daily. Oddly named but popular fast-food place for kebab & shawarma. **$$**

Restaurant Mnekbi Av Habib Bourguiba; 10.00–21.00 daily. Serving delicious rotisserie chicken & kebabs; you can't miss the bright-red signage. **$$**

Ben Youssef 12 Av de la République; m 98 238 497; 08.00–19.00 Mon–Sat, 08.00–14.00 Sun. Bakery serving fresh juices & a cheap place to grab b/fast if staying nearby at the Hotel Phenix. **$**

Boulangerie Sidi Mansour Rue Abri Zarrouk; 06.00–18.00 daily. Tucked away on a back street on the walk to the medina, this black & silver-fronted bakery does delicious fresh bread. **$**

Café el Marouani Av de France; 07.00–late daily. Beautiful old building with a porticoed front, looking out over a square featuring a fountain with dolphins. Very popular spot for shisha & coffee. **$**

ENTERTAINMENT AND NIGHTLIFE

There are plenty of coffee and shisha joints which stay open later in the centre of town, especially on Avenue Habib Bourguiba. As with many governorate capitals away from the coastal tourism resorts, you will struggle to find establishments serving alcohol, although the higher-end hotels (such as Hotel Phenix) do serve drinks at their bars. In the east of town, the **Complexe Culturel de Béja** (Rue de Ghana; 78 440 411; COMPLEXECULTURELBEJAOfficiel; 07.00–19.00 daily) hosts films, art exhibitions, live music events and dramatic performances in a modern space that includes an outdoor amphitheatre.

SHOPPING Those looking for gifts should try picking up some of the speciality cheeses for which the town is renowned. Your best bets are **Boutique Borj Lella** (56 Av de la République; m 93 203 103; w borjlella.com; 07.00–19.00 daily), which has a delicious assortment of sheep's-milk cheeses from the Borj Lella Farm just outside Béja (page 116), and **Maison du Fromage Béja** (Av Habib Bourguiba; m 28 776 588), though this was being renovated at the time of writing.

OTHER PRACTICALITIES **Banks** are located throughout the centre, especially near Place 11 Janvier 2011 and along Avenue Habib Bourguiba. For medical emergencies, head to either the **Hospital Regional Béja** (Av Habib Bourguiba; 78 455 431; 24/7) in the southwest of town, or the private **Clinique El Amen** (Bd de l'Environnement; 78 443 443; w beja.amensante.com; 24/7) in the northeast. For medical supplies, try **Pharmacie Boulakbèche** (Av Farhat Hached; 78 459 731; 08.00–20.00 daily). The **police station** is at the south end of Avenue Habib Bourguiba.

WHAT TO SEE AND DO Most public transport arrives in the north of Béja, near the motorway flyover. Just before you reach town, notice the **Pont Cinquième de Béja** (36.760888, 9.195074), a 38m-high, 350m-long arched railway bridge, constructed in 1915 to connect the Tunis to Béja railway line. The road passes directly underneath it. A few hundred metres from the bridge is the slightly mad **Vaga Land** (Pont 5ème, Rte de Tabarka; m 50 547 702, 98 154 800; VagaLandBeja; by appointment), an ATV recreational park and horseriding ranch that hopes to soon become Tunisia's first dedicated theme park (unless you count Carthage Land in Lac 1, which I do not!). Still under construction at the time of writing, it is hard to miss as you drive by, given the huge dragon statue overlooking the road. Until the park is finished, visitors will have to content themselves with horseriding and sand buggy treks in the picturesque surroundings.

Once you have made it to the bus, louage and railway stations by the flyover, take the main Avenue de Habib Bourguiba southwards to the heart of town. Before doing so, however, be sure to wander 200m northwest to the **Béja War Cemetery** (36.727440, 9.186480), which contains 396 Commonwealth burials from World War II, including 87 unidentified soldiers.

Turning right on to Place 14 Janvier 2011, note the large **Église Notre Dame du Rosaire de Béja**. The result of 40 years of competition between French and Sicilian congregations, this structure was inaugurated in 1938 when the French community finally outdid its rival. The church was closed at the time of writing, but is sometimes used for cultural events. To the west of here is Place de l'Indépendance, which is overlooked by the **Béja Municipal Government Building**, an amazing colonial-era structure built in 1933 with a unique balcony featuring a mixture of Classical, Islamic and more modern European architectural influences. Just south of here is the town's main **cemetery**, with the **Zlaoui Mosque** at the northern end, featuring distinctive blue-glass and yellow tiling.

Head back northwards through Place 14 Janvier 2011 to reach the **medina**, home to the **Great Synagogue of Béja** (⊕ 36.724307, 9.183301). There are records of a Jewish community in Béja since the 16th century, when Hebrew poet Rabbi Fraji Chaouat moved to the area (today he is buried in nearby Testour). This population peaked between the world wars, reaching 1,140 people according to the 1921 census. However, Tunisian independence in 1956, the Bizerte Crisis of July 1961 and the Six-Day War in 1967 led to the majority of the community emigrating to Europe or Israel. The synagogue was abandoned and today the building is used by the Tunisian Scouts (f scouts.beja). Slightly further north is the distinctive **Great Mosque**, built in AD944 by the Fatimids on the footprint of an earlier Christian basilica. It has brown terracotta tiles up the side of a square minaret, embellished with Moorish arches. A hundred metres further north is the **Zaouia of Sidi Abdel Kader**, an 1843 Sufi religious structure that was restored in 2009, but is currently not open to the public. If you then wander eastwards, you hit the **main market** area of the medina, with all manner of exotic and not so exotic foods on offer. Continuing out of the medina along Rue Caid Jaouhar you reach the 1737 **Marabout of Sidi Bouteffaha**, a small blue-and-green domed tomb commemorating a holy man, Sidi Ali Ben Sliman Bouteffaha, who came to Béja in 1621.

The **Kasbah of Béja** sits to the west of the medina overlooking the old town. Built on the site of 2nd-century BC Carthaginian fortifications, the structure here has been destroyed and rebuilt numerous times over the past 2,000 years. Today, what you see is mainly elements of the Husseinid Kasbah, with some later French colonial additions. The site was closed at the time of writing, but it sometimes hosts live music events during the Festival International de Béja (f festivalbeja) in August and September.

For those driving out of town, look out for the **old railway building** (⊕ 36.723219, 9.193556) if you cross the tracks following Avenue de La République eastwards towards the P6. Although abandoned and derelict, this imposing wooden structure with a tile roof must have been quite impressive back in its day. North of here is the **Stadium Boujemaa Kmiti**, home of Olympique de Béja, who at the time of writing are in the CLP-1 (Championnat de la Ligue Professionnelle 1), the Tunisian Football Federation's top division. For those heading south on the P6, there is a beautiful public park and forest, **Parc d'Amitié**, at ⊕ 36.714756, 9.180446.

AROUND BÉJA

Oued Zarga War Cemetery

(⊕ 36.677070, 9.413372) This cemetery, 20km east of Béja on the P6, contains 247 Commonwealth burials from World War II, including a small set of six graves orientated towards Mecca for the members of the British Indian Army interred here. The cemetery is 1km down a dirt track (turning at ⊕ 36.683646, 9.416833), overlooking the Sidi Salem Dam and reservoir. You will see the ruins of Oued Zarga church just outside.

Trajan's Bridge

(⊕ 36.639811, 9.200942) In the town of Mastutah, 15km south of Béja on the C76, this incredibly well-preserved, 12m-high three-arched bridge over the Oued Medjerda was constructed in AD129 under Emperor Hadrian, but his predecessor, Trajan, received the credit as he commissioned it. The bridge linked Carthage to Bulla Regia, which is 40km west of the site.

Thibar

Founded by Roman general Marius in the 1st century BC, this agricultural town is 30km south of Béja on the P6. Originally called Pagus Thibaritanus, it was populated by military veterans from the Jugurthine War (112–

105BC). More recently in 1895, the Society of the Missionaries of Africa (a group of French missionaries from Algiers more commonly referred to as the White Fathers) established a model farm and clinic, the **Domaine St-Joseph de Thibar** (⊕ 36.526124, 9.108752), which stretched over almost 2,000ha. The land was going quite cheaply as the area had a serious problem with leopards and malaria (both now gone). The missionaries did not let that hold them back: they steadied their resolve by inventing Thibarine liqueur, a strong digestif based on a secret blend of botanicals (claimed to contain dates) that is today enjoyed across Tunisia. The White Fathers also planted vineyards, turning Thibar into one of Tunisia's wine regions. Finally, they bred a new kind of sheep (the Noire de Thibar or Black Thibar) that was more suited to the conditions in the area. The mission was quickly nationalised by President Habib Bourguiba upon independence, although the White Fathers remained until 1975. The site is now the Lycée Sectoriel de Formation Professionnelle Agricole en Élevage Bovin de Thibar, an agricultural college specialising in cattle, although the buildings are very well preserved and if you ask at reception you can have a look around the grounds.

Just behind the mission is the **Thibar Seminary War Cemetery** (⊕ 36.527618, 9.105065), accessible via a dirt track and containing 99 Commonwealth burials from World War II, of which 98 are British and one is Canadian. Next door is a derelict colonial-era **Christian cemetery**, which features graves from the 19th century and at least one French serviceman.

BÉJA'S NORTHERN COASTLINE

Béja has a rugged 20km stretch of Mediterranean coastline which, though lacking in any major settlements, is perfect for hiking, camping and kayaking. The gateway to this region is **Nefza**, a quiet market town on the P7 that is built around agriculture (mainly fruit, vegetables, honey and cork from the cork-oak forest). Every April, the town hosts the Shitana Ultra Trail ultra-marathon (@shitana.tn), which features almost 3,000m of elevation change on the route through the coastal mountains.

One site of historical interest along this coastline is the former French colonial outpost of **Cap Negro** (formerly Tamkart; ⊕ 37.103575, 8.984793). From around 1970 to 1973, it was the site of an experimental French nudist colony run by Jean-François Parnaudeau; however, everyone was wearing their clothes when I visited in 2022, so presumably the experiment was not a success. Ten years ago, this peninsula could only be accessed by a rocky trail, but today there is a signposted, tarmacked road all the way from the turning off the P7 (⊕ 37.035844, 9.101896), just south of Tamera. On the way down, you pass **Camping Bellif/Maison Nature des Mogods** (5 rooms; ⊕ 37.060962, 9.048312; m 20 965 195; e ecotope.mastouri@yahoo.fr; f Maison-Nature-des-Mogods-101620704908933; **$**), an ecotourism project offering double rooms, a campsite with wash facilities and a signposted hiking trail. Check on its Facebook page for details of organised hiking trips in the area.

Unchecked development of holiday homes has somewhat spoiled the Cap Negro peninsula, although there is still a picturesque cove on the southern side of the promontory, mainly frequented by local fishermen. There is currently no hotel in town, although you can grab a coffee or a soft drink at **Escale du Cap Negro** (⊕ 37.103669, 8.984884; 08.00–17.00 daily; $), by the main car park.

MEDJEZ EL BAB AND AROUND

Like nearby Testour, Medjez el Bab was founded on the banks of the Oued Medjerda by Andalusian immigrants in the 17th century, on the site of a former Roman settlement (in this case, ancient Membressa). The Andalusians arrived in 1611, building the **Great Mosque** (⊕ 36.649700, 9.611700) in 1631, which was designated a Tunisian Heritage Site in 1915. The mosque is very architecturally distinctive, especially the 22.5m-high minaret in the northwest corner. The upper octagonal tower is richly decorated with colourful ceramics, and there is even a clock tower, which is very unusual in mosques from this period.

Mourad II, Bey of Tunis, built the **old bridge** over the Medjerda in 1677, so that he could move troops more easily in his wars against the Regency of Algiers. There is also an abandoned **synagogue** (⊕ 36.649253, 9.608301), a relic of the small Jewish community that used to live in this area (for more details, see page 26).

The plains around Medjez el Bab saw heavy fighting during World War II, beginning with an attempted German attack on the Allied forces here on 6–10 December 1942, and by February 1943 the Allied line had been pushed east of the town, at the cost of many lives, especially from the British 1st and 8th Armies. Today, Medjez El Bab hosts one of the largest **Commonwealth war cemeteries** in Tunisia, on the P5 4km southwest of town (⊕ 36.626249, 9.570775; w cwgc.org). It contains 2,903 Commonwealth burials, including 385 unidentified soldiers, as well as five World War I burials brought in from the Tunis (Belvedere) Cemetery and the Carthage (Basilica Karita) Cemetery in 1950.

Some 9km northwest of Medjez el Bab is the village of **Chaouach** (⊕ 36.711485, 9.540934), built on the site of a Byzantine fort and offering commanding views over the river valley. There are remains of the 2nd-century AD Roman site of Sua up here, as well as some *haouanet* (Libyco-Numidian rock tombs). Just west of

LONGSTOP HILL

Trevor Sheehan (w africanstalingrad.com)

Sitting on the C50 road, about 10km northeast of Medjez el Bab, is Longstop Hill (⊕ 36.735906, 9.649632), from which you can see Tunis and multiple battlefields in the nearby valleys and hills. One such significant fight was the Battle of Longstop Hill, which took place from 21 to 23 April 1943 and involved bitter fighting between British and German troops, with hundreds of casualties on each side. This was a significant victory for the Allied forces, as the hill represented the last great natural barrier that the Axis forces could use to delay the Allied advance on Tunis (which took place two weeks later).

Longstop dominates the Oued Medjerda Valley which flows past Medjez el Bab. Tunisia's only permanently flowing river, the Medjerda has created a hugely fertile area which is now dominated by extensive farms. Longstop Hill was nicknamed by the British Army as its position resembled a position in the game of cricket. The Germans called it Christmas Hill after they captured it from the British and Americans on Christmas Day 1942. There is a British war memorial at the foot of the hill (⊕ 36.726473, 9.666269) on the road in the village of El Herri. From this memorial it is easy to drive through the village up a dusty but passable track to near the top of the hill. The hill was fought over a number of times during the war. Many of the British dead from these battles are buried at the nearby Commonwealth military cemetery (⊕ 36.626249, 9.570775).

Chaouach is the site of the Roman town **Thuccabor** (⊕ 36.708519, 9.520796), where you will find a few remaining cisterns. It is also home to the award-winning **Ben Ismaïl Family Reserve** ✷ (⊕ 36.709692, 9.509398; m 23 801 064, 52 899 999; e triomphebensmail@gmail.com; f maherbensmail; ⌚ 10.00–18.00 Mon–Fri), where Triomphe Thuccabor organic olive oil is made. They offer three different olive-oil tasting experiences, and the farm shop stocks all their delicious organic products.

TESTOUR

Halfway between Teboursouk and Medjez el Bab on the P5, Testour is a worthwhile stop en route to or from Dougga, thanks to its unique Spanish history and architecture. Originally called Tichilla by local inhabitants (meaning 'green grass'), the modern town was founded on the south bank of the Oued Medjerda by Andalusian Muslim and Jewish settlers who moved here following their expulsion from Spain in 1609. The town soon became prosperous, but the settlers remained distinct from their Tunisian neighbours for a long time, both in terms of their architectural choices and language. When French physician and traveller Jean-André Peyssonnel visited Testour in August 1724 he noted that:

> All the inhabitants of that town were Granadians. They had shaped their city on the model of Granada and had given the squares and streets the same names as that of their old city.

Testour's inhabitants have long since assimilated into Tunisian society, but a few hints at their origins remain, such as their traditional roof-tile production, the architecture of the Grand Mosque, and some local dishes, such as *sfenj*, a light breakfast doughnut popularised in Al-Andalus in the 12th century.

GETTING THERE AND AWAY Testour is 80km west of Tunis along the P5 (an 80min drive), on the main louage route between Tunis and El Kef. Most SNTRI buses between El Kef or Thala and Tunis pass by town, as do louages between Medjez el Bab and Teboursouk. Your nearest SNCFT train station is in Oued Zarga, 14km north, although it is probably easier to get here from the much busier train station at Medjez el Bab, 20km east.

WHERE TO STAY Though there are no decent hotel options in Testour itself, there are two strong choices just north of town.

✷ **Les Vergers des Montagnes** (3 rooms) ⊕ 36.569349, 9.438442; m 52 830 909; e vergerdesmontagnes@gmail.com. This family-run guesthouse on a working farm offers basic but comfortable rooms & a hilltop pool, from where there are great views of Testour. The main attraction is the *table d'hôte*: delicious home-cooked lunches & dinners using local ingredients in very generous portions, all served out on the terrace overlooking the hillside. Try the coq au vin. **$$$$**

Camping Testour (Up to 100 pitches) ⊕ 36.564931, 9.437583; m 24 320 425; e Anisgammar50@gmail.com; f campingtestour. An idyllic campsite with swimming pool on the south banks of the Oued Medjerda. Meals available on request, including a b/fast of delicious fresh local produce. **$**

WHERE TO EAT AND DRINK There are a number of street vendors and cafés at the western end of the main street. For a sit-down meal, head to **Pizza Feu du Bois**

(m 20 256 019; f SalemOuelhaz; 11.00–late Fri–Wed; $$), which does delicious wood-fired pizzas right on the town's main square.

SHOPPING

L'Artigiano Testour Opposite the public library; m 27 774 801, 54 059 959; f FromageHamadii; 08.00–20.00 daily. A fantastic artisanal cheese shop selling all sorts of regional & Italian varieties.

Mazraa Market Av Habib Bourguiba; 78 570 707; 07.30–22.00 daily. A small supermarket with a selection of chilled & frozen goods. Also has rotisserie chicken.

WHAT TO SEE AND DO Starting on the west side of town near the louage stop, you first pass the amazing building of the **Farmacie De Nuit Nadhem Rgaya** (Av Habib Bourguiba; 78 571 076; 20.00–08.00 daily), which is well worth a visit even if you are not sick, with blue tiling and ornate decorated columns on the porticoes. Three hundred metres further east along the main road, if you swing northwards up Rue 2 Mars 1934, is the **Maison de Culture** (78 570 497; f MaisonDeCultureTestour; 09.00–18.00 Tue–Sat). The house was formerly owned by a wealthy Jewish merchant who burned his lover, Tunisia's most famous singer at the time, to death in 1930 (see below). Beautifully restored, the residence now serves as a cultural centre for art exhibitions and other events, which are listed on its Facebook page. It is also a good source of information on the annual **Festival International du Malouf**, which has been held in Testour since the 1960s. *Malouf* is a form of Andalusian classical music that was brought to North Africa by the Muslim Spanish refugees after their expulsion by King Philip III in 1609.

Coming to the main square, you pass the **Abdellatif Sahli Mosque** to your right. Tucked away down a back street, this small and unassuming 17th-century structure

THE FLAMES OF PASSION

The Hara, the Jewish quarter of Tunis, gave the demi-monde of 1920s Tunis a tragic figure in the form of minor diva, Habiba Msika (1895–1930), chiefly remembered today for such classics as *Ala sarir en-nawm dallani* ('On the bed of sleep he spoiled me, he gave me beer and champagne'). Her fan club, the *sakirel-lil* ('soldiers of the night'), followed her from concert to concert. She was dubbed *habibat el kul* ('beloved of all').

Habiba also conquered the heart of an elderly Jewish merchant from Testour, one Elyaou Mimouni. The bargain was the usual one: beauty for monied attentions. But Habiba was cruel, and Mimouni found himself rejected by his family and hometown. The besotted merchant eventually went wild with jealousy at his diva's varied loves, and burned down Msika's townhouse on Rue de Bône (today's Rue 2 Mars 1934) with the songstress inside.

Such a tragedy could not go undocumented and, in the late 1990s, Tunisian film producer Selma Baccar turned the fiery tale of the diva's life and loves into a film, *Habiba Msika ou la danse du feu*. Msika's former home in Testour is now the Maison de la Culture (see above), down a side street on the right as you head away from the Great Mosque.

But Habiba Msika was also touched by the political currents of the time. At La Marsa's Le Saf Saf café (page 83), at a famous concert in 1925, she struck a blow for liberty, turning the final song *Baladi, oh baladi* ('My homeland') into *Baladi tounis ou fiha el hurria* ('My homeland is Tunisia, where there is freedom').

tends to get overshadowed by the nearby Great Mosque. If you pause in the square near Pizza Feu du Bois, you will see a **stone plaque** built by the Testour Heritage Association commemorating Ettijani Belharcha, who was born in Testour in the interwar years. He served two terms as mayor of the town (1966 and 1972) before becoming one of the founding members of the Tunisian League for the Defence of Human Rights in 1976.

From the main square, you will see signs for the **Great Mosque**, whose high minaret, built in a distinctive style reminiscent of the Italo-Spanish renaissance, is visible as you enter Testour from the east. The clock face is said to be unique, allegedly not found on any other minaret in the world. The square tower is topped with two octagonal blocks and expert opinion is that the small pinnacles decorating the square tower and sundial hark back to the mosques of Aragon or Castille. The other key feature of the mosque is the tiled roof of the prayer hall, set with an unusual dome feature placed over the *mihrab* or prayer niche.

Heading south from the Great Mosque, back to the main road, if you walk down the hill to the east you rejoin the P5 at **Testour Cemetery**. Follow this road westwards round the bend and you eventually reach a turning for the **Jewish cemetery**. There are records of a small Jewish community in Testour from 1814 onwards, reaching a peak of 156 individuals in 1909. The cemetery became a pilgrimage site for Jews as far away as Algeria as it housed the tomb of a revered 16th-century Hebrew poet, Rabbi Fraji Chaouat. In 1924, local newspapers reported that 6,000 Jews arrived on pilgrimage that year, particularly during Sukkot. But how did Rabbi Fraji Chaouat end up in Testour, when he lived in Béja while in Tunisia? Legend has it that his dying wish, while in Béja, was for his body to be tied to the back of a donkey, and for him to be buried wherever the donkey stopped walking. The poor 17th-century donkey would have had to have walked at least 50km to get to Testour – unless it found some way of wading across the Oued Medjerda!

Heading northwards again from the Jewish cemetery to the southern end of Rue 26 Février 1953, you come to the 1733 **Zaouia Sidi Nasser Garouachi**, which features a typically Andalusian interior courtyard and painted ceramics.

AROUND TESTOUR

Aïn Tounga (⊕ 36.523840, 9.359587) Located halfway between Teboursouk and Testour on the P5, without clear signposting to the ruins, this 30ha site is often bypassed by travellers on their way to or from Dougga. This is a shame, as it hosts not only one of the most impressive Byzantine fortresses in Tunisia, but also the remains of the Roman town of Thignica. The 5,670m² fortress is very early Byzantine, dated by an inscription on the site to Domitius Zenofilus, proconsul of Africa Proconsularis from AD328 to 332. Sitting just 200m east of the road up a dirt track are the **baths**, a number of **temples** (including to Mercury and Neptune), **cisterns**, a **housing** complex, a well-preserved Roman **triumphal arch** and, further east in the site, the outer walls of a **theatre** (⊕ 36.522780, 9.362406). If you are feeling energetic, walk 500m northwards to ⊕ 36.527785, 9.361812 across the fields (or along the P5) to find the remains of an **amphitheatre**, set 125m east of the road.

Domaine Shadrapa (⊕ 36.612668, 9.532451; 78 599 300; w domaine-shadrapa.blogspot.com; f domainshadrapa; ⊙ 08.00–15.30 Mon–Thu, 08.00–14.30 Fri, 08.00–13.30 Sat) North of Testour on the P5 to Medjez el Bab is this wine estate, home of perennial favourite Désir Rosé. It offers excellent wine-tasting sessions and is well worth a day trip, even from Tunis (which is just over an hour away on the A3).

DOUGGA

(⌚ winter 08.30–17.30 daily, summer 08.00–19.00 daily; 8/5DT non-resident/resident) Dougga is one of Tunisia's eight UNESCO World Heritage Sites, and rightly so. When reaching their decision in 1997, the UNESCO judges noted: 'Dougga is the best-preserved Roman small town in North Africa and as such provides an exceptional picture of everyday life in antiquity'. Spread across nearly 75ha and set against an epic backdrop in the foothills of the Atlas Mountains, this place feels much bigger than it is. It is incredible that so much Roman architecture should have survived in such good condition for this long, including a 3,500-person capacity theatre that is still in use today. The site feels especially impressive given that it is empty outside peak season, meaning you can explore the alleyways and temples in complete privacy. Only 2 hours from Tunis, this is a site that every visitor to the country should consider adding to their itinerary.

HISTORY Dougga is situated on a plateau and down the side of a hill, overlooking the fertile valley of the Oued Khaled, from which it derives its name. In Latin it

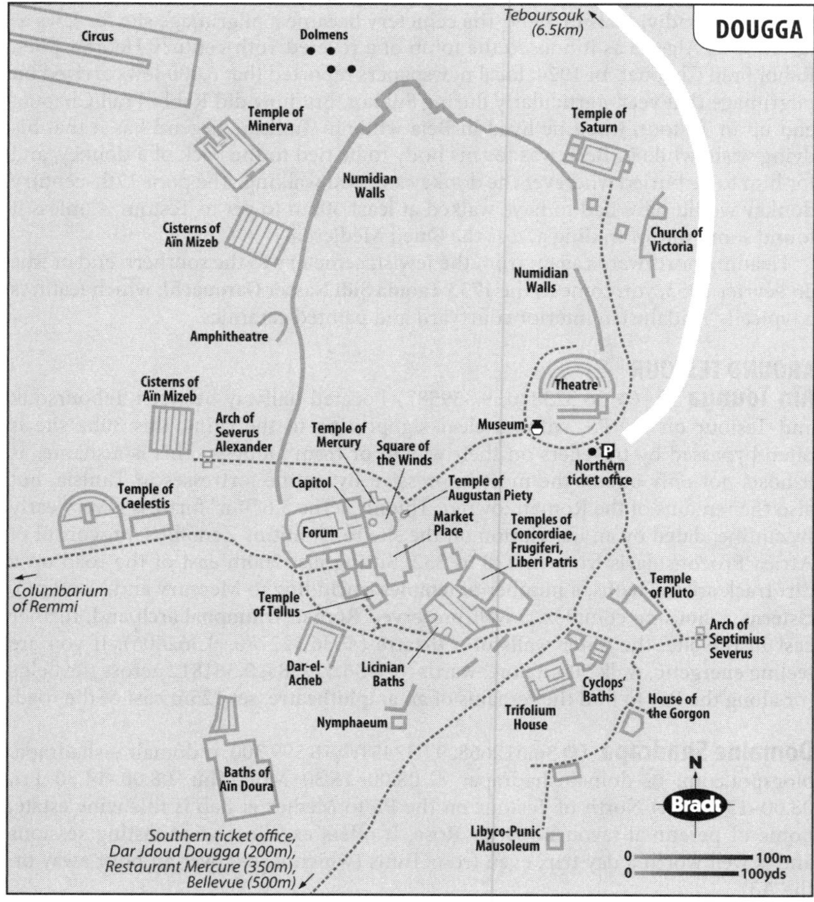

was called 'Thugga', which appears to be a Romanisation of earlier Phoenician and Amazigh names referring to its high, well-defended position. A quick glance at a map of the site shows that it does not conform to the usual Roman architectural norms of orthogonal grid planning and only building on flat ground. This hints at the site's earlier history, which may have begun as far back as the 6th century BC. By the 2nd century BC it had become the well-developed capital of Numidian King Massina, who used it as a base from which to support the Romans in their war against Carthage during the Second Punic War (or, at least, he did from 206BC after he had switched sides).

Although the region came under nominal Roman control following Julius Caesar's victory at the Battle of Thapsus in 46BC, it did not become fully Romanised for another 250 years. It even maintained a rather confusing overlapping dual administration up until AD205: one for the Roman citizens and another for the Peregrini (free provincial subjects without Roman citizenship). This was ended when Emperor Septimius Severus granted Thugga *municipium* status under the new name Colonia Licinia Septima Aurelia Alexandriana Thuggenses. The event was celebrated through construction of the large triumphal arch in the southeast of the site. The city was at its most prosperous in the 2nd century, which is why many of the most impressive surviving structures date to this period. Over the next 200 years, however, the city's fortunes would decline, and by the time the Vandals invaded in the 5th century, most of the inhabitants of Thugga had already moved to nearby Teboursouk, although the site was still occupied in the 19th century until local authorities forced the last remaining Tunisian inhabitants to move down the hill to Nouvelle Dougga or Nour Dougga (the name for the modern town).

GETTING THERE AND AWAY Dougga is 115km west of Tunis along the P5 (just under a 2-hour drive), just off the main louage route between Tunis and El Kef. To get here on public transport, take a louage to the quiet farming town of Teboursouk, 4.5km northeast, then get off at Nouvelle Dougga or Nour Dougga and walk the final 3km to the archaeological site. SNTRI buses between El Kef or Thala and Tunis also pass through Teboursouk. The nearest SNCFT train station is in Gaâfour, 16km to the southeast. If driving, there are car parks at the northern and southern ticket offices, although note that in low season there might not be anyone on duty at the southern one.

WHERE TO STAY AND EAT Your nearest decent hotel options are in Teboursouk, though Dougga can also be reached in under 2 hours from Aïn Draham and Tunis, or under an hour from El Kef, Siliana and Béja, all of which have plenty of good hotels. Two restaurants by the south gate of Dougga, Restaurant Mercure and Bellevue, were closed at the time of writing, but would certainly offer commanding views of the archaeological site if they ever reopened.

Hotel Thugga P5; 78 465 713, 78 466 647; e hotel-thugga@hotmail.fr; f Thugga.tour. Refurbished in 2020, the Hotel Thugga is a surprising find in Teboursouk. Rooms are spotless & modern, built around a glass-covered, astroturfed central courtyard with a mural of a wild-boar hunt on the wall. Dinner here is great, although the bar gets lively at night. **$$$**

Dar Jdoud Dougga m 97 306 697/678; e darjdouddougga@gmail.com; f darjdoudthugga; 09.00–20.00 daily. Opposite the car park by the southern entrance & mainly catering to organised tour groups, this is a solid restaurant overlooking the ruins. The wood & thatch design is great & it has a swimming pool. Menu features some excellent local dishes. Be sure to book in advance for food. **$$$**

EXPLORING THE SITE

Theatre From the northern car park, the first major monument you reach is the well-restored theatre. Originally built in AD168–69 and paid for by local bigwig Publius Marcius Quadratus, it is a typical example of a Roman theatre from the period. Though quite modest in size, it could nevertheless seat 3,500 people on its 19 semicircular tiers, in three stages, cut into the hill slope. This ensured the stability of the structure and simplified construction. The seating was closed off at the top by a portico, since destroyed, and it is suggested that a temporary screen or blind was erected over the seating to protect the spectators from the sun. Some of the columns have been re-erected on the stage but, now that the back wall is no more, a person seated in the *cavea* (seating) can enjoy a splendid panoramic view of the plain below. The theatre (today smaller) is still used for live music every July and August during the **Festival International de Dougga** (f Festival-international-de-dougga-424328987705689), which began in 1920.

Central area At the heart of ancient Thugga was the Capitol, with the temples of Augustan Piety and Mercury adjoining and the Forum and market close by. These were the public buildings and places where the men who ran the city would have been able to meet, arranging to discuss matters at the Forum or participating at the various rituals held in the temples.

Approaching the Forum and the great mass of the main temple, you reach the **Square of the Winds**, named after a compass-based inscription naming 12 winds cut into the paving. This square has, in fact, a semicircular wall at its east end, behind which stand the **Temple of Fortune** and **Temple of Augustan Piety**. The latter was a small, raised sanctuary with a smaller vestibule entered from the west by a stair. The engraving on the architrave supported by columns with Corinthian capitals indicated its name and use. This part of the archaeological site contains the **Temple of Mercury**, constructed in AD180–92 and composed of three chapels: a larger, rectangular central one, with much smaller lateral chapels, almost semicircular in plan. All three are dedicated to the same god, Mercury, who – among other things – was god of trade. It is therefore significant that the temple faces the market (see also Thuburbo Majus (page 218) where a similar arrangement exists).

The **market** is bordered on its two longer sides by a series of small shops, each exactly the same size, which were built under the portico – now vanished. In the centre of the market stood a fountain, and at the south end was a large alcove which probably held a statue of Mercury. To the right and the left of this alcove, a doorway leads out to separate stairways which descended to rooms below.

You cannot miss the **Capitol**, with its impressive set of steps and six huge, fluted monolithic columns over 8m high on the edge of the portico. These towering columns feature extensively in tourism promotional materials for the site. Built in AD166–69, it was dedicated to Jupiter, Juno and Minerva. The Corinthian capitals on these huge columns support an architraved frieze, bearing a dedication to the Triad for the salvation of the emperors Marcus Aurelius and Lucius Verus. The pediment features a bas-relief of an eagle making off with a human figure. Behind the portico is a 182m² *cella* (inner chamber), entered by a central doorway and divided into three parts, each with a niche in the end wall. The central, largest niche once held a white marble statue of Jupiter and the smaller side niches statues of the other two deities. Beneath the podium constructed to lift this capitol to its elevated position is a crypt, in three compartments, used at one time as a fort and at another perhaps as a church. A model of the Capitol area is on display in the Dougga Room at the Bardo in Tunis (page 108).

The $912m^2$ piazza in front of the Capitol at the base of the staircase opens on the west side to the **Forum**, also dating from the end of the 2nd century. It was the centre of public life and administration. Few of the original 35 columns (red-veined marble from Chemtou with white capitals) and bases remain. The floor beneath the porticoes which once surrounded three sides of the building was covered with mosaic tiles.

When fortunes became less secure in Byzantine times, the centre of Dougga was extensively remodelled for defensive reasons. At the Forum, traces of the Byzantine fortifications can be seen to the north (a rectangular tower) and south (a rectangular support). The fort, covering some $2,800m^2$, enclosed both the Forum and the Capitol and the gateways to the north and south. Much of the stone used to construct this fort was taken from older buildings on this site.

Also close to the central area is the small **Temple of Tellus**, the goddess of crop fertility, nearby which are the remains of a building referred to today as the **Dar el Acheb** (entry via a grand doorway with two Corinthian columns). Probably a temple originally, the four rectangular basins enclosed in the larger rectangular building were accessed from a door to the north. These basins could have been used for the storage of oil or even ritual washing.

Around the Arch of Severus Alexander Close to the central area are two pleasant ruins not to be missed. The first of these is the **Arch of Severus Alexander** (not to be confused with the similarly named arch on the southeastern side of the site; see page 128). Latin sources tell us little about Emperor Severus Alexander (AD222–35), but the citizens of Dougga clearly felt he had been generous enough to them to commission this arch in his honour. Tastefully placed among the olive trees, the 4m-wide arch once spanned a road that would have been one of the main access points to the city.

Nearby, look out for the **Temple of Caelestis**, also constructed during the reign of Alexander Severus, a few years before Christianity began to take hold in this part of North Africa. This rectangular sanctuary, once entirely enclosed by columns, is approached by an elegant flight of steps. There is a large, closed semicircular courtyard with a portico on the curved side.

Around the Licinian Baths This 3rd-century gift to the city by the Licinii family is a very large and complicated building, of which the furnace room, the hot room with the pipes visible in the walls, the cold room and the *palaestra* or exercise room remain. To the northeast, the **temples of Concordia**, **Frugifer** and **Bacchus** (**Liber Pater**) were constructed in AD128–38. The Temple of Bacchus is the largest and has a large square central area flanked by porticoes; on the northwest side are five rooms, the largest in the centre, while in the opposite direction was a small theatre, seats still present.

Below the Licinian Baths, heading away from the Forum, is a complex area of ruined housing where you can also see sections of the ancient **Numidian walls**, part of the same fortifications running north of the theatre and west of the Temple of Saturn. Although frequently labelled as of Numidian origin (partly because they contain two Numidian-era towers and other masonry from the period), archaeologists now believe that these walls were added in late antiquity, possibly by the Byzantines. In this neighbourhood, look out for the well-preserved **House of Dionysus and Ulysses**, where part of the first floor still survives. Now in the Bardo (page 108), the great mosaic of Ulysses, tied to the mast of his ship as he sailed past the Sirens, comes from this house.

WHO WERE THE SEVERANS?

The names of emperors **Septimius Severus** (AD193–211) and **Severus Alexander** (AD222–35) pop up regularly at Roman sites throughout Tunisia such as Dougga, where there are triumphal arches to both. But what was so special about them? In the late 2nd century, Rome went through a particularly difficult patch under Emperor Commodus, who lived a life of debauchery, renaming the city Commodiana and spending his time showing off his brute force fighting with wild beasts in the Colosseum. Eventually, he was strangled by a wrestling partner. In the power struggle that ensued among the military, one Septimius Severus, an aristocrat born in Leptis Magna (in present-day Libya), came out on top after four years of civil war.

Septimius Severus was the right strong man at the right time. He realised that the Empire faced some formidable enemies, notably on the eastern frontier, and hence was to rule from the frontier provinces. He added Mesopotamia to Rome's dominions, expanded the army and opened the career structure to soldiers from the ranks. His dying words to his sons are said to have been 'Do not quarrel with each other, pay the troops and despise the rest.'

Septimius Severus did not forget his African origins, and in 202–03 he overwintered in Africa. He had huge works undertaken at Leptis Magna, and Leptis, Carthage and Utica were given immunity from provincial taxes. The emperor had acquired huge properties in Africa Proconsularis, the lands of senators executed for their support of his rival Clodius Albinus. This no doubt gave him the resources for his considerable largesse towards Africa's cities, recognised by the construction of triumphal arches.

Unfortunately, Septimius Severus' sons, Caracalla and Geta, were not made of the same stuff as their father. Dynastic infighting followed, with Caracalla murdering Geta, only to be murdered by his own troops. Elagabalus, rumoured to be an illegitimate child of Caracalla, was also murdered after a short reign decadent even by Rome's standards, and his cousin, the young Severus Alexander, born in Lebanon, was to succeed in AD222. Severus Alexander, too, was eventually murdered by the army. The Severan Dynasty disappeared, and 26 emperors followed in 50 years. Although the mid 3rd century proved to be a time of chaos in Rome, the provinces of Africa prospered. Septimius Severus had broken the power of the warlike desert tribes, Numidia had been made a separate province and the defences reorganised.

Despite the vast sums spent on building programmes and the army, the Severan period saw a development which was to have long-lasting effects for Europe. Septimius Severus named Papinian praetorian prefect. Along with jurists Ulpian and Julius Paulus, he laid the basis of the Roman law that was eventually codified by the emperor Justinian in the 6th century. And, under Caracalla, an edict was issued granting Roman citizenship to virtually all free men in the Empire.

Lower residential area Below the Licinian Baths is an area where city homes and a further, smaller bath complex have been excavated. The **House of the Trifolium** here is usually presented by guides as Dougga's brothel, owing to the nearby relief of a penis and two breasts allegedly pointing the way to the structure. It dates from the 3rd century and is the best-preserved and largest house discovered on the site. It is built on two levels with the entrance at street level and the rooms on the floor below. The stairs on the north side of the house lead to a rectangular central garden or *viridium*. There was a small semicircular pool at one end, surrounded by a portico with a mosaic floor. The private quarters to the southwest have the vaulted, trefoil-shaped room from which the house was given its present name.

Next door, the **Cyclops' Baths** are named after the magnificent, extremely realistic mosaic taken from the floor of the cold room here and now on display at the Bardo (page 108). Dating from the 4th century, it shows three Cyclops working at the forge in the cavern belonging to Vulcan, the god of Hell. It is unusual to find figures of such gigantic proportions (well, they were giants) or with such dark skins depicted on Roman mosaics. The baths are not in a very good state, except for the communal latrine, which makes for a good photo opportunity. Further down towards the Libyco-Punic Mausoleum is the **House of the Gorgon**, named after the mosaic discovered here showing the Gorgon's head held in the hand of Perseus, also in the Bardo.

Libyco-Punic Mausoleum In the lower part of the city, looking for all the world like a lost piece from a giant's chess game, the Libyco-Punic Mausoleum is perhaps Tunisia's most famous pre-Roman ruin. In its day it no doubt belonged to a series of similar monuments being put up in the nascent towns of the Numidian tribal monarchy. Dating from the late 3rd/early 2nd century BC and drawing stylistic inspiration from archaic Greece and ancient Egypt, the monument hints at a faint influence of Hellenistic models. (The 3rd and 2nd centuries BC were a time when massive building works were undertaken in the Hellenistic kingdoms of Asia Minor.)

The mausoleum is dedicated to the Numidian Prince Ateban, son of Lepmatath, who was himself son of Pallu, according to the bilingual Libyic and Punic inscription, which also gives the name of the architect as Abarish. It is thought Ateban was a contemporary of Masinissa. The three-storey tower rises from a plinth of five steps and culminates in a pyramid, while the central section is reminiscent of a Greek temple. Originally, the pyramidal roof would have been flanked by birds with female faces, all set to guide the deceased's soul through the labyrinths of the afterlife. Take a minute to place this in context: it was a historic building when the Romans were building Dougga.

Having survived over 2,000 years, the 21m-high building was virtually destroyed by the British Consul in Tunis, Sir Thomas Reade, in 1842, who took the stones bearing the bilingual inscriptions back to the British Museum. Happily, in 1908–10 Poinssot and his team were able to reconstruct the mausoleum. With its simple silhouette, today it is one of the most elegant monuments at Dougga.

Retracing your steps up towards the House of the Trifolium and turning right, you come to the **Arch of Septimius Severus** (AD193–211), put up in this emperor's honour in AD205 after Thugga was made a *municipium* at his command, giving the community partial rights of Roman citizenship. The arch marked the eastern entrance to the city, sitting astride a 5m-wide road made of large limestone pieces set in a herringbone pattern. This was the main road to Carthage.

Behind the theatre to the Temple of Caelestis If you have time, you could go up to the back of the theatre's seating area and explore the plateau beyond, tracing a circle to come out close to the Arch of Severus Alexander. The remains here are not spectacular but give an idea of the extent of the city.

Moving away from the theatre, the ground drops away on a steep cliff and offers views on your right towards Teboursouk. To your right, as you approach the Sanctuary of Neptune, is a small Christian cemetery in which stands the

4th–5th-century AD **Christian basilica**. Many stones taken from the theatre and the Temple of Saturn were used in its construction. There are three aisles separated by two rows of columns; the central aisle is wider and longer ending in an altar. Two sets of stairs lead down to the crypt. The **Sanctuary of Neptune** itself is a small, rectangular sanctuary down off the plateau built near the now non-existent road that led to the Temple of Saturn. (Entrance is via a door in the east wall and a niche in the west wall opposite.)

Further on is the **Temple of Saturn** (AD195), its dominant position overlooking the valley signalling the importance of the cult. Apparently, it was built over the site of an earlier Baal-Hammon-Saturn sanctuary and is aligned almost east–west. The outer vestibule (some of the original Corinthian columns still stand) leads into the rectangular central courtyard, which originally had a gallery on three sides. At the west end are three equal-sized chapels, the central one of which once contained a marble statue of Saturn and, to the left, a statue of a man dressed in a toga, the benefactor.

Retracing your steps to the basilica, return to the top of the plateau and follow the line of the Numidian walls. There is one small section, only 130m in length, of very ancient walls with parts of two towers on the outer side. You may also be able to pick out some **dolmens**, stones set up as funerary monuments in some distant pre-Libyic past. Little remains of the **circus**, a very large rectangular area aligned east–west on the edge of the plateau, used for chariot racing. It is dated to AD214, with additions made some ten years later. Down the centre is the *spina*, a raised 190m-long area that ends in semicircles. Perhaps this is where spectators sat on the rocks to watch the charioteers race round this central strip.

To the southeast of the circus, the **Temple of Minerva** (AD138–61) remains only in outline. Enter by a central door into a large rectangular courtyard with a line of columns at each side. The sanctuary (outer and inner) at the northwest was reached upstairs. South further still, we find the **Cisterns of Aïn Mizeb**, which were a vital part of the town's survival. They are made up of seven long (175m^2) reservoirs set 1m apart, which stored water from the spring to the west. The method of construction and the lining to prevent leakage can still be examined where these cisterns are exposed. Having separate compartments prevented total loss if one part was damaged, and permitted cleaning and repairs without cutting off the supply. Further north are the similar **Cisterns of Aïn el Hammam**, five parallel reservoirs (each 102m^2) and one short one across the end, all fed from a spring in the southwest.

After the cisterns, the **Arch of Severus Alexander** is clearly visible and the **Temple of Caelestis** is on your right; turn left to head back towards the central part of the city.

Other buildings Down below the Dar el Acheb there are a number of minor ruins to look out for, including a **private chapel to Juno** (the Exhedra of Juno Regina), the **Columbarium of the Remmii**, a large funerary monument containing the tombs of the Remmii family, and the **Baths of Aïn Doura and cistern**. From these baths, heading towards the House of the Trifolium, you will come to a small **nymphaeum** or fountain on your left. The water for this came from Aïn el Hammam.

SILIANA GOVERNORATE

Like neighbouring Béja (page 112), Siliana Governorate encompasses some of Tunisia's most fertile arable land, and this wealth is reflected in the archaeological record, through sites such as Maktar and Mustis. Beyond extensive archaeology, Siliana is also home to Tunisia's highest town (Kesra), a nature reserve housing the extremely rare Cuvier's gazelle, and the site of the one of the most significant battles in ancient history: the Battle of Zama.

SILIANA Siliana is another quiet northern governorate capital, a farming town and hub for the region's agricultural produce. There has been a settlement here since at least the 4th century AD, although the modern town was only founded in 1905. Surrounded by olive, almond and apricot groves, it is a useful base from which to explore the archaeological sites to the south and east, as well as Jebel Serj National Park.

Getting there and around Siliana is 130km southwest of Tunis (around a 2-hour drive on the P3 and P4); SNTRI buses run between the two (2hrs 15mins; 9.50DT one-way); the bus stop is on Boulevard de l'Environnement. Louages connect with Béja, El Kef, Kasserine, Kairouan and Tunis, with most based at the louage stop where the C49 meets the C43. Given the grid pattern, the town centre is flat, compact and easily walkable.

Where to stay and eat Accommodation options are currently very limited in Siliana, with one hotel undergoing renovations (**Hotel Zama**) and the other closed (**Dar Askri**) at the time of writing. For now, your nearest good accommodation options are in Kesra, Tebersouk or Maktar. Food-wise, there are many cheap eats to be had in Siliana, particularly in the area around the Jardin Publique in the centre of town, where the 'I Love Siliana' sign is.

Sam's Fast Food Opposite Délégations Siliana Sud; m 99 455 333; f Sams-fast-food-106058654481907. ⏲ 11.00–19.00 Mon–Sat. A stylish, modern fast-food restaurant offering pizza, burgers, grilled meats & Tunisian favourites. You can book a table via its Facebook page. $$–$$$

Pizza Mamma Mia Jardin Publique, Bd de l'Environnement; ☎ 21 442 059; ⏲ 11.00–21.00 Mon–Sat. Good wood-fired pizza oven with outdoor seating in park by the fountain. $$

Ramirez Fast Food Bd de l'Environnement; ⏲ noon–late daily. Delicious fast-food joint offering pizza, kebab & makloub, though the purple décor is somewhat gaudy, with light bulbs hanging from ropes. $$

Why Not Café & Resto Bd de l'Environnement; m 98 776 990; ⏲ 08.00–22.00 Mon–Sat. Good spot to enjoy a fresh fruit juice or decent coffee under the orange umbrellas on the beautifully manicured lawn. $$

Café Panorama Rue Bizerte; ⏲ 08.00–late daily. On the roundabout opposite Oil Libya, notable for the Roman columns outside providing a shaded area. Does good grilled food. $–$$

Shopping The **main covered market** (Souq Al Baladi) is just behind Rue Ahmed B Abi Eddiaf and offers a variety of fresh produce, while the **fruit market** and **food and clothes market** are further north on Rue 18 Janvier 1952.

Those looking for gifts should head to **Wachma Siliana** (Rue Palestine; ☎ 95 055 260; f وشمة-wachma-824172284295946), a fair-trade and women's empowerment project supported by the German Embassy in Tunis and Les Aventuriers Siliana (page 138), who should be able to tell you where its products are sold, in Siliana and further afield. It sells magnificent local pottery and tapestries made by rural craftswomen. Its products are also available to buy via the Artisans d'Art Tunisie network (page 63), in locations such as the gift shop of The Residence in Tunis (page 80).

Other practicalities A number of **banks** are clustered on the P4 heading west out of town to Maktar. The **Pharmacy Bayrem Hamdi** is also on the P4, while the **Siliana Regional Hospital** is at the southern end of town.

What to see and do Siliana itself is light on tourist attractions. The **Jardin Publique** seems to be the centre of the action, surrounded by cafés and restaurants. It is a pleasant place for a stroll and features the ubiquitous 'I love Siliana' sign by the fountains, for those keen to post all over Instagram. If approaching the town from the west on the P4, note the green-and-white **Rahma Mosque.** For some impressive views, head 7km north of Siliana to the **Siliana Dam** (Barrage de Siliana; ⊕ 36.159646, 9.354823), which has a road running along the top of it.

ZAMA REGIA (AKA ZAMA MINOR) (⊕ 36.112117, 9.285928) Famously associated with the clash between Hannibal and Scipio Africanus that ended the Second Punic War in 202BC (see below), this site sits 8km northwest of Siliana and is easily accessible via the P4, signposted as Jema. Zama Regia was likely originally a Numidian settlement, with Roman historian Sallust talking about the settlement being involved in the Jugurthine War (112–106BC). Although there are no information boards, the archaeological ruins are still very impressive, sitting on a hill that gives commanding views of the Al Jamah countryside to the north. You can even walk down a surviving stone staircase into the site that includes column-lined walkways and a temple, all of which date from the Roman times.

WHERE EXACTLY WAS ZAMA?

On 19 October in 202BC, Scipio Africanus defeated Hannibal at the Battle of Zama (although even this is contested by some revisionist historians who claim the battle never took place). Following this victory, Roman hegemony across the Mediterranean was cemented, paving the way for the expansion of the Roman Republic and eventually the Roman Empire. However, despite the significance of this battle, archaeologists are still unsure where it took place.

One of the problems archaeologists face is that Zama appears to have been quite a popular name for settlements in this part of North Africa. Epigraphic evidence indicates that there were a number of cities called Zama, at least one of them 'major' (Maior) or 'royal' (Regia), and others 'minor' (Minor). One Zama Regia is mentioned in Sallust's *The Jugurthine War*, written in the 1st century BC (a good half-century after the events in question, although Sallust did actually live in that part of North Africa). The settlement was promoted in status for its loyalty to Julius Caesar during Caesar's Civil War. Emperor Hadrian seems to have further promoted the settlement, with one engraving recording the name as Colonia Aelia Hadriana Augusta Zamensis Regia. It then pops up again in the 13th-century Tabula Peutingeriana. However, none of the ancient authors are specific enough in their writing about the settlement for historians or archaeologists to geolocate it today: Polybius, Vitruvius, Sallust and Pliny the Elder all give us tantalising clues, but nothing specific.

For detailed discussions on the likely locations of key military sites around the Battle of Zama, see the Facebook group 'Kbor Klib – A site for the battle of Zama?' f groups/618157743397051.

GAÂFOUR ⚑ Also signposted as Qa Afur, this railway town is located 35km north of Siliana, up the C73 and C47 roads, sitting on the Oued Siliana and the main line that connects Tunis to Kalaât Khasbah. Those interested in colonial-era architecture might enjoy a walk through the former railway workers' quarter at the northern end of town around Rue Farhat Hached (⊕ 6.324433, 9.325600), with neat rows of old French housing facing the railway sidings, where old carriages can still be seen rusting in the sidings. Just to the west, the old Catholic church (⊕ 36.324500 9.324983), once used as a cultural centre, now sits abandoned with storks nesting in the steeple.

MUSTIS ⚑ *With Time Travel Rome (w timetravelrome.com)* (⊕ 36.335565, 9.143346) Located 35km northwest of Siliana and only 12km south of Dougga, this Roman archaeological site is just off the P5 at the northern entrance to the modern town of El Krib. Situated on the Roman road between Carthage and Tébessa, Mustis was an important Roman city, a centre for trading and a military deterrent against provincial unrest, as the town was initially settled by veteran soldiers of Gaius Marius's legions around the end of the 2nd century BC. The city obtained the rank of municipium under either Julius Caesar or Marcus Aurelius, while under the Byzantine Empire it became a fortress for defence against the Vandals. Rebuilding for this purpose destroyed some of the Hellenistic Roman architecture, though some still remains.

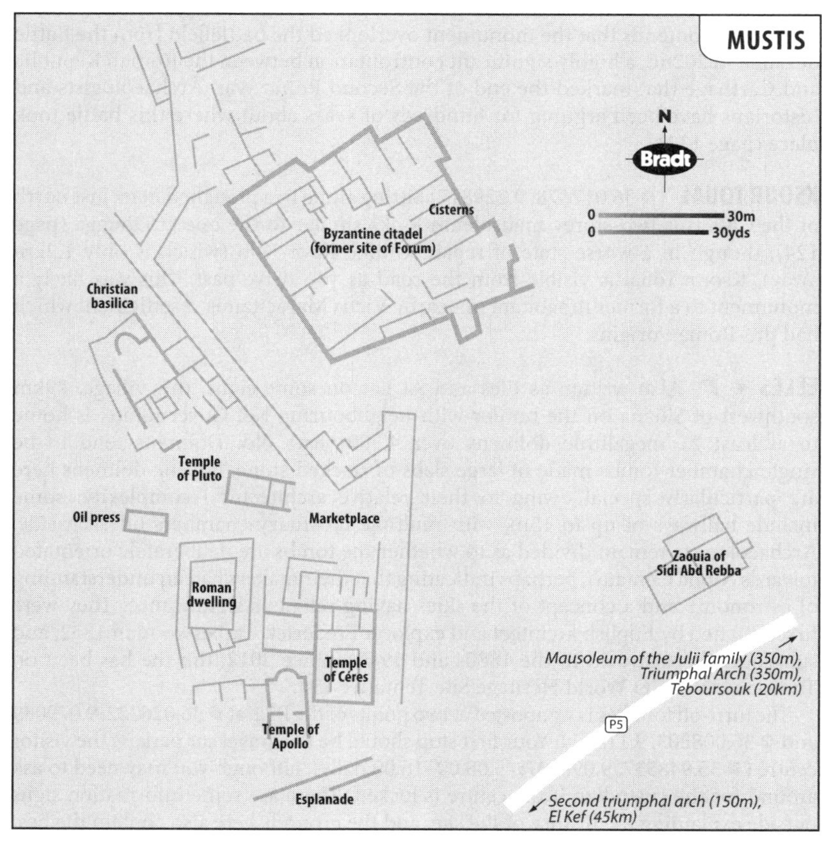

The Northwest SILIANA GOVERNORATE 4

The city became a bishopric through the 7th century, but after that is not mentioned in historical records.

The site boasts two triumphal arches, one of them having been largely restored, which mark the borders of the ancient city. Another structure which has seen extensive restoration is the impressive **mausoleum** of the Julii family. Partial remains of the city walls sit on the outskirts of the site, and a little way from a gate are the foundations of shops, a 4th-century AD **Christian basilica**, and temples to **Ceres**, **Pluto** and **Apollo**. Several other temples, cisterns, a Roman dwelling, the forum and marketplace have also been identified, as have scattered mosaics which form the floors of some of these buildings. Parts of the forum were lost, however, when the Byzantines built their substantial **citadel** over portions of it.

KBOR-KLIB ⚑ (⊕ 36.012525, 9.218703) The original purpose of this huge slab of masonry (45m long, 6m high and 15m deep) remains a mystery to archaeologists. Today it sits alone, isolated in a farmer's field on the south side of the C80. This ruin is best approached from the east or west along the C80, rather than from the south or north along the smaller country roads, as they are in poor condition. Theories as to its origins include it being a Numidian sanctuary or royal monument, or perhaps a work commissioned by Julius Caesar at some stage during his battles in Africa during the late Roman Republic. However, the most intriguing hypothesis comes from Duncan Ross's 2005 book, *Kbor Klib and the Battle of Zama*, in which the author contends that the monument overlooked the battlefield from the Battle of Zama in 202BC, a highly significant confrontation between the Roman Republic and Carthage that marked the end of the Second Punic War. Archaeologists and historians have been arguing for hundreds of years about where this battle took place (page 132).

KSOUR TOUAL (⊕ 36.017678, 9.229817) Sitting alone in a ploughed field, just north of the C80, this two-storey mausoleum looks similar to the one at Dougga (page 124), though in a worse state of repair. Unlike Kbor-Klib (which is only 1.2km away), Ksour Toual is visible from the road as you drive past. This was likely a monument to a former inhabitant of nearby Vicus Maracitanus, a settlement which had pre-Roman origins.

ELLÈS ✱ ⚑ Also written as Eles and Al Las on some signs, this village, 29km southwest of Siliana on the border with neighbouring Kef Governorate, is home to at least 71 megalithic dolmens over 4,500 years old. Dolmens tend to be single-chamber tombs made of large slabs of stacked stone, but the dolmens here are particularly special owing to their relative architectural complexity: some include hallways of up to 15m, with multiple mortuary chambers off each side. Archaeologists remain divided as to whether the tombs are deliberately orientated towards Alpha Centauri, perhaps indicating that their makers had an understanding of astronomy and a concept of the skies having religious significance. They were first sketched by English architect and explorer Frederick Catherwood in 1832, and subsequently excavated in the 1880s and 1940s. Since 2012, the site has been on Tunisia's UNESCO World Heritage Site Tentative List.

The turn-off for Ellès is signposted at two points of the P12: at ⊕ 36.026222, 9.079089 and ⊕ 36.008203, 9.113464. Your first stop should be the gravel car park by the visitor centre (⊕ 35.948537, 9.098137; ⏱ 08.00–16.00 daily), although you may need to ask around for the custodian if the centre is locked. There are some information signs outside explaining the history of the site, and the grounds here also contain the best excavated dolmen (which has metal beams reassuringly holding up the ancient, heavy capstones). From here, you can explore the 8ha site to the south of the road, where the dolmens are located. The nearest set is only 150m away (⊕ 35.947190, 9.098752), with others stretching all the way up the hill to the south. The farmers here cultivate the fields around the dolmens, so be mindful of crops as you wander.

MAKTAR (MACTARIS) Originally a Numidian settlement, Maktar (also written as Makthar and sometimes Mactar) was the site of numerous skirmishes between the Numidians and the Carthaginians, likely founded in an easily defensible position by the Numidians to prevent further Carthaginian expansion to the southwest. After the Roman sack of Carthage at the end of the Third Punic War in 146BC, a number of Carthaginian residents moved southwards, over time giving a more Punic flavour to the public architecture in Maktar. By 45BC it had been incorporated into the Roman Republic's province of Africa Nova and, by the middle of the 2nd century AD, it was a full Roman settlement, having been granted colonia status under the reign of Emperor Marcus Aurelius (161–80); an inscription from 198 identifies the settlement as Colonia Aelia Aurelia Mactaris. Fortunately for archaeologists, the site was completely abandoned in the 11th century following a raid by the Banu Hilal, a confederation of tribes from the western and central Arabian Peninsula. This meant that much of the Roman-era architecture survived without being recycled or built over, and remains in very good condition today.

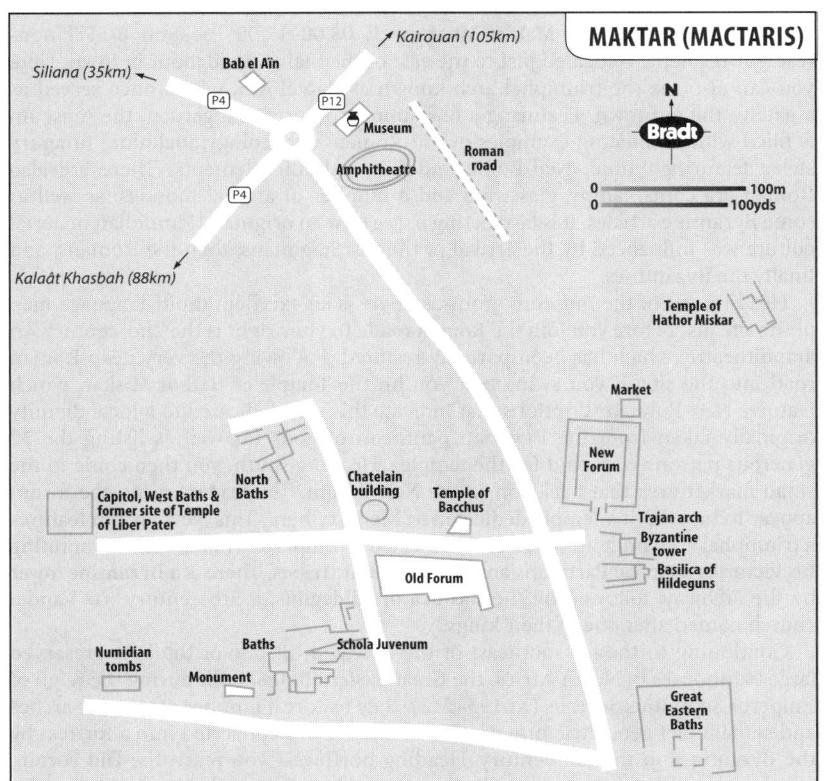

Getting there and away Maktar is 33km southwest of Siliana on the P4. On the drive down, note the collapsed tower, likely Byzantine, to your east (⊕ 35.930255, 9.224796). The town is on the main louage and bus route between El Kef (70mins) and Kairouan (2hrs), and SNTRI buses connect to Tunis (3hrs; 12.20DT one-way) and down to Kasserine (2hrs; 9.10DT). The louage stop is in the centre of town, just northwest of the archaeological site.

Where to stay and eat Although at the time of writing a new hotel was under construction in the south of town (⊕ 35.854139, 9.202768), there is currently only one accommodation option: the good-value **Hotel Maktharis** (5 rooms; Av Habib Bourguiba; ☎ 78 826 465; m 98 507 619, 98 473 319; e dr.bouhija@gmail.com; f HÔTEL-Maktharis-115970363110173; **$$$**). With its faux-ancient stone fascia and bright signage, it features modern and clean rooms with air conditioning, TV and high ceilings, with shared bathrooms, all opening out on to a shared living room area by reception. Downstairs, the **Barbara Bar** (⌚ 08.00–late daily; $$–$$$) seems to be the only place in town to find beers, making it very popular and very smoky in the evenings. To the right of the bar is a café and restaurant decked out in 1950s US diner style, offering fast food and a few Tunisian dishes. Otherwise, there are numerous cafés nestled in the porticoes around the main market, such as **Café Al Nasim** (⌚ 07.00–late daily; $), which is a good spot for a cheap coffee and some people-watching.

Exploring the site The **Maktar Museum** (⌚ 08.00–17.00 Tue–Sun; 8/5DT non-resident/resident) is located just to the east of the main roundabout in town. Here you can also see the triumphal arch known as **Bab el Aïn**, which once served as a gate to the old town. Featuring a few simple rooms and a garden, the museum is filled with fascinating examples of pre-Roman archaeology, including funerary stelae featuring Punic, Neo-Punic and Libyco-Punic elements. There are also Roman-era coins, lamps, glassware and a number of animal mosaics, as well as some Byzantine articles. It is fascinating to see how an originally Numidian material culture was influenced by the arrival of the Carthaginians, then the Romans, and finally the Byzantines.

Heading out of the museum grounds, there is an excellent multi-language map of the site just before you join the **Roman road**. To your right is the 2nd-century AD **amphitheatre**, which has been partially restored. Following the very deep Roman road into the site, if you swing east you hit the **Temple of Hathor Miskar**, which features Neo-Punic inscriptions that indicate this was dedicated to a local divinity originally taken from the Egyptian pantheon of gods (as well as listing the 32 generous patrons who paid for the temple). Heading south, you then come to the small **market** area that backs on to the **New Forum**. The traders using the forum appear to have built a temple dedicated to Mercury here. This New Forum features a triumphal arch built in AD115 and dedicated to Emperor Trajan, commemorating his victories over the Parthians and the Germanic tribes. There is a **Byzantine tower** by the archway, followed by the **Basilica of Hildeguns**, a 5th-century AD Vandal church named after one of their kings.

Continuing to the far southeast of the site, you hit one of the best-preserved large bathhouses in North Africa: the **Great Eastern Baths**. Built during the reign of Emperor Septimius Severus (AD193–211), they feature a number of massive arches and some intact geometric mosaics. This building was converted into a fortress by the Byzantines in the 6th century. Heading northwest you reach the **Old Forum**, which was probably situated here by the original Numidian inhabitants. The paving has not survived as well as that in the New Forum, meaning the meadow is able to fill with wild flowers in spring. The forum site also incorporates the remains of the **Temple of Liber Pater**, which was later converted to a Christian church. Opposite the Old Forum on the other side of the road is the **Temple of Bacchus**, although little of the above-ground structure remains. Next door, the **Chatelain building** is an unidentified temple, named after French archaeologist Louis Chatelain who excavated it in the early 20th century. Continuing westwards, you come to the Byzantine-era **North Baths** and finally the **West Baths**, which were built in the 2nd century AD and later converted into a church.

In the far southwest of the site are the **Numidian Tombs**, megalithic chambers that were subsequently used as an early Christian cemetery. Swinging back east from here, you reach a complex of ruins that includes the **Schola Juvenum** (an ancient Roman YMCA, but without the Christian element), more **baths** and a **monument** that is likely funerary in nature.

KESRA Sitting at an altitude of 1,078m, this is the highest town in Tunisia, located 20km southeast of Maktar on the P12. The drive down here is beautiful, heading through pine forest and past rugged, rocky outcrops that are reminiscent of the southwestern USA. If you are approaching Kesra from the southeast, the P12 passes through some picturesque rock formations (⊕ 35.776422, 9.466492) and then a tunnel through the mountain face (⊕ 35.771855, 9.447485) in the village of Dechret el Garia. Any louage or SNTRI bus plying the route from El Kef to Kairouan will pass through the new town of Kesra, which sits at the foot of the mountain by the P12, 1.75km south of the more tourist-friendly old town (Kesra Supérieur). There is a small car park in the centre near the post office and Seyadi Mosque, which is a really handy place to leave your vehicle before continuing on foot.

Where to stay and eat

Dar Hlima (3 rooms) ⊕ 35.813101, 9.367607; 78 892 523; m 21 967 206; e darhlima.kesra@gmail.com; f Dar-Hlima-1949586965163026. Opened in 2018, this former oil mill has been given a new lease of life by the NGO Kolna Tounes, in collaboration with the Swiss Embassy in Tunis. Old stone walls incorporate modern wooden touches, giving this boutique hotel a unique style. The shared living room features a large archway & open fireplace, while the views from the dbl bedrooms out over the plains below are stunning. It can organise meals for guests on request. **$$$**

Delices de Kesra ⊕ 35.813592, 9.366517; ⊕ noon–20.00 Sat–Thu. A basic 1-room canteen serving delicious local fare. Look out for the yellow-&-red sign on the wall as you head up the hill to the museum. $$

Café La Source ⊕ 35.813729, 9.365341; m 97 462 185, 22 191 966; e zgaya2017@gmail.com; f Kesra.Cafe; ⊕ 08.00–late daily. A cool café offering snacks, with coloured painted bricks out front. $–$$

What to see and do Heading on foot to the northeast of the car park, passing a number of street vendors selling local pottery, you reach the **fortifications**, built by the Romans in the 2nd century AD and then used by the Byzantines, which have a graveyard to the northeast. However, continuing along the main road that runs parallel to the water, you pass **Café La Source**, then the **'I love Kesra' sign** and the **natural spring** which flows down behind it. The hill begins to get steeper as you pass the **Delices de Kesra** restaurant on your right and then, further up, the **Museum of Customs and Traditions** (⊕ 08.00–17.00 Tue–Sun; free). Inaugurated in 2009, this imposing stone building is home to over 175 artefacts detailing traditional mountain life in the area, organised around three themes: the lives of women; rites of passage; and jewellery 'and the prophylactic symbolism attached'(!). It is a very well-organised exhibition, with displays in English, French and Arabic. Finally, no visit to Kesra would be complete without dragging yourself all the way up the mountain (via a steep cobbled street) to the **scenic viewpoint** which offers fabulous views over the valleys and town to the south. Just try not to disturb the donkeys under the rocky overhang!

Those keen to take home a gift could contact the team behind **Dar Sayar**, a rural, artisanal beekeeping co-operative supported by the International Labour Organization and the Dutch Embassy in Tunis, which sells sustainable honey and other natural produce. Further details are available from **Les Aventuriers Siliana** in Siliana (see below).

JEBEL SERJ NATIONAL PARK Straddling the border with neighbouring Kairouan Governorate in the far southeast of Siliana, this 1,720ha park, established in 2010, is home to the 1,357m Jebel Serj, Tunisia's sixth-highest peak. Jebel Serj is probably the highest mountain you can climb safely at the time of writing, owing to the security situation in some rural parts of Kasserine Governorate where the five higher peaks are located. The forest here includes Montpellier maple, which is extremely rare for Tunisia, while wildlife includes the rare striped hyena, wild boar, African golden wolf and North African hedgehog, as well as birds such as the short-toed snake eagle. The park also has some amazing caving opportunities, including the 3km-long La Grotte de Ain Dhab. If you are looking for a guide to explore the caves, contact **Club des Recherches Écologiques et de Spéléologie de Siliana** (m 95 144 355; e contact@speleo-siliana.com; f cress.tn).

In October 2016, the Spanish Consejo Superior de Investigaciones Científicas (CSIC-EEZA) and the Tunisian Direction Générale de Forêts (DGF), with the co-operation of the NGO Tunisia Wildlife Conservation Society (TWCS), began a project to reintroduce the vulnerable Cuvier's gazelle to the park. This dark-coated antelope is endemic to the hills and mountains of Algeria, Morocco and Tunisia, but by the 1970s had been hunted almost to extinction in Tunisia. Forty-three individuals (12 males and 31 females) were released, and the population is now closely monitored. You can visit the project (⊕ 35.944861, 9.546813; +34 95 095 1120, +34 95 028 1045; w rgct.eeza.csic.es), which includes an eco-museum and viewing platforms.

Local tour operators

Les Aventuriers Siliana Rue Palestine, Siliana; m 95 055 165; e aventurierssiliana@gmail.com; f aventuriers.siliana. Set up in 2014, this NGO offers ecotourism tours & outdoor activities such as hiking, climbing & caving in Jebel Serj National Park.

Association de Spéléologie Siliana (ASS) m 95 144 355, 24 495 545; e contact@speleo-siliana.com; f Association.Speleo.Siliana. Organises some incredible caving expeditions in the south of the governorate, especially in Jebel Serj National Park.

Where to stay It is possible to arrange camping trips in the park via the tour agencies listed above, or you could speak to the CSIC-EEZA team in the park itself. For higher-end accommodation options, head to Siliana or even Kairouan, which is only 35km to the southeast. Otherwise, the closest roof over your head outside the park is probably **Dar Khlifa** (m 54 263 796; f darkhlifa; **$**), a simple cottage on the C73 between Siliana and Al-Waslatiyah, at the southern end of the Jebel Serj range. They are able to arrange hiking and caving trips into the park.

TARF ECH-CHENA (AKA TARFCHNA) On the border with Zaghouan Governorate, this small settlement on the C47 is home to a rather dilapidated cemetery (⊕ 36.343716, 9.712865) for Muslim soldiers who died in the Free French Army during World War II. The area is filled with wild flowers during spring.

EL KEF AND AROUND

Meaning 'the rock' in Arabic, El Kef spills down the southern face of Jebel Dyr, with the old town occupying the highest ground. Sitting at 780m, this is the highest governorate capital in Tunisia. The hilltop is dominated by the Kasbah, which offers sweeping vistas across the fertile plains below. Here you will find Jewish, Christian and Muslim places of worship, all jostling for space in the narrow, winding streets of the old town. Steeped in thousands of years of history and offering some excellent museums and ancient sites, El Kef is a worthwhile addition to any Tunisian itinerary. It also serves as a central base from which to explore the bounty of regional archaeological attractions such as Hammam Mellegue, Ellès, Maktar, Assuras and Jugurtha's Table, all 90 minutes away by car.

SECURITY WARNING

At the time of writing, the FCDO advised against all but essential travel within 30km of the Algerian border in Kef Governorate. Some of the archaeological and other sites highlighted in this text fall within this zone.

HISTORY The area around El Kef has a history stretching back thousands of years. Archaeologists in the 1950s found Mousterian and Acheulean stone tools 11km south of the city in Sidi Zin, dating to Palaeolithic times. The nearby megalithic tombs (dolmens) at Ellès date to around 2500BC.

El Kef was a population centre and strategic site for the Carthaginians, who founded a settlement called Sicca here in the 5th century BC in order to control one of the main trading routes from the west into Carthage. In Roman times, it served as a frontier town on the main road to Theveste (modern-day Tébessa in northwestern Algeria). In 241BC, following the end of the First Punic War, the Carthaginians unwisely decided to billet a group of up to 20,000 unpaid mercenaries in Sicca while they negotiated a reduction in their pay for services already rendered. Unsurprisingly, this group of Libyans, Numidians, Greeks, Iberians, Celts and Ligurians was not best pleased with General Hanno's attempts to renege on their contract, and instead rose up to start the bloody five-year Mercenary War (page 70). This inspired French novelist Gustave Flaubert's controversial 1862 masterpiece, *Salammbô*.

During the Jugurthine War (112–106BC), Numidian King Jugurtha managed to ambush and almost kill his Roman adversary General Gaius Marius at Sicca, although Marius managed to escape the trap and eventually defeated Jugurtha, helping to subjugate the area to Roman rule. The town was renamed as Sicca Veneria by the Romans, who added the Veneria epithet because of the Carthaginian temple there dedicated to the Phoenician goddess Astarte, whom the Romans identified with Venus. Astarte represented fertility to the Carthaginians, and the town may have served as an important site for the cult of Astarte, which involved sacred prostitution, although the famed Temple to Astarte (Venus) where this prostitution took place has not been identified by archaeologists as it may have been destroyed by subsequent occupiers.

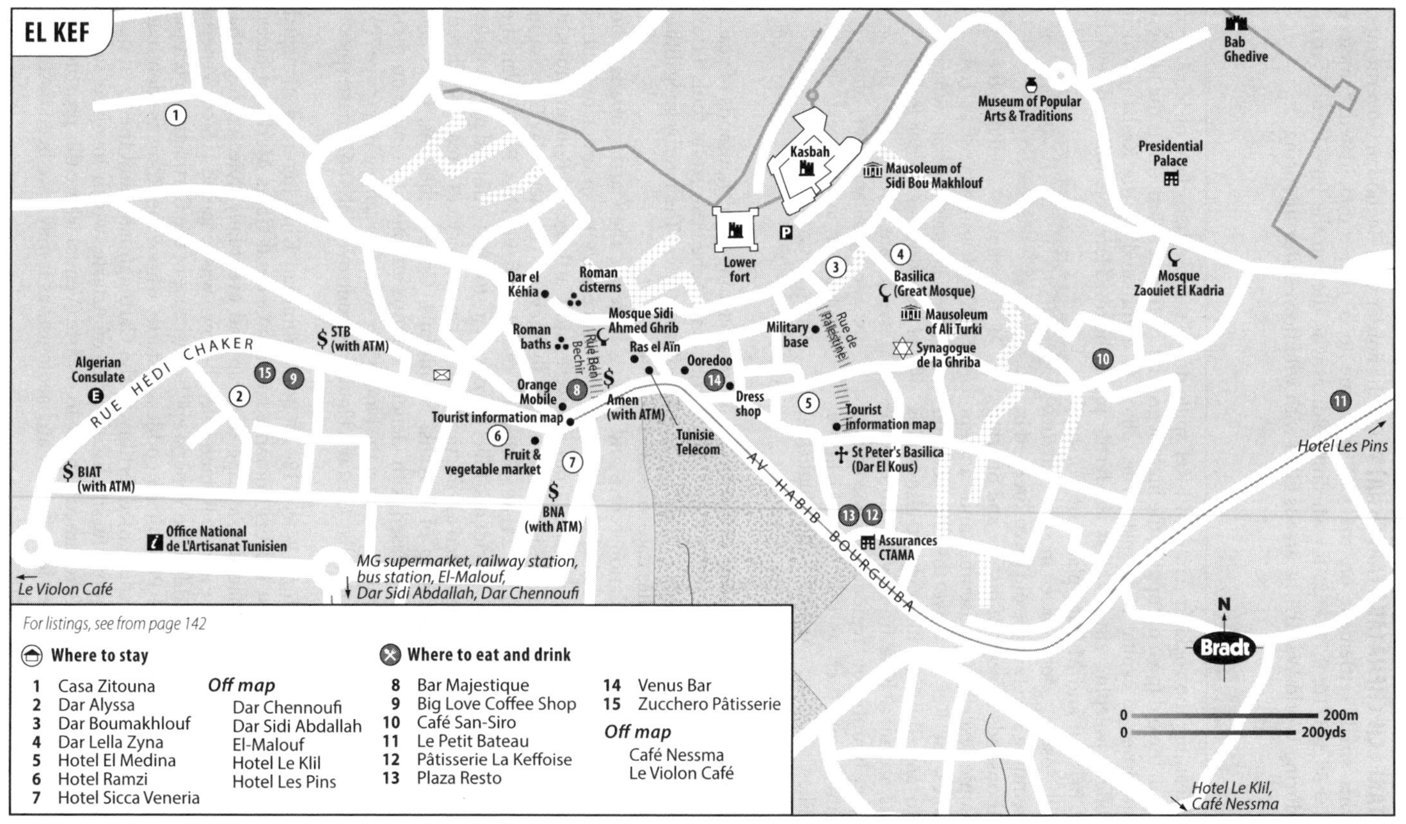
EL KEF
Bab Ghedive
Museum of Popular Arts & Traditions
Presidential Palace
Kasbah
Mausoleum of Sidi Bou Makhlouf
Lower fort
P
Mosque Zaouiet El Kadria
Basilica (Great Mosque)
Mausoleum of Ali Turki
Synagogue de la Ghriba
Military base
Rue de Palestine
Dar el Kéhia
Roman cisterns
Mosque Sidi Ahmed Ghrib
Roman baths
Rue Ben Bechir
Ras el Aïn
Ooredoo
Dress shop
Orange Mobile
Amen (with ATM)
Tunisie Telecom
Tourist information map
Fruit & vegetable market
BNA (with ATM)
STB (with ATM)
Algerian Consulate
RUE HÉDI CHAKER
BIAT (with ATM)
Office National de L'Artisanat Tunisien
Tourist information map
St Peter's Basilica (Dar El Kous)
Assurances CTAMA
AV HABIB BOURGUIBA
Hotel Les Pins
Hotel Le Klil, Café Nessma
Le Violon Café
MG supermarket, railway station, bus station, El-Malouf, Dar Sidi Abdallah, Dar Chennoufi
N
Bradt
0 200m
0 200yds
For listings, see from page 142
Where to stay
1 Casa Zitouna
2 Dar Alyssa
3 Dar Boumakhlouf
4 Dar Lella Zyna
5 Hotel El Medina
6 Hotel Ramzi
7 Hotel Sicca Veneria
Off map
Dar Chennoufi
Dar Sidi Abdallah
El-Malouf
Hotel Le Klil
Hotel Les Pins
Where to eat and drink
8 Bar Majestique
9 Big Love Coffee Shop
10 Café San-Siro
11 Le Petit Bateau
12 Pâtisserie La Keffoise
13 Plaza Resto
14 Venus Bar
15 Zucchero Pâtisserie
Off map
Café Nessma
Le Violon Café

THE ONE-WEEK EMPEROR

Time Travel Rome (w timetravelrome.com)

In AD265, Sicca Veneria held a Roman emperor for just seven days. At the time, Emperor Gallienus was proving to be more interested in luxury than ruling, and pretenders to the throne sprang up in all corners of the empire; Vibius Passienus, proconsul, and Fabius Pomponianus, general of Libya, decided to sponsor their own bid for the throne. They chose a man named Titus Cornelius Celsus, who had never risen high in rank but was of good character and capable of command. They clothed him with a royal robe taken from the statue of a goddess and proclaimed him their emperor. Unfortunately for Celsus, his reign was short-lived. After only a week, Galliena, cousin to the true emperor, killed Celsus. The people of Sicca were loyal to Gallienus, and in disgust they left Celus's body to be devoured by dogs. They then made an image of Celsus, placed it upon a cross, and danced about it in triumph.

The town fell to Vandal, Byzantine and finally Arab rule in AD688, when it became known as Shakbanaria (a corruption of the Roman name). The Ottomans arrived in the 16th century and were responsible for many of the impressive fortifications still visible in the town today. Al-Husayn I ibn Ali was born here in 1669, the founder of the Husseinid Dynasty that ruled Tunisia in 1705–1957. The town became a strategic centre in the power struggles between the Beylik of Tunis (ruled by the Husseinids) and the neighbouring Beylik of Constantine, under the Regency of Algiers, with four separate wars between them in the 18th century alone. The residents of El Kef also caused plenty of headaches for their Husseinid rulers back in Tunis, rising up in rebellion on a number of occasions, most significantly during the Mejba Revolt of 1864–65.

Despite the solid fortifications of the Kasbah, El Kef's defences were no match for colonial French forces in the 19th century, and it became the first town occupied by the French when they invaded eastwards from Algeria in early April 1881. Under French rule, El Kef was also one of the first municipalities set up in the new French Protectorate of Tunisia, on 8 July 1884. However, any hopes that French rule would bring prosperity to El Kef were quickly dashed. The railway line linking Tunis to Algeria was completed in 1884 and bypassed El Kef completely, instead crossing the border further north at Ghardimaou. Owing to its strong defensive positioning, El Kef became an Allied supply base and the provisional capital of Tunisia during World War II, but this was only to last until the end of the war.

El Kef was one of the first Tunisian towns to rebel against French rule during the struggle for independence, and became a major command centre for the Algerian National Liberation Army (ALN) in the 1950s, used to co-ordinate raids into eastern Algeria from a series of ALN bases in Tunisia. However, the construction of the Morice Line in 1957 reduced the significance of this location in the Algerian liberation struggle. Continuing this fiery tradition of political activism, in January 1984 El Kef's streets saw running street battles between the police, army and demonstrators, following riots over the removal of government flour subsidies.

GETTING THERE AND AROUND El Kef is 170km southwest of Tunis (around a 2½-hour drive down the A3 and P5). SNTRI **buses** connect the two (3hrs; 11.70DT one-way), while **louages** connect with Tunis, Tajerouine, Ad Dahmani, the border at Sakiet Sidi Youssef, Jendouba, Subaytilah, Thala, Kalaât Khasbah, Kalaât Senan, Al-Jarissah, El Ksour, Sfax and Gafsa.

Taxis congregate by the louage stop on Avenue Mongi Slim, ready to pick up arrivals, as well as by the main bus stop on Rue Dr Dhaoui Hnabila to the south of town.

The main **train** station is to the south of town, at the intersection of Rue de la Libie and Avenue de la Liberté (⊕ 36.166913, 8.703217). This stop is a cul-de-sac on the main route down from Tunis to Kalaât Khasbah, so it is not very frequently served, only receiving the irregular express train, arriving at 19.32 and departing at 05.00 (but even this is subject to change). Be sure to check dates of departures at the station

TOURIST INFORMATION AND LOCAL TOUR OPERATORS There are a number of useful **tourist information maps** dotted about town (marked on the map on page 140).

ASM El Kef Dar el Kéhia; t 78 200 476; e asm.kef@gmail.com; f ASM-El-Kef--807574972683023; ⌚ 09.00–16.00 Mon–Fri. Created in 1978, the Association de Sauvegarde et de Développement de la Médina du Kef aims to promote the sustainable development & use of El Kef's historic spaces, especially the medina. It is based in the 18th-century Dar el Kéhia & is a useful source of information about cultural events & exhibitions in the city.

Cirta Nova Touristica Dar el Kéhia; t 78 205 955/619; w cirtanovatouristica.com; f cirtanova; ⌚ 09.00–16.00 Mon–Fri. This social & economic solidarity programme, partly funded by the Dutch government, provides information about the main sites in town, online maps of tourist sites & hiking trails across the governorate, including to lesser-visited areas such as the Sidi Ahmed Caves (Grotte de Sidi Ahmed). It can also help with booking local dars, hosts local cultural events & also has a restaurant & gift shop selling artisanal products. It has an excellent website, full of useful information.

Office National de l'Artisanat Tunisien 21 Rue Taieb M'hiri; t 78 203 510; w artisanat.nat.tn; f Délégation-régionale-de-lartisanat-Kef-1821891928078802; ⌚ 08.30–16.30 Mon–Fri. Featuring an exhibition space for local handicrafts, this is a good place to come to find out about upcoming arts-related events in & around El Kef.

Siccaveneria 2 Rue de la Kasbah; w siccaveneria.com; f Siccaveneria.Kef; ⌚ 09.00–18.00 Mon–Fri, 10.00–17.00 Sat–Sun. This regional cultural promotion organisation runs a number of festivals in Kef Governorate, as well as running its own artisanal shop by the Kasbah.

WHERE TO STAY El Kef has a refreshing breadth of hotel options, both in terms of quality and price.

Upmarket

Dar Boumakhlouf (3 rooms) 13 Rue Kheireddine Becha; m 20 447 116, 53 026 634; w dar-boumakhlouf.com; f Page.Dar.Boumakhlouf. Perfectly located facing the Kasbah on one side & the old town on the other, the rooftop terrace here gives panoramic views of the old town to enjoy over b/fast or drinks. Features a beautiful 2-storey atrium in green & yellow, built in the Moorish style. The rooms are ornately decorated, especially the beds, & each named after a different regional song. Bathrooms are shared & there is a kitchen & lounge area in the basement for use of the guests. An incredible piece of architecture. **$$$$**

✷ ⚑ **Dar Sidi Abdallah** (6 rooms) Rte de Hammam Mellègue; m 51 892 053; w darsidiabdallah.com; f darsidiabdallah. Set in a rustic farmhouse in the countryside just outside El Kef, this is the perfect retreat after a busy day in town, especially given the 20m pool & beautiful outdoor areas. Rooms are spacious with good natural light, & some include en suites. The food served features Keffoise cuisine with locally sourced ingredients (including some grown on the farm itself). The owner Hamza is very knowledgeable about the local ecotourism scene & is able to organise activities such as hiking & clay pigeon shooting. **$$$$**

Zaafrane Le Verger [map, page 113] (2 rooms) ⊕ 36.203727, 8.834176; m 98 447 147; e myriambarbouchefphm@gmail.com; f. 10km northwest of El Kef, this modern farmhouse with open fireplace & pool is a comfortable setting from which to enjoy various agro-tourism activities such as helping with the olive harvest. Delicious meals using ingredients from the farm are also available. **$$$$**

Mid-range

Casa Zitouna (3 rooms) ⊕ 36.182583, 8.705582; m 54 461 577; e barbouche_fatma@yahoo.fr; f Casa.Zitouna.KEF. An oasis of calm only a few hundred metres from the centre, this cosy dar features a beautiful green garden filled with birds, chickens, cats & dogs. The hosts are known for their warm welcome & can cook Keffoise cuisine with locally sourced ingredients & organise tours of town. **$$$**

Dar Alyssa (6 rooms) Rue des Fleurs; m 97 926 050/1; e chernimajdileila@hotmail.fr; f ChambresDhotesDarAlyssa. In the centre of town but in a very quiet neighbourhood, Dar Alyssa's unassuming exterior hides a quirky guesthouse with a fishpond in the living room & all sorts of weird & wonderful décor hanging from the walls. The welcome is warm, Keffoise dinners can be arranged & there is a pool & a b/fast area with a view. **$$$**

Dar Chennoufi (6 rooms) ⊕ 36.1170768, 8.6916875; m 52 502 053; w dar.chennoufi.com. A beautiful, renovated farmhouse 10mins south of El Kef, set in a 6ha olive grove. Rooms are centred around a Moorish patio, with a pool in the garden. Meals (including packed lunches) can be prepared for guests, using many local ingredients. Local tours can also be arranged. **$$$**

Dar Lella Zyna (4 rooms) 9 Rue du Soudan; m 50 012 131; e zynalella@gmail.com; f LellaZyna. Up in the medina, this offers views of the Kasbah from the roof terrace. A cheaper option than Dar Boumakhlouf if you want to be in the centre of the old town. **$$$**

Hotel Le Klil (44 rooms) Rue Harrouch; m 78 204 747; e leklil.hôtel@gmail.com. Situated in the pine forest east of town, the décor here feels a little dated but large rooms, friendly management & surrounding nature make up for this. Also featuring a terrace & a pool, this is a convenient option for those with their own transport who do not wish to be in the centre of town. **$$$**

Budget

Auberge du Lac [map, page 113] (7 rooms) ⊕ 36.315103, 8.705826; m 96 974 003; e hoteldulac.lekef@gmail.com; f hoteldulac.lekef. Just east of the Mellegue Dam, 15km north of El Kef, this has simple rooms renovated in 2020 & is a great base for those seeking a quieter retreat, from which you can explore the reservoir & surrounding countryside. Popular with wild boar hunters, it also has a restaurant serving good grilled freshwater fish. The dam was built on the Oued Mellegue between 1949 & 1956 to produce electricity & regulate water flow for agricultural activities occurring in the lower part of the Medjerda Valley. **$$**

El-Malouf (8 rooms) Cité Elons, Rte de Tunis; m 78 225 768; f Bejikarim6. A relatively new budget hotel located at the far south end of town. Bright yellow & hard to miss. Only convenient if you have a late arrival or early departure from the bus station, which is 500m away. **$$**

Hotel Les Pins (21 rooms) Rue Mouldi Khamessi; m 78 204 300; f. Located overlooking the pine forest to the east of town, the central courtyard here features a great swimming pool. Not much to differentiate this place from nearby Hotel Le Klil, apart from price. **$$**

Hotel Sicca Veneria (34 rooms) m 78 202 389. If the receptionist can drag themselves away from their phone, you might get a room in this basic, budget hotel slap bang in the centre of town. Rooms only start on the second floor, which cuts out some of the traffic noise, but it is still on a busy intersection. Rooms are clean & larger than at Hotel Ramzi & even have TV & a desk, so an OK budget option if you need to work. Rooms with AC cost 10DT extra. **$–$$**

Shoestring

Hotel El Medina (17 rooms) 18 Rue Farhat Hached. The cheapest clean bed in town. Very basic rooms with shared bathroom facilities. Excellent central location in the heart of the medina. **$**

Hotel Ramzi (13 rooms) 44 Rue Hédi Chaker; m 78 203 035; f Ramziouefi. A basic budget option in the centre of town next to a fish market. Cheapest rooms have shared bathrooms, some offer en suite. **$**

WHERE TO EAT AND DRINK El Kef is full of small pâtisseries and cafés that offer quick and cheap snacks. For higher-end cuisine, consider booking an authentic Keffoise meal at **Dar Sidi Abdallah, Dar Alyssa** or **Cirta Nova Touristica** in the Dar el Kéhia.

Le Petit Bateau Av Habib Bourguiba; m 29 426 246; f; 11.00–late daily. The finest wood-fired pizzas in town, served in cosy dark wooden panelled surroundings. $$$

Big Love Coffee Shop Rue Hédi Chaker; m 26 460 190; e biglovecoffeeshoo123@gmail.com; f Big-love-coffee-shop-110776913784517; 07.00–late daily. A bright, modern, yellow-&-black coffee shop offering an excellent selection of pizza, savoury pastries & Tunisian fast-food favourites. $$

Café Nessma Rue Harrouch; m 25 338 486; 10.00–late daily. Large outdoor café on the outskirts of town offering great views of the surrounding countryside. Basic menu featuring fast food & non-alcoholic drinks. Sadly, had a monkey in a cage at the time of writing. $$

Le Violon Café Rue Taha Hussein; m 58 122 412; 07.00–late daily. As the name suggests, this café has violins all over the walls. Offers a good selection of non-alcoholic drinks & fast food. $$

Plaza Resto Av Habib Bourguiba; m 53 277 061; 11.00–late daily. Has a good pizza oven & also offers crêpes. $$

Bar Majestique Pl de l'Indépendance; noon–late Tue–Sun. Very central location for beers in a faded old colonial building. $

Café San-Siro Rue Farhat Hached; m 20 701 411, 78 282 520; 07.00–22.00 daily. Free Wi-Fi & good Italian coffee. $

Pâtisserie La Keffoise Av Habib Bourguiba; m 90 664 159; f; 08.00–18.00 daily. El Kef's most famous pastry shop, offering delicious filled sweets & custom-baked occasion cakes. $

Venus Bar Rue Farhat Hached; 11.30–22.30 Sat–Thu. Once a thriving restaurant, the only choice you need to make here now is whether you want Celtia or Heineken. Hint: choose Heineken. $

Zucchero Pâtisserie Rue Hédi Chaker; m 52 733 604; f; 08.00–18.00 daily. Another delicious pastry shop. Take-away only. $

SHOPPING There is a great daily fresh **fruit and vegetable market** on the street near Hotel Ramzi (Rue Hédi Chaker). For gift ideas, El Kef's **jewellery quarter** is located on Rue Bahri Babrouch near the Synagogue de la Ghriba. This narrow street is packed with small artisanal vendors offering gold and silver products, which were traditionally sold by the town's Jewish residents. There is also an impressive **dress shop** near Venus Bar, with a distinctive blue balcony and traditional tiling. **Cirta Nova Touristica** also offers a good selection of handicrafts in its shop in Dar el Kéhia (page 142), and there are often items on display at the **Office National de l'Artisanat Tunisien** (page 142). **Dar Sidi Abdallah** also sells a range of local organic farm produce, but be sure to call and confirm before driving out there.

OTHER PRACTICALITIES **ATMs** are easily found across the governorate capital, with a number along Rue Hédi Chaker. **Pharmacies** are located all over town, with a cluster to the immediate east of the Hôpital Régional du Kef. The **Algerian Consulate** on Rue Hédi Chaker (78 200 169, 78 203 880; 08.00–15.00 Mon–Fri) can process tourist visas for those able to prove residency in Tunisia.

WHAT TO SEE AND DO

Kasbah (07.00–19.00 daily) There's no better place to start your exploration of El Kef than the Kasbah, situated in the highest and most easily defended part of town. It is a slog to reach on foot, although heading up there through the medina area is a reward in itself. The local vendors are very laid back, and there are plenty of spots to grab a mint tea before you continue your ascent. For those keen to avoid the staircases and uphill climbs, there is a car park just to the south of the

EL KEF'S FESTIVAL SCENE

As the unofficial capital of western Tunisia, El Kef hosts a number of cultural events throughout the year that attract artists from near and far. Every summer (usually mid-July or early August) El Kef's Kasbah hosts the **Bou Makhlouf International Festival** (f festivalboumakhlouf), featuring live music, while the **Sicca Jazz Festival** (w siccajazz.siccaveneria.com; f SiccaJazz) runs every March and is very popular, attracting jazz artists from all over the world. In February 2020, the town hosted the first edition of its new comedy festival, **Festival International du Rire du Kef** (w festivaldurire.tn; f FDRTunisie), an offshoot of the well-established Festival du Rire in Tunis.

Kasbah on Rue de la Kasbah, which also makes for a convenient way of accessing Dar Boumakhlouf.

The larger, higher fortification was built in the early 17th century under Ottoman rule, and the lower fortification was added 200 years later by Hammuda ibn Ali, the fifth ruler of the Husseinid Dynasty. In April 1881, the French managed to seize control of these forts without a shot being fired by being let in through **Bab Ghedive** (Gate of Treachery), 400m northeast; the governor of Kef had been ordered by the Bey not to resist the French incursion. Adding insult to injury, the French colonial occupiers then converted part of the Kasbah into a prison for nationalist Tunisian leaders. Today, there is no charge to tour the fortifications, which include a number of well-preserved early-18th-century cannons.

The old quarter With some sturdy walking shoes, you can tackle Kef's hills and tick off many of the main historical sites in around 2 hours. Starting at the top of the hill at the northeastern end of town, where it is easy to park or get dropped off, your first stop should be the **Museum of Popular Arts and Traditions** (Rue de la Kasbah; ⌚ winter 09.30–16.30 Tue–Sun, summer 09.00–13.00 & 16.00–19.00 Tue–Sun; 8/5DT non-resident/resident). Founded in 1970, this ethnographic museum focuses on regional Amazigh culture, with a series of displays spread across four rooms including jewellery, pottery, horseriding equipment and a model tented encampment. The museum building itself is somewhat of a historical site, housed in the former zaouia of Sidi Ali Ben Aïssa. Built in 1784, it was the headquarters of a Sufi order that strongly opposed French colonial occupation of the area. Look for the large cannon on the roundabout out front. Also on top of the hill, opposite the Presidential Palace, you will also find **Mosque Zaouiet El Kadria**, founded as part of the Kadriya/Qadriya brotherhood, one of the oldest Sufi brotherhoods, originally set up in Algeria in 1824. It features 12th-century Almohad Caliphate architectural influences.

From the museum, head 150m to the southwest to the 17th-century **Mausoleum of Sidi Bou Makhlouf**, with its beautiful octagonal minaret and ribbed domes. Dedicated to the patron saint of El Kef, it is the headquarters for El Kef's Aïssawa Sufi order, which is famed for its spiritual music. The mausoleum sits just to the east of the **Kasbah**, which you can visit if you have not done so already (page 144).

Looking down from the Kasbah's ramparts, you can see the large **Basilica (Great Mosque)** on Rue du Soudan. This large mosque is of uncertain origins, although it was used as a place of worship for hundreds of years. It used to house a small museum of local artefacts, but this was closed at the time of writing. Just to the south, at the intersection of Rue de Soudan and Rue Marakit Karama, is the **Mausoleum of Ali Turki**, which is surprisingly small given the significance of its occupant. Kef-born Ali Turki was the father of Al-Husayn I ibn Ali, the founder of the Husseinid Dynasty that ruled Tunisia from 1705 until 1957.

El Kef's old quarter is home to historic Muslim, Christian and Jewish places of worship, and continuing for another 70m southwest from the mausoleum you hit the **Synagogue de la Ghriba**. The Jewish neighbourhood here (known as Hara el Yahud) is believed to date to the 1740s, peaking in the early 1900s at around 800 individuals. The synagogue is one of seven *ghriba* (isolated) synagogues dotted across North Africa that are believed to be especially holy, and once served as a pilgrimage site for Jews from across Tunisia and Algeria during the festival of Sukkot. Sadly, following World War II, El Kef's Jewish community shrank to just over 300 people. In 1984 the final Jewish resident and caretaker of the synagogue left the city, handing the keys to ASM El Kef (page 142). Though the synagogue is closed at the time of writing, ASM El Kef can arrange access. It is home to a number of important artefacts such as a wooden circumcision chair, a set of 600-year-old sheepskin Torah scrolls and rare examples of the Judaeo-Arabic script.

Opposite the synagogue, on the other side of the main Rue de Makthar, is **St Peter's Basilica (Dar El Kous)**. In 1897, French archaeologist Paul Frédéric Gauckler decoded some inscriptions showing that this 4th-century structure was a basilica to St Peter, making it the first basilica ever to be identified in Africa. Built on the site of an earlier pagan monument, it features some unique pieces of re-used classical architecture, likely scavenged from nearby Roman ruins (such as the door lintels with ocean-themed engravings). Closed at the time of writing, ASM El Kef (page 142) can arrange access. From the basilica, head back up to the main road and follow it westwards for 250m to hit Avenue Habib Bourguiba, right in the town centre, home to the **Roman baths** (Temple des Eaux) and **Roman cisterns** (Cisternes Romaines). They are partially excavated and can be viewed from Rue de la Source. They were fed by **Ras el Aïn**, the ancient spring that sits in the centre of town, just off Place de l'Indépendance. Towering over these baths is the green-and-white minaret of **Mosque Sidi Ahmed Ghrib**, which is still in use today.

Also on Avenue Habib Bourguiba is the highly visible, Art Deco blue-and-white **Assurances CTAMA** building, which serves as a useful landmark for when you are navigating around town. Likewise, at the northern end of town, the luxurious looking **Presidential Palace** (a post-independence structure used by President Bourguiba, on the former site of the city's ancient Cheifaine Gate) is a useful waypoint.

AROUND EL KEF With your own transport, El Kef makes an excellent base from which to explore the rest of the governorate.

Archaeological sites There are two archaeological sites close to El Kef, attesting to the lengthy human occupation of this part of Tunisia. In the caves by the village of **Sidi Mansour** (⊕ 36.19766, 8.728131), 3km northeast of El Kef, are Neolithic rock paintings, and if you climb up on to the plateau above the village you will also find a dolmen. Meanwhile, 8km southwest of town on the P5 is the Lower Palaeolithic site of **Sidi Zin** (⊕ 36.117852, 8.639554), one of the oldest in Tunisia. This site was excavated in 1950 by French archaeologist Dr E G Gobert, who found Palaeolithic tools associated with both Acheulean and Mousterian cultures, although there is little to see here today.

K/T boundary (⊕ 36.154000, 8.648767) Just 1.5km west of Dar Sidi Abdallah on the road to Hammam Mellegue is a site of global geological significance: the Cretaceous/Tertiary (K/T) boundary stratotype. This represents the world's most complete sedimentary record of the mass extinctions that occurred after a meteorite impact created the Chicxulub crater and wiped out the dinosaurs 66 million years ago. So significant is the site to scientists that it is on Tunisia's UNESCO World Heritage Site Tentative List – which is odd, given that there is only a small sign as you drive past!

Hammam Mellegue (⊕ 36.183313, 8.575397) Sitting on the floodplain of the Oued Kseub, these remarkably well-preserved Roman baths are 12km west of El Kef on a good-quality, signposted road. You pass a military base (⊕ 36.163035, 8.597800) before the road drops steeply down the hills to the level of the river below. The roof of the baths is missing from many sections, so you can peer down from above and get an idea of the scale during Roman times. The exterior swimming pool is particularly impressive. This is well off the beaten track, so if you would like to follow in the 2,000-year-old tradition and enjoy the 42°C waters here, be sure to bring your own kit. As you stand facing the river, the functional bath section is on your right. Be sure to ask a local if it is OK to go in, as men and women from the surrounding villages use the facilities at different times. There is also a recently constructed wooden chalet by the car park, which was intended to be a restaurant for visitors but closed because of the pandemic. At the time of writing, Dar Sidi Abdallah (page 142) was considering taking over management of this restaurant, so contact them to find out if it is open now.

Saddine Nature Reserve Created in 2009, this 2,610ha reserve was designated as a wetland site of international importance under the Ramsar Convention in 2015. The site is bounded in the north by the RN5 and in the west by the Oued Kseub. The reserve is covered by dense Aleppo pine forest and is dotted with permanent rivers and seasonal streams, as well as three mountains between 500m and 600m: Jebel Ettarabia in the north, Jebel Gasâa below that and finally Jebel Essaddine. There is a diverse assortment of flora and fauna including 20 species of mammals, 60 species of birds and 14 species of reptiles and amphibians. Some of the more notable inhabitants include golden eagle, Egyptian vulture, red fox, wild boar, golden jackal, striped hyena and viperine snake. The park also has a small eco-museum by the RN5 (⊕ 36.115762, 8.511465), which is the best place from which to access the rest of the park. Guides are not compulsory, but if you would like one, this will need to be arranged in advance from El Kef.

Sakiet Sidi Youssef This border town, 40km west of El Kef, connects to El Haddada on the Algerian side, though it is not as frequently served by louage services from El Kef as the more common border crossing point is Ghardimaou, 25km north. The town is sadly known as the site of an infamous massacre on 8 February 1958, when 25 French military aircraft strafed and bombed the town for 80 minutes. According to official Tunisian accounts at the time, the town was crowded because it was market day, leading to the deaths of 79 people, including 20 children; a further 130 people were wounded. Many of the town's buildings were levelled. The French authorities, already three-and-a-half years into the brutal Algerian War of Independence, claimed at the time that they had attacked an Algerian National Liberation Army (ALN) base a few kilometres from Sakiet Sidi Youssef, which had been used to ambush their troops in Algeria on 11 January.

This attack led to widespread condemnation in the international community, internationalising the Algerian conflict through debates in the UN. It also seriously damaged Franco-Tunisian relations, barely two years into Tunisian independence, contributing to the later Bizerte Crisis (page 179). Today there is a large white arch **monument** to commemorate those who died, near the graveyard at the southern end of town (⊕ 36.218680, 8.358128). Here you can also ask around for a guide to show you the nearby **Sidi Ahmed Caves** (Grotte de Sidi Ahmed), which are to the south, right by the Algerian border (although be sure to seek local advice on the security situation first).

Jugurtha's Table ⚑ (⊕ 35.744812, 8.377895) At 1,255m above sea level, Jugurtha's Table is visible for miles around, rising some 600 vertical metres above the surrounding farmland of Kalaât es Senam. It was the scene of Numidian King Jugurtha's last stand against Roman occupation during the Jugurthine War (112–106BC) and proved to be such an effectively defendable position for guerrilla warfare that Roman general Gaius Marius had to resort to bribing King Jugurtha's allies to betray him, rather than successfully conquering his forces up on the mountain. Today, it is still possible to see the steps on the side of the cliff face which were chiselled by Jugurtha's men 2,000 years ago. More recently, in the 18th century, a local warrior (Senam) used the mountain as a base from which to resist subjugation of the area by the Beys in Tunis, hence the name of the local settlement ('Kalaât es Senam' is literally 'Fortified Place of Senam').

A road out of town leads to the foot of the northern cliffs, from where you can climb a carved staircase all the way to the flat top, which stretches almost 1.5km from east to west. The raptors that perch on the cliff face tend to take off when you arrive at the foot of the stairs, adding to the incredible scene. From the top you can see over into Algeria. There is a small shrine at the summit and, if you explore, you will find many other historical remains, including ruined underground grain silos, Numidian cisterns for catching rainwater and the foundations of walls.

Jarissah Nine kilometres southeast of Tajerouine on the P18, this mining town expanded in 1899 when the Société du Jebel-Djérissa (SDD) began extracting haematite (an iron ore) from the 850m-high Jebel Djérissa, which sits to the south. In 1938, before World War II interrupted production, it exported 647,551 tonnes of ore back to Europe. Production levels would not recover for ten years as a result of the war, and the mine was eventually nationalised in 1961. Today, it remains the main employer in town. For those with an interest, the **Djérissa Geological and Mining Museum** is located in the old colonial-era church (Église Sainte-Barbe de Jérissa) in the southeast of town (⊕ 35.839881, 8.634268). It is easy to spot from the road as there is a big, rusting mining cart with a lump of iron ore at the front.

Althiburos ⚑ *With Time Travel Rome (w timetravelrome.com)*

This 9km² archaeological site running parallel to the road is fenced in but free to enter and always open. The turning is off the P18 (⊕ 35.904804, 8.778648), signposted as Mdayna. Originally founded as an Amazigh town, Althiburos lay at a strategic trading point on the confluence of the oueds Oum-El-Abid and Medenine on the border with Numidia. A Punic inscription found on site indicates that the city fell under Carthaginian control, and it subsequently came under Roman influence after their eventual defeat of Carthage. It remained a smaller civitas until the reign of Hadrian, when it was granted the status of municipium and several traditional Roman architectural structures were built. Though a prosperous

Roman city from the 2nd to 4th centuries AD, and becoming a bishopric during the emerging Christian era, the city was abandoned sometime after the 7th century in favour of nearby Ebba Ksour and remained largely unseen until the 18th century.

Thanks to being off main travel routes (and poorly signposted), Althiburos remains relatively well preserved, boasting a number of interesting ruins, mainly from the Roman and Byzantine eras. The forum, still paved, is surrounded by porticoes and various buildings, including some with religious purposes. Nearby, the façade of the capitol, Corinthian in design, remains mostly intact and still quite high. The fragments of two temples have been identified, as have several private residences and villas, with traditional peristyle construction and baths, though their rooms and mosaics have been damaged. A large peristyle building, dedicated to Asklepeia but whose purpose is still unknown, is one of the more unusual ruins. It consists of a long, windowed gallery with turrets at each end, opening on to a large room with a full hydraulics system, and possessing a series of symmetrically placed rooms, all with beautiful mosaic floors. Another unique discovery at Althiburos is believed to have been a factory. Its walls are constructed from larger, rougher stonework and it consists of a round main room and two courtyards with basins. Perhaps the most imposing of the structures, however, is the theatre. Though unexcavated, several sections of its walls remain to an impressive height. Archaeological teams working at the site have expressed a desire to excavate, catalogue and hopefully work to restore the theatre complex. Alongside these identified structures, the site contains a large number of paved streets, columns and scattered remains of ancient structures – an excitingly large collection to be explored.

Driving south towards the site, you first pass the **Complexe de Loisirs Jugurtha** (m 54 931 444, 25 088 450; ⌚ noon–18.00 daily; $$), a basic restaurant with a swimming pool attached, which is popular with families. Next door is the castle-like complex of the **Restaurant Touristique Althiburos Medeina** (m 99 452 436; ⌚ 13.00–late daily; $$$), a large, modern restaurant that seems very out of place here in the countryside, but has a good selection of Mediterranean and Tunisian cuisine, a green lawn and a beautiful pool. To the south of the archaeological site is the **La Grotte d'Althiburos** (⊕ 35.854586, 8.783155; ☎ 78 281 236; m 29 179 905; e althiburos.imagination@yanhoo.fr; f Grotte-dAlthiburos-768502339858048), an underground gallery and cultural centre run by local artist Ammar Belghith, who studied in France and Saudi Arabia but returned to his native region and now displays artwork both in and around his grotto. You can even see one installation from space, in Google Earth's photography of the area!

Assuras ⚑ The ruins of this Roman town lie near the village of Zannfour (which is spelled in many ways on Tunisian road signs, adding to the difficulty of finding it). Originally a Numidian settlement, it came under Roman control following the Battle of Thapsus in 46BC and was settled well into Byzantine times in the 8th century AD. The main archaeological attraction is the large arch on top of a hill (⊕ 35.994514, 9.020350) which the authorities are in the process of reconstructing, so it was covered in scaffolding at the time of writing. There are also a series of unexcavated remains to the west of the archway. Access to the site is via the dirt track at the farm entrance (⊕ 35.991269, 9.024947).

JENDOUBA

Jendouba town (known as Souk El Arba until 30 April 1966) is quiet by governorate capital standards but remains a significant transport hub, sitting on the main train line connecting Tunis to Algeria. It also serves as a useful base for day trips to Bulla Regia (9km away), Chemtou (25km away) and Thuburnica (30km away). Today, the town's main focus is on agricultural activity based on the production of cereals (especially wheat), as well as herding livestock, arboriculture and horticulture.

HISTORY Called Libertina under Roman rule, this whole area was very wealthy thanks to agriculture, as attested by the stunning archaeological remains at nearby Bulla Regia (page 152). The surrounding area is the alluvial plain of the Oued Medjerda which still flows through the town today, making the area very well suited to growing wheat. The town has had historical political significance too, with residents of nearby Oued Mliz organising an early protest against French rule on 4 April 1934, kicking off a chain reaction that eventually culminated in the massacre of protesters in Tunis on 9 April 1938, commemorated to this day as Martyrs Day.

During World War II, the town contributed to the Allied war effort by being a major airbase. On 16 November 1942 during Operation Torch, the airfield in the southeast was captured by the British 1st Parachute Brigade and immediately put to use by No 255 Squadron RAF. US military engineers also built Engle Field to the southwest of town, which was used by the Twelfth Air Force during the North Africa campaign, although today this is all cultivated farmland.

Post-independence, the town contributed troops to the Tunisian efforts to dislodge the French during the Bizerte Crisis in 1961 (page 179); there is a monument to the men that died at the Jardin Mémorial des Martyrs. More recently, Jendouba was the birthplace of the one and only Tunisian NBA player, Salah Mejri.

GETTING THERE AND AROUND

By road Jendouba is 155km southwest of Tunis (around a 2½-hour drive on the P6). The SNTRI bus station is in the southern end of town, near the Hotel Simitthu, with services east to Tunis via Béja (2hrs 30mins; 10.90DT) or north to Aïn Draham (1hr; 3.20DT). Louages congregate around Place 7 Novembre, although at the time of writing this roundabout was in chaos owing to construction of a flyover heading west on the P17. Louages for Aïn Draham and Tabarka are usually found on the stretch of the P17 closest to Place 7 Novembre, but are now spread out down towards the SNTRI bus stop.

For short journeys around town, yellow taxis can be flagged down. I would not trust either of the hotels listed to sort out a vehicle. You will find a lot of taxis waiting by Place 7 Novembre, ready to pick up arrivals from the louages and inter-governorate bus services.

Given the tourist facilities available in Tabarka, Jendouba would be a strange place to rent a vehicle. However, if you do need to hire one, try **Issaoui Location De Voitures** (Av de l'Environnement; 36 489 061; m 20 531 575; e issam.rentalcar@gmail.com; Issaoui Location De Voitures). You are more likely to get a response to a Facebook message than an email or phone call.

By rail The main Gare Ferroviaire de Jendouba is in the town centre, next to a Monoprix and the post office. There are usually four trains per day to Tunis (3hrs 25mins; 8.45DT), with an early departure at 04.54 and the last one at 15.40. Trains also run to Ghardimaou (25mins; 18.0DT), with departures at 09.58 and 16.12.

WHERE TO STAY Considering that Jendouba is the governorate capital and a business hub for the large agricultural sector in the area, it is surprising that the hotel choices are so poor. My honest advice is to stay elsewhere, with Aïn Draham (40km north), Béja (50km east) and El Kef (55km south) all good options. But if for some reason you are forced to stay here, choose the undeniably dated **Hotel Atlas** (Rue du Premier Juin; 24 rooms; ☎78 603 217; **$$**), which is tucked away next door to the police station.

WHERE TO EAT AND DRINK Aside from the following, Avenue Habib Bourguiba and the streets around Jardin Mémorial des Martyrs are filled with cafés and shisha joints, which tend to be busy until at least 22.00. Some places, such as Belle Vue, also have live music from time to time. Alcohol-licensing laws are quite strict in Jendouba, so if you want a beer you will need to brave the rowdy bars at either the Hotel Atlas or the Hotel Simitthu (and I would strongly recommend the former).

Pizzeria Farés Pl Farhat Hached (just off Pl de la République); ⏰ noon–21.00 daily. This interesting little restaurant serves great pizza, with a décor that feels like a mixture of Sicilian & Tunisian. $$$

Belle Vue Bd de l'Environnement; ☎78 613 367; ⏰ 09.00–22.00 daily. Cheap & cheerful café with a large outdoor seating area offering pizzas, some Tunisian dishes & the occasional live band. $$

Cléopâtre Pizzeria Al Habib Bourguiba; f Cléopâtre-Café-Resto-298196427662747; ⏰ 08.00–21.00 daily. Featuring Ancient Egyptian hieroglyphs on the façade, this place serves good pizza in relaxed surroundings. The outdoor seating is also popular for a morning coffee. $$

La Palma Salon de Thé & Restaurant 3 Av Habib Bourguiba; m 54 898 884; e amineyak@yahoo.fr; f LaPalma2015; ⏰ 07.00–23.00 daily. Set behind high walls to shield you from the nearby traffic, this place has a shaded grass outdoor area that is perfect for enjoying a fruit juice or burger. Try the deliciously fresh baguette farcie. $$

Oscar Café Al Habib Bourguiba; m 58 697 160; f Oscar-Jendouba-591745884513825; ⏰ 08.00–21.00 daily. An impressive assortment of meats & seafood on offer, as well as sweets, juices & coffee, all in spacious surroundings. The take-away sandwiches are great. $$

Café 7 Novembre Al Habib Bourguiba; ⏰ 07.00–22.00 daily. One of the most popular cafés in town with older Jendoubians. Normally already packed by 07.30 with men drinking coffee, playing dominoes & generally watching the world go by. Very basic facilities but fast service & good hot drinks. $

Restaurant Istanbul Pl 7 Novembre; ⏰ 07.00–22.00 daily. This large, hectic Turkish kebab joint offers grilled meats, rotisserie chicken, coffee & freshly baked bread. Gets very busy at lunch. $

SHOPPING There is a daily **covered market** at the south end of the railway station which sells a wide variety of fresh produce, and a **street market** selling many of the same items slightly further west.

OTHER PRACTICALITIES What Jendouba lacks in decent hotels, it more than makes up for in terms of **banks**, making this a useful spot to stop and get cash out on your travels. The majority are found on Place Farhat Hached and along Av Ali Belhaouane, where you'll also find Thabraca Exchange (⏰ 07.00–14.30 & 17.00–21.00 daily).

There are two well-stocked **pharmacies** conveniently located opposite one another on Rue Habib Thameur: Pharmacie Fatma Abichou (⏰ 08.00–20.00 Mon–Fri, 08.00–13.30 Sat) and Pharmacie de Nuit (⏰ 20.00–08.00 nightly).

WHAT TO SEE AND DO Jendouba is a pleasant place to stroll around for a few hours, with most of the sights found on the east side of the railway line that cuts through town. There were plans to develop the P6 road (Avenue de l'Environnement) in the southeast of town into a wide boulevard filled with public spaces and eateries, but the pandemic has delayed this. Until that happens, though, begin your walking tour in the centre of town, northeast of Place 7 Novembre. Starting at this roundabout, head 250m up Al Habib Bourguiba to see the abandoned **Le Casino cinema**, the exterior of which is still in a good state of repair, including the signage. There was talk of restoring this beautiful colonial-era building to a functional cinema and cultural centre in 2018, but this had yet to happen at the time of writing. The walls nearby have some striking graffiti on them, featuring pro-Palestinian images that are a familiar theme throughout the country's street art. After another 300m if you turn left up Avenue Ali Belhaouane you will eventually reach the **Jardin Mémorial des Martyrs**, a low-key garden which commemorates those Tunisians who lost their lives in the independence struggle, in particular during the efforts to dislodge the remaining French colonial forces during the Bizerte Crisis in 1961 (page 179).

ARCHAEOLOGICAL SITES AROUND JENDOUBA

Bulla Regia ⚑ (🕘 winter 08.30–17.30 daily, summer 08.00–19.00 daily; 8/5DT non-resident/resident) Around 8km northeast of Jendouba, this popular archaeological site is best known for its unique and excellently preserved underground villas built during the reign of Emperor Hadrian. Archaeological evidence indicates that the site was occupied as early as the 4th century BC, well before Punic settlers arrived. The name 'Bulla' appears to be a Romanisation of the name for Carthaginian god Ba'al Hammon. As with much of Jendouba, the land around is very fertile (especially in the Medjerda Valley), so the area's wealth was linked to grain trading. King Masinissa, who ruled Numidia from 202 to 148BC, profited greatly from Bulla Regia's fertile farmland, sending shipments of grain in 200 and 198 to feed the Roman Republic's armies in Macedon and Greece. By 2BC, Bulla Regia had become the capital of one of the three Numidian client kingdoms set up by the Romans after the death of Masinissa. Emperor Hadrian promoted the town to the status of colonia in AD177 and gave it the somewhat lengthier title of Colonia Aelia Hadriana Augusta Bulla Regia.

Evidence of the colony's continued wealth can be seen in the fantastically preserved private houses, which mainly date to the 3rd century AD. Continued occupation after this time is attested by the presence of Byzantine ruins. The distinctive underground homes were first discovered in 1879 by a French railway construction crew (who actually used some of the structures as lodgings during construction work), with archaeological excavations beginning in 1906. It was opened to the public in the 1940s. Sitting in the shadow of 617m-high Jebel Rebia, the area has significant temperature variations between summer and winter, explaining why the Roman architects decided to build downwards, digging into the soft rock below ground.

Getting there and away Bulla Regia sits on the C59 and is best accessed by private vehicle as it is awkward to reach on public transport. You can take a louage northwards from Jendouba to Firnanah and ask to be let out at the P17 intersection, then walk or hitch the final 2.5km along the C59 to the site. Alternatively, you could negotiate a taxi fare from Jendouba, which should be around 5–10DT.

Exploring the site Arriving from Jendouba, the car park and ticket office are on your right, along with a small café and gift shop, which stocks maps of the site, on the other side of the road. The **museum**, on the ticket office-side of the road, is sadly closed, with no indication of a reopening date at the time of writing.

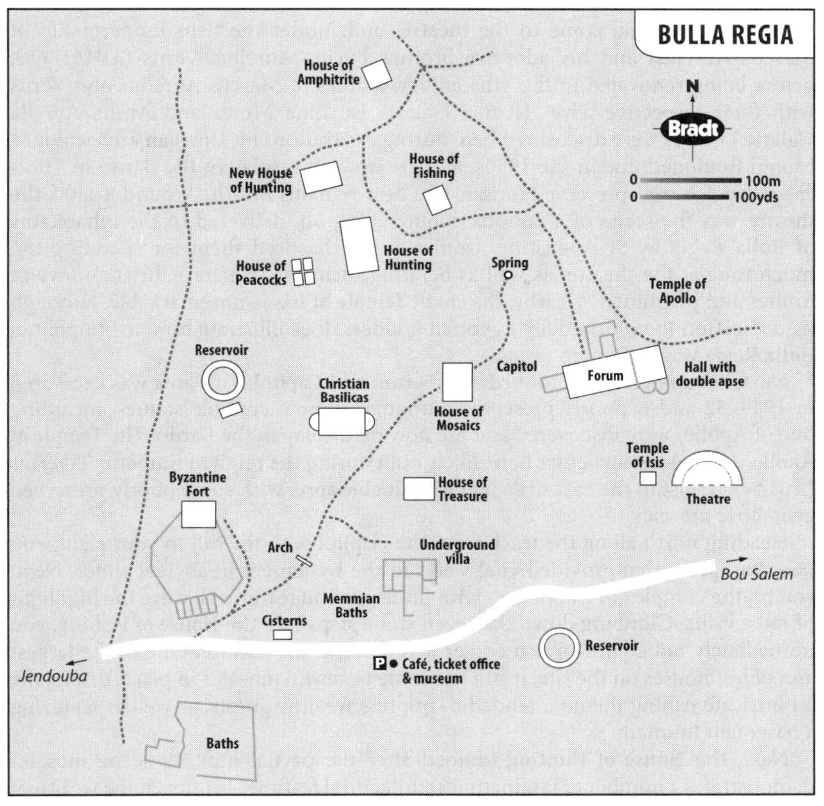

Entering the site proper, you will immediately see the **Memmian Baths** on your right. These are the highest structures surviving on the surface, visible as you drive up to the site, although they have suffered from earthquake damage over the years. They were named after Julia Memmia, daughter of local Roman consul Gaius Memmius Fidus Julius Albius, as she paid for their construction. Julia dedicated the baths to the wife of Septimius Severus, the first African Roman emperor who ruled the Roman Empire in AD193–211.

Looking to your left, the **Byzantine Fort** sits in the far southwest of the site, by the road. First erected in the 6th century AD, it is an archaeological mishmash of masonry cannibalised from other parts of the site. There are also some **cisterns** nearby, which in all likelihood were originally intended to supply the **baths** that are now on the other side of the road. They were converted into a food-storage depot in later years. The water source for these cisterns and baths was located at Aïn et Tolba (⊕ 36.553600, 8.762200), which lies 800m southeast of Bulla Regia.

Just to the north of the Memmian Baths is the **House of Treasure**, so named due to the hoard of 7th-century Byzantine coins that archaeologists uncovered here in 1942. Just to the northeast is the **House of Mosaics**, known to archaeologists as Maison no. 3, one of the largest villas on the site, although it is not as well preserved as some others. A staircase of eight steps provides access to the three underground rooms (a *triclinium* (formal dining room) and two bedrooms).

Heading east you come to the **theatre**, built under the twin Emperorship of Marcus Aurelius and his adoptive brother Lucius Aurelius Verus (AD161–69), before being renovated in the 4th century. Statues of Marcus Aurelius and Verus with their respective wives (Annia Galeria Faustina Minor and Annia Aurelia Galeria Lucilla) were discovered here during excavations by Tunisian archaeologist Mongi Boulouednine in the 1950s, and are now on display in the Bardo in Tunis (page 108). A well-preserved mosaic of a bear remains *in situ*. Around AD400, the theatre was the scene of a famous public telling-off, delivered to the inhabitants of Bulla Regia by St Augustine. Ironically, he chastised them for spending too much time at the theatre, as well as berating them for their un-Christian love of mimes and prostitutes. Nearby, the small **Temple of Isis** is unremarkable, although its dedication to an originally Egyptian goddess does illustrate how cosmopolitan Bulla Regia was in Roman times.

Next, head northwards towards the **Forum** and **Capitol**. This area was excavated in 1949–52 and is poorly preserved, although some incredible statues, including one of Apollo, were discovered and are now on display in the Bardo. The **Temple of Apollo** is the oldest structure here, likely built during the reign of Emperor Tiberius (AD14–37). Just to the east sits a **hall with double apse**, with some poorly preserved geometric mosaics.

Heading north along the track from the Capitol with the hill to your right, you pass the **spring** that provided vital water to the settlement in ancient times. Next, you hit the complex of five houses with underground features that are the highlight of most visits. Climbing down the seven stone steps into the **House of Fishing**, you immediately notice how much cooler it is than on the surface. One of the largest and oldest houses on the site, it still has some beautiful mosaics in place, displaying an intricate fishing theme intended to impress wealthy guests, as well as featuring a basement fountain.

Next, the **House of Hunting** (named after the partial hunting scene mosaic) demonstrates a number of fascinating architectural features, hinting at the wealth of the original owner. The above-ground columns are dug from the luxurious marble quarries of Simitthus (modern-day Chemtou, page 155), and the house features a separate double toilet and bathroom (unusual at the time) as well as private baths. It also has an underground colonnaded courtyard, with hollow terracotta tubes used to construct the vaults to reduce total weight. Despite much of the house being underground, the main courtyard receives a surprising amount of sunlight.

The **House of Peacocks** is named after a mosaic that has now been moved to the Bardo. Peacocks were symbolic of Christ's resurrection in early Christian art, thanks to St Augustine's writings about them in his book *The City of God* in AD426. The mosaics found here are another piece of evidence demonstrating just how long Bulla Regia was continuously occupied for. North of this, the **New House of Hunting** is home to an above-ground mosaic featuring a lion hunt. Other items depicted include a *kantharos* (Greek-style drinking vessel), a wild boar, horses and a hare. Below ground, five of the supporting columns are still standing.

The northernmost excavated house is the **House of Amphitrite**, home to the best-preserved mosaic on the site in the *triclinium*. Despite the house being named after Amphitrite (goddess of the sea), the main image actually depicts a nude Venus (goddess of love and victory). Two cupids are crowning her as she is transported along by the brother *ichthyocentaurs* (sea centaurs), Aphros (right) and Bythos (left), who represent the sea foam and sea depths respectively. The actual mosaic is roped off to prevent footsteps damaging it, but you can still get very close and the lighting at midday is excellent for photography.

Heading south back towards the entrance, you pass the **Christian Basilicas**, two 6th-century Byzantine churches. The *quadratum populi* (meeting area for the faithful) is made up of three naves, which include mosaics of birds (including peacocks) and geometric shapes, although these are not as well preserved as other elements of the site.

Chemtou (Simitthus) (78 602 143, 71 909 264; **w** patrimoinedetunisie.com.tn; summer 08.00–18.00 daily, winter 08.30–17.30 daily; 7/5DT non-resident/resident) Once the largest ancient Roman marble quarry in North Africa, Chemtou was prized for its valuable yellow marble (*marmor numidicum* or *giallo antico*) used in high-status architectural projects across the Empire for hundreds of years. Today, Chemtou is the site of one of the largest (1,500m^2) and most impressive archaeological museums in Tunisia, as well as an expansive 80ha archaeological site that you can tour on foot or in a 4x4. Note that in 1997 the Tunisian authorities changed the Arabic–English transliteration of the site's name from 'Chemtou' to 'Chimtou'; however, most maps have not followed this change.

The site was originally the Numidian settlement of Simitthus, founded in the 4th or 5th century BC. The Numidians first began exploiting marble from this area in the 2nd century under King Micipsa, son of King Masinissa. Micipsa used the marble here to build a monument to his father on top of Jebel Chimtou, and also exported the marble westwards, where it was used in the Mausoleum of Massinissa at Cirta (modern El Khroub, Algeria) in 130BC. Pliny the Elder tells us in his *Natural History* that this luxurious marble eventually made its way to Rome. Marcus Lepidus, famed consul in the final years of the Roman Republic, was the first person to use Numidian marble in his house in 78BC. After Julius Caesar won the Battle of Thapsus in 46BC, he took control of the quarries here; following his assassination, a column of marble from Simitthus was put on display in Rome in his honour. By 27BC, Rome's

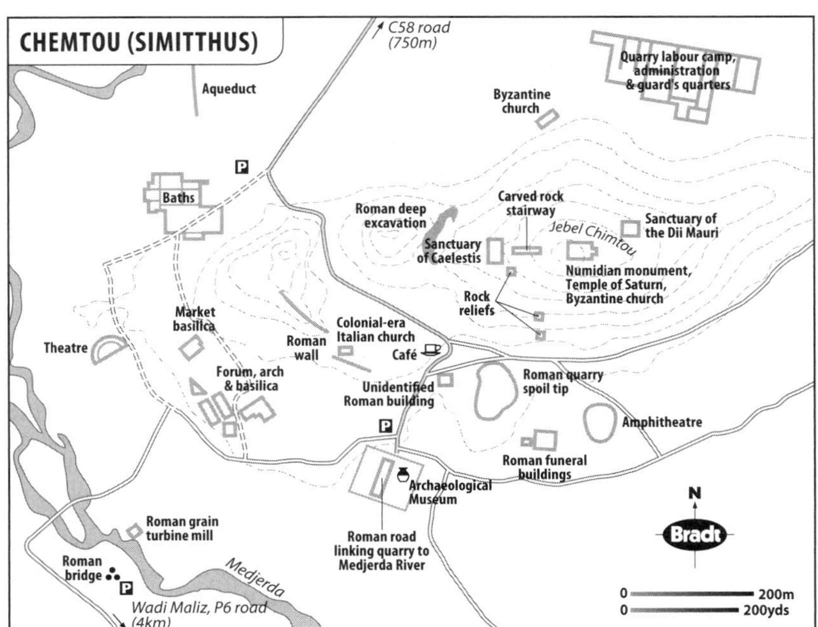

first Emperor, Augustus, had taken control of the quarry via his right-hand man, Marcus Vipsanius Agrippa, changing the settlement's name to Colonia Iulia Augusta Numidica Simmithensium. Agrippa was responsible for a massive series of public building works in Rome in the 1st century BC, and incorporated this marble into both the Forum of Augustus and in the colonnade of the Forum of Caesar.

By the 2nd century AD, Simitthus marble exports were flourishing as it became a favourite of later emperors, even being incorporated into Emperor Hadrian's private residence (Villa Adriana) in Tivoli. By 154, a large six-hall prison labour camp needed to be built to house the thousands of slaves who worked in the quarries to keep up with demand. These slaves were either captured as spoils of war, traded from elsewhere or sometimes prisoners, specifically sentenced to hard labour in the marble quarries. Unfortunately for these slaves, it was around this time that sections of the Oued Medjerda silted up, meaning it was no longer possible to float the excavated marble blocks eastwards along the length of the river to the port of Utica. Instead, the blocks needed to be hauled on Roman roads all the way to Tabarka, over 50km away and through the Khroumirie Mountains, before being loaded on to ships and sailed across the Roman Empire. The quarries remained in use throughout Byzantine times, but were abandoned following the Arab invasion, around the 9th century.

Getting there and away Chemtou is 22km from Jendouba, from where you can get a taxi – expect to pay around 30DT if you want to have them wait for you. The site is also accessible from Ghardimaou, 15km to the west. There are no direct public transport links, although you can jump on a louage from Jendouba to Ghardimaou (ensuring it is going northwards via Ouergech not southwards via Wadi Maliz) and get dropped off at the signposted turning (⊕ 36.499616, 8.579175), from where it is a 1.5km uphill walk to the museum.

Exploring the site Between 1965 and 1996 the Tunisian National Heritage Institute (L'Institut National du Patrimoine: INP) and the Rome Section of the German Archaeological Institute (Deutsches Archäologisches Institut: DAI) worked on a collaborative archaeological project in the area, inaugurating the site in October 1990. During the construction process, workers discovered a hoard of 1,647 gold coins, some of which are on display at the Finance Museum in Tunis.

The best place to start your exploration of the site is at the **museum**, which includes captivating displays (fully labelled in Arabic, French and German) outlining the history of the site and the marble that sits here. The museum is divided into four main sections, with maps available as you come into the main entrance. The first section covers the geology of the area and the Numidian period, with displays about the kings of Numidia and their famous Numidian cavalry, the economy, funerary rites, gods and language. You then walk out into an open-air courtyard, which features a life-size reconstruction of the eastern façade of a Numidian shrine that was found on the summit of one of the nearby hills. The third section gives information about the famous marble of Chemtou, including how it was excavated, how and where it was transported and what life was like for the slaves who worked in the quarry. The final section covers the Roman colony of Simitthus, housing a number of impressive funerary monuments as well as mosaics and other statues. There is also a room where informational films are projected. Once you have explored the museum, you can then drive or walk around the site itself and see the remains of the prosperous settlement that grew up around the valuable yellow marble quarry.

Starting in the south, head along a dirt track to the remains of the Roman **bridge** across the Oued Medjerda. The bridge you see today was commissioned by Emperor Trajan in AD112 and stood as the largest bridge in Africa Proconsularis, although there was a smaller bridge on the site before this. Trajan's bridge eventually collapsed in the 4th century. Next to the bridge are the remains of the Roman **grain turbine mill**, which is almost identical to the turbine mill discovered at Testour, 80km to the east. Back on the north side of the river is the Roman **Forum**, under which are some well-preserved Numidian tombs. Northwest of this are the **market basilica** (of which little is left) and the **theatre**. Much of the theatre structure has also been lost, although it is still possible to make out the arches supporting the stands and some of the terraced seating. Directly north of the market basilica are the remnants of the **baths**. These are one of the first structures you see if you drive into the site from the C58. They were clearly large, with a small section of a two-storey structure remaining. Behind to the north you can see the remnants of the **aqueduct** that fed them.

Heading southeast up the main road back into the site, you pass a Roman **wall** on your right, which divided the colony of Simitthus (to the south) from the imperial property (to the northeast). Just to the north of the wall, you will see a **colonial-era Italian church** from the 19th century; although the roof is completely gone, the walls and church front are well preserved. Continuing along the road, you hit a large, unidentified Roman building, which is thought to be connected to the administration of the marble quarry. Behind this you find the Roman **quarry spoil tip**, the **amphitheatre** and some Roman **funeral buildings**. The spoil tip is an unexciting hill, but there are some larger broken blocks of rejected marble dotted around. There is some evidence of the amphitheatre and other buildings above ground, but they are not as well preserved as the theatre.

Heading north up the side of Jebel Chimtou from the amphitheatre, you first hit the **rock reliefs**; carved directly into the red stone, they are easy to miss unless the shadows fall correctly. Many of these reliefs depict humans making sacrifices of rams to the god Saturn. Traversing northwest along the hillside, you next see the ruins of the **Sanctuary of Caelestis**. Known as Tanit before she was adopted into the Roman pantheon of gods, she was one of the most important deities in the Punic world. Looking out over the sanctuary ruins, you can see evidence of Roman deep excavation on the western flank of Jebel Chimtou. Walking up the **carved rock stairway** will bring you to the summit, home to the ruins of the **Numidian monument** built by King Micipsa (using local marble) to honour his father King Masinissa in the 2nd century BC. (A fine reconstruction of this monument is in the archaeological museum.) The original structure was 10m high, but little remains of it today as it was converted by the Romans into a Temple of Saturn, and then by the Byzantines in the 4th century into a church.

From here, looking down the north face of the hill you can see the limited remains of the **Sanctuary of the Dii Mauri**. Literally translated as 'Moorish Gods', these deities, much like Tanit, were important North African gods before being adopted into the Roman pantheon. There is a damaged relief carving of eight of them on the side of Jebel Chimtou. Looking to the base of the hill, you will also see the walls of a ruined **Byzantine church** and the massive footprint of the **quarry labour camp, administration and guard's quarters**. This was a six-hall prison labour camp built in AD154, at the height of the Roman Empire's yellow marble craze.

Thuburnica A further 10km west of Chemtou on the C58 near modern-day Ouergech is this Numidian and Roman archaeological site. In 1949, an inscription was found here indicating that the general Gaius Marius had founded Thuburnica as a colony for his military veterans during the late Roman Republic (1st century BC). It was then expanded by Emperor Augustus with more of his veterans a few decades later. There is an impressively preserved mausoleum, an archway, ruined Byzantine fortifications and a Roman bridge from the 2nd or 3rd century AD (⊕ 36.525567, 8.468860) that is in such good condition it is still in use by vehicles today. However, the overall level of preservation here is less impressive than at Bulla Regia and Chemtou, and it is a difficult site to reach without your own transport as most of the louages passing between Jendouba and Ghardimaou tend to stick to the main P6 road, rather than looping via Thuburnica on the C58. At the time of writing, parts of the Thuburnica site were being used by the Tunisian military as a forward operating base, so access was restricted.

GHARDIMAOU AND EL FEÏJA (EL FEDJA) NATIONAL PARK

Sitting on the Oued Medjerda, **Ghardimaou** is the last major settlement on the P6 before you hit the Ouled Moumen border crossing into Algeria, 11km further down the road. It was one of the headquarters of the Algerian National Liberation Army (Armée de Libération Nationale; ALN) in the 1950s, used to co-ordinate raids into eastern Algeria from a series of ALN bases. However, the construction of the Morice Line in 1957 reduced the significance of this location in the Algerian liberation struggle. There is a small military museum in town, the **Museum of Tuniso-Algerian Shared Memory** (Rue de l'Armée de Libération Nationale Algérienne; ☎ 78 662 077; w defense.tn/la-musee-de-la-memoire-commune-tuniso-algerienne-a-ghardimaou; ⏲ 09.30–17.00 Mon–Sat; 5DT), which tells the story of this time.

The only real reason to come here today, other than in transit to Algeria, is to visit nearby **El Feïja National Park**, 15km to the northwest. A national park since 1990, this 2,765ha forest area was added to the UNESCO Tentative List in 2008. The park serves as a reserve for the Barbary stag, but the forests are also home to a variety of other species including North African boar, crested porcupine, African golden wolf and African wildcat. It is a site of great archaeological significance, having been continuously occupied by humans since Neolithic times. Archaeologists have discovered stone tools here dating back thousands of years, as well as 2,000-year-old remains of Numidian settlements. More recently, the densely forested area served as a hideout for Algerian freedom fighters in the early 1960s, including Algeria's second president, Houari Boumédiène.

The park is popular with hikers, with the 1,150m-tall **Jebel Statir** (⊕ 36.521944, 8.313333) and the 712m-high **Le Rocher de Kef Negcha** (⊕ 36.488963, 8.305263) the star attractions. The latter was once a site of indigenous worship, with evidence of artwork in some of the caves below from thousands of years ago. Today there is a lookout tower on the top, accessed by a staircase carved into one side of the rock, which offers excellent panoramic views of the surrounding countryside and is a popular destination for Tunisian hiking groups. The Association Tunisienne Des Randonneurs (page 40) organises hikes into the park, using the nearby **Camping Aïn Soltane** (⊕ 36.526195, 8.336961; ☎ 78 668 501; f Centre-De-Camping-Ain-Soltan-Gh/318924018292039; **$**) as a base. Note there are no tourism facilities in the park, so you will need to bring your own supplies.

GETTING THERE AND AWAY Ghardimaou marks the end of the SNCFT train line from Tunis (3hrs 40mins), and it is easy to reach via car or louage on the P5 from

Tunis. You will need to arrange your own private transport to get from the town to the national park.

NORTH TO TABARKA

BOU SALEM This large market town on the P6, 23km northeast of Jendouba, is where agricultural traders gather cereals from the surrounding countryside. From a tourist perspective it is mainly useful as a transit point, with many louages passing through between Béja, Jendouba and Firnanah. It is known to ancient historians as the site where the Saltus Burunitanus was discovered in 1879. Dating to AD182, this stone inscription was of a petition to Emperor Commodus, which contains a complaint from a peasant spokesperson, Lurius Lucullus, about the abuses local peasants were suffering at the hands of their managers. Amazingly, the find also included a response from Emperor Commodus himself – he prohibited further abuses from the managers, but did not dish out any punishments.

FIRNANAH (FERNANA) Firnanah sits 22km north of Jendouba on the P17. Much like Bou Salem, it is an agricultural settlement that is likely only of interest to tourists as a transit point, with many louages passing through between Jendouba and Tabarka. The settlement takes its name from a mythical oak tree, which marked the furthest point that the bey of Tunis's tax collectors would dare to venture into Khroumirie territory. Apparently, each year the Khroumirie tribal leaders would gather under the tree and consult it as to how little tax they should pay to the Bey's collectors, with any rustle of the branches taken to indicate a response. Legend has it that the tree's poor tax-planning advice was what led to the French invasion of the area in 1881.

Just to the east of town is a lake created by the **Sidi Bou Huertma Dam**, where there is an excellent campsite and ecolodge, **Bouhertma Outdoors** (⊕ 36.647206, 8.773840; m 52 423 256; w bouhertmaoutdoors.tn; f BouhertmaOutdoors; **$–$$**), which offers camping spots by the edge of the lake as well as log cabins, from which you can enjoy kayaking, hiking, archery and local food.

BENI M'TIR The least-populous municipality in Jendouba Governorate, Beni M'Tir is a quiet town, and far less developed in terms of tourism infrastructure than nearby Aïn Draham (page 160). Nevertheless, it still serves as a popular weekend getaway spot for hikers and campers eager to explore the surrounding cork-oak forest and those wishing to admire one of Tunisia's largest reservoirs. The dam that created this body of water, the 483m-wide, 78m-high **Bni M'tir Dam** (Barrage Bni Mtir), was built on the Oued el Lil, a tributary of Tunisia's longest river, the Medjerda. Designed by Swiss engineer Alfred Stucky, the dam took around eight years to build and was completed in 1953. There is a car park on the western side of the dam with a small snack bar, from where you can admire this feat of engineering. You can also rent kayaks to explore the water from Bni M'tir Outdoors (page 160). A few kilometres out of town is a waterfall known locally as the **Cascade de Beni M'tir** (⊕ 36.728758, 8.705834). It is signposted from the road, and there is a wooden series of stairs down to the waterline. Be sure to visit in winter to ensure it is actually flowing.

Where to stay

Green Hill Resort (12 rooms, 18 chalets) ⊕ 36.745523, 8.738147; 70 548 125; w greenhill-tn.com. This new resort is built on top of natural hot springs & aims to be carbon neutral through the use of geothermal & solar energy, as well as using sustainable building materials. The resort offers guests access to 8 thermal treatment cabins as well as a hammam, sauna & 2 outdoor swimming pools. **$$$$**

Plan L Concept Tunisie (2 rooms) Rue Salah Zarouk; ⊕ 36.737170, 8.735224; m 24 933 666; e pascale@planlconcept.com; f planlconcept.tunisie. This youth hostel is an incubator for rural economic development projects in the area. It has a dorm set-up, 1 room with 4 beds & the other with 8, & offers guided botanical walks, yoga & meditation sessions. FB & HB options available. **$$–$$$**

✷ **Bni Mtir Outdoors** (9 rooms) Barrage Bni Mtir; m 93 513 272; f BniMtirOUTDOORS. This beautiful outdoor adventure centre sits on the shore of the reservoir. It has space for camping & also wooden chalets that can be rented, along with 4 tree-houses. This is also the only location on the water where you can rent kayaks. A clean, comfortable & safe base from which to explore. **$–$$**

Centre des Stages et des Vacances de Beni Metir (7 rooms) Av de l'Environnement; ☎ 78 649 200; e csv.benmetir@gmail.com. This basic youth hostel & training centre is centrally located & probably the cheapest bed in town if you are not camping. **$**

Where to eat and drink

Green Hills Food & Beverage m 96 570 247; f Green-Hills-Food-Beverage-Beni-Mtir-589947121418522; ⏲ 10.30–18.30 Tue–Sun. This smart new pizzeria attached to the Green Hills Resort has a sun deck looking out over the reservoir. Offering fast-food favourites with a wood & stone interior setting, it is a great spot for lunch while visiting the reservoir. **$$–$$$**

Beni M'Tir Café Av de l'Environnement; ⏲ 07.00–20.30 daily. Simple café offering coffee, tea & some Tunisian cooked dishes. **$–$$**

AÏN DRAHAM Sitting at 800m up in the Khroumirie Mountains, Aïn Draham is a remarkable town. Although ancient in origins, the modern town started out as a French colonial military base, set up in 1882, and a decade later it was designated a municipality – one of the first in Tunisia (along with El Kef, to the south). In 1930, French colonial architects decided to take advantage of the cooler weather up in the mountains, and fashioned Aïn Draham from an ancient market town into some sort of mountain retreat. Many of the old buildings would not be out of place in a Swiss ski resort, and thanks to the high average rainfall it is surrounded by forest and blessed with abundant snowfall most winters. Today it offers plenty of outdoor activities to enjoy, including camping, hiking and mountain biking. Aïn Draham is also a popular hub for wild boar hunters during the hunting season (Oct–Jan), attracting hunters from across Europe.

Getting there and around Aïn Draham is a 185km (3hrs) drive west from Tunis. The fastest routes take you via Béja, from where you approach the town along the good-quality, scenic, winding P17. Note that this mountain road becomes treacherous during heavy snows. Louages connect to Tabarka, Jendouba, Béja, Mateur, Sajanan, Nefza and Tunis (12.35DT one-way). SNTRI buses also connect to Tunis (3hrs 50mins; 14.50DT) via Jendouba and Béja. Both buses and louages stop at the northern end of town by the taxi ranks. The nearest border crossing into Algeria is at Babouche, 15km to the northwest (see page 42 for details on Algerian border crossings in the north-west subregion).

The nearest airport is Tabarka-Aïn Draham, 40km to the northeast, which is connected to Tunis via a 30-minute Tunisair Express flight (page 54). You will likely need to get a taxi into Tabarka and then find a louage heading south, unless you are happy to take a taxi for the entire journey.

Most of the main sights in Aïn Draham are located along the 1.5km Avenue Habib Bourguiba, which is very walkable if you do not mind slogging uphill.

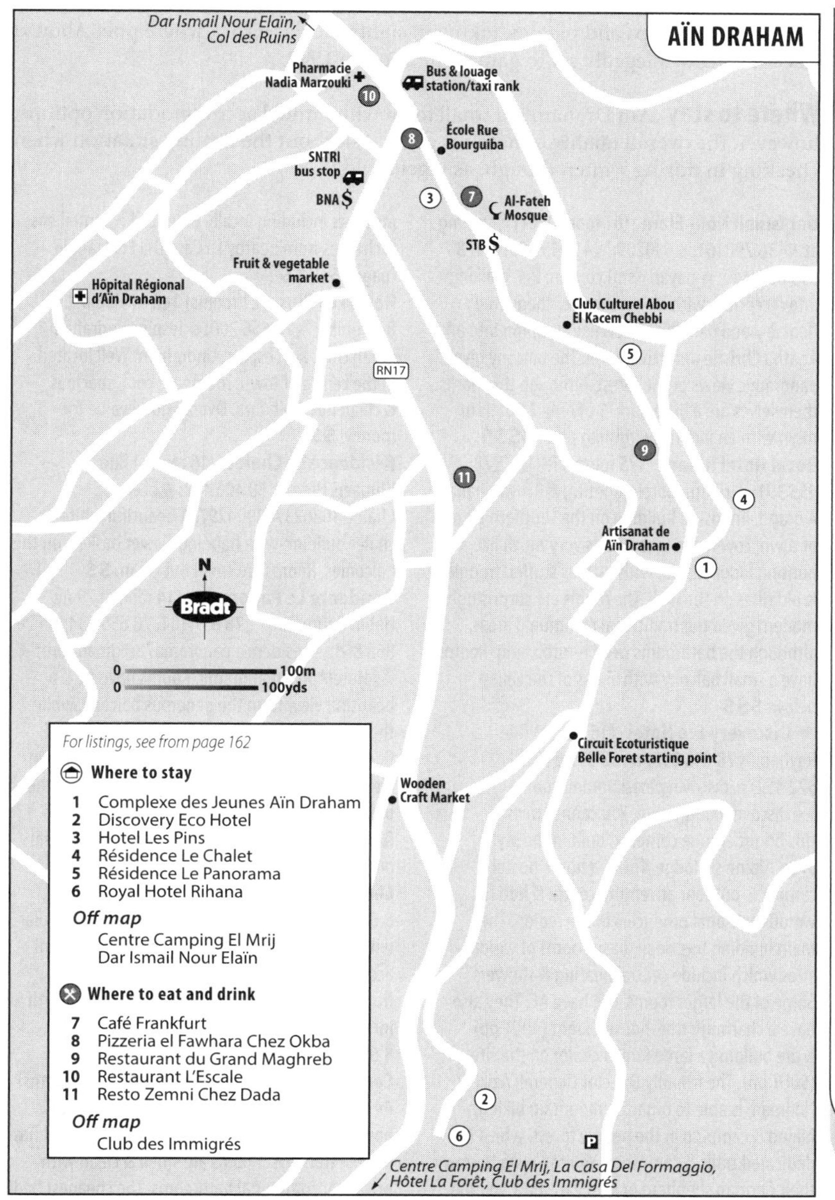

Otherwise, yellow taxis can be flagged down or found parked on the roundabout at the north end of town.

Local tour operators Hiking, mountain biking, camping and other outdoor activities can be arranged via the travel agencies in nearby Tabarka (page 168) or via the **Discovery Eco Hotel** (page 162). Local guide **Yahya** (☎ 53 541 350) can also arrange hiking trips and picnics, taking in sights such as a rock where poet Abou el Kacem Chebbi allegedly sat to gain inspiration in 1932.

Where to stay

Aïn Draham is a small town with limited accommodation options; however, the overall quality of hotels is good. Ask about the heating situation when checking in during winter, though, as it gets cold!

Dar Ismail Nour Elaïn (61 rooms) RN17, turning at ⊕ 36.790161, 8.690209; ☎ 41 535 595; m 78 655 000/440; e bayari@shti.com.tn; f. Walking into reception, with its roaring fire, chequered floor & wood panelling, feels like stepping into an Agatha Christie detective novel. The balcony gives panoramic views of the forest, although the rooms themselves are a little dark. 1 of only 2 hotels in town with an indoor swimming pool. **$$$$**

Royal Hotel Rihana (75 rooms) RN17; ☎ 78 655 391; e rihana.hotel@gnet.tn; f royalrihana. A grand, imposing building on the southern edge of town, covered in vines. Feels very much like a hunting lodge inside, with various stuffed trophies & old rifles on the wall. The rooms are surprisingly modern given the traditional communal areas, although the bathrooms need refurbishing. Rooms have a small balcony with views of the valley below. **$$$**

✷ **Discovery Eco Hotel** (16 rooms) Rue Rayhan; ☎ 78 655 055; m 98 912 519, 21 522 452; e discovery.azizi@gmail.com; f Discoveryaindrahem. You cannot miss this bright orange complex, built in the style of an Alpine ski lodge. This is a hotel, hostel, campsite, outdoor adventure centre & hub for various artisanal producers in the region. The main building has clean, basic rooms of various sizes which include central heating & showers. Some of the larger rooms also have AC. They also have a charming tree-house to rent (40DT pp) & are building a large family chalet on the site (50DT pp). The friendly Director General, Azizi Noöman, is able to organise mountain biking, hiking & camping in the nearby forest, which has dedicated trails & campsites. You can even borrow their German shepherd or husky to show you the way! The restaurant offers fast-food favourites & local cuisine, & the shop sells various artisanal products including locally produced essential oils & cheeses from nearby La Casa Del Formaggio (page 163). **$$**

Hotel Les Pins (21 rooms) 148 Av Habib Bourguiba; ☎ 78 656 200; e lespinsaindraham@gmail.com; f Lespins.Aindrahem. Well located in the centre of town, rooms are cool, spacious & clean but a bit dark. Overall good value for money. **$$**

Résidence Le Chalet (16 rooms) Rue Khmaeis Hjri; m 50 406 412; f Le-Chalet-108623763904297. A beautiful white chalet building with hanging flower baskets on the balconies. Rooms are small but clean. **$$**

Résidence Le Panorama (14 rooms) 79 Av Habib Bourguiba; ☎ 78 657 101, 78 655 434; m 20 868 868; e residence.panorama78@gmail.com; f HotelAppartPanorama. Rooms have AC & a beautiful view from the generous balcony, while the suites are up a steep set of stairs on the 3rd floor, featuring 5 beds each & access to their own kitchen, although views are not as good from the balcony. Also has a popular pizzeria downstairs, & a shop selling local artisanal honey & essential oils. **$$**

Centre Camping El Mrij ⊕ 36.755363, 8.688918; m 22 030 879. This campsite is popular with Tunisian hiking groups & provides excellent access to the surrounding forest. It is accessed from a turning just north of the Complexe Sportif International Aïn Draham at ⊕ 36.748284, 8.681366. **$**

Complexe des Jeunes Aïn Draham (20 rooms) Av Habib Bourguiba; ☎ 78 655 087. This youth hostel sits on top of a hill on a spacious site but has seen better days. Rooms are small & clean with private or communal bathrooms. The cheapest bed in town. **$**

Where to eat and drink

Club des Immigrés ⊕ 36.729863, 8.678807; m 21 614 888; e jbouslimi@hotmail.com; f CLUB-DES-Immigres-1386493991571407; ⊙ variable, call to book. A truly special find to the south of Aïn Draham along the P17, this restaurant is in a cobbled-together wooden encampment in the forest. With a rustic outside seating area & flag-draped interior, it offers excellent Mediterranean cuisine, making this a great pit stop for those hiking in the surrounding area. Be sure to book in advance to avoid disappointment! $$$$

Resto Zemni Chez Dada Av du 14 Janvier 2011; 51 446 710; e restozemnichezdada@gmail.com; 11.00–22.00 daily. In a quiet location to the south of town, this quirkily designed restaurant has some good local cuisine. Also offers a home delivery service. $$$

Café Frankfurt Av Habib Bourguiba; 09.00–late daily. Opposite the mosque, this café is pretty basic inside, but offers free Wi-Fi & some good fast food. $$

Pizzeria el Fawhara Chez Okba Av Habib Bourguiba; 96 898 989; 11.00–22.00 daily. Mainly offering take-away pizzas & grilled meats, this cheap & cheerful spot gets very busy at lunchtime. $$

Restaurant du Grand Maghreb Av Habib Bourguiba; 96 649 747, 98 513 792; 11.30–22.00 Mon–Sat. A great selection of traditional meat recipes including grills & stews. $$

Restaurant L'Escale Av Habib Bourguiba; 08.00–late daily. A popular spot to watch the world go by with a coffee from the terrace. Also offers rotisserie chicken in a large indoor seating area. $$

Shopping The main **fruit and vegetable market** is part way down Avenue du 14 Janvier 2011 and sells a great variety of fresh local produce daily. To the south of town is **La Casa Del Formaggio** (m 53 926 771; e fromagedeterroir@gmail.com; f lacasadelformagio; 10.00–16.00 daily), an agricultural co-operative owned by master cheese-maker Haykel Abidi, who produces some excellent cheeses that make good gifts. It can also offer alfresco eat-in breakfasts featuring locally sourced ingredients. Those looking for arts and crafts will find items on sale at the **Wooden Craft Market** (Av du 14 Janvier 2011; 09.00–19.00 daily) or at the **Artisanat de Aïn Draham**, also known as the Artisanat de la Khroumirie (Av Habib Bourguiba; 10.00–late daily), which both sell a variety of olive-wood handicrafts at reasonable prices.

Other practicalities Both the **BNA** (Av des Martyrs; 78 655 814; 08.00–16.00 Mon–Fri) and **STB** (146 Av Habib Bourguiba; 78 656 496, 78 655 140; 08.00–16.00 Mon–Fri) have ATMs. For medical emergencies or anything that cannot wait for you to drive to the larger hospitals of Jendouba (page 149) or Tabarka (page 173), head to the **Hôpital Régional d'Aïn Draham** (36.777556, 8.683928; 78 655 047; 24/7). The well-stocked **Pharmacie Nadia Marzouki** (78 655 376; 08.00–20.00 daily) is at the north end of Avenue Habib Bourguiba, on the roundabout.

What to see and do Aïn Draham's main draw is the surrounding countryside, but there are a few worthwhile sights in the centre, which is hilly but easily walkable in a few hours. Occupying the old French Catholic church built in 1931, the **Club Culturel Abou El Kacem Chebbi** (Av Habib Bourguiba) opened in 2014 and was refurbished in 2017 with the help of an EU grant. Named after the famous Tunisian poet who spent some time in Aïn Draham in 1932, this beautiful, whitewashed building hosts various exhibitions and cultural events on an irregular schedule. In the very centre of town on Avenue Habib Bourguiba, both the colonial-era **Al-Fateh Mosque** and **École Rue Bourguiba**, refurbished in 2020, stand out for their distinctive Islamic architecture. A few kilometres south of town is the eerie **Hôtel La Forêt** (36.740136, 8.679722), which was abandoned in the 2010s and now feels like the set of *The Shining*, with grand staircases and rusting wrought-iron gates.

For those wishing to explore the surrounding forest, the marked **Circuit Écotouristique Belle Forêt** (36.772078, 8.691492), at a road junction south of town, is a good starting point. The walk takes around 90 minutes and traverses both eucalyptus and cork-oak forest, as well as passing a freshwater spring and a number of artisanal craft areas which produce local pottery and essential oils. More details on the route can be obtained from **Fikra-Tounisiya** (☎ 70 819 013; e amina.bf@gmail.com; f FikraTounisiya), the Tunisian NGO that helped set it up. Note that the viewpoint marked on Google Maps and other mapping software to the east of town is not actually accessible, as the road is blocked after ⊕ 36.771129, 8.696105 owing to the presence of a military base. The 5km route up to **Col des Ruines** is signposted from the main road (⊕ 36.793819, 8.689611). As the name suggests, this hill is home to the ruins of a colonial-era three-storey structure, although the panoramic views are what really draws hikers up here.

If you're keen to strike out on your own, it is possible to hire camping equipment and mountain bikes from the **Discovery Eco Hotel** (page 162), though it can also arrange local hiking guides.

Oued Zen National Park A national park since 2010, this 6,700ha forest area east of Aïn Draham is the most humid national park in the country, home to a variety of species including Eurasian otters and Barbary stag as well as North African boar. Park infrastructure is limited, so you will need to bring everything you require with you, but the opportunities for hiking and wild camping are excellent. The park is most easily accessed from Aïn Draham, where you can also organise guides with local tour agencies (page 161), although it can be accessed from Beni M'Tir (page 159) as well. If you would like to explore independently, in May 2018 the International Trail Running Association published a 32km GPS trail run (w itra.run/race/13449-o2-trail-2018&2018) which leads all the way from the park into Aïn Draham. It is possible to complete this trail in a long day, but note that it involves 1,180m of positive elevation change.

HAMMAM BOURGUIBA ⚑ Hidden up in the hills by the Algerian border are some natural hot springs, some of which heat up to 50°C, which have been in use since ancient Roman times. The high levels of sulphur in the water are believed to be good for alleviating respiratory problems and attract Tunisian and foreign tourists alike. While the town itself is small, the allure of the hot springs has led to the construction of an incongruous luxury hotel and spa complex, **El Mouradi Hammam Bourguiba** (151 rooms; ☎ 78 654 055/8; w elmouradi.com; f elmouradihotels; **$$$$**), which is your only sleeping option. This white-and-red palatial complex is a very unexpected find out here. You have the choice of a regular room, suite, a bungalow or even the presidential suite. It offers an excellent range of spa treatments, making full use of the natural hot springs, and there is also a beautiful covered pool and jacuzzi area with a large skylight, as well as extensive sports facilities on the grounds. Non-guests can also pay to use the spa facilities. For those on a budget, the local hammam (⊙ 24/7) in the northwest of town is easily walkable from the centre, and only costs 1DT! It is usually quite busy and the local attendant also offers massages. Louages from Aïn Draham and nearby Firnanah connect to Hammam Bourguiba.

TABARKA ⚑

For many tourists, Tabarka is the main attraction of Jendouba Governorate, and for good reason. As you drop down from the tree-lined hills to the coast, one of the first sights to appear is the imposing 16th-century Genoese fort, sitting proudly on the

Tabarka peninsula, overlooking the town. Tourism infrastructure is well developed here, with a defined Zone Touristique and a walkable town centre filled with sights. The sandy beaches rival anything on offer in Hammamet, with the added bonus of having the Khroumirie Mountains as a backdrop. Diving is popular here thanks to the reef and underwater caves, and it's also one of the few places in the country where you can surf.

HISTORY The Phoenicians established a settlement here called Thabraca (meaning 'place in the shade') in the 5th century BC, although there is some evidence of earlier Amazigh occupation. The ancient Romans took control of the town in the 2nd century AD and it flourished as an export site for many high-value goods from the surrounding region, such as marble from the quarries at Chemtou, wild animals from the forested hills to the south as well as lead and iron from nearby mines. During the early Christian period, Thabraca was famous as a centre for high-quality mosaic work and has left us more surviving mosaic tomb covers than any other site in former Africa Proconsularis, some of which can be seen in the Bardo in Tunis (page 108). The site remained prosperous for hundreds of years throughout Vandal, Byzantine, Fatimid, Hafsid and Ottoman rule. In 1542 the Lomellinis, an aristocratic Genoese family originally from Lombardy, managed to purchase the Tabarka peninsula as a concession from the Ottoman bey of Tunis. The Genoese garrisoned here for the next 200 years, building the magnificent fort that you can still visit today and slowly encouraging migration from mainland Italy (especially Genoa).

In 1741 Tabarka was seized by Sidi-Younes, eldest son of Ali Pacha. He also seized Cap Negro, a French colonial possession 25km northeast. Tabarka was destroyed (though the fort was left intact), and much of the population (known

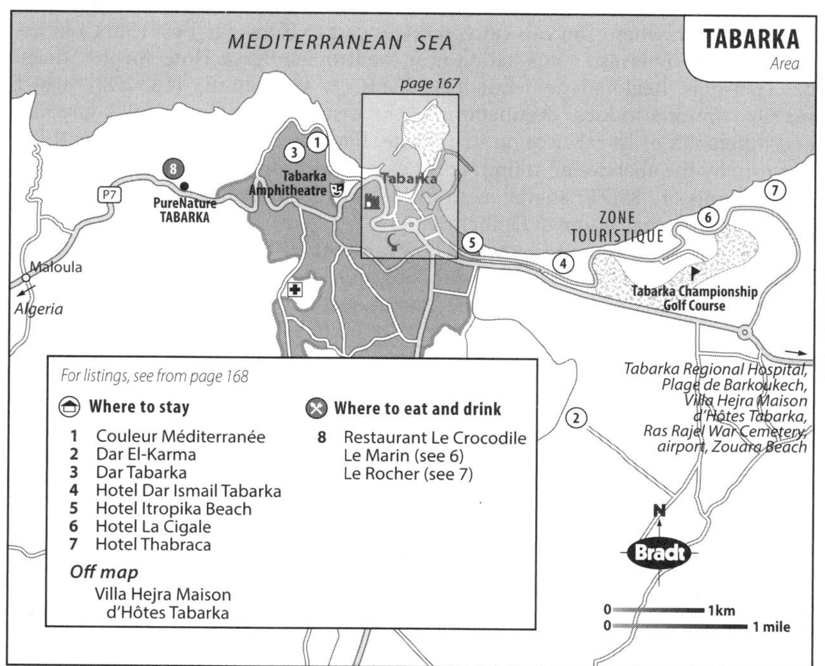

as Tabarquins) were rounded up and shipped back to Tunis. Many managed to narrowly avoid this fate, having emigrated to San Pietro and Sant'Antioco islands off Sardinia in 1738, in search of richer fishing grounds. A legacy of this migration can be found in the language of these islands today: they speak Tabarchino, which is a dialect of the Ligurian language spoken in Sardinia filled with 17th-century Ligurian archaisms.

Like the rest of Ottoman Tunisia, Tabarka was incorporated into a French protectorate in 1881, and quickly became a popular hunting spot for wealthy French officials looking to shoot wild boar or lions. Sadly, in 1891 the last Barbary lion ever recorded in Tunisia was killed in Babouch, between Tabarka and Aïn Draham. Like much of northern Tunisia, Tabarka experienced fighting during World War II between the Allied and Axis powers, from November 1942 to May 1943. Some of the losses during this fighting are commemorated to the east of town in the Ras Rajel War Cemetery.

After the war, in 1952, the region was still considered remote enough by the French colonial authorities that they exiled Habib Bourguiba here (although he was eventually moved to the more remote Galite Islands). Bourguiba's time in Tabarka is commemorated by the roundabout near the park in the centre of town.

GETTING THERE AND AROUND

By road Tabarka is a 180km (3hrs) drive west from Tunis on good-quality tarmac roads. It is also possible to access the Algerian border crossing at Oum Tboul from town (page 43). The tourist information office and agencies such as Vaga Tours (page 168) can help with car rental if you would like to explore the surrounding area. Most of the higher-end hotels can also arrange vehicles with drivers upon request.

The SNTRI bus station is on the western side of town [167 B6], near Tunisie Telecom, from where you can catch services east to Tunis via Béja (3hrs 15mins; 10.27DT). There is also a bus station near the Itropika Beach Hotel for the Société de Transport Régional de Jendouba (SRTJ) (w srtj.com.tn) [167 D7], which mainly connects to local destinations to the east. You can find a full route map and timetables of its services on its website. Louages congregate in the southeast of town, by the abandoned train tracks behind the Itropika Beach Hotel. Services run to Tunis (12.85DT) as well as to El Kef, Medjez el Bab, Béja, Nefza, Bizerte, Jendouba, Firnanah and Aïn Draham.

For short journeys around town, yellow taxis can be flagged down, although the centre is so compact that walking is probably quicker, unless you are staying in one of the resorts further east in the Zone Touristique.

TABARKA

For listings, see from page 168

Where to stay

1 Corail Royal Apart Hotel.....D7
2 Hôtel de France.....B5
3 Hôtel de la Plage.....C5
4 Hotel Novelty.....B6
5 Les Mimosas.....C7
6 Marina Prestige.....C5

Where to eat and drink

7 Barberousse.....D6
8 Belle Vue.....D6
9 Black and White Salon de Thé.....C6
10 Café Andalous.....B6
11 Café Chahrazed.....C5
12 Café du Port.....C5
13 Café La Marina.....D6
14 Crêp'eat.....C5
15 L'Esplanade.....D6
16 La Reine.....C5
17 Le Mondial.....C6
18 Le Vieux Port.....B5
19 Les Palmiers.....C6
20 Luna Mare.....C5
21 Restaurant Le Pirate.....D6
22 Ristorante Dolce Vita.....C5
23 Salon de thé Baya.....C6
24 Touta.....D5

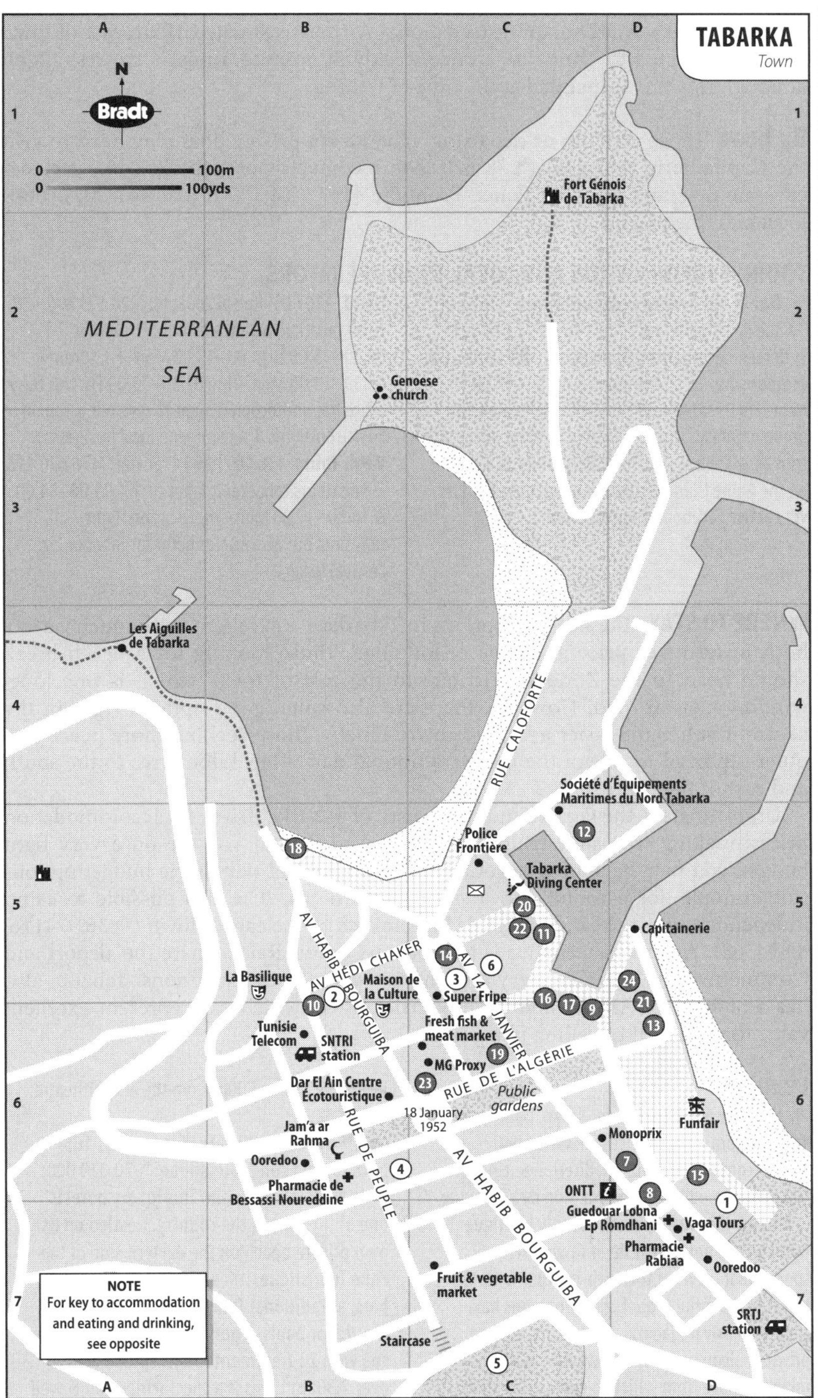

TABARKA
Town
Bradt
N
0 100m
0 100yds
MEDITERRANEAN SEA
Fort Génois de Tabarka
Genoese church
Les Aiguilles de Tabarka
RUE CALOFORTE
Société d'Équipements Maritimes du Nord Tabarka
Police Frontière
Tabarka Diving Center
Capitainerie
AV HABIB BOURGUIBA
AV HÉDI CHAKER
AV 14 JANVIER
La Basilique
Maison de la Culture
Super Fripe
Tunisie Telecom
SNTRI station
Fresh fish & meat market
MG Proxy
RUE DE L'ALGÉRIE
Dar El Ain Centre Écotouristique
Public gardens
18 January 1952
Jam'a ar Rahma
RUE DE PEUPLE
Ooredoo
Pharmacie de Bessassi Noureddine
Monoprix
Funfair
ONTT
Guedouar Lobna Ep Romdhani
Vaga Tours
Pharmacie Rabiaa
Ooredoo
Fruit & vegetable market
SRTJ station
Staircase
NOTE
For key to accommodation and eating and drinking, see opposite

By air Tabarka-Aïn Draham International Airport is situated 10km east of town and is connected to Tunis via a once-weekly 30-minute Tunisair Express flight, although this was suspended at the time of writing.

By boat Those arriving or departing Tabarka via private boat may need to visit the Capitainerie [167 D5] (78 670 599; e contact@port-tabarka.com, gerard@chassain.net) and also the Police Frontière [167 C5] (78 670 461/207), both located in the marina.

TOURIST INFORMATION AND LOCAL TOUR OPERATORS

✷ **Dar El Ain Centre Écotouristique** [167 B6] 19 Rue de l'Algérie; m 20 002 409 & 22 674 821; e darelain.ecotourisme@gmail.com; f DARELAIN.ecotourisme; 09.00–noon & 14.00–17.00 Mon–Fri, 09.00–14.00 Sat–Sun. This ecotourism group organises some incredible outdoor adventure trips across the region, including camping & hiking on the Galite Islands (summer only). Check out its very active Facebook page for more.

ONTT [167 C6] Rue al Zouaoui; 78 673 496/428; e crt.tabarka@ontt.tourism.tn; winter 08.00–13.00 & 14.00–17.00 Mon–Fri, summer 07.30–14.00 Mon–Thu, 07.30–13.00 Fri. This busy office has photocopied maps to give out & can offer advice on sights & recommend local businesses.

Vaga Tours [167 D7] Av 14 Janvier; 78 670 416; e vagatours.tabarka@planet.tn; 08.00–14.00 & 16.30–19.00 Mon–Fri. Focus on flight ticketing, but also a sales point for Tabarka Jazz Festival tickets.

WHERE TO STAY

The sleeping options in Tabarka are excellent, with much variety both in terms of price and type of lodgings. Those looking for a beach break should head to the Zone Touristique to the east of town, which is one long, winding coastal road. However, there are also some good options right in the centre if you want easier access to town. Finally, those seeking more peace and quiet can head to one of the more traditional dars a few kilometres to the south and east of the centre.

Unfortunately, the year-round popularity of Tabarka drives up accommodation prices, making true shoestring options hard to find. If you are on a very tight budget, you may be able to negotiate a reduced rate at one of the budget options (for example, for a room with a shared bathroom). It is also possible to camp independently at the sandy **Plage de Barkoukech** to the east of town (36.974116, 8.834368). Another alternative is to head east to Ras Rajel, where the airport and Commonwealth War Cemetery are, and ask about cheaper options. Tabarka also has a number of Airbnb holiday properties listed, which can represent excellent value for money if travelling in a group.

Luxury

✷ **Couleur Méditerranée** [map, page 165] (5 rooms) Rte Touristique; m 52 040 314; e contact@couleur-mediterranee.com; w couleur-mediterranee.com. Run by Véronique & Johnny, this beautiful adults-only boutique hotel on the northwest tip of town offers spectacular views of the 16th-century Genoese fort from its infinity pool. 2 of the rooms have their own private jacuzzi, & all rooms enjoy a private balcony with sea views. This is a very relaxing space from which to explore Tabarka, located less than 500m from the amphitheatre. **$$$$$**

✷ **Hotel La Cigale** [map, page 165] (248 rooms) Zone Touristique; 70 019 000; w lacigaletabarka.com. This luxury hotel is one of the best in the country. Nestled on its own private beach on the eastern side of the Zone Touristique, it features 5 restaurants, 5 bars, a traditional Tunisian tea house, indoor & outdoor pools, a golf course & an expansive spa with 23 treatment rooms spread across over 2,300m². This is a spectacular find & well worth a visit, even if driving all the way from Tunis! **$$$$$**

✷ ⚑ **Hotel Thabraca** [map, page 165] (308 rooms) Zone Touristique; 78 670 000; e contact@magichotels.com; w thabraca.magichotelsandresorts.com. Known as the Thabraca Thalasso & Diving, this is a strong offering from the same company that runs the excellent Palm Beach Palace Tozeur (page 348). It has all the facilities you would expect from an upmarket AI resort, & also a dive centre for those wanting to explore the nearby coral reef. The rooms are clean & spacious, with some offering sea views from the balcony. There is an extensive spa with saunas, hammam & an indoor swimming pool. Also home to the Le Rocher Restaurant & Bar which is a popular restaurant in Tabarka (page 170). This hotel also hosts the annual Thabarca Trail Challenge (thabarca_trail_challenge), one of the hilliest ultra-marathons in Tunisia. **$$$$$**

Dar Tabarka [map, page 165] (7 rooms) Cité Rmel; e dartabarka@yahoo.fr; f Dar-Tabarka-Tunisia-480106052016307. This well-appointed dar has a main house with 4 bedrooms, a bungalow with 2 bedrooms & a studio with 1 bedroom. The large windows of the main house offer fantastic views down the hill to Tabarka's main beach & marina. The traditional stone features, such as the fireplace & bar in the main living area, are great. The open-plan kitchen is also fantastic for entertaining large groups. **$$$$–$$$$$**

Upmarket

Dar El-Karma [map, page 165] (10 bungalows) m 27 845 281; w dar-elkarma.com. This dar is in the countryside 6km southeast of Tabarka's centre on the banks of the Oued El Kebir, from where you can kayak for 2.8km all the way to the sea, coming out near the Hotel Itropika Beach. Built in 2019, the wooden bungalows have 2 separate bedrooms, a kitchenette, shower, AC & a wooden terrace overlooking the 17m-long pool. Lots of options for outdoor activities include kayaking, pedalos & boats, as well as hiking & mountain biking in the surrounding countryside. **$$$$**

Hotel Dar Ismail Tabarka [map, page 165] (215 rooms) Rte Touristique; 78 670 188/820; w darismailhotels.com; f dar.ismail.tabarka. A similar set-up to the Itropika Beach, but slightly further out of town & with a unique pool design that loops around the grounds. Rooms are spacious & some have balcony. If you are looking to relax on the beach & do not mind the extra 1km distance from the town centre, then this place might be worth booking over the Itropika Beach given the slightly lower price. The food is also average. **$$$$**

Hotel Itropika Beach [map, page 165] (150 rooms) Rte Touristique; 78 673 300/429; w itropika.com. Conveniently located as the only large resort technically in town, this hotel has a grassy area around its pools, & direct access to a private beach with a lifeguard. The food is average, however, and you will need to be strategic about your room choice: normally those with a sea view are most desirable, but if the hotel is hosting one of its many weddings on the grass by the sea, then music from the event will keep you awake into the early hours. **$$$$**

Marina Prestige [167 C5] (49 rooms) Av 14 Janvier 201; 78 673 124; m 29 530 632; w marinaprestige.com; f. Recently refitted, this clean & modern hotel in the centre of town has some massive rooms with minibar & fridge, including some with balcony. It also has 10 apts featuring large living rooms, dual hob & microwave, fridge-freezer, 2 generous bedrooms & 2 full bathrooms. Represents serious value for money, especially if you book as a group. Its excellent café, Le Lido, is next door. **$$$$**

Villa Hejra Maison d'Hôtes Tabarka [map, page 165] (3 rooms) P7; m 58 005 008, 98 366 745; e villa.hejra.tab@gmail.com; f. A large, richly furnished country home to the east of town, surrounded by forest. Able to organise hiking, horseriding, quad biking & mountain biking in the area. Great pool area & excellent food. **$$$$**

Mid-range

Corail Royal Apart Hotel [167 D6/7] (59 apts) 78 671 000; w corail-royal.com. AC apts with sea views & a kitchen with oven, hob & microwave. Property has a pool but no direct beach access. Basic set-up but clean & good value for money. Not to be confused with Résidence Corail Royal Marina Tabarka, which shows up on Google Maps but is not recommended. **$$$**

Hôtel de France [167 B5] (16 rooms) Junction of Av Habib Bourguiba & Hédi Chaker; 78 670 600. Featuring an eye-catching wood & green-tile interior, rooms are basic, small & dark but clean. Given that the property dates to colonial times, I was surprised to find a lift. Great location if you want to be in the heart of the action. **$$$**

Les Mimosas [167 C7] (72 rooms) Av Habib Bourguiba; e reception@hotel-lesmimosas.com; ☎ 78 673 028/018; w hotel-lesmimosas.com. Sitting high up on a wooded hill overlooking Tabarka, this green, yellow & white building was originally a manor house, constructed in 1895. The pool area has views of the sea & the surrounding mountains, as do some of the room balconies. Some of the rooms themselves are showing their age & could do with renovation, but this remains a popular spot for tour groups, hunting parties & the occasional wedding. **$$$**

Budget

Hôtel de la Plage [167 C5] (56 rooms) 11 Av 14 Janvier, opposite the beach; ☎ 78 670 039. Most of the rooms are clean but quite small & the combined shower/toilets are cramped. It has bigger rooms with sea views higher up, but they are double the price. Despite this, it represents good value for money & offers a nice sea breeze. **$$–$$$**

Hotel Novelty [167 B6] (26 rooms) 68 Av Habib Bourguiba; ☎ 78 670 176, 78 673 176; f. The cheapest clean bed in town. Rooms are small but have AC, & though there was no hot water when I visited it is usually available. All room windows open out on to a shared courtyard so not much privacy. Watch the low ceilings as you climb the stairs. **$$**

WHERE TO EAT AND DRINK Tabarka has an understandably seafood-heavy selection of restaurants, meaning your main decision is likely to be what sort of view you would like while eating your grilled fish or calamari! All the cafés on the marina walkway seem to offer the same menu of non-alcoholic drinks, shisha and snacks; the **Black and White Salon de Thé** [167 C6] (☎ 78 674 628; f blackandwhitetabarka; ⏲ 08.00–23.00 daily) is probably the most modern.

Expensive

Le Marin [map, page 165] Zone Touristique; ☎ 70 019 000; w lacigaletabarka.com; ⏲ noon–late daily. While Hotel La Cigale (page 168) offers 3 à la carte restaurants, this is the one that really stands out. Perched up on umbrella-covered decking overlooking the Mediterranean, you can enjoy exquisite (if a little pricey) seafood here, including fresh lobster. **$$$$–$$$$$**

Le Rocher Restaurant & Bar [map, page 165] Zone Touristique; ☎ 78 670 000, 78 671 318; w thabraca.magichotelsandresorts.com; ⏲ 19.00–21.30 daily. At Hotel Thabraca (page 169) & with panoramic views of the Mediterranean, an extensive seafood menu here & outdoor bar (sometimes featuring live music), this is a perfect location to watch the sun set. **$$$$–$$$$$**

Above average

Le Mondial [167 C6] Porto Corallo; m 22 764 296; e mehdi.rezaigui@gmail.com; f LeMondial.1997; ⏲ 08.00–midnight daily. Excellent seafood served in the large dining room or tree-covered outdoor seating area. Very popular during football matches. **$$$$**

Touta [167 D5] Porto Corallo; ☎ 78 671 018; m 20 155 733; f Toutaresto; ⏲ 11.00–23.45 daily. Great seafood selection with views of the marina. Fish is charged by weight & can get expensive, but this is probably the best restaurant in this waterfront area. **$$$$**

Mid-range

Barberousse [167 D6] Av 14 Janvier 2011; ☎ 78 674 463; m 26 691 030; ⏲ 11.30–23.30 daily. Great seafood restaurant with a very wide variety of fresh fish on the menu, as well as beers on tap. **$$$**

Restaurant Le Crocodile [map, page 165] On the P7; m 53 297 746; e versoix@outlook.fr; f larmelmaloula.tn; ⏲ variable. Visible from the town as the building with the huge Tunisian flag painted on its tile roof, this restaurant is perched up on a hill en route towards the Algerian border. Mainly offering fish, it has a thatched outdoor seating area which offers breath-taking views of the Mediterranean below. Be sure to contact them & ensure they are open before driving up. **$$$**

Restaurant Le Pirate [167 D6] Porto Corallo; ☎ 78 670 061; ⏲ 11.30–23.00 daily. Seafood restaurant with good fresh fish right by the marina, but not much of a view because of the low seating. $$$

Ristorante Dolce Vita [167 C5] Porto Corallo; 78 671 640; m 52 640 309; noon–23.30 daily. Small Italian restaurant by the waterfront with emphasis on seafood, but also offers platters. No outdoor seating. $$$

Café Chahrazed [167 C5] Porto Corallo; f Chahrazed-487258281485061; 08.00–midnight daily. A beautiful tea house with traditional architectural features – such as a carved stucco ceiling & colourful stained-glass lighting fixtures – in its large main dining room. Has great outdoor seating overlooking the waterfront. Probably the best place for a drink by marina. Also offers meals, with emphasis (unsurprisingly) on seafood. $$–$$$

La Reine [167 C5] Porto Corallo; e messiayoub09@yahoo.com; f; noon–23.45 daily. Mixed Mediterranean fare, including pizzas, meats & whole grilled fish. $$–$$$

Cheap & cheerful

Belle Vue [167 D6] Av 14 Janvier 2011; m 97 872 200; f; noon–midnight daily. Excellent Italian restaurant offering pizza, pasta & seafood options. $$–$$$

L'Esplanade [167 D6] Kornich; noon–22.00 Tue–Sun. A basic seafood restaurant on the main roundabout for the seafront walkway, offering fish & meat dishes. Has a pleasant, grassy outdoor seating area which is good for people watching. $$–$$$

Les Palmiers [167 C6] Av 14 Janvier 2011; 10.00–midnight daily. A low-key BBQ joint with a huge smoker outside, offering great grilled fish & lamb. $$–$$$

Luna Mare [167 C5] Porto Corallo; 78 674 535; e restaurantlunamare@yahoo.fr; f; noon–midnight daily. Tasty thin-crust pizzas overlooking the waterfront. $$–$$$

Café La Marina [167 D6] Porto Corallo; 78 670 640; e ghanmimajed@gmail.com; 07.00–midnight daily. This smart & popular café has a large outdoor seating area overlooking the sea. If it contains sugar, you can bet Café La Marina has it on the menu: extensive range of pastries, ice cream & crêpes. It also does a great b/fast. $$

Rock bottom

Crêp'eat [167 C5] 11 Av 14 Janvier; 17.00–22.00 daily. Crêperie & gelateria with some delicious sweet offerings. $–$$

✱ **Café Andalous** [167 B6] Cnr Av Hédi Chaker & Rue du Peuple; 78 673 536; 08.00–late daily. This is a Tabarka institution, & rightly so. The fascinating Ottoman-themed interior is full of carved wooden features & trinkets dangling from the walls, including some old muskets. Very popular with the local gentlemen, who will while away the hours here playing cards & dominoes. Limited drinks menu & shisha only. $

Café du Port [167 C5] Porto Corallo; 08.00–late daily. A basic café offering drinks & shisha. Has a massive outdoor seating area with the water on 2 sides. Good place to stop on a walk around the marina. $

Le Vieux Port [167 B5] m 54 699 123; e mouss9@yahoo.fr; f; 08.00–late daily. Your view will not get much better than from this café on the waterfront in the quieter old port, overlooking Les Aiguilles de Tabarka & the Genoese fort, serving coffee, pastries, shisha & snacks. $

Salon de thé Baya [167 C6] Rue de l'Algérie; 08.00–late daily. Central café with a slick, modern interior. Does good take-away coffees. $

ENTERTAINMENT AND NIGHTLIFE Considering how many Western tourists frequented Tabarka before the pandemic, it's surprising that there is not much of a bar scene in town. Many of the coffee and shisha bars on the waterfront do not serve alcohol, and you are far more likely to find Tunisian and Algerian families wandering around the marina area at midnight than drunken Europeans, which sets Tabarka apart from many resort towns on the other side of the Mediterranean. If you are looking for drinks with a sea view in the evening, head to one of the resort hotels on the Route Touristique such as **La Cigale** (page 168) or **Hotel Thabraca** (page 169). If you like your music turned up slightly beyond the capacity of the speakers, then head to **Cubano Club** at the Hotel Itropika Beach [map, page 165] (Rte Touristique; f cubano.club; 10.00–03.00 daily), which may have changed its name by the time we go to print, or for live music try **Le Rocher Restaurant & Bar** (see opposite).

TABARKA'S MUSIC FESTIVALS

Tabarka has a solid reputation as one of Tunisia's premier live music locations, mainly thanks to the internationally renowned Tabarka Jazz Festival. However, it also hosts a number of smaller annual events that cater to a diverse range of music tastes.

TABARKA JAZZ FESTIVAL (w tabarkajazzfestival.com f TabarkaJazzFest) Since 1973, this five-day annual event held in July or August has been the highlight of Tabarka's cultural calendar. Originally held in the grounds of La Basilique [167 B5], a Roman cistern repurposed as a church in 1891, it moved to the purpose-built Tabarka Amphitheatre in 2018 before confusingly moving back to La Basilique in 2019. Over the years the festival has played host to a disparate group of jazz legends including Miles Davis, Dizzy Gillespie, Kool & the Gang, Diana Krall and Manu Dibango, and it draws crowds from across the country as well as further afield. Tickets can be purchased online via the official website and are sometimes also available from the tourist office (page 168) or the venue itself.

TABARKA SKY LANTERN FESTIVAL (FESTIVAL HELMA) (f HelmaTabarkaSkyLanternFestival) This three-day open-air cultural festival runs annually in September, and takes place both on the main beach and throughout the port. Featuring live music from Tunisian and international acts, street art and, of course, lanterns, it attracts a young crowd.

PLUG'N'PLAY FEST TABARKA Started in 2014 by the Association Tabarka Art Center (f TABARKAARTCENTER), this week-long summer music festival takes place between June and August and features an eclectic mix of different musical genres, hosted at various hotels and cultural spaces around the town.

Even though the courtyard of **Maison de la Culture** [167 B6] (Av Habib Bourguiba; 78 670 022; e maisondelaculturetabarka@gmail.com; f MaisonDeLaCutlureTabarka; 08.30–12.30 & 13.30–17.30 Mon–Fri) looks abandoned from the outside, if you wander in past the rusting old film projectors you will find a vibrant community arts centre hosting live music events, art exhibitions and film screenings. Look for details on its very active Facebook group.

SHOPPING There is plenty of fresh local produce available in the centre of town, especially around the gardens. You will also find **fresh fish and meat** [167 C6] stalls on Rue Farhat Hachad, where they will grill it right in front of you on hot coals, and a **fruit and vegetable market** [167 C7] over on Rue Ali Chaawani. Those looking to pick up used clothing at bargain prices should head to **Super Fripe** [167 C5] on Rue Mongi Slim (f; 09.00–18.00 daily).

OTHER PRACTICALITIES There is no shortage of **banks** in Tabarka, mainly around the 18 January 1952 roundabout. The five main banks in town (BNA, Banque de Tunisie, STB, UIB and Zitouna) all have ATMs that accept international Visa and MasterCard withdrawals. There is also an ATM at **La Poste Tunisienne** [167 C5] (Av Hédi Chaker; 78 673 419, 78 674 275; 08.00–17.30 Mon–Fri, 09.00–12.15 Sat, til 21.30 in summer).

For medical emergencies, **Tabarka Regional Hospital** (78 672 555, 78 673 653; HopitalRegionalTabarka; 24/7) is around 6.5km east of the centre on the P7 towards the airport. Town pharmacies include **Pharmacie Rabiaa** [167 D7] (Av 14 Janvier 2011; 78 673 900; m 52 374 302; 08.00–20.00 daily), **Guedouar Lobna Ep Romdhani** [167 D7] (Av 14 Janvier 2011; 20.00–08.00 nightly) and **Pharmacie de Bessassi Noureddine** [167 B6] (25 Rue de la Constitution; 78 673 996; m 98 357 146; 08.00–20.00 daily).

SPORTS AND ACTIVITIES

Surfing

Tabarka is the best place in the country to surf, although you will find occasional good swells around Carthage & La Marsa in the capital. Despite this, there are no board-rental shops in town so you will need to come fully prepared (see page 184 for details of where to obtain a board in Tunisia). During winter you will find some swell gets pushed into the harbour around Les Aiguilles de Tabarka, & there are also some beach breaks along the Route Touristique, but Tabarka has so many points west of town that a bit of exploring is bound to yield results.

Diving

Tabarka is also one of the best places in the country for diving. A few of the most popular dive sites along the coast include Cap Tabarka & Grouper Rock, both home to some very large specimens of grouper. Tunnels Reef features a series of caves & passageways stretching up to 30m in length, while other sites include the underwater caves at La Grotte a Pigeons, La Piscine, Le Sec de Cernie & Cap Galena. Even further afield, it is possible to organise dives off the Galite Islands (page 174), 62km northeast of Tabarka, where you will find a colony of Mediterranean monk seals plus a number of shipwrecks, sunk mainly during the world wars. **Tabarka Diving Center** [167 C5] at the marina has a café and is home to a number of dive companies that run day trips on their own boats. There are also 2 dive shops over in the eastern corner of the marina where you can rent or buy gear, near the Société d'Équipements Maritimes du Nord Tabarka [167 C5] (m 98 906 663).

Club Nautique Tabarka Yachting Club 78 671 352; m 98 553 803, 92 017 746; e clubnautiquetabarka60@gmail.com; w clubnautiquetabarka.tn. Operating since 1972 & the best-established club in Tabarka, this offers CMAS diving certification, snorkelling & dives with equipment rental. It also offers discounts for purchases of 6 or 10 dives.

Étoile de Mer m 26 965 321, 98 911 462; e etoiledemer.tabarka@gmail.com; etoile.de.mer.diving.center. Offers trips to 8 principal dive sites around Tabarka, ranging in depth from 2m to 42m. Also offers CMAS diving certification.

Boat trips

For those keen to stay on the surface of the water, 2 companies offer pirate boat excursions from the marina: the ***Albatross*** (m 22 833 901) & the ***Hannibal*** (m 92 400 251; Balha-Quad-et-Bateau-Pirate-Tabarka-125925167592028), both of which charge around 25DT for a 2hr trip including non-alcoholic drinks & an opportunity to swim & snorkel off the coast. Those feeling more ambitious may be able to charter a boat through **Dar El Ain Centre Écotouristique** (page 168) to the Galite Islands.

Golf

Tabarka Championship Golf Course La Cigale; 78 671 031, 70 029 900; w lacigaletabarkagolf.com; winter 08.00–18.00 daily, summer 07.00–19.00 daily. Reopened after extensive renovations in 2017, this par 72, 6,080m, 18-hole golf course was designed by Californian course architect Ronald Fream, & incorporates the hills, beach & surrounding forest. There is also a clubhouse with a driving range, golf shop, restaurant & bar.

Cycling

Raid VTT de Tabarka Started in 2016, this cycling race takes place in Dec and features a mixture of road & off-road sections between Tabarka & Aïn Draham. More details are available from the Fédération Tunisienne de Cyclisme (FTC; 71 235 277; w ftcyclisme.tn). Those wishing to hire bikes in Tabarka should speak to one of the travel agencies in town or visit Dar El-Karma (page 169).

WHAT TO SEE AND DO Perched precariously on a hillside overlooking the town, **Fort Génois de Tabarka** [167 C1] is the town's most impressive sight and main attraction. Constructed in 1542 by the wealthy Genoese Lomellini family, who made their fortune in banking, the fort was built on land granted to them by the King of Sicily, Charles II, as part of a complex debt repayment programme. The Lomellinis then purchased a grant from the Hafsid caliphs of Tunis for a monopoly on coral fishing. This rather profitable arrangement lasted until 1742, when the Genoese upset the bey of Tunis, Abu l-Hasan Ali I (Ali Pasha), by trying to cede the fort to the French without his prior approval. Ali Pasha besieged the fort and added it to the Husseinid territory in Tunisia. The fort was briefly shelled by the French frigate *Surveillante* during the French occupation of Tunisia in 1881, but remains in good condition today.

After a short walk up the hill, you are rewarded with panoramic views of the surrounding town and beaches, as well as getting to admire the impressively preserved fortifications. The interior museum was closed at the time of writing and is only open on select dates throughout the year. However, you can request a permit to enter from the Commissariat Régional du Tourisme Tabarka-Aïn-Draham (ask at the tourist office, page 168).

Another fantastic viewpoint is at **Les Aiguilles de Tabarka** [167 A4], about 500m northwest of the centre. These impressive sea stacks, some of which are 20m high, have been carved out of the coast by the wind and waves, and can now be accessed by a newly refurbished walkway. Around 300m south of Les Aiguilles, on a hilltop at ⊕ 36.957505, 8.751948, is another **fort** [167 A5], built during colonial times on older foundations, which has previously been used as a golf hotel and a diving base. Today, however, it is a military base, so is not possible to visit. Over on the west side of Île de Tabarka you will find the **ruins of a Genoese church** [167 B2] (⊕ 36.963837, 8.756697). Dilapidated and somewhat overgrown, the two-storey surviving structure dates to the 16th century.

The town centre itself retains a certain faded charm and is easily walkable in an hour. Tabarka runs a strong line in nautical-themed roundabouts, including a blue anchor, red coral and a mermaid, all of which serve as useful waypoints for navigating on foot. Near the **public gardens** is the **18 January 1952 roundabout** [167 C6], which features a statue of Habib Bourguiba and commemorates the date the father of the nation was arrested by French authorities and eventually transferred to Tabarka. There are some very photographer-friendly sites around town, such as the colonial-era **staircase** leading towards Les Mimosas Hotel, the imposing green-and-white **Jam'a ar Rahma Mosque** [167 B6], which is still in use, and the **graffiti** of a Tunisian woman playing music on the front of the abandoned colonial building on Avenue Hédi Chaker (⊕ 36.956489, 8.756833). Fans of street art should also go and check out the front courtyard of the **Maison de la Culture** off Avenue Habib Bourguiba (page 172).

AROUND TABARKA

Galite Islands Out in the Mediterranean, about 60km from Tabarka, lies this archipelago of seven small islands, of which La Galite (Jalta in Arabic) is the largest ($10km^2$), clearly visible from Cap Serrat on a clear day. The island was a stopping-off point for Phoenician mariners and was inhabited in Roman times, and today there are abandoned quarries, caves, remains of Roman tombs and Punic relics to explore, not to mention a wealth of bird and marine life that earned the islands' nature reserve status in 2001. Significant bird species include Audouin's gull, the Sardinian warbler and Eleonora's falcon.

During colonial times, the islands were inhabited by a few fishermen and their families, most of whom were Tunisian but of Italian origin (from the island of Ponza to the northwest of Naples). Italian troops occupied the islands during World War II, although there was no fighting here. Interestingly, despite being ostensibly Italian, the local population was quite hostile to the occupying troops and espoused greater loyalty to Free France. Habib Bourguiba was exiled here from 1952 to 1954, free(ish) to move around the islands and mingle with the local inhabitants, often playing pétanque with the fishermen. He was followed at all times by a French gendarme, maintaining a respectful 50m distance behind him.

The islands were abandoned in the 1960s, with many of the inhabitants relocating to France. Generally the islands are off-limits today, in order to protect the rare monk seals living on Galiton; however, a limited, sustainable tourism season is slowly being developed over the summer months, with permits for groups of up to 20 people at a time now being issued. Visitors can expect crystal-clear waters for snorkelling in the coral, cliffs similar to those found along the Bizerte coastline (great for kayaking) and an abundance of beautiful, natural camping spots.

These islands are administratively part of Bizerte Governorate, but most frequently reached from Tabarka. Permits are given only to tour groups – see page 173 for a list of operators. Visits tend to last for three days (with two nights of camping) and are reliant on good weather for the boat crossing.

Hiking and activities around Tabarka The hills around Tabarka make for excellent hiking, either independently or as part of an organised group. Founded by Dalinda Medini, **PureNature TABARKA** (⊕ 36.957618, 8.730161; m 96 375 115, 96 213 591; e purenaturepure.tk@gmail.com; f PurenatureTabarka) is an ecotourism group with a beautiful forest base just west of town (near Restaurant Le Crocodile), from which it offers day hikes and mountain-biking trips into the surrounding forest. It also offers traditional meals as part of its excursion packages. You can also venture into the forest and experience the local apiculture with **Api Pro Tabarka** (m 23 897 313, 22 776 209), a group of local beekeepers who organise tours of their beekeeping facilities. The wooded hills are also very popular for wild boar hunting, attracting hunters from across Europe every season (Oct–Jan). **Round Table Tunisia** (m 20 040 408; w roundtable.tn/hunting) offers hunting trips based out of Les Mimosas Hotel (page 170).

Beaches and viewpoints The coast around Tabarka is blessed with some beautiful beaches, although you will require private transport to reach them. Six kilometres west of town is the quiet village of **Maloula** where, if you turn down an unmarked track (⊕ 36.949636, 8.711406) and follow it for 2km (it turns into a decent, if steep, concrete road after the initial bumpy section), you will arrive at a beautiful, secluded rocky beach. In the summer months this is home to **Restaurant Chez Mouldi** (☎93 903 851), a thatch and tarp hut arrangement offering basic seafood and great views. In the other direction, **Zouara Beach** (⊕ 37.048876, 8.938460) is a 4.5km stretch of perfect sand to the northeast of Tabarka, named after the Oued Zouara that flows out into the Mediterranean here. At the northern end of this beach is a rocky outcrop called El Megaseb (⊕ 37.065554, 8.956419) which is popular for wild camping. Note that as soon as you cross to the east side of the Zouara you are in Béja Governorate.

Jendouba is the wettest governorate in Tunisia, and the authorities here are taking full advantage of the abundance of water by filling the area with dams. One such construction is 13km southwest of Tabarka: **Zarga Dam** (Barrage Ezzarga;

⊕ 36.882486, 8.699062), which has an eerie feel thanks to the abandoned buildings flooded out with turquoise waters. It's worth pausing here if you are heading down the RN17 to Babouch and Aïn Draham.

Ras Rajel War Cemetery (⊕ 36.95336, 8.86642; w cwgc.org; ⌚ 24/7) Ten kilometres from Tabarka on the P7, this Commonwealth war cemetery is home to 441 identified and 60 unidentified casualties from the World War II. It is open 24/7, although if you would like to sign the register and visitors' book it is advisable to visit during office hours, so that the custodian can fetch it for you.

5

The Northeast

Telephone code: +72

Encompassing the governorates of Bizerte, Nabeul and Zaghouan and Africa's northernmost point at Cap Angela, the northeast features a rugged coastline and several isolated beaches accessible only by 4x4. Those wanting to relax by the coast, only a stone's throw from Tunis, can enjoy the tourist-friendly and easily accessible beaches of RafRaf, which also offer some great hiking opportunities in the hills behind. The agriculturally fertile Cap Bon Peninsula features the very well-established tourist hot spots of Hammamet and Nabeul, as well as less-visited but equally stunning beaches at Kélibia, El Haouaria and Korbous. Birders will delight at UNESCO-listed Ichkeul National Park, an important stopping-off point for migratory species such as pink flamingos.

As the first area of Tunisia to be settled in ancient times, the northeast is also home to worthwhile archaeological sites such as the Roman town of Thuburbo Majus and the UNESCO World Heritage Site of Kerkouane, a unique Punic site. The picturesque port town of Bizerte, the northernmost city in Africa, is also a highlight for its seaside charm and old architecture.

BIZERTE

Only 70km from Tunis, Bizerte is a historic port with plenty of attractions: from the old port to the corniche to the striking colonial-era architecture. Happily, it has somehow managed to avoid the overdevelopment seen on some of the east coast, and still retains its small, seaside town charm. As the governorate capital, it is well connected in terms of public transport and serves as a comfortable base from which to explore the region's wild beaches and archaeological and World War II sites.

HISTORY One of the first places in Africa settled by the Phoenicians, Bizerte's history stretches back at least 3,000 years. Having founded Utica in either the 12th or 9th century BC (depending on whether you believe modern archaeologists or ancient historical sources), the Phoenicians soon expanded their control northwards to found the harbour of Hippo Zarytus, which is modern-day Bizerte. With excellent natural harbours and the lush farmland that surrounded them, the Phoenician and later Carthaginian society that developed in this area flourished. However, the natural wealth and strategic positioning of settlements such as Bizerte was not always a blessing, as often they would tempt foreign invaders who brought destruction across the centuries.

The town was destroyed with the fall of Carthage, but later rebuilt by Julius Caesar in the 1st century BC and known as Hippo Diarrhytus. Conquered by the Arabs in AD661, Bizerte expanded during the Hafsid dynasty. The arrival of the Moors from Spain in the 17th century, as in other cities in Tunisia, gave it a new lease of life and guaranteed its fortune. The opening of the Suez Canal in 1869, and

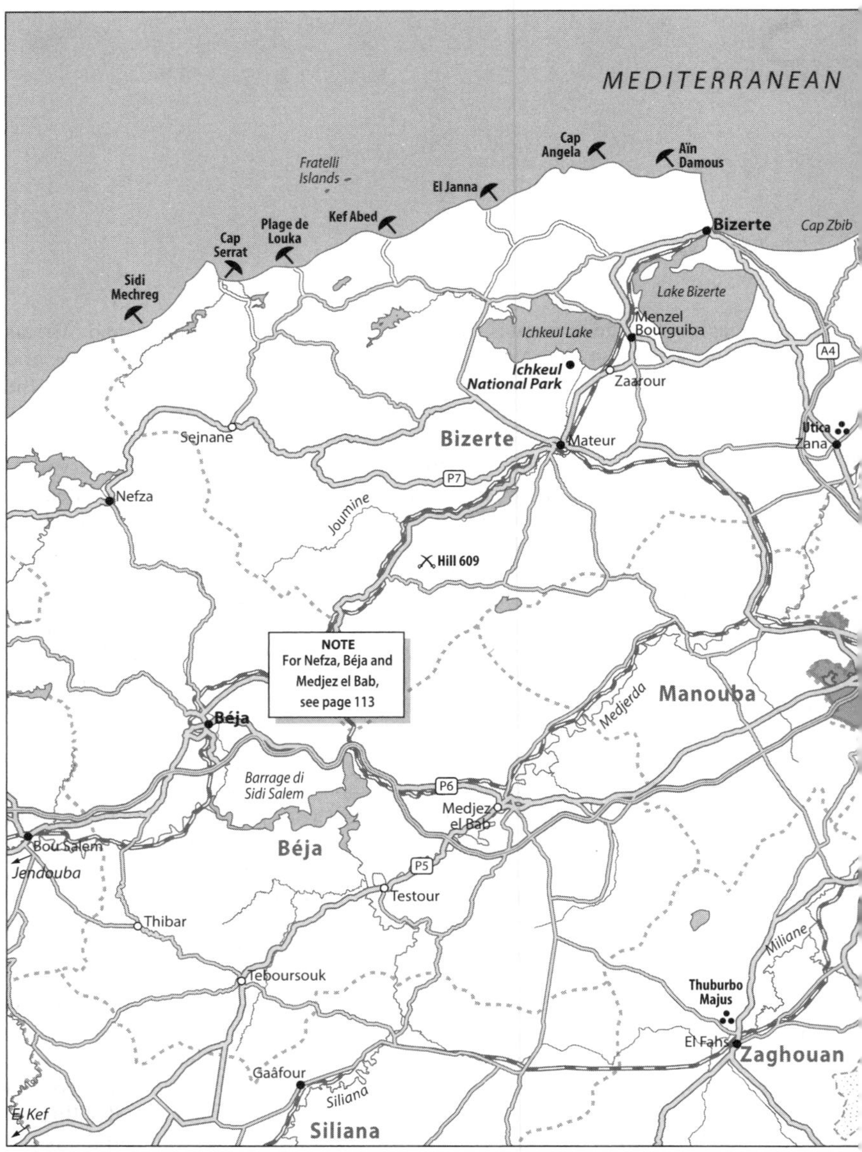

the 1881 arrival of the French, who appreciated its strategically important position and turned the town into a naval arsenal controlling the Straits of Sicily, were significant in Bizerte's development.

In the 1930s, the naval base was the second largest in North Africa, after Mers el Kébir in Algeria, and was thus a major objective of the Axis armies. During World War II, the Germans occupied Bizerte in 1942, before the Allies took it back again the following year. Upon Tunisia's independence in 1956, France somehow managed to keep control of the naval base, despite agreeing in an exchange of letters on 17 June

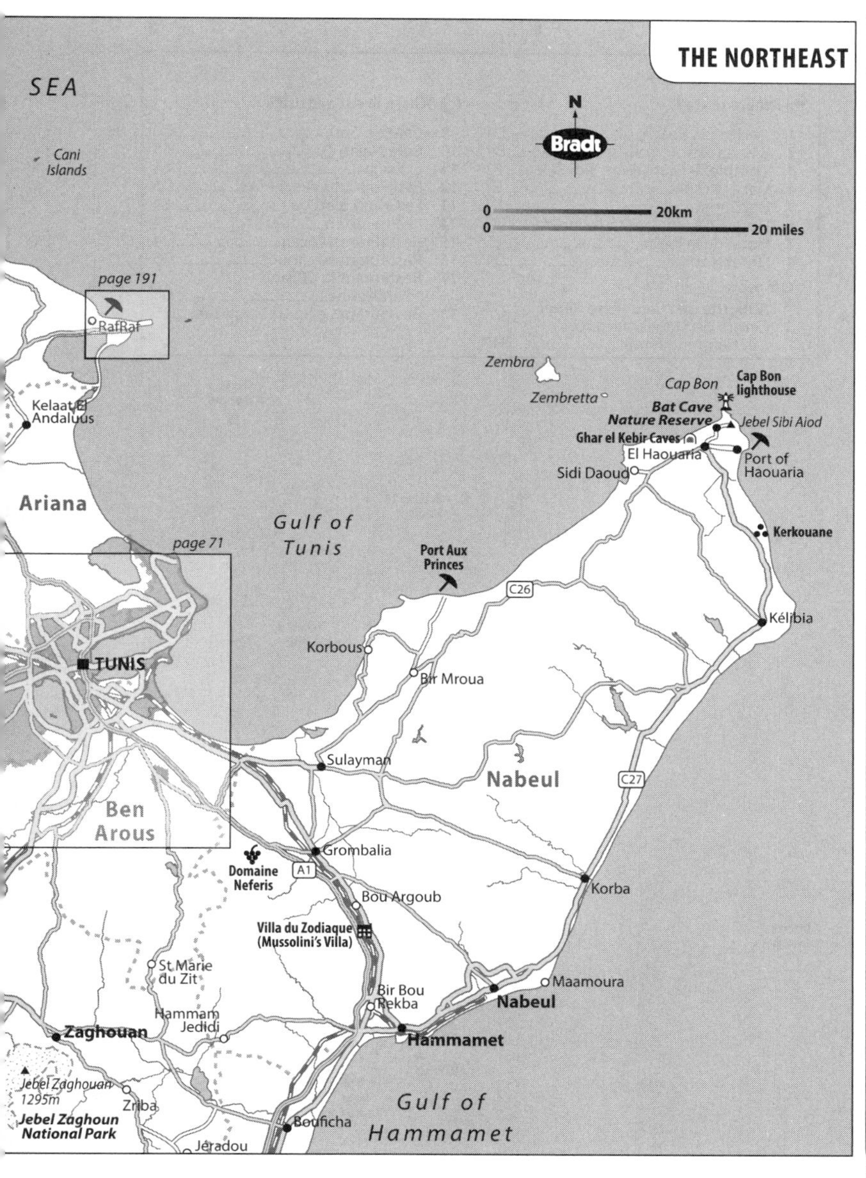

1958 to a complete withdrawal of French troops within four months. Resolution of this issue was somewhat complicated by President Bourguiba's insistence on linking the French presence in Bizerte to an ongoing border dispute between Tunisia and French Algeria in the south of the country (page 369).

In the late 1950s, relations between France and Tunisia deteriorated and President Bourguiba soon began considering a blockade of the naval base to force the French out. Open hostility broke out in July 1961 during the Bizerte Crisis, following the imposition of a Tunisian blockade which resulted in French paratroopers storming

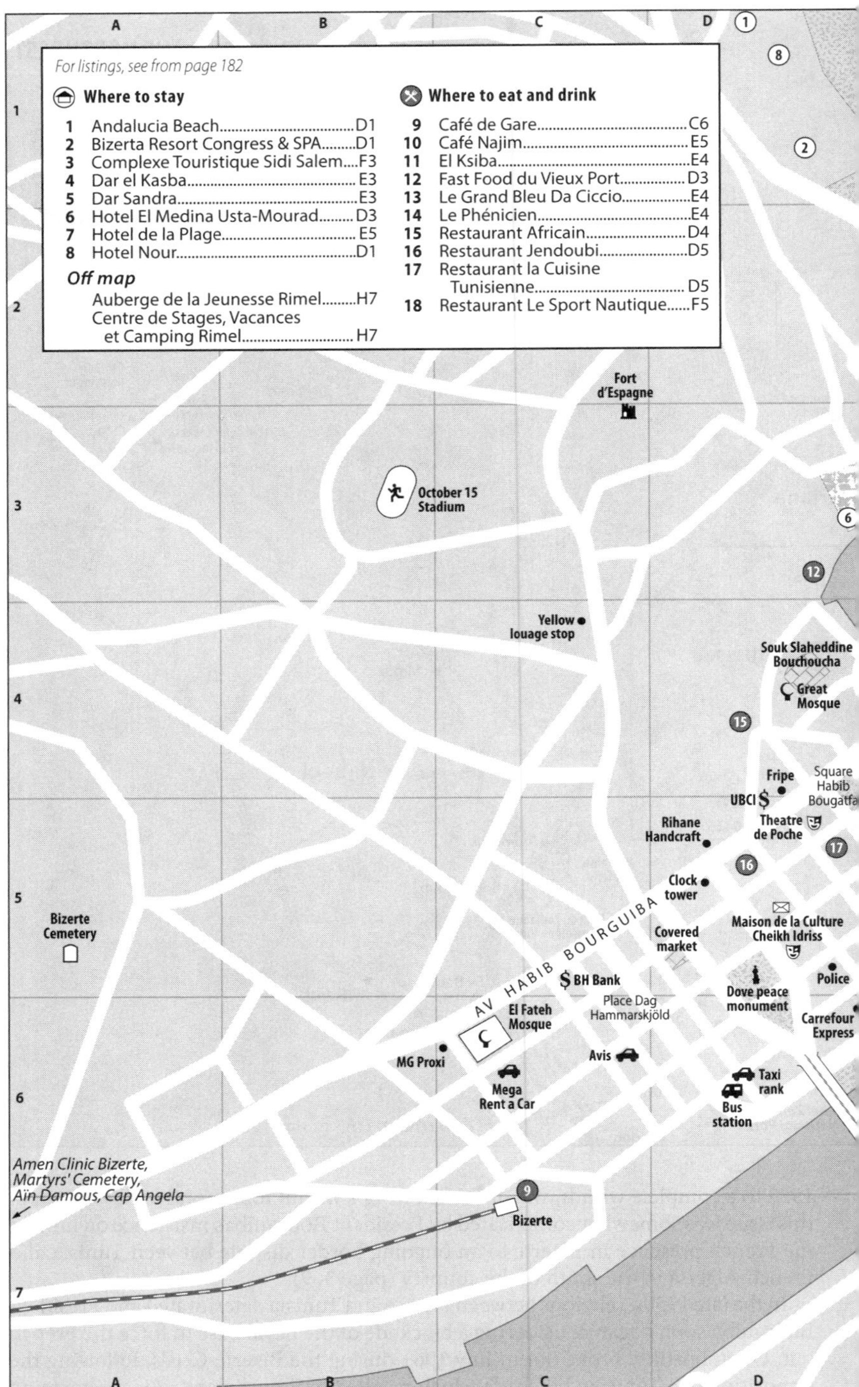
For listings, see from page 182
Where to stay
1 Andalucia Beach D1
2 Bizerta Resort Congress & SPA D1
3 Complexe Touristique Sidi Salem F3
4 Dar el Kasba E3
5 Dar Sandra E3
6 Hotel El Medina Usta-Mourad D3
7 Hotel de la Plage E5
8 Hotel Nour D1
Off map
Auberge de la Jeunesse Rimel H7
Centre de Stages, Vacances et Camping Rimel H7
Where to eat and drink
9 Café de Gare C6
10 Café Najim E5
11 El Ksiba E4
12 Fast Food du Vieux Port D3
13 Le Grand Bleu Da Ciccio E4
14 Le Phénicien E4
15 Restaurant Africain D4
16 Restaurant Jendoubi D5
17 Restaurant la Cuisine Tunisienne D5
18 Restaurant Le Sport Nautique F5
Fort d'Espagne
October 15 Stadium
Yellow louage stop
Souk Slaheddine Bouchoucha
Great Mosque
Fripe
Square Habib Bougatfa
UBCI
Theatre de Poche
Rihane Handcraft
Clock tower
Maison de la Culture Cheikh Idriss
Covered market
AV HABIB BOURGUIBA
BH Bank
Place Dag Hammarskjöld
Dove peace monument
Police
Carrefour Express
El Fateh Mosque
MG Proxi
Avis
Mega Rent a Car
Taxi rank
Bus station
Bizerte Cemetery
Amen Clinic Bizerte, Martyrs' Cemetery, Aïn Damous, Cap Angela
Bizerte

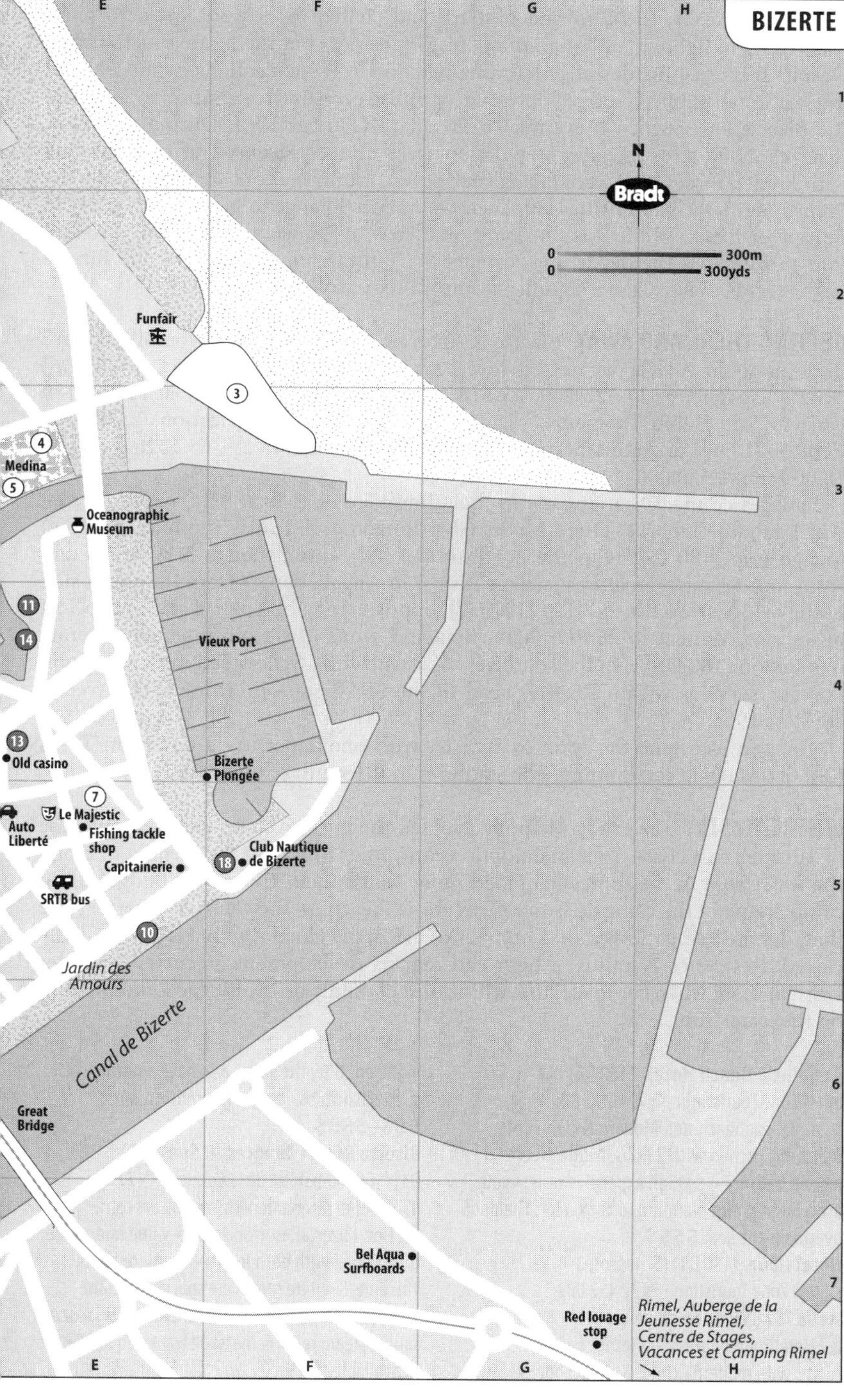
BIZERTE
E
F
G
H
1
2
3
4
5
6
7
N
Bradt
0 300m
0 300yds
Funfair
3
4
Medina
5
Oceanographic Museum
11
14
Vieux Port
13
Old casino
Bizerte Plongée
7
Le Majestic
Auto Liberté
Fishing tackle shop
Club Nautique de Bizerte
18
Capitainerie
SRTB bus
10
Jardin des Amours
Canal de Bizerte
Great Bridge
Bel Aqua Surfboards
Red louage stop
Rimel, Auberge de la Jeunesse Rimel, Centre de Stages, Vacances et Camping Rimel

the city. Officially, 630 Tunisian military and civilian lives were lost across five tragic days of fighting, although many historians now put the figure much higher. Despite this crushing defeat, a damning reaction to French actions by the UN and international public outrage increased populist pressure for France to evacuate the Bizerte base, which it eventually did on 15 October 1964. During the crisis, Bizerte's 2,000-strong Jewish population were unjustly accused of collaborating with French forces, and were facing such severe recriminations that eventually the French and Israeli authorities launched Operation Solange to get them to safety in Europe or Israel. While it is the traditional view in Tunisia that the 1967 Six-Day War precipitated the departure of many of Tunisia's remaining Jews, the Bizerte Crisis seems to have had a significant impact six years beforehand.

GETTING THERE AND AWAY Bizerte is 70km northwest of Tunis (around an hour's drive along the A4). If you need to hire a car in town, try **Mega Rent a Car** [180 C6] (Rue d'Espagne; m 29 575 220, 25 818 129; ⌚ 09.00–16.00 Mon–Sat), **Avis** [180 C6] (33 Rue Habib Thameur; ☎ 71 205 347; w avis.com/en/locations/tn/bizerte; ⌚ 08.30–17.00) or **Auto Liberté** [181 E5] (Rue Garibaldi; m 29 365 532; ⌚ 08.00–18.00 Mon–Fri, 08.00–12.30 Sat).

Louages connect to many towns including Medjez el Bab, Béja, Nefza, El Kef, Aïn Draham, Tabarka, Oued Meliz, Ghardimaou and Tunis. The main (yellow) louage stop [180 C4] is to the northwest of the centre, though services to and from more remote locations such as near Cap Angela depart from the south side of the bridge from the red stop [181 G7], opposite the Total petrol station. SNTRI **buses** also connect to Aïn Draham, Béja and Tunis; the main inter-governorate bus station [180 D6] is in the southwest of town, with a yellow taxi rank next door. For bus services within Bizerte, head to the SRTB station [181 E5] on Avenue 20 Mars 1956.

You can also take the **train** to Bizerte, with one departure a day from Tunis (3hrs), usually in the evening. The station is in the south of town [180 C7].

WHERE TO STAY Bizerte has happily avoided the overdevelopment seen on some of Tunisia's east coast. Your main options are either to stay in the medina or along the waterfront in the somewhat faded Zone Touristique. Those on a budget could camp at one of the campsites on nearby Rimel beach, to the south of Bizerte. Note that, despite being marked on a number of maps, the Hôtel Zitouna is permanently closed. Residence Nautilus, a high-end marina development, is currently under construction; when complete, this will almost certainly be the best accommodation on the waterfront.

Andalucia Beach Hotel [180 D1] (32 apts) Zone Touristique; ☎ 72 421 182; w andaluciabeach.net. Modern & clean apts featuring kitchen with 2 hobs, fridge-freezer & a good balcony – though expensive unless you are a large group planning to cook a lot. The pool overlooks the sea. **$$$$**

Hotel Nour [180 D1] (57 rooms, 3 suites) Zone Touristique; ☎ 72 452 003; m 98 782 653; w hotelnour.com; f HotelNourCongressAndResort. Large rooms with modern fittings & great showers in the en suite; the suites also have amazing jacuzzi bathtubs. It hosts live music nights. **$$$–$$$$**

Bizerta Resort Congress & Spa [180 D1] (100 rooms) Rte de la Corniche; ☎ 72 436 966; e reservation@bizertaresort.com; f HotelBizertaResortSpa. Good-value mid-range resort hotel with both indoor & outdoor pools. The blue-&-white rooms are spacious & come with balcony. The on-site Caraïbes Spa has jacuzzi, sauna, steam room & massage treatments. B&B & AI available. **$$$**

Dar el Kasba [181 E3] (4 rooms) Medina; 72 431 082; m 23 311 219; e darelkasba.bizerte@gmail.com; f DarElKasbaTunisieBizerte. These traditionally decorated rooms open on to a courtyard with a fountain. Excellent b/fast included with eggs, fruits, cheeses & *mlewi* (Tunisian flatbread). Look for the plant pots outside to know you're in the right place! **$$$**

* **Hotel El Medina Usta-Mourad** [180 D3] (17 rooms, 2 apts) Medina; m 54 605 923; e intersoco@gmail.com. Beautiful hotel situated in a renovated 16th-century building, with a roof terrace offering views of the old port. Apts have kitchens for those looking for a longer stay. Great value. **$$$**

Complexe Touristique Sidi Salem [181 F3] (40 rooms) Zone Touristique; 72 420 365; m 23 905 801; e hotel.sidi.salem@gmail.com; f BungalowBizerte. Large, clean rooms with bath & shower, with 2 rooms per bungalow. Pretty basic & might get noise from neighbours sat on their porch if you have someone else in your bungalow. The main attraction is the big pool & direct access to the beach. **$$**

Dar Sandra [181 E3] (3 rooms) Medina; m 99 666 888. This traditionally decorated house has large, comfy beds & views of the port, though it is difficult to find – look for the blue door with blue writing above it. Confusingly, there is another Dar Sandra just outside Bizerte listed on Facebook, so be sure you are contacting the correct one. **$$**

Hotel de la Plage [181 E5] (30 rooms) 34 Rue Mohamed Rejiba; 72 443 560; m 24 052 927. Very basic, but great location 100m back from the beach/marina & the staff are also very friendly. More expensive rooms have AC & en suite with shower, or you can get a discount for using communal toilet. **$$**

Auberge de la Jeunesse Rimel [181 H7] (15 rooms) Plage de Rimel; 37.254516, 9.910464; m 28 368 859, 98 472 863. Underwent extensive refurbishment during the pandemic. Rooms are still basic but have en suites & AC, or you can camp, with access to toilets & showers. Excellent location, 100m from the beach. **$**

Centre de Stages, Vacances et Camping Rimel [181 H7] (100 beds) Plage de Rimel; 37.252069, 9.919659; 72 440 819; e ccrimel7080@gmail.com. Very basic campsite with communal toilets & showers, but well positioned close to Rimel beach. **$**

WHERE TO EAT AND DRINK

Le Phénicien [181 E4] Vieux Port; 72 424 480; e restaurant.phenicien@gmail.com; f Lephenicienpageofficiel; noon–late daily. If you like your seafood overpriced & served in a kitsch replica of a Phoenician galley, then you will love Le Phénicien! Might be fun with children, otherwise best admired from the outside. **$$$–$$$$**

* **El Ksiba** [181 E4] Vieux Port; m 55 630 703; 11.00–23.00 daily. On a sunny day, this is a great spot for alfresco dining with views of the port. Menu of the day features delicious traditional Tunisian cuisine (usually with a fish option). **$$$**

Le Grand Bleu Da Ciccio [181 E4] Rue Ahmed Tlili; 72 423 584; f LeGrandBleuDaCiccio; noon–22.00 Mon–Sat, noon–16.00 Sun. Authentic Sicilian cuisine with a fantastic self-service buffet of appetisers. Also has occasional live music. **$$$**

Restaurant Le Sport Nautique [181 F5] Quai Tarak Ibn Ziad; 72 432 262; f; noon–15.00 & 19.00–23.00 daily. Good fish restaurant in the marina. Attached to a sailing club (Club Nautique de Bizerte) with a swimming pool. Also offers rentals of various boats to enjoy in the Mediterranean. **$$$**

Fast Food du Vieux Port [180 D3] Rue de la Regence, Vieux Port; 09.00–21.00 daily. Popular fast-food outlet offering pizza, sandwiches & kebabs with seats overlooking the water. **$$**

Restaurant Africain [180 D4] Rue 2 Mars & Mongi Slim; 11.00–late daily. Fresh couscous every day; next door to El Hamdani jewellery store. **$$**

Restaurant Jendoubi [180 D5] Rue du 1 May; f; 11.00–21.00 daily. Amazing graffiti artwork outside & delicious fish couscous every day. **$$**

Restaurant la Cuisine Tunisienne [180 D5] Rue d'Espagne; m 22 790 429; 11.00–23.00 daily. Cheap & cheerful Tunisian staples (shawarma, grilled fish, couscous, etc). Usually busy – this place has a good reputation. **$$**

Café de Gare [180 C6] Rue Pasteur & Rue de la Gare; m 95 215 149; 07.00–late daily. A comfy spot to wait for the train (or bus) with a coffee, sat under the red-tiled, plant-decked roof. **$**

Café Najim [181 E5] Jardin des Amours; ⌚ 07.00–late daily. On the grass by the waterfront, this basic café is a great spot to watch the boats coming in & out of the harbour. $

SHOPPING You will find plenty of fresh produce in the **covered market** [180 D5] (Marché Centrale; ⌚ 07.00–19.00 daily) as well as in **Souk Slaheddine Bouchoucha** in the old town [180 C4] (Rue de la Regence; ⌚ 07.00–19.00 daily). There is also a **fripe** [180 D4] (Av Habib Bourguiba; ⌚ 08.00–16.00 daily) for all your used clothing needs. If you are looking for gifts, **Rihane Handcraft** [180 D5] (Av Habib Bourguiba & Rue Mongi Slim; m 24 724 646; e rihanehandcraft@gmail.com; f rihanemajdi; ⌚ 09.00–19.30 Sun–Fri, 09.00–17.00 Sat), established in 1963, sells high-quality custom-made traditional jewellery, clothing and handicrafts.

ACTIVITIES The main sporting attractions here are based around the wonderful coastline. Fishing from the quaysides and beaches is very popular; if you head to the area around Rue Jules Ferry and Rue de Tunis (near the Majestic Cultural Centre) you will find plenty of fishing-tackle shops to kit you out for the day.

✷ **Bel Aqua Surfboards** [181 F7] Rue de Tunis; m 52 248 420; w belaqua.tn; f BelAquaSurfboards; ⌚ by appointment only. Those into surfing can pick up a custom-made Tunisian surfboard here – as far as I am aware, the owner of the brand, Mohamed Bellakhoua, is the only Tunisian surfboard shaper in the country! Great-value, quality products.

Bizerte Plongée ☎ 72 420 411; m 98 441 419; e bizerteplongee@planet.tn. One of the various dive clubs based out of the port; can arrange all sorts of day trips, including to the Cani Islands (page 185).

Club Nautique de Bizerte [181 F5] Attached to Le Sport Nautique Restaurant, page 183; e snbizertin@gmail.com; f sportnautiquebizertin. Offers rentals & lessons on all sorts of watercraft.

OTHER PRACTICALITIES For cash, head to Place Dag Hammarskjöld [180 C6], where there are at least four ATMs. For medical issues, the private **Amen Clinic Bizerte** [180 A7] (Cité Jalaa; ☎ 70 246 800; w bizerte.amensante.com; ⌚ 24/7 for emergencies) is to the west of the centre.

WHAT TO SEE AND DO ⚑ By day, the charming **old harbour** (**Vieux Port**) [181 F4] is a place of calm, its pastel-coloured houses overlooking the fishing boats bobbing up and down. It comes to life in the evening, however, when the restaurants and cafés spring into action. To the north, with its ramparts overlooking the water, is the 17th-century **Kasbah**, which was built to guard the **medina** behind. The medina's labyrinth of little streets is fascinating to explore, offering glimpses into doorways where craftsmen work using centuries-old techniques. The octagonal minaret of the **Great Mosque** [180 D4], built in 1652, serves as a useful navigational aid. Above and behind the Kasbah is **Fort d'Espagne** [180 C3], built between 1570 and 1573 by the pasha of Algiers to plans by Gabriel Serbelloni, and completed under the Spanish. After 400 years of use, it has been sufficiently restored to serve, on occasion, as an open-air auditorium. Across the modern bridge from the medina is the old neighbourhood of **Ksiba**, or 'little kasbah', where you'll find the sleepy little **Oceanographic Museum** [181 E3] (known locally as Aquarium Sidi El Henni; ⌚ 09.30–12.30 & 14.00–18.00 Tue–Sun; 1DT), where a small collection of Mediterranean sea-life is housed in tanks set into the 17th-century walls.

To the south of the medina but still on the north bank of the Bizerte channel, the new city is pleasant with its squares and cafés. Located in the former colonial-era church, the **Maison de la Culture Cheikh Idriss** [180 D5] (Rue de Turquie; ☎ 72 434 390; e gmb.live1978@gmail.com; f) stands out as an architectural feature, with the most incredible stained-glass windows – check its Facebook page for details of upcoming exhibitions and performances in this unique space. Another cultural centre further east is **Le Majestic** [181 E5] (Rue de Tunis; m 98 782 630/1; e cult.majestic@gmail.com; ⏲ 11.00–22.00 Tue–Sun), a colonial-era cinema that still shows films alongside hosting other cultural events. Fans of Art Deco should also make time to visit the nearby **Theatre de Poche** [180 D5], dating to 1923, with its incredible exterior, and the equally impressive **old casino** [181 E4] on Rue Ahmed Tlili, although neither building appeared to be open at the time of writing. Perhaps the most striking feature of the Bizerte skyline is the **Great Bridge** [181 E6] – Bizerte's answer to Sydney Harbour. Climbing 15m above the channel, it came into service in 1980. Until 1904 there was a swing bridge, subsequently replaced by two ferries. The present bridge has a middle section that opens up to allow large boats into the port.

At the western end of town is the **Bizerte Cemetery** [180 A5], which contains 26 identified Commonwealth war graves from World War I, mainly from the Indian Labour Corps and the Royal Navy, as well as several French and Serbian war graves. Over 41,000 members of the Serbian armed forces were treated in Tunisian and Algerian hospitals during the war, with over 3,000 ultimately losing their life in North Africa. Even further out of town is the **Martyrs' Cemetery** [180 A7] (⊕ 37.275508, 9.854598), a memorial to the hundreds (potentially thousands) of Tunisians who lost their lives in fighting with French colonial troops during the Bizerte Crisis in July 1961 (page 179).

AROUND BIZERTE

Beaches There are some great beaches on either side of town, but the most popular is at **Rimel**, about 4.5km over the bridge to the south. The white, sandy beach is backed by pine forest, and there are a couple of large, wrecked vessels rusting away, partially submerged in the water just off the coast. Two are Greek transport ships: MV *Ydra* and MV *Tarpon Sentinel*, both wrecked in 1983. A third ship, the Togolese-flagged MV *Hamada S*, ran aground in 2019. If you are driving to Rimel, head towards the car park at ⊕ 37.254182, 9.920249.

If you have your own transport, you could also check out the sandy and forested **Aïn Damous** (⊕ 37.326872, 9.795075) to the north of Bizerte, which is great for camping and also has caves nearby, or Africa's northernmost point at the rocky **Cap Angela** (⊕ 37.346909, 9.742312), known as Ras Ben Sakka locally, which is marked by a monumental metal map of the continent.

Cemeteries There is a large set of **Serbian WWI war graves** in Menzel Bourguiba (⊕ 37.168888, 9.781549). This cemetery contains the graves of more than 1,790 Serb soldiers. There is also an ossuary with the remains of an unknown number of French and Serb soldiers. Over the road is a Jewish Cemetery.

Cani Islands Around 10km northeast of Cap Zbib are these two islands: Grande Île Cani (⊕ 37.355143, 10.122823) and Petite Île Cani (⊕ 37.353360, 10.119754). The area is an unspoilt marine environment which is ideal for diving, where you can see the likes of octopus, the massive dusky grouper and the brightly coloured swallowtail sea perch. It is possible to charter boats from Bizerte Harbour; head to the Capitainerie (⊕ 37.272391, 9.879517; ☎ 72 425 786; f marinabizertetunisia) and ask for further details, or contact Bizerte Plongée (see opposite).

Ichkeul National Park Lying west of Lake Bizerte and the town of Menzel Bourguiba, Lake Ichkeul is a unique biotope created by the shifting seasonal balance of salt and fresh water in a large and shallow inland lake. It is the last of a chain of great freshwater lakes which stretched across the length of North Africa hundreds of years ago. The lake is unique in that while it has fresh water in winter, its waters turn saline in summer. High evaporation levels mean that the water level falls to 1.5m or less during the summer months, leading to inflow from saline Lake Bizerte via the 5km-long Oued Tindja, and salinity rises to 20g per litre. In winter, with the seasonal rains, the balance shifts, with the rivers supplying fresh water; the depth rises to 3m and salinity falls to 5g per litre.

Today the lake and its surrounding marshes make up the 12,600ha UNESCO-listed Ichkeul National Park, described by UNESCO as 'the most important single wetland in North Africa'. It is arguably the most interesting of Tunisia's national parks for birdwatchers as it is a vital stopover point for various species of migratory birds who spend the winter here (the best time to visit is between November and February). Thanks to the warm winter, large seasonal beds of water plants can grow, thus providing food for huge flocks of migrant birds.

The greylag goose is the emblem of the park and remains the most famous migrant visitor, feeding on club rush. However, numbers have dropped significantly over the past 30 years, owing to increased pressures on the park's water supply caused by dam building, demand for drinking water and irrigation. Other water birds seen here include purple gallinule, coot, the retiring marbled teal and maybe even white-headed duck. Of the waders, the easiest to spot are black-and-white avocets and white storks. Wild boar, porcupine, otter and jackal also roam the park, along with Asian water buffalo (see opposite).

However, there are concerns that poor hydrological management (mainly excessive damming of freshwater sources feeding into the lake) is having a negative impact on this delicate ecosystem, reducing the numbers of wintering waterfowl. For example, in the 1990s the government constructed a large dam on the Oued Sejnane, west of Ichkeul, which sharply reduced freshwater inflow. The effect of this can be seen round the lake: the once extensive reedbeds have receded, and there is far less cane than there used to be. Given the changes in the ecosystem, the question remains as to whether it will continue to merit its UNESCO classification. The authorities are keen to maintain the water balance in the lake by artificial methods; however, the International Union for Conservation of Nature's latest (2020) Conservation Outlook Assessment for the site still categorises it as 'of significant concern' owing to water-management issues in the park.

In the mid 1990s, Ichkeul Lake was considered sufficiently similar to Japan to be used as the setting for a film version of *Madame Butterfly*. A mock-up Japanese village was constructed on the edge of the lake, with Oriental accessories and extras flown in from Paris's China Town.

Practicalities The entrance to the park is off the P11 by the far southeast corner of the lake (⊕ 37.113587, 9.727036). It is quite difficult to reach on public transport, although you might be able to get dropped off by a louage plying the route between Zaarour (the nearest town) and Mateur on the P11, or Zaarour and Menzel Bourguiba. There is a small **eco-museum** on the lakeshore (⊕ 37.138321, 9.692636), which highlights the park's flora and fauna as well as the conservation efforts under way. Otherwise, there is little infrastructure in the park, so bring everything you need (including a guide if you want one).

ICHKEUL'S WATER BUFFALO

One of the most surprising sights at Ichkeul are the small herds of Asian water buffalo grazing on the plain below Jebel Ichkeul. The origins of these animals are obscure. According to one story, they descend from a pair given to the bey of Tunis by the king of Sicily in 1729. Another version runs that they were imported by Ahmed Bey (1837–55), a modernising monarch, who felt they would be the ideal solution to towing his field artillery around. When the buffalo proved unequal to the task, they were released at Ichkeul. When the French took over in 1881, there were over 1,000 of these animals at Ichkeul, who presumably found the seasonal marshes like the rice-paddies of their homeland. The buffalo were the personal property of the bey, who would grant the occasional buffalo-hunting licence. In World War II, American troops stationed in the area nearly wiped out the herd in search of fresh meat, but it has since recovered.

Where to stay and eat

Dar Ichkeul (7 rooms) ⊕ 37.032836, 9.708577; m 27 595 239; e support@darichkeul.com; f dar.ichkeul. Just outside the large market town of Mateur & very convenient for the national park, this country home has elegant, modern rooms & a stunning garden with a large pool. Horseriding is also offered & they serve excellent food using local ingredients. **$$$$**

Utica Traditionally recognised as the first colony to have been founded by the migrating Phoenicians as they expanded their settlements westwards into North Africa, Utica straddles the border between Bizerte and Ariana governorates, 2.5km northeast of Zana on the C69 road. Today this is all agricultural land, and it is strange to imagine that 3,000 years ago this would be the site from which Carthaginian civilisation would arise. There are few options in the area in terms of accommodation or dining, so you are best off treating this as a day trip from Bizerte or even Tunis.

History Like many ancient cities in Tunisia, Utica was first a Phoenician and then Punic city founded at some stage between the 8th and 12th centuries BC, and later developed by the Romans. As a reward for not supporting Carthage in the Third Punic War (149–146BC), Utica was made the first capital of the new Roman province of Africa Proconsularis. The settlement prospered as a garrison for Roman troops and the residence of many rich and powerful Roman citizens. As such, it was very rich in public monuments. Utica was originally a port, exporting agricultural produce from its rich hinterland. Today, the Oued Medjerda has silted up the bay on which Utica stood, leaving it around 15km from the shore. Before the Punic Wars, however, Utica's superb strategic location was second only to that of Carthage. Utica's collapse, like that of other Roman cities, came with the invasions by the Vandals and the Byzantines. The final fall came after the Arab conquest in the 7th century.

Getting there and away This is a difficult site to reach on public transport, as buses and louages between Bizerte and Tunis tend to bypass it completely on the A4 or P8. From Tunis, you are best off heading to Kelaat El Andaluus, then taking a taxi 5km east to the site. From Bizerte, you could get dropped at the Péage Utique toll booth (⊕ 37.074708, 9.999947) and then try to hitch a lift 6km east to the site, but note that this is quite a rural spot.

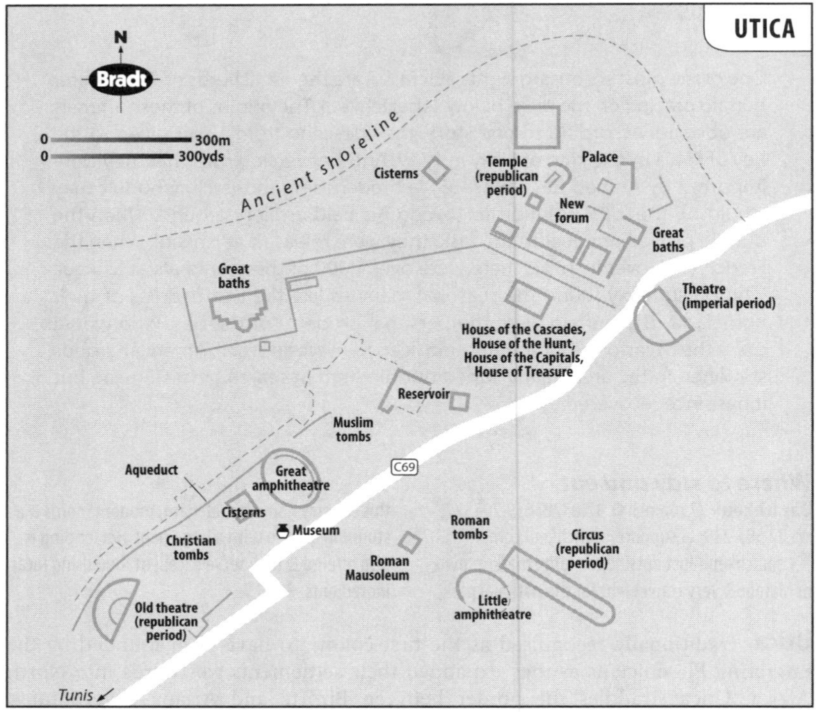

The site The Roman site is not extensive and has been only partially excavated. There is evidence of the replacement of smaller buildings by something much larger and grander (owing to a more important role as capital, perhaps) and in some cases of duplication (two theatres). In 2011, a joint team from Paris-Sorbonne University and the National Heritage Institute of Tunisia carried out an excavation to find out more about the Phoenician and Punic periods of occupation of this site.

Visitors should begin at the **museum** (⊕ 37.051971, 10.058499; ⏲ winter 08.30–17.30 Tue–Sun, summer 08.00–19.00 Tue–Sun; 8/5DT non-resident/residents), where displays include an assortment of Punic items, including gold brooches and earrings from the 4th to 3rd centuries BC, oil lamps from the 7th to 1st centuries BC, vases from Greece and Italy that indicate trade links, and small sarcophagi for the bones and ashes of children who, according to (mainly subsequent Roman) legend, were sacrificed here. Roman finds include statues, a building inscription from the 1st to 2nd centuries AD, a mosaic of a hunting scene and an interesting diagram of the excavations of the House of Cascades.

Heading north from the museum to the top of the site, you reach a residential area containing houses, built in the classical style and often named after the mosaics discovered there. The most impressive is the **House of the Cascades**: a large dwelling centred round a patio, on to which opened the imposing triclinium as well as smaller chambers, many with basins and fountains. The adjacent **House of the Hunt** had a large garden surrounded by a patio and numerous rooms, one of which contained the famous mosaic now in the Bardo (page 108). The **House of the Capitals** had capitals representing human figures, while the **House of the Treasure** produced a hoard of coins. Look out for the use of yellow Chemtou marble in the house construction, as well as the white-and-green marble from Greece.

At the foot of the hill to the west are the **great baths**, covering over 26,000m². The cisterns and conduits to service this were fed from an aqueduct and water tower, which came in at the highest point where the remains of the water tower, sometimes referred to as the citadel, can be found. Further south, around the **amphitheatre** (which was likely originally built during the Roman Republican period of the 1st century BC) are some **Muslim**, **Roman** and **Christian tombs**, all within a few hundred metres of each other – evidence of the multiple occupancy of the site.

BIZERTE'S NORTHERN COASTLINE

West of Bizerte, the coastline is wild and remote all the way to Tabarka and this is a very rewarding part of the country to explore if you have your own 4x4 and are keen on hiking and camping. This is an area of Tunisia that I know very well, having kayaked the 250km stretch from Tunis to Tabarka (page 106). Some of the beaches are extremely isolated with zero tourist infrastructure, so you will need to be self-sufficient, but others have both restaurant and accommodation options.

EL JANNA (⊕ 37.297508, 9.592250) The road down to this beach is rocky, but the sweeping views from the hills as you descend to sea level are worth the wear and tear on your tyres. This seems to be a popular spot for well-to-do Tunisians to build their holiday homes, and just to the west of the main beach you will find **Dar el Janna** ✱ (10 bungalows; ⊕ 37.293064, 9.589018; m 95 557 728, 58 864 278; e accueileljena@gmail.com; f DarElJanna). Each of the stone bungalows has two bedrooms, a large open-plan living area with full kitchen, bathrooms with shower and its own barbecue set-up outside. The furthest north bungalow is right on the water, with steps down into the surf. There is also a large pool and a stable, which can offer horseriding tours of the area, as well as mountain biking, hiking and snorkelling.

KEF ABED (⊕ 37.265199, 9.466316) This beach may be beautiful, but it has no facilities so you will need to be self-sufficient. Also note that there is a village behind it, so do not expect much privacy while camping! Just to the west (at ⊕ 37.261062, 9.457676), however, there was a three-storey structure under construction at the time of writing, which locals indicated may end up as a hotel.

PLAGE DE LOUKA (⊕ 37.231381, 9.330700) This sandy fishing beach is home to **Résidence Louka** on the west side if you wish to spend the night (5 rooms; ⊕ 37.230914, 9.328845; m 98 442 510. **$$**). Rooms are quite basic but have air conditioning and a restaurant that is right on the water. It can also organise watersports gear rental. Some 3.5km further east up the coast you will find **Camping Shiri** (⊕ 37.244406, 9.367624; m 92 155 018) offering cheap pitches set about 200m back from the sea.

CAP SERRAT (⊕ 37.216068, 9.237612) The beach to the east side of this peninsula is particularly sandy and as such Cap Serrat is quite well set up for tourism, offering at least two decent accommodation options and a restaurant. Despite being 7km from Kef Abed, the Fratelli Islands (⊕ 37.304465, 9.408582 and ⊕ 37.299853, 9.393129) can be visited by boat from Cap Serrat. Although you can't land on these rocky islands, the surrounding waters are good for snorkelling and you might spot both Eleonora's falcon and Cory's shearwater, as the islands are home to two colonies.

Where to stay and eat

Le Pirate (8 rooms, 1 suite) ⊕ 37.218621, 9.222339; m 22 600 733; e jamel.cap@hotmail.fr; f aubergelepirate. Clean & modern with AC, brand-new bathrooms & sea views from the beds. Offers boat trips out to empty beaches, remote BBQ lunches & visits to the Fratelli Islands just offshore. **$$$$**

Résidence Ennejma (10 rooms) ⊕ 37.218892, 9.222474; m 23 335 916, 28 650 480; f. Cheaper than Le Pirate but still of a good standard & with AC, though note the bathrooms are only wet rooms. Also has a nice grassy area overlooking the beach. **$$$**

Galet Café-Restaurant ⊕ 37.218738, 9.222488; ⊕ 09.00–late daily. Offers shakshuka, crêpes, pastas, grilled meats & fish. Great views of the sea. **$$$**

SIDI MECHREG (⊕ 37.163478, 9.123363) It is possible to drive all the way from Cap Serrat to Sidi Mechreg along the rocky coastline, but this is for experienced 4x4 enthusiasts only, ideally in convoy, as the track is a sandy disaster in sections. Some tall Roman ruins – possibly the remains of an aqueduct or baths complex – stretch right down to the waterline on the beach to the southwest of town. Just to the east of the main beach is **Eco-Rand Sidi Mechreg** ✷ (⊕ 37.174297, 9.138374; m 27 874 811; e imed.ecorand@gmail.com; f EcoRandSidiMechreg; **$$**), an ecotourism site offering camping, snorkelling, hiking, local gastronomic experiences and all sorts of other outdoor activity. On Sidi Mechreg beach itself, **Restaurant La Cabane** (⊕ 37.163963, 9.124682; m 98 784 651; ⊕ 10.00–20.00 daily; **$$$**) serves some great seafood.

SEJNANE Heading to Tabarka along the P7, you pass through this former railway town where a series of abandoned mining carts, rusting on their rails perilously high off the ground, are today filled with stork's nests. A truly tranquil scene, but the town was not always this peaceful. During the North African campaigns of World War II, the Allied drive eastwards to Mateur and Bizerte passed by Sejnane, then just a wayside hamlet. Here the so-called Bald Hill and Green Hill were of key strategic importance. In the winter of 1942–43, in bitter cold and rain, the Argylls and the Germans fought it out, shelling each other until the hillsides were pocked with craters of red mud. Later the British parachutists were brought in, where they were used as ordinary infantry. According to Australian war correspondent Alan Moorhead's account, they were feared by the Axis troops as 'the most terrible animals'. As he put it in *The End in Africa*, the last part of his published chronicles of the African campaigns, the parachutists 'had become so well acquainted with death they had no fear of it any longer…It was not that pity or grief had gone out of them, but that they were living in a well of danger.'

HILL 609

Trevor Sheehan (w africanstalingrad.com)

Named after a military map reference, Hill 609 (⊕ 36.901999, 9.494052), 27km southeast of Sejnane, entered the history books as the US Army's first major victory against the Germans in World War II. From 27 April to 1 May 1943, it was the site of a major battle between the US 34th Infantry Division and the Afrika Korps to secure the route into Bizerte. The closest village to the summit is Tahint, from where it is a 300m walk up some tracks to the top. The adjoining hills were fought over a number of times during the war, but it was the Americans who finally captured the dominating peaks, major roads and the city of Bizerte.

The modern town, which grew significantly around the railway line in colonial times, is better known today as a centre for traditional female artisanal potters, and their skills were inscribed in 2018 on UNESCO's Representative List of the Intangible Cultural Heritage of Humanity. The women manage every step of the pottery-making process, producing terracotta cooking utensils, dolls and animal figurines inspired by the environment, which are then sold by the roadside (and make excellent souvenirs). Some examples of the work can be seen at @sejnane_pottery.

RAFRAF PENINSULA

Visible from the capital across the Bay of Tunis, about 32km north of La Marsa's beach, the RafRaf Peninsula is a very popular spot for day trips or weekends away from the capital during the summer, owing to the long sandy public beach, great hiking, plentiful accommodation options and a series of private-beach day resorts. The little town of RafRaf is divided into two parts: RafRaf Ville, the town proper at the top of the hill, and RafRaf Plage, the beachside suburb where many wealthy Tunisois have second homes. A steep tarmac road dips down between the two.

GETTING THERE AND AWAY You can drive to RafRaf from Tunis in around 75 minutes. Be sure to check online mapping to see whether it is quicker to take the A4 or the more scenic coastal route through the towns of Raoued and Kelaat El Andaluus. It is also possible to take a louage from Tunis's Gare Routière Nord. For

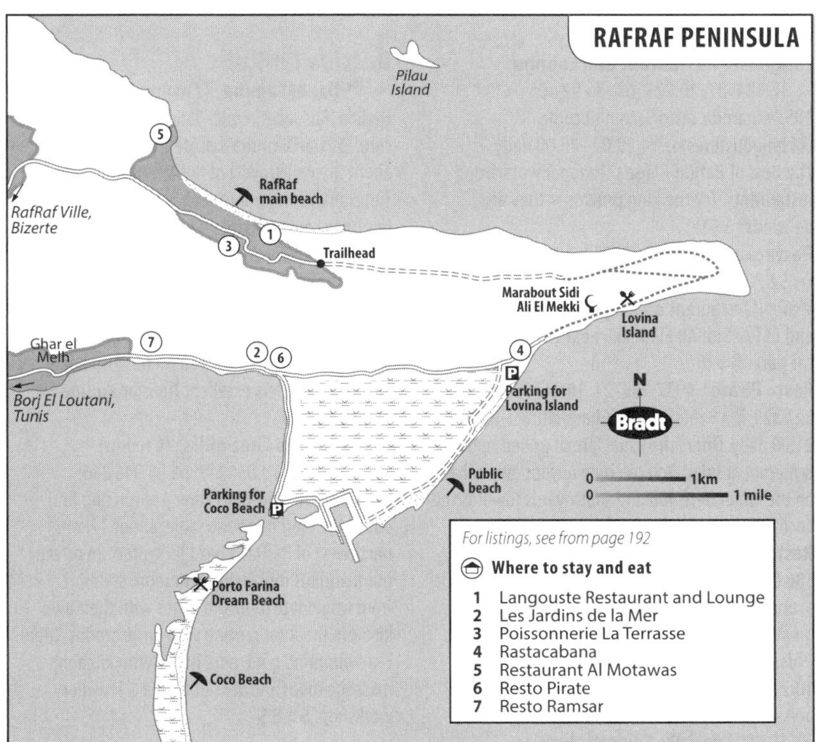

a day on the beach, you can park your vehicle in the RafRaf main beach car park, which costs 2DT. Note that to enter and exit this car park you must drive all the way through the town's narrow streets, which get snarled up with traffic at busy times. You are then only a stone's throw from the seasonal waterfront restaurants that set up shop here for the warmer months.

If you are heading to one of the private beach resorts on the peninsula (which can be reached only by boat), then your hosts will likely direct you to the car parks to the south of RafRaf Peninsula. Each beach has its own dedicated parking spot, so check with your hosts before setting out. You will then be collected from the nearest relevant public beach and taken to your respective resort for the day (usually only a 10–20-minute boat ride). Some of the private beaches are also reachable by foot along a sandy track that runs parallel to the coast, but arriving by boat is much easier.

WHERE TO STAY AND EAT

In RafRaf *Map, page 191*

✵ **Les Jardins de la Mer** (7 bungalows, 1 villa) 37.170549, 10.215332; m 22 251 279; e belazzi_rm@yahoo.fr; w ljdlmgharelmelh.com; f lesjardinsdelamergharelmelh. Modern private bungalows have en suite & AC plus decking overlooking Ghar el Melh lake & the Mediterranean beyond. There is also a restaurant, pool & a trail out the back of the property that you can follow all the way over to RafRaf Ville. **$$$$**

Langouste Restaurant and Lounge 37.184187, 10.223163; m 92 505 105; e hamda.resto.3@gmail.com; f langousteresto; 10.00–20.00 daily. The best of RafRaf Plage's seasonal waterfront restaurants. Try the king prawns – they are delicious! **$$$**

Rastacabana 37.170514, 10.253444; m 52 707 032; 11.00–21.00 daily. A good seafood restaurant on the public beach at the end of Rte Sidi Ali El Mekki, next to the public car park. **$$$**

Resto Pirate 37.169321, 10.217684; m 99 821 325; f PirateParadiseGharMelh; 11.30–21.00 daily. Offers the usual fare of grilled seafood & *méchouia* salad. You can dine in your own cabana on the water here, looking southwards towards the Coco Beach peninsula. **$$$**

Resto Ramsar 37.170667, 10.203692; m 22 586 643; noon–21.00 daily. Seafood restaurant overlooking Coco Beach with wooden decking & great views of the water. **$$$**

Poissonnerie La Terrasse 37.182584, 10.218284; m 95 412 592; f restaurant.poissonnerie.la.terrasse.rafraf.lahmeri; 10.00–late daily. Situated above a fishmonger in RafRaf Ville, this offers simple but delicious grilled catch of the day. The fishmonger is also ideal for loading up your cool box with fresh fish before driving back to Tunis. **$$–$$$**

Restaurant Al Motawas 37.192937, 10.209097; m 97 613 644; 09.00–21.00 daily. Good wood-fired pizza on the far western side of RafRaf Plage. **$$**

Outside RafRaf

✵ **Dar el Lamma** (7 rooms, 2 villas) Rte Ain Hadida, Ras Jebel; m 55 355 000; w darellamma.com; f DarEllamma. Located in Ras Jebel, about 8km northwest of RafRaf, this traditional Tunisian country home with expansive grounds has been converted into a boutique hotel. Each room is uniquely decorated (& priced), with names like 'Chambre Andalouse' & 'Chambre Africaine' illustrating the different geographic themes. You can even take a virtual tour of each room on the website to decide which you prefer. Also has a large pool & offers excellent Tunisian cuisine for dinner. **$$$$**

✵ **Du Côté de Chez Blili's** (9 rooms) 37.219755, 10.050249; m 95 946 846; w sejours-tunisie-blilis.com. A surprising find out in the Metline countryside, about 14km northwest of RafRaf. Chez Blili's offers an eclectic but luxurious mix of different room styles, from troglodyte rooms to suites with their own kitchen. Great for renting with large groups, there is a swimming pool, pool house with kitchen, massage room, outdoor BBQ area & jewellery workshop. **$$$$**

WHAT TO SEE AND DO The most popular hiking route in RafRaf is the 7.5km U-shaped trail around the peninsula, which loops from the end of RafRaf town into the town of Ghar el Melh on the southern side of the peninsula. From here you can either hitch a lift back into RafRaf or head back over the peninsula via a goat track to retrace your steps. You can leave your vehicle at the trail head (⊕ 37.180389, 10.226761), then head eastwards up a sandy track through the forest. Looking northwards as you head up the track, you can see **Pilau Island** (⊕ 37.201286, 10.239757) 2km offshore, which briefly turns golden every sunset as it catches the light. Once you reach the end of the peninsula, you descend to the southern side towards the former pirate stronghold of **Ghar el Melh**, but not before passing the **Marabout Sidi Ali El Mekki** (⊕ 37.176129, 10.261237), a tomb built into the caves for a local holy man, which has been used for religious ceremonies such as circumcisions since at least the 17th century. The end of the hike takes you past two decent waterfront restaurants (page 192) before passing through Ghar el Melh with its well-preserved Ottoman fort, **Borj El Loutani**, and the fortifications around the old port. This complex was built in 1659 and served as a stronghold for Barbary pirates.

If all that sounds too strenuous, head for one of the peninsula's private beach resorts, which are built into sandy coves and will provide lunch from a set menu (usually seafood), bottled water and a choice of non-alcoholic drink (though you can bring your own alcohol). You get your own private cabana and can then spend the day swimming and exploring the rocky peninsula. Bathroom facilities tend to be limited. The best of the bunch on the eastern peninsula is **Lovina Island** (m 58 040 000; e lovinaisland@gmail.com; f Lovina.island; $$$$), while on the slightly more crowded southern spit (Coco Beach), go for **Porto Farina Dream Beach** (m 20 551 733; e waloo1974@gmail.com; f capfarina; $$$$).

CAP BON PENINSULA

Nabeul Governorate encompasses the entirety of the Cap Bon Peninsula, marking the beginning of Tunisia's eastern coastal tourism developments that stretch as far south as Sfax. Easily reached from Tunis-Carthage or Enfidha-Hammamet international airports, Cap Bon is a safe bet if you are looking for a coastal holiday while avoiding the all-inclusive resorts. Highlights include taking a dip in the hot springs of Korbous, lounging on the idyllic white-sand beaches of Korba and Kélibia, shopping for beautiful ceramics in Nabeul and enjoying the culinary options in El Haouaria.

NABEUL One of the first places to attract tourist development on Cap Bon, Nabeul has long featured in the holiday brochures thanks to its long clean beach, large hotels, attractive medina and swathes of new estates of second homes. The town also makes some of the best harissa paste in Tunisia. However, despite being the governorate capital, it is not the tourism hub of the region (that title clearly goes to nearby Hammamet), making it an appealing choice for those wishing to avoid the crowds.

History The name Nabeul is a corruption of the ancient 'Neapolis' ('new town'). Writing in *History of the Peloponnesian War* in the early 4th century BC, Athenian historian Thucydides described the town as Carthaginian. The original town was occupied by Roman troops during the Third Punic War in 148BC; under Julius Caesar it became Colonia Julia Neapolis, with the Romans building over the earlier Punic

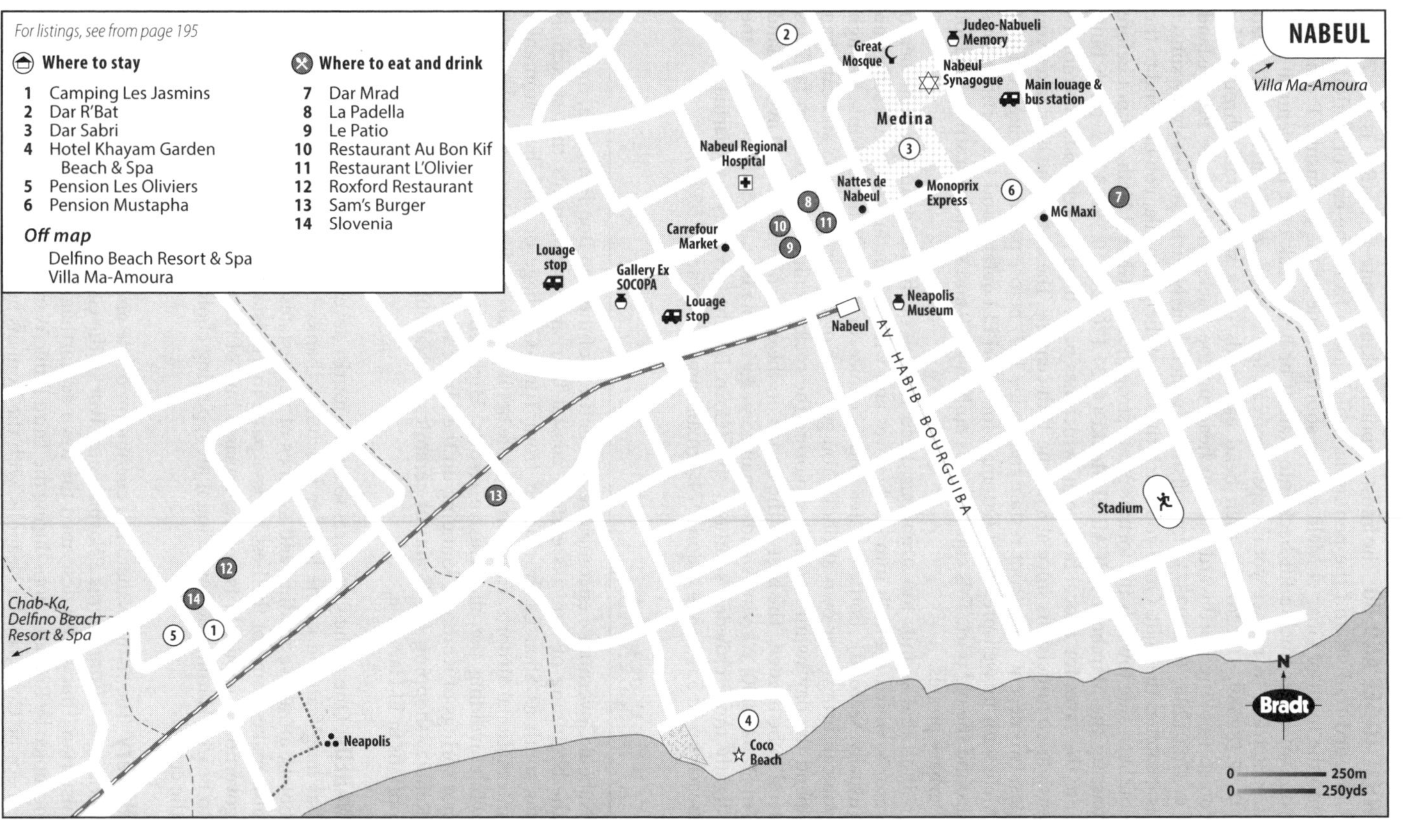
NABEUL
For listings, see from page 195
Where to stay
1 Camping Les Jasmins
2 Dar R'Bat
3 Dar Sabri
4 Hotel Khayam Garden Beach & Spa
5 Pension Les Oliviers
6 Pension Mustapha
Off map
Delfino Beach Resort & Spa
Villa Ma-Amoura
Where to eat and drink
7 Dar Mrad
8 La Padella
9 Le Patio
10 Restaurant Au Bon Kif
11 Restaurant L'Olivier
12 Roxford Restaurant
13 Sam's Burger
14 Slovenia
Great Mosque
Judeo-Nabueli Memory
Nabeul Synagogue
Main louage & bus station
Medina
Nabeul Regional Hospital
Nattes de Nabeul
Monoprix Express
MG Maxi
Carrefour Market
Louage stop
Gallery Ex SOCOPA
Louage stop
Nabeul
Neapolis Museum
AV HABIB BOURGUIBA
Stadium
Villa Ma-Amoura
Chab-Ka, Delfino Beach Resort & Spa
Neapolis
Coco Beach
N
Bradt
0 250m
0 250yds

The Kerkennah Islands are known for their traditional *charfia* fishing methods, which use palm fronds PAGE 264

above (DD/A)

Guellala on Djerba island is renowned for its pottery PAGE 325

right (At/S)

Tozeur is one of the best places in the country to sample dates PAGE 345

below right (PE/S)

Sfax's medina has a good selection of souks, including Souk El Haddadine, which is dedicated to metal and woodwork PAGE 262

below (CC/S)

above (LA/S) The amphitheatre at El Djem is the third-largest ever built by the Romans PAGE 253

below left (AB/A) The remarkably preserved mosaic of Venus at the House of Amphitrite, Bulla Regia PAGE 154

below right (JK/S) Tunisia's most famous statesman, Habib Bourguiba, lies in rest in his hometown of Monastir PAGE 244

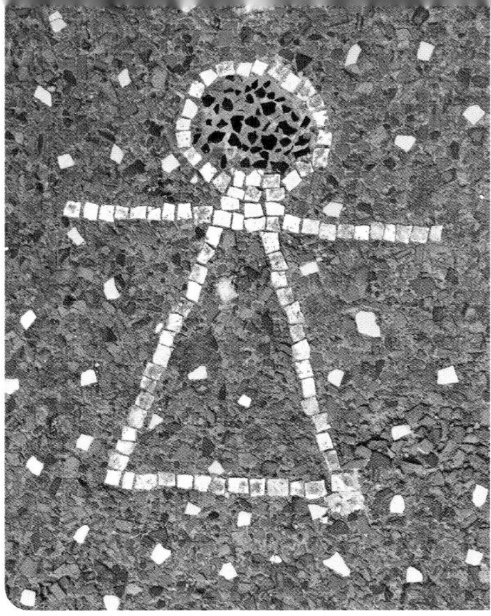

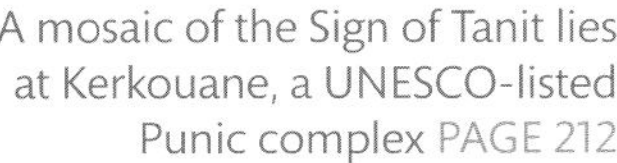

A mosaic of the Sign of Tanit lies at Kerkouane, a UNESCO-listed Punic complex PAGE 212 — above (W/S)

Despite being one of Tunisia's most impressive Roman sites, the ruins of Sbeïtla remain little visited PAGE 284 — above right (j/S)

Built by the French in 1936–40, the Mareth Line was intended to protect Tunisia against an Italian invasion PAGE 303 — right (OS)

Southern Tunisia is home to many ruined *ksour* (fortified granaries), such as here at Ksar Ouled Debbab PAGE 332 — below (GB/S)

above (AW/S) Sousse's ribat (fort) is one of the oldest in North Africa PAGE 230

below left (SS) The imposing Fort Génois de Tabarka is perched precariously on a hillside overlooking the town PAGE 174

below right (LL/S) Meaning 'the rock' in Arabic and sitting at 780m, El Kef is the highest governorate capital in Tunisia PAGE 139

bottom right (SS) Since 2014, the whitewashed walls of Er Riadh have been taken over by the Djerbahood project, created by artists from across the world PAGE 324

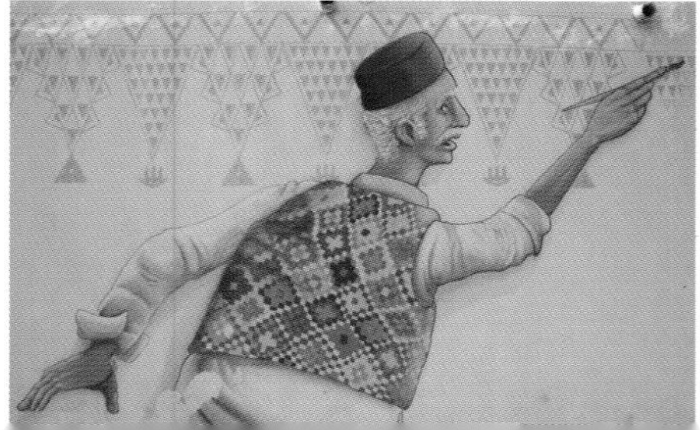

Located high above the arid plain, Chenini is the most famous of Tunisia's hilltop Amazigh villages PAGE 333

above (LA/S)

Djerba's Synagogue of El Ghriba is Tunisia's most significant Jewish site PAGE 323

right (JK/S)

Home to the venerated Great Mosque, Kairouan is the spiritual and religious capital of Tunisia PAGE 279

below (F/S)

above (JK/S) The deep south is where you'll find Tunisia's section of the Sahara, home to a number of isolated campsites PAGE 367

below left (SS) Tourist-friendly Hammamet offers some of the finest beaches on the Cap Bon Peninsula PAGE 198

below right (SS) A trip through dramatic Seldja Gorge on the historic Lézard Rouge is a highlight of any visit to the south PAGE 344

bottom right (s/S) Tozeur's 17km^2 Palmeraie is one of the country's most spectacular oases PAGE 349

Almost 600m high, Jugurtha's Table was the scene of Numidian King Jugurtha's last stand against Roman occupation PAGE 148

above (DG/S)

The easily accessible coast around Tunis offers many opportunities for watersports PAGE 189

top right (BH)

The ancient Midès gorge and oasis, by the Algerian border, was a filming location for *The English Patient* PAGE 352

right (SS)

Chott el Djerid is the most spectacular of Tunisia's salt lakes PAGE 345

below (IM/S)

above left (rc/S) Eleanora's falcon is just one of the significant bird species spotted on the Galite Islands PAGE 174

above right (SS) Bou-Hedma National Park is home to the endangered addax antelope PAGE 291

left (NPL/A) Known for its oversized ears, the fennec fox is native to the deserts of North Africa PAGE 6

below (Ag/S) Perhaps surprisingly for Tunisia, Lake Ichkeul is home to a herd of Asian water buffalo PAGE 187 site. Under Augustus it grew in importance, and by AD258 it had obtained the status of a full-blown colonia (the highest-ranking Roman city). The Roman site of Neapolis (page 198) has been excavated not far from the beach, and in 2017 archaeologists also discovered major Roman ruins stretching for 20ha just off the coast, likely submerged following a tsunami caused by a massive earthquake in Crete in AD365. This discovery included around 100 tanks used to produce garum (a fermented fish-based condiment that was a favourite of ancient Romans), confirming that Neapolis was a key production centre for this stinky Roman delicacy.

Getting there and away Nabeul is less than 70km southeast of Tunis (around an hour's drive along the A1 toll road). As the governorate capital it is well connected in terms of public transport, with **louages** to Zaghouan, Sousse, Kairouan, Monastir, Kélibia, El Haouaria and, of course, Tunis. The main inter-governorate louage and bus station is just south of Avenue Habib Thameur; louages to and from other areas of Cap Bon depart further east, off Rue al Arbi Zarrouk.

For **bus** services within Nabeul, head to the Société Régionale de Transport de Gouvernorat de Nabeul (SRTGN) station just north of Avenue Habib Thameur (⊕ 36.451635, 10.726214). SRTGN also runs buses to Tunis (the 102 and the 140), which take between 60 and 90 minutes and depart every half-hour from 06.00 until 18.30 daily.

There are around five daily SNCFT **trains** between Tunis and Nabeul (90mins, although you will usually have to change at Borj Cedria). The station is on Avenue Jedeida Maghrebia. The town is relatively walkable, but there is a taxi rank near the SRTGN bus station.

Where to stay *Map, page 194*

In town

Dar R'Bat (4 rooms) 20 Rue Ibn Chara; m 28 310 610; w darrbat.com. Beautifully restored Tunisian home, with rooms around a central courtyard. Great rooftop lounge area with white awnings & small pool. Also offers delicious home-cooked meals for 50DT pp, bookable 24hrs in advance. **$$$$**

✷ **Dar Sabri** (4 rooms) Av 7 Impasse Farhat Hached; m 23 949 327; w dar-sabri.com/en. An elegant, modern, bright white dar in the heart of the medina, with a small rooftop infinity pool surrounded by walls topped with Barbary fig trees. **$$$$**

Hotel Khayam Garden Beach & Spa (360 rooms) Mohammed V St; w khayamgarden.com. Beach resort with a solid reputation for good customer service. Lots of sports on offer (tennis, minigolf, football, volleyball) & a number of pools (including 1 with flumes) to keep the kids entertained. **$$$–$$$$**

Pension Les Oliviers (6 rooms) ⊕ 36.443442, 10.714111; ☎ 72 286 865; m 98 274 817, 20 273 173; e pensionlesoliviers@yahoo.fr. One of the oldest-established family-run hotels in Nabeul. Guests come back year after year because of the convenient location near a beach, friendly hosts & beautiful garden. Reservations essential for summer. **$$**

Camping Les Jasmins ⊕ 36.443123, 10.714723; m 98 366 041; e hotel.jasmins@gnet.tn; f 348841758550582. Large campsite in an orange grove 300m from the beach. Clean shower blocks, 3 restaurants, a pool & individual power sockets for parked vehicles make this a solid choice for overlanders & backpackers alike. **$–$$**

Pension Mustapha (5 rooms) ⊕ 36.453399, 10.740937; ☎ 72 286 729. Clean, basic hotel close to the souk with basic rooms featuring sink, shared toilet & bath. Street-facing rooms are noisy. **$**

Around Nabeul

Villa Ma-Amoura (5 rooms) ⊕ 36.486366, 10.801347; m 23 186 806; e villamaamoura@gmail.com; f villamaamoura. Guesthouse & creative residency set within 7ha of olive & almond groves. Offering some of the best vegetarian cuisine in the country, with vegan meals also available on request. Rooms are tastefully decorated with artwork & brick-vaulted ceilings, some with direct terrace access. Overall, a very well-designed space. Prior booking essential. Can be rented by the room or as an entire property. **$$$$**

Delfino Beach Resort and Spa (321 rooms) ⊕ 36.427055, 10.682847; ☎ 72 285 400; w ttshotels.com.tn/delfinobeach. Halfway between Nabeul & Hammamet, this highly rated AI resort features a private beach, 2 outdoor pools, gym, tennis courts & a minigolf course. **$$$**

Where to eat and drink *Map, page 194*

Slovenia ⊕ 36.443772, 10.714340; ☎ 72 285 343; ⏱ noon–15.00 & 18.00–late daily. Owned by celebrated Tunisian chef Rafik Tlatli, this restaurant puts interesting Spanish & Asian twists on some traditional Tunisian seafood recipes. The menu is eclectic & you can dine in the olive grove outside (attached to Camping Les Jasmins). Also has a good wine list. **$$$–$$$$**

Dar Mrad Rue Khmais Hajri; m 20 859 220; e moez.mrad@gmail.com; f NABEUL1973; ⏱ noon–16.30 Mon–Sat, 09.00–17.00 Sun. Great Tunisian lunch spot that also does delivery. Menu of the day is on a chalkboard, which you can check on the Facebook page. Try the delicious *kamounia* (liver & beef stew) & the excellent tuna brik. **$$$**

Le Patio Rue de Marbella; ☎ 72 233 433; e farhathatem@hotmail.fr; f; ⏱ 10.00–23.00 daily. Bright, modern Tunisian restaurant with an emphasis on seafood & national classics. **$$$**

Restaurant Au Bon Kif Rue de Marbella; ☎ 72 222 783; m 98 309 089; e hbzayed@gmail.com; f Bonkif.nabeul; ⏱ noon–15.00 & 19.00–22.00 daily. Step through the towering blue doors to find seafood, couscous au mérou (with grouper) or well-cooked paella. **$$$**

Restaurant L'Olivier Hédi Chaker; m 99 382 700; e farhathatem@hotmail.fr; f Restaurant.lolivier.Nabeul; ⏱ noon–late daily. Very popular Franco-Tunisian restaurant with a great variety of seafood dishes. **$$$**

La Padella Rue de Marbella; m 98 762 300; e la.padella20@gmail.com; f; ⏱ 10.00–22.00 daily. Tasty fast-food joint serving pizzas, burgers, tacos, makloub & baguette farci. **$$–$$$**

Roxford Restaurant Av Hédi Nouira; ☎ 72 288 222; f RoxfordNabeul; ⏱ 10.00–23.00 daily. Mediterranean restaurant & fast-food place with pizzas, sandwiches & fresh pasta. **$$–$$$**

Sam's Burger Av Jedeida Maghrebia; m 27 094 449, 22 999 133; f samsburger.nabeul; ⏱ 10.00–23.00 Tue–Sun. Good-quality fast-food joint serving mainly burgers, but also pizza & filled baguettes. **$–$$**

Entertainment and nightlife Nabeul is much quieter than neighbouring Hammamet when it comes to nightlife. If you don't fancy trekking west in a taxi, many of the larger beach resorts have bars serving alcohol that are open to non-residents. For daytime drinking, get yourself over to **Coco Beach** (at Hotel Khayam Garden; m 29 285 596/7; e cocobeach@khayamgarden.com; f CocoBeachKhayamGarden; ⏱ summer 09.00–19.00 daily), which allows non-guests as day visitors. Part of the Hotel Khayam Garden Beach and Spa, this reservation-only beach bar has loungers, parasols and waiter service. A great place to lounge all day while sipping cocktails and eating tapas.

Shopping Nabeul is noted for its pottery, as well as its mats woven from rushes and esparto grass (page 197). Also found in town is *zhar*, a fragrant essence distilled using jasmine, wild orange flowers and roses, and prized by the local people for its soothing qualities.

If you are looking for gifts, head to the **medina**, with its large and imposing refurbished gate at the end of Avenue Habib Thameur. Wandering along the main Rue Farhat Hached, you'll likely be offered all sorts of Tunisian artisanal goodies (of varying quality). This is a great place to pick up some of the pottery for which Nabeul is renowned (page 197) and the local harissa is also known for its quality.

NABEUL'S CRAFT INDUSTRIES

Its largest industry after tourism, **pottery** is Nabeul's speciality. The art of polychrome ceramics was introduced in the 15th century by the Andalusians, but it is Nabeul's more recent history of pot-making that is interesting – though there is little written on the subject.

Under the French protectorate, a special department encouraged the revival of different crafts. The Chemla brothers, Victor and Mouche, were ceramists from a local family who owned a pottery factory at the turn of the 20th century. They developed the art of tile-making, and their fine tile panels, generally signed, can be seen even today on various façades in Tunis (such as at the base of the mosque at Bab Jazira). Spanish models were copied too, possibly thanks to immigrants fleeing the political turmoil in Spain in the late 1930s. With the ready availability of high-quality clay, the pottery industry at Nabeul has never looked back. The quantities of pottery were such that the French writer Jean Genet, when visiting Tunisia back in the 1970s, worried that the country would be quarried away to nothing for its clay!

All along Avenue Farhat Hached in the medina you will see stalls of pottery: blue-and-white standard Mediterranean tourist ware, alongside slightly more upmarket stuff with simple floral or fish motifs. Production covers a whole range of ornaments, from the simplest earthen water jar to white and gilded pot pineapples. Sadly, little actual pot-making can be observed today, as the potteries are now industrial concerns located on the outskirts of town (and much of the clay is in fact now imported).

A craft that has taken off in a big way since the mid 1980s is **stone-carving** at the neighbouring town of Dar Chaâbane el Fehri, a few kilometres to the northeast of the city, but now effectively part of the greater Nabeul area. The Tunisian construction industry boomed in the 1990s, and new homeowners were in need of signs of distinction for their façades. What could be easier than sandstone columns and facing, cut to measure at Dar Chaâbane? These stone features, once limited to the immediate area, can now be seen on hotels and villas across Tunisia.

More threatened by technology is the craft of **rush-mat** (plant-based floor covers) making. Until the 1970s, no self-respecting mosque would be without its rush mat or *hassira* (plural *hsur*). The vast size of the mats, plus the need to renew them regularly, meant that generations of Nabeulians were kept busy at their horizontal floor looms. After independence, a number of trendy tourist products, including small floor mats, trays, baskets, lampshades and seating, were created. Traditionally styled cafés started using rush mats too, to put round the walls behind stone benches. In the 1990s, however, the industry was dealt a severe blow in the form of large, cheap plastic floor mats imported from China via Libya, and now only a few workshops remain. One good-quality vendor is Nattes de Nabeul (84 Av Hédi Chaker; f Nabeul. Nattes; ◷ 09.00–20.00 daily).

A little way out of town there is also a great concept store, **Chab-Ka** (⊕ 36.439079, 10.703175; **m** 29 567 719; **e** chabkaleconceptstore@gmail.com; f ChabakaLeConceptStore; ◷ 10.00–19.00 Mon–Sat, 11.00–17.00 Sun), full of Tunisian handicrafts from local artisans.

Other practicalities The main **Nabeul Regional Hospital** is at the junction of Avenue Habib Thameur and Rue de la République (☎ 50 724 345; ⏲ 24/7).

What to see and do As with many places in Tunisia, the best place to start exploring the town is the medina. One of its most striking buildings is the **Great Mosque** (⏲ closed to non-Muslims), with its ornately carved main entrance and the fine green *qubba* (dome). Nearby is the **Judeo-Nabeuli Memory**, a space dedicated to the memory of Nabeul's Jewish community, displaying photographs and artefacts. The exhibition is housed inside the historic Bibliothèque Gaston Karila, built by the prominent Jewish Karila family in 1919 to commemorate family member Gaston Karila, who died at the age of 25 in 1918 from the Spanish flu. Prior to the outbreak of World War II, Nabeul was a centre of Jewish culture in Tunisia, with some sources claiming that one in four residents were Jewish. Today, however, the community is limited to a handful of residents, represented by Albert Chiche, head of the Jewish Committee of Nabeul. Chiche oversaw the restoration of the Bibliothèque Gaston Karila in 2022. About 200m to the northwest of the library on the other side of the mosque is the **Nabeul Synagogue**, though like many of Tunisia's remaining synagogues it is securely locked up most of the time and only partially operational. There is also a good art gallery nearby, **Gallery Ex SOCOPA** (93 Av Habib Thameur; ☎ 72 223 578; f artisanatdenabeul) which showcases local talent. Listings and opening times are published via the Facebook page.

Neapolis (Rue Hassan Hosni Abdelwahab Jasmin; ⏲ 08.00–18.00 Tue–Sat, 08.00–17.00 Sun) Originally founded by the Phoenicians, under Roman rule Neapolis developed into a trading town with many wealthy *navicularii* (shipowners). Much of the site is in need of renovation and only some ruins have information signs, but it is still worth a visit to see some of the mosaics *in situ*, as well as the **House of Nymphs**, from which seven beautiful mosaics were removed to be exhibited in the Neapolis Museum. It is also said to be the place where Artemonis, a superb horse doted on by his Roman master, was buried.

Neapolis Museum (44 Av Habib Bourguiba; m 24 178 773; ⏲ 09.00–17.00 Tue–Sun; 8/5DT non-resident/resident) Located in a park near the railway station and the much-photographed roundabout adorned with a giant ceramic jar, this small museum is built around a traditional square courtyard and displays the best of the local remains from nearby Neapolis, as well as from Kerkouane and Kélibia. Artefacts include an extensive display of pottery and oil lamps through to the 3rd century AD, and some rather touching terracotta statuettes from the Punic necropolis and shrine of Thinissut, near Bir Bou Regba (Hammamet). One represents the goddess-mother breastfeeding her baby, while another is of a sinister lion-headed goddess; the figurines were probably made as grave-furniture. There are also some fine mosaics from the archaeological site, the best of which is a life-size mosaic showing the vanquished Chryses kneeling before a seated Agamemnon, with Ulysses and Achilles standing behind them; another shows Mars standing behind a reclining Neptune.

HAMMAMET Tourism in Tunisia would not be where it is today without Hammamet. Known as Pupput to the Romans, the settlement was a stopping point on the Roman road linking Carthage to Hadrumetum (now part of Sousse). The city developed as a result of the expansion of agriculture and maritime trade as well as the generous sponsorship of a wealthy local patron, the 2nd-century AD jurist Salvius Julianus, who was very influential in Emperor Hadrian's government. Subsequent 'visitors' included the Sicilians, the Spaniards and the Ottomans.

In the first half of the 20th century, Hammamet was a tiny medina, with the Mediterranean lapping its honey-coloured walls. The pleasant local climate was popularised by European aesthetes in the early 1900s. Swiss-born German artist Paul Klee visited in 1914, painting a famous watercolour of the town with a minaret (imaginatively named *Hammamet with Its Mosque*), and soon Hammamet welcomed a flood of Western artists, such as Irish poet and playwright Oscar Wilde, French artist Jean Cocteau and Italian actress Sophia Loren. Many wealthy Europeans indulged themselves with homes of cool vaulted rooms and gardens of cypresses, orange trees and plunge pools. The first tourist hotels were built in this spirit, their silhouettes carefully concealed behind the treeline.

Sadly, the 1990s saw construction on an unprecedented scale and Hammamet is now a sprawling tourist town, welcoming visitors in their thousands. Today, development spans a full 20km along the coast from Plage de Hammamet to the Yasmine Hammamet Marina, which straddles the governorate line between Nabeul and Sousse. Despite this overdevelopment, Hammamet offers visitors some excellent luxury hotel options, fine dining and one of the coolest beach bars in the country, as well as some interesting historical sites dating to colonial times and World War II. Visit during the summer and you can also catch live music during the month-long International Festival of Hammamet.

Getting there and away Most visitors access this subregion via Carthage International Airport, but Enfidha-Hammamet International Airport, 40km south of Hammamet, is also sometimes useful – though its services are mainly seasonal or charter, linking to cities across Europe and the UK.

Hammamet is less than 70km southeast of Tunis (around an hour's drive along the A1 toll road) and is well connected in terms of public transport. **Louages** run to Nabeul, Zaghouan, Sousse, Kairouan, Monastir, Kélibia, El Haouaria and Tunis. The main louage station is at Baraket Sahel along with a number of yellow taxi ranks; another is located just north of the medina on Avenue Mongi Slim. SRTGN **buses** (the 105, 145 and 246) run from Hammamet to Tunis, taking between 60 and 90 minutes and departing every half-hour from 06.30 until 18.30 daily. The station is on Avenue de la Republique, near the tourist information office.

There are around five daily SNCFT **trains** between Tunis and Hammamet every day (1hr 25mins, although you will usually have to change at Borj Cedria). The station is on Avenue Habib Bourguiba.

Tourist information

Inspiring Tunisia Av de la République; 72 286 737; e crt.nabeul@ontt.tourism.tn; winter 08.00–13.00 & 14.00–17.00 Mon–Fri, summer 07.30–14.00 Mon–Thu, 07.30–13.00 Fri

Where to stay *Map, page 200*

Hammamet's higher-end hotels tend to be located further north along the coast, while the package-holiday resorts cluster along the beaches of Hammamet Sud, extending into Yasmine Hammamet. Note that Hammamet's medina is not to be confused with the Disneyland-style faux medina of Yasmine Hammamet, located 10km further south down the coast.

✱ **Les Orangers Beach Resort & Bungalows** (391 rooms) Rue Nevers; 72 280 144; w orangershotel.com. A 4-star AI resort set in 12ha of beachfront orange groves,

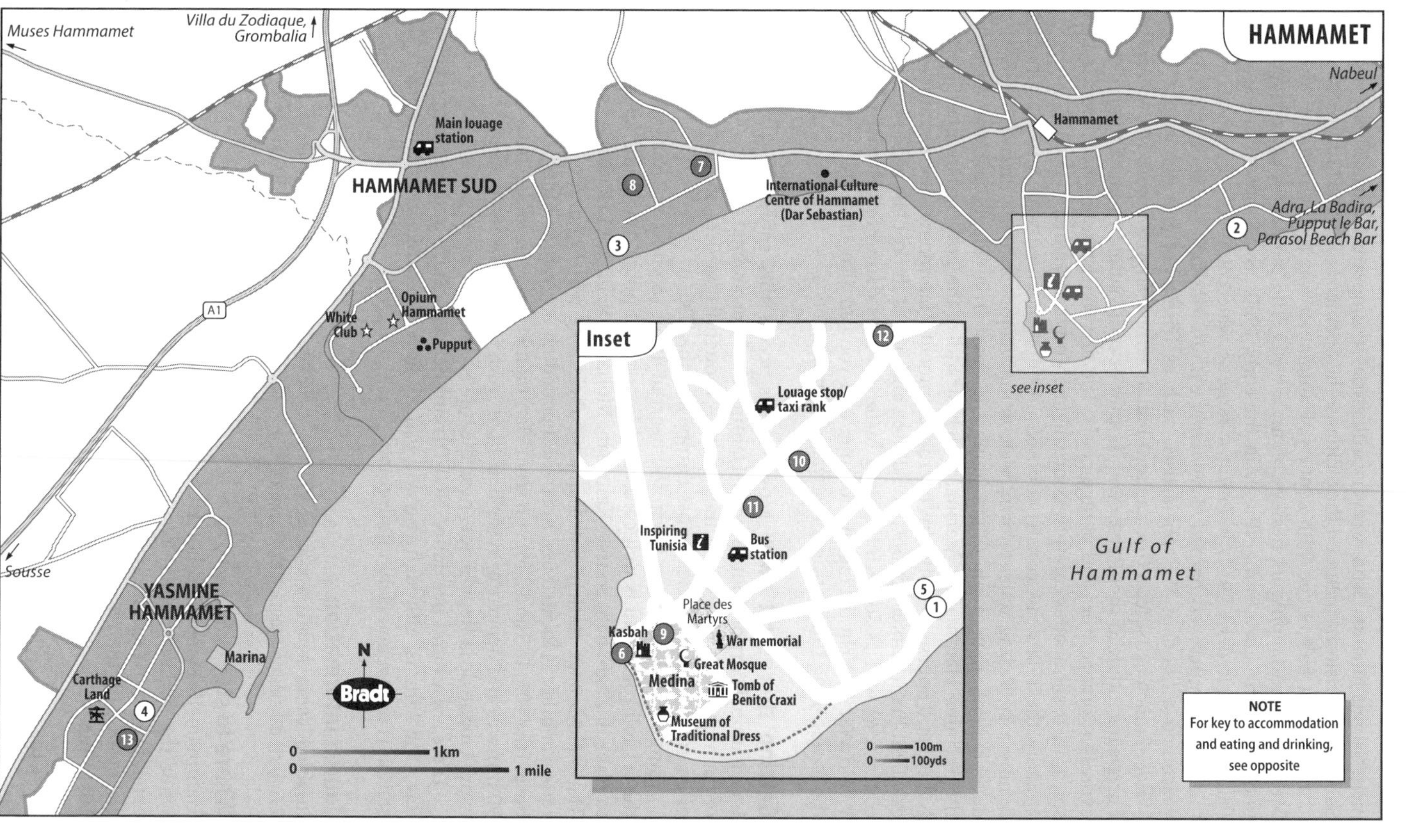
HAMMAMET
Muses Hammamet
Villa du Zodiaque, Grombalia
Main louage station
HAMMAMET SUD
Hammamet
Nabeul
International Culture Centre of Hammamet (Dar Sebastian)
Adra, La Badira, Pupput le Bar, Parasol Beach Bar
see inset
A1
White Club
Opium Hammamet
Pupput
Inset
Louage stop/ taxi rank
Inspiring Tunisia
Bus station
Place des Martyrs
Kasbah
War memorial
Great Mosque
Medina
Tomb of Benito Craxi
Museum of Traditional Dress
100m
100yds
Gulf of Hammamet
Sousse
YASMINE HAMMAMET
Marina
Carthage Land
N
Bradt
1km
1 mile
NOTE
For key to accommodation and eating and drinking, see opposite

HAMMAMET

For listings, see from page 199

Where to stay

1 Hotel Bellevue
2 Hôtel Sol Azur Beach
3 Les Orangers Beach Resort & Bungalows
4 Medina Solaria & Thalasso
5 Villa Phoenicia

Off map

La Badira
Muses Hammamet

Where to eat and drink

6 Café Sidi Bouhdid
7 Chez Robert
8 La Bella Marina Restaurant
9 Le Barberousse
10 Le Petit Pêcheur 2 Hammamet
11 Movida Club Ristorante
12 Restaurant El Tahrir (Liberation)
13 Rovers Return

Off map

Adra
Parasol Beach Bar
Pupput le Bar

with modern but standard rooms. Where this place really shines is in the facilities & the levels of service: multiple outdoor & indoor pools, hammam, gym, highly attentive waiters (both food & drink) on the beach & excellent food quality, especially in the buffets. The walk-in rates are pretty outrageous, but if you can find a discounted deal online this is a brilliant place to spend the w/end. **$$$$$**

Muses Hammamet (5 rooms) Rte Hammam Bent, 14km west of Hammamet; m 29 455 550; w muses-hammamet.com. Sitting in an olive grove with sea views, this secluded farmhouse makes for a relaxing countryside retreat from the hustle & bustle of Hammamet, featuring an outdoor pool, gym, billiards table, tennis court, roaring open fireplace & sauna. **$$$$$**

✷ **La Badira** (130 rooms) Rte Touristique Nord; 70 018 180; w labadira.com. This adults-only luxury hotel is a favourite among business & leisure travellers alike. Its aim is to recreate the glamorous universe of travel from the 1930s, & has done an excellent job of fusing the charm of yesteryear with modern architectural & artistic touches. Some rooms have private pools, there are 5 restaurants (offering both excellent Tunisian & Mediterranean cuisine) & the only Clarins spa in Tunisia. Very good value for the quality, especially in low season. **$$$$–$$$$$**

Medina Solaria & Thalasso (239 rooms) Rue de la Médina, Yasmine Hammamet; 72 241 959; w medinasolaria.website. Conveniently located next to CarthageLand (page 204), this 5-star AI resort is the best of the bunch on the Yasmine Hammamet strip. With a 3-tier swimming pool, multiple bars, generously sized rooms & a private beach, it is a solid choice for a lazy beach holiday in Hammamet. **$$$$**

Hôtel Sol Azur Beach (302 rooms) 145 Rte Touristique; 72 279 550; e marketing@azurhotels.net; f Sol.Azur.Beach. Spread over 15ha of beachfront gardens, this hotel represents good value on Hammamet's Route Touristique & has a reputation for good customer service. **$$$**

Villa Phoenicia (4 rooms) Rue du Stade; 72 262 381; e info@villaphoenicia.com; f. A centrally located B&B with a beautiful internal courtyard & generously sized bright rooms (some with balconies) & en suites. **$$$**

Hotel Bellevue (10 rooms) Bd Ibn el Fourat; 72 281 121; f bellevuehammamet. Not the most attractive of buildings but very close to the beach & the medina, with clean rooms (most with a sea view). The cheapest decent bed in town. **$$**

Where to eat and drink *Map, opposite*

Adra Rte Touristique Nord; 70 018 180; w labadira.com; 19.00–midnight Tue–Sun. Inside La Badira hotel (above), this features both classic Tunisian dishes & newer recipes prepared by its chef, Slim Bettaieb. The 7hr slow-cooked lamb is mouth-wateringly good. **$$$$$**

Chez Robert 119 Av des Nations Unis; 72 280 403; m 98 476 873; e ghrairi.m@gmail.com; f chez.robert.hammamet; 18.00–midnight Tue–Sun. Upmarket Mediterranean cuisine (mainly French & Italian influences) in an intimate dining environment. **$$$$**

Le Barberousse Medina; m 27 280 037; e hellocastle@restaurantbarberousse.com; f barberoussehammamet; noon–midnight daily. Fine Mediterranean dining on the ramparts of the medina with a good wine list & extensive selection of seafood. **$$$$**

✷ **Movida Club Ristorante** Rue de la Republique; m 94 851 230, 24 260 275; noon–

midnight daily. Delicious Italian & Sicilian dishes including crowd-pleasing desserts such as fresh cannoli & tiramisu. $$$$

✷ **Rovers Return** Hotel El Mouradi, Yasmine Hammamet; m 56 203 465; f roversreturnhammamet; ⌚ 10.00–23.30 daily. Restaurant & sports bar serving international & British cuisine. Make the trek out to Dawn's place for a fully cooked English b/fast with a properly poured pint while watching the Premier League. $$$$

Le Petit Pêcheur 2 Hammamet Rue Salah Ben Youssef; m 29 989 971; f lepetitpecheur2; ⌚ noon–late daily. Popular Tunisian seafood restaurant with classic dishes such as *ojja aux fruits de mer* (seafood shakshuka). Reservations recommended at w/ends. $$$–$$$$

✷ **Parasol Beach Bar** In front of Hôtel Hammamet Beach; f parasolbeachbar; ⌚ summer noon–19.00 Tue–Sun. Run by the team from Gingembre & Tangerine in Tunis (page 86), Parasol features the same winning mixture of good music, tempting cocktails & a delicious international menu, with the added bonus of being right on the beach! Reservations essential. $$$–$$$$

La Bella Marina Restaurant Rue Dag Hammarskjöld; ☎ 72 261 374; e labellamarina@hotmail.fr; f LaBellaMarina; ⌚ noon–04.00 daily. Part Mediterranean restaurant, part sports bar, this place does good seafood & is also popular for watching international football; live music at w/ends. $$$

Pupput le Bar Bd de l'Environnement, Hammamet Nord; ☎ 70 021 988; m 23 554 433; w cooeepresident.com/pupputlebar.php; ⌚ noon–late daily. Pizzas, burgers, pasta & some Asian dishes in this popular gastropub located inside the Hotel COOEE President, which often shows live football or hosts karaoke. Reservations recommended for non-residents of hotel. $$$

Restaurant El Tahrir (Liberation) Av de la Liberation Hwanet; m 23 196 530; f RestaurantElTahrir; ⌚ 11.00–midnight daily. Good-value Tunisian seafood restaurant. $$$

Café Sidi Bouhdid Medina; ☎ 72 280 040; w sidibouhdid.net; ⌚ 06.00–22.00 daily. Somewhat kitsch tea joint in the medina, with a lovely cushion-filled outdoor seating area, offering pizzas, panini, crêpes, sweets & shisha. $$

Entertainment and nightlife Almost all the resort hotels in Hammamet have bars that serve alcohol. If you are looking for an actual nightclub, head to Hammamet Sud, which is packed with discos such as **White Club** (Av de la Paix; m 22 617 905; f whiteclub1; ⌚ 22.00–04.00 daily) and **Opium Hammamet** (Rue Moncef Bey; m 55 285 020; f opiumhammamet; ⌚ 15.00–05.00 Tue–Sun); at the latter you will be encouraged to buy a generous fruit platter to accompany your drinks. Licensing rules are pretty loose – a very different situation from the rest of the country – and many places do not close until 04.00. Note that owing to Tunisian promoters' obsession with having grand openings, many of the nightclubs and bars frequently close and then reopen each season with a different name. Although a nightmare for us travel writers (and mapping software), you will still find the same club, with the same staff, year after year – just under a different name.

Shopping Hammamet is not a good place to shop for souvenirs. Items tend to be overpriced, and it is one of the few places in the country where you run the risk of being hassled by hard-selling vendors. Better to head down to Nabeul to find something more authentic (page 197).

What to see and do

The medina The small (but perfectly shaped) medina is the main landmark in Hammamet, built right on the beach. Originally constructed in AD904, and frequently damaged and restored, most of what you see today is from the 15th century. Its walls practically rise out of the water and protect a network of narrow, winding streets of numerous stalls intent on attracting the tourists. Its focal point is the **Great Mosque**, rising out of the medina and obvious by its white square tower, where the upper part and just below the crenellations are covered with black-patterned yellow tiles. The rest of the medina is made up of private dwellings; the impressive doors set into the otherwise blank walls are an attraction in their own right. The most exclusive homes tend to be on the sea-facing side of the medina – no longer do waves lap the walls, as a walkway has been constructed.

Dominating the western corner of the medina is the **Kasbah**, first constructed between AD893 and 904 under the Aghlabid Dynasty. The building you see today was developed over the original between 1463 and 1474 while the Hafsids were in power. There are some splendid views from the walls to the northwest over the Gulf of Hammamet and the beach, and to the southwest over the Mediterranean, while to the west you might pick out the Jebel Zaghouan (1,295m). In the north corner is a squat tower, while the inner courtyard is bare apart from a few trees which provide welcome shade in the summer. Here there are three cannon and several horse-drawn ploughs on display.

The medina contains many reminders of the holy men who spent time in Hammamet, among them **Sidi Bou Hadid** who may have come from Morocco, perhaps Sakiet el Hamra. It is said that, shortly before he died in the 12th century, he instructed his family to put his corpse into a coffin and throw it into the sea. He wanted the waves and currents to decide on his final resting place, and his tomb was to be built where his coffin was washed ashore. Legend has it that the sea spirits built his tomb in the town walls, under the ramparts, from where he can keep watch over the Gulf of Hammamet. For this reason, he has become the saint of the fishermen who make offerings to him and, in times of real danger, call on his assistance. Like the former entrance to the shrine of Sidi Bou Saïd in Tunis, Sidi Bou Hadid's alleged final resting place today functions as the very popular Café Sidi Bouhdid (see opposite) and is a romantic place to watch the sun go down over the sea.

In the southwest corner of the medina is the three-room **Museum of Traditional Dress (Dar Hammamet)** (⌚ 09.00–17.00 daily; 1.5DT), featuring an interesting collection of traditional female clothing and wedding garments. One room is set out as a bedroom, and there are additional costumes in the cabinets. It is worth the entry fee just to watch the sunset from the roof. Enter from the square by the cemetery or follow the signs by the seafront.

Next to the car park outside the medina, in Place des Martyrs, a tall white modern **memorial** (⊕ 36.394750, 10.614360), sweeping skywards, which commemorates the dead of World War II. Adjacent to it, on the wall forming the boundary with the small Christian cemetery (⊕ 36.393528, 10.614450), is a high-relief frieze depicting the horrors of war. A little further south along Rue Imam Sahnoun, nestled in the cemetery, is the **tomb of Bettino Craxi** (1934–2000), a former Italian Prime Minister and leader of the Italian Socialist Party. He was a polarising figure in Italian politics, who lived out his final years in a villa in Hammamet in self-imposed exile in order to avoid serving a corruption sentence back in Italy. He is the subject of the excellent 2020 Italian biographical drama *Hammamet*, which was released just before the 20th anniversary of Craxi's death.

International Cultural Centre of Hammamet (Dar Sebastian) ☗ (97 Av des Nations Unis; ☎ 72 280 410; w ccih.gov.tn; ⌚ 08.30–16.00 Mon–Sat; 5DT) Originally built in 1927, this is the former party villa of millionaire Romanian aesthete, Georges Sebastian. Throughout the 1930s, Sebastian used it to entertain all manner of famous guests, including English writer Somerset Maugham and Swedish-American actress Greta Garbo; the villa even featured in American *Vogue* in August 1935. Having abandoned the property during World War II, Sebastian eventually sold it to the Tunisian state in 1959, but stayed on to help transform it into a cultural centre. It has now been beautifully refurbished and frequently hosts everything from live music events and poetry recitals to children's pottery workshops, with full events listings published on its website and Facebook page.

Inside the property, the original lounge is worth seeing, with its long table and simple wrought-iron chairs and the walls hung with contemporary Tunisian paintings. The novel four-seater sunken bath is in the shape of a cross (presumably mixed bathing – all very avant-garde) rather like four hip baths. The rather small guest bedroom can also be viewed, where Von Arnim, Rommel, Montgomery and Churchill were accommodated according to the fluctuations of World War II, no doubt making maximum use of the beach in between bouts of moving counters around on a large map of North Africa.

In the warmer months, you might want to try to get to a show at the 1,100-seat open-air theatre, built 150m to the west of the main house in the 1960s. The theatre was the brainchild of Cecyl Hourani, one of President Bourguiba's advisers, and Ali Ben Ayed, the country's leading actor and descendant of a noble family. Bourguiba, who had enjoyed amateur dramatics in his youth, approved the project. The annual **International Festival of Hammamet**, usually held in the theatre in July/August, began in 1964 as a summer showcase for the performing arts, with dance, theatre and music all on view. In its heyday, the festival attracted North African dramatists such as Saddiki and Kaki, and productions by Peter Brook, Littlewood and Béjart. More recently, the theatre has seen festival performances from Césaria Evora, the barefoot diva of Cabo Verde, various jazz bands and Marseillais hip-hop group IAM.

Pupput (⊕ 36.392917, 10.562448; ⌚ summer 08.00–13.00 & 15.00–19.00 daily, winter 08.30–17.30 daily; 5DT) Lodged in between the Samira Club and the Hawaii Beach Club hotels in Hammamet Sud, the ancient town of Pupput is recorded as being settled since at least the 1st century BC and, like many later Roman settlements in this part of the world, may have had Punic origins. It was a staging post on the road from Carthage to Hadrumetum (modern Sousse), and today it is a dusty and not-very-well-developed archaeological site. The remains are slight but significant – there are some fine late-Roman mosaics here, including some unusual black-and-white swastikas and a lighthouse, which is very rare in ancient Roman iconography.

CarthageLand (Rue de la Médina, Yasmine Hammamet; ☎ 72 240 111; w hammamet.carthageland.com.tn; ⌚ 10.00–18.00 daily; adult/child 26/16DT) Who wouldn't want to go to a Carthaginian-themed amusement park? Here you can explore ancient mazes, zoom down slides in the waterpark and even jump on a (very small) replica of the Lézard Rouge train from Gafsa (page 344). I am not sure how the Carthaginian supreme god Baal-Hammon would feel about being immortalised in a swinging boat ride, but it's all good fun!

AROUND HAMMAMET

Villa du Zodiaque (Mussolini's Villa) ⚑ (⊕ 36.507672, 10.562924) If you have your own transport, it is worth stopping off at this incredible piece of Tunisia's architectural heritage, sat completely unmarked by the side of the A1 about 16km northwest of Nabeul. Perched on top of a hill overlooking the motorway, this rare piece of modernist architecture was built by Italians in 1935 and was so extravagant that locals assumed it must have been built for Italian dictator Benito Mussolini once he inevitably conquered Tunisia from the French. This is an urban legend, as it was in fact built by the Garsia family, who were wealthy Italian farmers in the area. The structure was designed by Italian architect Ugo Chiarini, who was a prominent figure in Tunisia's colonial architectural scene.

Although the structure is currently occupied by local squatters, they will show you around if you ask politely. The villa is constructed to a perfectly round floorplan: the curve is queen here. A splendid circular galleried hall is topped by a simple dome set with tiny skylights, as in an old-style Turkish bath. Access to the first-floor rooms (which have magnificent views over the countryside) is via a staircase housed in a cylinder topped with a green-tiled dome. Inside, the most interesting feature is the mosaics. On the ground floor are animals (a giraffe, a wounded gazelle, an eagle) and people (a Roman soldier, an archer, a dancing woman, a Bedouin woman, a Corsican head). On the first floor are mosaic star signs – hence the name Villa du Zodiaque.

Grombalia With around 25,000 inhabitants, Grombalia (Roman Colombaria) is the focal point for the surrounding agricultural region. Nothing is left from Roman times, and today the oldest remains here (a mosque built by Mustapha Cardenas) date from the 16th century, the time of the evacuation of Andalusia by the Moors. The olive presses, which also date from the 16th century, indicate the quick growth in prosperity of the region.

Since the turn of the 20th century, Cap Bon's main vineyards have been centred around Grombalia. In the late 19th century, the spread of phylloxera on vines in mainland Europe encouraged grape-growing in Tunisia, though in the interwar years phylloxera took its toll on Tunisian vineyards too. New grafted stocks were subsequently introduced and, until the 1960s, much of the wine was exported to France for blending. Unlike the terraced fields of France and Germany, the vineyards here are generally planted on flat ground. Today, wine production runs at 30–40 million litres per year, the majority of which is consumed in Tunisia. According to the World Health Organization, Tunisians are the heaviest alcohol drinkers in northwest Africa; however, their preference is beer, so wine production has failed to grow since the revolution.

Nevertheless, in August/September Grombalia has its annual moment of glory: the **Festival of the Grapevine**, with a parade and an agricultural fair. The town is also home to many roadside stalls during wine season and there are also some good local vineyards where you can take part in wine tastings throughout the year. One such is **Domaine Neferis** (2 Rue Yasmine El Menzah; m 22 534 556; w neferis.com), a 200ha vineyard set up in 2000 on the site of a colonial vineyard dating to 1878. It produces many local favourites such as Selian, Magnifique, Château Defleur, Diamant Rosé and Terrale, and offers a tour of the facilities with wine tasting and a substantial lunch for 90DT (booking essential).

At the time of writing, the EU Council of Europe was hoping to restart its European wine route, the **Iter Vitis Wine Route**, which incorporates vineyards in Tunisia. Be sure to check its website and social media (w coe.int/en/web/cultural-routes/the-iter-vitis-route; f itervitis) for announcements. Grombalia is also well known for its *merguez*, a spicy red sausage made with beef (or sometimes lamb).

SULAYMAN Dating to the 17th century, this market town is the gateway to Cap Bon's northwest coastline. Like many other small towns in Tunisia, it takes great pride in its Andalusian heritage. It is named after its patron, a rich Turkish farmer who came to this area around 1600 and began the construction of a new town. The subsequent influx of immigrants from Al-Andalus left their mark in the form of building style, irrigation methods and even culinary preferences.

The town centre, with its trees, arcades and cafés, is a pleasant sort of place. Sulayman's most outstanding architectural feature is its **Malikite Mosque**, whose solid square minaret dominates the town centre; parts of the building are roofed with Spanish-style rounded tiles. (The main mosque in Testour has a similarly strong Andalusian identity – see page 123.) While the town itself is set back around 4km from the sea, there is a decent 3km stretch of sandy beach on offer if you follow Rue 14 Janvier to the coast.

KORBOUS A small spa resort, Korbous is set on a wild, rocky coast in a tiny narrow valley. The Romans called the town 'Aquae Calideae Carpitanae' ('the warm waters of Carpis') after the springs in the area; they are thought to have built some pleasure baths here, though no traces of these have survived. In the early 19th century, reforming ruler Ahmed Bey had a pavilion here for enjoying the thermal springs. Later, Korbous was home to one Edmond Lecore-Carpentier, who in 1889 set up a company to market the curative powers of the hot springs to a wider audience. After his death, he was buried in a mausoleum on top of a hill overlooking Korbous. His burial site became a place of prayer and pilgrimage, and he became known as Sidi Karbanti to the locals; the irredentist French settler terrorist group, La Main Rouge, exhumed him in the early 1950s, refusing to admit that a Frenchman could have been integrated into local society to the point of being considered a holy man. Tunisia's first president, Habib Bourguiba, had palaces and residences in all the right places, and Korbous was no exception – the now-disused villa on the hilltop was one of his summer homes.

Korbous's other claim to fame is the **Zerziha Stone**, visible on your left through an arch as you head up the street for the Hotel des Sources. Women in search of a cure for sterility may slide down it. All Korbous children have played on this 'slide' at one time or another in their childhood.

Note that the coastal C128 road from Sulayman to Korbous was closed at the time of writing due to a rockfall (although this still makes for spectacular hiking, or a great cliff-jumping spot if you sail over from Sidi Bou Saïd harbour – see page 77), so continuing northwards from Sulayman involves heading inland at the roundabout north of Marisa, 2.3km after coming off the C26.

The springs The waters off the coast around Korbous are used for treating arthritis, rheumatism, obesity, cellulite and hypertension. They come boiling out of the earth at a hefty 60°C, are faintly radioactive, contain calcium, sodium and sulphur, and sometimes smell of rotten eggs. Approaching Korbous from the Sulayman direction, **Aïn Oktor** is the first spring you reach. Overlooking the sea, the site is home to a hotel complex of the same name (⊕ 36.794851, 10.561299; ⌚ 24/7), which dates from 1966 and was designed, like so many other public buildings of the period, by President Bourguiba's then-favourite architect, Olivier Clément Cacoub. The water emerges slowly, hence its name – 'Oktor' means 'the spring which emerges drop by drop' in Arabic – and contains a high proportion of chlorine and sodium hydrogen carbonate, used in the treatment of kidney disorders and urinary problems.

Aïn Echfa (☎ 72 284 585; ⌚ 08.00–16.00 daily; 2–3DT) is the main spring in Korbous. There is a thermal station at ⊕ 36.816893, 10.567441 that uses the spring waters to offer such delights as *fangiothérapie* (mud baths) and other treatments that will leave you feeling squeaky clean. The main, everyday baths fed by the spring are called the Arraka (from the Arabic 'arak', meaning 'sweat') – an apt name, as in the underground grotto you will really get a sweat going.

The best of the three springs is **Aïn Atrous**, 1km north of Korbous on the main road (⊕ 36.827432, 10.569192). The spring gushes out of a duct in the hillside at 50°C and runs across the rocks for a few metres before tumbling down some 3m into the sea. You can sit with your feet in a small concrete basin while wisps of steam and whiffs of rotten eggs rise from the nearly scalding water. There is a car park and a few small cafés and restaurants close by. Note that it is a favourite spot for local visitors, so it gets very busy at the weekend.

PORT AUX PRINCES (⊕ 36.878485, 10.670981) Getting from Korbous to the beautiful, isolated beach at Port Aux Princes involves an inland detour. The road down to the beach forks off the main C26 at Bir Mroua (⊕ 36.796152, 10.626132), which you then follow for 11km. On the west side of the bay is an abandoned castle-like structure said to have belonged to President Bourguiba's second wife, Wassila. If you come down here at sunset, you will see that she had good taste – the fading light creates spectacular views across the water. There are a couple of shacks on the beach selling seafood during high season, but otherwise facilities are non-existent.

SIDI DAOUD (⊕ 37.021396, 10.910384) This small fishing port, 37km north of Korbous, is no tourist hot spot, but its name will be familiar to Tunisian residents as it is seen on the many cans of tuna consumed across the country. With views looking out to the steep cliffs of the uninhabited islands of Zembra and Zembretta (page 209), Sidi Daoud has an isolated, end-of-the-world feel. In late May to early June each year, local fishermen take part in the *matanza* ('slaughter' in Spanish, although it is unclear why they describe it in Spanish!), when shoals of large tuna fish (at times weighing more than 200kg), migrating from the Atlantic Ocean via the Straits of Gibraltar, are caught in carefully positioned nets, only to be dragged towards the shore and then harpooned between the boats. Unlike the Taiji dolphin hunt in Japan or the Grindadráp whale hunt in the Faroe Islands, the *matanza* has thus far managed to stay off the radar of animal rights groups, perhaps as video footage of the hunt does not seem to exist.

EL HAOUARIA Approaching from the south, sleepy El Haouaria appears in the bare landscape as an expanse of low, flat-roofed houses below the gently rising mass of the djebel, with only the tall, onion-domed Cap Bon minaret penetrating the skyline. For the tourist, there are excellent accommodation and dining options, and attractions include the bizarre underground Roman quarries and the low-key beach at Rass Eddrek. The scenery is rugged, and birdwatchers will have much to enjoy during the annual trans-Mediterranean migrations, which include the likes of sparrowhawk and white stork.

In Roman times, El Haouaria was referred to as 'Aquilaria' – 'the place of eagles'. The capture and rearing of falcons, still part of local life today, was no doubt an important activity in ancient times. A great time to visit is during May or June for the Festival de l'Épervier, when people bring their hawks to put them through their paces in front of other bird handlers. Live prey are used for these flying displays, and the falconers operate their birds with no mean skill.

El Haouaria and the surrounding islands (page 209) are also popular for diving. Located in the town centre, Ras Adar Diving Club (⊕ 37.047183, 11.019383; m 56 500 233; f plongee.el.haouaria.club.ras.adar) is a Scuba Schools International official dive centre; in 2020, divers from this club discovered the remains of the

French submarine *Ariane*, sunk by a German submarine during World War I on 19 June 1917, killing 21 of the 29 submariners on board.

Where to stay

✷ **Villa Zembra** (6 rooms) ⊕ 37.056596, 11.010410; m 21 162 698; w villa-zembra.com. Perched at the base of the hill at the northern end of town, this dar offers incredible views of the islands of Zembra & Zembretta (page 209). The traditionally decorated internal courtyard is used for aerial yoga & the dar hosts various retreats involving Qigong, meditation, hiking, diving, kayaking & art workshops. Rooms are cosy, the host is very welcoming, there is a pool & meals are served in a separate building with views of the Mediterranean. **$$$$**

Hotel & Restaurant Les Grottes (16 rooms) ⊕ 37.056255, 10.999302; ☎ 72 297 296; w les-grottes.e-monsite.com. Basic motel-like set-up with rooms around a communal pool. The restaurant does pretty good seafood, although you are better off walking up the hill to La Daurade. **$$**

Dar Toubib (5 rooms) ⊕ 37.053078, 11.012850; ☎ 72 297 163. The cheapest decent bed in town. Blue-&-white tiled en-suite rooms open out on to a leafy courtyard with communal kitchen & private parking. **$**

Where to eat and drink

La Daurade ⊕ 37.058896, 10.995069; m 23 269 080; e waliddaurade@yahoo.fr; f restoladaurade; ⏲ 11.00–23.00 daily. Excellent seafood restaurant on a terrace overlooking the waves. **$$$$**

✷ **Restaurant Bella Riva Dalla Luna** ⊕ 37.050223, 11.014785; ☎ 72 269 969; m 21 882 411; f; ⏲ 11.30–16.00 & 19.00–22.30 daily. One of the best Italian restaurants in Tunisia for fresh pasta, in a very low-key setting. Ask host Lina for her recommendations of the day. You will not be disappointed! **$$$**

Restaurant Les Grottes ⊕ 37.056255, 10.999302; ⏲ 11.00–23.00 daily; ☎ 72 297 296; m 24 248 281; f les.grottes.resto. Seafood dining with a setting that can feel worryingly close to the coast when the waves are big. Has a plunge pool overlooking the water, which is great on a sunny day. **$$$**

What to see and do

Falconry (Nadi el Bayazara) (⊕ 37.056933, 11.000758) El Haouaria's gleaming white falconry centre is situated up on the hill on the road to the Roman quarries. The centre was closed at the time of writing, but does open up to the public during the annual Festival de l'Épervier (page 61). Two sorts of bird are used for falconry: the sparrowhawk (*épervier* in French, *essaf* in Tunisian Arabic) and the peregrine falcon (*faucon pélérin* or *el burni*). Sparrowhawks are captured up on the mountain during the April migration from Africa, and after around three weeks' training are ready to hunt in time for the festival. Quail is the favourite prey. Generally, after the festival, most of the sparrowhawks are released. Takes of the much rarer peregrine falcons are very closely controlled: only one or two nestlings may be taken each year, and the young birds are reared in capacity, and permits are issued to bona fide falconers only.

Ghar el Kebir Caves (⊕ 37.059432, 10.996066) Three kilometres from the centre, on the shore near the extremity of the Cap, are these Roman quarries. They are easy to reach as the road all the way down to La Dourade restaurant is paved (although they may ask you to pay a few dinars for parking there). It is thought that the rock quarried here was used to build parts of Carthage and even the Colosseum in Rome. The question is, why did the Romans opt for quarrying on this remote stretch of coast? One major factor must have been the accessibility of such a large amount of easily worked soft sandstone right on the waterline – the stone could be easily shipped to Carthage and other settlements across the Bay of Tunis. And then there is the matter of how they worked the stone. As they cut down from above, the quarry workers created pyramid-shaped underground chambers. The operation was a skilled one, especially when it came to hoisting the blocks out through the 'skylights'. Getting the blocks on the fragile ancient ships would have been another skilled manoeuvre using simple cranes. Depending on the demand for the stone, there must have been a sizable population living out at ancient Haouaria.

There are said to be 97 caves in total; the main ones are interlinked and have small openings in the roof, originally for the exit of the quarried stone, so daylight can now enter. Caper plants grow in the sandy stone, hanging down through the openings. At the time of writing, the caves were closed; however, this does not stop local guides from prying open the fence and taking visitors in anyway. If you are accompanied by a guide, they will point out the camel-shaped stone in the big hall – a female, we are told. There is a small **museum** by the entrance to the site (⊕ 37.059195, 10.995355), which details some of the quarrying techniques used in ancient times; signage is in Arabic, French and English.

AROUND EL HAOUARIA

Jebel Sidi Abiod This 375m-tall promontory in the forest at the tip of Cap Bon offers great views of the Cap Bon lighthouse and the islands of Zembra and Zembretta. From here, the Italian island of Pantelleria is only 80km to the east (although not visible at this elevation). Note that there is a radio transmission tower guarded by the military up here (⊕ 37.071677, 11.046139), so do not drive all the way to the end of the tarmac road; best to park on the curve at ⊕ 37.069866, 11.042163. This area is also a favourite for birdwatchers in spring, catching the migrations between Europe and Africa; to organise a birdwatching tour, speak to one of the specialised birding outfits listed on page 41.

On your way up the hill, you will pass Tunisia's smallest nature reserve, the **Bat Cave Nature Reserve** (⊕ 37.064864, 11.030222). If you can set aside any lingering pandemic-based concerns about hanging out with flying, cave-dwelling mammals – and can get past the large and rather scary-looking bat statue at the entrance – you will find five species of bat in this network of caves: Mehely's horseshoe (*Rhinolophus mehelyi*), Blasius's horseshoe (*R. blasii*), greater horseshoe (*R. ferrumequinum*), common bent-wing (*Miniopterus schreibersii*) and the rather cute lesser mouse-eared bat (*Myotis blythii*). The reserve was closed at the time of writing; ask in town for details of potential reopening.

Zembra and Zembretta These small, steep-cliffed islands are 17km and 12km offshore from El Haouaria, respectively. The islands and their waters have been designated a national park since 1977 with no fishing – professional or sports – allowed. There was once a hotel and a diving centre on the islands, but today there is only a military base – and a colony of Cory's shearwater.

Zembra rises straight out of the sea to its summit at 435m, and the island's most notable resident is a subspecies of wild rabbit (*Oryctolagus cuniculus*), with distinctive genetic markers not found in nearby wild rabbit populations. They are thought to descend from animals introduced by Phoenician sailors, perhaps to ensure a source of meat if they were forced to spend time on the island. The smaller of the two islands, Zembretta's main feature is a lighthouse.

It is possible to access the islands, but only with a permit. In Tunisia's ever-shifting Byzantine bureaucracy, access to national parks (at the time of writing) was handled by the Direction Générale des Forêts, which is part of the Ministry of Agriculture (⊕ 36.828936, 10.184066; ☎ 71 786 833; e bo.dgf@iresa.agrinet; f DirectionGeneraleDesForetsAladartAlamtLlghabat). However, you are far better off asking a tour agency in Tunis to secure a permit (page 40) or sailing to the islands with a charter vessel that has experience securing the permits (page 77). Otherwise, Zembra is clearly visible from El Haouaria's Roman quarries (page 208), and the view at sunset is magnificent.

KERKOUANE (w tunisiepatrimoine.tn/musees/le-musee-de-kerkouane; ⊙ winter 09.00–16.00 daily, summer 09.00–18.00 daily; 8/5DT non-resident/resident) Although not as spectacular as the great inland Numidian and Roman towns, the UNESCO-listed ruins of Kerkouane have a certain isolated charm of their own, sited on the edge of a low cliff overlooking the Mediterranean, backed by a hinterland of dark, windswept pines and heath. Unlike so many other ancient sites, Kerkouane was never built upon by subsequent peoples, a feature that makes it very exciting to archaeologists. The original Phoenician-Punic town buildings decayed into a jungle of briars, gorse and tamarisk, until they were unearthed again, first by a local teacher in the 1920s, then – to much more fanfare – by archaeologists Charles Saumagne (born in Sousse) and Pierre Cintas (born in Tabarka). They consequently spent years arguing about who had actually discovered it first. Visitors today can enjoy a glimpse at the streets, ramparts, port, shops, residential districts and religious structures in the same configuration as they were in the 3rd century BC.

History Kerkouane is thought to have been built in the 6th century BC. M'hamed Hassine Fantar, Professor of Archaeology at Tunis University and leading authority on Kerkouane, sees the town as being a sort of ethno-cultural melting pot of Libyco-Punic and Greek influences. Excavations of the houses have not brought to light any material later than the 3rd century BC, which would suggest that the town was pillaged and abandoned at the time of Roman consul M Atilius Regulus's invasion of Africa in 256BC. It was certainly abandoned before the fall of Carthage to the Romans in AD146. The settlement had a small port, and it is likely that its people made their living both from the sea and farming.

In 1929, several decades before the discovery of the actual town of Kerkouane, a local teacher happened upon a necropolis, called Arg el Ghazouani, some 1.5km northwest of the ancient town (⊕ 36.955988, 11.086219), with vaults carved into a hillside looking out over the sea. On discovering that the hundreds of tombs contained scarabs, jewellery and black-figure ceramics, he mined his discovery for all it was worth, selling off the most valuable finds to treasure hunters. Other funerary objects and pottery that were too cumbersome were broken up to fill in already ransacked tombs.

The 'official' discovery of the necropolis, however, was not made until one J Combre, an officer appointed to conduct a local murder enquiry, met the teacher later that year. He noted that the teacher's wife was wearing a superb pair of gold earrings, obviously of great age. The teacher eventually told the tale of the tomb robberies, but official awareness does not seem to have put an end to local pillaging of the site, which continued for the next 20 years.

In the early 1950s, archaeologists Pierre Cintas and Charles Saumagne began to research tombs elsewhere in the region. Kerkouane town itself was discovered almost by accident – the sort of scoop that archaeologists dream of. In fact, the area could all too easily have gone the way of so many other sites, the land subdivided for villa development, with building too far advanced for anything to be done.

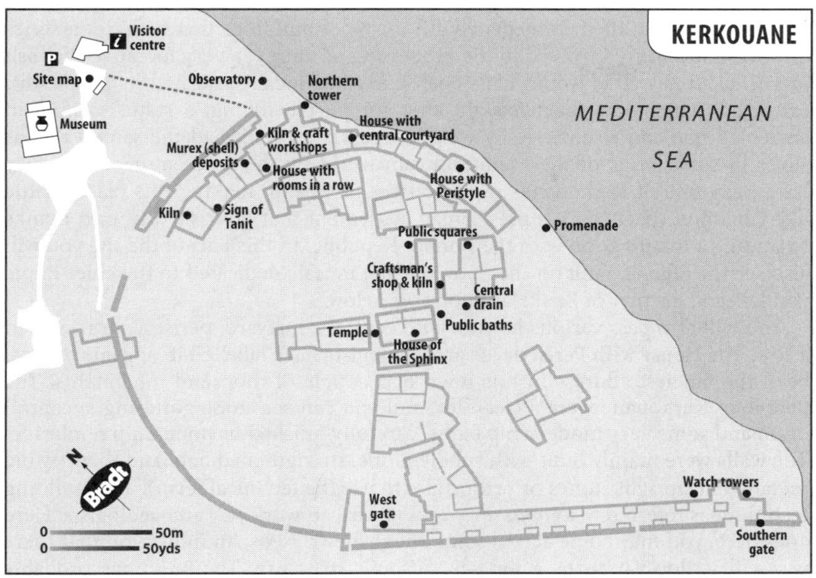

One (highly disputed) version of the story goes that, one afternoon in 1952 while sitting on the cliffs of Kerkouane, Charles Saumagne noticed some black-glaze pot shards and fragments of stucco in the soil. As an archaeologist, he immediately gave this loose surface material a closer inspection, realising that it was probably pre-Roman. The Department of Antiquities was informed, and test trenches were dug. The results were conclusive given that, with almost the first shovelful, a Punic mask was brought to light. Despite all the pillaging in the area, there were tombs which survived unopened into the 1960s and later. In July 1970, a tomb at Arg el Ghazouani was found to contain a wooden sarcophagus, its lid carved with the bas-relief image of a woman, thought by some to be Astarte, protector goddess of the dead. This piece can be viewed today in the site museum.

Getting there and away The site is less than 1.5km off the main C27 road. To get there on public transport, you could jump on a louage between Kélibia and El Haouaria and ask to get off in Kerkouane, by the town of Dar Allouche.

The site today The best place to start any exploration is the **museum**, which offers insight into the everyday goings-on in ancient Kerkouane with displays of weights and obsidian objects, murex shells and basalt grindstones, pottery, both local and imported, stelae and altars. There are also amulets, toilet requisites, scarabs and glass-paste decorative items. The museum's most unusual item, however, has to be a wooden sarcophagus carved with the image of the goddess Astarte, protector of the dead (known as the Lady of Kerkouane). The robed goddess is almost complete, with only the feet missing. The find is unique – no other example of Punic wood-carving has survived. After the discovery in July 1970, wood-conservation experts were flown in from Switzerland and, in the event, the statue had to be flown off to Zurich for treatment before being returned to its home.

Heading into the site proper from the museum, you first see the **northern tower**, which appears to have been built in preparation for the impending First Punic War

(264–241 BC). You then immediately hit a row of buildings that includes a series of **workshops**, likely involved in the processing of murex, a very lucrative shellfish in ancient times. This would have been harvested locally and had its purple dye extracted, which was much sought-after for purple robing, a status symbol in ancient Rome and elsewhere. By weight, this luxury item had the same value as silver in some parts of the Mediterranean world by the 4th century BC. It may have been one of Kerkouane's main sources of wealth, making this place a little like Chemtou (page 155): a pre-Roman settlement that flourished in part thanks to trading a luxury good with the Roman Republic. In this part of the site you will also see the **Sign of Tanit** on the floor, a white mosaic dedicated to the chief Punic goddess and partner of Ba'al Hammon (see below).

You will also pass various **houses**, with central courtyard, peristyle or rooms in a row. The **House with Peristyle**, as archaeologists have labelled it, appears to have been the fanciest address in this town of a couple of thousand inhabitants. The people of Kerkouane were a clean lot, and you can see stone guttering, a central drain and some very modern hip baths, carefully finished in stone-chip rendering. The walls were mainly built with rubble-stone, strengthened here and there by big rectangular upright stones or orthostats (to use the technical term). This building technique is referred to as *opus africanum* ('African work') by archaeologists. Here and there, you may come across some rough-hewn steps, an indication that there was a first floor, perhaps a light wood-built structure. The buildings probably had flat, terrace roofs, and there were stone waterspouts to ensure that water did not accumulate on the roofs. The Kerkouanese liked to have their homes well finished. A form of stucco was in use, and you can see occasional layers of stucco flaking on the clay-and-gravel walls. It was the floors that had the most elegant finish, however. The preferred paving technique, referred to by archaeologists as

OUR LADY TANIT

At Carthage, Tanit, a chief Punic goddess of Phoenician origin, was referred to as 'lady'. The mother goddess and symbol of fertility, her name often precedes that of Baal-Hammon on the stelae of Carthage. In all probability, Tanit and Baal-Hammon formed a sort of divine couple. One of the earliest sacred motifs known in North Africa, the Tanit sign is formed by a triangle topped by a horizontal line on which rests a circle. The general theory is that it is a stylised representation of a female figure, shown in long, flowing robes. At Kerkouane, a famous example of the Tanit sign is found in a proto-mosaic pavement, picked out in white against a dull-red ground. It has also been found decorating funerary chambers, stamped on the handles of amphorae and on terracotta medallions.

What was the function of the Tanit sign? It may be that the Tanit is derived from the Egyptian ankh, the hieroglyphic symbol for life. Thus, when it is placed on the doorstep of a home it has a great protective force, while in funerary chambers the Tanit would seem to promote the forces of life over death. Today, Tunisians tend to use the fish (*hout*) and the *khomsa* (the so-called Hand of Fatima) more frequently in everyday symbolism, but some see the Tanit still very much present in contemporary Tunisia. Feminist film-maker Nadia El Aunt created a dream-like short feature film, *Tanitez-moi* (1992), emphasising the Carthaginian side in the identity of post-independence Tunisian women.

opus signinum, involved setting white marble chips in a hard mix of old pottery and primitive cementing. The resulting overall colour is terracotta pink, flecked with white.

Towards the centre of the site are many of the public buildings, such as the main **temple** (with priest's accommodation), the somewhat functional **baths** and the **square**. Here is also the **House of the Sphinx**, a large space with at least ten rooms dedicated to all sorts of domestic and craft activities including glass blowing, named after a terracotta altar with a sphinx that was found inside, and is now on display in the museum.

KÉLIBIA Too far from Hammamet to have attracted developers' interest and a full 2-hour drive from Tunis thanks to the lack of motorway on the peninsula, Kélibia remains quite far off the established Cap Bon tourist trail. It is a working town, with fishing, farming and furniture the main industries, but for the visitor there are some beautiful beaches and an impressive fortress, a symbol of the 18th-/19th-century Husseinid Dynasty's authority over the area. Though nothing swish, the town is perfect for a siesta-like break from Tunis.

History The settlement and fortress here go back to Punic times. Phoenician traders no doubt appreciated the defensive value of the site: Kélibia holds the key to the straits separating Africa from Sicily. Greek historians referred to the town as Aspis (Greek for 'shield') and the Romans adopted the same term but this time in Latin, redubbing it Clupea. The remains of a large Punic necropolis, including 28 tombs, were discovered in 1984–85 near the former Hotel Mansoura. In the early 20th century, the area saw extensive Italian settlement, thanks to the rich farmland. A pleasant white wine, the Muscat sec de Kélibia, is a legacy of these influences; unfortunately, the grape juice is sent up to the main production unit in Tunis for fermentation, so you cannot go for jolly tastings in the local winery.

Getting there and away There are frequent **buses** between Kélibia and both El Haouaria and Nabeul, while bus and **louage** services from Tunis leave from Gare Routière Sud (Bab Alioua). The main SRTGN bus and louage stop is at the junction of Rue Taieb Sardouk and the main C27 road, a good 3km from the beach area, so you may want to jump in a taxi.

Where to stay *Map, page 214*

Beit el Houta (10 rooms) Aïn Grinz; m 26 638 631; w beitelhouta.com. The most architecturally striking of the accommodation options on Aïn Grinz beach. Host Nejib Ridène has created a plant-filled environment that employs a lot of wood & fish motifs (look at the window frames, the pool shape), as well as frequent splashes of yellow & blue paint. Room types are very different (inc 1 penthouse with a private pool), so check on the website before selecting. Difficult to book as not very responsive online. **$$$$**

Dar Gino (7 rooms, 2 suites) Aïn Grinz; 72 274 343; m 22 692 700; w dargino.weebly.com. Upmarket dar with whitewashed walls & an elegantly decorated roof terrace topped by a calligraphy-covered dome. Good pool & very close to the beach. **$$$$**

✷ **Dar Kenza** (10 rooms) Aïn Grinz; 72 273 140; m 27 740 779; e darkenzakelibia@gmail.com; f darkenzakelibia. Another upmarket dar with whitewashed walls & a good pool plus hammam on Aïn Grinz beach. Richly furnished, traditionally decorated rooms, with a fair amount of variation in room size. What really sets this place apart is the panoramic views from the upstairs restaurant, with open log fire. **$$$$**

Kelibia Beach Hotel (251 rooms) Mansoura Beach; 72 277 774; w kelibiabeachhotel.com. A very popular 4-star AI resort on the beach, aimed mainly at the Italian market. 4 pools, spa,

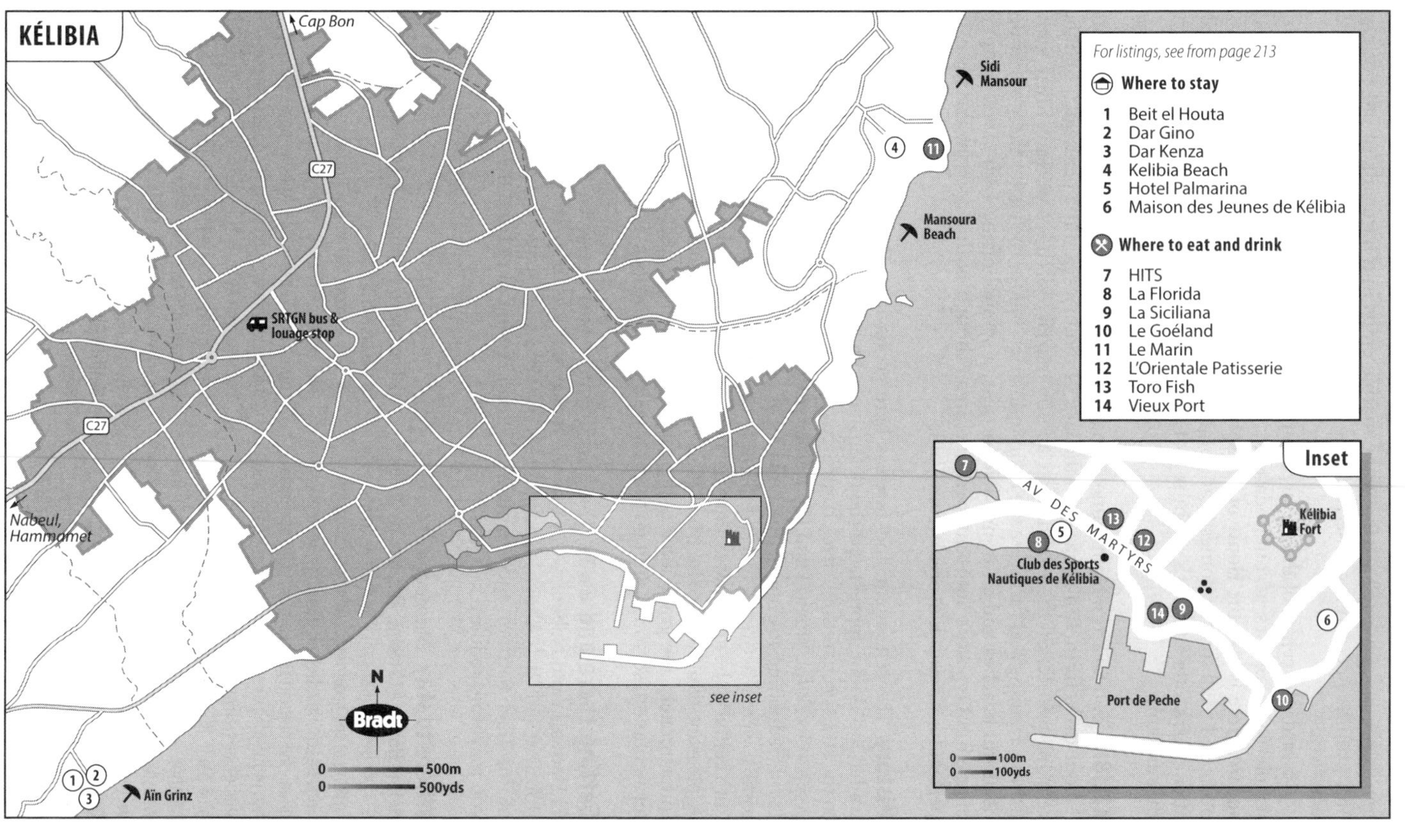
KÉLIBIA
Cap Bon
Nabeul, Hammamet
C27
SRTGN bus & louage stop
Sidi Mansour
Mansoura Beach
Aïn Grinz
see inset
N
Bradt
0 500m
0 500yds
For listings, see from page 213
Where to stay
1 Beit el Houta
2 Dar Gino
3 Dar Kenza
4 Kelibia Beach
5 Hotel Palmarina
6 Maison des Jeunes de Kélibia
Where to eat and drink
7 HITS
8 La Florida
9 La Siciliana
10 Le Goéland
11 Le Marin
12 L'Orientale Patisserie
13 Toro Fish
14 Vieux Port
Inset
AV DES MARTYRS
Club des Sports Nautiques de Kélibia
Kélibia Fort
Port de Peche
0 100m
0 100yds

extensive sports facilities & access to the white sands of Mansoura Beach. **$$$$**

Hotel Palmarina (11 rooms) Rue Ennasim; 72 274 063; m 55 905 643. Tired hotel in need of renovation down by the port. Should only consider for a budget night if the youth hostel is full. **$$**

Maison des Jeunes de Kélibia (16 rooms) Av de la Mansoura; 72 296 105. Very well-run youth hostel, here since 1974. Most dorms have 4 beds & sea views, some with TVs. Communal toilets are spotless. Whole place is very nice & clean. **$**

Where to eat and drink *Map, opposite*

Toro Fish Av de Martyrs; m 28 777 536/427; f fishtoro123; 10.00–late daily. Probably the best seafood restaurant in town, overlooking the water, with a sign that looks suspiciously like the Red Bull logo. Try the *ojja fruits de mer* & the delicious sorbets. **$$$–$$$$**

La Siciliana Port de Peche; m 23 810 682; f; 11.30–late daily. Italian-Tunisian-run seafood restaurant with a simple but ever-changing chalkboard menu of the day. Similar to nearby Vieux Port, but cheaper & with a more secluded outdoor seating area, though less impressive views. **$$$**

Le Goéland Port de Peche; 72 273 074; m 98 343 538; f; 11.00–22.00 Mon–Sat. Nothing screams 'classy seafood restaurant' more than entering through the mouth of a giant replica prawn. But if you can get over the kitsch doorway, the seafood is actually pretty good, as are the views. **$$$**

Le Marin Bit Al Assa, Mansoura Beach; 72 208 072; e reservation.lemarin@gnet.tn; f; 09.00–21.30 daily. About 2km north of town on the delightfully sandy Mansoura Beach, this seafood restaurant has an excellent location on the water, with grassy outdoor seating area – & you can basically park on the beach. Convenient for walking northwards to Sidi Mansour. **$$$**

Vieux Port Rue Chandhly Khaznadar; m 52 940 440; f vieuxportt; 11.30–late daily. Up a cobbled street overlooking the fishing port, this unassuming seafood restaurant has a terrace decorated with amphorae & various flotsam & jetsam. Also hosts live music events. **$$$**

HITS 93 Av de Martyrs; m 29 535 477; e contact@hits.com.tn; f Hits.Tunisie; 09.00–midnight daily. Bright, modern fast-food restaurant offering pizzas, burgers, filled sandwiches, chicken & juices. Also does delivery. **$$**

La Florida Kélibia beach; m 25 296 248; 09.00–late daily. Billed as a restaurant but probably more a pub, with good views of the water. **$$**

L'Orientale Patisserie Av de Martyrs; m 52 074 448; f; 09.00–19.00 daily. Delicious fresh ice cream & a wide variety of cakes & cupcakes. **$$**

What to see and do The town's main sight, **Kélibia Fort** (summer 08.00–19.00 daily, winter 08.30–17.00 daily; 5DT) looms prominently over the centre atop a 150m-high hill. The present Byzantine fortifications date to the 6th century AD, although these were likely built on Punic foundations and have been changed and rebuilt many times since. The crenellated walls, almost complete, are made of huge blocks of stone and are reinforced with square towers at the corners. The fortress surrounds the remains of a much more ancient fort and some deep wells. Inside the fortress are several vaulted rooms, one of which, with three naves, was probably a chapel. The fortress is accessible by car or on foot up a steep road which is thankfully now run as a one-way system. It is an impressive structure, offering magnificent views of the surrounding coastline, and is well worth the slog up the hill. The fort is also the setting for **FIFAK** (Le Festival International du Film Amateur de Kélibia; w ftcafifak.com), quite possibly Africa's oldest amateur film festival, inaugurated in 1964.

At the base dotted among the modern city is an **archaeological site** from Roman Clupea, although there are no information boards on offer. Today you can see a few foundations and a house with a small peristyle, dating from between the 1st century BC and the 2nd century AD. A bust of Emperor Marcus Aurelius and some prominent mosaics were found here, but these have long since been moved to the museum in Nabeul or the Bardo.

North of Kélibia, **Mansoura** is a pleasant little corner, despite the growing number of mediocre concrete bunker-villas behind its graceful beach. The water is crystal-clear, the sand fine and white, and there is even a restaurant, Le Marin, with chairs around the rock pools. This stretch of beach gets very crowded during summer, however, as the car park makes it easy to drive to; if you head a little further north to **Sidi Mansour** you are more likely to find a private stretch of sand. Those looking to partake in watersports while in Kélibia should contact the **Club des Sports Nautiques de Kélibia (CSNK)** (Av des Martyrs; m 20 275 550; f CsnkClubDesSportsNautiquesKelibia), which rents various dinghies, sailboards and kayaks.

KORBA A small town on the Oued Bou Eddine, just 20km north of Nabeul, Korba sits at the centre of a perfect white-sand beach that stretches 13km southwards to Maamoura and 30km north to the outskirts of Kélibia. Large flocks of greater flamingos hang out in the two long bays behind Korba's beach in the winter months, but beyond that there aren't many sights. Almost nothing of this Roman city (known then as Julia Curubis) remains, although you might see traces of the aqueduct. Curubis is thought to have been the seat of an archbishop associated with the presence of St Cyprien here in AD275. From the Islamic period there are remains of the mausoleum of Sidi Moaouia and a mini ribat to protect the settlement from attacks by pirates. Every other year, usually in the summer, there is a week-long national festival of amateur theatre. Details are available from the Association Étoiles du Théâtre de Korba (f EtoilesTheatreKorba).

Where to stay and eat

Africa Jade Thalasso Hotel (257 rooms) ⊕ 36.560354, 10.858560; ☎ 72 384 633; w africajadethalasso.com. If you can get past the frankly ridiculous pastiche décor, this is a high-quality 4-star beach resort with good customer service that is very family-friendly. The steak in the à la carte restaurant is excellent & access to their beach alone is worth the price of a room for the night. **$$$$$**

✱ **Sawa Gite Rural** (2 rooms, 1 bungalow, camping) ⊕ 36.609196, 10.712879; m 22 605 555; e lamia.temimi@sawa.com.tn; f Sawagiterural. This working farm near a lake offers rooms in the main house, a separate bungalow with space for up to 10 guests & camping with outdoor bathrooms & solar showers. Among the activities are farm work (including checking on the snail farm!), cooking classes, cycling & donkey rides. There is a shop selling local produce in association with The Next Women Tunisie (w thenextwomentunisie.com), a local co-operative focusing on female empowerment. A fantastic option for a quiet, rural escape. **$$$–$$$$**

ZAGHOUAN AND AROUND

Some 55km south of Tunis and an excellent spot for day or weekend hikes from the capital, Zaghouan is dominated by the towering 1,295m-high Jebel Zaghouan, which sits southwest of town in the Dorsale Mountains and is a designated national park. Known as Ziqua in Roman times, the town was the starting point of the complex system of cisterns and aqueducts which carried fresh water over 132km to Carthage in the 2nd century AD. The spring and the start of the aqueduct can still be visited, about 2km out of town, but the real interest is the natural beauty of the national park. Zaghouan also serves as a useful jumping-off point for the nearby Roman ruins of Thuburbo Majus.

GETTING THERE AND AWAY Zaghouan is 55km south of Tunis on the C133 or C36 (about an hour's drive). SRTGN runs a number of local **buses**: the 841 links Zaghouan to Nabeul, the 842 to Enfidha and Sousse, and the 802 and 840 go to Tunis (Bab Alioua station). **Louages** connect Zaghouan to Hammamet, Nabeul and Tunis. The main louage and bus stop is on Avenue 14 Janvier, next to the BNA Bank.

The national park is to the south of town, with the water temple around 2km from the town centre. You will need your own car to explore.

WHERE TO STAY

Dar Aida (2 rooms) 9 Rue Hédi Chaker; m 98 379 449; e aidaham@gnet.tn; f maisondhotezaghouan. Traditional dar in the heart of the old town, opposite the Zaouia of Sidi Ali Azouz, offering some dbls with a balcony overlooking the garden. Excellent food; also has BBQ facilities. **$$$$**

Dar Zaghouan (15 rooms) Rue Errouaiguia, near Zaghouan Regional Hospital; m 26 309 103, 23 724 000; e darzaghouan@gmail.com; f DarZaghouan. Wooden ecohotel in the countryside northwest of town. Eclectic mix of room types, from Scandi-style wooden bungalows to grand old Tunisian décor in stone rooms. Lots of family activities, among which are visiting the farm's various animals (including ostrich), zip-lining, archery, high ropes course & kayaking. Very popular at w/ends. Pool & hammam sometimes open to non-residents. **$$$$**

Hôtel Les Nymphes (80 rooms) Zone Touristique Ras El Ain; 31 106 318/9; m 58 205 555; e lesnymphes.zaghouan@gmail.com; f hotel.les.nymphes. Recently renovated hotel in the forest less than 1km from the water temple. Great pool & outdoor seating areas overlooking the mountain. Rooms are clean & spacious with AC. **$$$**

Maison des Jeunes (85 beds) 36.399754, 10.141265; 72 675 265. In the government quarter to the west of town. Shared dorms are basic but clean; also offers meals. **$**

WHERE TO EAT AND DRINK

Dar Zaghouan Rue Errouaiguia, near Zaghouan Regional Hospital; m 26 309 103; f DarZaghouan; noon–21.00 daily. This ecohotel serves good-quality Tunisian cuisine using home-grown ingredients in green surroundings – eat under the vine-covered pergola or in the restaurant itself. Booking highly recommended. **$$$–$$$$**

La Jaconde Rue Kherredine; m 99 846 808; 10.00–16.00 Mon–Sat. Great little lunch spot serving fresh, tasty Tunisian classics in a small stone-&-wood restaurant. **$$$**

La Comida Cité el Bostene; m 54 517 101; 09.00–21.00 daily. Fast-food joint offering salads, makloub, pizzas, omelettes, baguette farci & tacos. **$$**

WHAT TO SEE AND DO Most of Zaghouan's attractions lie out of town, but there are a couple of places of note in the centre. Opposite the **municipal market** (Av 14 Janvier; 07.00–13.00 Mon–Sat) stands a **honorific arch**, dating from the 2nd century AD when Zaghouan was Roman Ziqua. Climb up the steps to the well-preserved arch, noting the bull's head on the keystone. Continuing along a street lined with cheap eateries and shops, turn sharp right uphill to come to a small square with a café. Close to the square is the former church of **St Helena Church of Zaghouan**, which opened in 1902 and is now used as a private school. If you continue about 300m uphill along Rue Sidi Ali Azouz, on your right you will see the **Zaouia of Sidi Ali Azouz**, noted for its intricately tiled walls and colourful stained-glass windows. Originally a 17th-century tomb, it is now a centre for Koranic studies.

Temple des Nymphes (36.386914, 10.131233; 24/7; free) Dating from the reign of Hadrian, this 2,210m^2 water temple is built into the hillside in the shadow of Jebel Zaghouan. It was intended to keep the gods happy and ensure continuous water flow along the 132km Zaghouan Aqueduct, which started in Zaghouan and flowed all the way to Carthage. Steps (safe to climb) lead to a semicircular wall of 12 alcoves, which once held life-size statues indicating the months of the year, though unfortunately all have now gone. The pool in the centre has been restored and again (occasionally) holds water. Contemplate the panoramic view, north and east over the plain towards the sea, as the Romans would have done. The site is easily walkable from Zaghouan, only around 2km from the town centre.

Jebel Zaghouan National Park Created in 2010 and centred by the 1,295m-tall Jebel Zaghouan, this national park is forested with holly oak and Aleppo pine and is home to various fauna including wild boar and Egyptian vulture. Little-visited Jebel Zaghouan is an incredibly diverse massif, with a lush forested north side and dramatic limestone cliffs on the southern side. On a clear day, you can see as far as Tunis and the Mediterranean Sea from the summit. But it's the connecting shepherd paths that wind their way along the slopes and gorges that make this small national park a true outdoor gem.

If you have your own vehicle, follow the tarmac road to Sidi Medien Mosque (⊕ 36.334783, 10.088153), park up and then hike northeast into the park on the gravel track. From here it is a 7km round-trip to the summit plateau (⊕ 36.352131, 10.111258), with an elevation gain of 820m, or a full 15.5km loop around the entire mountain. As long as you know where you are going it is not particularly technical and there is little exposure to heights. More details (and GPS trails) for these routes can be found on Jan Bakker's website (w tunisiatrails.blogspot.com) or in his book *Hiking in Jebel Zaghouan*. If you are looking for a guide to the mountain (or the various cave systems in the area, all of which require accredited guides to explore), contact the Association de Spéléologie et d'Escalade de Zaghouan (w speleo-tunisie.com). More details on hiking Zaghouan can also be found on my YouTube channel, YouTube Scafidi Travels. The park has no infrastructure, signage, official trail markings or accommodation options, so be sure to bring everything you need with you.

Thuburbo Majus (⊕ 36.402657, 9.902084; ⊕ 08.30–17.30 daily; 5DT) One of Tunisia's largest archaeological sites, the vast complex of Thuburbo Majus occupies a hilltop location above the town of El Fahs, 60km south along the P3 from Tunis (the turn-off is signposted). Covering some 40ha in its heyday, this wealthy Roman city was founded in AD27 by Emperor Augustus as a colony for veterans and grew to between 7,000 and 12,000 inhabitants by the 2nd century. It sat at an important trade crossing, encircled by hills except to the west, permitting a close watch on movement of people and trade between the plain and the coast along the route of the Oued el Kebir. The fertile hinterland produced cereals, olives and wine in abundance, providing a further boost to the economy in addition to that of toll/tax collection. However, the town declined as the Romans' authority waned, and once the Vandals were in power in the mid 5th century the town reverted to a village.

The site was first excavated by French archaeologist Charles-Joseph Tissot in 1857. The scale of the finds was so significant that they were still digging a century later, under the direction of Louis Poinssot, who was also involved in the excavations at Dougga (page 124). The level of preservation of some monuments (especially the Capitol), the lack of visitors and the proximity to Tunis make this a must-see on any archaeology enthusiast's itinerary.

There is a car park at the entrance, a small café and a clean toilet.

Exploring the site The **Forum** and the **Capitol** dominate the ruins and are a good starting point for exploring the site, as they offer a great vantage point from which

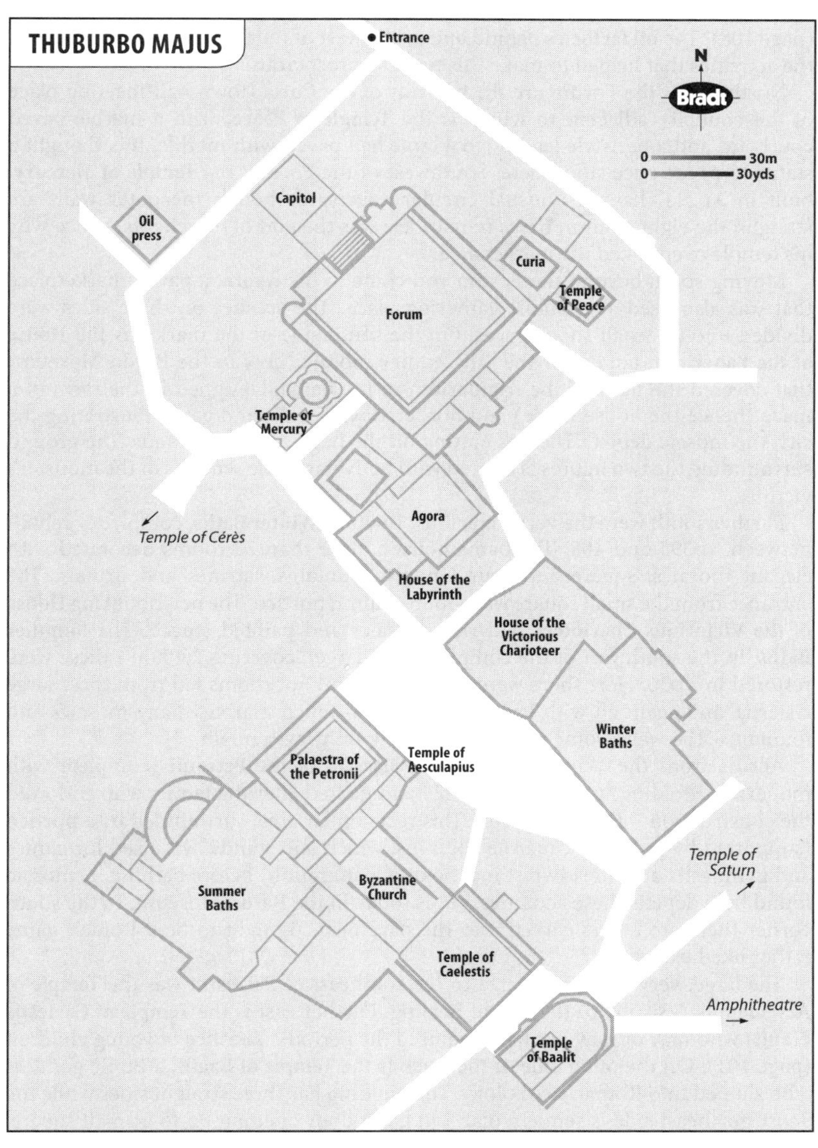

to view the complex. Built between AD161 and 192 and restored with some layout changes in around AD376, the well-preserved, $49m^2$ Forum is bordered by a portico on three sides. The fourth side leads, by means of a broad flight of stairs, to the Capitol, built in AD168. Great efforts were made to raise the level of this building to give it the height it needed for its imposing position overlooking the town. Six fluted Corinthian columns, each 8.5m high, stand tall today. The building includes carved Latin dedications to Emperor Marcus Aurelius, Commodus and the triad of Jupiter, Juno and Minerva. All that remains of the statue of Jupiter is the head and foot, once an impossible 8m high, and today these are in the Bardo Museum (page 108). The **oil factories** behind and to the west of the Capitol are a reminder of the activities that helped to make this town so prosperous.

Northeast of the Forum are the remains of the **Curia** (town hall/meeting place of the council), adjacent to which is the **Temple of Peace,** with a marble-paved courtyard and a peristyle leading to a large hall paved with marble. It is thought a statue to peace once stood here. Southwest of the Forum, the **Temple of Mercury**, built in AD211, has an unusual circular courtyard though the outer walls are straight; the eight column bases remain. He was the god of merchants, hence why his temple overlooked the market area.

Moving south beyond the Forum you come to the **Agora**, a paved marketplace that was also used as a public gathering place. The arcades on three sides were divided into 21 small shop spaces. On the south side of the market is the **House of the Labyrinth**, famed for the 4th-century mosaic (now in the Bardo Museum) that covered the floor of the frigidarium in the baths. Designed in the form of a maze (hence the house name) and bordered with walls and gates, illustrating the city, the mosaic depicts Theseus cutting off the head of the Minotaur. The ground surrounding the two figures is littered with body parts, the remains of the monster's victims.

Further south were the very luxurious, 1,600m^2 **Winter Baths**, completely rebuilt between AD395 and 408. The baths housed more than 20 rooms decorated with elegant mosaics, square and round pools, fountains, latrines and urinals. The entrance from the small square was a four-column portico. The neighbouring **House of the Victorious Charioteer** had rich mosaics and painted stucco. The **Summer Baths**, in the southwest of the complex, were larger, covering 2,400m^2; these were restored in AD36. Here there were cold, warm and hot rooms fed from three large cisterns, and again all with lavish decoration – much marble, many mosaics and fountains. The walls, some mosaics and a few archways remain.

Across from the Winter Baths, the **Palaestra of the Petronii** (complete with modern scaffolding) was built in AD225 and named after the family who endowed the construction – Petronius Felix. This rectangular area, surrounded by a portico (supported by grey/black marble columns, which still stand), was used for games and gymnastic activities (wrestling, boxing, pankration) before bathing. A mosaic found here depicts these activities, but is today in the Bardo Museum. In the south corner there are letters carved into the pavement, thought to be a Roman game rather like Lexicon.

The large, very overgrown area to the southeast of Palaestra was the **Temple of Aesculapius**, a shrine to the god of healing. Further east is the **Temple of Caelestis (Tanit)** who may or may not have required the periodic sacrifice of young children (page 101). On the other side of the track is the **Temple of Baalit**, a Punic goddess who slipped into Roman mythology. The building has three straight sides while the short northeast side is semicircular and has a door opening on to a small square, smaller than but similar to the square by the Winter Baths.

To the northeast of the site and at the highest point in town, the **Temple of Saturn** later became a church, though there is not much left here. Again, as with the Capitol, there is evidence of 'building up the land' before constructing the temple. The ruins of the **amphitheatre**, hollowed out of the hillside, can be found to the very edge of the site. Nearby is one of the cisterns for water supply. The remains of this cistern to the south of the site are huge and show it was large enough to have an inner gallery constructed on the inside rim.

The **Temple of Cérès**, to the west of the site on sloping ground, had a 900m^2 courtyard, the centre decorated with mosaics and a portico with three gateways.

Later this portico was turned into a church, using half of the courtyard, of which little remains today. A number of tombs were found in the church, one containing jewels.

St Marie du Zit This small village on the C35, about 15km northeast of Zaghouan, will be of interest to World War II enthusiasts as the site where Afrika Korps commander, General Jürgen von Arnim, was captured by/de facto surrendered to Allied forces on 12 May 1943, the day before Marshal Giovanni Messe, commander of the Italian First Army, surrendered unconditionally to the British Eighth Army, thereby ending the battle for North Africa.

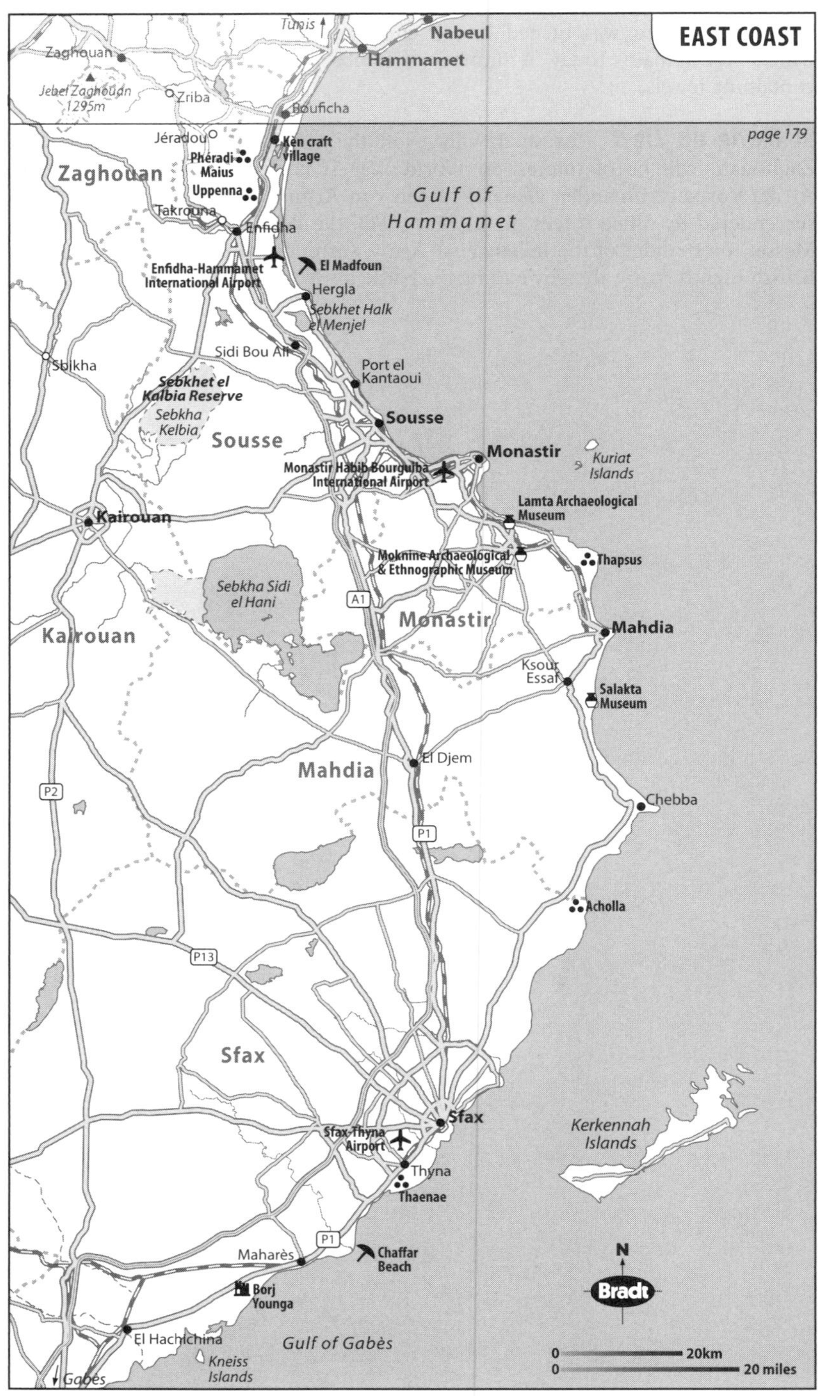
EAST COAST
Tunis
Nabeul
Hammamet
Zaghouan
Jebel Zaghouan 1295m
Zriba
Bouficha
page 179
Jéradou
Kèn craft village
Pheradi Maius
Uppenna
Zaghouan
Gulf of Hammamet
Takrouna
Enfidha
Enfidha-Hammamet International Airport
El Madfoun
Hergla
Sebkhet Halk el Menjel
Sidi Bou Ali
Sbikha
Port el Kantaoui
Sebkhet el Kalbia Reserve
Sebkha Kelbia
Sousse
Sousse
Monastir
Kuriat Islands
Monastir Habib Bourguiba International Airport
Kairouan
Lamta Archaeological Museum
Moknine Archaeological & Ethnographic Museum
Thapsus
Sebkha Sidi el Hani
A1
Monastir
Mahdia
Kairouan
Ksour Essaf
Salakta Museum
El Djem
Mahdia
P2
Chebba
P1
Acholla
P13
Sfax
Sfax
Kerkennah Islands
Sfax-Thyna Airport
Thyna
Thaenae
P1
Maharès
Chaffar Beach
N
Bradt
Borj Younga
El Hachichina
Gulf of Gabès
Kneiss Islands
Gabès
0 20km
0 20 miles

6

The East Coast

With its fine beaches, turquoise sea and grand white hotels, this part of Tunisia is often associated with package holidays, and it is true that much of the coastline – from Sousse (known as the Pearl of the Sahel) to Monastir (birthplace of former president, Habib Bourguiba) – is densely developed with hotels and tourism infrastructure squarely aimed at the European market. But there is much more to detain you than just sun, sea and sand. Owing to good natural harbours, this stretch of coast was a highly desirable spot for ancient settlements and evidence of Roman cities is found across the region, notably at El Djem, one of Tunisia's most impressive UNESCO World Heritage Sites.

In the south is entrepreneurial and energetic Sfax, an industrious city with an enchanting medina and the jumping-off point for the unique and unspoilt Kerkennah Islands, which should also be on any itinerary. Elsewhere, wildlife lovers will want to seek out the turtle-nesting grounds at Chebba and the important bird habitat of the Kneiss Islands, while those with an interest in World War II will find much to explore around Enfidha and the hilltop Amazigh settlement of Takrouna.

SOUSSE *Telephone code: +73*

The third-largest city in the country after Tunis and Sfax, Sousse is best known for its wonderful Mediterranean coastline, luxurious beach hotels and excellent seafood restaurants. But it is more than just a beach resort, and the city also boasts thousands of years of fascinating history. The UNESCO-listed medina throws up a new surprise every time you explore it, while the archaeological museum is one of the finest in the country. The diversity of Sousse's population is reflected in its religious architecture, with ancient mosques, churches and even the odd synagogue jostling for position on the city's busy streets.

Today, Sousse serves as a regional cultural hub, with numerous spaces for live performances and a selection of annual arts festivals. Sousse is also a great base from which to explore the wider region. The two former Tunisian capitals of Kairouan and Mahdia, as well as the birthplace of Tunisia's founding father, Habib Bourguiba, are all within easy reach.

HISTORY Sousse was founded as a Phoenician trading post in the 9th century BC, making it one of the oldest ports in the Mediterranean. A 2015 study in the *Journal of Human Genetics* showed that the people of Sousse have a more diversified genetic structure than any other studied Tunisian population, a testament to the influence of successive waves of migration to this town since its foundation. When Carthage became the leading city in the area in the 4th century BC, Sousse entered its sphere of influence, mainly through trade. During the Second Punic War, Hannibal used Sousse as his base, but was defeated in 202BC. Then, during the Third Punic War,

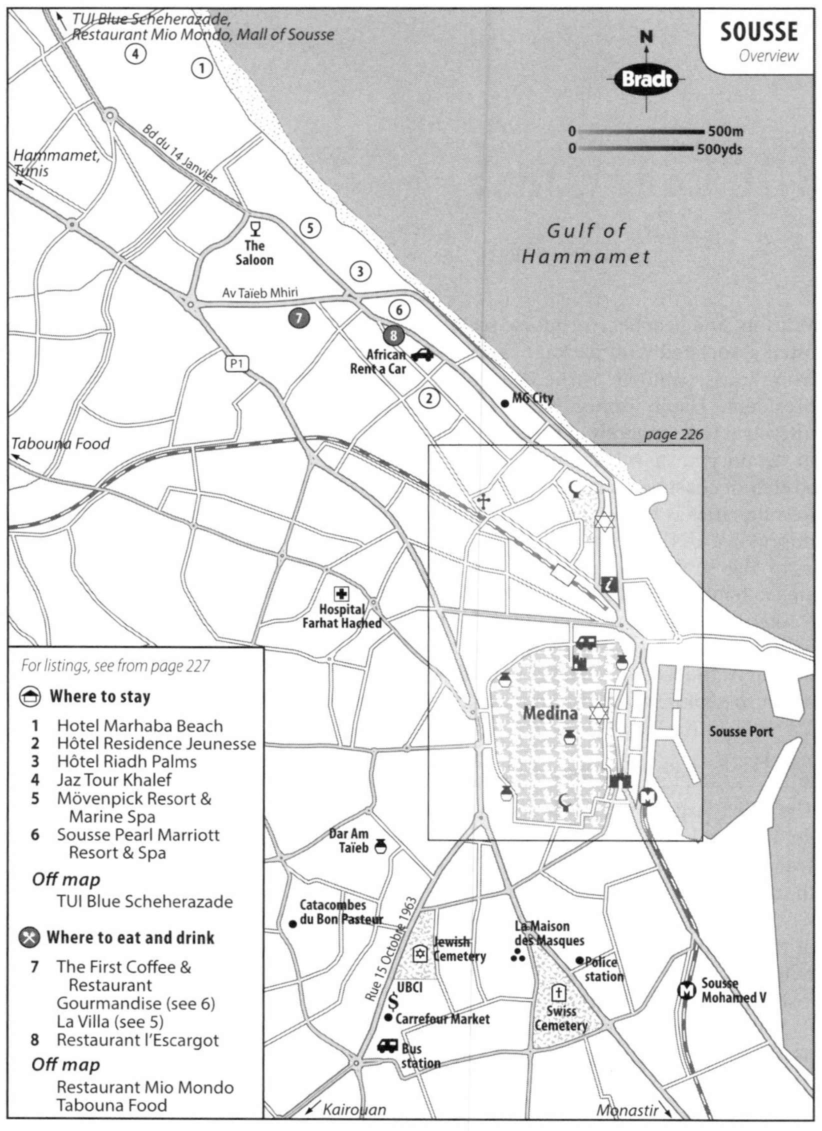

Sousse's savvy residents switched allegiance to Rome, thereby avoiding destruction and gaining the status of free town, acquiring the Latin name of Hadrumetum. Unfortunately, in 46BC Caesar defeated the armies of Pompey in Thapsus (50km down the coast from Hadrumetum), and Sousse found itself on the wrong side of this conflict, with Caesar imposing heavy taxation on the town as punishment. Nevertheless, under the rule of Trajan (AD98–117) the city became an important commercial centre thanks to its natural harbours.

Under Diocletian (AD284–305), Sousse became capital of the new province of Byzacium, and was the home of a flourishing Christian community, as evidenced by the catacombs (page 233). Under later invasions, Sousse had a few name changes: it was renamed Hunericopolis under the Vandals; and when retaken by the Byzantines, it was redubbed Justinianopolis. With the Arab invasions of the 7th century, it was destroyed.

In the 9th century, with the coming of the Aghlabid Dynasty to Kairouan, it was again rebuilt and prospered as that inland city's main port; it was from Sousse that the Muslim armies heading for Sicily would have embarked. Sousse was taken in the 12th century by the Sicily-based Normans, the mid-Mediterranean regional power of the day, and in the 16th century by Spain. With its port installations, the city was a target in World War II, and was seriously damaged in 1942–43.

Since the 1960s, Sousse has become a major town, with service industries and tourism important in the local economy: an almost unbroken strip of hotels, some of which are now mothballed since the pandemic, runs the whole way up to Chott Meriem and Akouda. Further north, Port el Kantaoui, Tunisia's first purpose-built marina, has been a great success, still popular nearly 20 years after it was opened, despite being the location of the 2015 terror attack.

GETTING THERE AND AWAY

By air The nearest airport is Habib Bourguiba, only 15km (20 minutes' drive) away at Monastir, while Enfidha-Hammamet and Tunis-Carthage are 50km/155km away respectively. See page 54 for details of routes servicing these airports.

By road Tunis is 155km to the north (about 1 hour 45 minutes' drive along the A1 toll road). SNTRI **buses** run from Tunis (Moncef Bey) to Sousse (2hrs 15mins; 10.8DT one-way) and **louage** services depart from Gare Routière Sud (page 94). The main louage and bus station in the centre of Sousse is on Boulevard Yahia Ibn Omar, just north of the medina, where buses from Monastir and Mahdia tend to arrive. Most other routes (including Tunis) use the louage stop on Rue el Masjed el Aksa at Sousse's southern end. There is also another in the east of the city by the massive Hospital Sahloul (Gare Routière Sahloul), at the end of Rue Salim Ammar, which services more local routes such as to the Mall of Sousse or Hammam Sousse. Buses and louages covering more local destinations within Sousse Governorate tend to run from the bus stop on Avenue 15 October.

By rail There are generally around five SNCFT trains per day between Tunis and Sousse (2hrs 20mins), with the first departure before 06.00 and the last departure after 21.00. The main train station is very central and close to the marina.

There is also a metro line (the Sahel Metro, which connects Sousse to Mahdia with a spur for Monastir.

GETTING AROUND Sousse's city limits stretch almost 10km along the coast. Many of the large beach hotels sit on a strip of coastline at the northern end of town off Boulevard du 14 Janvier, while the medina and port are at least 1.5km south of here.

By road Route maps for regional **bus** networks can be seen on the well-designed Commune de Sousse Open Géo Data website (**w** sousse-plus-open-data-sousse.hub.arcgis.com). These services will get you as far north as Hergla, as far inland as Sidi Al-Hani (about halfway to Kairouan on the P12) and as far south as Zaramidin. Sousse also has a hilariously kitsch **road train** plying the hotel strip to the north of town all the way up to Port el Kantaoui (5DT return).

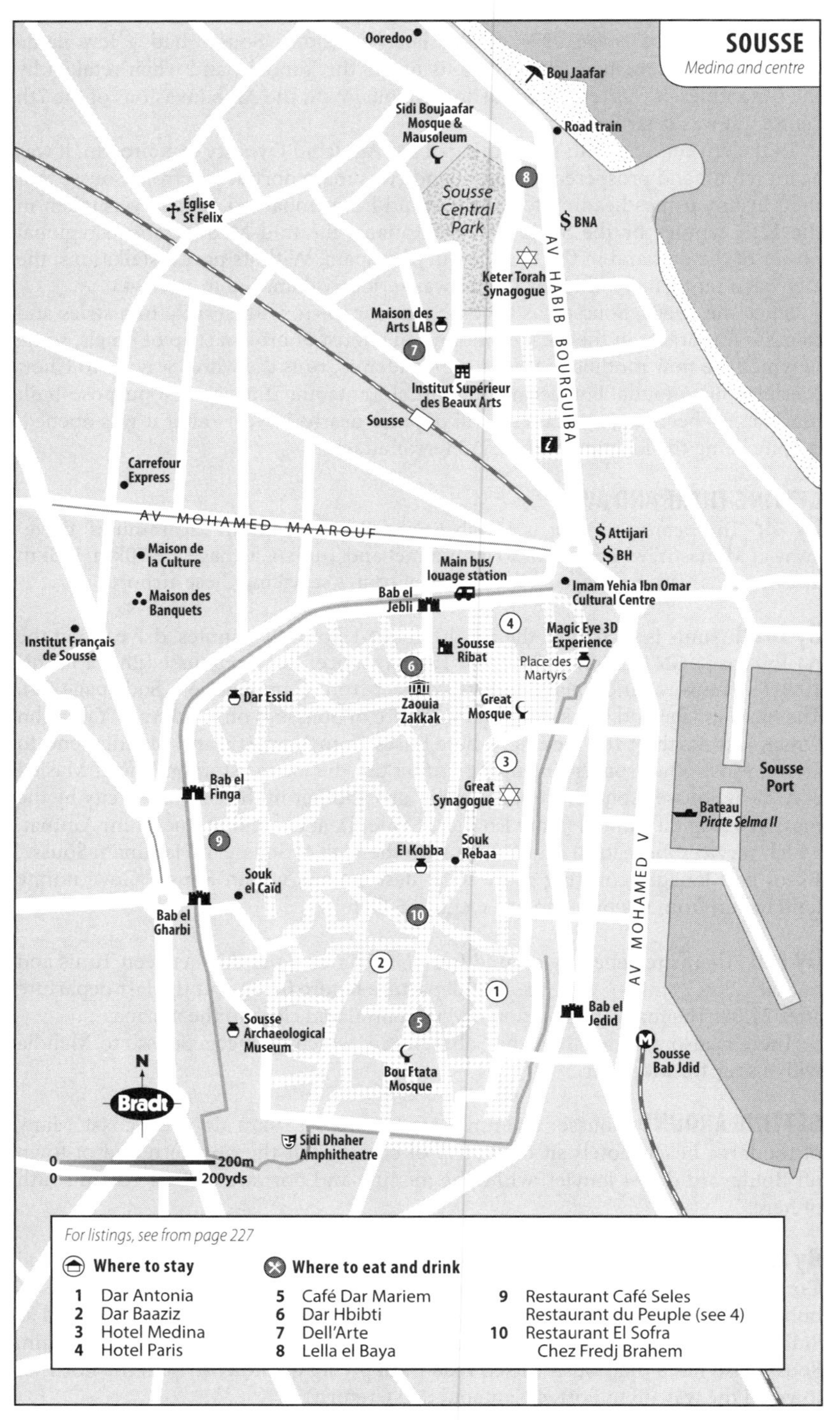
SOUSSE
Medina and centre
Ooredoo
Bou Jaafar
Road train
Sidi Boujaafar Mosque & Mausoleum
Sousse Central Park
$ BNA
Église St Felix
Keter Torah Synagogue
AV HABIB BOURGUIBA
Maison des Arts LAB
Institut Supérieur des Beaux Arts
Sousse
Carrefour Express
AV MOHAMED MAAROUF
$ Attijari
$ BH
Maison de la Culture
Main bus/ louage station
Imam Yehia Ibn Omar Cultural Centre
Maison des Banquets
Bab el Jebli
Magic Eye 3D Experience
Institut Français de Sousse
Sousse Ribat
Place des Martyrs
Dar Essid
Zaouia Zakkak
Great Mosque
Sousse Port
Bab el Finga
Great Synagogue
Bateau Pirate Selma II
El Kobba
Souk Rebaa
Souk el Caïd
Bab el Gharbi
AV MOHAMED V
Bab el Jedid
Sousse Archaeological Museum
Sousse Bab Jdid
Bou Ftata Mosque
N
Bradt
Sidi Dhaher Amphitheatre
0 200m
0 200yds
For listings, see from page 227
Where to stay
1 Dar Antonia
2 Dar Baaziz
3 Hotel Medina
4 Hotel Paris
Where to eat and drink
5 Café Dar Mariem
6 Dar Hbibti
7 Dell'Arte
8 Lella el Baya
9 Restaurant Café Seles
Restaurant du Peuple (see 4)
10 Restaurant El Sofra Chez Fredj Brahem

For short journeys around town, yellow **taxis** can be flagged down. Rather helpfully, the Bolt ride-hailing app (page 55) operates in Sousse.

If you are renting a **car**, it is better to do so from one of the international agencies at Monastir Habib Bourguiba International Airport (page 241). There are, however, a number of rental outfits in town clustered around Avenue Taïeb Mehiri, such as **African Rent Car** (m 27 775 662, 20 733 000; e africanrentcar1212@gmail.com; f; ⌚ 08.30–17.30 Mon–Sat), but they are of varying degrees of quality. Traffic can get bad during rush hour and finding street parking in the centre can also be an issue.

By metro Running roughly every 40 minutes from 05.00 to 22.00, the Sahel Metro from Sousse to Mahdia has a couple of stops in town, the main being Sousse Bab Jdid, right next to the port (⊕ 35.823039, 10.641536). It then heads south to Sousse Mohamed V and Sousse South before continuing to Skanes-Monastir airport station and eventually Mahdia. Schedules are available on w sncft.com.tn.

TOURIST INFORMATION

Commissariat Régional au Tourisme de Sousse 1 Av Habib Bourguiba; ☎ 73 225 157; e crt.sousse@ontt.tourism.tn; ⌚ 08.00–13.00 & 14.00–17.00 Mon–Fri

WHERE TO STAY

You have two main options in Sousse: the strip of beach resorts that stretch northwards from the town centre towards Port el Kantaoui, or the medina itself. You will generally get a much larger room for your money in the resorts, but there are some incredible properties available in the medina if you are interested in a more authentic stay.

Along the beach *Map, page 224*

Jaz Tour Khalef (500 rooms) Bd du 14 Janvier; ☎ 73 241 844; e sofien.cherif@jaztourkhalef.com; w jaztourkhalef.net; f. A larger, more expensive version of the Hotel Marhaba Beach. With a reputation for good customer service, this family-friendly resort has a spa, large pool, private beach & a very enthusiastic animation team. **$$$$$**

Mövenpick Resort & Marine Spa (618 rooms) Bd du 14 Janvier; ☎ 73 202 000; w movenpick.com/en/africa/tunisia/sousse/hotel-sousse.html. Luxury 5-star resort in an excellent location: has a private beach & spa but still close enough for town centre (medina) to be walkable. The buffet-style Mosaique Restaurant serves a great selection of cuisine including Japanese & Spanish, & there's also a highly rated Mediterranean restaurant (page 228). **$$$$$**

Hotel Marhaba Beach (259 rooms) Bd du 14 Janvier; ☎ 73 243 869; w marhabahotels.tn. Probably the best AI resort of the bunch on the beach to the north of the town centre: great customer service, pristine beach, large pool with swim-up bar, & rooms with balconies & sea views available. **$$$$**

Sousse Pearl Marriott Resort & Spa (222 rooms) Abdelhamid El Kadhi Av; ☎ 73 104 000; e reservations.soussepearlresort@marriott.com; f SoussePearlMarriott. Billed as a 'lifestyle beach resort', this Marriott feels very upmarket & elegant. Rooms are large & bright with modern fittings (go for one with a sea view). Access to the beach is via an underground tunnel from the pool area (⌚ 06.00–22.00 daily). **$$$$**

TUI Blue Scheherazade (221 rooms) Bd du 14 Janvier; ☎ 73 241 433; w tui-blue.com/en/en/hotels/tui-blue-scheherazade. Adults-only AI hotel intended for couples, with private beach, 3 restaurants & spa. **$$$$**

Hôtel Riadh Palms (650 rooms) Bd du 14 Janvier; ☎ 73 225 700; m 29 550 000; e info@hotelriadhpalms.com; w hotelriadhpalms.com. Boasting the same great views of the beach as its Mövenpick neighbour, this dated hotel also has a nice pool area. Some issues with maintenance but cheap for the location when it offers discounted rooms. **$$–$$$**

Hôtel Residence Jeunesse (21 rooms) Rue Mongi Slim; ☎ 73 213 373; e residencejeunesse21@outlook.fr; f ResidenceJeunesse21. Variety of rooms at this basic hostel: most expensive have en suite (a small wet room), representing great value for money, but even rooms with shared bathrooms only share with 1 other room. Rooms on 2nd floor upwards have better light from large windows. Most also have AC. Has a loyalty stamp scheme: 12th night free! **$**

Medina *Map, page 226*

✱ **Dar Antonia** (4 rooms) 21 Rue Kaabar; ☎ 73 232 122; **m** 25 502 008; **w** darantonia.com. Set around a central courtyard in a restored 400-year-old medina home, rooms here are well designed, combining minimalist architecture with the odd Tunisian flourish. The décor mixes historical elements with local craftsmanship & the communal spaces are gorgeous, especially the library & rooftop terrace. At the time of writing the dar was being expanded to include a neighbouring building, which should increase the number of rooms available & also enlarge the rooftop space. Can also organise cookery classes & trips into the souks of the medina to shop for meal ingredients. **$$$$**

Dar Baaziz (5 rooms) 7 Rue Sidi Baaziz; **m** 98 400 154; **f** darbaaziz.sousse. Dating from 1775, this traditional home offers rooms with fantastic big dbl beds with elaborate wooden frames, set around a plant-filled courtyard with fountain. **$$$**

Hotel Medina (12 rooms) 15 Rue Othman Osman; ☎ 73 221 722; **w** hotel-medina.com. Good-value budget hotel right next to the Great Mosque. Variety of room types, but recently refurbished so all now have AC & heating. **$$**

Hotel Paris (36 rooms) 15 Rue des Remparts Nord; ☎ 73 220 564; **w** hotelparis-sousse.com. Clean, comfortable, basic rooms in the medina, above an excellent restaurant. Cheapest rooms have shared bathrooms or you can pay more for an en suite; all have AC, TV & shower. **$–$$**

WHERE TO EAT AND DRINK *Map, page 226, unless otherwise stated*

La Villa [map, page 224] Mövenpick Resort, Bd du 14 Janvier; ☎ 73 202 000; ⌚ 19.00–midnight Tue–Sun. Excellent selection of Mediterranean haute cuisine with an extensive wine list. **$$$$$**

Restaurant l'Escargot [map, page 224] Av Taïeb Mhiri; ☎ 73 224 779; **f** restaurant.escargot.sousse; ⌚ noon–23.30 daily. Recently renovated old-style French restaurant in a cosy setting, packed to the rafters with antiques (including various firearms on the wall). Good selection of fish & meats – & yes, there are snails on the menu. **$$$$**

Dar Hbibti Restaurant 14 Rue de Secile; **m** 98 622 218, 52 291 653. Hard to miss thanks to its bright-yellow doors, this very popular Tunisian restaurant in the medina does great couscous (lamb, fish or vegetable) in traditional surroundings. **$$$**

Dell'Arte Pl de la Gare Centrale; **m** 54 523 921; **f**; ⌚ noon–22.00 Mon–Sat. Authentic Italian restaurant with great risotto & tortellini. **$$$**

The First Coffee & Restaurant [map, page 224] Av Taïeb Mhiri; **m** 29 825 000; **e** cafe@firstclass.com.tn; **f** thefirstcofferesto; ⌚ 07.30–midnight daily. Renovated in 2021, this slick café serves an assortment of decent Meditteranean fare including seafood, pastas & pizzas. But Italians be warned: it serves a pizza with a crust made of hotdogs. It is truly an abomination! **$$$**

Restaurant Café Seles 42 Rue Abounawas; **m** 98 562 847; **w** cafeseles.weebly.com; ⌚ 09.00–21.00 Mon–Fri, 09.00–22.00 Sat–Sun. Here since 2000, Sami & Fuzia serve up delicious home-cooked Tunisian cuisine in this family-operated restaurant & café. House specials include traditional couscous (fish or lamb), Moroccan kebab & grilled fish. **$$$**

✱ **Restaurant du Peuple** 15 Rue des Remparts Nord; ☎ 73 220 564; **m** 99 199 300; **f** restaurantdupeuple; ⌚ noon–17.00 Mon–Thu, noon–18.00 Sat–Sun. You will be lured in by the delicious smells wafting off the charcoal grill of this small restaurant, located inside the medina's Hotel Paris. Great authentic Tunisian cuisine; try the *cocotte berbère* (Berber casserole), which can come with chicken, beef or lamb. **$$$**

Gourmandise [map, page 224] Abdelhamid El Kadhi Av; ☎ 73 104 006; **w** gourmandise.com.tn; ⌚ 07.00–20.00 daily. Expect high-quality pastries, coffees & sandwiches from this well-established Tunisian patisserie chain, in the base of the Marriott building (but with a separate entrance). **$$–$$$**

Restaurant Mio Mondo [map, page 224] Bd du 14 Janvier; ☎ 73 273 243; **e** medina.city@gmail.

com; f miomondo.coffeeandmore; ⌚ 07.00–late daily. High-quality café & restaurant serving mainly Mediterranean fare, with all sorts of mezze options. Also a good brunch spot. $$–$$$

Tabouna Food [map, page 224] Av Imam Mouslem; m 27 771 105; ⌚ 11.30–late daily. Small wooden-fronted restaurant with chalkboard daily menus of great, authentic Tunisian cuisine. $$–$$$

Lella el Baya 5th fl, Ahla Centre; m 21 181 781; f cafe.lella.beya; ⌚ 08.00–20.00 daily. Centrally located café serving the usual assortment of drinks, sweets, fast food, pasta & grilled items, with great views of the water. $$

Restaurant El Sofra Chez Fredj Brahem 6 Rue El Soffra; m 40 508 488, 23 372 001; ⌚ 10.00–late daily. A hidden gem tucked down a back street in the medina (look out for the red sign & blue gate). Does especially good seafood options, such as couscous or *calamars farcis* (stuffed squid). $$

Café Dar Mariem Bd el Arbi; m 21 475 378; f cafe.dar.mariem. This café is easy to spot with a bright-yellow wooden front with 2 (rather sad) painted turtle shells outside. Great place for a coffee (with free Wi-Fi) while exploring the medina. $

ENTERTAINMENT AND NIGHTLIFE Much of the partying in Sousse happens inside the all-inclusive resorts, which are generally kitted out with their own bars and nightclubs. However, if you wander down the side streets between Avenue Taïeb Mhiri and Avenue Hédi Chaker (by the corniche) in high season you will find all sorts of less-than-reputable (but still safe) pool halls, bars and faux Irish pubs. Another option is **The Saloon** (Bd du 14 Janvier; m 28 636 636; f Saloontn; ⌚ 11.30–late daily), a bizarre Wild West-themed steak restaurant and disco, with a large outdoor seating area in front of a stage which features live music and belly dancing.

SHOPPING The **medina** has a number of interesting souks, mainly situated around the north end of the Rue d'Angleterre. On the west side is **Souk Rebaa**, specialising in fabrics and perfume, while those entering from the western Bab el Gharbi will wander straight through **Souk el Caïd**, selling mainly fresh produce and household goods.

Otherwise, the truly enormous **Mall of Sousse** (☎ 70 555 880; w mallofsousse.tn; ⌚ summer 09.00–23.00 daily, winter 09.00–21.00 daily), 15km north of town on the P1, has a Carrefour supermarket, food court, kids' play area and Pathé cinema.

OTHER PRACTICALITIES The **Hospital Farhat Hached** (Rue Ibn El Jazzar; ☎ 73 102 500) is the main university hospital in town, attached to the Ibn El Jazzar Medical Faculty of Sousse. ATMs can be found all over town, including in the medina.

WHAT TO SEE AND DO The main draw in Sousse is clearly the UNESCO-listed medina, but the areas immediately to the north, south and west also make for rewarding exploration, with all manner of fascinating historical sites interspersed with modern attractions. **Bou Jaaafar**, located just north of the marina, is the city's main beach, where many of the popular waterfront hotels are also located.

The medina ⚑ Unlike its counterpart in Tunis, Sousse's fine old medina is still surrounded by long stretches of the original walls, first built in AD859 by the Aghlabids (although incorporating some parts of a previous Byzantine fortress) and restored in 1205 by the Almohads. Those entering from the west side do so via **Bab el Gharbi** (Western Gate) or **Bab el Finga** (Gate of the Blade, named after the French guillotine that was set up here in colonial times), two of the six surviving gates. On the east side you can enter via **Bab el Jedid** (New Gate), or through **Place des Martyrs** in the north, on which stands a **monument** by Tunisian sculptor Hédi Selmi (1934–95) of seven figures holding up a man, dedicated to those who died in World War II. To the northeast of the medina is an attraction you might not expect in such a historic part of town. The **Magic Eye 3D Experience** (Soula Centre, Rue Habib Thameur; m 23 635 000; e magiceye3dsousse@gmail.com; f magiceye3dsousse; 09.00–20.00 daily; 15DT) offers interactive displays filled with 3D optical illusions that you access via an app – plenty of good opportunities for weird Instagram selfies, and it now also has indoor glow-in-the-dark minigolf.

Continuing into the medina, your next point of interest is much more historically significant: the 9th-century AD **Great Mosque (Grande Mosquée de Sousse)** (Rue Al Madina Almounawara; w tunisiepatrimoine.tn/monuments/la-grande-mosquee-de-sousse; 08.00–noon Mon–Thu, Sat–Sun, 08.00–11.30 Fri, though non-Muslims are permitted only into the central courtyard). Built under the Aghlabid emir, Abou Abbas Mohammed, it was likely a conversion of a kasbah built a few years earlier. Further renovations and restorations took place during the Zirid period (972–1148), when the *mihrab* (a niche indicating the direction of Mecca) was added and a fourth portico in front of the prayer hall, and then later under the Muradites in 1675. On two corners, large, round towers dominate the marble-floored courtyard and make it look like the fortress it may originally have been. Overall, the monument is very simple, the courtyard being decorated solely by inscriptions around its sides.

Unusually, it is also lacking a minaret, so the call to prayer comes from the northeast corner tower or the **Sousse Ribat** (off Rue de l'Église; m 54 640 715; summer 08.00–19.00 Tue–Sun, winter 09.30–noon & 14.00–18.00 Tue–Sun; 7DT) to the northwest. The oldest ribat in Tunisia (and one of the oldest in North Africa), it is an integral element of the medina's claim to UNESCO World Heritage Site status. Constructed under Aghlabid ruler Ziyadet Allah I in AD820, the ribat was part of a series of 9th-century coastal strongpoints built to defend the coast of Ifrikiya against the Byzantines. Like most other early Islamic buildings in Ifrikiya, the ribat was built using materials from older sites, as can be seen at the entrance where antique columns are placed on either side of the door. The architectural approach here served as the model for the ribat in nearby Monastir (page 243). There is nothing particularly elaborate about the 38m^2 structure: it has towers at all four corners, the main one being the watchtower from where there is a good view over the city and sea. On the first floor, a vast prayer room (which non-Muslims can enter) takes up the entire south side of the building. The ribat has been much restored, and the buildings which once surrounded it have been cleared away so you can see the structure as an urban monument, isolated from context, much as it must have been when it was first built – although no doubt the sea came right up to the walls back then.

Heading west from the ribat, you reach one of the medina's more unusual buildings: the 17th-century **Zaouia Zakkak** (Rue el Aghalba), an Ottoman construction distinguished by its remarkable but rather bijou Hanefite octagonal minaret. Sadly it is closed to non-Muslims, as it is still an actively used religious building. Continuing west to the outer walls, you come to **Dar Essid** (65 Rue du Rempart Nord; t 73 220 529; m 96 923 470; f; summer 10.00–19.00 daily, winter 10.00–18.00 daily; 4DT), a privately owned museum that showcases what the life of a wealthy 19th-century family in Sousse medina might have been like. There are also some Roman artefacts on display here, and its tower gives panoramic views of Sousse.

Heading south from here towards **Bab el Gharbi**, you can then cut eastwards back into the medina along **Souk el Caïd**, taking in the sights and smells of this fresh-food market. Eventually you hit the building known locally as **El Kobba**, home of the Museum of Arts and Popular Traditions (Rue Laroussi Zarrouk, Souk des Orfèvres; 73 229 574; 08.45–16.45 Mon–Wed, 08.45–14.15 Sat–Sun; 2DT, plus 1DT to photograph or 3DT to film). A 10th-century structure with a unique swirl-patterned cupola, the only one of its kind in Tunisia, the museum has several displays on traditional dress and culture, but few information signs. There is also a cool, shady underground café which makes for some welcome respite from the heat of the medina in summer.

Just to the northeast of El Kobba, cutting through the Souk Rebaa (page 229), is the **Great Synagogue** (Rue de France; 35.825889, 10.639833). From the outside, there is absolutely no indication that this was once a synagogue, with the walls and even entrance obstructed by street vendors selling clothes. Inside, the place of worship is sadly derelict (practising Jews in the city instead use Keter Torah Synagogue, just to the north of the medina; page 232), though local tour guides (page 40) may be able to arrange access.

Heading southwards from the synagogue, you eventually hit the 9th-century **Bou Ftata Mosque** (Rue d'Angleterre; closed at the time of writing) at the far southern end of the medina. Built between 838 and 841, this is likely one of the oldest mosques in the city and may have been the private worship site for the Aghlabid emir, Abu Iqal al-Aghlab ibn Ibrahimand. It has been designated as a Tunisian cultural site since 1945, and may have served as the model upon which both the Great Mosque of Sousse and Tunis's Zitouna Mosque were based. Note the bright white, square minaret which was added during the Hafsid period, a good 400 years after the original construction. To the southwest is the **Sidi Dhaher Amphitheatre** (Av Soudan), a modern construction just behind the Kasbah that is one of the venues for the annual **Festival International de Sousse** (e contact@festivaldesousse.art; festivalSousse), a month-long (July/August) musical festival that has been taking place since shortly after independence. The amphitheatre is not open to the public outside live performance times.

The highest point of the historic centre of Sousse, the southwest end of the medina is dominated by the **Kasbah**, built in the 11th century and extended in the 16th around an old signal tower (the Khalef) dating to AD859. Today the fort is home to the **Sousse Archaeological Museum** (Rue Abou Kacem Echabi; 73 219 011; w tunisiepatrimoine.tn/musees/musee-archeologique-de-sousse; summer 09.00–18.00 Tue–Sun, winter 09.00–17.00 Tue–Sun; 10/5DT non-resident/resident), which has exhibits detailing the history of Carthage. Displays include finds from the Tophet of Hadrumetum (a Carthaginian cemetery), such as votive and funerary stones, sacrificial urns and Punic jars, some dating to the 7th century BC, as well as a detailed discussion on the Carthaginian practice of child sacrifice, which has been a topic of furious debate among archaeologists over the decades. Though the collection is smaller than that at the Bardo in Tunis, it has its fair share of very well-preserved Roman mosaics. The majority are from the 3rd and 4th centuries AD, the central theme being the sea (Neptune in his chariot, pictures of fish, etc). Particularly worth seeing is the 3rd-century Triumph of Bacchus, found in Sousse, which illustrates the victory of a young god over the forces of evil.

North of the medina Exiting the medina via Place des Martyrs in the northeast corner, you first come to **Imam Yehia Ibn Omar Cultural Centre** (Av Habib Bourguiba; 73 219 677, 73 227 782; e njahrachid@yahoo.fr; 08.00–18.00

Mon–Fri, 08.00–14.00 Sat). This beautiful 9th-century former mausoleum is today a library and cultural centre, so make sure there isn't a class going on before you walk in! No trip to this stretch of Tunisia's coastline would be complete without a **boat trip**, and 200m south of the medina exit is **Sousse Port**. During the summer, the port is overrun with 'pirates', all hoping to take tourists out on their kitsch ship for a swashbuckling half-day excursion. Trips include live entertainment, lunch, non-alcoholic drinks and snorkelling. One to recommend is the Bateau *Pirate Selma II* (m 50 401 530; f Bateau.Pirate.Selma), though best not to ask what happened to the *Selma I*.

Returning to the tour, head 650m northwards from Place des Martyrs until you reach the Corniche, where you will see the green-domed **Sidi Boujaafar Mosque and Mausoleum** (Bd de la Corniche; ⏲ closed to non-Muslims), dedicated to holy man Abu Jaafar Ahmad Ibn Saadoun who was originally from El Kef but spent much of his life in Sousse, where he died in AD935. Nearby, you could grab a coffee in one of the various cafés at the pleasant **Sousse Central Park (Star Gardens)**.

Just southeast of the park is **Keter Torah Synagogue** (Rue Amilcar), the only functional synagogue in Sousse (originally there were seven). Completely unmarked, it is noticeable only by the large plant pots blocking the street (presumably to stop vehicles ramming the building). It was built at the turn of the 20th century under Yossef Guez Guez, the Chief Rabbi of Sousse from 1906 to 1928, when he then went on to become the first native Chief Rabbi of Tunisia. Continuing southwest, next to the Institut Supérieur des Beaux Arts and the train station, you find **Maison des Arts LAB** (2nd fl, Pl de la Gare; m 52 878 878; e contact.mda.2022@gmail.com; f maisondesartslab; ⏲ 08.30–17.30 daily), a cultural centre, co-working space and café located in a very cool Art Deco building. A great spot if you need to catch up on some work or do some printing. Exhibitions are sometimes also held in the building, which they also share with **Didon** (m 52 878 878; e tunisie.didon@gmail.com; f DIDONTN1), a youth-focused Tunisian NGO doing great work in the area.

If you follow the train line to the northwest for 500m, you will reach the Catholic **Église St Felix** (1 Rue de Constantine (entrance on Rue de l'Église); ☎ 73 224 596; w soussechurch.org; ⏲ Mass celebrated 18.15 Mon–Sat, 09.30 Sun). Inaugurated in 1916 and with a 35m-high steeple, it managed to survive Allied bombing during World War II as well as a more recent Islamist arson attack in June 2011. The church is clearly visible thanks to its whitewash and terracotta tiling, and is still in active use today.

Northwest of the medina Leaving the medina via Bab el Gharbi or Bab el Finga along the P1, after 500m on your left you will reach the **Institut Français de Sousse** (Villa Marini, 4 Rue des Jasmins; ☎ 73 227 935; w institutfrancais-tunisie.com/sousse; ⏲ 09.00–18.00 daily), a language centre, library and cultural space which hosts numerous concerts, exhibitions and film screenings; see its website for listings. On the other side of the road, 150m to the northeast, is the **Maison de la Culture** (Av Mohamed Maarouf; ☎ 73 225 450; ⏲ 08.00–18.00 Mon–Sat), which has an amazing colonial-era 750-seat cinema, plus spaces for various arts clubs and exhibitions. Event listings are posted on a noticeboard outside.

Located just behind the Maison de la Culture is the **Maison des Banquets** (Rue Victor Hugo), a Roman site under excavation that can be viewed only through the gate. Discovered in 1968 and in use between the 3rd and 5th century AD, the house has a series of fine polychrome mosaics in a hypostyle courtyard. It was believed to be the headquarters of some sort of association or a banqueting house, rather than a private residence. Occasionally the Institut Français de Sousse organises tours with a local historical expert.

South of the medina

Dar Am Taïeb (Rue Ben Ghedahem; ☎ 73 234 081; ⏱ 09.00–19.00 daily; 10DT) Local sculptor and visual artist Taïeb Ben Hadj Ahmed has transformed his house in this quiet suburb into a 1,500m² collection of fascinating sculptures (mainly humans and animals) made of recycled materials: think bar-heater trolls, a driftwood horse and a car-parts donkey. Eclectic and truly unique. Note that Google Maps has this located on Rue 25 Juillet, which is incorrect.

Catacombes du Bon Pasteur (Rue Abdelhamid Lasska; ⏱ summer 09.00–18.00 daily, winter 09.00–17.00 daily; 5DT) Named after an engraving of the good shepherd found on the site, these catacombs are a good 20 minutes' walk from the southwestern corner of the medina. To get here, take Rue Commandant Béjaoui west from the Kasbah, then first left on to Rue Abdou Hamed el Ghazali; the catacombs are on a street on your left after 10 minutes' walk.

Unlike the Romans, early Christian communities did not practise cremation and, generally, they were too poor to buy land for burial. For the communities in Rome, Naples and North Africa, the solution was to dig down into the rock, creating tunnels where shrouded bodies could be placed on ledges (*loculi*) or in niches. In the days of anti-Christian persecution, catacombs provided a safer gathering place for Christians around chosen martyrs' graves, given the risk of being attacked by mobs. Later, when Christianity was accepted, basilicas were built above ground on the site of catacombs.

The catacombs were discovered in 1888 by Colonel Vincent, French commander of the Fourth Tunisian Tirailleurs Regiment. In total, the complex stretches for some 5km, with more than 250 galleries containing up to 15,000 tombs, testimony to the importance of early Christianity in North Africa. They were built and used between the 2nd and 4th centuries AD. In the more recently restored sections, there are a few hundred metres open for inspection, with some tombs fronted with glass to reveal the contents within.

Jewish Cemetery (Entrance on Rue 15 Octobre 1963) At the time of independence, Sousse had a Jewish community numbering in the thousands, though today it is estimated at less than 100. In 2018 the local government decided to pay homage to Sousse's Jewish heritage by naming four streets in the city after prominent 20th-century Jewish residents: Daniel Uzan (a doctor), Claude Sitbon (a lawyer), Yvonne Bessis (a midwife) and Ichoua Ghouila-Houri (a prominent philanthropist). The expansive cemetery, with its slowly decaying gravestones, is surrounded by a large wall to prevent vandalism following a series of incidents in 2013 and 2018. The gates are mainly locked unless it is a special religious event. A local guide (page 40) may be able to arrange access. Note that while there is a large hole in the southern end of the perimeter wall, this is guarded by a very aggressive dog on a chain, so do not walk through the gap.

La Maison des Masques (Rue El Masjed El Aksa) This 3rd-century AD Roman house was discovered in 1962 by French archaeologist Louis Foucher. It takes its name from a mosaic at the site depicting the masks used in Roman theatre, and is a good example of a wealthy home from this period. It is fenced off so you can look at it only through the bars, although there is some talk of restoring the site further and making it accessible to visitors. Just southeast of the house is the so-called **Swiss Cemetery** (Av Ibn Khaldoun), though it is unclear why it is called this, given that it is filled with mainly Tunisian Muslim graves.

WEST OF SOUSSE On the Sahel west of Sousse are various salt-lake wetlands (*sebkha*), such as **Sebkha Kelbia** and **Sebkha Sidi el Hani**, which are good for birdwatching; the wetlands to the south of Sebkha Kelbia, in particular, are excellent for spotting hunting raptors. Although Sebkha Kelbia is officially a natural reserve, and is signposted as such, there is no tourism infrastructure so, in order to make the most of your visit, you will need to bring a guide from Sousse or Hammamet (see page 41 for birding tour operators in Tunisia).

NORTH OF SOUSSE

The stretch of coastline north of Sousse makes for some excellent day trips, offering bird-rich wetlands, archaeological and World War II sites, and opportunities to learn more about local crafts, traditions and Amazigh culture. Those wishing to spend the night will find a fabulous dar in Hergla.

PORT EL KANTAOUI Some 10km north of Sousse, since being constructed in 1979 this purpose-built marina has been a resounding success, attracting luxury yachts from around the Mediterranean as well as golf enthusiasts. The 130ha, 36-hole, PGA-approved **golf course** (Tourist Rd; ☎ 73 348 756; w kantaouigolfcourse.com.tn; ⌚ tee times available from 07.00–15.50 daily) is set a few hundred metres back from the marina; choose from the Sea Course or the Panorama Course. Inside the marina (if you walk all the way around the left-hand perimeter) is the **Centre de Plongée d'El Kantaoui** (m 55 402 428; f elkantaouidivingcenter; ⌚ 08.00–16.00 daily, dive trip times 08.30 & 10.30 daily), where a team of CMAS-qualified scuba instructors offer everything from cave and wreck dives to CMAS certification training.

Getting there and away You can catch a Société de Transport du Sahel (STS) bus from Sousse (20mins) or jump in a local louage from the stop by the massive Hospital Sahloul (Gare Routière Sahloul), at the end of Rue Salim Ammar.

Tourist information The main tourist information office is on your right as you enter the marina (⌚ 08.00–18.00 Mon–Sat). It offers a selection of information in various languages and have a very useful large map outside with details in French, English, German, Italian and Arabic.

Where to stay Note that Port el Kantaoui is not cheap, so if you are looking for budget accommodation you are better off heading to Sousse (page 227). The main things differentiating the options listed here are price, whether you want the option of all-inclusive and how close to the golf course you want to be.

Iberostar Selection Kantaoui Bay (358 rooms) BP243; ☎ 73 246 477; f IberostarSelectionKantaouiBay. The best of the AI resorts on this strip, with the choice of 3 restaurants (Asian, Tunisian & Italian), 5 bars, a large spa & access to a private beach. **$$$$$**

Concorde Green Park Palace (452 rooms) BP95; m 25 452 220, 36 030 000; f. Popular beach resort, set in 5ha of gardens with 3 themed restaurants, 4 bars (including a swim-up bar), a large spa & private beach access. **$$$$**

Hotel Marhaba Palace (322 rooms) BP120; ☎ 73 347 076; w marhabahotels.tn; f Marhaba.

Palace.kantaoui. With 5 pools, a water-therapy & spa centre & no fewer than 7 different eating options during high season, this is a solid choice for a beach holiday. Offers AI rates. **$$$–$$$$**

Where to eat and drink

Coconut Island 73 348 479; CoconutIslandTunisia; 10.00–23.00 daily. Luxury French/Mediterranean restaurant on the beach behind the El Mouradi Club Kantaoui Hotel, with amazing views of the sea. **$$$$**

Hard Rock Café Zone Touristique; 73 347 300; e pek.info@hrctunisia.com; HRCPEK; noon–02.00 daily. The only Tunisian branch of this American chain, with rock memorabilia all over the walls. Good burgers & live music. **$$$**

✷ **New Fly** Zone Touristique; m 94 505 295; 09.00–19.00 daily. Though under renovation at the time of writing, once open this fried chicken restaurant inside the Hawaii Shopping Centre will mainly be of interest to Star Wars fans, thanks to its display of one of the real podracer engines from *Episode I – The Phantom Menace*, purchased from Mr Kamel Souilah's Star Wars shop in Nefta (page 355). There are planes, helicopters & engines inside too. **$$**

SIDI BOU ALI Some 10km north from Port el Kantaoui on the RN1 is this rural town, where in the surrounding countryside are a series of ecovillage developments that make for good day trips if you would like to do some hiking, mountain biking or horseriding. Some of them even offer accommodation.

Where to stay and eat

Le Domaine de l'Olivier Rouge (5 rooms) ⊕ 35.975815, 10.387445; m 28 304 303; e bo.bourg@yahoo.fr; f. Located in the middle of a quiet olive grove 12km west of Hergla, this dar offers spacious rooms, a large pool & horseriding on site. **$$$$$**

Ecovillage Wild Luxury (10 cabins, 2 chalets) ⊕ 35.935661, 10.490722; m 99 066 611; e gasunivers@gmail.com; Ecovillage.WildLuxury. Complete with castle gate & cannons out front, these wooden, AC chalets sleeping up to 4 feel quite Scandinavian. Activities include volleyball, paintballing & buggying, & there is a large pool. **$$$$**

HERGLA Known as Horrea Coelia during Roman times, this former fishing village, 30km north of Sousse, is located on a low rise overlooking the sea with some narrow fine-sand beaches to the north. The beach and nearby forest at El Madfoun is particularly beautiful, and there are also some worthwhile beaches to the south at Chott Meriem, as you head up the coast from Port el Kantaoui. This is a great place to spend the night to get away from the hustle of Sousse, and is easily reached via louage from Sousse, Port el Kantaoui or even Enfidha.

Where to stay and eat

✷ **Dar Khadija** (5 rooms) Rue 9 Avril; m 98 400 279; HeRgla.Tunisie. Tucked away down a back street in the old town, this beautiful Tunisian guesthouse is centred around a large courtyard with a pool that is overflowing with greenery. Each of the rooms is named after 1 of the children of the owners, & has a slightly different character, but all are tastefully decorated. Some have baths, some have baths & showers, & 1 even has a jacuzzi. There is also a hammam & a great rooftop terrace for watching the sunset. B/fast inc; other meals available by prior arrangement. **$$$$**

Artifex Restaurant 5 Bv Amor Maatoug; m 94 295 209; noon–19.00 daily. Delicious Mediterranean cuisine & a friendly welcome from a Milanese-trained chef, with views over the corniche. **$$**

What to see and do Just before entering Hergla from the south, you cross a bridge over the **Sebkhet Halk el Menjel** (⊕ 35.975463, 10.524061), home to a huge flock of greater flamingos. The availability of water here year-round makes it a favourite stopping-off spot for various migrating birds, including Eurasian spoonbill, common shelduck, northern pintail, Kentish plover, Eurasian curlew and common crane. There is an information sign by the side of the road explaining the significance of this bird habitat.

Hergla's most important building is an 18th-century **mausoleum** in honour of Sidi Bou Mendil, located just behind the port (⊕ 36.030523, 10.509752). Known as 'the saint with the handkerchief', Sidi Bou Mendil was a 10th-century holy man said to be able to transform any piece of cloth into a magic flying carpet to whisk him off to (or back from) the Holy Land of Arabia. The small blue-and-white structure is generally closed to non-Muslims, but local guides or accommodation providers can sometimes organise a quick visit.

Otherwise, Hergla is famous for its *esparto* grass weaving. Originally, woven and plaited esparto grass was the raw material for a whole series of utilitarian products, including donkey bags and *scourtins* (round mats used in olive-oil presses to filter the oil). Today, you can also find decorative fish and place mats in the shops around the main square, plus a couple of small restaurants catering to the tourist trade.

ENFIDHA AND TAKROUNA Around 25km north of Hergla, Enfidha (formerly Enfidaville) and the neighbouring hill-crest village of Takrouna were the scenes of some fierce fighting during the final week of the Tunisian Campaign in World War II, and today you will find a number of military cemeteries in the area relating to the conflict.

Getting there and away It is possible to reach Enfidha and Takrouna by **louage** from Tunis (1hr 15mins) or Sousse (50mins). Enfidha is also on the main SNCFT **train** line between Tunis and Gabès (1hr 35mins); five trains per day depart Tunis for Enfidha, with the first service at 06.15 and the final one at 17.20.

What to see and do

Takrouna Aside from its World War II significance (see below), it is also worth scaling the 375m-high hill (via a tarmac road) to the village of Takrouna simply for the breath-taking views from the top, best enjoyed from **Le Rocher Bleu Café** (⊕ 36.150195, 10.326943; 73 381 780; summer 07.30–20.00 daily, winter 09.00–17.00 daily; $). Next door, owner Dr Aida Gmach Bellagha has created a small

THE BATTLE OF TAKROUNA

Trevor Sheehan (w africanstalingrad.com)

The hilltop Amazigh village of Takrouna was one of the military objectives for invading Allied soldiers in April 1943 and as a result saw some bitter hand-to-hand fighting in the village streets and houses between the attacking Allies (mainly New Zealand soldiers), and the Axis (mainly Italian) defenders. Despite repeated counter-attacks by the Italians, the Allies finally captured the summit on 21 April but were kept under constant attack for another two weeks. The surrounding hills, which continue out to Hammamet, were heavily defended by the Germans and Italians until their final surrender on 13 May. A memorial to the Italians is in the valley by the road (⊕ 36.151153, 10.336163). There are also two nearby Allied cemeteries that are well worth a visit (⊕ 36.134071, 10.374079 and ⊕ 36.143425, 10.349893).

museum of traditional life (2DT), which is worth a look. Note that in February 2021 rockfall closed the entire top of the hill, and the site remained closed as of October 2022 (although it is still possible to walk up for the views). There is no indication of when the road up (or the café) will be reopened to the public. There are fears that some of the highest buildings may now need to be condemned.

Takrouna French Military Cemetery (⊕ 36.143305, 10.350178; ⌚ 24/7; free) This well-maintained 1ha cemetery by the side of the main road commemorates the 235 Christian, Muslim and Jewish soldiers who died fighting for the Free French Army (Forces Françaises Libres) against Axis forces in Tunisia between November 1942 and May 1943. It has a striking cenotaph, topped with metal insignia, in honour of the 1st Free French Division (1re Division Française Libre), as well as a memorial to General Diego Brosset, who successfully led his troops to take 28,000 prisoners from the German 90th Light Infantry Division and the Italian 101st Motorised Division 'Trieste' in this area.

Folgore Memorial (⊕ 36.150966, 10.336049) A relatively new memorial in Takrouna, inaugurated on 24 April 2018 via private funds raised by Italian parachute regiment veterans, this commemorates the fallen soldiers from Italy's 185th Paratroopers Division 'Folgore'. This division had the misfortune of facing heavy losses in October 1942 at the second battle of El Alamein, and then fighting on the Mareth Line before finally being defeated during the Battle of Takrouna (see opposite) on 20–21 April 1943. War correspondent Harry Zinder noted for *Time* magazine that 'the famed Folgore parachute division fought to the last round of ammunition'. The memorial is locked apart from on special occasions, but is still visible from outside the gates.

Enfidha Housed in the renovated former French St Augustin church, the **town museum** (⊕ 36.135154, 10.379618; ⌚ 09.00–16.00 Tue–Sun; 5DT) is worth a look for its well-presented collection of stelae and Roman mosaics, with information signs in Arabic, French and English.

Enfidha Commonwealth War Cemetery (⊕ 36.133972, 10.373913; ⌚ 24/7; free) This immaculately landscaped cemetery contains 1,551 Commonwealth graves from World War II, 88 of them unidentified. Most of the burials here died in the battles between March and May 1943, as Montgomery's Eighth Army captured Enfidaville amid strong resistance from Axis forces. Note that the register and visitors' book is only available during regular working hours.

Enfidha Christian Cemetery (⊕ 36.134555, 10.373425; ⌚ 24/7; free) Adjoining the Commonwealth cemetery is a large civilian Christian cemetery, filled with the graves of the mainly Italian settlers from the colonial period. Here you will also see large tombs to the likely wealthier Italian families based in the area, such as Famiglia Gusmano and Famiglia Proetto. There is even a memorial to the Italian soldiers who died fighting the Austro-Hungarians in the Dolomites during World War I, with the battles at Monte Pasubio (May 1916) and the Piave River (June 1918) commemorated.

UPPENNA (⊕ 36.172316, 10.413666) In the farming settlement of Henchir Chigarnia, 6km up the P1 from Enfidha, is the remains of this Roman basilica, discovered by French archaeologist René Cagnat in 1881. Inside, the well-preserved mosaics include Latin text, hinting that this is the burial place of several important people, including a Donatist bishop who participated in the Conference of Carthage in AD411, one of the most significant meetings of the Catholic Church's African leadership in its history. Entry is free, but you may need to ask a local person in the village to fetch the man with the key for the gate. Nearby (to the east) you will find the remains of a Byzantine fortress (⊕ 36.171299, 10.415825), which is sadly now used as a fly-tipping site.

KÈN CRAFT VILLAGE (⊕ 36.250259, 10.439381; m 98 209 960, 54 629 872; e villageken@yahoo.com; f le.village.ken) Some 65km north of Sousse, this craft village owned by civil engineer Slah Smaoui is a unique example of private money going into a carefully put together heritage project. The word 'kèn' means 'was' in Arabic, here referring to 'kèn min zaman' ('once upon a time'), as the village is intended to be a window into a past, rural way of life. You can watch the country's flat-weave or *kelim* carpets being produced and, on summer evenings, displays of local folklore with dinner under a tent are organised in an open area adjacent to the village. It also organises painting, ceramics and drawing classes for children and adults.

PHÉRADI MAIUS (⊕ 36.248627, 10.399762) Just west of Kèn and the A1 is this Roman site, where major excavations were first undertaken back in 1966. Evidence of the site dates to at least the 3rd century BC, likely making it of Punic origins, but it really flourished under the Roman Empire. The settlement was given colonia status under Emperor Marcus Aurelius, after which a number of fine public buildings were constructed. In 1972, the public baths were brought to light. Highlights include a satisfyingly intact triumphal arch and, up on the hill, the ruins of a temple to Venus, later transformed into a small fort (*castra*). The stone-flagged forum, with what must have been tiny lock-up shops around it, is particularly atmospheric. There is also a nymphaeum, which is entirely understandable given the quality of the spring water; bring a bottle so you can fill up at the spring of Aïn Khélifa, close to the site, which you should be able to spot by the concrete well-head and the presence of someone filling up a container of some kind.

MONASTIR *Telephone code: +73*

Situated on a headland some 2km south of Sousse, Monastir is an attractive fishing port with an elegant promenade along the bay. It could have been just another sleepy Sahel coastal town but, as the birthplace of Habib Bourguiba, things turned out rather differently. Tunisia's first president wanted a city to mark his country's accession to nation-state status and so quiet Monastir was extensively remodelled, acquiring a gold-domed mausoleum, some impressive modernist public buildings and an esplanade. The sandy coastline west of town saw some of the country's first mass-tourism hotels, including Tunisia's first five-star offering. Today, Monastir offers visitors a fine collection of ancient architectural features, and both the magnificent mausoleum and summer residence of President Bourguiba, the latter a 1960s design wonder by the French architect Olivier-Clément Cacoub.

HISTORY In Roman times, Monastir was called Ruspina (a corruption of the Punic name, Rous Penna), and it served as Julius Caesar's operations base for his African campaign. Part of the triple ramparts from this time still survive. During the 11th

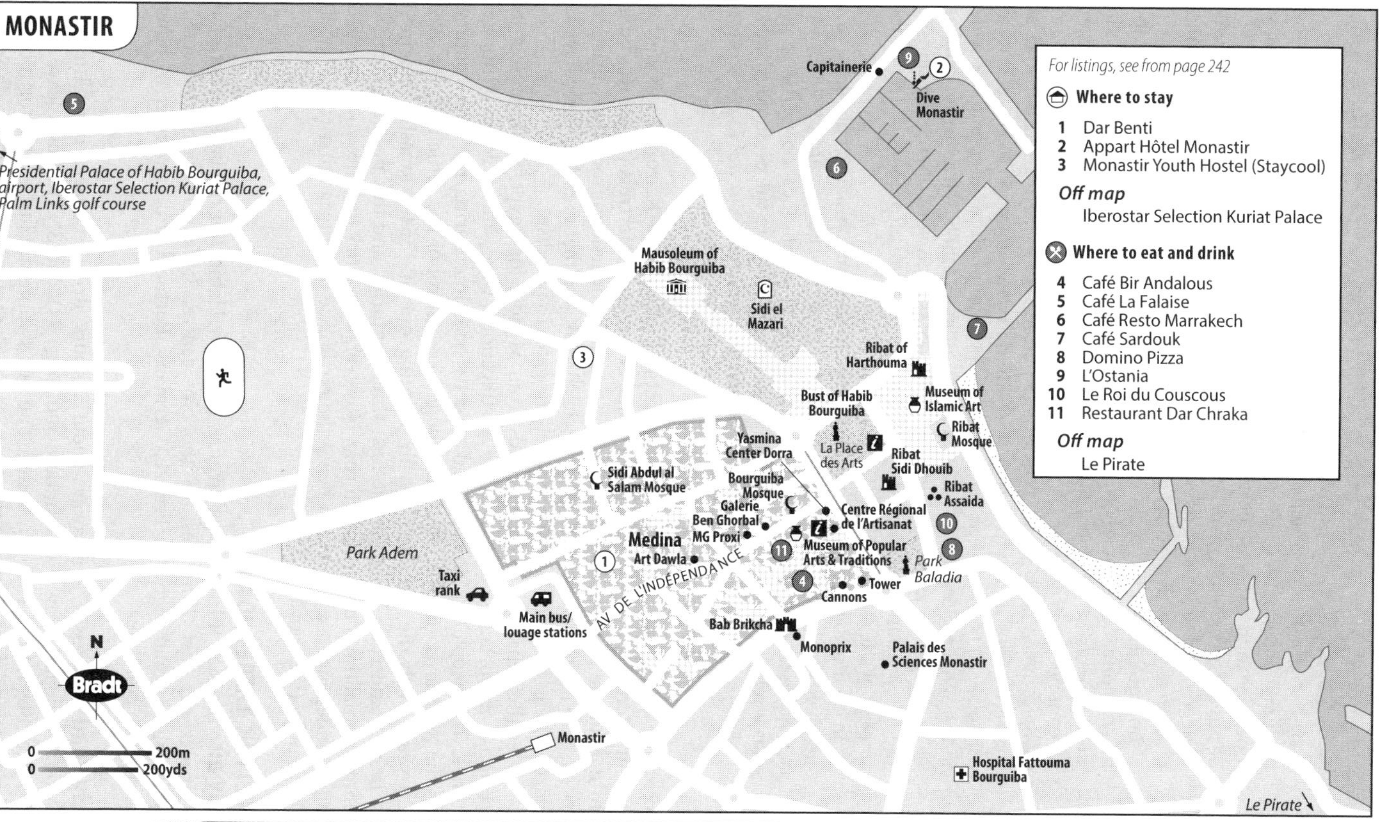
MONASTIR
For listings, see from page 242
Where to stay
1 Dar Benti
2 Appart Hôtel Monastir
3 Monastir Youth Hostel (Staycool)
Off map
Iberostar Selection Kuriat Palace
Where to eat and drink
4 Café Bir Andalous
5 Café La Falaise
6 Café Resto Marrakech
7 Café Sardouk
8 Domino Pizza
9 L'Ostania
10 Le Roi du Couscous
11 Restaurant Dar Chraka
Off map
Le Pirate
Presidential Palace of Habib Bourguiba, airport, Iberostar Selection Kuriat Palace, Palm Links golf course
Capitainerie
Dive Monastir
Mausoleum of Habib Bourguiba
Sidi el Mazari
Ribat of Harthouma
Museum of Islamic Art
Ribat Mosque
Bust of Habib Bourguiba
La Place des Arts
Yasmina Center Dorra
Ribat Sidi Dhouib
Ribat Assaida
Sidi Abdul al Salam Mosque
Bourguiba Mosque
Galerie Ben Ghorbal
Centre Régional de l'Artisanat
MG Proxi
Medina
Museum of Popular Arts & Traditions
Art Dawla
Park Baladia
AV DE L'INDÉPENDANCE
Tower
Cannons
Park Adem
Taxi rank
Main bus/ louage stations
Bab Brikcha
Monoprix
Palais des Sciences Monastir
Monastir
Hospital Fattouma Bourguiba
Le Pirate
N
Bradt
0 200m
0 200yds

THE FORMATIVE YEARS OF MONASTIR'S MOST FAMOUS SON

Born in Monastir on 3 August 1903, Habib Bourguiba is arguably one of the most influential figures in Tunisian history. Founder of the country's nationalist movement and first president of the Tunisian Republic (declared on 25 July 1957), he has left an indelible mark on Tunisian life, propelling the country from the rank of sleepy Mediterranean statelet under French protection to that of a pragmatic, modern nation with Arab nationalist credentials.

Bourguiba was the product of a particular environment. While Tunis, with its cosmopolitan population, had no real issue coping with French rule, the small farmers of the Sahel had a different attitude. Seeing few opportunities to continue their way of life owing to the encroachment by European farm owners, they quickly seized upon the importance of modern education and, in the early 1900s, began to send their children to newly founded bilingual private schools – 70 of the 90 *écoles franco-arabes* existing before independence were in the Sahel region. By the 1930s, sons of ordinary families like the Bourguibas were competing with the children of Tunis notables for jobs open to Muslims in the administration. Many, like Habib Bourguiba, were also going to France for university education.

In his memoirs, Habib Bourguiba tended to present himself as belonging to a deprived family, but in reality his father, retiring from the Beylical army in 1893, was a notable on the Monastir town council and held various local posts. The family was wealthy enough to send Habib's two elder brothers to the prestigious Sadiki College in Tunis and Habib almost followed the same track, but was forced to drop

century, when nearby Mahdia was the Fatmid capital and Kairouan was out of favour, Monastir was an important regional centre, and a fortress (*ribat*) was built to defend the Muslim coastal settlements against incursions from the Christian north. The fortress was said to hold special virtues, and that spending three days as part of the garrison in Monastir opened the gates to paradise.

After the departure of the Fatimids from Mahdia for Egypt, the town lost its regional importance, although the fortifications were improved in Ottoman times. The people of Monastir had a pretty bad time during the 16th century, as the Spaniards and the Ottomans fought for control of the settlement for over 20 years, with the Ottomans finally winning out in 1554. Monastir remained relatively underdeveloped for the next three centuries, and this neglect extended into colonial times under French rule. However, Monastir's fortunes soon changed upon independence, thanks to being the birthplace of Tunisia's first ruler: Habib Bourguiba (see above).

GETTING THERE AND AWAY

By air Tunisia's third-busiest airport, Monastir Habib Bourguiba International Airport sits just 7km west of the city centre. It is very well connected, offering seasonal flights to France, Germany, Portugal and a number of other European countries.

By road Tunis is 170km away (about 2 hours' drive). **Louages** from Tunis to Monastir depart from Gare Routière Sud (page 94), and SNTRI **buses** leave from Moncef Bey (2hrs). The main louage and bus stations are just to the north of the train station. The 316 bus connects to Sousse (35mins). The Commune de Sousse out through illness. He returned to schooling at the Lycée Carnot, switching from an establishment that trained members of the Muslim elite to one dominated by French students. This was a practical move; through professions such as law, accessible to those with a French education, social mobility was possible. In 1924, after completing his baccalauréat, Bourguiba headed for Paris and a law degree from the Sorbonne. He returned in 1927, marked by French culture, and bringing with him a French wife.

Despite this education, he was to remain an outsider in all the circles that counted in 1930s Tunisia, whether it was among the Tuniso-French administration or the traditional Muslim or cosmopolitan middle-class communities. The difficulties were both social and professional, and between 1927 and 1930 Bourguiba was to move from being a young lawyer trying to build a career to the unstable status of nationalist activist. One of his earliest forays into public political debate came in 1929 when he got involved in a discussion on gender equality and women's headscarves in Tunisia. The following year, he legally defended Tunisians arrested by French colonial authorities for protesting against the 30th International Eucharistic Congress of Carthage. This was a Catholic event that saw thousands of Europeans flood the streets of Tunis, causing much controversy among the Muslim-majority colonised population. This was a key event that spurred Bourguiba to join the Constitutional Liberal Party, Destour ('Constitution'), a nationalist party founded in 1920 to end French colonialism in Tunisia.

See page 17 for more details on Bourguiba's life.

Open Géo Data website (w sousse-plus-open-data-sousse.hub.arcgis.com) details routes in the region.

By rail and metro To get to Monastir by rail, you will need to get an SNCFT train to Sousse, change at Sousse Bab Jdid Station and then jump on the Sahel Metro which connects with Mahdia – it's a 30-minute journey from Sousse Bab Jdid to Monastir, with services running roughly every 40 minutes from 05.00 to 22.00. When you arrive in Monastir, the main train station is quite central, about 850m from the beach in front of Avenue 18 Janvier 1952.

GETTING AROUND Monastir's metro and louage stations are less than 1km from the beach, so everything is very walkable. For short journeys around town, yellow **taxis** can be flagged down and there is a taxi rank just to the north of the train station, by the louages and buses.

There are several international **car-hire agencies** based at Monastir Habib Bourguiba International Airport, including Avis (73 521 031; 08.00–20.00 daily) and Hertz (m 36 205 102; 08.00–20.00 daily). Driving around town is pretty straightforward and on-street parking (often paid) is not too hard to find.

TOURIST INFORMATION There are two tourist information offices in town: one on the eastern corner of La Place des Arts (09.00–18.00 Mon–Fri) and another on Avenue de l'Indépendance (08.30–18.00 Mon–Fri). In the medina, the Monastir branch of the National Office of Tunisian Handicrafts, **Centre Régional de l'Artisanat** (just off Av Trimeche; 73 461 290; w artisanat.nat.tn; 08.30–16.30 Mon–Fri), has information downstairs about relevant exhibitions and events in the area.

WHERE TO STAY *Map, page 239*

Monastir is surprisingly bereft of decent accommodation options, perhaps as a result of being so close to the massive tourism market in Sousse, where you will have a lot more choice in every price category. However, there are a few places in town and over by the airport that are worth considering.

✱ **Dar Benti** (5 rooms) Av Mahmoud Bourguiba; m 25 020 036; w darbenti.com. A breath-taking, immaculately restored dar in the medina by the Bab El Gharbi. The attention to detail in decorative elements like the stucco is very impressive, but unsurprising given that the owner is an architect. The upstairs rooms are even wheelchair accessible thanks to an integrated lift. 4 standard rooms have AC & central heating plus en suite, & there's a significantly larger royal suite. Also features a rooftop pool & hammam. **$$$$–$$$$$**

Iberostar Selection Kuriat Palace (382 rooms) Rte Touristique, Skanes; 73 520 100; w iberostar.com/en/hotels/monastir/iberostar-kuriat-palace. This 5-star beach resort is the best of the 20 or so AI resorts stretching from the airport up to Monastir golf course, featuring a private beach & aquapark. **$$$$–$$$$$**

Appart Hôtel Monastir (56 apts) Marina; 73 462 305; w marinamonastir.tn. Well-presented, if a little dated, studio apts with a balcony overlooking the marina, a small kitchenette at the foot of the stairs & an en suite with bath & shower. Very good value for money & includes parking for resident vehicles inside the grounds, in an area where it is otherwise very difficult to find spaces. **$$$**

Monastir Youth Hostel (Staycool) (18 rooms) Sidi Sree; m 26 210 612, 51 460 104; e daly_mat@yahoo.fr; f auberge.monastir. Refurbished in 2022, this place has a mishmash of different room sizes & configurations, but all are large, clean & with plenty of natural light. Some have en-suite wet room. Cheapest decent bed in town, in a very good location. **$**

WHERE TO EAT AND DRINK *Map, page 239*

Le Pirate Port de la Peche, El Ghedir; 73 468 126; e contact@lepirate.net; f piratemonastir; ⌚ noon–16.00 & 19.00–23.00 Tue–Sun. A veritable Monastir institution, this seafood restaurant down by the old fishing port is worth the 1.5km journey from the centre of town. $$$$

Domino Pizza Immeuble Bab Essour; m 25 895 516; f DominoPizzaMonastir.officielle; ⌚ 11.00–23.00 daily. Not sure how Domino's Pizza feels about this outrageous copyright infringement (which includes stealing the logo), but the pizzas here are pretty good & offer delivery. The icing on the cake is the choice of Facebook URL. . . *officielle* indeed! $$$

L'Ostania Restaurant Marina; m 52 501 755, 28 635 700; ⌚ 11.00–late daily. Mediterranean restaurant in the marina serving tasty seafood, but with a smoky pub vibe (unless you choose to sit outdoors). $$$

Le Roi du Couscous Immeuble Bab Essour; m 98 277 380; e rhimmed83@gmail.com; f; ⌚ noon–21.00 daily. Delicious homemade couscous & tuna brik in this very popular local restaurant. Has pavement seating with views of the park. $$$

Restaurant Dar Chraka Houmet Trabelsia, Av de l'Indépendance; 73 460 528; Hidden through an archway in a square that sells mainly tourist tat, this quiet restaurant has an interesting menu of Tunisian & Mediterranean options, including a whole selection of Tunisian speciality dishes that need to be ordered 24hrs in advance. Generous portion sizes. $$$

Café La Falaise Rte de la Falaise; m 56 772 772; f lafalaisecafe; ⌚ 09.00–late daily. Glass-fronted café with a large outdoor seating area offering panoramic views of the shore below. $$

Café Resto Marrakech Marina; m 96 257 770, 25 886 625; f cafemarrakechmarina ⌚ 07.30–late daily. This is the first place that opens in the marina in the mornings, so a useful b/fast spot if you are staying here. Good coffee & pastries. $$

Café Sardouk Marina; m 22 777 410; ⌚ 09.00–23.00 daily. Well-situated café by the marina, with great views of the passing boats & the Garde National building. Pretty standard menu of grilled fish & pasta dishes, so probably better just for a fresh juice or coffee. $$

Café Bir Andalous Medina; m 92 197 570; f CafeBirAndalous; 07.00–late daily. The tree-covered courtyard away from the traffic makes a good spot for a coffee or shisha break. $–$$

SHOPPING Monastir's medina is an interesting area, though it lacks the associated small-scale manufacturing often found in Tunisia's other medinas. The artisanal crafts on offer tend not to be sold by the makers themselves, but by businesses aimed squarely at tourists.

Art Dawla Av de l'Indépendance; 35.773526, 10.829139; 10.00–16.00 Mon–Fri. Fascinating streetside art gallery in the medina where the owner welds bits of scrap metal into sculptures.
Galerie Ben Ghorbal Houmet Trabelsia, Av de l'Indépendance; 73 461 738; 08.00–20.00 daily. Opposite Restaurant Dar Chraka, this emporium of tourist tat includes scarves, pottery, paintings & rugs, but there are a few nice pieces dotted among their wares.
Yasmina Center Dorra Rue Sakka; 73 425 200; m 52 242 439; 08.00–20.00 daily. Mega emporium offering a large range of tourist gifts under 1 roof, including artisanal crafts, clothing, shoes, leather goods, etc.

SPORTS AND ACTIVITIES

Capitainerie Marina; 73 462 305; e capitainerie@marinamonastir.tn. Should be able to point you in the direction of boats in the harbour offering day trips to the Kuriat Islands (page 245).
Dive Monastir Marina; 73 462 509; m 98 457 393, 24 157 393; w dive-monastir.com. Offering 2 dives per day & night, plus dives on request; most sites are within a 15–30min boat ride from the marina. Should also be able to arrange boat trips to the Kuriat Islands.
Palm Links Skanes; 73 521 910/1; e direction@golf-palmlinks.com; 06.00–19.00 daily. Located a good 16km west of Monastir, this 18-hole golf course also has & driving range & clubhouse with bar & restaurant.

OTHER PRACTICALITIES The area around Park Baladia, surrounded by banks with ATMs, is useful if you are looking for cash. The **Hospital Fattouma Bourguiba** is on Rue 1 Juin 1955.

WHAT TO SEE AND DO

Ribat of Harthouma (summer 08.00–19.00 daily, winter 08.30–17.30 daily; 7DT) The walls and turrets of Monastir's most famous monument will be familiar to all who have seen Monty Python's *The Life of Brian*. The much-restored fortifications of the ribat were built in AD796 by Harthouma Ibn el Ayoune, as part of the coastal lookout system. One of the oldest and largest military structures built by the Arabs in North Africa, it was later refortified and surrounded by an additional wall during the 9th and 11th centuries, which gives the whole edifice an interesting mixture of contrasting styles and shapes. But the initial plan remains – a courtyard surrounded by primitive accommodation for the defenders and a prayer hall, now beautifully set out as the **Museum of Islamic Art** (summer 08.00–19.00 Tue–Sun, winter 08.30–17.30 Tue–Sun; 7DT). There is a separate entrance for the museum, at the foot of one of the towers on the west side of the ribat, where a corridor flanked by former guard rooms and now used as a ticket office leads into the central courtyard. The museum is well laid out, with good details about the exhibits: gravestones, glass, pages of Koran, pieces of pottery found here at the ribat, small pipes, pots and oil lamps, leather covers, exquisite old fabrics, a display of coins and a unique wooden Arab astrolabe (for measuring altitude), made in Cordoba and dating to the 10th century. In the courtyard there are more engraved stelae and tombstones dating from the 11th and 12th centuries.

Opposite the ribat, the **Great Mosque** was built in the 9th century and extended in the 11th century. It is still in use today and therefore closed to non-Muslims. Nearby, the **Ribat Assaida**, possibly named after a now unknown Aghlabid, dates to the mid 9th century and is today little more than some excavated foundations rising no more than about 1m from the ground. On the other side of the road, **Ribat Sidi Dhouib** is a 9th-century Aghlabid military barracks that today houses a Koranic school, but is not open to the public.

The medina Likely already in use during Aghlabid rule in the early 9th century, Monastir's medina lacks the scale of those in Sousse or Tunis, partly owing to some demolition work carried out in the 1960s by President Bourguiba and his favourite architect, Olivier-Clément Cacoub. The oldest eastern district, Houmet El Blad, saw major changes to make way for new access roads, monuments and roundabouts. Indeed, the section of town east of Avenue Trimeche, from Domino Pizza to the ribat and the park at La Place des Arts, all used to be part of the historic medina.

Entering from the southern **Bab Brikcha** (the late-17th-century gate off Avenue Habib Bourguiba), you will pass a **large tower** from the time of Ali Bey and what are presumably two Ottoman-era **cannons** on display at the entrance.

Taking a right on Avenue de l'Indépendance, you reach **Bourguiba Mosque**, built in the 1960s, mimicking the richly decorated traditional style of architecture of the buildings around it. The entrance to the prayer hall is through 19 intricately carved teak doors, made by the craftsmen of Kairouan. Once inside (off-limits to non-Muslims), the huge-vaulted prayer hall is supported by 86 pink marble columns. There is a large dome before the mihrab, inlaid with golden mosaics and decorated with small onyx columns. Opposite the mosque, the **Museum of Popular Arts and Traditions** (Av de l'Indépendance; 73 501 415, 73 461 272; 09.00–16.00 daily; 5/4DT non-resident/resident) is little more than a series of displays of traditional dress with very scant information beyond a name for each item in French and Arabic. It does, however, have a gift shop that sells some French-language books on archaeological sites in Tunisia.

The medina's only other site of note is the **Sidi Abdul al Salam Mosque**, just north of Rue de Tunis; dating to 1760, it has an impressive tower that serves as a useful landmark when navigating the north of the medina.

Habib Bourguiba As his hometown, Monastir boasts a number of sights relating to the former president. He lies in rest here at the **Mausoleum of Habib Bourguiba** (entry on Rue Mzali; winter 09.00–16.30 daily, summer 09.00–17.30 daily; free) situated at the north end of the Sidi el Mazari cemetery. An imposing affair, this huge square building has a resplendent golden cupola flanked by two matching minarets. Inside, there are an interesting series of displays of his personal effects (including his identity card and desk), as well as photographs of the president with various other heads of state throughout his lifetime. The tomb itself sits in a dedicated room in a sea of black marble. The former president's final resting place is an intricately carved white coffin, sat on what looks like nine stone rollers. The mausoleum also houses the bodies of his family members, including his first wife, brothers and parents. If you leave from the southeastern end of the mausoleum, you will pass a golden bust and (truly massive) painting of Habib Bourguiba on Place des Arts. Another golden statue is found in Park Baladia, some 600m south of the mausoleum.

The president's former summer residence, the **Presidential Palace of Habib Bourguiba** (09.00–17.00 Tue–Sun; 9/5DT non-residents/residents, photography

1DT) opened its doors to the public in April 2013 as a museum to the great man, giving a glimpse into his personal life via displays of photographs, artwork and a few rooms fully furnished in the way he once had them. Even setting aside the political context, it is an amazing piece of architecture, and the interior decoration is fascinating: think cubist antelope frescoes, painted velour tapestries and stained-glass windows – even Bourguiba's original stretched presidential Mercedes is on show.

Palais des Sciences Monastir (Av Farhat Hached; 73 463 556; 08.30–17.30 Mon–Fri) Though generally closed to the public, apart from during its science festival every April or scientific exhibitions, this is a fascinating example of mid-century hyper-modernism (also known as Googie architecture), with its angular porticoes, glistening silver sign lettering and bold geometric shapes on the exterior walls.

AROUND MONASTIR

Kuriat Islands About 15km offshore from Monastir, the two Kuriat Islands are the primary nesting site of Tunisia's loggerhead turtles, with over 45 nests recorded in 2020. The larger island is known as Kuriat el-Kabira ('Big Kuriat' in Arabic, or often just 'Kuriat') and the smaller island is Île Conigliera, meaning 'Island of Rabbits' owing to its rabbit-like shape.

Though inhabited since Phoenician times, the islands have no modern infrastructure beyond a lighthouse on Kuriat and a scientific monitoring station for turtles on Île Conigliera. Only day trips are allowed and they tend to be limited to the white-sand beaches of Île Conigliera, with all visitors having to depart by 15.00. Numerous operators run tours, departing from Monastir harbour between 08.00 and 09.00 during the summer season, returning around 17.00 and charging 40–60DT per person. The most comfortable and modern is probably ***Lac Majeur II*** (m 50 685 071; LacmajeurII), but you could also try the wooden **Bateau *Pacha II*** (m 22 757 414; e commercial.kuriat@gmail.com; kuriat2017). If you don't mind heading over on a pirate party boat, then contact **Bateau *Sultan*** (m 98 827 140; bateau_sultan_monastir).

For more information on Tunisia's sea turtles, contact Tunisian marine-conservation NGO **Notre Grand Bleu** (w notregrandbleu.org).

Lamta Archaeological Museum (Av Habib Bourguiba, Lamta; winter 09.00–17.00 Tue–Sun, summer 09.00–13.00 & 16.00–19.00 Tue–Sun; 5DT) This museum is set near the coast, among the ruins of the baths of Roman Lepti Minus, which was founded on a formerly Phoenician site. Displays include a Punic wooden sarcophagus from the 3rd century BC, a statue of Emperor Trajan and a series of well-preserved mosaics ranging from the 2nd to 4th centuries AD.

Moknine Archaeological and Ethnographic Museum (Rue de l'Indépendance, Moknine; 73 436 090; winter 09.30–16.30 Tue–Sun, summer 09.00–13.00 & 15.00–18.00 Tue–Sun; free) The town of Moknine is famous for its pottery, in particular unglazed coarseware ceramics such as the *gargoulette* (used for cooking traditional Tunisian recipes) and *nigueli* (amphora-like storage jars). This museum tells the story of this tradition, with displays of ceramic-making methods and ancient examples of pots dating to the 3rd century BC, alongside some unique archaeological pieces including a large 5th-century AD Vandal mosaic (Mosaic of the Auriga) – the only one of its kind in Tunisia. There is also a display of traditional jewellery with Jewish artisanal gold-working machinery, a testament to the town's diversity in modern times.

Thapsus In the modern-day settlement of Bekalta (also known as Ras Dimass) are a series of partially excavated archaeological remains from the Roman settlement of Thapsus, which was built on a previously Phoenician site. Thapsus is famous in history as the site of the Battle of Thapsus on 6 April 46BC, a key engagement in Caesar's Civil War. Eleven months after his success in this battle, Caesar had won the war, going on to declare himself dictator for life (which, unfortunately for him, lasted only two months before he was assassinated). The main ruin to visit is the Roman theatre (⊕ 35.619144, 11.042375), though it is not very well preserved. There are also a series of unexcavated ruins 350m to the north next to the greenhouses (⊕ 35.622671, 11.043340).

MAHDIA *Telephone code: +73*

Tunisia's second-largest fishing port, 60km south of Sousse, Mahdia is a charming little town which has (to some extent, at least) escaped the tourist mania of the rest of the coast. The town's name comes from an Islamic religious term meaning 'the rightly guided one' in Arabic. Today, Mahdia has some fine architecture and a small but busy fishing harbour. The medina is very small but still fun to get lost in; the Spanish fort is neat, not mean and brooding, and the Great Mosque feels proudly restored. Though in recent years Mahdia's dignity and repose has been somewhat disturbed by mushrooming beach hotels up the north coast, it remains a pleasant place to visit with some solid accommodation options.

HISTORY The history of Mahdia is closely linked with the Shi'ite branch of Islam, who believe that the Caliph must descend from Ali and Fatima (the Prophet's daughter). After a seven-year war with the Aghlabids, the founder of the Shi'ite Fatimid Dynasty, 'Abd Allāh – known as El Mehdi ('the rightly guided one') – finally secured victory and sought to establish his own capital. Mahdia was founded in AD912, following Carthage and Kairouan as the new capital of the land now known as Tunisia. It was sited on an easily defended promontory and El Mehdi settled in the still unfinished town in 921 in order to reinforce his power and protect himself. However, his enemies' hatred made peace short-lived. In 944, the city was besieged (unsuccessfully) for eight months by the army of one Abou Yazid. Eventually, the third Fatimid caliph moved the capital to a palace complex closer to Kairouan, Sabra el Mansouriya. The inhabitants of the abandoned capital turned to the sea for their livelihood: fishing, commerce and, more excitingly, piracy brought prosperous times.

In the medieval Mediterranean world, with its ever-shifting frontiers, reprisals were not slow in coming, with first an unsuccessful Christian expedition to dislodge the pirates in 1088, and then the occupation by Roger de Lauria, King of Sicily, from 1148 to 1160. Later, various other attempts were made to rid the town of the pirates, by a joint French-Genoese force in 1390 and in 1550 by Charles V of Spain. The Spanish were finally successful in 1550 but, when forced to evacuate four years later, resorted to blowing up the ramparts.

Eventually, Mahdia's inhabitants had to revert to more traditional ways of life, such as olive cultivation and the production and weaving of silk. Under the Husseinid beys, the town became home to a cosmopolitan population, with Albanians, Anatolians, Greeks, Italians and French. In the late 19th century, the

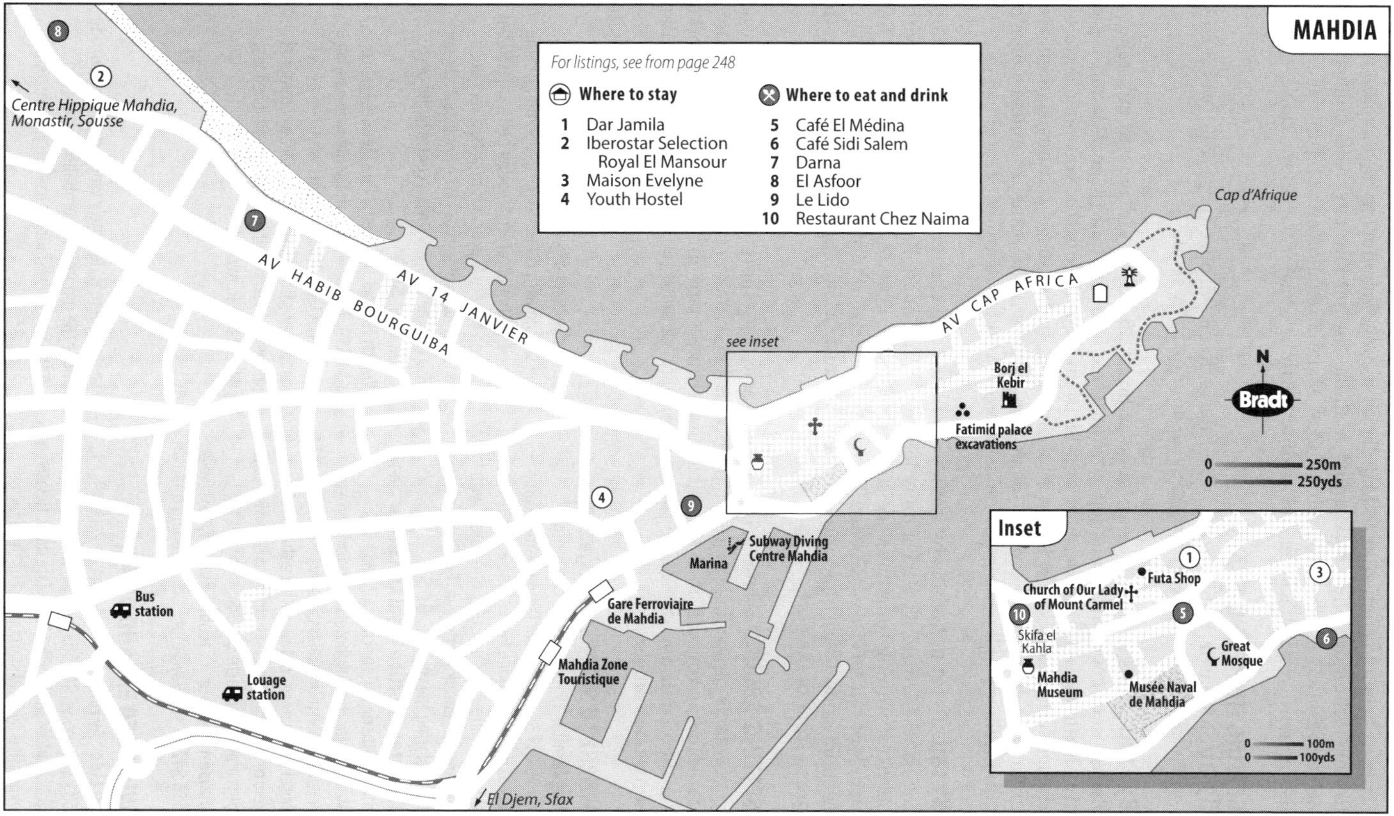

MAHDIA

For listings, see from page 248

Where to stay

1 Dar Jamila
2 Iberostar Selection Royal El Mansour
3 Maison Evelyne
4 Youth Hostel

Where to eat and drink

5 Café El Médina
6 Café Sidi Salem
7 Darna
8 El Asfoor
9 Le Lido
10 Restaurant Chez Naima

Centre Hippique Mahdia, Monastir, Sousse
AV HABIB BOURGUIBA
AV 14 JANVIER
AV CAP AFRICA
Cap d'Afrique
see inset
Borj el Kebir
Fatimid palace excavations
N
Bradt
0 250m
0 250yds
Subway Diving Centre Mahdia
Marina
Gare Ferroviaire de Mahdia
Mahdia Zone Touristique
Bus station
Louage station
El Djem, Sfax

Inset
Futa Shop
Church of Our Lady of Mount Carmel
Skifa el Kahla
Mahdia Museum
Musée Naval de Mahdia
Great Mosque
0 100m
0 100yds

Sicilians began to come over to Mahdia for fishing, introducing the *lamparo* night-fishing technique. They nicknamed Mahdia 'the sardine city', and built a new neighbourhood north of the port. Today, Mahdia remains one of Tunisia's largest fishing ports, with mackerel and sardines forming a major part of the catch.

GETTING THERE AND AWAY

By air Monastir Habib Bourguiba International Airport (page 240) sits 50km northwest of the city centre, roughly an hour away by road.

By land Tunis is 210km away (about 2 hours 35 minutes' drive without traffic). **Louage** services from Tunis depart from Gare Routière Sud (page 94), and there are also louages to Sousse, Sfax and El Djem. From Monastir, you often have to change louage at Ksar Hellal or Moknine. The main louage and bus stations are unfortunately not very central, located on Avenue Belhaouane, so unless you're a good walker you'll need to get a local bus or a taxi into the town centre.

By rail To get to Mahdia by train, you will need to change at Sousse and jump on the Sahel Metro – it's a 95-minute journey from Sousse Bab Jdid to Mahdia, with services running roughly every 40 minutes from 05.00 to 22.00. See page 225 for details of rail services to Sousse. There are two metro stations in the centre of town: Mahdia Zone Touristique and Gare Ferroviaire de Mahdia, the end of the line; both are in front of the port.

GETTING AROUND Mahdia is very walkable. For short journeys around town, yellow **taxis** can be flagged down, or there is a taxi rank in front of Gare Ferroviaire de Mahdia. You can find timetables and route maps for regional **bus** networks on the Commune de Sousse Open Géo Data website (w sousse-plus-open-data-sousse.hub.arcgis.com).

WHERE TO STAY *Map, page 247*

Dar Jamila (5 rooms) 1 Av Cap Africa; m 98 631 372; e cm.dar.jamila@gmail.com; f darjamilamahdia. Each of the en-suite rooms in this charming dar is uniquely decorated, with large balconies overlooking the sea. Excellent location for exploring the medina. **$$$$**

Iberostar Selection Royal El Mansour (447 rooms) Rte de la Corniche; t 73 681 100; w iberostar.com/uk/hotels/mahdia/iberostar-royal-el-mansour-thalasso. Large, very popular AI hotel to the north of town with a thalassotherapy centre including sauna, hammam & Turkish baths, plus a private beach. **$$$$**

Maison Evelyne (5 rooms) Borj el Rass; m 98 556 542; e subway@topnet.tn. Opening on to an attractive plant-filled interior courtyard, rooms are simple with colourful patterned tiling; some have traditional carved wooden bed frames. Great rooftop terrace & delicious b/fasts; a very good location for exploration of the peninsula. Owners also run the Subway Diving Centre in the port (page 249). **$$$**

Youth Hostel (60 beds) Rue Mendès France; t 73 681 559, 73 687 980; e maisonjeunesmahdia@yahoo.fr. Clean & basic dorms with 2–5 beds & good views from the rooftop. Clean communal showers. Meals available on request. Cheapest decent bed in town. **$**

WHERE TO EAT AND DRINK

Le Lido Av Farhat Hached, Port de Peche; t 73 681 339; m 96 049 583; e rest_lido@yahoo.fr; f LeLidoMahdia; ⏲ 10.00–late daily. Relatively expensive by local standards, but the delicious seafood here is definitely worth it. Sitting outside under the umbrellas is probably better than in the narrow restaurant itself. Try the octopus salad. **$$$$**

El Asfoor Rte de la Corniche; m 58 329 025/6; ⌚ 07.30–midnight daily. Fancy Mediterranean restaurant next door to the Iberostar, serving seafood & pasta, with a good wine list. 2 pleasant outdoor dining spaces. $$$–$$$$

✱ **Darna** Av 14 Janvier; m 54 676 088, 28 127 175; f; ⌚ 10.00–22.00 daily. A very simple concept: the menu of the day is on a chalkboard outside (& posted on Facebook), with a choice of 2 or 3 traditional Tunisian specialities. Salad & *chorba* starters usually included, & there is almost always a seafood & couscous option. Dishes are cooked in the open kitchen, so you can watch the food preparation as you wait. Fast service, low prices, tasty food. A must-visit for lunch! $$$

Restaurant Chez Naima Rue Mohamed Turki; m 93 627 617; f restaurantcheznaima; ⌚ 11.00–17.00 Mon–Sat. Great lunch spot offering a tasty traditional menu of the day, published on Facebook each morning. There are only a few choices, normally including a seafood, meat & vegetable option. $$–$$$

Café Sidi Salem Rue de Borj Othmani; ☎ 73 695 696; m 23 583 563; ⌚ 10.00–20.30 daily. Café up on the rocks with a spacious terrace overlooking the water below. Stick to ordering drinks, though, as food service is often slow. $$

Café El Médina Rue de l'Ancienne Poste; m 50 577 482; f cafeElMedina; ⌚ 08.00–23.00 daily. The tree-shaded terrace is a popular spot with locals & cats alike, where you can grab a shisha or coffee. Good views of the medina from the rooftop. $–$$

SHOPPING

Futa Shop Just off Av Cap Africa. Step inside to see owner Mohamed Ismail hard at work on the amazing looms used to make these thin-patterned cotton towels.

Musée Naval de Mahdia 41 Rue des Fatimides; m 97 712 651; f museenavalde.mahdia. This is not a museum but a shop selling wooden model boats, from a few centimetres long to over 1m. Very impressive craftsmanship.

SPORTS AND ACTIVITIES

✱ **Centre Hippique Mahdia** Cap Mahdia Hotel; m 24 751 464; e gabi_incisa@yahoo.com; w mahdiahorses.com; f centrehippiquemahdia. Italian founder Gabriella has been in Tunisia for over 30 years & runs this horseriding centre with a difference. Not only does it offer lessons for those wishing to learn to ride, but it also breeds rare Barb & Arabian horses as well as Mogod ponies. The centre offers animal-based therapy sessions for children too. A worthy cause & well worth a visit!

Subway Diving Centre Mahdia Port de Pêche; m 98 556 542; e subway@topnet.tn; w subway-mahdia.com; ⌚ 15 May–30 Oct, dives depart at 09.00 & 14.00 daily. A joint-owned Tunisian-German company with instruction available in Arabic, German, Italian, French & English.

WHAT TO SEE AND DO

A walk around the peninsula Start your visit to Mahdia by walking round the edge of the promontory. Beginning on the north side, head along Boulevard du Cap Afrique to the **lighthouse**, from where you can gaze across the turquoise waters fringing Cap d'Afrique, or back towards the ancient ruins of Borj el Kebir to your southwest (especially good at sunset). Just behind the lighthouse is a large **cemetery** where – on the most exposed, barren part of the peninsula – the Mahdois have buried their dead for centuries. Looking southwards from the cemetery, you will see the remains of the **Fatimid port** from which the 11th-century invasion of Egypt was launched, and today where local children often jump off the rocks to swim. It seems that the entrance was defended by two towers, linked by an arch. The port fell to Christian ships in 1088.

Walking back westwards along the south side of the peninsula, you pass Mahdia's impressive fortress, the **Borj el Kebir** (⌚ summer 09.00–19.00 Tue–Sun, winter 09.00–16.00 Tue–Sun; 7DT, photography 1DT), on your right. Built on the highest point of the headland and overlooking the sea, it was constructed around the same time as the Skifa el Kahla in the 10th century; the corner bastions were added in the 18th century. The view from the top is good, though the architectural interest is limited.

You will then pass an area of excavations of the **Fatimid palace**, just to the west of Borj el Kebir and likely commissioned by El Mehdi at the same time as the nearby Great Mosque. It is unclear why this structure did not survive, while the fortifications and mosque around it did. The **Great Mosque** itself dominates this southern side of the peninsula. There is something a bit too perfect about the honey-coloured walls, and indeed the mosque was totally rebuilt in 1963 following the original 10th-century plans. This was the first Fatimid mosque ever built, under the direction of El Mehdi, and its reconstruction must have had important symbolic value for the recently independent Tunisian state. In architectural terms, there are several interesting things that can be spotted by the non-Muslim visitor, even if the interior is off-limits. Note the splendid arched main entrance – possibly inspired by Roman triumphal arches – that was the grand ceremonial entryway for the Fatimid imam. The area separating the mosque from the new port, dating from the beginning of the century, is landfill created when the port was dredged.

The medina Enter the medina through the **Skifa el Kahla** ('The Black Passage'), the monumental passageway to the old town. During El Mehdi's reign, only troops and a few privileged people lived within the medina's walls; though their shops were inside, townsfolk lived outside. This reduced the prospect of rebellion, as to do so during the day when their shops were open risked them being locked within the Skifa el Kahla by the authorities, jeopardising the life of their families outside. Starting a rebellion at night, on the other hand, would mean them being locked out of their shops and workshops, leading to the loss of their livelihood. The present format of the gate was built in 1554, following the departure of the Spanish. Right next to the Skifa is **Mahdia Museum** (🕘 summer 09.00–13.00 & 15.00–19.00 Tue–Sun, winter 09.30–16.00 Tue–Sun; 8/5DT non-residents/residents), home to Punic, Roman, Byzantine and Islamic displays, including

THE MAHDIA WRECK

This early 1st-century BC Roman shipwreck, which sank en route from Attica in Greece to Italy, lies 5km off the coast of Mahdia. It was a luxurious shipment of artworks and house furnishings intended for purchase by the elites of ancient Rome with one customer believed to have been the famed Roman consul and dictator, Lucius Cornelius Sulla.

Archaeologists Merlin and Poinssot describe the wreck spotted by sponge divers in 1907:

> items of far greater value were discovered, the objects which filled the hold: noble effigies, fine statuettes and reliefs in bronze and marble, fragments of containers or utensils with delicate fittings, fragments of luxury decorative marble pieces, a whole set of items indicative of skilled craft techniques, thanks to which we have a reflection of high Hellenic art.

Sadly at the time of writing, dive centres in Mahdia do not offer this wreck as one of their dives.

some very well-preserved mosaics from El Djem (page 252) and a series of gold-coin hoards. The views from the roof over the coastal peninsula and the medina are also spectacular.

As you wander the medina, look out for cloth-weavers in action. Peering through a doorway of one of the numerous weaving workshops (such as that owned by Mr Mohamed Ismail, page 249), you may see someone involved in the elaborate foot-dance required to operate the typical weaver's loom. The products are high-quality striped silks for wedding costumes and cotton *futas* (towels). Curiously, when it comes to looms, there is a gender divide in Tunisia's cities: men operate horizontal cloth looms, while women work at vertical carpet looms.

You could finish your medina tour with a visit to the **Church of Our Lady of Mount Carmel**. With whitewashed walls and three simple glass windows, it looks pretty nondescript from the outside: it is likely that this was originally an oil press owned by Mohammed el-Sadik Bey, before it was donated to Mahdia's small Christian community (made up mainly of Italians and Maltese) in 1861 to be converted into a church. Like many other Catholic properties, it was handed over to the Tunisian state by the Vatican on 10 July 1964. It has now been restored and is occasionally open to the public as an exhibition space.

AROUND MAHDIA

Salakta Museum (⊕ 35.392392, 11.048701; 🕘 winter 09.30–16.30 Tue–Sun, summer 09.00–noon & 14.00–18.00 Tue–Sun; non-residents/residents 5/4DT) Some 14km south of Mahdia, just beyond the small town of Ksour Essaf in the coastal village of Salakta, are the remains of Roman Sullecthum. This was a moderately wealthy port town in ancient times, first occupied by the Phoenicians who, along with subsequent occupants, earned revenue from exporting wheat across the Mediterranean. Situated next to the ancient cemetery and the modern port, this museum has some interesting items including a splendid mosaic showing a lion (the emblem of a rich shipowner of the city at that time) and a funerary breastplate of a Carthaginian general. As English archaeologists did a lot of work on Roman pottery here, there are English captions in the museum.

Chebba Just under 40km south of Mahdia is Chebba, a pleasant seaside resort town with a beautiful, forested beach and some decent accommodation options. Known as Caput Vada in Roman times and then Justinianopolis under the Byzantines, little remains of the ancient site thanks to a massive battle between the Vandals and the Byzantines here in AD533 which levelled the entire town. The only thing left standing was the Byzantine **Borj Khadija** (⊕ 35.234786, 11.156448), an imposing four-storey defensive structure, situated just by the port, which dates to the 7th century AD – although local legend has it that the name 'Khadija' originates from a local 11th-century poet by the same name. Her father, Ahmed ben Kalthoum El-Maafiri, was a well-known figure living in Kairouan at the time. There is a small museum inside the tower, and it is possible to climb the stairs to the top for the views; however, it was closed indefinitely at the time of writing.

As the statue on the town roundabout implies, the town's beaches are a nesting site for loggerhead **turtles**, specifically Essir (the main beach in front of Restaurant La Barque) and Sidi Messaoud (the 200m stretch to the southeast of Borj Khadija, behind the port). Scientists count between 40 and 45 nests each season. The Chebba-based NGO Association des Fans de la Chebba (m 26 804 864; e fanschebba@gmail.com; f AFChebba) works to preserve the turtles and their habitats, and may be able to give some advice on spotting them during the summer months.

Chebba is a little tricky to reach on public transport, having no train or metro station. You could try to catch a louage the 37km south from Mahdia, but most services between Mahdia and Sfax do not use the coastal C82 road on which Chebba sits, as it is not the most direct route. Best to come in your own vehicle.

Where to stay and eat

Dar el Barka (6 rooms) ⊕ 35.246881, 11.128230; m 52 775 157; e elbarka_chebba@yahoo.com; f DelBarka. Northwest of town & only 30m from a beach, each of the rooms has a different colour scheme & is minimally decorated with driftwood & nautical-themed items. Dinners are made to order with fresh ingredients from the local market. **$$$$**

Centre de Camping et de Vacances Chebba (47 rooms, 120 beds total) ⊕ 35.267275, 11.094971; 73 643 815; m 98 590 730. Around 6km northwest of town in the forest, 300m from the beach, this youth hostel/campsite seems to have been recently refurbished. Rooms have twin beds, a large balcony & a toilet & shower in wet-room configuration. Some rooms have AC. Offers meals on request. **$**

Casino Chebba ⊕ 35.241774, 11.139471; m 22 093 365; ⌚ 08.00–21.30 daily. Thatched pizzeria & café overlooking the water with plenty of outdoor seating. **$$**

Restaurant La Barque ⊕ 35.238278, 11.144408; ⌚ 10.30–late daily. Fast-food joint doing burgers & wraps, with wooden benches outside overlooking the beach. **$$**

EL DJEM

This small town in the middle of a plain of olive trees would be of little interest to tourists were it not for its imposing Roman amphitheatre, one of Tunisia's most incongruous and surprising sights upon first approach. It is the third-largest amphitheatre ever built by the Romans (behind the more famous Colosseum in Rome and the now-destroyed amphitheatre of Capua), and the largest of all Roman monuments in Africa. The sheer size of the ochre stone walls and arches – and a thought for the simple technology that must have been used to build it – makes this a breath-taking monument, which is unsurprisingly one of Tunisia's eight UNESCO World Heritage Sites. The ancient city itself covered an area of 150–200ha, and the size of the remaining monuments gives a clear indication of the original scale.

HISTORY Ancient Thysdrus was founded as a Punic town, although the Latin name has Amazigh roots. It was under the Romans, in particular the rule of Hadrian (AD117–38), that the town prospered as an important centre for the manufacture and export of olive oil. By the 3rd century, the town reached its peak with a population of over 30,000; the ruins of luxurious villas testify to wealthy residents, but there was a large rural population too. Owing to political rivalries within the Empire, El Djem's fortunes gradually declined, and were finally brought to an end during the Arab invasion, when the olive groves were set on fire, definitively ending the area's commercial prosperity.

GETTING THERE AND AWAY Tunis is 205km away (about 2 hours 15 minutes' drive). **Louages** service Sousse, so you will need to change there if coming from Tunis, while SNTRI buses run to Tunis, Sfax and Sousse. The main louage and bus station is very central, only 350m south of the amphitheatre and 300m west of the train station. Around five **trains** per day run between Tunis and El Djem (3hrs–3hrs 45mins), with the first departure around 06.15 and the last after 21.00.

WHERE TO STAY AND EAT El Djem would be a slightly odd choice for spending the night, given the far superior (and cheaper) options available in Sousse, Sfax and Monastir (all an hour away) or even Mahdia (45 minutes away). However, there are a couple of good hotels catering mainly to the large tour groups that pass through during high season.

Hotel Dar Ammar (7 rooms) Rue Ibnou Badis; m 53 635 565; w darammar.com. A very modern hotel, 2.5km west of the amphitheatre on the C87. Restaurant, private parking, bar, outdoor pool & garden with BBQ facilities. Rooms have river views, AC & en suite with shower. **$$$$**

Hotel Julius (37 rooms) Av Taïeb Mhiri; 73 631 006; w julius.tn. A very convenient base for exploring El Djem, right next to the train station & only 400m from the amphitheatre – with views of the latter from your room. Rooms are relatively large with a lot of wood, & en suite including bath & shower. Pool & on-site restaurant. **$$$$**

Le Bonheur 1 Rte de Sfax; 73 630 306; m 22 976 655; 11.00–23.00 daily. Brik, makloub, chorba, tagine: all the classics in a simple setting near the train station. **$$$**

Restaurant Elyes Av Farhat Hached; 73 631 255; m 98 295 996; f RestaurantElyes; 11.00–late daily. Offers Tunisian classics such as *lablabi* (chickpea soup) alongside various fast-food options including rotisserie chicken. Delivery available. **$$–$$$**

Café-Restaurant El Hana Av Habib Bourguiba; m 96 576 417; 09.00–17.00 daily. One of the closest decent eateries to the amphitheatre, with amazing views. Serves good grilled items (including fish & meat kebabs) as well as freshly squeezed orange juice in season. **$$**

WHAT TO SEE AND DO

Main amphitheatre (summer 07.30–18.30 daily, winter 07.30–17.30 daily; 12DT, also includes museum entry) A good guide to the level of the 'Romanity' of a city was the presence of an amphitheatre, and the amphitheatre of Thysdrus was, after the Colosseum in Rome and the amphitheatre in Capua, the largest in the Empire. At 18,056m^2 and with a perimeter of over 425m, it had capacity for around 35,000 spectators, with tiers that rose to more than 35m. Lack of inscriptions prevents accurate dating, but construction is thought to have been between AD230 and 238 and is attributed to Emperor Gordian I, who owned land and property in the area. When one considers that the nearest quarries were over 30km away, the task must have been enormous. The building was never completed owing to lack of funds and political instability. The stone was too soft for fine sculpture, hence the simplicity of the decoration. The amphitheatre was used for some of the spectacular shows so dear to the heart of Emperor Gordian – wild beasts fighting to the death and martyrs or prisoners being thrown to the wild animals. All good family viewing. Some of the scenes were recorded in the mosaics found here.

In later years, the amphitheatre was used as a rebel stronghold. Despite a lack of archaeological evidence, many tour guides will happily tell you of the legend of underground tunnels leading from El Djem to the sea – even though the sea is over 30km away. It is said that the Amazigh leader Queen Kahena rebelled against Islamic rule in 693 and used the amphitheatre as a fortress. She apparently waved wriggling fish at the troops surrounding her stronghold, taunting them with her freedom of movement thanks to the hidden tunnels. In 1695, Mohammed Bey ordered a hole to be made in the amphitheatre's walls to prevent its use during any further uprisings by the local population, who protested about his heavy taxation. The breach in the walls was further enlarged in 1850 during another tax revolt, which is why you are now able to sit in the cafés on the north side of the amphitheatre and peer into the middle. The amphitheatre was thereafter used as a convenient source of building stones by the inhabitants of the town. Nevertheless, the bulk of the original building remains and it is a truly impressive sight.

Today's visitor to Thysdrus can clamber up into the highest parts of the seating and look down into the arena just as the Roman spectator would have done. Mercifully, the slaughter of people and beasts is no longer considered great entertainment (see opposite) and little disturbs the quiet of the great building apart from the clicking of camera shutters and cooing of pigeons nesting in the crumbling stonework.

Since 1986, the amphitheatre has hosted the annual **El Djem International Symphonic Music Festival** (w festivaleljem.tn) in late July/early August. It tends to feature European symphony and chamber orchestras, although there have been concerts of lyric music and the occasional opera too. Thousands of candles light the building, creating an incredible and unique atmosphere enhanced by El Djem's night-time echoes, such as the last call to prayer or the braying of a donkey.

Archaeological Museum (⌚ summer 07.30–18.30 daily, winter 07.30–17.30 daily; free with amphitheatre ticket) Set in a replica of a Roman villa, 500m from the amphitheatre on the road to Sfax, this houses some magnificent mosaics found in a villa that once stood beside the museum. In the main room is the famous Orpheus mosaic, showing him charming the beasts with his music, while in the end room are two lively scenes: lions devouring a wild boar and next a tiger attacking two wild donkeys. The careful detail of the mosaics is impressive: for example, one Dionysian scene in the main hall contains a border full of lurking grasshoppers, frogs, rats, snails and lizards. The entire pavement is trellised with vines and set with tiny birds, animals and cupids, including a ladder-carrying cupid, off to the grape harvest. In the central medallion, three chubby *putti* (cherubs), urged on by a naked woman, are tying up a bald, bearded and pot-bellied Silenus (Bacchus's father) with floral garlands.

Wealthy Romans liked to display their taste and status, and one way to do this was with wall paintings (which do not seem to have been widespread in ancient Africa) and mosaic pavings. Certain themes were more popular than others. The inhabitants of El Djem seem to have been good-time people and liked scenes of muses (to remind them of the arts), animals and boozy romps, liberally decorated with vine leaves and cupids. The museum has scenes of Minerva judging the musical contest between Apollo and Marsyas, for example

Another theme dear to villa owners was the four seasons. The countryside was close by, and the wealth of the city depended on farming. A small mosaic with a central medallion containing the bust of a bearded old man is a good example of this concern. Six circles contain the Sun (Apollo), the Moon (Artemis) and the four seasons: Spring in green, Summer in red, bare-breasted and vine-draped Autumn and darkly cloaked Winter.

Smaller amphitheatres and other excavations A short distance south of the main amphitheatre on the other side of the road from the archaeological museum are El Djem's two smaller amphitheatres, one built on top of the other. Dating from the 1st century, the older, more primitive theatre was simply cut into the rock, while the second one, which was to last until the building of the large amphitheatre, was erected in the early 2nd century against the hillside on top of the remains of the first. Today it is sadly neglected, in the shadow of its more impressive successor.

The large number of fine **Roman villas** excavated at El Djem is indicative of the considerable wealth of the town. The dwellings, built around an inner courtyard and surrounded by a colonnaded gallery, were paved with colourful mosaics

A TASTE FOR BLOOD

In his *Natural History*, Pliny tells the tale of the origin of the amphitheatre. In 53BC, in Italy, a candidate for the tribune's office in search of votes devised a new electioneering technique. Two semicircular wooden theatres were set up back-to-back, mounted on a swivel, so two plays could be put on at the same time. But the gimmick was revealed in the afternoon, when the two theatres were swung round on their pivots to form a circle where a *munus* (gladiatorial show) was held. *Munus* literally means 'duty' or 'obligation' in Latin, but in this context it refers to the obligation of high-status individuals to finance public works or entertainment for the benefit of the Roman people.

Under Emperor Augustus (27BC–AD14), the *munus* became an important (and sinister) way for rulers to interact with their subjects. The primitive wooden structures gave way to magnificent stone buildings and the word 'amphitheatrum' was coined to describe the settings for these various brutish 'sports'. In addition to the *hoplomachia* (gladiator) fights, there were re-enactments of various myths (Pasiphae and the bull, among others) and, in the later Empire, the followers of Christianity – then viewed as a dangerous sect with secret ceremonies – became a particular target.

Amphitheatres were also the setting for *Damnatio ad bestias* (a form of capital punishment in which a subject was condemned to the beasts), though this was reserved for common criminals and certain prisoners of war. To go by the evidence of the mosaics, those in the province of Africa preferred that their exotic animals be used for *venationes* – the exhibition of, and 'hunting' by, big cats and other wild beasts (as portrayed in the mosaic of the tiger attacking two wild donkeys in El Djem museum; see opposite). Nevertheless, the huge resources devoted to the shipping of rare beasts for slaughter is testimony to the importance of the amphitheatre shows, evidencing the wealth of the Empire and the extent to which this wealth could be squandered.

depicting mythological themes (now displayed in the Bardo Museum, in Sousse and at the museum here). In the more recently discovered villas, the mosaics have been left *in situ*.

Behind the museum, about 250m to the west of the small amphitheatre, there is a group of villas bounded by a Roman necropolis to the south and a well-preserved, paved street to the east. The houses are of the classic Roman style with a garden surrounded by a peristyle with richly decorated rooms.

SFAX *Telephone code: +74*

Tunisia's second-largest city and port, Sfax has a very different character from Tunis or Sousse, owing to its lack of reliance on tourism revenue, but it remains a cosmopolitan urban centre with a rich history that warrants exploring. Some highlights include some of the best-preserved medinas in the country, the archaeological museum and the Muslim, Christian and Jewish places of worship scattered across the city. There is a certain amount of light-hearted (and occasionally not so light-hearted!) rivalry between Sfax and the rest of Tunisia, especially nearby Sousse: Sfaxiens have a reputation for being hard-nosed businesspeople, but do not listen to what the detractors have to say. This is one of my favourite cities in the country, and an excellent jumping-off point for the idyllic Kerkennah Islands.

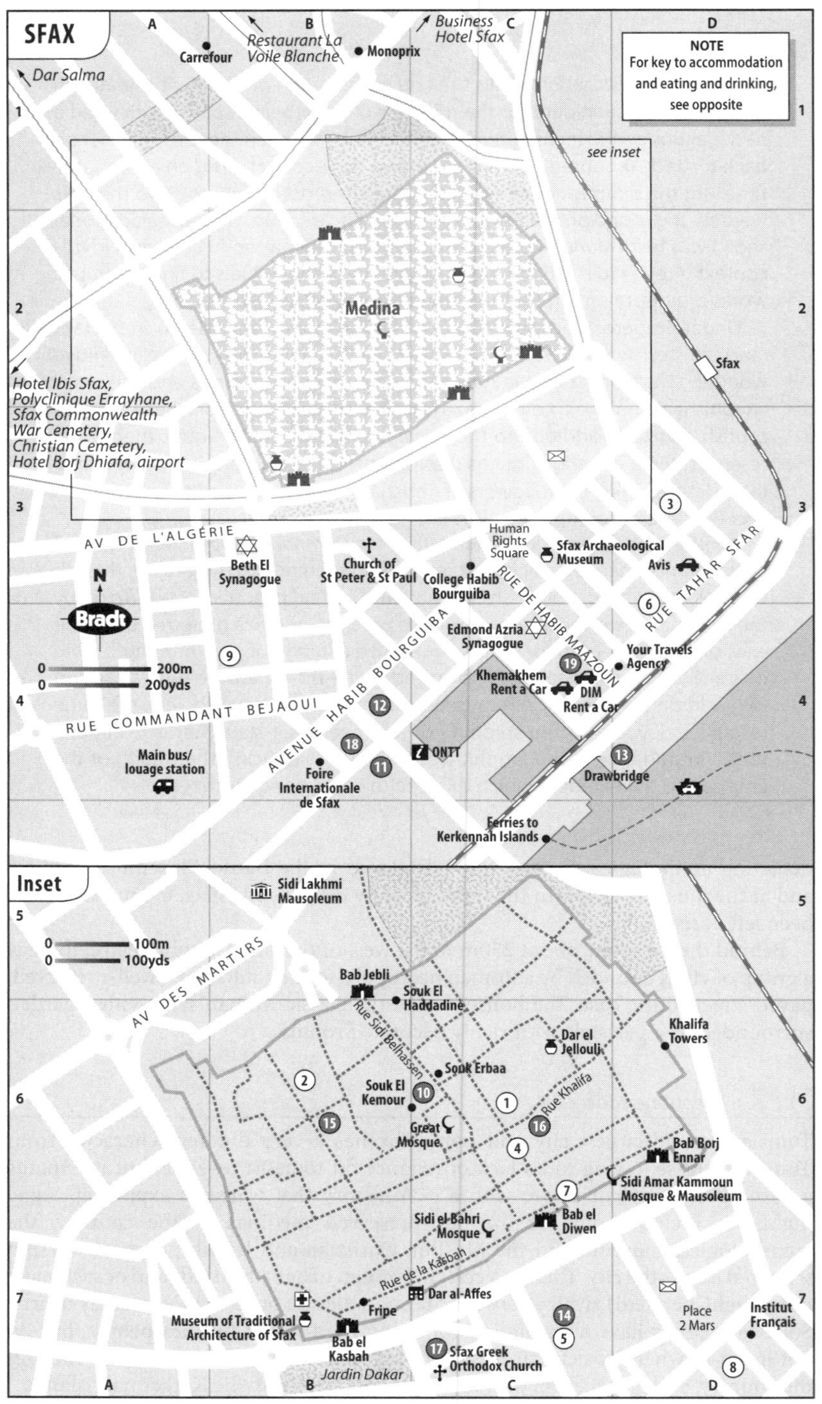
SFAX
NOTE
For key to accommodation and eating and drinking, see opposite
Dar Salma
Carrefour
Restaurant La Voile Blanche
Monoprix
Business Hotel Sfax
see inset
Medina
Sfax
Hotel Ibis Sfax, Polyclinique Errayhane, Sfax Commonwealth War Cemetery, Christian Cemetery, Hotel Borj Dhiafa, airport
AV DE L'ALGÉRIE
Beth El Synagogue
Church of St Peter & St Paul
College Habib Bourguiba
Human Rights Square
Sfax Archaeological Museum
Avis
RUE DE HABIB MAÂZOUN
RUE TAHAR SFAR
Edmond Azria Synagogue
Your Travels Agency
Khemakhem Rent a Car
DIM Rent a Car
200m
200yds
RUE COMMANDANT BEJAOUI
AVENUE HABIB BOURGUIBA
ONTT
Main bus/ louage station
Foire Internationale de Sfax
Drawbridge
Ferries to Kerkennah Islands
Inset
Sidi Lakhmi Mausoleum
100m
100yds
AV DES MARTYRS
Bab Jebli
Souk El Haddadine
Rue Sidi Belhassen
Dar el Jellouli
Khalifa Towers
Souk Erbaa
Souk El Kemour
Rue Khalifa
Great Mosque
Bab Borj Ennar
Sidi Amar Kammoun Mosque & Mausoleum
Sidi el-Bahri Mosque
Bab el Diwen
Rue de la Kasbah
Dar al-Affes
Fripe
Museum of Traditional Architecture of Sfax
Bab el Kasbah
Place 2 Mars
Institut Français
Sfax Greek Orthodox Church
Jardin Dakar

Since the turn of the century, the city has been constantly expanding: nine main roads radiate out in all directions like a spider's web, connecting Sfax to the rest of the country, while the port connects it to the rest of the world. Sfax is also the birthplace of legendary but controversial endurance open-water swimmer Nejib Belhedi. Belhedi holds some incredible records including swimming the English Channel at high tide, swimming from Sfax to the Kerkennah Islands and a 1,400km swim along Tunisia's coastline. However, he hit the headlines in June 2022 after claiming to have swum 155km between the Italian island of Pantelleria and the coast of Hammamet with some highly dubious GPS data as evidence.

HISTORY Sfax has its founding legend. The Arabic name of the town (Safakus) derives from the name of an Aghlabid prince's groom, Safa, and the Arabic verb *kus* ('to cut'). 'Cut, Safa,' said the prince, 'cut the cow hide into fine strips and mark out the limits of the city.' This, of course, is a repeat of the myth that recounts how Dido outsmarted the local king to found Carthage (page 101). More prosaically, however, it would seem the name Safakus is of Amazigh origin.

The ancient town of Taparura, likely originally Amazigh, sat on the site of present-day Sfax. In the 7th century, the town was already a trade centre, exporting olive oil to Italy and, by the 10th century, it declared itself an independent state, only to be conquered by Roger of Sicily in 1148. It later fought off the Venetians in 1785 and surrendered to the French only in 1881 after some fierce fighting – one of the few Tunisian towns to put up much resistance at all. In the early years of French rule, the Frankish and Jewish quarter, Rbat el Qibli, was replaced by the new Bab el Bhar neighbourhood, and several fine public buildings in the neo-Moorish style went up, including the town hall with its minaret, and the now-demolished municipal theatre. A modern port was completed in 1891.

Bombardment during World War II destroyed a large part of Sfax, but this created an opportunity to replan the centre. Neighbourhoods close to the medina's walls were cleared, and the resulting open spaces give central Sfax the feel of a Moroccan city, where new European areas were always built separately from the old medinas. Today, Sfax remains Tunisia's second-largest port; activities include exporting phosphates, and olive-oil processing continues to be a major industry.

SFAX

For listings, see from page 258

Where to stay

1	Andalusia	C6
2	Dar Baya	B6
3	Hotel Alexandre	D3
4	Hotel el Medina	C6
5	Hotel Thyna	C7
6	Les Oliviers Palace	D4
7	Maghreb	C6
8	Occidental Sfax Centre	D7
9	Radisson Hotel Sfax	B4

Off map

Business Hotel Sfax	C1
Dar Salma	A1
Hotel Borj Dhiafa	A2
Hotel Ibis Sfax	A2

Where to eat and drink

10	Café Kemour	C6
11	Chahia Chick'n Box	B4
12	La Renaissance	B4
13	La Sirene	D4
14	Le Corail	C7
15	Petit Déj Lemdina	B6
16	Restaurant Abid Saffoud	C6
17	Restaurant Baghdad	C7
18	Restaurant Cercina	B4
19	Tutti Frutti	C4

Off map

Restaurant La Voile Blanche	B1

GETTING THERE AND AWAY

By air Sfax-Thyna Airport sits 6.5km west of the city centre, but it is not particularly well served, connecting only to Tunis, Istanbul, Libya and (seasonally) to France. The much larger Enfidha-Hammamet International Airport (page 75) is 170km north (2 hours' drive), while Monastir Habib Bourguiba International Airport (page 240) is 130km to the north.

By road Tunis is 270km away (about 3 hours 10 minutes without traffic). **Louage** services from Tunis depart from Gare Routière Sud (page 94), and SNTRI **buses** run from Tunis (Moncef Bey) (4hrs 15 mins; 18.90DT one-way). The main louage and bus station is on Rue Commandant Bejaoui [256 A4], in the west of the town centre.

By rail There are generally around five SNCFT trains per day from Tunis to Sfax (4hrs 30mins), with the first departure before 06.00 and the last after 21.00. The main train station is behind the medina [256 D2].

GETTING AROUND Sfax is very flat, which certainly helps if you intend to do a walking tour of the city, and many of the sights are concentrated within the square kilometre encompassing the medina and the port, which is all very walkable.

For short journeys around town, yellow **taxis** can be flagged down; unfortunately, there is no ride-hailing app presence in the city. A number of **car-hire outfits** can be found on Rue Tahar Sfar, including Avis [256 D3] (74 224 605; 08.30–19.00 Mon–Sat), DIM Rent a Car [256 C4] (74 298 081; w dimrentacar.com; 08.00–13.00 & 15.00–18.00 Mon–Sat) and Khemakhem Rent a Car [256 C4] (74 200 463; m 22 630 455; e khemakhemrentcar@gmail.com; f KhemakhemRentCar; 08.00–19.00 daily). Traffic can get pretty bad at rush hour in Sfax, and parking can also be a problem, so plan your journey in advance.

Much like the main road network, the **bus** network tends to radiate outwards from the city centre like a clock face, so moving east–west (or vice versa) across town is usually best done in a taxi. You can find timetables, route maps and prices for regional bus networks on the SORETRAS website (w soretras.com.tn). Visitors will likely find the 16b route useful as it heads west towards the airport and Commonwealth War Cemetery (page 263).

There is a 70km **metro** (w metrosfax.tn) network currently under construction, which will include trams and rapid-transit buses, but this is not due to be completed until 2030.

TOURIST INFORMATION AND LOCAL TOUR OPERATORS

ONTT [256 C4] Av Mohamed El Hédi Kefacha; 74 497 041; e crt.sfax@ontt.tourism.tn; 08.00–18.00 Mon–Fri.

Your Travels Agency [256 D4] 49 Rue Tahar Sfar; 74 229 429; w yourtravelsagency.com; f Your.Travels.Agency; 09.00–17.30 Mon–Fri, 09.00–13.00 Sat. Can book Kerkennah Islands ferry tickets (& print them for you!).

 **WHERE TO STAY** Accommodation in Sfax is generally aimed at business visitors rather than tourists, but there are a few great dars in the city. If it ever reopens, the grand old **Hotel Les Arcades** would likely make a good budget choice near the centre.

Les Oliviers Palace [256 D4] (137 rooms) 25 Av Hédi Chaker; 74 201 999; e olivierspalace.sfax@goldenyasmin.com. Here since 1920, this grand 5-star hotel is part of the Golden Yasmin chain. Clean & modern rooms are large with a bath & shower, minibar & separate toilet. Some faded colonial charm in the communal spaces, but feels too expensive. **$$$$$**

Business Hotel Sfax [256 C1] (67 rooms) Av 5 Août; m 39 159 000; e reservation@businesshotelsfax.com.tn; f BusinessHotelSfax. As the name suggests, this smart business hotel north of the centre features modern, spacious rooms, a trendy bar & a hammam. **$$$$**

✱ **Dar Baya** [256 B6] (7 rooms) 112 Rue Al-Shaykh Al-Tijeni; 74 200 814; w dar-baya.com. If you are going to stay in the medina & your budget stretches to it, this restored traditional home is your best bet, all pink & white stone with green wooden doors & metalwork features. Rooms are individually designed, some with a dbl bed in a raised alcove, with a small bathroom & shower, & direct access to the interior courtyard where meals are served. Also has a rooftop café. A great base from which to explore the medina. **$$$$**

✷ **Dar Salma** [256 A1] (6 rooms, 1 studio) Rte de Gremda Bouzayane; m 22 135 446; f. Located in the affluent northern suburb of Gremda, Mme Salma's dar is a hidden gem. Recently refurbished, the Moorish architectural features (such as the carved stucco in the home's central dome) are astonishing. Rooms are all of different types, including 1 that is palatial in size & has a walk-in closet & direct access to a large balcony. There is also a studio in the sizeable garden. B/fast inc; other meals available if booked in advance. **$$$$**

Hotel Borj Dhiafa [256 A2] (50 rooms) Rte Soukra, km3; 74 677 777; w hotelborjdhiafa.com. West of the town centre near the airport, this castle-like hotel boasts beautiful interior architectural features such as Corinthian columns & intricately carved wooden doors. Good hammam, pool & restaurant. **$$$$**

Hotel Ibis Sfax [256 A2] (187 rooms) Av Majida Boulila; 70 241 000; f ibissfax. Excellent customer service & bright, immaculate rooms in this very centrally located Ibis property. A great base from which to explore the city. There is also a very popular bar downstairs. **$$$$**

Occidental Sfax Centre [256 D7] (130 rooms) Av Habib Bourguiba; 74 225 700; w barcelo.com/en-gb/occidental-sfax-centre; f OccidentalSfaxCentre. In a good location near the train station, this 4-star hotel offers 2 restaurants, a large spa & an outdoor swimming pool. Ignore the large 'Concorde' sign outside – that is the old name. **$$$$**

Radisson Hotel Sfax [256 B4] (88 rooms) Rue de Ribat; 31 231 001; w radissonhotels.com/en-us/hotels/radisson-sfax. This high-quality, centrally located hotel has a 9th-floor restaurant & bar (Younga Sky) & rooftop pool with panoramic views of the city. **$$$$**

Hotel Alexandre [256 D3] (34 rooms) Rue Alexandre Dumas; m 25 818 740. Good location in the quieter end of town; look for the silver sign which leads to a marble-clad reception. A very old-school, wrought-iron lift in a cage leads to the rooms, which are dark but clean with a bath & shower. **$$$**

Hotel Thyna [256 C7] (27 rooms) Rue Habib Maâzoun; 74 225 317; w hotel-thyna.com. Simple en-suite rooms with a large bed, AC & TV, plus balcony overlooking town. **$$$**

Andalusia Hotel [256 C6] (8 rooms) Rue Sidi Ali Karray; 28 304 298. Very old & in a state of disrepair, but one of the cheapest beds in the medina & a great location. **$**

Hotel el Medina [256 C6] (12 rooms) 53 Rue Mongi Slim. In a better state than the nearby Andalusia (& the same price); rooms are very clean (just a bed & a window), as are the communal bathrooms, plus the owner is friendly. **$**

Maghreb Hotel [256 C6] (20 rooms) Archway off Rue Borj Ennar. Here since 1963, rooms are grim but it has a big, open interior courtyard. Only worth considering if Hotel el Medina is full, as it is also slightly more expensive. **$**

WHERE TO EAT AND DRINK

La Renaissance [256 B4] 9 Av Mohamed Hédi Khefacha; m 25 762 616, 98 415 031; f; noon–15.00 & 18.00–22.00 daily. Grey stone-fronted seafood restaurant with a decent wine list. **$$$$**

La Sirene [256 D4] Rue Haffouz; 74 224 691; f ShtAlqraqnt; noon–15.00 & 19.00–23.00 daily. On the northeast side of the drawbridge in a rather unappealing-looking industrial section of the port is this very popular seafood restaurant. All fish is sold by the 100g, so things can get a little expensive, but it is as fresh as it gets with a great selection. **$$$$**

Le Corail [256 C7] 39 Av Habib Maâzoun; 74 227 301; m 22 260 213; e contact@restaurantlecorail.tn; f lecorailrestaurantettraiteur; noon–15.00 & 19.00–midnight Mon–Sat. Upmarket seafood restaurant attached to the Hotel Thyna, with live music at w/ends. **$$$$**

Restaurant La Voile Blanche [256 B1] Rte Teniour, km1.5; m 22 287 799; f; noon–16.00 & 18.30–22.00 daily. Excellent seafood restaurant in the north of town. **$$$$**

✷ **Restaurant Baghdad** [256 C7] 63 Bd Farhat Hached; 74 223 856; e saifk@hotmail.fr; f Restaurant.baghdad; noon–15.00 & 19.00–

23.00 Sat–Thu. A veritable Sfax institution, this place has been serving up traditional Sfaxienne cuisine since the early 1960s. $$$

Restaurant Cercina [256 B4] 19 Rue Ibn Majed; 74 229 241; f; noon–15.00 & 18.00–22.00 Sat–Thu. It's easy to miss this tiny place squashed against the neighbouring garage, but look out for the red-&-blue sign as it serves simple, tasty local seafood. $$$

Chahia Chick'n Box [256 B4] Av Ali Bach Hamba; m 24 060 085; e info@chahiachicknbox.com; 09.00–18.00 daily. Chicken butchers that also has a take-away place next door, selling good rotisserie chicken & chips. Great option for a packed lunch. $$

Restaurant Abid Saffoud [256 C6] Rue Khalifa; m 22 116 655; 10.30–22.00 daily. Small restaurant in the backstreets of the medina serving cheap & cheerful meat skewers, grilled to perfection on the charcoal. Also plates of heaped seafood on offer, with a variety of specialist Sfaxienne sauces. $$

Tutti Frutti [256 C4] Rue Tahar Sfar; m 98 289 319, 50 583 387; f; 09.00–18.00 daily. Good fresh fruit juices in this bright-green café. If you are lucky, it might be serving *jwajem*, a traditional Sfaxien yoghurt dessert with dried fruits. $$

Petit Déj Lemdina [256 B6] 52 Rue Cheikh Tijani; 10.00–16.00 Tue–Sun. Simple café in the medina with good fresh juices, coffee & pastries. $–$$

Café Kemour [256 C6] Souk El Kemour; e achraftrigui@yahoo.fr; f CafekemourSfax; 07.00–18.00 Tue–Sun. Very popular café right next to the Great Mosque. The rooftop seating has good views. $

ENTERTAINMENT AND NIGHTLIFE Outside the larger hotels and resorts, Sfax is surprisingly lacking in bars and nightclubs for such a big city. However, you should be able to hunt down some nightlife during festival season (page 61), or check Tunisian ticketing sites such as w teskerti.tn for live music events.

Built in 1957, the impressive black-and-white **Foire Internationale de Sfax** [256 B4] (Av Habib Bourguiba; w foiredesfax.com; f AssociationDeLaFoireInternationaleDeSfax) hosts all sorts of trade fairs, exhibitions and live events. Check its website or Facebook page for up-to-date listings.

SHOPPING Sfax's medina has a good selection of souks. Upon entering through the northern Bab Jebli you soon hit **Souk El Haddadine** [256 B5], which is traditionally dedicated to those who work with metal and wood – blacksmiths and joiners. In the centre of the medina, near the Great Mosque, **Souk El Kemour** [256 C6] was historically the spice and dried food market, although today you will find all sorts of other modern products on sale here. Just to the north is **Souk Erbaa** [256 C6], the oldest and most prestigious of the souks, hence the covered space, which now sells all manner of consumer goods.

OTHER PRACTICALITIES For medical issues, the well-regarded **Polyclinique Errayhane** [256 A2] (Rte Menzel Chaker; 74 404 404; e contact@errayhaneclinic.com; w errayhaneclinic.com) over near the Ibis has an emergency department.

WHAT TO SEE AND DO

Along Avenue Habib Bourguiba Our 2-hour walking tour of Sfax begins at the **Institut Français** [256 D7] (9 Av Habib Bourguiba; 74 224 745; w institutfrancais-tunisie.com/sfax; 08.00–18.00 Mon–Fri). Known locally as Maison de France, this lovely old colonial building with decorative battlements and intricate wrought-iron railings houses a language centre, library, exhibition space and some consular services.

Walking southwest, you soon hit **Place 2 Mars** [256 D7] on your right which is home to some fascinating architectural treasures: a blue pavilion that looks like it once hosted live music (but sadly does not seem to any more), a four-storey abandoned colonial building overlooking Rue Victor Hugo, and a silver-domed structure that is home to the post office (🕘 08.00–17.00 Mon–Fri).

Continuing westwards, you come to **Human Rights Square** [256 C3] on your right with a large fountain. At the southern end of this square is the imposing, castle-like Sfax municipal government building, which houses the **Sfax Archaeological Museum** [256 C3] (33 Av Habib Bourguiba; 🕘 closed at the time of writing, but usually winter 08.30–13.00 & 15.00–17.45 Tue–Sun, summer 08.00–14.00 Tue–Sun; 5DT). The oldest museum in the country, founded in 1907, it houses a varied collection across seven rooms. Artefacts cover prehistory and the Punic, Roman, Byzantine and Islamic periods, including mosaics, glass products and coins excavated locally (from here in Sfax, known as Taparura in ancient times) as well as regionally (from Thaenae, La Louza, Acholla and even the Kerkennah Islands).

Further along Avenue Habib Bourguiba is the palm-fronted **College Habib Bourguiba** [256 C3], still a functional educational institution but under renovation at the time of writing. Here, turn left (south) on to Rue de Habib Maâzoun to reach **Edmond Azria Synagogue** [256 C4]. With a prominent stone Star of David on the wall, the blue exterior iron doors are inscribed with the initials 'A E' in memory of the son of the founder, Makhlouf Azria, who died in 1943. At the time of the synagogue's construction in 1948, the Jewish population of Sfax was over 4,200, although this had plummeted to only 205 by 1976. The synagogue was renovated in 2010 by a member of the Azria family. It is still functional, though not open to casual visitors; you may be able to organise a tour through a guide (page 40).

Sfax's other synagogue, **Beth El Synagogue** [256 B3] (Av de l'Algérie), is north of here close to Jardin Dakar. This imposing, monolithic structure was opened in June 1955, and intended not only as a place of worship but also to provide accommodation for Jewish pilgrims visiting the area during religious holidays (hence why it is so large). Today, however, it is not immediately obvious from the outside that this sadly abandoned structure was once a synagogue. In fact, looking up at the colourful stained-glass windows from the Avenue de l'Algérie, one might guess it was a church of some kind, but the Stars of David on the iron gate on Rue Imam Boukhari and the main entrance give it away. The synagogue has been vandalised on a number of occasions since the Tunisian Revolution and is locked up securely.

Just east of the synagogue is the ancient **Church of St Peter and St Paul** [256 B3]. This is not the original location of the church; it once sat on the north side of Boulevard de France (now Avenue Farhat Hached), but was completely destroyed during an intense Allied bombing campaign of Sfax from 12 December 1942 until 28 January 1943. This newer church was completed in 1953, and it was ceded to the Tunisian government by the Vatican in July 1964. From then on it was used as a sports hall and cultural centre, although at the time of writing it has been closed by the Ministry of Culture for an ambitious set of renovations.

Over the road, opposite Jardin Dakar, is the **Sfax Greek Orthodox Church** [256 C7] (Av Habib Achour). Greek emigration to the city began in the mid 19th century and by 1882 the community was large enough to warrant its own Greek consulate, and by 1887 there were 600 members, mainly trading in olive oil and grain, but also sponge fishing. A plaque on the church commemorates the visit of Mélétios II (a very senior religious leader within the church) in the summer of 1931. The church was locked at the time of writing, although it is still in use for special religious ceremonies. If you can find a local tour guide to arrange access (page 40), there is a series of beautiful frescoes inside.

The medina 🏴 One of the best-preserved and most authentic in Tunisia, Sfax's medina has souks that are primarily aimed at locals, who do a lot of their shopping here. Many artisans and craftsmen still work here and earn a living in a traditional way. This all makes the medina very interesting for visitors, particularly as its walls are still intact and the difference in atmosphere between the old and new cities is clear.

Entering via **Bab Jebli** [256 B5] at the northern end (the most intact and impressive of the six main gated entrances), you are immediately thrust into the bustle of the medina's souks, in this case mainly fresh fruit and vegetables. Wandering straight down Rue Sidi Belhassen leads to the **Great Mosque** [256 C6], built in 849 during the rule of Muhammad I ibn al-Aghlab and altered in 988 and 1035. Though it is closed to non-Muslims, from the outside you can admire the minaret, made of three superimposed square sections. Though similar to the minaret at the Great Mosque of Kairouan (page 279), there is far more decoration here, including horizontal bands and religious inscriptions. There is a large courtyard, though this is considerably smaller than it once was, part of it having been built upon during an extension of the prayer hall. The roof terrace of neighbouring Café Kemour (page 260) gives alternative views. There is also a small information sign on the northeast wall if you care to walk the perimeter.

Threading east from the mosque down Rue Khalifa, you reach the museum of **Dar el Jellouli** [256 C6] (Rue Sidi Ali Ennouri; ⌚ 09.30–16.30 Tue–Sun; 5DT). Under refurbishment at the time of writing, it was set up by French academic Lucien Camille Golvin in 1939, in the 17th-century home of a wealthy Sfaxienne family. It showcases traditional male and female clothing, toiletries and jewellery alongside a Sfaxien wedding scene depicting a bride jumping over a fish, which is said to bring good luck.

Continue following Rue Khalifa eastwards as far as it will take you, until you reach the **Khalifa Towers** [256 D6], defensive structures which were under refurbishment at the time of writing. It remains unclear if the intention is to open up a gate here, but right now it is not possible to walk the interior perimeter of the walls because this section is a dead end. Instead, head south along the walls until you are forced to curve westwards, past the **Bab Borj Ennar** [256 D6], and eventually you reach the four-storey **Sidi Amar Kammoun Mosque and Mausoleum** [256 D6] (⌚ closed to non-Muslims). Started in 1630 under the orders of Murad II Bey (confusingly the third Muradid Bey of Tunis), it was completed thanks to Sidi Amar Kammoun (who is buried here), as he managed to cure the bey of a disease caught while visiting the city. Continue past **Bab el Diwen** to **Sidi el Bahri Mosque** [256 C7], a 19th-century structure incorporating fine stone quarried from Gabès; note the engravings on the plinth above the green doorway.

Head east on Rue de la Kasbah for 150m to reach **Dar al-Affes** [256 C7]. Built by wealthy Sfaxienne Mohamed al-Affes, it was destroyed by Allied bombing during World War II, but subsequently reconstructed according to the original architectural designs. It is now sometimes used as a cultural centre for poetry recitals. Continuing through the lively **fripe** [256 B7] at Nahj al Qasabati, near the Bab el Kasbah, you come to the **Museum of Traditional Architecture of Sfax** [256 B7] (⌚ 09.30–16.30 Tue–Sun; 5DT). Housed in the restored kasbah, it hosts an outdoor display of various construction tools and techniques, while inside the ramparts you will find detailed information panels and artefacts relating to the architecture of the region.

Other sights As you exit the medina through Bab Jebli, look out for the **Sidi Lakhmi Mausoleum** [256 B5] on Avenue des Martyrs. With a distinctive white rutted dome, this is a monument to an 11th-century religious figure, Sidi Abu El

Hassan El Lakham (although it was not built until the 17th century), and remains an important local religious site where people come to pray for blessings. It was closed at the time of writing, and will likely be closed to non-Muslims if it reopens.

Accessible by private vehicle (or by hopping on the number 16b bus), the **Sfax Commonwealth War Cemetery** [256 A2] (Rte de Gabès; w cwgc.org; 24/7, although if you wish to access the visitors' book you need to visit during office hours) is 3.5km west of town. The cemetery contains 1,253 Commonwealth graves from World War II, of which 52 are unidentified. Interestingly, it also contains a single World War I grave to sub-assistant surgeon Jan Muhammad, who died on 25 June 1917 and was transferred from the smaller Bizerte Muslim Cemetery in March 1983. There is also one Greek soldier (Major Gregorios Bourdakos) buried here from World War II. Next door is the civilian **Christian Cemetery** [256 A2]; though in a significantly poorer state of repair than the Commonwealth cemetery (as is always the case across Tunisia), it still features a fascinating series of mainly French and Italian graves from colonial times.

AROUND SFAX

Acholla (35.079483, 11.020844; 24/7; free) Right on the northern boundary with Mahdia Governorate, this archaeological site is probably for serious archaeology enthusiasts only. Located just outside the modern settlement of Henchir Botria, it was originally founded by settlers from Malta, possibly as early as the 8th century BC, and then absorbed into the Carthaginian Empire, but rather sensibly sided with the Romans in the Third Punic War (149–146BC) and again during the Caesar's Civil War at the end of the Roman Republic (49–46BC). Upon arrival, you will likely be accompanied by the site guardian (although entrance is free); as you wander around the cultivated fields, you will see that small patches of excavation, which took place mainly between 1947 and 1955, have revealed all sorts of remains, including baths, private villas and even some Christian tombs.

Thaenae (34.649892, 10.684295; 24/7; free) Around 14km south of town near present-day Thyna, this archaeological site is in average condition but worth a visit if you have your own transport. Founded as a Phoenician colony before transitioning to Carthaginian then Roman rule, Thaenae sat at the coastal end of the line marking the limit between Numidian and Roman territories. It has suffered from thoughtless pillaging over the centuries, and the necropoli on the town's periphery were all destroyed by tomb raiders. Later excavations produced evidence of a huge square enclosure having a side over 2km long with semicircular towers. Baths were discovered nearer the coast, and it was suggested that the bathing facilities, originally of individual ownership, had been changed into public use. The Baths of the Months, excavated in 1961, had walls several metres high, and roofing with barrel vaults. Some noteworthy mosaics and a treasure hoard of gold coins dating to the 3rd century AD were discovered at the site, but most objects were taken to the Bardo and Sfax Archaeological Museum.

To get to the site, head south on Route de Gabès for 10km to a turn-off for **Park Tyna** (34.668048, 10.683113). Do not let Google Maps route you through the port, unless you have an amphibious vehicle! The park itself is unremarkable apart from the odd flock of birds drifting in and out from the nearby salt farms. Continue along the road until it becomes a track to reach the impressively tall **Thyna lighthouse** (34.651818, 10.685566). Carry on to the small **museum** (34.649892, 10.684295; closed at the time of writing) where you can park; the archaeological site is a 100m walk west from here.

Chaffar (⊕ 34.528838, 10.566678) Around 25km south of Thyna, this beach is made up of two spits of white sand, radiating almost 5km in each direction like a hammerhead. On the western end of the spit there is often a flock of greater flamingos. This is a relaxing beach on which to spend the day in the summer, as there is more than enough sand to escape the crowds that tend to congregate on the section most easily reached on foot from the car park. Local lads will charge you 1DT to park, ostensibly for keeping an eye on the vehicle.

Maharès Another 8km down the coast, this coastal town has a reputation for public art. From the four-lane main street (Avenue Habib Bourguiba, as usual), fun metal structures can be spied on the beachside gardens, including a wire horse similar to the one in Zarzis and a huge robot figure. Also note the reconstructed skeleton of a small whale in the sculpture promenade near the harbour.

Borj Younga (⊕ 34.467296, 10.411255) Following the P1 south for 10km from Maharès, through fields and fields of olive groves, you reach the turn-off for this Byzantine fortress at ⊕ 34.494176, 10.390023. Originally built by the Byzantines on the site of a former Punic and then Roman settlement (Macomades Minores), the 40m-wide fortifications were restored and used by the Aghlabids. The fort, which is in a relatively good state of repair, has information signs outside. A few hundred metres east of the site are some scattered Roman remains, and 450m west is a Byzantine church (⊕ 34.464161, 10.407259) that is currently under excavation.

Kneiss Islands In the Gulf of Gabès, this archipelago is made up of tiny islands connected to one another by shallow waters that turn into mudflats with the tides, and form a significant waterbird habitat. Tens of thousands of migrating and wintering birds (mainly seabirds) pass through, including common crane, great cormorant, great crested grebe, Eurasian spoonbill and greater flamingo. Even if you are not into birdwatching, the islands themselves are a beautiful natural site to explore, with plenty of unspoilt coastline to enjoy, and make for a fun day out on a boat.

To get here, where the P1 passes through El Hachichina (⊕ 34.420688, 10.179285) take the signposted turning for the La Réserve Naturelle des Îles Kneiss. Follow this road towards the coast, heading left at the fork and, at the sharp corner (⊕ 34.389802, 10.246113), you will reach a sign with a map of the reserve (in French and Arabic) with details of an eco-trail that you can hike. If you continue down to the coast you will reach a jetty (⊕ 34.378891, 10.270909) with another information sign, from where the free boat to the islands departs – usually around 05.00–06.00, depending on tides, returning around 15.00. There are always plenty of fishing boats around, however, so theoretically it should be possible to pay someone to take you over to the islands even when the boat is not available, although it is unclear whether you are allowed to enter the natural reserve in this way.

KERKENNAH ISLANDS

Little has happened to disturb the tranquility of the Kerkennah Islands throughout Tunisia's turbulent history. Legend goes that they are named after Circe, a nymph who tried (but failed) to keep the Greek hero Odysseus here during his Mediterranean travels. Other famous exiles on the islands include Hannibal and

Habib Bourguiba. Lying off the coast of Sfax, the archipelago's two main islands are Gharbi (western) and Chergui (eastern), and its 15,000 residents go quietly about their business, extending the sort of welcome to visitors that you really only find in small island communities. None of the tourism overdevelopment that has impacted Djerba to the south has made its way here, and you could spend a pleasant few days on the archipelago, cycling, birdwatching, exploring the historical sites and splashing in the shallows. Note that Kerkennah is one of the few places on the planet where you can buy stretches of the sea (see below).

HISTORY The Kerkennah archipelago was originally settled by the Phoenicians, with archaeologists confirming Phoenician origins at the site of Borj el Hsar, on Chergui's northwest coast (page 270). The Romans called the islands Cercina or Cercinna, and they were mentioned in the texts of Greek geographers such as Strabo (1st century BC) and Ptolemy (2nd century AD).

In ancient times, the Kerkennah archipelago was a good place to hide. Following his defeat at the Battle of Zama in 202BC, the Carthaginian general and statesman Hannibal is thought to have spent the night on the islands before sailing off into voluntary exile in Tyre. The Roman historian Livy tells us that in order to avoid being betrayed by any sailors heading to the mainland to alert the Romans, Hannibal hosted a massive feast, got them all drunk and sailed off before they had recovered from their hangovers. Almost 200 years later, Emperor Augustus exiled the Roman aristocrat Sempronius Gracchus to Kerkennah for 14 years for sleeping with his (then married) daughter, Julia the Elder.

In AD293, during the reign of Emperor Diocletian, the islands were annexed to the newly created Roman province of Byzacena. Like much of the Tunisian coastline, the islands would spend hundreds of years with ownership passing to whichever was the dominant power at the time, namely the Muslim conquerors, the Normans, the Spanish and the Venetians, before finally being folded into the Ottoman Empire.

During the colonial period, Kerkennah was a stopping-off point for future president Habib Bourguiba, as he fled French-controlled Tunisia in a fishing boat to Egypt via Libya in March 1945. Oil was discovered in the Gulf of Gabès in 1971, with oil and gas deposits found very close to Kerkennah's coast in 1992. You can see

OWNING THE SEA

The practice of local fishermen owning sections of Kerkennah's shallow sea dates to Ottoman rule in the 15th and 16th centuries, when locals wrote to the bey of Tunis to complain about outsiders coming in and exploiting their waters. He issued a decree allowing them to 'own' tracts of the water, holding honorary ownership contracts that allowed them to kick trespassers off their patch of sea. Today this tradition continues, with families exploiting their section of the sea, handed down through the generations via male heirs, using age-old fishing methods of *charfia* (page 270).

The use of *charfia* requires a permit from the local authorities. However, there are also some unwritten rules that have developed around this traditional fishing practice, mainly to aid sustainability. For example, it is customary to leave at least a 500m gap between each set of traps, and to not install more than six traps per *charfia*. Fishing usually only happens between the autumn equinox and June to give fish stocks a chance to recover.

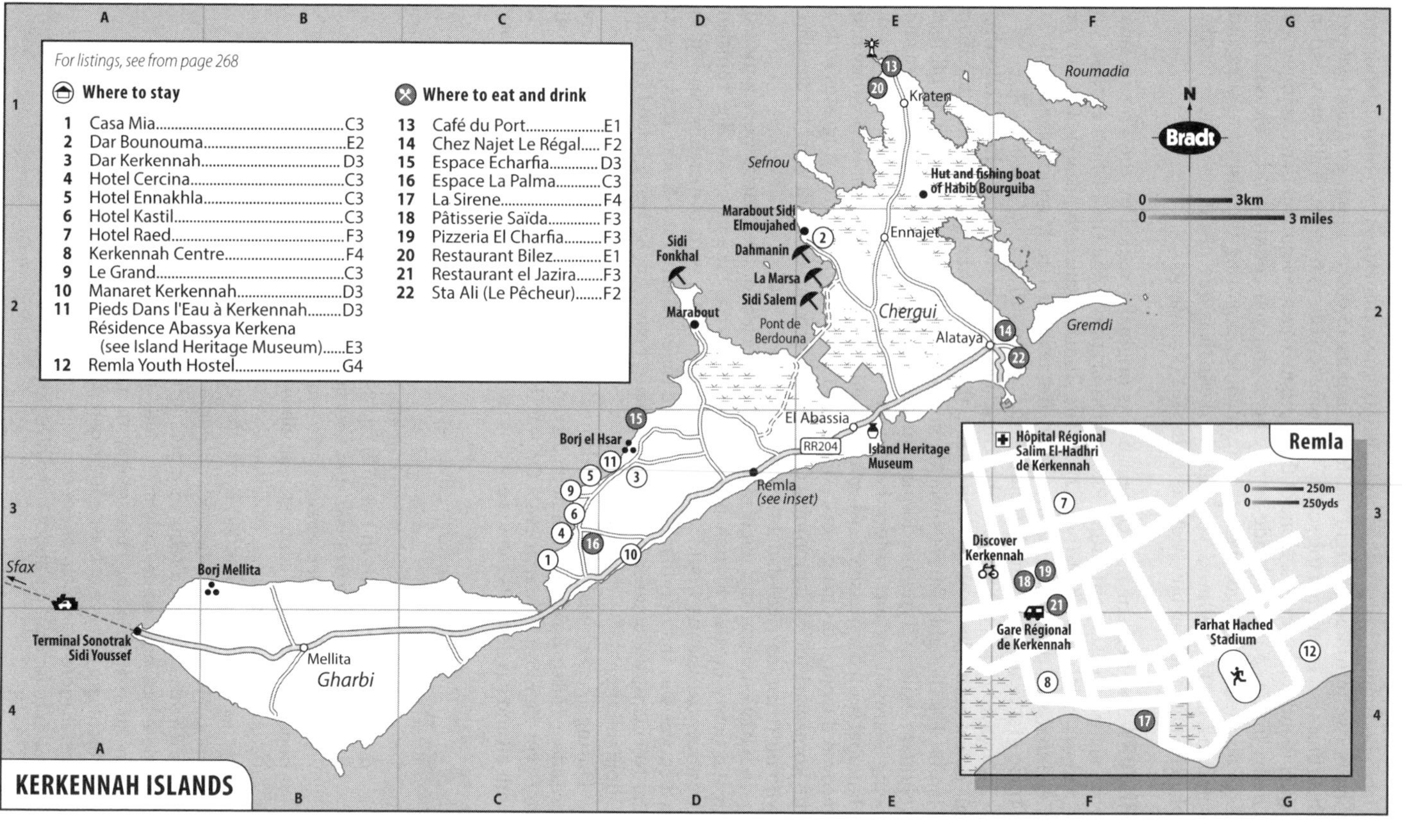
KERKENNAH ISLANDS
For listings, see from page 268
Where to stay
1 Casa Mia........C3
2 Dar Bounouma........E2
3 Dar Kerkennah........D3
4 Hotel Cercina........C3
5 Hotel Ennakhla........C3
6 Hotel Kastil........C3
7 Hotel Raed........F3
8 Kerkennah Centre........F4
9 Le Grand........C3
10 Manaret Kerkennah........D3
11 Pieds Dans l'Eau à Kerkennah........D3
Résidence Abassya Kerkena (see Island Heritage Museum)......E3
12 Remla Youth Hostel........G4
Where to eat and drink
13 Café du Port........E1
14 Chez Najet Le Régal..... F2
15 Espace Echarfia........D3
16 Espace La Palma........C3
17 La Sirene........F4
18 Pâtisserie Saïda........F3
19 Pizzeria El Charfia........F3
20 Restaurant Bilez........E1
21 Restaurant el Jazira......F3
22 Sta Ali (Le Pêcheur)......F2
Bradt
N
0 3km
0 3 miles
Roumadia
Kraten
Sefnou
Hut and fishing boat of Habib Bourguiba
Marabout Sidi Elmoujahed
Ennajet
Sidi Fonkhal
Dahmanin
La Marsa
Sidi Salem
Marabout
Pont de Berdouna
Chergui
Gremdi
Alataya
El Abassia
RR204
Island Heritage Museum
Borj el Hsar
Remla (see inset)
Sfax
Borj Mellita
Terminal Sonotrak Sidi Youssef
Mellita
Gharbi
Remla
Hôpital Régional Salim El-Hadhri de Kerkennah
0 250m
0 250yds
Discover Kerkennah
Gare Régional de Kerkennah
Farhat Hached Stadium

some of the extraction platforms offshore from the northwestern coastline. Luckily, all the processing happens in Sfax, so there has been little impact on the islands.

Unsurprisingly, fishing is the islands' main industry – Kerkennian men have a great reputation as skilled fishermen and are often recruited by mainland fishing fleets. However, the industry has suffered considerably since the early 1990s. Pollution, possibly caused by phosphate processing in Sfax and Gabès, has led to a sharp reduction in the fish stock, while the Cap Bon fishing fleet – under severe competition from Italian boats illegally fishing with more sophisticated methods in Tunisian waters – now fishes further south, in areas traditionally fished by Kerkennah's people. Their modern trawling methods are harmful, as the heavy weights used on trawler nets rake up the sea bottom, destroying the weed that is source of food for the fish. See page 270, for more on the islands' unique fishing methods.

In 2017 Kerkennah made headlines in the (admittedly very limited) circle of Arabic linguistic academics, following the identification of three different dialects of Tunisian Arabic on the islands. One of these dialects was described by Arabic sociolinguistics expert Bruno Herin as 'the missing link between the highly innovative pre-Hilalian dialects of present-day Maghreb and Maltese'.

GETTING THERE AND AWAY The only way to reach Kerkennah is by **ferry** from Sfax (1hr). The Sonotrak terminal is on the southwest side of the drawbridge by the port [256 C5]. Up to nine ferries per day make the crossing, with the earliest departing Sfax at 04.15 and the last at 20.00. It is possible to simply turn up and board the ferry (either as a foot passenger or in a car) but this will involve queueing, as those with pre-booked tickets get priority. It is possible to pay online (w sonotrak.tn/fr) using an international credit card, but you must print your ticket for inspection at the ferry terminal (Your Travels Agency in Sfax can also do this for you; page 258). Foot passengers pay 1DT one-way whereas vehicles are charged by weight, ranging from 5DT up to 25DT for a vehicle over 17 tonnes. Ferries arrive at the far western tip of Gharbi, at Terminal Sonotrak Sidi Youssef [266 A4].

GETTING AROUND The two main islands are linked by a Roman-built causeway, so it is possible to **drive** from Gharbi (where you arrive on the ferry) to Chergui (where 99% of the sites of interest are). The main roads on the islands are good-quality tarmac. The Sidi Youssef **bus** terminal is a few metres away from where the ferry docks, with regular buses via Mellita to Remla on Chergui. The bus stop in Remla (Gare Régional de Kerkennah [266 F4]) is right in the centre of town, walking distance from all the main restaurants, banks and hotels. **Hitchhiking** is also pretty standard on the islands, so you could try to hitch a lift into town from one of the vehicles on the ferry. **Louages** and **taxis** connect more rural areas to the main settlements.

The islands are very flat, so ideal for **cycling**; bikes can be rented from some hotels. **Discover Kerkennah** [266 E3] (w discoverkerkennah.com) also offers guided bicycle tours and rental.

TOURIST INFORMATION There is no official government tourist office in Kerkennah, but you can get information about the islands before you arrive from the ONTT office in Sfax (which is conveniently near the port, page 258). The local government website in Kerkennah also has an excellent interactive map with recommendations for tourist sights. It can also be downloaded as a PDF w communekerkennah.tn/tourisme-alternatif.

Run by an Italian NGO, **Slow Food Kerkennah** (w fondazioneslowfood.com) works with traditional fishermen in Kerkennah to highlight the importance of preserving artisanal fishing and local gastronomy. It hosts various events, both on the islands and abroad, to showcase artisanal Kerkennian produce, such as Adas lentils or dried octopus.

WHERE TO STAY Overall, Kerkennah has a good selection of accommodation options. The best are clustered around the beach at **Sidi Fredj**, but there are a few cheaper places to stay in **Remla**, the largest town on Chergui island. **Mellita** is the largest settlement on Gharbi, but there is little here of tourist interest beyond some handy ATMs and the odd streetside café.

✷ **Dar Bounouma** [266 E2] (4 rooms) Plage Dahmanin; ⊕ 34.772810, 11.224648; m 98 344 876, 25 356 605; e darbounouma@gmail.com; f. Immaculately restored dar with ornate yellow doors featuring fish carvings. Largest room upstairs has a jacuzzi-bath & generous balcony overlooking the outdoor pool. The roof terrace looks down into the glass-roofed atrium, & there are 2 outdoor BBQs & a pizza oven. Also has 2 traditional fishing boats moored out front that can take guests sightseeing or fishing with a local guide. **$$$$$**

✷ **Casa Mia** [266 C3] (6 rooms) Zone Touristique, Sidi Fredj; m 98 529 206; w casamiakerkenna.com. An absolute paradise, just over the road from the clear, shallow waters of Plage Sidi Fredj. Mme Monia makes you feel completely at home: AC rooms are modern with en suite, some with sea views, & the glass-walled dining area is gorgeous, with views over the water. The biggest attraction is dinner (arranged in advance), especially the fresh seafood. An absolute feast. **$$$$–$$$$$**

Manaret Kerkennah [266 D3] (4 rooms, 2 apts) Borrouss, Ouled Yaneg; m 22 707 809; w manaret-kerkennah.com. With an amazing castle-like design, this hotel on Chergui's south coast boasts a large courtyard with all sorts of ramparts & a large wooden fire. Regular rooms have wooden ceilings & floors, fridge, large windows & brand-new bathroom with shower, while apts also include full kitchen with 2 hobs, double sink & a mezzanine living room area with small balcony overlooking the sea. **$$$$**

Hotel Kastil [266 C3] (8 rooms) Zone Touristique, Sidi Fredj; ☎ 74 489 884; m 29 535 000; e hotelelkastil@yahoo.com; f elkastil. Under renovation at the time of writing, with large, bright & airy en-suite dbl rooms. Great terrace & restaurant space right on the water. Also a deep pool with a bar on the waterfront. **$$$**

Le Grand Hotel [266 C3] (83 rooms, 3 bungalows) Zone Touristique, Sidi Fredj; ☎ 74 489 857/9; e somvik@grand-hotel-kerkennah.com.tn; f GrandHotelKerkennah. Though regular rooms are a bit dated & noise from neighbours might be an issue, the large 3-bedroom bungalows represent excellent value for money with sea views, full kitchen & outdoor BBQ. **$$$**

Pieds Dans l'Eau à Kerkennah [266 D3] (3 rooms, 1 bungalow) Zone Touristique, Sidi Fredj; m 24 343 431; e fethi.kebaili@tlf.com.tn; f. Basic rooms are large & bright with views over the water; the bungalow has a kitchen & waterfront terrace that can sleep 4. Not much of a sandy beach here, but they have created their own small sandpit for children. **$$$**

Dar Kerkennah [266 D3] (17 rooms) Zone Touristique, Sidi Fredj; ☎ 74 489 017; e contactdarkerkennah@gmail.com; f hotel.darkerkennah. Looking out over the sea & the nearby Borj el Hsar archaeological site, this large hotel has some lovely colourful tiling. Rooms are very big with plenty of natural light & bathrooms have shower with half-length bath; some rooms have terraces with sea views. Indoor pool is also a big draw. Very good value for money. **$$**

Hotel Ennakhla [266 C3] (10 rooms, 19 bungalows) Zone Touristique, Sidi Fredj; ☎ 74 489 022/3; e residenceennakhla@gmail.com; f ENNAKHLA.HOTEL. Also known as Hotel du Palmier, this has a great pool area but is set a little back from the sea. Rooms are well presented with AC; bungalows have full kitchen. Solid budget option. **$$**

✷ **Kerkennah Centre** [266 F4] (37 rooms) Remla Plage; ☎ 74 481 514. Recently refurbished, this pristine option is an absolute bargain. Rooms are clean & bright with balconies overlooking the sea; note the bathroom is a wet room. Also has an outdoor café overlooking water with olive trees for shade, & they set up a pizzeria right on the waterfront in summer. **$$**

Hotel Cercina [266 C3] (28 bungalows) Zone Touristique, Sidi Fredj; 74 489 600; e hotel.cercina@planet.tn; Hotel.cercina. A varied selection of normal, residence & mini-suite bungalows near the coast. Very good location & the gardens & restaurant are pleasant, but the bedrooms are a little dated & some smell of smoke. Probably a good choice for those on a very tight budget. **$–$$**

Hotel Raed [266 F3] (11 rooms, 6 apts) Remla; 74 482 427; m 98 587 889; e raedaubergekerkennah@gmail.com; . A cross between a youth hostel & a motel, with large & clean AC, en-suite rooms opening out on to a central courtyard where pizza is served, so probably quite noisy in evenings. Good budget choice if you want to be in Remla. **$**

Remla Youth Hostel [266 G4] (19 rooms) Next door to Farhat Hached Stadium, Remla; 74 481 148. The cheapest bed in town: simple whitewashed rooms with access to communal toilet. Also allows camping. **$**

Résidence Abassya Kerkena [266 E3] (30 beds) El Abassia; m 52 131 611, 22 379 354; e cecerim2002@gmail.com. Located inside the Island Heritage Museum (page 271), this hostel has beds split across 11 clean & simple rooms with Wi-Fi but no AC or TV. Probably the cheapest decent beds on the islands. **$**

WHERE TO EAT AND DRINK

✷ **La Sirene Restaurant** [266 F4] Remla Plage; 74 481 118; e restaurantlasirene@gmail.com; restaurantlasirenne; 11.00–23.00 daily. Mountains of fresh seafood, with both Heineken & Celtia draught on tap. Partially covered outdoor seating area overlooking the water. Delicious food, attentive service. **$$$$**

Sta Ali (Le Pêcheur) [266 F2] Vieux Port, Alataya; m 98 519 060, 22 355 150; 10.00–midnight daily. Fresh fish & pasta dishes with views of the water. **$$$$**

✷ **Chez Najet Le Régal** [266 F2] Rte el Kraten, Alataya; 74 484 100; m 98 291 235; ChezNajetleRegal; 10.00–16.00 & 18.00–midnight daily. Look out for the blue anchors & fishing gear all over the walls in this excellent seafood place near the east coast. Try the *salade Kerkennienne* (octopus salad) or the *tchich au poulpe* (barley & octopus soup); for the very popular *couscous aux calamars farcis* (stuffed squid couscous), contact the restaurant to order 24hrs in advance. **$$$**

Espace Echarfia [266 D3] 34.721433, 11.156760; m 25 313 145, 26 486 000; ESPACEECHARFIA; 10.00–late daily. Seafood restaurant on an amazing peninsula overlooking the water. The beachfront bar area is popular in the evenings. **$$$**

Espace La Palma [266 C3] Zone Touristique, Sidi Fredj; m 99 518 842; 10.00–23.00 daily. Big Italian pizzeria in a castle-like structure with thatch roof overlooking the roundabout. Top floors give good views of the sea. **$$$**

Pizzeria El Charfia [266 F3] Rte el Kraten, Remla; 74 482 644; 09.30–23.00 daily. Very popular, delicious Italian thin-crust pizzas, served under a thatched roof overlooking the centre of town. **$$$**

Restaurant el Jazira [266 F3] Rond Point, Remla; m 51 015 333; 11.00–late Sat–Thu. Good seafood restaurant, weirdly hidden away down a side street near the government buildings in Remla. Great value for money, but not the most inspiring of settings. **$$$**

Restaurant Bilez [266 E1] Plage de Kraten; m 97 897 999; wwwayadibilez; 10.00–23.00 daily. Grilled fish joint with plastic chairs right on the beach, with shade provided by palm fronds. **$$–$$$**

Café du Port [266 E1] Port du Kraten; 07.00–late daily. Right on the northern tip of Chergui island, this is a very basic café full of fishermen. Cool for watching the octopus catch landing. **$**

Pâtisserie Saïda [266 F3] Rte el Kraten, Remla; 74 481 167; m 29 914 141; patisserieSAIDA; 09.00–18.00 daily. Good café with sweet & savoury offerings. **$**

ACTIVITIES A number of outfits run leisure cruises around the islands, usually including lunch and fishing/swimming opportunities.

Al Mahras Pirate Boat Port du Kraten; m 92 329 030; e bateaupiratekerkennah@gmail.com; f bateaupiratemahres. Departs 3 times a day during high season from the Kraten port.

Captain Azzedine's Tourist Boat Zone Touristique, Sidi Fredj; m 55 071 043, 21 746 199; f tourisme.marin.a.kerkennah. Departs from the jetty in front of the Hotel Cercina.

Captain Mohamed Haj Sassi's Tourist Boat Vieux Port, El Attaya; m 28 565 701; e hadjsassi.med@gmail.com. Departs from the jetty in front of the Sta Ali (Le Pêcheur) restaurant in the far east end of Chergui island.

OTHER PRACTICALITIES For medical emergencies, the **Hôpital Régional Salim El-Hadhri de Kerkennah** is in Remla [266 F3] (74 421 006; e abousajeddebaya@gmail.com; f; 24/7), although you will probably need to head back to Sfax if there is a serious problem.

WHAT TO SEE AND DO

Gharbi The minute you step off the ferry, you will see one of Kerkennah's unique features: its traditional **charfia fishing traps**, long avenues of palm fronds stuck into the mud of the shallow waters. Around 3km northeast of the port down an unmarked agricultural track is one of the few other tourist sites on this small island: the Ottoman-era **Borj Mellita** [266 B3] (34.669520, 10.997540), sometimes also called the Tower of Sidi Youssef. The watchtower, likely used to spot potential hostile shipping approaching the Sfax coastline, is in a good state of repair, sitting isolated in a farmer's field. There is an entrance but it is around 4m off the ground, so you will have to admire the structure from the outside unless you are a good climber!

Chergui Just north of the Roman-era causeway connecting the two main islands is the incredible archaeological site of **Borj el Hsar** [266 D3] (34.710364, 11.153428). With elements dating to the 7th century BC, this is a rare find in Tunisia: a truly Phoenician set of ruins (similar to Utica in Bizerte, page 187) that have not been

FISHING TECHINQUES ON KERKENNAH

The shallowness of the sea around Kerkennah has led its people to develop unique fishing techniques, the best known of which is *charfia*. Using palm branches and fronds, fishermen and women construct fences out into the water which form a sort of hedge, curving or zigzagging away from the coast. At high tide, shoals of fish swim in between the hedge and beach and, when the tide goes out, it becomes impossible for them to swim back. Stuck in the increasingly shallow water, they take refuge in the special fish-traps (*drina* in Arabic, *nasse* in French).

Another primitive but fairly efficient Kerkennian fishing technique involves a team of people and a sort of floating barrier made of *dhriaâ* seaweed (Neptune grass). The team walks slowly through the shallows, moving away from the coast, each individual pushing a floating section of twisted seaweed. The frightened fish swim back landwards between the individual fishers. Once they are 1km from the shore, the team turns back, gradually moving closer together and trapping the fish in the shallows.

If you want to go out fishing, many fishermen will take a passenger with them for a small fee, while some hotels and dars can also arrange for you to rent a *felouka* (traditional fishing boat) with a captain for a day trip.

destroyed by subsequent Punic or Roman occupation. This area served as the capital of the islands in Phoenician times, known as Cercina or Cercinna (confusingly, a label often also used by ancient writers to refer to the whole archipelago). Much of the site has ended up underwater owing to shifting sea levels, but it is still remarkable to walk the grounds and find intact mosaics, cisterns, roads and walls, all completely open to the elements and with no protection save for a small fence. There is a large Aghlabid and then later Spanish fort on the site (the Borj itself), which is currently being converted into a visitor centre.

Continuing eastwards along the northern coastline, you reach the Sidi Fonkhal peninsula. Passing a **marabout** (Muslim shrine) [266 D2] (⊕ 34.749226, 11.177900) that is in the process of being restored, it's another 1.2km north to one of the best remote beaches on the island, **Plage Sidi Fonkhal** [266 D2]. There is nothing here apart from palm trees, the odd fisherman's boat and a vast stretch of white sand – an excellent spot for a picnic.

At this stage, unless you have a 4x4, you will need to head back to Remla (page 266) and use the main R204 road to continue your journey eastwards, as there is no decent tarmac road that runs from here up the northern coast of the island. But if you are feeling brave, you could try driving over the single-track **Pont de Berdouna** [266 E2] causeway which links these two stretches of northern coastline together. Having done this drive, it is not recommended at high tide or during a storm! Once across, continue off-road to **Plage Sidi Salem** [266 E2] and rejoin a tarmac coastal road to cut through La Marsa beach and then Dahmanin beach (home to Dar Bounouma; page 268). You will eventually reach the 18th-century **Marabout Sidi Elmoujahed** [266 E2] (⊕ 34.776928, 11.219887); though in a rather poor state of repair, you can enter and see the palm-wood roof and grave.

Heading back to the main road and then northwards through Ennajet, you reach a right turning for a dirt track (⊕ 34.792555, 11.258664) which, after 1.2km, leads to the abandoned **hut and fishing boat of Habib Bourguiba** [266 E1] (⊕ 34.787754, 11.268636). Having been denied permission from the French colonial authorities to leave the country legally, the country's founding president sought shelter here before escaping to Egypt via Libya in March 1945, travelling from the mainland in a traditional *loud* fishing boat that used to be on display at this very spot. Sadly, at some stage following the Tunisian Revolution, the *loud* was set on fire and destroyed (either by mischievous teenagers or by Islamists, depending on who you ask). Today the hut is still there, but only a burnt-out hull of the boat remains under the display roof.

Chergui's northwestern peninsula, home to the port town of **Kraten** [266 E1], has several sites of interest. The town's **beach** has a great stretch of white sand and ankle-deep water, with a good restaurant (page 269) at the southern end. In the centre of the settlement is the **Al Qaratin mosque** (⊕ 34.816804, 11.256158), with whitewashed walls and a pastel-green-and-white minaret, while at the peninsula's very northern tip is the **lighthouse**, oddly painted black and still in use today.

In the southeastern corner of Chergui, the town of **Alataya** [266 E2] has some of Kerkennah's best restaurants (page 269). Swinging back towards Remla along the RR204, you pass the **Island Heritage Museum** [266 E3] (El Abassia; ☎ 74 482 728; m 21 765 176, 97 899 560; e cecerim2002@gmail.com; ⏲ winter 09.30–16.00 Wed–Sun, summer 09.30–18.00 daily; 3DT), opened in 2006 by Tunisian university professor Abdelhamid Fehri. It showcases many aspects of island life, with displays on traditional fishing and rites of passage such as wedding ceremonies. There is also a *loud* on display out front.

7

The West

Though one of the poorest parts of Tunisia, the western region (encompassing the governorates of Kairouan, Kasserine and Sidi Bouzid) is culturally very rich. Here you will find the Great Mosque of Kairouan, a UNESCO World Heritage Site dating to the 7th century and situated in the most ancient Arabo-Muslim base in the Maghreb, alongside one of the most impressive sets of Roman archaeological remains in the country at Sbeïtla. This part of Tunisia also hosts the country's only surviving savannah relicts in Parc National Bou-Hedma, where you can embark on a Tunisian 'safari'. Note, however, that there are travel advisories relating to security in some areas of these three governorates – look out for individual warnings throughout the chapter.

KAIROUAN

Isolated on featureless steppe and founded in the 7th century by Arab conquerors, Kairouan is the spiritual and religious capital of Tunisia. Still surrounded by its historic walls, the town has a strong character and is an excellent place to understand the evolution of Islam in North Africa. Getting a hold on names of places and rulers, you begin to understand how the Muslim religion took root, developing with the dynasties into the religion as it is lived today. The city is also a lesson in just how fragile the medieval Muslim state was in North Africa. For a leading city, it was actually very small and totally dominated by its vast mosque – similar to how English wool towns developed in the shadow of huge churches. Around the top of the austere sandy-coloured minarets run friezes with the wording 'There is no god but Allah and Muhammad is his prophet' picked out in brick. Here and there, green doors indicate the presence of tiny neighbourhood *msejed* (prayer rooms).

The city's highlight is undoubtedly the UNESCO-listed Great Mosque, built of tawny brick and pillaged ancient masonry, but there is much more to see besides: wander the streets of the medina and explore the sleepy souks, observe the industrious weavers at work (the city is Tunisia's carpet-making capital), buy some *makroud* (sticky date cakes) or meditate on vanished dynasties at the Palace of Rakkada.

HISTORY The Romans, who knew a thing or two about city planning, never considered the inhospitable plain at Kairouan as a suitable location, with their closest settlement 25km northwest at Aïn Jelloula. Siting a city in such a barren place therefore takes some explanation, but fortunately there is a founding legend for just this purpose. Back in AD671, Okba ibn Nafi, companion of the Prophet Muhammad and warrior leader, was leading an army into Byzantine Africa. He halted his troops at the edge of an arid, wild-beast infested valley (which no longer seems to exist), and called out 'Inhabitants of the valley, depart, for we are stopping

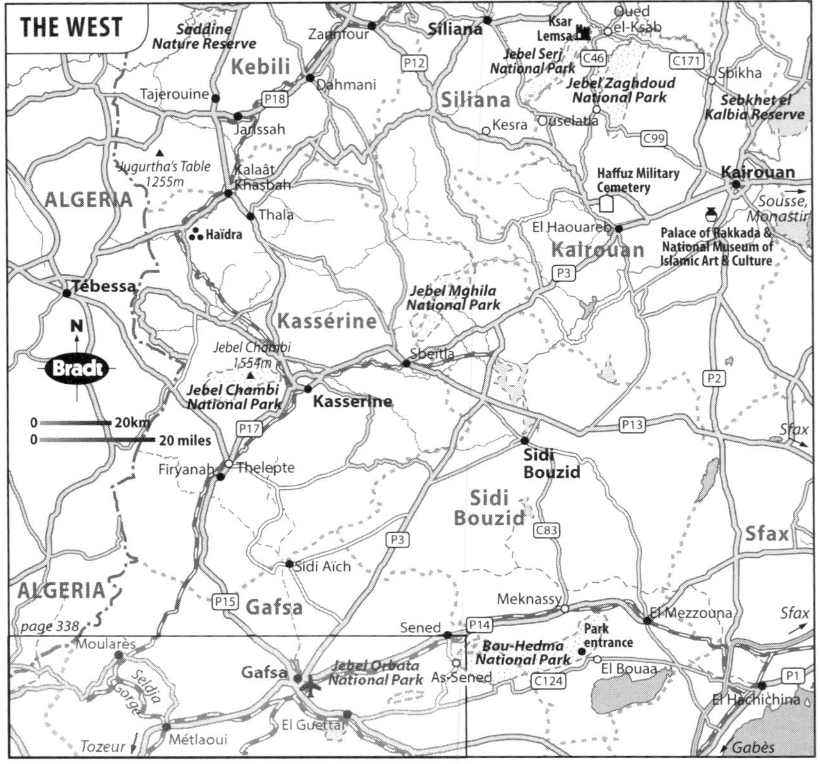

here', at which point the various snakes, scorpions and creepy-crawlies emerged from their hiding places and headed out of the valley, allowing Okba's troops to camp in complete safety. Extra reassurance was provided for the Muslim forces when Okba's horse stumbled across a goblet which had been lost in Mecca. Water flowed from this miraculous cup, directly from the sacred spring of Zemzem in Mecca. The site was clearly ripe for a holy city, and Kairouan was founded.

During the 9th century, Kairouan prospered as home to the local Aghlabid Dynasty, achieving independence from the Caliphate of Baghdad. The city saw much building activity under the Aghlabid emirs, notably Ziyadet Allah I. Kairouan also developed into something of a medical research centre, with Jews and Muslims working to develop a heritage of medical knowledge passed down from ancient Greece. One of the leading scholars of the 8th century was Malik ibn Anas, and many Ifrikiyans travelled here to attend his seminars. With Islam laying down so many rules for life, it was inevitable that a major body of legal knowledge should emerge to interpret the grey areas. At Kairouan, the Malikite school emerged, winning the support of the people through its rigorous approach: only Koranic prescriptions and the traditions of the Prophet could be valid bases for law. The scholarly Imam Sahnoun produced a comprehensive digest of Malikite law, Al Mudawwana.

As opposed to the Malikite scholars, the Aghlabid princes followed the more intellectual Hanafite school of Islam and were seen by the people as decadent and oppressive. Things went horribly wrong for them in the late 8th century. Mohamed II, who came to the throne aged 13, quickly developed a taste for dissipation and frivolity and died prematurely. His governor in Kairouan (the future Ibrahim II) won a reputation for fairness but later turned into a tyrant, massacring members of the Arab military caste and crucifying an Arab aristocrat. In 876, he began building a vast royal residence at Rakkada, near Kairouan, recruiting a corps of slave troops. The military aristocracy saw its influence declining, and this, combined with various exactions, explains the success of the Shi'ite Fatimids in overthrowing the last Aghlabids in 910. Aghlabid rule had lasted little more than a century.

Fatimid rule was to weigh heavily on the Sunni Muslims of Ifrikiya, and Kairouan became a focus for major rebellions. The Malikites were persecuted, and although the Fatimids were not a decadent lot, nor did they spend on religious buildings; tax revenues went into campaigns against the Sunni caliphate in Egypt. Rebellion was inevitable, and came in the form of Kharijite leader Abou Yazid, who easily won control of Kairouan with Sunni support. All of Ifrikiya – bar Mahdia – was lost in 944. Abou Yazid failed to take the Fatimid capital and the revolt failed, with a new Fatimid caliph, El-Mansour ('the victorious') defeating Abou Yazid at a key battle in Kairouan in 947. In 953, he began the construction of a new capital, Mansouriya, just 2km away from Kairouan. This meant the older settlement was bypassed commercially, most trade being done in the new city.

The real decline of Kairouan came with the invasion from Egypt in the 1050s, when the city changed its allegiance from the Fatimids in Cairo to the Sunni Abbasids in Baghdad. By way of vengeance, the Shi'ite Fatimids allotted Ifrikiya as booty to the warlike Banu Hilal, who had been stirring up trouble in southern Egypt for some time. Opinions are divided as to the actual extent of the devastation caused by the Hilalian invasion: Ibn Khaldoun, for one, who was writing in the following century, attributes a severe economic decline in Ifrikiya to the havoc caused by the Banu Hilal.

Under the Hafsids, the centre of power shifted in Ifrikiya. Relations changed with Europe, trade with the Italian merchant cities developed, and it became important for the capital to be on the coast. Kairouan was thus left by the Hafsid court in favour of Tunis, which after all had a far more agreeable climate. The development of the coastal cities continued in the 17th and 18th centuries, as first Ottoman deys and beys, and subsequently Husseinid beys, became involved in profitable piracy. Kairouan thus became a backwater, albeit an important one. It maintained a holy aura, and the tradition went that seven visits to Kairouan were equivalent to the *hajj*, the pilgrimage to Mecca which every Muslim is supposed to perform once in their lifetime. When French troops arrived in 1881, however, the town surrendered without a shot being fired. No doubt rumours of what the French had done in Algeria's cities were fresh in the minds of Kairouan's notables.

Based on its bygone theological glories, Kairouan today has some claims to be an important religious centre, the leading holy city in the Maghreb region, preceded in status only by Mecca, Medina and Jerusalem. As such, the city has been a focus for Islamist groups in modern times. Although marginalised by former President Ben Ali, who considered the Salafist Islamic fundamentalist groups here a threat to his power, these groups briefly took control of the city after his overthrow in 2011. This included Ansar al-Sharia, which was soon designated a terrorist organisation by the Tunisian state in August 2013. Today, in the post-revolution period, Kairouan is perfectly safe, and is a major focus for regional tourism.

GETTING THERE AND AROUND Kairouan is 160km from Tunis (2 hours 10 minutes on a fully tarmac road). SNTRI also runs buses from the capital (3hr; 11.90DT).

Buses and louages from El Kef, Makthar, El Fahs, Sousse, Sfax and Gabès arrive at the main bus and louage station, located northwest of the medina.

Kairouan has quite a compact centre, with the narrow streets of the old quarter much more suitable for walking than driving. If you wish to get to the museum at Rakkada, 10km southwest of town, you will need to either jump in a louage down the P2 towards Sidi Amor Bou Hadjila, or arrange a private taxi. Most hotels and dars in Kairouan are able to help with this.

TOURIST INFORMATION

ONTT Pl des Martyrs; 77 231 897; e crt.kairouan@ontt.tourism.tn; 08.00–13.00 & 14.00–17.00 Mon–Fri

WHERE TO STAY *Map, opposite*

Dar Alouini (9 rooms) 34 Rue Oum Iyadh; 77 231 321; w dar-alouini.com. Nestled between the medina walls & the Grand Mosque, this meticulously restored traditional Kairouan house features Andalusian, Ottoman & European influences. Each room is individually designed, & there is a hammam & indoor pool. An expensive but luxurious way to spend a night in Kairouan. **$$$$$**

Kasbah (97 rooms) 3140 Rue de la Kasbah; 77 237 301; w goldenyasmin.com/fr/la-kasbah. Set in a former barracks a stone's throw from the medina & the Great Mosque, this Golden Yasmin hotel is a fascinating mix of original & modern architectural features. All the luxuries one would expect in this category, including a pool & very handy free guest parking. **$$$$$**

Dar Hassine Allani (3 rooms) 37 Rue El Kadraoui; 77 235 760; m 25 258 684; f darhassineallani. 18th-century townhouse converted into a boutique hotel in the heart of the medina, with a beautiful rooftop terrace. Rooms decorated with traditional furniture. **$$$$–$$$$$**

Continental (100 rooms) Rue Ibn Al Jazzar; 77 232 006, 77 231 135; w hotelcontinental.tn. Located in front of the Aghlabid pools, this high-end hotel was renovated a few years ago, & features a beautiful swimming pool. Popular choice for business travellers. **$$$$**

Amina (106 rooms) Av de l'Environnement; 77 274 555; w hotelamina.tn. Near tourist office & Aghlabid pools, otherwise not very central. Rooms have bath, AC & balcony; grounds include 2 restaurants & large pool. **$$$**

Splendid (35 rooms) Av du 9 Avril; 77 227 522. Housed in a 1920s building, rooms are clean & basic with AC, heating & en suite. Has a popular but noisy bar that serves alcohol. **$$**

Sabra (30 rooms) Rue Ali Belhouane, Pl des Martyrs; 77 230 263. A budget choice near the Bab Ech Chouhada southern entrance to the medina. Basic 2- & 3-bed rooms with washbasins spread across 2 floors, with hot showers in shared bathrooms along the corridor. No heating; rooms at back are quieter. Clean-ish, friendly staff & great views from roof terrace. **$**

Youth Hostel (70 rooms) Av de Fès; 77 228 239. Opposite the Ali Zouaoui stadium, 200m down the road from Aghlabid Hospital. Very cheap & with a kitchen, but inconveniently located & mixed reviews in terms of cleanliness. **$**

WHERE TO EAT AND DRINK *Map, opposite*

Aside from the following, if you are looking for decent cheap eats then head to Avenue Ibn El-Jazzar, where you'll find dozens of roadside grills (10.00–late daily) serving local fish to the truck traffic passing through town. Smells delicious!

Dar Abderrahman Zarrouk Rue Mohamed Bouhaha; m 94 670 670; e restaurant@darzarroukairouan.com; f DarAbderrahmenZarrouk; noon–16.00 & 19.00–22.00 daily. Traditional Tunisian food, often with an haute-cuisine twist. The building is the refurbished 18th-century home of a former governor, set in the heart of the medina, with a beautiful courtyard for summer dining. **$$$$**

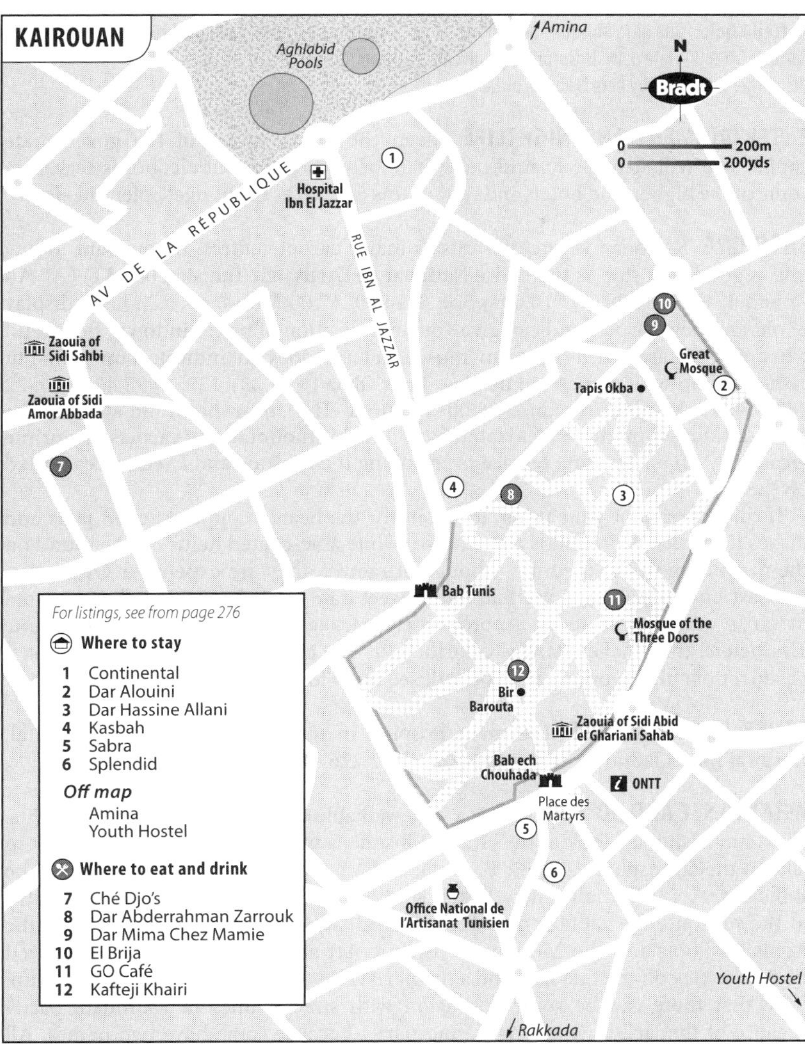

El Brija Av Okba ibn Nafi; 77 229 019; e info@resto-elbrija.com; f ElBrija.laClasse; 08.00–22.00 daily. Perched on top of the city walls, offering views of the Grand Mosque from a large terrace. Typical menu including Mediterranean & Tunisian options with plenty of sweets. Note: it is up a flight of stairs so not wheelchair accessible. $$$

Ché Djo's Av de la République; m 51 300 050; noon–22.00 Wed–Mon. Delicious grilled-meat joint, also offering delivery. $$–$$$

GO Café Rue Mouley Taieb; m 24 101 831; e gocafe@gomarket.com.tn; f Gocafe.tn; 07.30–20.00 daily. Opposite the GO community co-working space, offering delicious coffee, tea & local dishes. Striking black-&-white exterior décor makes it hard to miss! $$–$$$

Dar Mima Chez Mamie 270 Av Okba ibn Nafi; m 50 333 411, 55 777 770; e gares.mediheb@gmail.com; f Dar.Mima.Chez.Mamie; 08.00–23.00 daily. Hipster café in an old building serving crêpes, drinks & meals within a stone's throw of the Grand Mosque. $$

Kafteji Khairi Rue de la Mosquée des Trois Portes; ⌚ 09.00–late daily. Unsurprisingly given the name, the speciality here is kafteji but it also does excellent tabouna bread. Good cheap eats. $

ENTERTAINMENT AND NIGHTLIFE Given the pious nature of the governorate capital you will struggle to find pubs, bars or nightclubs, but alcohol is served in some of the higher-end hotels and restaurants (as well as the budget Splendid Hotel).

SHOPPING Kairouan is one of Tunisia's major carpet centres. If you want to buy one, a good first stop is the **Office National de l'Artisanat Tunisien (ONAT)** (Av Ali Zouaoui; ☎77 231 897; ⌚ 10.00–noon & 14.00–17.00 Mon–Fri), as it has a display of old and new carpets and can give you an indication of prices in town. Be careful when walking around, as the term 'musée du tapis' does not indicate a museum but rather a shop with carpets on display. **Tapis Okba** (☎77 231 129; m 98 451 486, 22 780 064; f Tapisdekairouan; ⌚ 08.00–14.00 Sat–Thu), near the Grand Mosque, is a good option; proprietor Saket Habib has set up his mountains of carpets in a prime location, with an amazing terrace overlooking the mosque and fixed prices posted on the wall.

If carpets are not your thing, look out for the beaten copper kitchen pans and dishes for which Kairouan is also known, while zinc-coated items can be found on the main drag in the medina – though attractive, they are expensive. Otherwise, the best buy in Kairouan are *makroud*, sweet date cakes basted in oil and coated in syrup and sesame seeds. Appropriately packaged in boxes labelled *pâtisserie Tunisienne*, they make a sticky, calorific gift. The city is also the leading national producer of chilli peppers, and you will see them for sale by the roadside.

OTHER PRACTICALITIES The main hospital in town is the university hospital, **Hospital Ibn El Jazzar** (Rue Ibn El Jazzar; ☎77 226 300; ⌚ 24/7).

WHAT TO SEE AND DO Kairouan is a very walkable city in terms of the main sights. For many visitors, a look at the Grand Mosque, a wander down the main street to take in the atmosphere and Bir Barouta, and a peek in at Sidi Abid Zaouia will be sufficient. A 12DT multi-entry ticket, sold at the Grand Mosque, includes entry to the mosque, the zaouias of Sidi Sahbi, Sidi Abid and Sidi Amor Abbada, the Aghlabid Pools and the Museum of Islamic Art at Rakkada; you probably need 2 hours to tick off the first five, and a further 1½ hours for a trip out to the museum. Note that there can be some confusion with street names in Kairouan, partly because of the lack of street signs, and partly because some have two names. All part of the challenge when it comes to exploring!

The medina Compared with Tunis or Sousse, Kairouan's medina is small, so it is difficult to get totally lost. A large part of the medina's walls have survived, notably the section near the Great Mosque. The medina dates to the founding of the city in the 7th century AD and stood in for the streets of Cairo during filming of *Raiders of the Lost Ark* (1981). The main street (Avenue Habib Bourguiba) leads from Bab ech Chouhada to Bab Tunis, on which you will find stalls selling the *makroud* sticky date cakes, various everyday shops, carpet emporia and Bir Barouta, after which, on the right, there is a small covered souk. Further up, again on the right, is a small busy market.

If you enter the medina through Bab ech Chouhada in the south, you might start your culture hunt with a look in at the **Zaouia of Sidi Abid el Ghariani Sahab** (take the second street on the right after the gate and look for a fine doorway on your right). This burial place of Sidi Abid, a 13th-century saint, was constructed in the 14th century. The building is a good example of the courtyard style that dominated in Kairouan, used for both religious buildings and homes. Of particular interest is the room with the mausoleum; the ceiling is extremely finely worked wood, with superb plasterwork all around. Today, the zaouia houses the office of the Association de Sauvegarde de la Médina de Kairouan (☎77 228 126), an organisation founded in 1977 to help to preserve the medina.

Continuing up the main drag, turn right just before Bir Barouta, up the Rue de la Mosquée des Trois Portes, and you will eventually come to the **Mosque of the Three Doors (Jamaâ Thelethe Bibene)** on your right. Founded by an immigrant from Cordoba in AD866, the mosque has an interesting façade with carved inscriptions. If you look at the column capitals, recycled from Byzantine monuments, you will see some much-eroded birds, their beaks broken or heads removed – testimony to the fact that Islamic art prefers to avoid the representation of living beings. Nearby, you may hear goldfinches tweeting in the weavers' workshops.

At the end of Rue de la Mosquée des Trois Portes, turn left down a narrow street and you will come to Rue Tahar Zarrouk. Turn right here, then left at the end of it on to the wide Boulevard Ibrahim ibn Aghlab, which leads to the imposing, buttressed, ochre walls of the **Great Mosque**. Founded with the city by Okba ibn Nafi in AD671 and constructed by master builder Sidi Cherif ibn Hindu (who is buried in the city, see page 280), the building includes much ancient masonry recycled from earlier Roman and Byzantine structures. The oldest mosque in western Islam, it was severely damaged during the rebellion of 688, was virtually rebuilt in the 9th century and then later enlarged in the same severe style. The age of the minaret is open to debate, although the bottom section is thought to date from 730. The main dome is of ribbed brick in a herringbone design. The top section is thought to date from 836. The square, 31.5m-high minaret rises in three sections, each diminishing in size towards the top, where there is a ribbed dome. (Ask if it is possible to climb the 128 steps for a superb view.) One theory goes that the minaret was inspired by the Lighthouse of Alexandria, a 100m-high structure that once stood in Egypt's main port and was one of the Seven Wonders of the Ancient World.

Although it is not obvious to the visitor, both the prayer hall and sloping courtyard are trapezoid in shape. Here, there are pillared cloisters with easily missed wooden ceilings. Both the east and west porticoes have two aisles supported by three lines of arches. The vast courtyard, one of the largest in any mosque in Tunisia, is half-paved in white marble, the remainder paved with limestone blocks in which there is a differentiated path, not quite central, which leads to the minaret. Towards one corner is a sundial indicating the times of the five daily prayers. Close to the sundial, rainwater was collected in a cistern for use in ritual ablutions.

The prayer hall is filled with numerous imposing red-granite and white-and-green marble columns brought from vanquished Roman cities. Unfortunately, non-Muslims are unable to view the internal wooden ceilings, the lavishly decorated and carved doors, woodcarving on the pulpit, nor the 9th-century tiles from Baghdad in the niche which faces Mecca. You can, however, see that red mergoum Kairouan carpets overlay the woven reed mats (*hsur*) used to cover the floor. Further reed mats wrapped around the columns stop worshippers from getting a cold back.

So why is the Great Mosque laid out like it is? Compared with the Byzantine basilicas that the Arab conquerors would have found when they took towns such as Sbeïtla, the mosque marks a sharp break. Gone are the high-vaulted ceilings of the basilicas as Roman building technology got lost in the conquest. Rather, the new occupiers needed a large, ritually pure space. Islamic worship is based on the principle of facing Mecca. The worshippers face the *mihrab*, the niche indicating the direction of Islam's holiest city. The 70m width of the mosque allows long lines of worshippers to form parallel to the mihrab wall. If the number of worshippers grew, the covered area could easily be extended by adding further colonnades across the courtyard and roofing them. There was no need for a prayer hall much larger than the one in existence as medieval Kairouan was a small town. When large numbers of people gathered for the prayers on great occasions, the overspill could be easily contained in the courtyard.

One final point of interest in the medina is **Bir Barouta (Barouta's well)**, a domed building just off Avenue Habib Bourguiba, down Rue Barrouta. The story goes that a dog called Barouta came across the spring, an answer to his pious master's prayers some time back in the 13th century. Up the steep stairs are a small café and a large piece of functioning medieval technology in the form of a waterwheel activated by a blinkered camel.

Aghlabid Pools (🕘 winter 08.30–17.30 daily, summer 08.00–noon & 15.00–19.00 daily) Unfortunately for the early inhabitants of Kairouan, there were no useful bits of Roman aqueduct to be brought back into service. The solution to the water-supply problem was found by sultan Abou Ibrahim Ahmed in the 9th century, who had 14 large *fesquiyet* (reservoirs) constructed. Of these, only two survive today, to the north of town on the P12. The pools were seemingly part of a much more elaborate water system. The Cherichera aqueduct (now partially collapsed) was constructed to carry water from over 36km away to the west. The smaller pool was used to settle the silt carried in the water and the clear water was stored in the big pool (diameter 128m, depth 5m). Although the pools may have resolved Kairouan's recurring water-supply problem, they also added a health risk as they proved to be a superb breeding ground for mosquitoes. Today the pools are probably not worth driving out to unless you are a true aficionado of ancient hydrology.

Zaouia of Sidi Sahbi (🕘 08.00–20.00 daily) The burial place of one of the Prophet's companions, Abou Djama el Balaoui, this is also known as the Barber's Mosque and labelled as Mausolée Abi Zâmaa on the multi-entry tickets. This is because Abou el Balaoui carried about with him three hairs from the Prophet's beard, from which he would never be parted. Dating to the 17th century, the present building, with its elegant minaret, is beautifully decorated with the usual ceramic tilework. To reach the mausoleum, you first pass through a small room and continue through an open-air corridor. The next small room, with a finely worked plaster ceiling, opens on to the delightful main courtyard (square in shape and bordered on three sides by colonnades) with the mausoleum which houses the tomb – but access is reserved for Muslims only. Another small room off to one side houses a different tomb, this time of Sidi Cherif ibn Hindu, master builder of the Great Mosque (page 279). Notice the painted wooden ceilings under the arcade surrounding the courtyard. It gets busy on Fridays, when circumcision ceremonies take place, and during the Mouled (the Prophet's birthday).

Zaouia of Sidi Amor Abbada (🕘 winter 08.30–17.30 daily, summer 08.00–noon & 15.00–19.00 daily) Closed at the time of writing, this is another fairly peripheral monument. This zaouia is the burial place of a 19th-century blacksmith who had a penchant for designing large Tolkienesque metal objects, including huge anchors and immense swords fit for a dragon slayer. A number of these items are on display in his seven-domed tomb, although some seem to have been stolen. It's all rather curious, and there is little to tell you about how and why such an obviously expensive building was put up by a blacksmith around 1860. However, the lack of information illustrates Tunisian attitudes to saints' shrines in the post-independence period. In the 19th century, the beys and their ministers frequently sponsored the construction of new zaouias, but in the 1960s, with Tunisia becoming a modern nation state, the practice of visiting saints to seek blessing was severely stigmatised.

AROUND KAIROUAN

Palace of Rakkada and National Museum of Islamic Art and Culture

(⊕ 35.592811, 10.052946; 77 323 337; e zchehaibi@yahoo.fr; ⊕ 09.00–16.00 Tue–Thu & Sat–Sun, 09.00–13.00 Fri; 5/4DT non-residents/residents, or included in multi-entry ticket) Once ex-president Habib Bourguiba's official Kairouan residence, this palace 10km southwest of Kairouan on the GP2 today houses Tunisia's most important collection of Islamic art. The palace was designed by architect Jacques Marmey and constructed between 1963 and 1970. Marmey was a proponent of the Sahel architectural style, a product of his early experiences in Morocco and affection for North Africa. Rakkada was the second royal town of the Aghlabid Dynasty, where ruler Ibrahim II built himself a vast royal residency in AD876, which was also very briefly used by the Fatimids. In the 1960s archaeological excavations took place here and found a trove of fine pottery, confirming the high status of the previous occupants. Perhaps this is why Bourguiba chose to construct a palace on this site – he was seeking to confirm his place in the pantheon of Tunisian rulers.

The palace became a museum in 1986, and the collections here are very different from those at the Bardo in Tunis (page 108). Islamic art rejects representations of the living form, so there is neither sculpture nor painting of humans. There are, however, some fine 10th-century manuscripts, leather bindings, coins, pieces of minor ceramics and glassware, as well as a display of well-crafted glass flasks from Mansouriya. The walls are hung with old painted views of the ribats in Monastir and Sousse. One of the most significant pieces is the famous Blue Koran, a 9th- or 10th-century manuscript written in gold Kufic script that is a masterpiece of calligraphy. The blue dye for the pages came from Egypt or India and each letter, made from gold leaf, is carefully glued on with egg-white. Pages of this document have ended up dispersed across the world by Islamic art collectors, fetching hundreds of thousands of dollars each at private auction. Though the exact provenance of the manuscript is debated by many historians, with some arguing for as far afield as Spain or Iran, it is generally accepted to have come from just down the road: the ancient library of the Great Mosque of Kairouan.

Sebkhet el Kalbia Reserve (⊕ 35.887286, 10.299689) On the P2 around 30km northeast of Kairouan, this 8,000ha nature reserve is dominated by the Sebkhet el Kalbia, an 18km-long salt lake. Clear paths and viewing points are rare as the water level varies, falling dramatically in summer when you might spot squacco herons, purple gallinules or the fan-tailed warbler. In winter, migrating birds such as flamingos and cranes pass through.

Jebel Zaghdoud National Park This 1,792ha park is dominated by Jebel Zaghdoud (⊕ 35.898691, 9.774621) and the Aleppo pine forest around it. There are two main roads through the park: the C171 in the north, which connects Sbikha to Oued el-Ksab; and the C99, which forms the park's southeastern border. The park's southwestern border is formed by the C46. The park is home to all sorts of

TUNISIA'S CHALLENGING TERRAIN

Trevor Sheehan (w africanstalingrad.com)

Formerly known as Fondouk, the town of El Haouareb, 33km southwest of Kairouan, is a good place to fully understand the difficulties the Allied and Axis forces faced when it came to navigating Tunisia's terrain during World War II. Given the poor network of tracks and roads, moving heavy artillery and tanks was a huge challenge and mule trains were commonly used to carry ammunition. Both sides, at various times throughout the war, tried to cross the pass at El Haouareb (⊕ 35.548669, 9.755922) either from or to Kairouan, but were unable to do so because of the treacherous hilly terrain and the risk of being ambushed by enemies hidden above the pass. There were particularly intense battles here in late March 1943 between Allied and Axis forces and the nearby military cemetery at Haffuz (⊕ 35.634129, 9.686685) is a poignant reminder of their struggles. It is in a rather sad state of repair, on the south side of the road, and is dedicated to Allied troops (North African and Senegalese soldiers from the Free French Army) who died here.

exciting flora and fauna, including wild boar, jackal, porcupine, mongoose, wildcat and even the very rare striped hyena. However, there is little infrastructure so be sure to bring everything you need, possibly including a guide.

Ouselatia This agricultural settlement has little to attract tourists beyond making a good base from which to explore the surrounding countryside, where you'll find some Neolithic cave paintings at Aïn Khanfous (⊕ 35.743025, 9.732928). If you wish to visit independently, park your car at the western end of Bir Nahal village (⊕ 35.760489, 9.752686), from where it is a 3km hike westwards (there is no marked trail after it departs from the river), with a 175m elevation change, part way up the side of Jebel Ousselat. Spread across over 40m of cave walls, the paintings showcase human figures with bows and arrows hunting a variety of animals, including ancient buffalo and gazelle. Researchers do not agree on the age of the paintings, giving estimates of 8000–4000BC.

A great place to base yourself here is **Dar el Henchir** ✷ ⚑ (4 rooms; ⊕ 35.827881, 9.631966; m 23 302 239; e hichem_gassab@yahoo.fr; w darelhenchir.tn; **$$$$**), set on a 120ha former colonial farm. Rooms are decorated with antique furniture and have high ceilings with large windows offering views over the working farm as well as Jebel Serj and Jebel Ousselat. You can buy their organic products such as honey, olive oil, rosemary essential oil and soaps produced on the farm. The restaurant serves delicious, local food. They can also organise a guide to explore the wider countryside, as well as providing 4x4, moped and bicycle rental.

Ksar Lemsa ⚑ (⊕ 36.035941, 9.691961) Just west of the C46 between Ouselatia and Oued el-Ksab, this Byzantine fortress dates from the 6th century BC (the reign of Justinian), though re-use of older building stones complicates dating. Like most Roman cities, it was situated in a position of strategic importance on a low plateau backed by the Jebel Bargou, overlooking the valleys of Oued el Kebir and the smaller, closer Oued Maarouf. It controlled movement from the plains of the west to the coast and was itself protected by its location. The battlements of the well-preserved fortress remain; inside was a large and deep water cistern fed by a conduit from outside – a supply in times of siege. Around the fortress are many Byzantine ruins, though few are excavated, while on the opposite side of the road is a pocket-sized amphitheatre.

KASSERINE GOVERNORATE

'Kasserine' means 'two *qasrs*' (castles), a reference to this governorate capital's twin Roman mausoleums (one of which, to the Petronii, is destroyed). Though the surrounding region in the high steppes lacks urban tourist attractions, it more than makes up for this with its archaeological treasures, including one of Tunisia's most impressive Roman sites at Sbeïtla. This is also where you'll find the country's highest mountain, Jebel Chambi, which, at 1,554m, towers over the governorate capital and surrounding national park. The settlement of Kasserine itself feels like a frontier town: there is a heavy security forces presence, owing to the ongoing insurgency in the surrounding mountains, and you may well see armoured vehicles driving around.

SAFETY WARNING

At the time of writing, the UK Foreign, Commonwealth and Development Office (FCDO) advised against all but essential travel to Kasserine Governorate and against all travel to Jebel Chambi National Park and the peak itself. See page 49 for further information or visit w gov.uk/foreign-travel-advice/tunisia.

GETTING THERE AND AROUND Kasserine is 280km southwest of Tunis (4hrs 15mins, mainly along the P2 and P3). SNTRI buses run between the two (5½hrs; 19.60DT one-way); buses and louages arrive at the main station just over 1km east of the town centre (⊕ 35.177832, 8.847848). A train line once linked Sousse with Kairouan and Kasserine, but this is no longer in use.

All major roads in the area are in good condition. For security reasons, it is better to arrive and depart using your own private transport. However, take note of security advisories before departure, as no matter which direction you drive from Kasserine, you are likely to pass through an area where travel is not advised by certain embassies.

WHERE TO STAY AND EAT Kasserine is not a great option as a base to explore the region, long deprived of the kind of tourism income that has helped other towns' hotel scenes thrive. Nearby Sbeïtla is better set up for overnight stays (page 286).

Hotel Amaidra (33 rooms) Rue 18 Janvier 1952; ☎ 77 412 606. Large & clean with AC & big en suite including a full bath & shower. On a busy road, so traffic noise might be an issue on ground floor. B/fast inc. **$$**

Maison des Jeunes (30 rooms) Av Habib Bourguiba; ☎ 77 474 053; m 94 682 023. Cheapest bed in town. Very basic but run-down en suites or bunks with shared bathrooms. **$**

Restaurant Avenir Sportif de Kasserine Av Taieb Mhiri; ⊙ noon–late daily. Named after the local football team, this offers a short fixed menu changing daily, including fish, grilled meats & couscous. **$$–$$$**

The Twins Coffee 14 Rue 18 Janvier 1952; m 99 452 925; f TheTwinsCoffee; ⊙ 08.00–late daily. Slick, modern coffee spot offering drinks, b/fast plates & sweets. Very popular. **$$**

Café Place des Martyrs Maroon awnings are easy to spot, in the thick of the action by the station. Good coffee & pastries. **$**

KASSERINE ⚑ The capital's main draw is **Cillium**, the ancient Roman remains on the western side of town by the university. The settlement was fairly prosperous if judged by mosaics discovered here in the 19th century, some of which are now in the Bardo in Tunis. The best known of these is a panel with Venus surrounded by tritons, nereids on sea-monsters and putti on dolphins. Much of the wealth came from the development of olive presses in the 2nd century AD, when the capital achieved municipium status. The site is most easily accessed from the north, and there is a car park at the superbly restored Roman theatre. On the complex's western side, near the back gate, is the 3rd-century AD triumphal arch, with a dedication mentioning the Colonia Cillitana, the Roman settlement from which the town derives its name.

There are a few other impressive Roman remains dotted across town, including the 2nd-century AD **Mausoleum of the Flavii** (⊕ 35.173967, 8.798097), opposite the stadium on the main road. This three-storey humblebrag was commissioned by wealthy olive-oil producer Titus Flavius Secundus and is inscribed with such modest lines as 'Who would not marvel at this work and from seeing the riches that were spent / Stand too awestruck to comprehend such wealth for himself?' It also throws shade on the quality of competing Spanish olive-oil producers, an activity that some Tunisian olive farmers still love to partake in over 2,000 years later!

Also in town is a small **monument** (⊕ 35.168819, 8.790270) to the US troops who died in the Battle of the Kasserine Pass in February 1943. This was the first major engagement between US and Axis troops in North Africa during World War II. Rommel's Afrika Korps killed over 3,000 US troops, an event that led to George S Patton replacing Major General Lloyd Fredendall as commanding general of the US II Corps. The actual monument is obscured from view of the main road by a military building; to get there, take the dirt track at ⊕ 35.167398, 8.790418. Be careful where you point your camera, however, as there is an active military base near the monument.

SBEÏTLA ✷ ⚑ The most distant major settlement from Carthage, Sbeïtla (Roman Sufetula) is today also one of the best preserved. Whereas many Roman cities were quarried for building stone down the centuries, Sbeïtla remained relatively untouched, apart from a little refortification under the Byzantines. For a short time it was even an imperial Christian capital. Regardless of when you visit this impressive ruined town, you are likely to have the site almost to yourself, apart from the odd local teenager. The best time to come, however, is early in the morning or evening when the sunlight is softer on the golden stones of the temples, giving them an otherworldly feel.

History Sufetula was thought to have been built in the 3rd century BC, but little is known about the settlement until the period under the rule of Emperor Vespasian (AD69–79). Judging by the remains of the public buildings, the town was very prosperous during the 2nd and 3rd centuries, but it wasn't until the early 7th century that Sbeïtla emerged into history. At the time, Byzantine Africa was supplying corn and olive oil to Constantinople which, under the leadership of Emperor Heraclius, defeated the Sassanid Persian Empire in the east. But a new enemy was emerging in the form of the tribes of Arabia, united by a new revealed religion: Islam. Egypt was invaded, leading to a flood of refugees. In 642, the Arabs took Cyrenaica, and a year later they besieged Tripoli. In 646, in a bold move the exarch Gregory declared himself independent from Constantinople, proclaimed himself emperor and moved his administration from Carthage to Sufetula, which

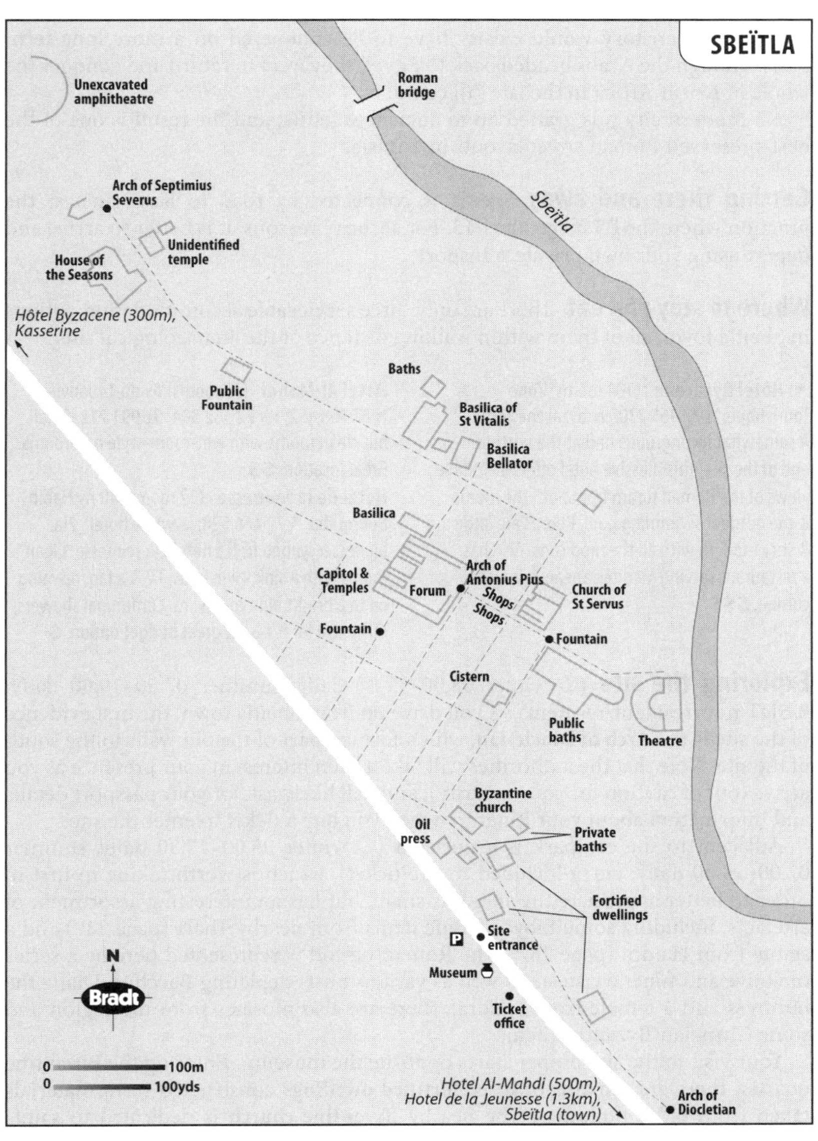

he considered to be a better centre from which to defend the country against the new and energetic enemy from the east.

However, this proved not to be the case. Abdallah ibn Saâd launched an invasion in 647 and Gregory's forces were annihilated by the mobile Arab cavalry, and Gregory himself was killed. The remaining Byzantine forces withdrew northwards, abandoning southern Byzacena, but they made a fatal error after their defeat: they offered a huge bribe to the Arabs to leave. Surprised by the quantity of coins put before him, Abdallah ibn Saâd asked where all this wealth came from. The Byzantine representatives explained that it came from the sale of olive oil to Constantinople.

Such a rich territory would clearly have to be conquered on a more long-term basis. Though the Arabs headed back to Egypt, they were to return and conquer the whole of North Africa in the late 7th century.

No modern city was grafted on to ancient Sufetula, and the result is one of the best-preserved Roman street layouts in Tunisia.

Getting there and away Sbeïtla is connected by road to Kasserine, at the junction where the P3 meets the P13. For security reasons, it is better to arrive and depart using your own private transport.

Where to stay and eat There are only three serviceable accommodation options in Sbeïtla town, all of them within walking distance of the archaeological site.

✱ **Hôtel Byzacene** (104 rooms) Zone Touristique; ☎ 77 465 230; w byzacene.com. A somewhat incongruous find at the northern end of the site, this massive hotel offers incredible views of the Roman forum from both the rooms & the outdoor swimming pool. Rooms are large & very modern with all the mod cons. Also has a restaurant serving Mediterranean & Tunisian cuisine. **$$$**

Hotel Al-Mahdi (33 rooms) Av du 14 Janvier; ☎ 77 468 452; m 22 562 504, 92 991 212. Small but clean rooms with wet-room-style bathrooms. Great location. **$$**

Hotel de la Jeunesse (12 rooms) 40 Av Habib Bourguiba; ☎ 77 466 528; e www.hotel_2la.jeunesse@yahoo.fr; f hotel.2la.jeunesse. Clean rooms with a sink, twin beds, TV & a fan, opening on to a bright blue courtyard. Communal showers; 6DT extra for b/fast. A great budget option. **$**

Exploring the site (⏱ winter 08.00–17.30 daily, summer 07.00–19.00 daily; 8/5DT non-resident/resident) As you drive up from Sbeïtla town, the first evidence of the site is the **Arch of Diocletian**, which formed part of the old walls to the south of the site. Note that the authorities will take a keen interest in your presence as you arrive (out of caution for your security), and will likely ask for your passport details and information about your itinerary when you buy a ticket to enter the site.

Adjacent to the car park is a **museum** (⏱ winter 08.00–17.30 daily, summer 07.00–19.00 daily; entry included in site ticket), which is worth taking in first in order to better appreciate the site. It is small, but has an interesting assortment of artefacts, including some Libyco-Punic items from nearby Thala (page 289) and a statue from Haïdra (page 287). The Roman period is represented here by a series of votive and funerary stelae as well as various busts depicting Bacchus, Diana the huntress and a female from Haïdra. There are also mosaics from the region and some Christian/Byzantine items.

Your visit to the site proper starts opposite the museum. Entering the Byzantine quarter, there are remains of three **fortified dwellings** constructed from materials taken from older buildings. The nearby **Byzantine church** is dedicated to saints Gervais, Protais and Tryphon; the badly damaged **private baths** have been partially rebuilt with a mosaic of fish and crustaceans and an oil press (originally there were two presses and a windmill).

Turning right down the street taking you towards the central area, you reach a large **cistern** which supplied water to the city, the rainwater being perhaps supplemented by an underground canal. Close by are the remains of the large **public baths**, with hot and cold rooms and a geometric mosaic decorating the room dedicated to exercise. You can see evidence of the hypocaust underfloor heating system very clearly. The nearby **fountain** is one of three public fountains dating from the 4th century. To the right here, overlooking the Oued Sbeïtla, is the **theatre**, which has now been restored and occasionally plays host to modern performances, with magnificent views over the dry river course. Turning back to the baths and heading towards the main temples, the **Church of St Servus**, built in the courtyard of a Roman temple, is on your right. Today only four stone columns mark the corners of the building.

Head west along the main street, which originally had shops on either side, to the magnificent **Capitol**, entered through the **Arch of Antonius Pius**. This gateway was built in the style of a triumphal arch and formed part of the ancient walls, and can be dated to AD138–61 thanks to an inscription which refers to the Emperor Antonius Pius and his two adopted sons, Marcus Aurelius and Lucius Verus. The three massive **temples** which stand side by side opposite this gate, across the vast, almost square Forum, are assumed to be dedicated (from right to left) to Juno, Jupiter and Minerva. The central temple dedicated to Jupiter, accessible only by steps from the side, was the most opulent of the three, though the temple of Minerva has more elegant columns. The **Forum**, paved with huge stone slabs, is surrounded by a wall which shows evidence of several restorations. The whole complex is highly impressive, and offers some fantastic photo opportunities. Close to the Forum is another **basilica** constructed on the site of an older building. Though in poor condition, the central aisle and two smaller side aisles separated by a double colonnade are visible.

The group of buildings to the northeast, known as the episcopal group, comprises two churches, a baptistery, a chapel and some small baths. Excavated in 1907, the **Basilica Bellator** is named after a fragment of inscription found there. Covering an area of 520m^2, the building has a central nave, two side aisles and a double apse. The mosaic floor in the choir room still remains. The baptistery was converted into a chapel dedicated to Bishop Juncundus, a 5th-century religious leader who is believed to have been martyred by the Vandals. The adjacent **Basilica of St Vitalis** is a later, larger building with five naves, double apses and, like the Basilica Bellator, evidence of long occupation. A marble table decorated with biblical themes that was found here is now in the Bardo in Tunis (page 108). If time and enthusiasm permit, you could explore the northwest of the site past houses and an unidentified temple to the unexcavated **amphitheatre** and across to the much-restored **bridge**. The poorly preserved Arch of Septimius Severus nearby is dedicated to the emperor and his two sons Geta and Caracalla. It was probably built to commemorate their victories over the Parthians at the end of the 2nd century AD.

HAÏDRA (🕘 24/7; free) Well off the main tourist track and sitting less than 8km from the Algerian border, these lonely Roman ruins are scattered over an arid hillside sloping down to a river. Known as Ammaedara, the settlement stood at the western end of one of the oldest Roman roads in Africa (inscriptions record it as having been built in AD14), which ran inland from Tacapae (modern Gabès) on the coast. Later, under Emperor Hadrian, a road from Carthage to Theveste, some 40km southwest in modern-day Algeria and a major Roman military base, passed through Ammaedara. Under Augustus, Ammaedara became the Third Augustan Legion's headquarters in the 1st century BC. When Emperor Vespasian moved the legionary base west to Theveste in AD75, a colony of veterans was settled at Ammaedara.

Ammaedara remained an important centre in Christian times, and there are the remains of no fewer than five basilicas on the site. Under Justinian in the 6th century, with Africa temporarily reconquered by the Byzantines, the town acquired a vast citadel, which in all probability continued in use under the early Arab rulers. It was in part restored and altered in Husseinid times.

There are all the usual features, including a triumphal arch and the basilicas, plus the massive masonry of a Byzantine fort. In Roman times, either the climate must

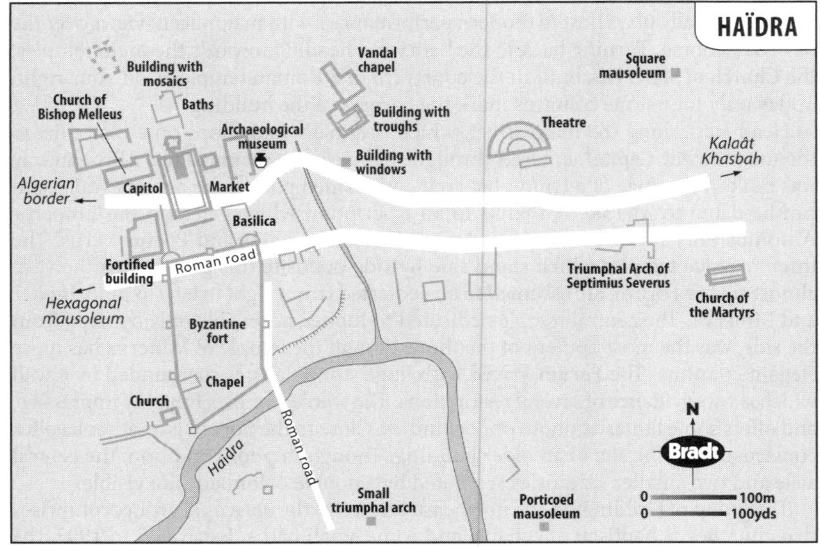

have been wetter or the water infrastructure very efficient to support such a grand military base on this stony site.

Getting there and away Haïdra is easily reached by louage from Kalaât Khasbah, a mining town 18km northeast which is on the train line to Tunis (a journey of over 5 hours). Louages also run from Firyanah, 80km to the south, and Sbeïtla, 95km southeast.

Exploring the site The remains are located north and south of the main road, with the more spectacular sights on the south side. Approaching from the east, you first come to the **Triumphal Arch of Septimius Severus**, which once spanned the Roman road to Carthage. The arch was dedicated in AD195 as can be seen from the frieze. It was incorporated into a small Byzantine fort in the 6th century, meaning it has stacks of bricks obscuring some original features. Southeast of the arch are the remains of the Byzantine **Church of the Martyrs**, dedicated to those who perished under the persecution of Diocletian. It has three naves, and excavations show that it was built on a more ancient church; in both, the apse faced east.

About 300m to the south is a beautiful, well-preserved **porticoed mausoleum**, with a façade of four columns supporting a pediment. The second storey is still intact, in the style of a small temple. Any statues which stood between the columns, however, have long since been removed, with at least one of them ending up on display in the museum in Sbeïtla (page 286).

To the northwest of the mausoleum is without doubt Haïdra's finest structure: the **Byzantine fort**, built at the time of Justinian (AD527–65). Covering a vast 22,000m^2 area and with 10m-high walls, these massive fortifications have claims to be the largest Byzantine fort in Africa. Nine square towers can be clearly seen. A small chapel with three naves was incorporated into part of the west wall against one of the towers, and just outside the walls to the southwest is yet another small basilica. Renovations to the north elevation of this fortress were undertaken by the Ottoman beys. To the west of the site is a two-storey, 2nd-century **hexagonal**

Roman mausoleum, sadly looted many years ago, and currently being undercut by floodwaters in the wadi.

On the north side of the main road, the ruins are rather less well preserved. Opposite the Church of the Martyrs is the **square mausoleum** decorated with Corinthian pillars and stylised garlands. The **theatre** is a bit of a disappointment as the restorations of AD299 have not prevented it from being now just a pile of stones on hard-to-distinguish foundations. With three naves, the nearby **Vandal chapel** refers to these invaders from the 5th century who left funerary inscriptions. Further west, the jumbled ruins are thought to be those of the **capitol**. Between this and another basilica, the so-called Church of Bishop Melleus, is a discernible square with miscellaneous stones that was probably the market. The **Church of Bishop Melleus** was a most distinguished building with two massive columns supporting an arch at the perimeter of the courtyard. Inside there were three naves and a semicircular apse, on either side of which was a sacristy. It is said relics of St Cyprien were kept here in the 6th century. There is also a small **archaeological museum** on the north side of the road, which has a number of statues and other artefacts from the site, with labels in English, Arabic and French.

THALA Some 50km north of Kasserine, Thala has been occupied since Palaeolithic times, with the etymology of its name hinting at its popularity for human habitation. 'Thala' means 'source' in Amazigh, likely a reference to the various natural springs in the surrounding area. In the time of the Roman Republic, the town sided with King Jugurtha in his rebellion against the Romans, leading to Thala being besieged by General Quintus Caecilius Metellus Numidicus in 108BC. Today it is a quiet market town, with little hint of its long and historically significant past beyond the excavated ruins of a Byzantine church, which sit in the middle of the main street (⊕ 35.576116, 8.669677).

JEBEL CHAMBI NATIONAL PARK Part of the Monts de Tébessa forest massif that spreads all the way from the Algerian frontier, this park, 11km south of Kasserine, is home to Tunisia's highest point – the 1,554m-tall Jebel Chambi – as well as wildlife such as Cuvier's gazelle, Barbary sheep, short-toed snake eagles, Egyptian vultures and gundis (comb rats). Unfortunately, since December 2012 Tunisian security forces have been engaged in counter-insurgency operations here against Salafist jihadist groups that move back and forth between this mountainous region and Tébessa Province in neighbouring Algeria. The pace of military operations in the park intensified during the Covid-19 pandemic, with IED explosions targeting security patrols and a number of suspected militants killed in military operations. The park is currently designated as a military zone, meaning it is off-limits to tourists. Hopefully this will change once the security situation stabilises, and tourists will once again be able to scale the country's highest mountain.

THELEPTE Close to the Algerian border, 35km southwest of Kasserine on the P17, is this small, quiet frontier town. It is of little tourist interest, though it does have a beautiful blue, abandoned **French colonial station house** (⊕ 34.975417, 8.595550), as well as a **Byzantine archaeological site** at the south end of town (⊕ 34.966783, 8.587488), of which none of the remaining ruins are much above waist height. If you find yourself stuck here for the night, the **Hotel Dora** in the north of town is a safe bet (22 rooms; 77 431 222. **$$$**), and the owner can recommend all sorts of remote archaeological sites in the area. World War II enthusiasts will note the presence of **Thelepte Airfield** to the north of town (⊕ 35.003737, 8.595761), which was built and occupied in December 1943 by USAAF XII Fighter Command as part of the Allied advance across North Africa. Today it is in use by the military and is not accessible to tourists.

SIDI BOUZID GOVERNORATE

Normally warranting little more than a one-sentence entry in most guidebooks (if covered at all), this governorate is home to a unique natural reserve in Tunisia: Parc National Bou-Hedma, boasting savannah plains that you might expect to see on safari somewhere in southern Africa. Sidi Bouzid town itself is short on tourism offerings, serving mainly as a semi-convenient base from which to explore Bou-Hedma and the agricultural settlement of Meknassy, known for its horse breeding.

> **SAFETY WARNING**
>
> At the time of writing, the national park around Jebel Mghila on the border with Kasserine Governorate was designated as an area of military activity owing to the presence of Islamic State-affiliated insurgents in the mountains. This means that Tunisian security forces will not allow you near the area. It looks unlikely that this designation will change in the immediate future.

HISTORY The governorate played host to Amazigh and then Roman settlements, as evidenced by the archaeological remains discovered at Henchir-Simindja (Roman-era Simingi), now an olive-growing area. During World War II it was the scene of a serious mauling of US troops by Axis forces in the Battle of Sidi Bouzid (14–17 February 1943), which served as a precursor to the disastrous Battle of Kasserine Pass a few days later (page 284). The governorate capital hit international headlines on 17 December 2010, when street vendor Mohamed Bouazizi set himself on fire in front of the governor's office, following a confrontation with local police where they confiscated his scales, allegedly for trading fruit and vegetables without a permit. His death, 18 days later, was to prove a catalyst for the Tunisian Revolution in 2011, and the wider Arab Spring. The main street in Sidi Bouzid is now named after Mohamed Bouazizi, and there is also a monument to his fruit cart on display.

GETTING THERE AND AROUND Sidi Bouzid is some 275km south of Tunis (4hrs, mainly along the P2 and P3). SNTRI buses run between the two (4½hrs; 18.70DT one-way), and buses and louages arrive at the main station, 1km northeast of the centre.

WHERE TO STAY AND EAT Aside from these options in Sidi Bouzid, Bou-Hedma also offers basic camping and accommodation (see opposite).

Hotel Ksar Dhiafa (35 rooms) Bd Mohamed Bouazizi; 76 630 800/900; e contact@hotel-ksardhiafa.com; f hotelksardhiafa. An oddly luxurious hotel to find in a place with almost zero tourists. From the black-&-white façade to the marble hallway, it all feels a bit out of place, but this is definitely the best hotel in town – though with a price tag to match. Note that the architects appear to have forgotten the toilets in some of the rooms, then retro-fitted them in the small hallway between the bedroom & the shower room, so check before you accept a key. **$$$$**

Horchani Hotel (28 rooms) C83; 76 630 855. Rooms with either en suite (wet-room-style shower) or communal facilities. Long, dark blue hallways with cases displaying local crafts. Rooms are dark but have small balconies. Has large outdoor space, though now mainly used by local lads drinking beers. This is OK as a last resort if Hotel Ksar Dhiafa is full. $$

Balance Café & Restaurant Bd Mohamed Bouazizi; m 93 613 528; e cafebalance05@gmail.com; ⌚ 08.00–20.00 daily. With a huge orange-&-black façade, this serves a mixture of Mediterranean cuisine & popular sweets & cakes. $$–$$$

Restaurant Oscar Bd Mohamed Bouazizi; ⌚ 10.30–23.00 daily. Menu featuring traditional Tunisian cuisine (including grilled fish) as well as pizzas. $$–$$$

Pizzeria Roxy Bd Mohamed Bouazizi; m 23 263 929; ⌚ 11.00–late daily. Good thin-crust pizzas to eat in or take away. $$

WHAT TO SEE AND DO

Bou-Hedma National Park ✷ In the far south of the governorate, straddling the border with neighbouring Gafsa along the southern Tunisian mountain ranges that are extensions of the Saharan Atlas, this park is unique to both Tunisia and North Africa as it is home to relicts of the region's pre-Saharan savannah (for instance, forests of *Acacia raddiana* – a short, umbrella-shaped desert tree). Looking out over the distinctive acacia silhouettes you would be forgiven for thinking you were in South Africa or Botswana. Although lions are long gone from North Africa, the remaining fauna is characteristic of the African savannah that used to stretch across this part of the world. Endangered species in the park include the addax antelope and the critically endangered dama gazelle, and you are also likely to see southern ostrich running about – a very strange sight in Tunisia! Those with their own 4x4 can drive along the very rocky trails, but you are likely better off on foot so as not to disturb the herds. The park has marked hiking trails, signs with maps and organised campsites, details of which you can collect at the eco-museum when you first arrive.

Practicalities Entry to the park is free, though you will need to organise a permit from the Ministry of Agriculture (specifically the Direction Générale des Forêts, see page 209). This can be collected in Tunis or in the nearby town of El Mezzouna, which you drive through en route to the park (entrance from the Gafsa end of the park is forbidden, see page 49). The Direction Générale des Forêts office in El Mezzouna is at ⊕ 34.575139, 9.84276, near the train station. Once you have your permit in hand, head south out of El Mezzouna until you hit a roundabout (⊕ 34.53623, 9.860806), from where the park is signposted. The park gates are just after El Bouaa (⊕ 34.479643, 9.668212), from where a gravel track leads west into the park until you hit the eco-museum (⊕ 34.47522, 9.64892), where there is a car park. The eco-museum is well worth a visit, with displays outlining the history of the park and the wide variety of species that live in it.

There are three accommodation options in the park (all free, but requiring prearranged permits). If you are happy without any facilities, you can camp in designated spots around the park. You can also stay in the park observatory (⊕ 34.47902, 9.613456), still occasionally used by scientific teams. This is a solid stone structure with solar power and hot water. Alternatively, as a third option, you can arrange to stay in the accommodation block next to the eco-museum, which has basic rooms, running water and toilets.

Meknassy This agricultural settlement, 55km south of Sidi Bouzid on the C83, is famous for breeding purebred Arabian horses. Since 1975 it has hosted the annual Festival International du Cheval Arabe de Meknassy, which features racing as well as displays of traditional horsemanship. The dates of the festival alternate between July and November.

8

The Southeast

Incorporating the governorates of Tataouine, Medenine and Gabès, this diverse region offers an eclectic mix of attractions, whether you are keen on early Islamic architecture or just lounging on a beach. Its most famous name is Djerba, North

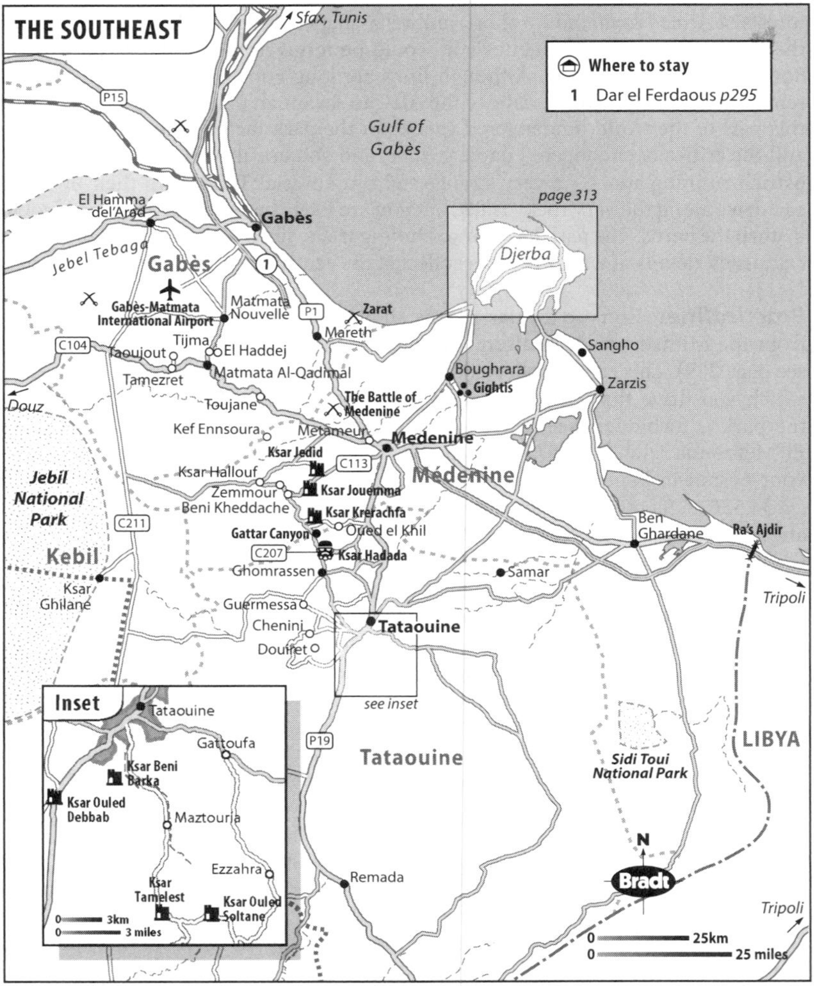

Africa's largest island and one of the best places to kitesurf in the Mediterranean. Here, old meets new as luxurious beach resorts jostle for space with an ancient and distinctive island community that includes a Jewish population that is over 2,000 years old. Inland, the coastal plains give way to the Dahar Mountains, dotted with abandoned Amazigh settlements, historic *ksour* (fortified granaries) and troglodyte dwellings now transformed into hotels. Further north sits Gabès, the only oasis by the sea in Tunisia (and possibly the world); a former terminus for the region's trans-Saharan caravans. The region is also famous for its wealth of Star Wars filming locations, most notably at Matmata, and the site where Axis troops were pushed back from the Mareth Line by the Allies during World War II. Finally, adventurous travellers can venture into Tunisia's slice of the Sahara proper, in the remote far south where rolling sand dunes flow over the border from eastern Algeria.

GABÈS

Home to Tunisia's only oasis by the sea, Gabès has been a place for weary travellers to rest and replenish for thousands of years. As the terminus for a regional trans-Saharan caravan route, the oasis would have been a welcome sight to Arab and Amazigh traders, appearing out of the desert after weeks of walking from as far afield as Agadez in Niger and Timbuktu in Mali.

Today, downtown Gabès is a mixture of old quarters, 19th-century colonial buildings and some significant post-World War II modern developments. Traditionally, there were two ancient quarters: El Menzel, the area south of the present louage station, which straddles the eastern border of the oasis; and Jara, which is divided into Petite Jara, north of the Oued Gabès, and Grande Jara. The French established a small new town and a large military base east of Jara, towards their new port. The military base remains in use today, and separates the older sections of Gabès from the coast. On the southern banks of the Oued Griaa, just south of the oasis, is another old quarter, called Boulbaba. Much of the town looks relatively new and industrial, with large sections having been rebuilt after bombardment in World War II (mainly in Jara), as well as after the serious flooding in 1962. Despite the long beaches and fine sand the coast is not very developed, especially compared with nearby Djerba and Zarzis. This is likely because of the water pollution caused by the state-owned phosphate processing plant in Ghannouch, around 3km north of the city centre. But even if you cannot whip out your swimming trunks, there is plenty to see in the oasis, the historic neighbourhoods with their traditional architecture, and even an ethnographic museum.

HISTORY Thought to be of Phoenician origins, by 161BC Gabès was part of the Carthaginian domain, an important trading link with the south. Under Roman rule it was known as Tacapae. Destroyed during the Arab invasions, the rebirth of the town was linked to the arrival of Sidi Boulbaba, the Prophet's companion (now revered as the town's patron saint), in the 7th century AD. Gabès later became an important halt on the caravan routes from the south.

After colonising Tunisia in 1881, the French quickly turned Gabès into a garrison town. Concerned about potential Italian interference from neighbouring Libya, they set up their largest base in the south here. During World War II, the Afrika Korps had its headquarters in the town, using it as a strategic point on its supply lines back to Libya. Gabès was retaken in March 1943 by British and French troops, but only after extensive damage had been done.

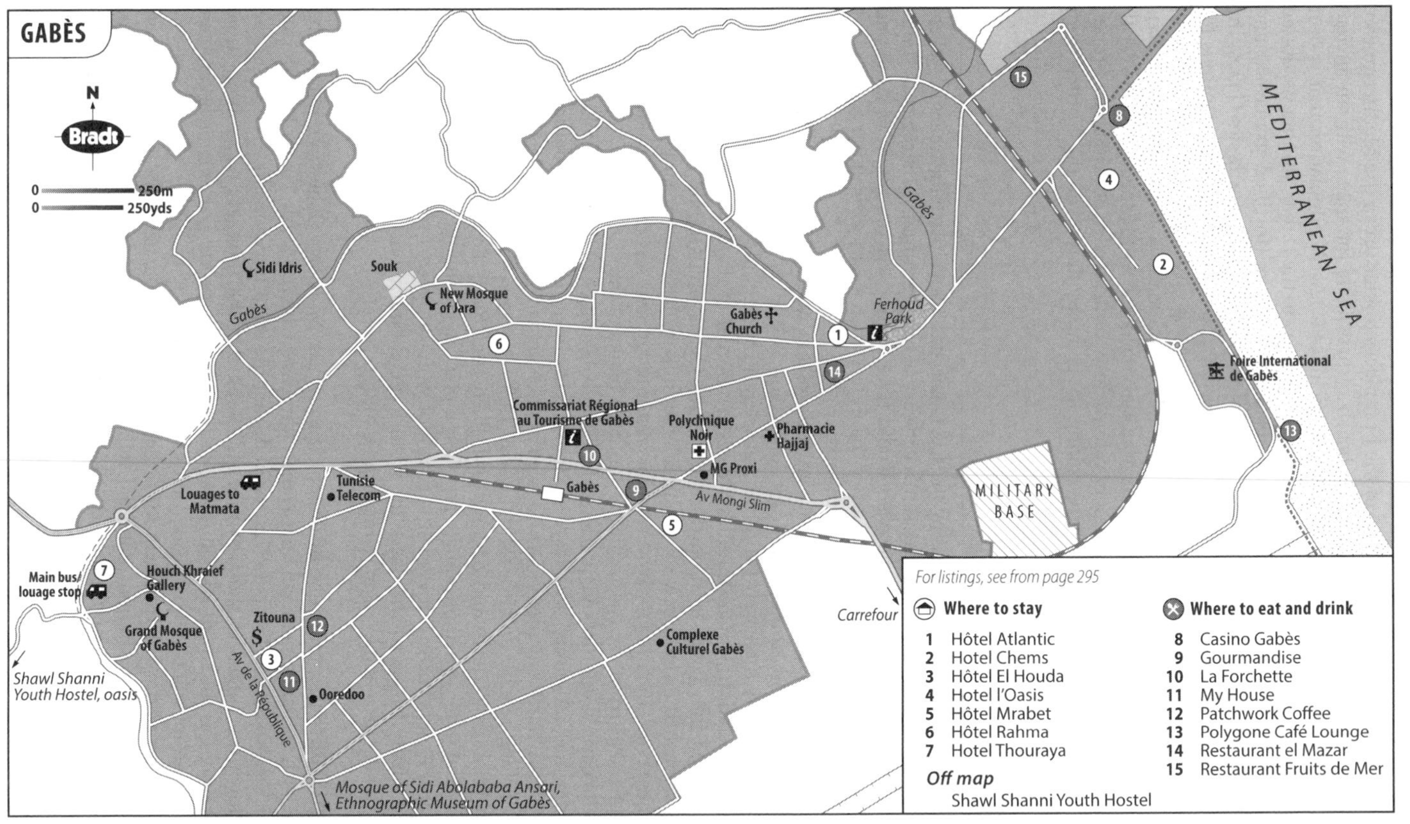
GABÈS
N
Bradt
0 250m
0 250yds
MEDITERRANEAN SEA
Sidi Idris
Gabès
Souk
New Mosque of Jara
Gabès Church
Ferhoud Park
Foire International de Gabès
Commissariat Régional au Tourisme de Gabès
Polyclinique Noir
Pharmacie Hajjaj
MG Proxi
Gabès
Av Mongi Slim
MILITARY BASE
Louages to Matmata
Tunisie Telecom
Main bus/louage stop
Houch Khraief Gallery
Grand Mosque of Gabès
Zitouna
Ooredoo
Av de la République
Complexe Culturel Gabès
Carrefour
Shawl Shanni Youth Hostel, oasis
Mosque of Sidi Abolababa Ansari, Ethnographic Museum of Gabès
For listings, see from page 295
Where to stay
1 Hôtel Atlantic
2 Hotel Chems
3 Hôtel El Houda
4 Hotel l'Oasis
5 Hôtel Mrabet
6 Hôtel Rahma
7 Hotel Thouraya
Off map
Shawl Shanni Youth Hostel
Where to eat and drink
8 Casino Gabès
9 Gourmandise
10 La Forchette
11 My House
12 Patchwork Coffee
13 Polygone Café Lounge
14 Restaurant el Mazar
15 Restaurant Fruits de Mer

GETTING THERE AND AWAY Around 30km southwest of town, Gabès-Matmata International Airport has once-weekly flights from Tunis with Tunisair Express on Wednesdays (1hr; 130.70DT). The airport is a bit of a pain to reach on public transport, being in such an isolated location. If you do not want to take a taxi, you could try taking a louage from Gabès to Matmata Nouvelle, and then hop on any vehicle plying the route between Matmata Nouvelle and El Hamma, which goes past the airport.

Gabès is 415km from Tunis (just over 4 hours on the A1 toll road). **Louages** connect with Tunis and the neighbouring settlements of El Hamma, Kebili, Sfax, Medenine, Gafsa, Kasserine, El Mazouna, Sidi Bouzid, Meknassi and Regueb, and SNTRI **buses** connect with Tunis (6hrs; 27DT one-way). Both louages and buses depart from the very west end of town, except those louages to/from Matmata, which are parked slightly northeast.

There are three daily **trains** from Tunis to Gabès (7hrs), departing at 06.15, 13.05 and 21.20. The train station is in the centre of town on Avenue Mongi Slim.

Overall, Gabès is quite a flat, walkable city, although if you are staying in one of the beachfront hotels to the east of town, you may want to drive into the centre.

TOURIST INFORMATION There is a **tourist information office** by Ferhoud Park in the eastern end of town (Av Habib Thameur; ⌚ 09.00–17.00 Mon–Fri, 10.00–13.00 Sat), with a great map of the town outside. You will find the larger **Commissariat Régional au Tourisme de Gabès** further west (159 Av Farhat Hachad; ☎ 75 279 050, 75 275 055; e crt.gabes@ontt.tourism.tn; ⌚ 08.00–13.00 & 14.00–17.00 Mon–Fri), with a selection of maps and other materials in various languages. They may also be willing to issue permits here for Tunisia's extreme south. However, you are better off heading to the commissariats in Tataouine, Kebili or Tozeur, who are more used to dealing with these requests (see *The Deep South*, page 367).

WHERE TO STAY *Map, opposite, unless otherwise stated*

✷ **Dar el Ferdaous** [map, page 292] (5 rooms) m 29 298 823; e dar.elferdaous@yahoo.com; w agoubiabdel.wix.com/el-ferdaous; f MaisonDhoteDarElFedaous. One of the best accommodation options in the governorate is this traditional Tunisian country home on a farm, 17km south of Gabès near El M'Dou. You know you are arriving somewhere special when you pull into the palm-lined driveway & there are horses grazing by the entrance! Converted into a boutique hotel, rooms are spacious with AC & en suite. The grounds are extensive, & there is a swimming pool & terrace. **$$$$**

Hotel Chems (120 rooms) Av Habib Thameur; ☎ 75 270 547; w hotelchems.com.tn. Much more modern facilities than the next-door Oasis for roughly the same price (unless you eat lunch or dinner in the very expensive restaurant). Beautiful outdoor swimming pool. **$$$$**

Hotel l'Oasis (115 rooms) Av Habib Thameur; ☎ 75 270 381; w hoteloasisgabes.com. Large, well-situated beachfront hotel with clean rooms & a lively bar. Solid mid-range choice. **$$$$**

Hôtel Atlantic (40 rooms) 4 Av Habib Bourguiba; ☎ 75 220 034. Opened in 1923, this colonial-era relic once housed General Rommel in 1943. The exterior façade does not look too shabby given its age, but rooms could do with renovation. Basic furnishings with no AC but spacious, with high ceilings & a small balcony overlooking the park. **$$**

Hôtel El Houda (6 rooms) Av de la République; ☎ 75 220 022; m 52 356 681; e hotelhoudagabes@gmail.com; f Hotel.Houda.Gabes. Here since 1988, this hotel has a cool black-&-white coffee shop downstairs. Small but clean & modern rooms with en-suite wet room with shower. A bargain for such a central location. **$$**

Hôtel Rahma (30 rooms) 26 Rue Boulbaba Mrabet; ☎ 75 275 385. Clean but basic; AC, TV & en suite, but very tired compared with Hôtel El Houda, which is the same price. Only benefit is walking distance to train station for late arrival or early departure. **$$**

Shawl Shanni Youth Hostel (43 rooms) ⊕ 33.864876, 10.054460; ☎75 228 728. This immaculately landscaped campsite & eco-hostel features individual green-roof wood-&-stone bungalows plus space to pitch tents, with shower blocks, communal cooking facilities & even a pool under construction. A great base from which to explore the oasis & nearby waterfall. Taxi drivers might still know it by the old name of Hotel Chela Club. **$$**

✷ **Hôtel Mrabet** (24 rooms) Rue Ali Zouaoui; ☎75 270 602; m 98 203 577. Bright, spacious, simple rooms with AC, bath, shower & decent-sized balcony. Communal spaces have southern-themed décor including desert frescoes on walls – note the hilarious stuffed camel toy as you walk in. All very basic but great value & in a quiet spot. **$–$$**

Hotel Thouraya (7 rooms) Next to the louage/bus station; m 96 853 246. One of the cheapest beds in town, conveniently located by the main louage stop at the western end of town. Great if you arrive late or are leaving early. Very basic – rooms with not much more than a clean sgl bed & 4 walls. Restaurant serves cheap brik & other mains. **$**

WHERE TO EAT AND DRINK *Map, page 294*

Restaurant el Mazar 39 Av Farhat Hachad; ☎75 272 065; ⊕ noon–15.30 & 18.00–late daily. With various qualifications from a German hotelier school proudly displayed on wall plaques outside, el Mazar offers an intimate & refined dining experience. Serves a mixture of Mediterranean & Tunisian cuisine, with a focus on meats. **$$$**

Restaurant Fruits de Mer Av Hédi Chaker; m 98 507 323; ⊕ noon–23.00 daily. Large, modern seafood place by the port that is reliably packed at lunch & dinner time. Best fish in town. **$$$**

Gourmandise 27 Av Mongi Slim; ☎75 265 538; m 29 836 216; ⊕ 07.00–20.00 daily. Expect high-quality pastries, coffees & sandwiches from this well-established Tunisian pâtisserie chain. **$$–$$$**

✷ **Polygone Café Lounge** Corniche; m 26 752 100; e fawzi-fessi@live.com; f polygone.Gabes; ⊕ 07.00–01.00 daily. As the name suggests, this is a polygonal wooden structure offering panoramic views of the beautiful (if empty) beach, via floor-to-ceiling glass windows. Offers non-alcoholic drinks & a fast-food menu. Also has live music & shows live sports (check the Facebook page). **$$–$$$**

La Forchette 61 Av Mongi Slim; ☎75 238 977; m 97 869 564; f restaurant.pizzeria.la.fourchette; ⊕ 10.00–late Mon–Sat. Very popular pizzeria that also churns out all manner of weird & wonderful creations involving pizza dough & toppings (think *lahmacun* – the classic Turkish flatbread – baguette farcie & everything in between!). **$$**

My House Av de la République; m 50 148 832; f MyHousecafeloungerestaurant; ⊕ 11.30–23.30 Mon–Sat. Billed as a café-lounge-restaurant, offering coffees, sweets & fast food including tasty pizzas. **$$**

Patchwork Coffee Av Béchir El Jaziri; m 22 100 996, 21 849 893; ⊕ 06.00–19.00 daily. Opened in 2020, this red-brick-fronted coffee shop is very popular. Offers a selection of hot & cold drinks plus good crêpes. **$$**

Casino Gabès Av Habib Thameur; m 55 106 122; ⊕ 08.00–late daily. Large café with outdoor seating, offering the usual assortment of hot & cold drinks plus sweets. **$–$$**

OTHER PRACTICALITIES In a medical emergency the enormous, silver-panelled **Polyclinique Nour** has a separate A&E entrance (96 Bd Mohammed Ali; m 31 301 212; e contact@polycliniquenour.tn; f Polyclinique.Nour.Gabes; ⊕ 24/7). For non-emergencies, **Pharmacie Hajjaj** is very well stocked (39 Bd Mohammed Ali; ☎75 271 152; ⊕ 08.00–20.00 Mon–Fri, 08.00–13.30 Sat).

WHAT TO SEE AND DO

The oasis (⊕ 33.881661, 10.085895; ⊕ 24/7; free) Gabès's main attraction is undoubtedly its large oasis, around 7km west of town near the village of Chenini, not to be confused with its namesake in Tataouine Governorate (page 333).

Covering 10km², it is home to an estimated 300,000 palm trees sheltering hundreds of olive and fruit trees, plus numerous vegetable gardens. Owing to its unique microclimate, the oasis is on Tunisia's UNESCO World Heritage Tentative List. Much of this is thanks to the three-tier cropping system which has been used to make the land productive for thousands of years: fruit trees, palm trees and annual crops share the space and water. This system was referred to as far back as in the 1st century AD by Pliny the Elder. Beyond enjoying the pleasant shade among the trees, the oasis is worth exploring for its birdlife; notable species include the commonly seen Spanish sparrow, the Western orphean warbler, common kestrel, Eurasian hoopoe and grey heron.

It's possible to visit by car, but a more picturesque way to get to the oasis is to take a *calèche* (traditional horse-drawn cart) from the end of Avenue Farhat Hached (although these are only around during peak tourist season). At the southwest corner of the oasis is the **Association de Sauvegarde de l'Oasis de Chenini (ASOC)** (⊕ 33.869700, 10.067053; w asoc.org.tn), an NGO that can provide excellent maps as well as other information to help you explore independently. Note that there are no marked walking trails, so you will need to bring a guide or have a map handy.

In front of ASOC is the golden-domed **Great Mosque of Chenini**; although it is still in active use, ASOC may be able to find someone to give you a tour. Also nearby is the **Southern Tunisia Nature Museum** (⊕ 33.863814, 10.059958; ☎75 228 877). Closed at the time of writing, this used to be a zoo complete with crocodiles and a selection of desert creatures. It is unclear if the live animal displays will return upon reopening.

In town One of Gabès's most important old buildings is the 11th-century **Mosque of Sidi Idris** in Petite Jara, one of the only buildings to survive the damage inflicted on town during World War II. Although it is closed to non-Muslims, a considerable amount of Roman masonry was recycled into the building and is visible from the outside.

In El Menzel, look out for the **Grand Mosque of Gabès**, dating to 1938. Refurbished in the late 1990s, the bright-yellow doorway is highly photogenic, and the square around it has also been repaved.

More spectacular is the **New Mosque of Jara** on Avenue Bourguiba in Grande Jara, which has an impressive five-tiered tower with black religious calligraphy up the side, built shortly after the Tunisian Revolution. The 47m-high minaret is the tallest in the country, with decorative calligraphy on the side designed by El Seed, a French-Tunisian artist who was born in Gabès. El Seed's work is also on display on the walls of Djerbahood (page 324). Opposite the mosque is a **souk** selling local handicrafts including basketwork items and hats made of plaited palm, plus jewellery, food and spices. Also on show are powdery green volcanoes of henna, Gabès's real speciality. This powerful dye has three strengths: neutral, which strengthens hair; red, used as hair dye; and black, used for geometric temporary bridal tattoos. The strength of the henna depends on how long the leaves were left on the plant.

Continuing east from here is the sadly abandoned **Gabès Church** (⊕ 33.888232, 10.105697) on Rue Alger. Commissioned in 1886, but not finished for another 25 years, it managed to survive World War II (although it was badly damaged), only to be shut down by the nationwide flooding of 1962. The east end of town also features many green spaces, such as **Ferhoud Park** (Av Habib Thameur; m 20 528 795; f manegefarhoudpark), which has a small children's funfair, and the **Foire International de Gabès** by the coast, home to a bigger funfair and café area.

Finally, there are a couple of cultural spaces in town: the **Houch Khraief Gallery** (m 98 660 854; e ezzedineo@gmail.com; f daralfounoun.gabes), next door to the Grand Mosque, which runs events including live music and photography exhibitions; and **Complexe Culturel Gabès** (☎ 75 275 220; f complexeculturel.gabes), which hosts various exhibitions and events including film screenings.

Boulbaba Around a 30-minute walk south from the centre is the ancient quarter of Boulbaba, named after Sidi Boulbaba – the Prophet's barber who came from Kairouan. He died in Gabès and is buried in the elegant 7th-century **Mosque of Sidi Abolababa Ansari** (⊕ 33.869033, 10.091280), which remains one of the most important religious monuments in the area. Today the town's patron saint is still the object of much veneration, and on Friday afternoon the smell of incense wafts around the mausoleum. Only the inner courtyard is open to visitors, but the portico is crowded by people drinking tea kept hot on small charcoal braseros. Pilgrims come to ask Sidi Boulbaba's intercession for success in exams, a happy marriage or to bring about a much-awaited pregnancy.

Just over the road from the mosque is the **Ethnographic Museum of Gabès** (⊕ 33.868553, 10.090833; ☎ 75 281 111; ⏲ 09.30–16.30 daily), housed in a former *madrasa*. Built during the reign of Mohammed Bey, it once provided student accommodation and today the rooms contain a collection of everyday objects demonstrating the traditional way of life in Gabès. There are four main themes to the displays: domestic crafts, marriage, oasis cultivation, and food preparation and storage.

AROUND GABÈS

Aside from the capital, Gabès Governorate has a number of other interesting attractions, most notably the unique troglodyte caves of Matmata which are today better known for their Star Wars credentials. The governorate is also a must-see for World War II history enthusiasts, as the home of the amazingly preserved Mareth Line and military museum, as well as the site of significant battle sites at Wadi Akarit and El Hamma. Owing to the positioning of Axis forces and the geography of Tunisia, the countryside around Gabès became the scene of some of the bloodiest fighting in Tunisia during World War II. The Germans and Italians made their last stand here in the south, before rapidly losing control of the whole country only a few days after their defeat at Wadi Akarit in April 1943.

EL HAMMA DEL'ARAD Situated between the salt flats to the north and the foothills of Jebel Tebaga to the south, this settlement, 40km west of Gabès on the P16, has grown up around its ancient sulphurous hot springs. (Note there is another El Hamma, also with hot springs, near Tozeur, called El Hamma du Djerid.) There are various hammams dotted around town, the most central one being the **Hammam Sidi Abdelkader** (⊕ 33.884596, 9.793894; ⏲ 08.00–19.00 Tue–Sun; 1DT), which locals say has been in use since Roman times. There is a separate entrance for women at the side of the building.

Just southeast of the hammam on the main road is a **bust of Mohamed Daghbaji**. A local folk-hero, he led a guerrilla campaign from the hills surrounding town to rid his land of French rule between 1915 and 1924, when he was finally captured and executed. Another local hero, **Rabbi Yousef el-Ma'arabi**, is buried further east still at ⊕ 33.881746, 9.801465. While El Hamma's Jewish community has long since departed (an exodus prompted in part by the 1961 Bizerte Crisis, page 179), an

THE BATTLES OF EL HAMMA AND WADI AKARIT

Trevor Sheehan, (w africanstalingrad.com)

The **Battle of El Hamma** was one of the most decisive battles in Tunisia during World War II, taking place as part of the wider advance on the Mareth Line in March 1943. It took place on 21–28 March, concurrently with the nearby Battle of Mareth (page 304). It is also known as the left-hook, as it involved the Allied forces going around the Matmata mountains in a left-flank movement through the desert, parallel to today's pipeline road, in order to get into position to attack the Germans and Italians through the gap in the mountains between Jebel Tebega and the northern tip of the Matmata mountains towards El Hamma. The battle was led by troops from New Zealand along with the British Army; the Royal Air Force conducted what was, until then, the world's biggest air attack on ground targets. Over three days and nights, the Axis forces were defeated, with surviving German and Italian troops withdrawing to the coast. While exact casualty figures were never collected, there were at least 200 dead from the Allies (New Zealand and Britain) and likely 600 dead from the Axis side (Germany and Italy).

Many Roman ruins dot the landscape, testament to the timeless military importance of this area. There are the remains of a Roman defensive wall across the gap at ⊕ 33.684414, 9.605601, and it was here that the Allies formed up their troops for the advance to El Hamma. You'll need a 4x4 to explore the area.

Soon after this Axis defeat came the **Battle of Wadi Akarit** on 6–7 April 1943. This was the final battle of World War II to take place in southern Tunisia and resulted in a crushing defeat for the Germans and Italians by the British Eighth Army. The Axis troops suffered significant casualties and had 7,000 prisoners taken. Wadi Akarit had strategic importance as the wadi and adjoining hills formed the last natural barrier before the coastal road up to northern Tunisia. The battle involved a massive artillery bombardment and determined bayonet attacks resulting in the mainly Italian defenders surrendering to the British in vast numbers. The German and Italian units with transport quickly withdrew along the coast road up to the hills above and beyond Enfidha, taking their tanks and artillery with them for the final battles around Tunis.

The battle area stretches east from the hills around ⊕ 34.093809, 9.856230 across to the coast, and the area is best explored on foot. Be prepared for some spectacular views of the coastal plain and the sea, which is 15km away, from the hilltops.

annual pilgrimage to the tomb still takes place during the month of Tevet (usually December or January in the Gregorian calendar). Sadly, on 31 January 2011 (a few weeks after the end of the Tunisian Revolution) the tomb was attacked by arsonists. The site remains locked outside Tevet owing to the threat of vandalism.

MATMATA AL-QADIMAL (OLD MATMATA) The underground pit-homes and arid hills of Matmata Al-Qadimal were never destined to become a major day-trip destination. Then along came George Lucas, whose vision converted a traditional troglodyte structure into Luke Skywalker's home for the original *Star Wars* film, and Matmata found its place on Tunisia's tourist trail.

Formerly known as Āthweb by the local Amazigh residents (meaning 'good land' in Tamazight), Matmata's population has likely been living in troglodyte houses for over 700 years, although the earliest evidence for pit dwellings in the village dates to the 1630s. The soft ground made the construction of homes underground possible and, provided there was no excessive rainfall, troglodyte living provided the best protection from heat and marauders. However, you will find many abandoned homes dotted about town, especially to the south of Ksar Matmata, a testament to the impacts of the terrible flooding across Tunisia in 1969.

Getting there and away Matmata is well connected to surrounding settlements, 43km south of Gabès on the C107 and 65km northwest of Medenine on the snaking, mountainous C104. SNTRI runs **buses** from Tunis (7hrs; 27.90DT one-way); be sure to get off at the correct Matmata (Matmata Al-Qadimal, also indicated as Matmata Ancienne (Old Matmata) on some bus services); confusion could arise as some buses terminate at Matmata Nouvelle, which is 15km north of Matmata Al-Qadimal on the C107, and very short on tourist sights. **Louages** terminate at the northern end of town (⊕ 33.545269, 9.968593) and connect to most nearby settlements, including Tamezret, Toujane and Matmata Nouvelle, as well as some further-afield destinations such as Medenine and Gabès.

Tourist information There is an **ONTT office** at the northern end of town next to the main louage stop (Av Habib Bourguiba; ☎75 240 075; ⌚ 08.00–13.00 & 14.00–17.00 Mon–Fri). Most of the hotels in town, as well as the Ksar Matmata, can also arrange tour guides and vehicle hire for their guests.

Where to stay *Map, opposite*

Many visitors to Matmata only stay for the day, stopping off en route between Gabès and Douz. However, there are a few accommodation options should you wish to overnight.

Hotel Diar Matmata (165 rooms) ⊕ 33.548660, 9.950037; ☎75 240 074; **e** contact@diarelbarbar.com; **f** diarelbarbar1. 500m west of town, this more upmarket take on troglodyte living offers the choice between traditional underground or regular hotel rooms. Large pool & restaurant with excellent views of the surrounding hills. Popular with tour groups. **$$$**

Hotel Marhala (45 rooms) ☎75 240 015; **m** 98 468 178; **e** marhala.matmata@gmail.com; **f** hotelmarhala.tn. The best of the troglodyte hotels in town – very clean (but very basic) rooms, with communal bath/toilet. Excellent Tunisian food in restaurant, composed of 5 interior courtyards around which the rooms are located – it's neither humid/cold in winter, nor hot in summer. Cheap & very friendly management. **$$**

Hotel Matmata (50 rooms) ☎75 240 066. Although the stuffed crocodile (with its rear leg stuck on with tape) in reception does not inspire confidence, the clean, vaulted rooms in this above-ground hotel have AC/heating & en suite. There's an incredibly deep pool in the courtyard. Popular with Italian overlanders. **$$**

✱ **Hotel Sidi Idriss** (20 rooms) ⊕ 33.542754, 9.967254; ☎75 240 005; **m** 50 549 908; **w** hotel-sidi-idriss.com. Nicknamed the 'Star Wars Hotel' (page 302), this is the largest & most popular of the underground hotels, thanks to its Hollywood heritage. The troglodyte rooms themselves are small & simple, but cool in the desert heat & relatively comfortable. Expect multiple corridors & courtyards, communal bath/toilet, a restaurant & a bar, allowing you to have a drink in the same location as Luke Skywalker all those years ago – though bring your own blue milk! **$$**

Chez Abdoul ☎75 240 189; **m** 95 039 703; ⌚ 10.00–21.00 daily. This restaurant serving standard Tunisian fare (all quite tasty) also allows camping in its large car park, opposite the louage station. Understandably popular with overlanders. **$**

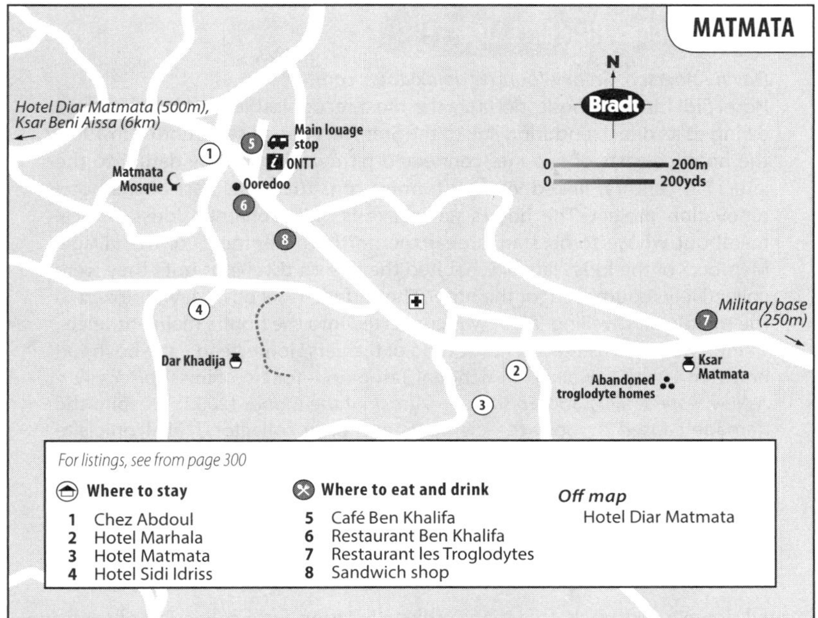

Where to eat and drink *Map, above*

Your best options for lunch or dinner are in any of the hotels dotted about town, which do a large proportion of their business catering to tour groups; Hotel Marhala has particularly good food. Be sure to book in advance during the high season.

Restaurant les Troglodytes ⊕ 33.542055, 9.976585; ⏲ 11.00–21.30 daily. A new restaurant with tasty traditional food including tagine, grilled fish & assorted meats. Owner speaks good English. $$$

Restaurant Ben Khalifa ⊕ 33.544536, 9.968116; ✆ 75 240 183; ⏲ 09.00–22.00 daily. Low-priced Tunisian staples as well as grilled chicken. $–$$

Café Ben Khalifa ⊕ 33.54505, 9.968116; ✆ 75 250 183; ⏲ 08.00–late daily. Great spot to grab a tea or coffee under shady trees by the main square. $

Sandwich shop ⊕ 33.54389, 9.968895; ⏲ 08.00–late daily. Very good fresh flatbreads filled with potato & harissa. $

What to see and do Even if you are not a Star Wars fan, Matmata has a number of sites to offer. At the east end of town is **Ksar Matmata** (m 28 333 025, 25 521 077; e mariem1gnouma@gmail.com; ⏲ 08.00–late daily; 2DT), a museum dedicated to Amazigh culture set in a troglodyte home. Each of the rooms around the main courtyard is thematically decorated with traditional furniture and contents. In the courtyard itself are a number of Italian and German World War II artefacts salvaged from the nearby battlefields, hinting at the significance of this area during the war. The museum also serves tea and traditional bread and can organise full meals for groups with advanced notice, as well as 4x4 trips and guided hikes in the surrounding area.

To the south of town is another Amazigh cultural museum: **Dar Khadija** (m 28 333 025; ⏲ 10.00–18.00 daily; 3DT). Slightly less polished than Ksar Matmata, and

THE REAL LARS HOMESTEAD

Davin Anderson, Galaxy Tours (w galaxytours.com)

Hotel Sidi Idriss is unquestionably the most recognisable landmark in town, owing to its direct, enduring link to the Star Wars franchise. Founded in 1968, the hotel consists of five interconnected pit dwellings (likely dating to the late 17th century) linked via four tunnels constructed as part of the hotel renovation project. The hotel's namesake is Sidi Mohamed Idriss, a local marabout whose tomb stands near the northern perimeter of the village. Members of the Idriss family inhabited the five pit dwellings until they were collectively repurposed for the hotel. The surface-level passageway linked to the middle pit dwelling (Pit 3) was converted into the hotel's main entrance.

Pit 2 was used as the interior setting of the Lars Homestead – the boyhood home of Luke Skywalker on fictional Tatooine – for two films: *Episode IV – A New Hope* (1977) and *Episode II – Attack of the Clones* (2002). Despite the damage caused by both the elements and prop collectors, this iconic site remains overtly recognisable to Star Wars enthusiasts, with many of the *Attack of the Clones* set dressings (such as the yellow metal fixtures) still in place. Non-guests are welcome to visit the hotel to have a drink in the bar and wander the sets.

located down a dirt track, this is an unlikely location for a collection of traditional artefacts including farming equipment, clothing and food-storage items, but still worth a visit.

Six kilometres northwest of town is the abandoned **Ksar Beni Aissa** (⊕ 33.562015, 9.906112), one of the fortified granaries more commonly found in southern Tataouine (page 330). Its location on the summit of a hill makes for a great half-day hike from Matmata.

EL HADDEJ Known for its cave dwellings, the settlement of El Haddej is 7km from Matmata, southeast of the main C107. Though similar to Matmata, El Haddej is not on the main tourist trail and so it is possible to see what Matmata must have been like before the influx of visitors. Still visible are the typical troglodyte houses (though many sadly abandoned now), the oil press (formerly powered by a camel), various zaouias and a cave used for marriage ceremonies. Most notable, however, is the hilltop location where they filmed the famous scene from Monty Python's *Life of Brian*, in which Eric Idle sang 'Always Look on the Bright Side of Life'. Local guides will often volunteer their services if you arrive without a guide from Matmata; bargain and arrange the price in advance.

If you'd like to stay in the area, the **Au Trait d'Union Tijma Matmata** (5 rooms; ⊕ 33.580203, 9.980249; m 98 279 609; e autraitdunion_tijma@yahoo.fr; f autraitdunion.tijma; **$$$**) is a smart maison d'hôte in a traditional troglodyte dwelling. Rooms open out on to the inner courtyard and have carpets, plug sockets and electric lighting. It also does good traditional meals, sometimes catering for tour groups.

TAMEZRET Tamezret sits just 12km west of Matmata, on the C104 to Douz. Along with neighbouring Taoujout, it is one of the few places in Tunisia where a variety of Tamazight, the Amazigh language, is still spoken by some older residents. The relative isolation of the settlement enabled the language to survive through the 20th century. The village has a striking position above stony hills to the east, while to the west the arid land levels off into desert. Cut into the side of the mountain, the **Amazigh Museum** (⊕ 33.536862, 9.864510; m 98 567 266; e monjibouras.mazigh@gmail.com; f museetamezret; ⏲ 09.00–17.00 daily) has fascinating displays depicting the story of traditional life in Tamezret, from clothing and marriage ceremonies to food preparation and storage.

Ignoring power cables, the scenery on the C104 looks like a mixture of the moon and the Grand Canyon, with the occasional troglodyte house thrown in for good measure. Though many houses have been abandoned, a few business owners are investing in trying to draw tourists here, and there are two excellent hotels available.

Where to stay and eat

✷ **L'Auberge de Tamezret** (3 rooms) ⊕ 33.537300, 9.863510; 75 244 026; e info@tamezret.com; f aubergedetamezret. Hosts Patrick & Sabrine have managed to bring a little slice of luxury to this ancient hillside. The property features troglodyte rooms dug into the hillside, each with unique architectural & decorative features. The luxurious 6-course dinner (included in HB rates) would be the gastronomic highlight of any trip to Tunisia. There is also a monthly culinary class if you would like to learn how they make such great food! **$$$$$**

✷ **Dar Ayed** (10 rooms) ⊕ 33.532736, 9.862252; m 55 267 409; w dar-ayed.com; e darayed2007@gmail.com; f DarayedTamezret. A tourism complex on the western edge of town with both a pool & indoor jacuzzi that offer breath-taking views of the desert. Stone rooms are

THE MARETH LINE

Built by the French between 1936 and 1940, this system of fortifications was intended to protect Tunisia against an Italian armoured invasion from its colony in Libya. (Italy, only involved in the colonial race from the late 19th century, had always felt that the French had acquired their protectorate over Tunisia in 1881 unfairly.) The Mareth Line ended up being occupied by Axis forces during World War II and was the site of a key battle during the Allied invasion of North Africa in March 1943 (page 304). The final version of the line, as repaired by the Germans after the Battle of El Alamein in late 1942, comprised 40 infantry emplacements, 8 large artillery bunkers, 15 command posts and 28 support points.

The entire Mareth Line is the property of the Tunisian military, and any tours of the fortifications should, in theory, be organised via the military museum in Mareth (page 304). In practice, however, private tour guides often independently take clients to the more remote sections of the line without permits. Using Toujane as a base, it is possible to hike all the way from the German anti-aircraft installations at Kef Ennsoura (⊕ 33.410610, 10.156110), southeast of Zmerten, to the military museum in Mareth, a journey of over 40km if you follow the lines. The route takes you via General Rommel's Afrika Korps command bunker (⊕ 33.483700, 10.164060), as well as the bunker that many other guidebooks mistakenly assume was his command bunker (⊕ 33.573630, 10.249210).

NOTE: There remains an issue with landmines and unexploded ordnance (UXO) along sections of the line, especially east of Mareth, so be sure to seek expert advice before hiking.

spacious with all mod cons. Also a restaurant, gift shop, small museum, café & panoramic lookout tower. **$$$$**

Café Ben Jemma ⊕ 33.537018, 9.864988; **m** 53 093 494; **w** cafebenjemma.com; ⊕ 08.00–20.00 daily. Here since 1932 but recently renovated, this offers breath-taking vistas over Tamezret's desert surroundings – try the almond tea. **$$**

TOUJANE This picturesque Amazigh mountain village, 27km east of Matmata or 66km west of Medenine, is accessed via the snaking C104. Although sections of the old ksar are abandoned, it is still very much an active village, with residents living in a mixture of modern brick homes and more traditional dwellings dug into the rocky hillside. Toujane has three things to offer potential visitors: amazing hiking up in the Matmata hills, top-quality locally produced carpets, and access to some of the highest sections of the Mareth Line (page 303). Coming in from the west, down the hill past the large 'Welcome to Toujane' sign, is the one-stop shop for all your carpet needs: the **Belle Vue Café** (⊕ 33.470524, 10.128091; **m** 97 773 095, 24 409 809; **e** toujane.info@yahoo.fr; **f** toujane.carpet; ⊕ 08.00–18.00 daily), where you can enjoy a coffee or a freshly squeezed fruit juice while browsing the extensive rug collection. If you wish to stay the night, **Chez Ben Ahmed Fathi** (2 rooms; ⊕ 33.463393, 10.135132; **m** 96 958 004; **f** chezbenahmed; **$$$–$$$$**) is an excellent place to experience sleeping in a simple troglodyte home, and at the time of writing it was expanding, adding two modern rooms with panoramic views over the mountainside. Host Fathi has a wealth of historical and hiking knowledge about the local area and is able to organise hikes along the Mareth Line and to other sites of interest in the surrounding hills.

MARETH Though normally bypassed by tourists en route to Djerba or the deep south, this mid-sized settlement is of historic significance owing to the battle that occurred near here on the Mareth Line during World War II (see below). It is worth setting aside an hour or two to visit the superb **Mareth Military Museum** (⊕ 33.596180, 10.311290; 75 306 433; ⊕ 09.00–16.00 Tue–Sun), situated right on Italian general Giovanni Messe's command bunker. It has a detailed map of the Axis defensive positions along the Mareth Line (page 303), along with displays of uniforms, weapons and equipment from German, Italian, British and French troops involved in the battle. You can clamber into Messe's bunker and the surrounding trenches, and view some of the artillery pieces used during the fighting.

THE BATTLE OF MARETH

Trevor Sheehan (w africanstalingrad.com)

Despite its name, the Battle of Mareth did not actually take place in Mareth, but to the northeast in Zarat (⊕ 33.648296, 10.389194). On 16–27 March 1943, it was here that the British Eighth Army attempted to cross the deep and wet wadi when their tanks got bogged down – and the Italians and Germans counter attacked, with the British Eighth Army receiving 850 casualties on 20–23 March alone. The British withdrew and decided instead to mount an attack around the Matmata mountains through the Tebaga Gap to get past the Mareth defences. There are extensive bunkers and trenches to explore all around the site, but be careful of unexploded ordnance.

MEDENINE AND AROUND

Although the governorate capital, Medenine is seen as little more than a transit point for most visitors, either en route to Ben Ghardane and the Libyan border, or northwards to Djerba, the region's real tourism draw. This is a shame, however, as a quick walk around town reveals some fascinating relics hinting at what was once a major urban hub, attracting traders from Algeria and elsewhere in West Africa. Those with more time could enjoy a morning or afternoon in town, while Star Wars fans should also add Medenine to their itinerary thanks to the presence of a key filming location. Medenine Governorate also features Tunisia's easternmost national park, Sidi Toui, an important bird habitat and a site where the Scimitar-horned oryx has been reintroduced, having become extinct in the wild in 2000.

HISTORY Medenine was once the capital city of the Ouerghema League, formed in the 16th century by an alliance between the Ouderna (from Jebel Abiadh, Tataouine), the Touazin (from the semi-arid plains between Medenine and Ben Ghardane), the Khezour (from around Beni Kheddache) and the Mehabel and Akkara tribes, based on the coast opposite Djerba island. This tribal grouping was very powerful and caused major headaches for the Bey's security forces

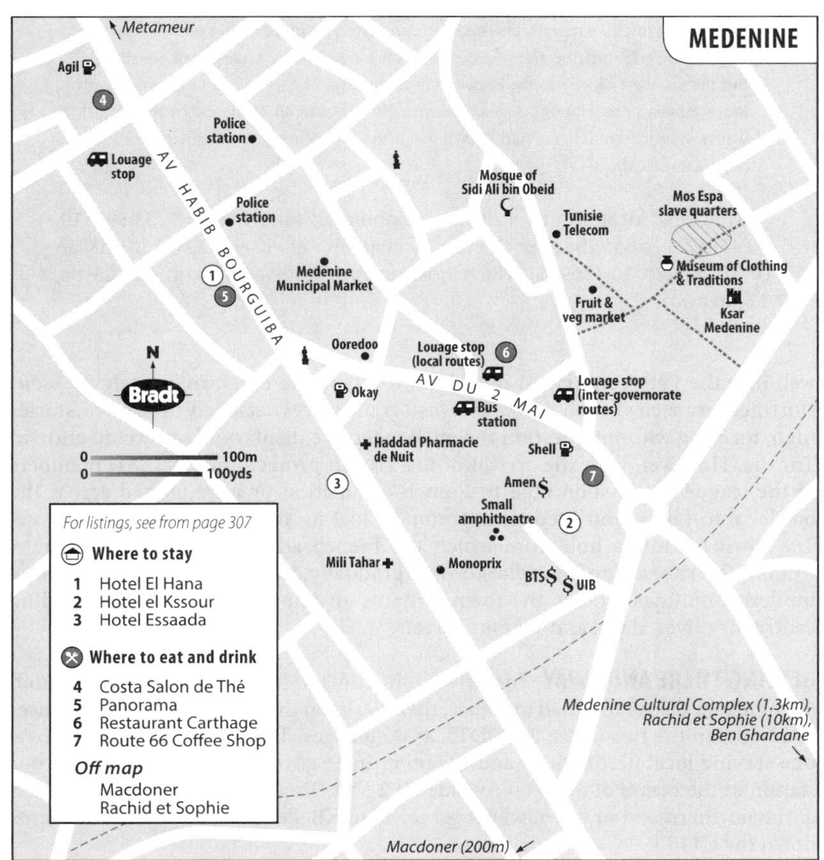

THE BATTLE OF MEDENINE

Trevor Sheehan (w africanstalingrad.com)

If you can visit only one battlefield in southern Tunisia, make it this one – if only for the views. Fought on 6 March 1943 just outside Medenine, off the P1 road near the village of Metameur, this was the largest tank battle to take place in Tunisia during World War II. It was also the last battle by General Rommel in Tunisia. He drove his German Afrika Korps tanks out of the Matmata mountains down on to the coastal plain to attack the British Eighth Army, led by General Montgomery. The British were forewarned of the attack, however, and had a massive quantity of anti-tank guns waiting for Rommel. In just a single day, Rommel lost over 50 tanks in front of the hill that dominates the area (nicknamed 'Edinburgh Castle' by the British, given its similarity in appearance to the castle hill in the Scottish capital).

Rommel noted after the attack:

> The attack began extraordinarily well, but soon came up against strong British positions in hilly country, protected by mines and anti-tank guns…Attack after attack was launched, but achieved no success…it soon became clear that the attack had failed and there was nothing more to be done about it…The British commander had grouped his forces extremely well and had completed his preparations with remarkable speed…We had suffered tremendous losses, including forty tanks totally destroyed. But the cruellest blow was the knowledge that we had been unable to interfere with Montgomery's preparations. A great gloom settled over us all. The Eighth Army's attack was now imminent and we had to face it. For the Army Group to remain in Africa was now plain suicide.

The best locations to visit are Edinburgh Castle itself (⊕ 33.393510, 10.412670) and the spectacular viewpoint at Ksar Ouled Abdallah (⊕ 33.368820, 10.436966), which looks northwest towards Edinburgh Castle, 3.5km away.

well into the 19th century. At its height, it was home to approximately 25 *ksour* (fortified granaries) with 6,000 *ghorfas* (grain stores) stacked up to five stories high, forming without question the most extensive display of *ksar* architecture in Tunisia. However, with the arrival of the French protectorate in 1881, members of the league either submitted to French occupation or were chased across the border into Libya, and Medenine gradually lost its significance as a tribal base. The town became a hub from which the French administered their Southern Military Territories, and the *ghorfas* were gradually demolished in favour of more modern buildings. Today, the town remains an important agricultural trading centre for olives, dates and various cereals.

GETTING THERE AND AWAY The drive from Tunis to Medenine is 485km (around 5½ hours on the A1 toll road to Gabès, then south on the C107 or P1). SNTRI **buses** run between the two (7hrs; 29.50DT), as do **louages**. There are two louage stops – one serving local destinations and the other inter-governorate routes – and a bus station in the centre of town on Avenue du 2 Mai. There is a further louage station at the northern end of town, which serves Beni Kheddache and other settlements down the C113.

WHERE TO STAY *Map, page 305*

With tour groups generally opting to stay 55km south in Tataouine or 65km west in Matmata, there has been little pressure on Medenine's hotels to up their game since the Revolution. If you spend the night here, be prepared for it to be quite basic.

Hotel el Kssour (45 rooms) Pl de la Liberté; 75 643 878, 75 164 378/9; w hotel-kssour.com. Relatively modern rooms with TV, desk, AC & en suite, but some issues with maintenance & soundproofing. Good central location. **$$$**

Hotel El Hana (21 rooms) Av Habib Bourguiba; 75 640 690. Basic rooms with bed & sink, most with communal showers. **$–$$**

Hotel Essaada (25 rooms) 91 Av Habib Bourguiba; 75 640 300. The pricier rooms have clean showers, are repainted & open out into a communal courtyard. No b/fast, although the restaurant next door does dinner from 7.50DT. A bargain & definitely the best in the shoestring category. **$**

WHERE TO EAT AND DRINK *Map, page 305*

Panorama Av Habib Bourguiba; 75 630 162; e panoramacontacts@gmail.com; Panoramamedenine; 06.00–19.00 Mon–Sat, 06.00–16.00 Sun. The large green sign is hard to miss; as the name suggests, it has upstairs seating with window views. The menu is mixed Tunisian & Mediterranean fare, including grilled fish. Offers home delivery. **$$$**

Rachid et Sophie 33.359187, 10.551776; m 20 946 915; noon–15.00 & 18.00–22.00 Tue–Sun. Formerly located on Djerba, this popular Tuniso-French restaurant comes with a solid reputation but is a bit of a drive out of town on the road to Ben Ghardane. **$$$**

Macdoner Rte Tataouine, P19; m 50 075 617; noon–late daily. Featuring the golden arches & a cavalier attitude towards spelling, this fast-food joint continues in the fine tradition of Costa Salon de Thé when it comes to intellectual property rights. Try the burgers. **$$**

Restaurant Carthage Rue du 18 Janvier; 10.00–20.00 Sat–Thu. Good rotisserie chicken, grilled fish & Tunisian dishes. **$$**

Route 66 Coffee Shop Pl de la Liberté; m 26 073 229, 20 356 888; 07.00–22.00 daily. Striking yellow walls & chalkboard menu, serving good coffee & take-away sandwiches. Plexiglas seating area outside. **$$**

Costa Salon de Thé Rue de Gabès; 06.00–late daily. A good modern coffee shop that is almost certainly not affiliated with the British coffee-house chain. **$**

WHAT TO SEE AND DO Medenine's main sights can easily be covered on foot in half a day. A good place to start is around the **Mosque of Sidi Ali bin Obeid**; its minaret is a useful landmark and is garishly lit up at night. The narrow streets in the surrounding area, still home to various street traders, give you an idea of what Medenine must have been like before the French-driven modernisations of the early 20th century. Nearby, tucked away behind a palm-wood gate in a restored section of the old *ghorfas*, is the **Museum of Clothing and Traditions** (Ksar Lobbeira; m 96 315 753, 21 873 204; 09.00–16.00 daily; 3DT), with displays of traditional clothing, pottery and a modelled desert encampment. Just south of here is **Ksar Ommarsia**, used as a filming location in *Star Wars: Episode I – The Phantom Menace* (page 308). Further south still is **Ksar Medenine**, the only remaining section of the 17th-century warren of *ghorfas* built by the Ouerghema League. Many of the *ghorfas* are still occupied by traders hawking pottery, local food products, clothing and even the odd souvenir. This *ksar*, along with the wider troglodyte habitats and other *ksour* in southern Tunisia, was added to Tunisia's Tentative List for UNESCO World Heritage Status in 2020.

AROUND MEDENINE

Gightis

Gightis (33.532497, 10.676844; winter 08.30–17.30 Sat–Thu, summer 09.00–13.00 & 15.00–19.00 Sat–Thu; 5DT entry to site & museum) Situated 30km

KSAR OMMARSIA

Davin Anderson, Galaxy Tours (w galaxytours.com)

Medenine once had 25 *ksour*. While many have since collapsed or been demolished, a few in Medenine's open market district were immortalised in George Lucas's Star Wars universe: Ksar Ouled Brahim, defined by its large 2,250m^2 courtyard; the adjoining Ksar Lobbeira, which houses the costume museum (page 307); and Ksar Ommarsia. The last is aesthetically the most impressive of the three, defined by a narrow, 70m-long alleyway (Rue le Théâtre) that opens on to a nearly rectangular compact courtyard (300m^2). The alley is populated with roughly 120 *ghorfas* stacked three storeys high (in most cases) and over 40 rickety concrete stairs leading to the upper levels; though the original number of levels and stairs was likely higher.

The *ksar* itself, which continues to function as a pedestrian walkway with three unenclosed exterior entrances that link the historic city centre to the busy open market district, served as the filming location for the Mos Espa slave quarters street scenes in *Episode I – The Phantom Menace*. Amplifying the authenticity of the historic Amazigh site to create a futuristic setting, crews dressed all four of the *ksar*'s walls with fresh plaster and paint, added faux doors for the majority of the *ghorfas*, as well as door-frame ribbing, door control panels, cooling/heating pipes and other fixtures. Crews also stationed one moisture evaporator prop in the southwest section of the narrow courtyard and covered the flat stone courtyard floor with sand, to depict the desert Tatooine climate.

northeast of Medenine on the C108, this Roman archaeological site is a convenient stopping point for those heading from Tunis to Djerba by road, regardless of whether you are taking the ferry from Jorf or planning to drive across the causeway at Al Qantarah. First identified by the French explorer and amateur archaeologist Victor Guérin in 1860, the site was originally established by the Phoenicians in the 6th century BC and, in turn, ruled by the Numidians, Romans (following Julius Caesar's conquests in North Africa) and Byzantines, becoming a highly prosperous trading post. It was eventually sacked by the Vandals and, by 1307, when the Arab chronicler Abu Muhammad Abd Allah al-Tijani visited the site, it had long since been in ruins.

The ruins stretch all the way down to the coast, and you can often see flamingos wading in the shallows. Visible today are the remains of Romano-African-style buildings, plus a capitol, forum, temples and two sets of baths. Try to get here early, as the wind kicks up in the afternoon and it is quite exposed. There is also a small museum on site.

Metameur Nestled on the semi-arid Jeffara Plain, this 13th-century Amazigh settlement is about 7km northwest of Medenine on the P1. Legend has it that the settlement was founded by a local marabout called Sidi Ahmed Lahjel, who first set up shop in a cave in the vicinity. His tomb is located in the town mosque, which is named after him. Although some scholars sceptically suggest that *ksour* might have existed in Metameur as early as the 14th century, the earliest archaeological confirmation of *ksour* in the village dates to the 18th century. The main *ksar*, Ksar Ouled Abdallah (⊕ 33.368891, 10.436985), was considered but ultimately rejected as a filming location for *Episode I – The Phantom Menace*. This *ksar* is impressively well preserved, and offers commanding views to the northwest of one of Tunisia's most significant World War II battlefields: the site of the Battle of Medenine on 6 March 1943 (page 306).

The road west of Medenine Heading west from Medenine, the C113 offers epic views, winding along the Jeffara Plain and up into the Jebel Haouaia mountains on the Dahar Plateau. Just before you head up off the plains, you will reach a turn-off for **Ksar Jedid** (⊕ 33.301278, 10.294186), a very modern example of a *ksar*, built in 1916 and still in use today as a market. Three kilometres further west, the road begins to wind up into the mountains; note the **panoramic viewpoint** at the top of a pass at ⊕ 33.259169, 10.276725. Atop this plateau is **Ksar Jouemma** ✷ (⊕ 33.251359, 10.258694; 10 rooms; m 98 433 847; f gite.rural.ksarjouamaa; **$$$**), a unique *ksar* perched up high on a clifftop with steep drops on two sides, offering unrivalled views of the arid scenery below (and epic sunrises/sunsets). Built at some stage between 1763 and 1773, it has been recently refurbished; owner Rachid has big plans for further refurbishments, but for now the troglodyte rooms are cosy and clean with electricity, and the outdoor dining experience is not to be missed, considering the views on offer.

Zemmour (⊕ 33.264738, 10.181649) Some 2.5km northwest of the C113 on the C207, this village has an excellent and extensive selection of accommodation options if you want to use it as a base to hike and explore the local area, although there is little of note to explore in Zemmour itself.

Where to stay

Dar Hayet (3 rooms) ⊕ 33.265471, 10.162722; m 22 183 382; w dar-hayet.com. A couple of kilometres west of the village centre, this new dar offers an excellent selection of local cuisine. Although the rooms are troglodyte, the high ceilings give a greater sense of space than you might find elsewhere. The owner, Mr Ayoub, is very knowledgeable about the local area & can organise outdoor activities such as hiking with a guide or mountain biking. **$$$**

Dar Jeddi Zammour (4 rooms) 500m north of the main road at ⊕ 33.269816, 10.183525; m 23 275 144; e maison.darjeddi@gmail.com; w dar-jeddi.com; f DarJeddi. The newest of the village's accommodation options, offering clean, simple rooms & access to a kitchen, making it popular with hikers & campers. **$$$**

Dar Saber (5 rooms) ⊕ 33.261306, 10.189705; m 98 232 818, 29 232 818; w darsaber.com. Sitting at the eastern approach to town, this features 3 troglodyte rooms decorated with Amazigh weaving & 2 modern rooms. Also offers guided tours of the area on foot or with donkeys. **$$$**

Gîte Rural Dar Ennaïm (11 rooms) ⊕ 33.261939, 10.181297; m 94 979 428; e commercial.darennaim@gmail.com; f ZammourDarEnnaim. To the south of town, the rooms here, although troglodyte, are quite modern & comfortable, with wooden floors & electricity; 3 of them even have en-suite facilities. The interior courtyard is spacious. The owner, Jalel, is very knowledgeable about the local area & can show you some hidden sights out in the hills, including World War II battlefield & fortification sites, as well as a cave that might also have been a synagogue. **$$$**

ZARZIS

On the mainland, a stone's throw from Djerba, Zarzis is Tunisia's most southerly resort town. Sadly nothing remains of the town's previous life as a Roman outpost; under the French, Zarzis had a small military garrison and there was much planting of olive trees in the region. In more recent years, there had been hope that as Djerba developed there would be spill over into Zarzis, and in many

CROSSING INTO LIBYA

Ben Ghardane is the last town before the Libyan border, which is 33km east along the P1 at Ra's Ajdir. The border is open and very busy, and it is possible to cross here as a non-Tunisian and non-Libyan citizen. However, at the time of writing, the FCDO advises against all travel to the town of Ben Ghardane and the immediate surrounding area, as well as within 20km of the rest of the Libya border area north of Dhehiba. Similar warnings have been issued by other foreign embassies in Tunis. Check before travel.

ways this made sense: it shares the same beautiful white-sand beaches as over the strait on the island. However, despite the fancy newer developments to the north of town, this feels like a seaside resort in decline. In most cases you are better off staying in Djerba, crossing the causeway to visit the sites around Zarzis from there.

GETTING THERE AND AWAY Zarzis is 540km from Tunis (6 hours on the A1 toll road and then the P1 and C118). It is well connected by public transport, with two SNTRI buses a day linking to Tunis (8hrs; 33.40DT). Louages connect to all significant nearby settlements, including Ben Ghardane, Medenine and Gabès.

WHERE TO STAY Accommodation in Zarzis falls into three main categories: budget rooms in Zarzis town itself, cheap seaside options on the main strip north of town, and then more luxurious resorts in the newer Sangho suburb, which begins about 9km up the coast towards Djerba.

Dar Selma (6 apts) ⊕ 33.580389, 11.088467; ☎ 75 705 328; m 27 374 035; e contact@darselma.com. These self-contained holiday apts have AC, most with outdoor spaces & access to a BBQ less than 50m from the sea. Great food. **$$$$$**

Dar Nesma (5 rooms) ⊕ 33.556478, 11.099385; m 55 900 708; w dar-nesma.com. Set 700m back from the touristy coastline, this is an oasis of calm created by hosts Catherine and Stéphane. 2 pools, hammam & treatment room, plus modern rooms with AC, TV & Wi-Fi, & good food. **$$$$**

Odyssee Resort & Thalasso (344 rooms) ⊕ 33.592561, 11.075686; ☎ 75 705 705; w odyssee-resort.com. The best of the large pack of 4-star AI resorts scattered around Sangho. Rooms are a minimum of 28m^2 with a balcony overlooking the pool, sea or gardens. Complex features 4 pools, gym, crèche, daily sports programmes & an amphitheatre hosting live performances. **$$$$**

Hotel l'Olivier (aka Hotel Zitouna) (20 rooms) Av Farhat Hached; ☎ 75 691 955. Budget hotel near police station at western end of town. Simple & clean – probably the best of the cheap hotels. **$**

WHERE TO EAT AND DRINK

Restaurant Le Mérou ⊕ 33.580617, 11.088289; m 50 370 757, 27 374 035; ⊙ noon–15.30 & 18.00–21.00 daily. Great seafood restaurant right by the beach. Look out for the blue longboard doubling as a sign & the driftwood/netting outside. **$$$$**

Marina Pizza and Café Residence La Corniche, Av de la République; m 93 634 624; f MarinaZarzis; ⊙ 08.00–late daily. Very popular waterfront restaurant serving mixed Mediterranean & Tunisian fare. **$$$**

Restaurant Le Petite Vague le Sfaxien Plage le Casino; m 50 846 356, 98 940 156; ⊙ noon–15.30 & 18.00–21.00 daily. Amazing grilled seafood with beach views – try the prawns. **$$$**

Riviera Lounge Port de Zarzis; m 27 138 600; e rivierazarzis@gmail.com; ⊙ 08.00–late daily.

Just inside the port entrance, with a beautiful covered wooden area – though unfortunately overlooking a very industrial port. Mixed Italian & Tunisian fare. $$$

Türk Sofra ⊕ 33.574733, 11.093092; m 20 456 287; ⏲ 11.00–21.00 daily. Wooden beachfront restaurant with a very Pacific vibe, though the menu features mainly Middle Eastern grilled meat dishes. $$–$$$

WHAT TO SEE AND DO There isn't a huge amount to see in Zarzis itself. The town's only historical building of note is the small **Synagogue Mishkan Ya'akov de Zarzis**, built in 1905 to serve the then-thriving Jewish community of over 1,000 members. It was burnt down in 1982 following an arson attack, but has since been rebuilt for use by the roughly 130 Jewish residents who remain. Elsewhere, the **Maison de la Culture Ibn Charaf** (75 692 775; f zarzis2016897; ⏲ 09.00–noon & 15.00–19.00 Mon–Sat, 09.00–13.30 Sun) is the town's cultural and artistic hub, with live music and theatrical performances plus art exhibitions.

South of town is the small **Zarzis Archaeological Museum** (Av Habib Thameur; ⏲ 09.00–16.00 Tue–Sun; free) established in 2003 in the former Catholic church of Notre-Dame de la Garde, which was built in 1920. There is a Punic wooden sarcophagus from the 4th century BC and some Roman pieces from various archaeological sites across the region, as well as a number of items taken from a Roman shipwreck in the area. Otherwise, interest is limited.

POIGNANT MEMORIALS

Since the beginning of the migrant crisis in Europe in 2015, Tunisia has become a major transit point for migrants hoping to head across the Mediterranean from Africa and start a new life in the European Union. Zarzis has tragically seen hundreds of fatalities from these small-boat crossings, and a number of local sites pay tribute to those who have been lost.

LE JARDIN D'AFRIQUE (⊕ 33.449406, 11.068829) The most high-profile of all the sites in Zarzis, this beautiful memorial was set up by Algerian artist Rachid Koraïchi. Inaugurated on 9 June 2021 in the presence of UNESCO Director General Audrey Azouley, it is not only a burial place: the site also has a DNA database with DNA information also recorded on the tombstones, in the hope that one day relatives and loved ones might be able to identify those lost.

MUSEUM FOR THE MEMORY OF MAN AND THE SEA (⊕ 33.545836, 11.105803; m 92 254 426; ⏲ 10.00–13.00 & 15.00–18.00 daily; free entry). This collection was set up by local poet Mohsen Lihidheb, who originally intended to display a collection of objects (mainly plastic) found in the sea as a comment on humanity's ecological impact on the marine environment. However, given that many of the items belonged to migrants, many of whom likely died at sea, the exhibition has become much more poignant (note the shoes and messages in bottles).

STRANGER'S GRAVEYARD (⊕ 33.443971, 11.066380) In 2003, local fisherman Chamseddine Marzoug began burying the bodies of migrants he found at sea in this site. There are now over 300 graves, each of them decorated with some of the items Marzoug found with the unidentified migrant.

SIDI TOUI NATIONAL PARK

Tunisia's easternmost national park sits 9km west of the C203 road, near the settlement of Bordj Sidi Toui. Established in 1993, this 6,315ha park is centred around the 172m-high Jebel Sidi Toui, which is surrounded by small sand dunes and dry wadis (riverbeds). The park is classified as an Important Bird Area (IBA), with notable species including the pallid harrier, Moussier's redstart and the Thekla's lark, and is also home to the rather common dorcas gazelle and the extremely uncommon Scimitar-horned oryx. The latter was reintroduced in 1999, having gone extinct in the wild, in a project run by Marwell Wildlife, a UK conservation NGO linked to the zoo of the same name in Hampshire, in collaboration with Tunisia's Direction Générale des Forêts (DGF). Their 2020 report noted that there were 74 Scimitar-horned oryx in the national park, with a further 100 in Dghoumes National Park and nearly 40 in Bou-Hedma National Park. Sidi Toui also has a small herd of rare slender-horned gazelles.

Unfortunately, given its location within 20km of the Libyan border, at the time of writing the FCDO advised against all travel to the park. Note that there are no paved roads in the park and little infrastructure for tourists, beyond a small building marked as an eco-museum (⊕ 32.696443, 11.222070) that is generally locked up, and a set of buildings used by the park rangers (⊕ 32.693523, 11.214502). If you do choose to visit, be sure to go in convoy with an experienced team of desert drivers, and check local security advice in Ben Ghardane or Bordj Sidi Toui. The Garde Nationale in these towns will want to know where you are going and for how long.

DJERBA

A low-lying expanse of sand and palm trees moored off Tunisia's southern coast, Djerba is the perfect holiday island. It is a slow-moving, seductive place – you can feel that life pulses quite a few beats slower than on the mainland. You could easily spend your time here lazing on the soft, sandy beaches or by the hotel poolside, but the island certainly merits some independent exploration. Architecture buffs will want to seek out its unique underground mosque as well as the oldest synagogue in North Africa, still in use by Djerba's remaining Jewish community (who will also cook you up some mean brik!). Star Wars fans have no fewer than three filming locations to visit, and there is also an impressive Roman archaeological site in the island's southeast.

Houmt Souk and its immediate surroundings are a good location to base yourself if you wish to explore Djerba's capital on foot, or if you are in town for kitesurfing. All the package holidaymakers tend to be concentrated along the northeast coast of the island, sometimes bus-tripping into the capital for half-day visits.

HISTORY Those with an interest in classics will know Djerba from Homer's epic, the *Odyssey*, in which the Greek hero Odysseus lands on the island and has great difficulty leaving, mainly because of the attractions of the lotus tree he found here. This tree, as yet to be identified by modern scientists, was said to produce a highly addictive narcotic fruit and flowers that, when eaten, made you sleepy. Greek historian Polybius refers to the people of Djerba as the 'lotus-eaters', implying that this myth was still believed by some over 500 years after the *Odyssey* was written.

Back in the less-fictitious realm of history, Djerba was in turn Phoenician, Carthaginian and Roman. To the Carthaginians, it was known as the island of Meninx, much appreciated for the safe anchorage it offered. The Romans were not about to leave such a pleasant island unsettled and they established a city in the southeast part of the island, close to where their causeway touched land (the archaeological site of Meninx, page 326). Djerba was finally conquered by the Arabs in AD667, but was later involved in the rivalries between the Kharijite sect and the orthodox Muslims.

By the 15th century, Djerba had become a den of Barbary corsairs (or pirates, depending on who you asked). Efforts were made to dislodge them, the most fateful being in 1560 when an attempt was made by stranded Spanish troops to fight off the fearsome Ottoman pirate Dragut. This failed, however, and Dragut built a tower with the skulls of the slain Christians near present-day Borj el Kebir. The unpleasant monument was demolished in 1848, though images of it survive in early prints. The French arrived in the late 19th century, a move welcomed by the commercially minded Djerbans who feared attacks from rebellious inland tribes, which had the potential to upset trade. For a few years post-independence, Djerba remained a quiet island, well off the beaten track for tourists seeking fun and sun on the Mediterranean. This did not last long, however, and by 1985 the country's ten-year tourism development plan had specifically identified Djerba as a location for major tourism investments. Visiting today it is hard to imagine that, only a generation ago, Djerba looked much like the Kerkennah Islands still do: remote, wild and largely unspoilt.

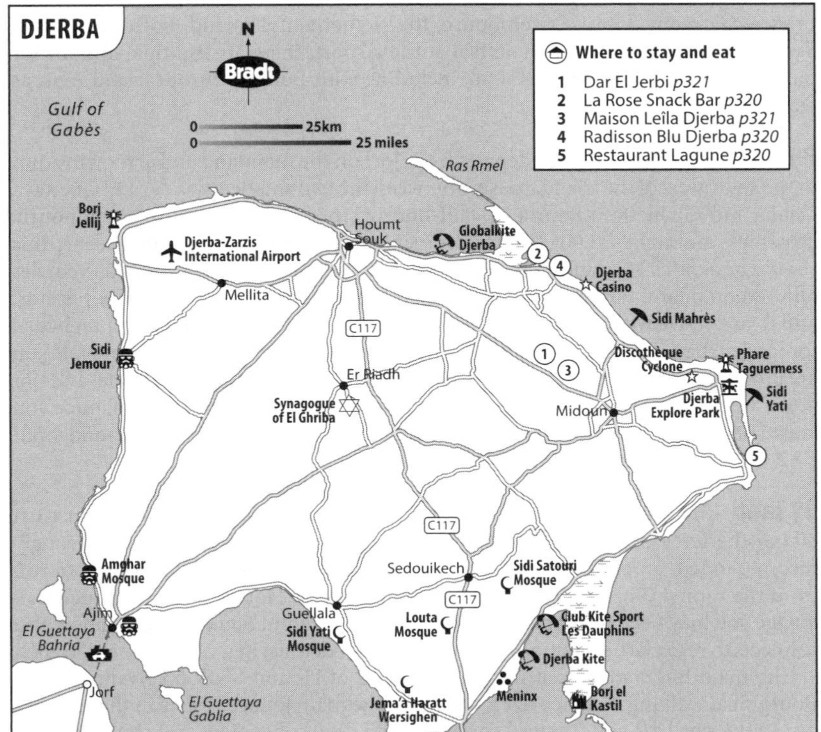

Djerba has always been quite isolated from the mainland, and has seen the development of a unique style of life and architecture. The population is now mostly Amazigh in origin but, until recently, there was also a significant Jewish population on the island (page 26), one of the oldest communities in the world, dating to 586BC and the fall of Jerusalem to Nebuchadnezzar. Now there are just over 1,000 Jewish people left here, a large number having emigrated to Israel and France, and the remainder having faced various periods of insecurity in Tunisia's post-revolution society. Djerba is also home to a population of Muslims who adhere to the conservative Ibadi branch of Islam, a moderate (and tolerant) offshoot of the 7th-century radical Kharijite movement. Ibadi Muslims likely migrated from Oman to Djerba as early as the 8th century.

Today, tourism has a considerable impact on the Djerbian population's lifestyle and, in many families, work in traditional farming and fishing continues alongside easier and better-paid jobs in tourism. Other residents have been forced to change jobs or leave due to the ever-increasing cost of living, making Djerba an island with a very high emigration rate. In major French towns, the ever-open corner shop is sometimes *un Djerbien*. However, after years abroad, this grocer will often return to their native island to live out retirement among family and friends.

GETTING THERE AND AROUND

By air In the far northwest of the island, Djerba-Zarzis International Airport is one of the largest and busiest in Tunisia. There are multiple weekly flights between Tunis and Djerba (on both Tunisair Express and Nouvelair), as well as seasonal direct flights connecting to Belgium, Bulgaria, the Czech Republic (Czechia), France, Germany, Libya, Luxembourg, the Netherlands, Poland, Portugal, Russia, Serbia and Switzerland. Upon arrival at the airport, there are multiple options for picking up hire cars at the terminal, including with Budget, Europcar and Avis, as well as in Houmt Souk.

By boat The ferry to Djerba departs from Jorf on the mainland and arrives in Ajim in the southwest of the island, passing between the two smaller islands of El Guettaya Gablia and El Guettaya Bahria (🕒 half-hourly crossings 05.00–midnight & hourly crossings midnight–05.00; 0.8DT/free vehicles/foot passengers). In theory, this should be a quick 30-minute crossing, with both pedestrians and around 20 vehicles allowed on board, but in reality the ferry is highly unreliable during busy periods, and if you arrive with a vehicle you will likely find yourself queuing to get on board for longer than it would have taken to drive across the causeway (see below). If you are crossing with a vehicle, aim to do so as early in the morning as possible, and not at the weekend, as queues get worse throughout the day. As a pedestrian, once you arrive on the jetty at Ajim it is a 1km walk to the bus stop off the main roundabout (⊕ 33.725369, 10.748394).

By land The drive from Tunis to Djerba is 520km (around 6½hrs) if you trust taking the ferry or 575km (7hrs) if you take the causeway. The latter is strongly recommended, especially during busy periods. **Louages** and SNTRI **buses** also run from the capital (9hrs; 38.10DT), both terminating in Houmt Souk (although in a louage you may need to change in Medenine first). Houmt Souk's louage station also connects to regional destinations such as Zarzis, Medenine, Ben Ghardane and Gabès.

The main bus station is at the southern end of Houmt Souk on Avenue Habib Bourguiba, walking distance from the souk. The main louage stop is in the car park just to the north. If you can find space, this is a very convenient and cheap place to park and then explore the town centre on foot. The main **taxi** rank is a few hundred metres north of the louage stop.

The roads on the island are generally excellent, and hiring a vehicle is advisable if you wish to explore some of the more remote locations, as reaching them on public transport is a pain. If you wish to pick up a **hire car** in Houmt Souk (as opposed to at the airport), try Budget (177 Av Abdelhamid El Kadhi; m 21 353 444, 22 130 821; ⏲ 09.00–18.00 daily) or La Colombe Rent a Car (Av Habib Thameur; ☎ 75 655 369; m 98 501 643; ⏲ 08.00–18.00 daily). Alternatively, there's Relax Rent a Car in Midoun (⊕ 33.807706, 10.993300; ☎ 75 733 555; m 98 318 733; e relax.rentacar@topnet.tn; ⏲ 09.00–18.00 daily).

HOUMT SOUK On the northwest coast, Houmt Souk ('the market quarter') is the largest settlement on Djerba, with over 75,000 inhabitants, and often referred to as the island's capital. The town has quadrupled in size over the past 20 years, thanks to the seemingly endless series of resort hotels popping up along the north coast. Here you will find a large and diverse souk with a pleasant assortment of boutique hotels and restaurants hidden down the narrow alleyways.

Tourist information The main tourist information office is at the **Commissariat Régional au Tourisme** (Bd de l'Environnement; ☎ 75 650 016; e crt.djerba@ontt.tourism.tn; ⏲ 08.00–13.00 & 14.00–17.00 Mon–Fri), with a selection of maps and leaflets available. There is also an **Office National de l'Artisanat** (3 Rue Habib Thameur; ☎ 75 652 557; ⏲ 08.00–17.00 Mon–Thu, 08.00–13.00 Fri).

Where to stay *Map, page 316*

✱ **Hotel Arischa** (16 rooms) Pl de l'Église; ☎ 75 650 384; m 22 421 908; e info@hotel-arischa.com; f arischahotel. Hidden away near the church, this converted traditional home has a beautiful courtyard with a pool in the middle. Rooms are large & vaulted (to stay cool) with massive shower & TV. Good value & location, plus it has an excellent Djerbian restaurant (page 317). **$$**

Hotel Marhala (40 rooms) 32 Rue 2 Mars 1934; m 96 704 088, 98 264 878; e helmiabdelli1@gmail.com; f. Recently renovated, 2-storey building opening out on to a bougainvillea-filled courtyard. Rooms have en-suite toilet & shower, plus AC & heating. Excellent value. **$$**

Hôtel Hadji (47 rooms) Rue Mohamed Badra; ☎ 75 650 630/421; e hotel.hadjires@gnet.tn. Good-value rooms with tiled floors, AC, TV, balcony & en suite. Friendly reception. **$$**

Hôtel les Palmes d'Or (35 rooms) 84 Av Abdelhamid El Kadhi; ☎ 75 653 370; w hotelpalmesdor.com. Modern rooms with AC, TV & en suite. OK value but poor location – especially given that they were building a noisy bar next door at the time of writing. **$$**

Hôtel Sindbad (16 rooms) Pl Mongi Bali; ☎ 75 650 047; e hotel.sindbad@topnet.tn. Clean rooms with private showers opening on to nice courtyard. Great location for exploring the souk, though no AC or b/fast. **$$**

Hotel Essalem (30 rooms) Rue de Remeda; ☎ 75 651 029. Thick-walled blue-&-white building stays cool in summer. Very basic but acceptable set-up: 2 sgl beds, a wardrobe & AC that costs extra to turn on; toilets are shared. **$–$$**

Auberge de la Jeunesse (40 rooms) 11 Rue Moncef Bey; ☎ 75 650 619. Cool, dark vaulted rooms, most of which contain 2 sgl beds & nothing else. Shared bathrooms & a nice courtyard with birds. Excellent value. Full mid-Jul–Aug, when a YHA card is required. B/fast can be provided for 5DT. **$**

Where to eat and drink *Map, page 316*

✱ **Restaurant Haroun** Port; ☎ 75 650 488; e msallemsalim@gmail.com; f Restaurant.Haroun; ⏲ noon–22.30 daily. For many years Houmt Souk's tourism development was held back by a lack of seafood restaurants with their own replica pirate ships. Thankfully,

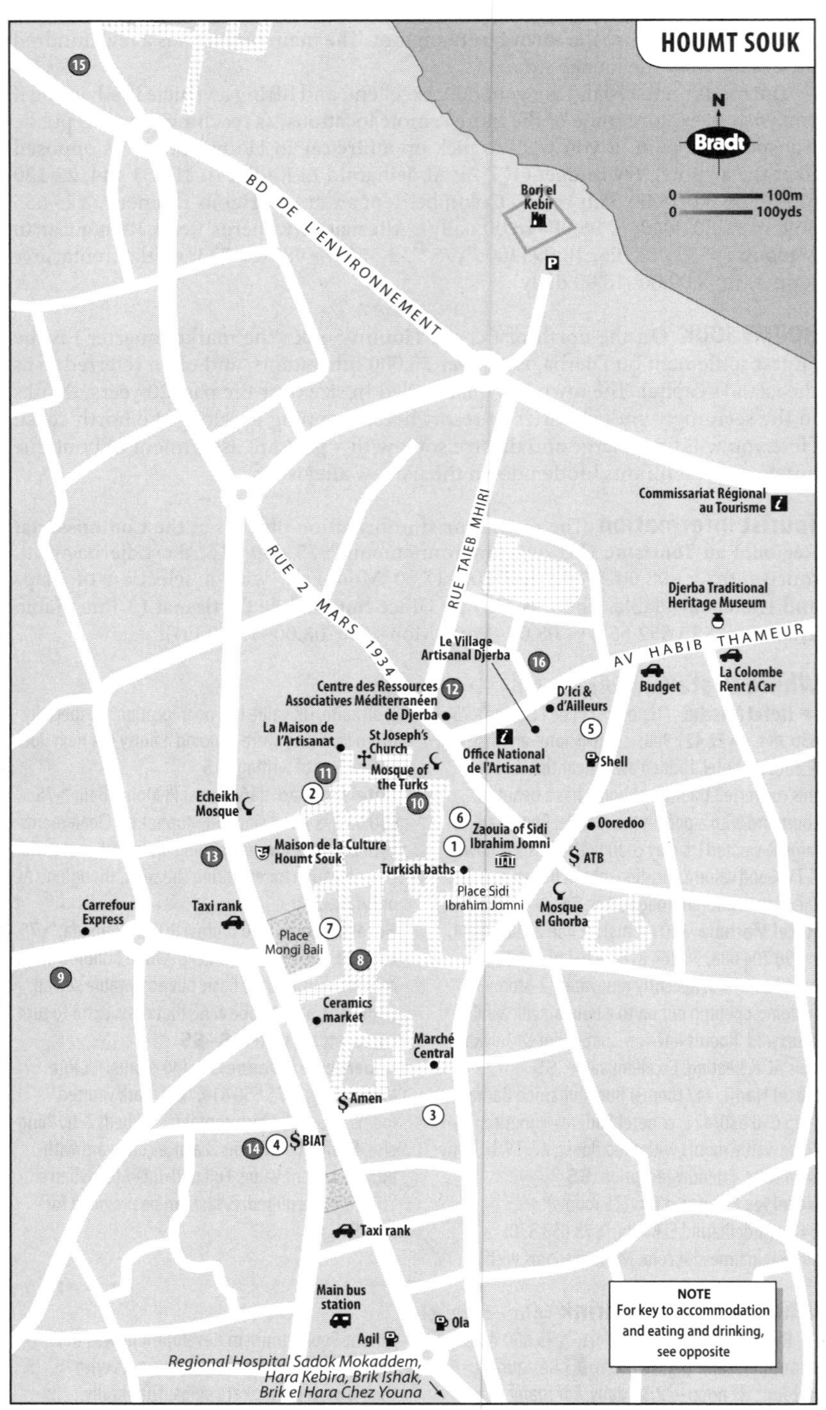
HOUMT SOUK
N
Bradt
0 100m
0 100yds
BD DE L'ENVIRONNEMENT
Borj el Kebir
P
Commissariat Régional au Tourisme
RUE TAIEB MHIRI
RUE 2 MARS 1934
Djerba Traditional Heritage Museum
AV HABIB THAMEUR
Le Village Artisanal Djerba
Budget
La Colombe Rent A Car
Centre des Ressources Associatives Méditerranéen de Djerba
D'Ici & d'Ailleurs
La Maison de l'Artisanat
St Joseph's Church
Office National de l'Artisanat
Shell
Mosque of the Turks
Echeikh Mosque
Ooredoo
Zaouia of Sidi Ibrahim Jomni
Maison de la Culture Houmt Souk
ATB
Turkish baths
Place Sidi Ibrahim Jomni
Carrefour Express
Taxi rank
Mosque el Ghorba
Place Mongi Bali
Ceramics market
Marché Central
Amen
BIAT
Taxi rank
Main bus station
Ola
Agil
Regional Hospital Sadok Mokaddem, Hara Kebira, Brik Ishak, Brik el Hara Chez Youna
NOTE
For key to accommodation and eating and drinking, see opposite

HOUMT SOUK
For listings, see from page 315

Where to stay
1 Auberge de la Jeunesse
2 Hotel Arischa
3 Hotel Essalem
4 Hotel Hadji
5 Hôtel les Palmes d'Or
6 Hotel Marhala
7 Hôtel Sindbad

Where to eat and drink
8 Ben Yedder
9 Dar Hassine
10 El Fondouk Djerba
11 El Hanout
12 Essofra
Hotel Arischa (see 2)
13 Matterello di Stevn
14 Pâtisserie Hannibal
15 Restaurant Haroun
16 Ristorante Scilla

Off map
Brik el Hara Chez Youna
Brik Ishak

Restaurant Haroun has stepped up to the plate. You can either eat in the very fancy dining room with views of the port, or you could take the sensible option & eat on the pirate ship, with the *Pirates of the Caribbean* soundtrack playing in the background. Excellent seafood, good service & it serves alcohol. A winning combination. $$$–$$$$

Dar Hassine Av Boumasouar; 75 650 406; e darhassine.restaurant@gmail.com; f RestaurantDarHassine; 10.00–22.00 Mon–Sat. Djerbian cuisine on a patio in a traditional *houch* (a Djerbian home designed to keep cool) built in the 1930s. Delicious local dishes with excellent fresh fish. $$$

✷ **El Fondouk Djerba** Fondouk Jomni, 30 Rue Moncef Bey; m 28 988 276; e info@elfondouk.com; f elfondoukdjerba; 08.00–21.00 daily. This immaculately restored 17th-century building is home to a cultural centre, boutique store & restaurant in the heart of the souk. Choose from a private table in one of the many alcoves or sit in the central courtyard under the glass roof. Mixed Mediterranean & Tunisian fare. $$$

El Hanout Pl de l'Église; m 54 307 604; f; 11.00–17.30 daily. Very popular lunch spot with a quirky rooftop terrace & a changing international menu, including Tunisian dishes, a variety of fish & everything from Indian to fast food. $$$

Essofra Rue Taieb Mhiri; m 98 281 049; 12.30–16.00 & 19.00–22.00 Tue–Sun. An eclectic but delicious menu of Tunisian cuisine, served in a barn-like space with walls adorned by agricultural & fishing tools. You might need to ask the waiters what some of the dishes are, but that's all part of the fun. $$$

Hotel Arischa Pl de l'Église; 75 650 384; m 22 421 908; e info@hotel-arischa.com; f arischahotel; 11.30–late daily. Djerbian & wider Tunisian cuisine including couscous, merguez, Fatma's fingers (Tunisian deep-fried egg rolls) & *kamounia* (beef & liver stew). It also does delicious desserts such as *makroud* (date-stuffed semolina cookies). $$$

Ristorante Scilla Av Habib Thameur; m 95 478 338, 55 759 262; noon–21.00 daily. Very popular restaurant serving fish & Italian cuisine in a relaxed setting. Also has outdoor seating. $$$

Matterello di Stevn Av Habib Bourguiba; m 21 642 426, 23 600 985; f matterellodistevn; noon–23.00 Tue–Sun. Truly excellent pizzeria. Easy to spot with a façade of rolling pins as a decorative entrance. $$

Pâtisserie Hannibal Rue Mohamed Badra; 75 653 669; m 24 653 000; e patisserie.hannibal@tunet.tn; 09.00–18.00 daily. Good selection of pastries, sweets & chocolates, many sold by weight. $$

Brik el Hara Chez Youna Rue des Amandes; m 23 482 349; 10.00–22.00 Sun–Fri. Another delicious brik place in the Hara Kebira Jewish quarter, also offering *kefta* (grilled minced meat on a stick) & *fricassee* (deep-fried sandwich with tuna & egg) $–$$

✷ **Brik Ishak** Rue des Amandes; m 27 345 117; f; noon–02.00 Sun–Fri. Located in the Hara Kebira Jewish quarter, this is a great place to load up on a bag of traditional brik. Also has a mosaic on the side depicting an alien riding a brik, created by French urban artist Invader. $–$$

Ben Yedder Pl Farhat Hached; m 29 940 548; 05.00–23.00 Sun–Fri, 05.00–21.00 Sat. A great spot for good coffee on the square; also has a mosaic by French artist Invader on the roof. $

Entertainment and nightlife If you are looking for bars and nightclubs, you will need to head east to the Zone Touristique along Plage de Sidi Mahrès (page 313). There are only a few places in Houmt Souk itself that serve alcohol, such as Restaurant Haroun (page 315), which will let you in for just a drink if it is not too busy. Most people entertain themselves in the evenings on the waterfront strip at Boulevard de l'Environnement, where the cafés and ice-cream parlours are packed out with families late into the night.

Shopping The central souk area around the **Marché Central** sells all manner of fresh produce as well as a fine assortment of gifts from traders who seem to have learned the language of every possible European tourist to have graced their store! Note that prices are on the high side. Djerba is noted for its alfalfa mats (originally made for olive-oil presses), pointy straw hats, blankets and silver jewellery (until relatively recently, much being Jewish-made). Outside you will find a **ceramics market**; pottery, chiefly from Guellala (page 325) is unglazed and made for practical use, such as for storing water, oil or foodstuffs. A **street market** is held around the Marché Central every Monday and Thursday. Next to the tourist information centre is **Le Village Artisanal Djerba** (Av Habib Thameur; m 54 405 669, 53 370 887; f; ⌚ 10.00–18.00 daily), a new, purpose-built market offering a variety of local craft stalls all under one roof.

For gifts, try the boutique shop in El Fondouk Djerba (page 317) for crafts, jewellery and prints, while **D'Ici & d'Ailleurs** (Av Habib Thameur; m 98 520 850; e arouayrari@gmail.com; f Djerba2; ⌚ 09.00–19.00 daily) is a modern épicerie selling everything from harissa to honey and even gluten-free *bsissa* (a breakfast paste of roasted barley flour with cumin, aniseed and sugar). For carpets, **La Maison de l'Artisanat** (Pl de l'Église; ☎ 75 623 889; ⌚ 09.00–19.00 daily) is popular with tourists.

Other practicalities For medical emergencies, the **Regional Hospital Sadok Mokaddem** (Av 14 Janvier 2011; ☎ 75 106 000) is 750m southeast of the town centre, near the Jewish quarter.

What to see and do

Borj el Kebir (The Great Tower) (☎ 75 653 786; ⌚ summer 08.00–noon & 15.00–19.00 Sat–Thu, winter 09.30–16.30 Sat–Thu; 8DT) On the seafront by the harbour, this is also known as Ghazi Mustapha Fort after the Turk who supervised its reconstruction. It was built on the remains of both a Roman building and a later 13th-century structure, which dates to the time of Roger of Sicily, who was at the time extending his influence along the Ifrikiyan coast and needed to build a strong point on Djerba for his forces. Later, in the 16th century, with Habsburg Spain and Ottoman Turkey fighting for Mediterranean supremacy, the fort was occupied by the Spaniards. In 1560, the Ottoman sea supremo and mega corsair/pirate Dragut wiped out a Spanish fleet, and a large number of Spanish troops were left defending the fort. When the borj fell, the Turks massacred the Spaniards, building a tower with their skulls – now marked by a small monument – as the tower itself was demolished in 1848. There is an interesting display inside on Dragut.

Djerba Traditional Heritage Museum (Av Habib Thameur; ☎ 75 650 540, 75 622 974; e contact@patrimoinedetunisie.com.tn; w djerbamuseum.tn/index.php; ⌚ summer 09.30–19.00 Sat–Thu, winter 09.30–16.30 Sat–Thu; 8DT) Set in a 12th-century zaouia dedicated to Sidi Zitouni, who used to come here and heal those with mental illnesses, this well-organised collection labelled in multiple languages includes displays on pottery, cooking, fishing, agriculture and traditional clothing, as well as rites and ceremonies.

Other notable buildings For those interested in religious buildings, the austere 17th-century **Zaouia of Sidi Ibrahim Jomni** was a centre of religious learning upon construction. Jomni was revered as a local theologian who defended Sunnism on the island against the influences of the Kharijites (an Islamic sect that emerged in the 7th century AD, page 11), and today the zaouia contains the saint's tomb. Nearby are the **Turkish baths** (🕘 to men 08.00–noon, then women 13.00–18.00; 1DT) and across the road is the Maliki-Sunni **Mosque el Ghorba**, also known as the Mosquée des Étrangers (the Outsiders' Mosque), distinguished by the large number of small domes around the main one. Built originally in the 15th century, this is where Sidi Ibrahim Jomni taught in the 17th century. Further north, the **Mosque of the Turks** is notable because of its splendid pointy minaret, recalling those built by the Ottomans further along the coast in Tripoli. In the west of town is the 16th-century **Echeikh Mosque**, its beautiful blue door with black studs reminiscent of something you would see on the streets of Sidi Bou Saïd in Tunis.

These monuments are generally closed to non-Muslims, although you may be permitted inside the Mosque el Ghorba by the caretaker outside times of worship if you ask nicely. Far easier in terms of access is the Catholic **St Joseph's Church** (Pl de l'Église; w eglisecatholiquetunisie.com/les-paroisses/eglise-saint-joseph). In the 19th and first half of the 20th centuries, Djerba, like other southern ports, had a fair-sized European population of Greek, Maltese and Sicilian origin, who were involved in fishing (for both sponges and fish) and trade, although today this population is very small. This community clubbed together to purchase the land and construct the church in 1848, under the direction of Capuchin Friar Gaetano de Ferrara. Today Mass is celebrated on Sundays at 10.30 in Italian, French and German, and at 09.00 Tuesday–Friday in French.

Cultural centres There are several cultural centres and exhibition spaces dotted about town for those hunting for arts or cinema events. **Maison de la Culture Houmt Souk** (also known as Maison de la Culture Farid Ghazi; Rue Moncef Bey; ☎ 75 651 346; e mcult@hotmail.com; f MCFGHS; 🕘 09.00–18.00 daily) is a large arts space with a boat in the courtyard, featuring exhibitions, live theatrical events and cinema nights; check its Facebook page for the latest events listings. Elsewhere, the **Centre des Ressources Associatives Méditerranéen de Djerba** (7 Rue 2 Mars 1934), inaugurated in June 2021 with the support of the UNDP, features a large exhibition centre and cinema room.

Hara Kebira (Jewish quarter) No visit to Houmt Souk would be complete without stopping by the Jewish quarter, which is about 1km southeast of the town centre, past the hospital. If driving into town, you will know you have arrived as you pass through well-fortified police checkpoints, a sad testament to the various attacks this community has suffered over the past decades (page 324). While the area is no more aesthetically pleasing than any other suburb of Houmt Souk, it is a great place to pick up some delicious brik while wandering around (page 317). The origins of this savoury pastry dish are much disputed, although there is an argument that it is the Jewish community here that brought it to Tunisia, possibly via emigrating Sephardic Jews from Moorish Spain, or possibly adapted it by adding egg from a pre-existing recipe. Either way, it is delicious and cheap!

THE NORTHEAST COAST The 15km stretch of coastline between the Ras Rmel sandbar and the Sidi Yati beaches features some of the best sand and bathing conditions on Djerba, centred around Plage Sidi Mahrès. As such, it is absolutely saturated with hotels, package-holiday resorts, bars and water parks. The sheer level of overdevelopment here is pretty shocking, and it is no surprise to see why the residents of Kerkennah (page 264) have no desire to replicate this economic model on their equally beautiful Mediterranean island. Despite this, there are a few decent beachfront options if you are looking to relax on the sand, as well as some good seafood restaurants in the area.

Where to stay

Djerba Plaza Thalasso and Spa (299 rooms) 75 731 230; e contact@djerbaplaza.com; f DjerbaPlazaThalassoSpa. Surrounded by a 14ha palmeraie, this highly rated hotel has a 1.5km private beach, a pool, a thalasso & spa centre, 5 restaurants & 3 bars. **$$$$**

Hotel Djerba Beach (246 rooms) 75 731 200; e info.djerbabeach@ttshotels.com.tn; f ttshotels.Djerbabeach. The highest-rated AI resort on the strip, & surprisingly good value, featuring spa, tennis courts & horseriding. **$$$$**

Iberostar Mehari (300 rooms) 75 745 240; e meharidjerba@iberostar.com.tn; f IberostarMehariDjerba. For a slightly more sustainable AI experience, this popular hotel is Iberostar Wave of Change certified, meaning it is free of single-use plastic & has a series of other measures in place to help protect the marine environment. **$$$$**

Les Jardins de Toumana (58 rooms) 75 757 187; w toumana.com. Stylish aparthotel with 4 room types, all of them with a living room, bathroom & kitchenette. **$$$$**

✷ **Radisson Blu Djerba** [map, page 313] (296 rooms) 75 757 600; w radissonhotels.com/en-us/hotels/radisson-blu-resort-djerba. A fantastic offering featuring indoor & outdoor pools, an immaculate private beach, various dining options, a very entertaining Irish pub (minus the Guinness) & fitness centre & sauna. Being the westernmost hotel on the strip, you can easily walk northwest along the Ras Rmel sandbar & enjoy some undeveloped sections of coastline. Also has a Globalkite Djerba rental for kitesurfing, kayaking, stand-up paddleboards & catamarans (see opposite). **$$$$**

TUI BLUE Palm Beach Palace (260 rooms) 75 758 989; e nfo.palmbeachpalace@tui-blue.com; f TUIBLUE.PalmBeachPalace. An adults-only AI hotel very popular with French & German tourists. **$$$$**

Where to eat and drink

If you are not a guest, it can be difficult to just walk into the hotels around Plage Sidi Mahrès and access the restaurants (the Radisson Blu Djerba and Djerba Casino being the exceptions). Elsewhere, **La Rose Snack Bar** [map, page 313] (⊕ 33.874266, 10.956418; m 97 380 449; ⌚ 11.00–18.00 Tue–Sun; $$), a shack on the public beach just west of the Radisson, serves a simple but tasty catch of the day, including king prawns. Nearby is **Les Palmiers Chez Neji et Catherine** (Av de l'Environnement; m 97 906 529; ⌚ 18.00–22.30 daily; $$$), offering a mixture of French and Djerbian cuisine (try the lamb or the grilled fish) with attentive service. Finally, there is an excellent seafood restaurant at the northern tip of Plage de la Seguia called **Restaurant Lagune** [map, page 313] (⊕ 33.788671, 11.058640; m 54 440 422; ⌚ 10.00–20.00 daily; $$$); they even cook up a special paella on Saturdays!

Entertainment and nightlife

Many of the resorts have their own clubs and bars, but for those venturing out, **Djerba Casino** (75 757 537; m 29 210 542; e casinodjerba@yahoo.fr; f casinodjofficiel; ⌚ 10.00–04.00 daily) has both the main gambling hall and the Primavera Lounge serving alcohol. For those keen to forget the days of Covid-19 restrictions, cram on to a smoky dance floor and sweat all over complete strangers, head to **Discothèque Cyclone** (Rte Touristique; m 50 818 282; e contact@cyclone-djerba.com; w resa.cyclone-djerba.com; f discocyclonedjerba; ⌚ 22.00–04.00 daily).

Sports and activities Almost every hotel in Sidi Mahrès can organise quad-bike tours, bike rental, horseriding along the beach, archery and any other activity you can think of. Watersports are the main draw, with the area being particularly suited to kitesurfing thanks to the shallow waters and protective cove at Ras Rmel.

✷ **Globalkite Djerba** ⚑ ⊕ 33.873359, 10.910022; m 22 792 515; e moez@globalkite.com; w kitesurfdjerba.com. With a main rental location on the coastal road between Houmt Souk & Sidi Mahrès & another within the grounds of the Radisson Blu Djerba, this very well-run school is ideal for beginners all the way up to advanced kitesurfers. Owner Moez speaks great English & is highly responsive when contacted, & there are some great instructors. Prices are also very competitive by European standards. They also rent stand-up paddleboards, kayaks & Hobie Cat sailing catamarans.

What to see and do If you get bored of the beach at Sidi Mahrès, head over to the **Djerba Explore Park** (☎ 75 745 277; w djerbaexplore.com; ⏱ summer 09.00–19.00 Tue–Sun, winter 09.00–17.00 Tue–Sun; 30/20DT adult/child), which treads the line between children's theme park, zoo and open-air museum. Inside are rows of shops in a traditional village set-up, an Islamic art museum, a number of heritage structures including an oil press, serviced rental apartments and a crocodile farm with over 400 Nile crocodiles. On the way here, note the 49m-high, red-and-white-striped **Phare Taguermess** (⊕ 33.822829, 11.042790), built in 1895. The tallest lighthouse in Tunisia, it also one of the first in the country built using concrete. Note that there is a military installation nearby, so be careful where you point your camera.

MIDOUN Djerba's second-largest town, 14km southeast of Houmt Souk, Midoun is not really somewhere you would want to stay (with two exceptions, both a few kilometres to the northwest of town), as it is really just a less-picturesque, non-coastal version of the island capital. However, it is very popular with tourists from the Sidi Mahrès resorts, heading on day trips to buy souvenirs.

The **weekly market** on Friday is worth a visit, selling a mixture of local produce and crafts aimed squarely at tourists. For a slightly more unusual gift, try **La Maison du Miel Safraou** (Av Ali Belhouane; m 50 904 209, 55 904 209; e maison_miel@yahoo.fr; ⏱ 09.00–17.00 Mon–Sat), which has been selling honey, pollen and royal jelly since 1988. Look out for the bee-keeper outfit out front!

Otherwise, the open-air **Théâtre Municipal Jerba Midoun**, just behind the police station in the pedestrianised centre of town, hosts musical events and other live performances, including a weekly event on Tuesday afternoons involving a mock marriage ceremony featuring the distinctive local musical tradition. Tickets are sold in front of the theatre (m 21 171 718, 54 388 699; e mounirzaghdidiutico@yahoo.com). For an authentic baths experience, the **Hammam El Baccouche** (Av Saleh Ben Youssef; ⏱ men 04.00–noon & 18.00–22,00, women noon–18.00 Tue–Sun) offers a scrub and a massage for 15DT.

Where to stay and eat

Dar El Jerbi [map, page 313] (6 rooms) ⊕ 33.836002, 10.943699; m 21 400 484; e dareljerbi@yahoo.com; f dareljerbi. A large, wonderfully refined dar with a palm-lined pool, good food & excellent customer service. **$$$$**

Maison Leïla Djerba [map, page 313] (7 rooms) ⊕ 33.824991, 10.960473; m 98 816 330; e maisonleila@topnet.tn; f maisonleiladjerba. A charming & tranquil dar with traditionally decorated rooms & a 15m pool. Some rooms have a kitchenette. **$$$$**

Ti Diwan Av Ali Belhouane; m 20 370 776; f creperietidiwan; ⏲ 09.00–18.00 daily. Great sweet & savoury crêperie, also offering good salads. Look out for the sign of a weird white ferret wearing a red hat & playing the bagpipes. $$$

Restaurant Lotophages Rond Point Central Midoun; ☎ 75 730 250; m 98 596 536; ⏲ 08.00–late daily. Hard to miss with the massive green sign & amphora on the side of the wall, this Turkish restaurant is popular for grilled meats. $$

SOUTH AND WEST DJERBA The west coast of Djerba, from Ajim up to the airport, is very underdeveloped in terms of tourist infrastructure, probably owing to its rocky terrain and windy temperament. However, there are a few sights to see if you are driving this way towards Houmt Souk.

Unless you're a Star Wars fan, **Ajim** village itself does not have much to offer tourists, although there are a few cafés and restaurants with large terraces, and rows of street stalls. The town is considered an Ibadi Muslim stronghold on Djerba, and the ancient Ibadi architectural style mixed with indigenous Amazigh design – a building style visible across the entire island – remains a distinctive defining element of modern-day Ajim. Lime-covered whitewashed rectangular structures with simplistic domes, barrel-vaulted roofs and weight-bearing external buttresses are visible on most streets inside the small city.

Located 14km up the barren coastal road from Ajim, **Sidi Jemour**'s sandy beach is very popular with picnicking Tunisian and Algerian families; it is not hard to see why, especially at dusk when you are treated to a spectacular sunset over the water. The best section of beach is just north of the mosque, where you'll find the excellent

DJERBA'S STAR WAR SITES

Davin Anderson, Galaxy Tours (w galaxytours.com)

AJIM (⊕ 33.723964, 10.750016) Djerba's otherworldly Ibadi/Amazigh architecture prompted the decision to select a small neighbourhood near Ajim's city centre as the setting for Mos Eisley on fictional Tatooine in *Episode IV – A New Hope*. Located three blocks southeast of the C116–C209 roundabout (Ajim's main interchange) in the Al-Hunit Mosque district, the most prominent feature of the area at the time of filming (1976) was an unnamed rectangular-shaped open space, lined to the north and south with several domed *ghorfas*. Lucasfilm crews transformed the square, its bordering structures and two unnamed side streets just to the north into the Mos Eisley setting, while the now-abandoned bakery on the east side of the square functioned as the exterior of famous Mos Eisley Cantina.

AMGHAR MOSQUE (⊕ 33.740849, 10.734973) Another iconic Star Wars site is found 2.5km north up the coast from Ajim. This small, isolated seaside structure resting along the Gulf of Gabès was originally built in the 10th century, and the Ibadi mosque served as both a place of worship and as part of the defensive network of coastal lookouts situated on promontories around Djerba's perimeter to warn the island of potential invaders. Square in shape (33m^2), the intentionally simplistic whitewashed stone edifice was constructed with a double barrel-vaulted roof, two interior rooms of roughly equal size, and a protruding sphere-shaped mihrab niche. Notably there is no minaret, an otherwise common characteristic among Ibadi mosques on Djerba. The mosque was repurposed likely in the early 20th century as a storage shelter used by local fishermen.

Also in *Episode IV*, Amghar was used as the original exterior for Old Ben Kenobi's secluded hermitage. No construction or set dressing enhancements

Le Petit Marin ✷ (⊕ 33.833414, 10.748568; m 44 575 759; f LePetitMarinDjerba; ⊙ noon–18.30 daily; $$$), a seafood restaurant right on the sand. Try the grilled prawns – they're delicious!

In the Djerba's northwest corner is the lighthouse of **Borj Jellij** (⊕ 33.886934, 10.746530), which was originally a 16th-century fort. There is a large traditional fishing installation off the coast here, as well as an active military base – so be careful where you point your camera.

Driving between the airport and Houmt Souk, you will pass through the modern town of **Mellita**. The etymology of the town's name suggests a Punic origin, and this ancient settlement is home to the oldest mosque on Djerba: **Jama el Kebir**, also known as **Bou Messouer Mosque** (⊕ 33.862178, 10.821269). Dating to the 9th century, it was an important centre of Kharijite scholarship.

CENTRAL AND EASTERN DJERBA

Synagogue of El Ghriba (⊕ 33.814238, 10.859133; ⊙ 09.30–noon & 14.30–16.30 Sun–Fri; ostensibly free, though a small (not really voluntary) donation will be requested in return for a postcard upon entry) After the introduction of Islam to the island in the late 7th century, most Jews moved to the town of Er Riadh, 7km south of Houmt Souk and originally known as Hara Sghira or 'Little Neighbourhood'. The town's original synagogue is said to have been built at the time of the first Jewish settlement in 586BC, shortly after the destruction of King Solomon's temple in Jerusalem, making it the oldest synagogue in North Africa. The story goes that the

were required; crew members filmed close-up plate footage of the mosque at low camera angles from different vantage points to hide views of the prominent Mediterranean coastline behind. A composited landspeeder model was added in post-production. The sequence was replaced in the *Episode IV Special Edition* (1997) with a Djerba-style miniature enhanced by CGI.

SIDI JEMOUR MOSQUE (⊕ 33.831420, 10.748173) Founded in the 16th century by a local marabout of the same name, Sidi Jemour Mosque was the original standalone structure in this remote area and, like its counterpart further south, was both a place of worship and defensive lookout. Rectangular in shape (123.5m^2), surviving original elements of the simple whitewashed mosque include a triple barrel-vaulted roof, a protruding sphere-shaped mihrab niche, one weight-bearing external buttress, the main entrance and the side entrance. Although it experienced periods of neglect and non-use, especially during the late 20th century, the structure has functioned as an active place of worship for the local Ibadi Muslim community since 2014.

The square fort-like building (42.25m^2) positioned on an elevated stone platform over the rocky coast directly southwest of the mosque is Sidi Jemour's mausoleum, likely dating to the 17th century. The edifice functions as the focal point of the Festival Sidi Jemour, an annual pilgrimage celebration held at the site in honour of the enshrined founder. While pilgrims no longer slaughter a cow at the site, they do still visit the mosque and light candles.

The mosque complex was used to create three separate sets at two different locations on Tatooine for *Episode IV*: the Anchorhead main road, Tosche Station's exterior and the Mos Eisley perimeter. No construction at the site was required.

DJERBAHOOD (*w djerbahood.com*)

Er Riadh hit the headlines in June 2014 when a collective of artists from around the world painted over 250 murals on the village's whitewashed walls, coordinated by Galerie Itinerrance, a contemporary urban art gallery in Paris. The original series included street art from 150 different artists from over 30 countries, but the total number today has grown significantly as people continue to add more. French urban artist Invader has even hidden a few of his *Space Invaders*-themed ceramic-tile mosaics on the walls! Visit the website to download a map of the artworks, or for a few dinars you can ask one of the local children to direct you to a particular piece you might have seen on social media. As you explore the warren of narrow streets, you will come across everything from Disney characters such as Aladdin and Princess Jasmine, to the great Palestinian poet, Mahmoud Darwish.

location was marked by a sacred stone falling from Heaven and by the arrival of a strange woman to supervise the construction. Should the Jews ever abandon Djerba, the story goes, then the key to the synagogue would be hurled back up to Heaven.

The present structure was constructed in the 1920s on the site of the original, and is a smart building made up of two main rooms, with outer walls freshly whitewashed each year. The huge studded wooden doors open on to a large, rectangular main room where the marble-paved floor is covered with rush matting. The walls are faced with blue tiles, the columns have had a good dose of pale-blue gloss paint, and there is coloured glass in the windows filtering the sun on to dark, heavy wooden furniture in which men recite from holy books. Some of the older men wear baggy trousers which fasten at a black band below the knee – the black signifies mourning for the destruction of Solomon's temple. The second room (where you will be invited to make your entry donation) holds what is said to be one of the oldest Torahs in the world. The synagogue has thus become a spiritual centre for the study of the Torah and makes an interesting stop in an Islamic country.

Ghriba means 'miracle', and on the 33rd day after the Passover there is an annual procession called Lag BaOmer to commemorate the miracles. The congregation, including many pilgrims, bears the holy books through the streets on a covered platform.

Note that to enter the synagogue today you will need to head to the car park 100m north of the entrance and go through an airport-style security check, including having any bags scanned. This is a result of an al-Qaeda suicide bomber who targeted the synagogue on 11 April 2002, killing 14 German, three Tunisian and two French citizens. Inside, both men and women will need to cover their heads (covers are provided if you do not have one).

Where to stay and eat If you wish to stay in Er Riadh, the best option is **Dar Dhiafa** (⊕ 33.821619, 10.854768; 16 rooms; ☎ 75 671 166; m 94 190 776; w dardhiafa.tn; **$$$$**), a lovingly renovated *houch* (traditional Djerbian house). Each of the rooms has a distinct character and features only traditional furniture, and there is a pool, hammam and an excellent restaurant serving traditional dishes.

For food, try **La Placette** (⊕ 33.821133, 10.853672; ☎ 75 671 169; m 94 190 718; f restaurantlaplacette; ⌚ noon–15.00 & 19.00–22.00 Tue–Sun; **$$$**), a surprisingly upmarket find in the centre of the village just off Place de l'Indépendance, serving mainly Tunisian and Mediterranean dishes.

Guellala Called Haribus in Greek and Roman times, this sleepy town on Djerba's south coast was once renowned for its pottery, both large white utilitarian clay pots and more delicate shiny terracotta. The latter, resembling cheap Roman tableware, has practically disappeared and much of the pottery now on sale is standard Nabeul issue. However, a number of old-style potters continue to work from semi-underground workshops.

Guellala's main attraction is the **Heritage Museum** ✷ (⊕ 33.732572, 10.865914; ☎75 761 114; f; ⏲ winter 08.00–18.00 daily, summer 08.00–20.00 daily; 10DT, plus 3DT for photography), an incredible 4,000m² museum filled with life-size models depicting traditional Djerbian and wider Tunisian rites and customs. You will see lots of interiors with waxwork models showing locals preparing to get married, such as the *barboura* – a rite during which the future husband would walk around a sacred olive tree to the squeal of the bagpipes (*mizoued*) to gain protection. Look out too for the bridal gear (particularly spectacular, with all its gold and sequins, is the costume from Bizerte), the traditional healer with a chameleon in his claws, and Yacoub Bchiri, the lutist, marked as Jewish by the black ribbon in his baggy pantaloons or siroual. My personal favourite is the Sufi rights section, including a man eating a scorpion while in a trance. There is also a threshing floor, where ancient camel-powered technology will be enthusiastically demonstrated. The final section of waxworks is devoted to 'typical Tunisia'; here the glassed-in waxwork dummies figure a lonely desert shepherd playing his flute, a Zlass tribal horseman, a nocturnal Ramadan drummer waking the faithful for their predawn meal, and a courting couple in a Sidi Bou Saïd street, which has an air of Romeo and Juliet about it. In fact, the fine views from the café terrace at the museum have given it the nickname 'the Sidi Bou Saïd of Djerba'.

At the southern end of town on the coast is the abandoned 10th-century Ibadite **Sidi Yati Mosque** (⊕ 33.706814, 10.861692), the perfect spot from which to watch the sun go down. Photo opportunities abound, especially as there is a stable nearby, so the local lads are often galloping up and down the coast on their horses. The beach here is also beautiful.

Down a dusty farm track 4km south of Guellala are the remains of a curious structure: **Jema'a Haratt Wersighen** (⊕ 33.697361, 10.884576). Archaeologists believe that through various periods of occupation this building went from being a Roman temple to a synagogue and then a Byzantine church, before it took its final form as a mosque.

Sedouikech Another village once well known for its pottery is Sedouikech, 3km east of Guellala on the road to Midoun. Today all that remains of this craft are long underground stores, but there are a couple of religious structures nearby that are worth seeking out. Just east of town is the 16th-century **Sidi Satouri Mosque** (⊕ 33.737042, 10.937047), named after a holy man who, legend has it, once turned an entire wedding party of women to stone after they refused to stop singing while he was trying to pray. Despite his problematic approach to female choirs, the mosque is today somehow a site of pilgrimage for women hoping to conceive.

A little further south of Sedouikech, about 2km along the C117 towards the causeway, is the **Louta Mosque** (⊕ 33.721586, 10.911892), with two domes and set underground to maintain a steady temperature all year round. This 12th-century Ibadite structure is very easy to miss from the road, down a 200m dirt track through a cultivated field. There is a theory among some local historians that this now-abandoned structure was originally a Byzantine Christian church, before being converted into a mosque hundreds of years later.

Meninx Situated at the southern end of Djerba, this site is of great significance to archaeologists because of the wealth of finds that paint a detailed picture of the island's economic life thousands of years ago. Although today there are no well-excavated monumental buildings visible from the viewing platform, it nonetheless makes a good stop-off if driving past, if only to check out the sea views and birdlife on the coast. Note that Meninx is also the ancient Greek name given to the entire island.

First established by the Carthaginians, the settlement was refounded in Roman times and was an important trading post, especially given its proximity to the great city of Leptis Magna in Libya. In the same way that Chemtou became wealthy thanks to vast reserves of a much-sought-after luxury item in the Roman Empire (in that case, golden marble, page 155), Meninx became the most prominent settlement on Djerba owing to the production of murex, a purple natural dye made by crushing the Muricidae sea snails that are prevalent off the coast. As the 1st-century historian Pliny the Elder explains in his *Natural History*: 'The best Asiatic purple is at Tyre, the best African is at Meninx…the best European in the district of Sparta.'

During excavations in 2017–18, German and Tunisian archaeologists discovered evidence of Punic occupation during the 4th century BC, and even back then there was a focus on the production of murex dye. Remnants of imported ceramics from Carthage itself, as well as from Sicily, Corinth and Malta, show the Mediterranean trade links that Djerba maintained over 2,000 years ago. The sea level in this area has risen 50–75cm since antiquity, so there is likely also a large amount of underwater archaeology just off the coast, waiting to be discovered – although the flamingos that currently hang out in the shallows are unlikely to appreciate this!

Borj el Kastil Strategically located at the end of the Djerba's southeastern spit, overlooking the causeway, Borj el Kastil has a similar story to the better-preserved Borj el Kebir (page 318) on the north coast. Likely originally built in 1289 by Roger of Sicily and then upgraded in the 16th century by the fearsome Ottoman pirate Dragut (page 313), its last occupants were the troops of Hammouda Pasha Bey in the 17th century. Today the 12m-high walls are slowly crumbling into the sea and can be reached only by boat, 4x4 or via a 6.5km walk along the beach from the road that connects Aghir to El Kantara. The turn-off is at ⊕ 33.740846, 10.972198, but be careful driving your 4x4 down here, especially after rain, as it can get very muddy.

This part of the coast is also good for kitesurfing – try either of the following: **Club Kite Sport Les Dauphins** (⊕ 33.722769, 10.952296; m 98 430 527; w wassersport-tunesien.de; ⏲ 09.00–18.00 daily, wind-dependent) or **Djerba Kite** (⊕ 33.712529, 10.946107; m 55 510 396; w djerbakite.fr; f DjerbaKiteTunisie).

TATAOUINE

Established by the French as an administrative centre for the surrounding villages and nomadic tribes, Tataouine still has something of a frontier feel to it. Though fleets of 4x4s pass through on their way to picturesquely abandoned villages and *ksour*, life goes on unperturbed with locals – settled, semi-nomads or government employees – coming in for the jolly weekly markets. The area is well known by palaeontologists for the wealth of fossil remains found in the rocky landscapes. The town makes a good base for exploring the hilltop villages to the west, such as Chenini, Douiret and Guermessa, and the *ksour* of the Jebel Abiadh (White Mountains). Here you will also find Neolithic cave paintings and dinosaur footprints around Ghomrassen, as well Ksar Hadada (made famous by Star Wars).

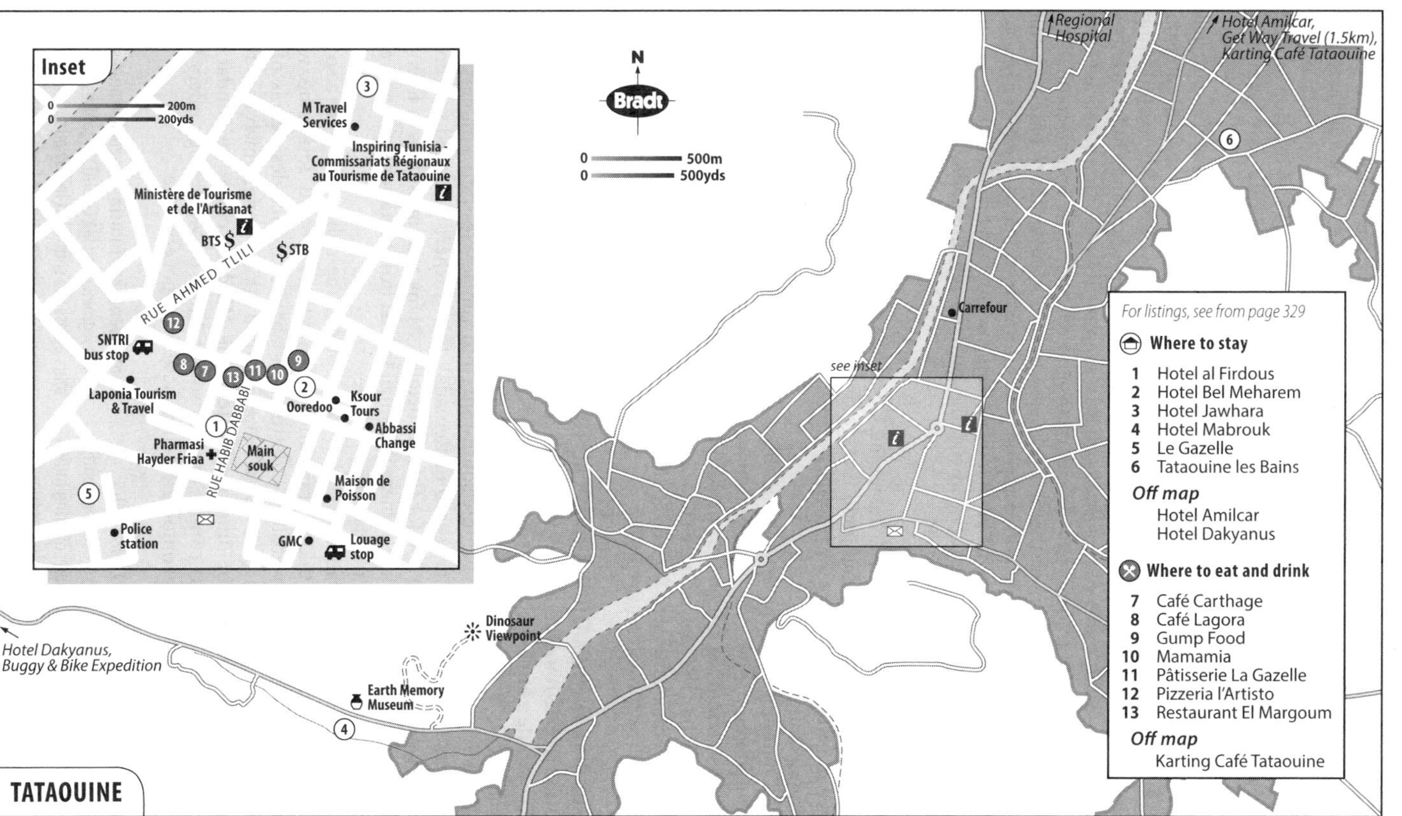
TATAOUINE
Inset
0 200m
0 200yds
M Travel Services
Inspiring Tunisia - Commissariats Régionaux au Tourisme de Tataouine
Ministère de Tourisme et de l'Artisanat
BTS
STB
RUE AHMED TLILI
SNTRI bus stop
Laponia Tourism & Travel
RUE HABIB DABBABI
Ooredoo
Ksour Tours
Abbassi Change
Pharmasi Hayder Friaa
Main souk
Maison de Poisson
Police station
GMC
Louage stop
N
Bradt
0 500m
0 500yds
Regional Hospital
Hotel Amilcar, Get Way Travel (1.5km), Karting Café Tataouine
Carrefour
see inset
Dinosaur Viewpoint
Earth Memory Museum
Hotel Dakyanus, Buggy & Bike Expedition
For listings, see from page 329
Where to stay
1 Hotel al Firdous
2 Hotel Bel Meharem
3 Hotel Jawhara
4 Hotel Mabrouk
5 Le Gazelle
6 Tataouine les Bains
Off map
Hotel Amilcar
Hotel Dakyanus
Where to eat and drink
7 Café Carthage
8 Café Lagora
9 Gump Food
10 Mamamia
11 Pâtisserie La Gazelle
12 Pizzeria l'Artisto
13 Restaurant El Margoum
Off map
Karting Café Tataouine

HISTORY Tataouine's name points to Amazigh origins, being the plural of 'tit', meaning 'spring', and until independence it was referred to as Foum Tataouine ('mouth of the springs'). The presence of water here clearly made it a useful stop on the caravan trails, but there is evidence of human habitation in the area dating back thousands of years, thanks to the Neolithic cave paintings near Ghomrassen.

In 1881, on the declaration of the French Protectorate over Tunisia, the southern tribes initially accepted the new authorities' rule; as there was only a small garrison left in Medenine, however, dissident tribes were not slow to revolt the following year. In 1883, the tribes submitted once more, with the Touazin and Ouderna tribes being given the status of *makhzen* – that is, exempt from taxation provided they protected the south from outside incursions and rebellion. The French colonialists developed Tataouine over the next 30 years from a small military base to a full garrison town, complete with hospital and school. It was a garrison for one of France's penal regiments, the *bataillons d'Afrique*, which had originally been set up in Algeria. Like many southern towns, the garrison remains today, although the troops inside are now Tunisian.

GETTING THERE AND AWAY Tataouine Governorate technically has an **airport** at the El Borma oil fields, but good luck getting permission to land there! In reality, the most useful airports for travellers are Gabès-Matmata and Djerba-Zarzis, both equidistant from Tataouine.

Tataouine is 540km from Tunis (6hrs 15mins by car). SNTRI **buses** connect to Tunis (9hrs; 36DT one-way), and **louage** services also run to the capital as well as the neighbouring settlements of Remada, Ben Ghardane, Medenine, Gabès, Douz and Djerba. The main louage stop is at the northern end of town, right next to the 'I Love Tataouine' sign (⊕ 32.948264, 10.456360), while the SNTRI bus stop is in the centre of town on the P19.

TOURIST INFORMATION AND LOCAL TOUR OPERATORS The main office of the **Ministère de Tourisme et de l'Artisanat** is on Rue Ahmed Tlili (⌚ 08.00–17.00 Mon–Fri), while a little further out of the centre is the office for **Inspiring Tunisia** (Av Hédi Chaker; ☎ 75 862 674; m 96 055 947; e crt.tataouine@ontt.tourism.tn; 09.00–17.00 Mon–Fri). If you wish to venture southwards into Tunisia's restricted military zone (ie: anywhere in the desert south of Remada), this is where you need to come to secure permits (see page 368 for further details). Many tour operators in town can also organise permits. Finally, there is a small **tourist information kiosk** on Avenue Habib Bourguiba with a painted map outside.

The **Géotourisme Dahar** website (w geotourisme-dahar.com) is also an invaluable resource for hiking trails and GPS locations around Tataouine, while the Destination Dahar website (w destinationdahar.com) includes details of the new 194km La Grande Traversée du Dahar regional hiking route, which runs from Tamezret to Douiret. For dinosaur hunters, the **Mindat** website (w mindat.org/paleo_loc.php?id=62292) run by the Hudson Institute of Mineralogy offers GPS locations of exciting palaeontological finds across the governorate.

Buggy & Bike Expedition ☎ 71 980 200/5; w buggy-bike.com. Portuguese off-roading outfit with locations in Tunis & Tataouine, offering multi-day quad-bike, motorbike & dune-buggy trips into the desert.

GeolAdventures Tunisia e geoladventures.tunisia@gmail.com; f GeolAT. Organises 4x4 tours across the southeast led by qualified geologists, for those who are keen to find out more about the 250-million-year history of the region.

Get Way Travel [map, page 327] Cité Mahrajene; ☎75 846 121; m 98 775 486; e mariem.l@getway.fr; ⌚ 09.00–17.00 Mon–Sat. One of the eight travel agencies in town able to apply for permits to head into the southern desert.

Ksour Tours [map, page 327] Rue Mosbah Jarboua; ☎75 862 338; e ksourtour@gmail.com; ⌚ 08.00–18.00 Mon–Thu, 08.00–13.00 Fri & Sat. This is one of the agencies in Tataouine that can apply for permits to visit the southern desert.

Laponia Tourism & Travel [map, page 327] Rue Jilani Marzougui; ☎75 863 914; e contact@laponiatours.tn; f laponia.agence.de.voyage; ⌚ 08.00–noon & 14.00-18.00 Mon–Sat. Another agency that is able to apply for permits for the southern desert.

M Travel Services [map, page 327] Rue Commandant Bjaoui; ☎75 862 123; e mtravel.services@gmail.com; ⌚ 08.00–17.00 Mon–Sat. One of the eight agencies based here that can apply for permits for the southern desert.

✷ **Mohamed Ghdiri** m 93 115 342; medghdiri. Excellent Tataouine-based guide who is very knowledgeable about the *ksour*, Neolithic, palaeontological & Star Wars sites in the region.

WHERE TO STAY *Map, page 327*

Your best options for a comfortable stay are a little way out of the centre. Many establishments in Tataouine allow camping on their grounds. The Ksotel (Auberge Ksour) on 8 Rue Habib Ghandour is best avoided.

✷ **Hotel Dakyanus** (100 rooms) Rte El Ferch; ☎75 832 199; e dakyanus@gnet.tn; f dakyanus.hotel. Large high-end hotel to the northwest of town on the road to Ghomrassen. Elegantly decorated communal spaces, cool vaulted rooms with AC/heating & en suites, large pool & good restaurant. **$$$$**

Le Gazelle (27 rooms) Av Hédi Chaker; ☎75 860 009; m 21 438 071; e kh1farhat@yahoo.fr. With a wooden reception straight from the 1970s, rooms here have AC, TV, shower & small balcony overlooking the secure car park. Camping is also allowed at 20DT per vehicle. A solid mid-range option. **$$$**

✷ **Tataouine les Bains** (3 rooms) Cité Mahrajène; m 98 438 056; w tataouine-lesbains.com. A bungalow home in Tataouine's northern suburbs with modern en-suite rooms opening on to a communal courtyard with kitchen. Has heating but no AC. It is possible to camp in garden & there are 2 caves the owner intends to turn into troglodyte rooms. Great for overlanders. **$$$**

Hotel Mabrouk (40 rooms) Rte de Chenini; m 98 438 115; e mabroukhotel@yahoo.fr. Basic, large rooms with baths, AC & Wi-Fi, or more traditional vaulted-brick rooms with showers. Lots of space for camping, with electrical sockets & shower blocks. Good for overlanders. **$$–$$$**

Hotel Amilcar (18 rooms) Opposite Nejib el-Khattab Stadium; ☎75 846 222; m 26 648 948; w hotelamilcar.tn. Rooms are large & bright with AC, TV, toilet & shower. Good value, but out-of-the-way location. Be sure to select non-smoking room! **$$**

Hotel al Firdous (7 rooms) 44 Av Habib Bourguiba; m 90 031 690. Selection of room types overlooking the market, from bunks in a shared room to en suites & smaller rooms with shared toilet facilities. Access to a small kitchen; communal areas have Wi-Fi. Very cool original HMV gramophone at reception. Great location. **$**

Hotel Bel Meharem (29 rooms) Rue 18 Janvier 1952; ☎75 860 104. Same pricing as Hotel al Firdous but much bigger space (especially if you want a bunk-bed in a dorm). Reduced prices if you do not use heating or AC in rooms. **$**

Hotel Jawhara (16 rooms) 82 Av Habib Bourguiba; ☎75 860 621. Cheapest bed in town if you split a quad 4 ways. Some rooms have TV & bathroom but no AC, others communal bathrooms. **$**

WHERE TO EAT AND DRINK *Map, page 327*

For high-end dining, head to one of the hotel restaurants such as at the Hotel Dakyanus. Most of the options in the centre of town are generally cheaper, fast-food places.

Restaurant El Margoum Souk; m 97 387 519; ⌚ 11.00–22.00 daily. Good rotisserie chicken & couscous dishes. $$–$$$

Gump Food 3 Rue de 18 Janvier 1956; ☎ 75 861 437; e gumpfood@hotmail.com; ⌚ 08.00–late daily. I do not understand the name, nor do I understand why there is a hedgehog logo. But setting the confusion aside, this offers good sweets, cakes & kebabs. $$

Karting Café Tataouine ⊕ 32.971868, 10.481663; m 25 400 448; f karting.Tataouine.page.officielle; ⌚ 18.00–late daily. If you enjoy copyright infringement & go-karting, then you will love this place, tagged on the front of a go-karting track & decorated in the style of the Hard Rock Café. $$

Pizzeria l'Artisto Rue Ahmed Tlili; ⌚ 10.00–late daily. Delicious cheese-slathered junk food. Quick service. $$

Mamamia Rue Habib el Missawi; ⌚ 10.00–21.00 Sat–Thu. Good pizzas & other fast food. Also does cheap sandwiches. $–$$

Café Carthage Av Habib Bourguiba; ⌚ 06.00–23.00 daily. Very popular café with green awning over the outdoor seating area. Good coffee. $

Café Lagora Av Habib Bourguiba; ⌚ 07.00–late daily. A bit quieter than nearby Café Carthage, in a pedestrianised section of road. Porticoes with purple vines growing overhead. Nice spot for a tea. $

Pâtisserie La Gazelle Rue de 18 Janvier 1956; ⌚ 08.30–17.00 daily. Named after Tataouine's signature pastry (*cornes de gazelle*), filled with assorted nuts & honey & shaped like a gazelle's horn. Delicious! $

A *KSOUR* CIRCUIT SOUTH OF TATAOUINE

If you have your own transport or are feeling very confident with the local louage timetable, there is an interesting 57km loop exploring the '*ksar* land' southeast of Tataouine. A *ksar* (*ksour* plural) is a fortified granary built in the Jebel Abiadh (White Mountains) by the local Ouderna tribe, generally between the 11th and 19th centuries, made up of high outer walls and an inner courtyard filled with *ghorfas* (vaulted rooms for grain storage). These ancient defensive structures are now all reasonably accessible thanks to the decent tarmac road on the loop. Some ksour are on mountains or hilltops and a few are on valley floors, though most are now abandoned, with a few having been destroyed by French colonial forces owing to local resistance to French rule. However, some of these incredible buildings have either been restored as historical sites, sites of pilgrimage for Star Wars fans or are in current use as housing, shops or even tourist accommodation.

Driving in a clockwise direction from southern Tataouine, the first series of ksour you hit are at **Gattoufa**, 8km away. **Ksar Beni Blel** is the furthest south (⊕ 32.897897, 10.525064), featuring a white-painted entrance and a small tea-shop inside; just to the north are **Ksar Gattoufa** (⊕ 32.902500, 10.524500) and **Ksar Jellidet** (⊕ 32.904103, 10.523750). Of the two, Gattoufa is in better condition, but the structures at Jellidet are much higher and more impressive.

The next stop is **Ezzahra**, 12km south of Gattoufa. Here, **Ksar Ezzahra** (⊕ 32.817200, 10.565472) is made up of two interconnected courtyards: the smaller one to the northeast is accessed through an iron gate and not in use, but beautifully preserved, while the larger adjoining one is used as both a market and tea-shop.

Continuing for 11km southwest, you hit **Ksar Ouled Soltane** (⊕ 32.788389, 10.514624), one of the best-preserved ksour in Tunisia and recognisable from various tourism promotion materials and postcards. Built on a slight rise allowing good views across the desert towards Libya, the ksar's circular outer wall is still virtually intact. Two superb courtyards of ghorfas survive, the older dating from the 15th century. Standing on the hillside below the ksar, you can understand how

SHOPPING Bizarrely for a desert location, you will find an excellent fishmonger, **Maison de Poisson** (Rue 02 Mars 1943; m 97 765 447; ⌚ 07.00–16.00 daily), as well as an excellent fruit and veg **street market** on Rue Habib Dabbabi. This extends all the way past the **main souk**, where you can pick up all manner of fresh produce, souvenirs and other items. The main market days in both locations are Monday and Thursday, although you will be able to find something for sale any day of the week. The souk offers some of the rather nice slippers made in Tataouine, which combine leather and pieces of kilim-type wool or plastic weaving. The area around the main souk also has some jewellery shops, and you might just be lucky and pick up an old silver ankle-bracelet.

OTHER PRACTICALITIES For medical emergencies, the **Regional Hospital** is on the P19 around 6km north of town (📞75 862 005, 75 870 114), and the modern, well-stocked **Pharmasi Hayder Friaa** is at 25 Avenue Habib Bourguiba (📞75 860 245; ⌚ 08.00–20.00 daily).

For money exchange, try the yellow-and-grey **Abbassi Change** (Rue Khaled Ibn Eloualid; ⌚ 09.00–17.00 daily), which is located next door to the supermarket of the same name.

easily defensible it must have been, at least against pillagers armed only with light firearms. Despite a barrage of misinformation suggesting otherwise, no Star Wars filming took place here.

The next stop is **Ksar Tamelest**, 5km west (⊕ 32.793836, 10.472660), accessed via a really rough track so either go in a 4x4 or walk from the road. This 13th-century structure was badly damaged during World War I when the Ouderna tribe based here aligned themselves with the Senussi leader, Khalifa Ben Asker. In 1915 he led an ultimately unsuccessful cross-border raid from Libya (then the Italian colony of Tripolitania) to encourage revolt against French rule. Authorities were busy reconstructing the ksar at the time of writing, making it the second most visually impressive ksar on the route, after Ksar Ouled Soltane.

The penultimate stop on the loop is **Maztouria**, 6km to the north, home to no fewer than four ksour. The first, just south of town, is the 15th-century **Ksar Daghara** (⊕ 32.840982, 10.473479), followed by the very finely restored **Ksar el Kadim** (⊕ 32.847736, 10.467736). With an inner courtyard almost 50m in diameter, this is by far the largest ksar on the loop. There is also an inscription outside claiming that this ksar was built in AD1072, which would make it an incredibly early example of Hilalian architecture given that they only got to Kairouan in 1057, following their invasion of Ifrikiya. A further 800m north is **Ksar Aouadid** (⊕ 32.854775, 10.471067), also well restored, with high stone walls like a fortress and a safe staircase you can climb on to the roof for panoramic views. There is also an 11th-century inscription at the entrance. Finally, 1km further north is **Ksar Ouled Aoun** (⊕ 32.863797, 10.472067), though it is only partially restored and down a very rocky track that is difficult to reach in a vehicle.

The final stop on the loop is **Ksar Beni Barka** (⊕ 32.886339, 10.434019), a good 800m west of the main road but easily visible, perched on a hilltop overlooking the valley floor. Consisting of over 500 ghorfas across four levels, plus a mosque and eight traditional olive-oil presses, this 15th-century site is on UNESCO's Tentative List for World Heritage Status.

WHAT TO SEE AND DO Tataouine, and southern Tunisia generally, is famous among geologists and palaeontologists as being very rich in dinosaur fossils. Tataouine plays host to some of the most diverse examples of Early Cretaceous vertebrate fauna fossils in Africa, including pterosaurs, sarcopterygians, actinopterygians, elasmobranchs, turtles and crocodyliforms. A good place to see some of these is the **Earth Memory Museum** (Rte de Chenini; ☎75 850 244; m 98 234 211; ⏱ 09.00–16.00 Mon–Fri), which has a small display of fossils from the area including bones of dinosaurs and prehistoric fish, plus some of the first dinosaur fossils identified in the area in 1955. The museum should also be able to arrange a guide if you wish to wander up into the surrounding hills and see dinosaur footprints, such as the ones at Ghomrassen, and other fossils *in situ*. Just east of the museum is a track (4x4 only) that leads northwards to the so-called **Dinosaur Viewpoint** (⊕ 32.921250, 10.422034). There were originally plans to add a big plastic *Stegosaurus* up here at one stage, but this seems to have ended up over at Ksar Ouled Debbab, 7km south. For now, it is simply a great viewpoint from which to watch the sun rise or set over Tataouine. At the southern end of town there is a hill with large Arabic script on the side saying **Marhaba Bikom** (Welcome Everyone) at ⊕ 32.924405, 10.449639.

AROUND TATAOUINE

The following are all best accessed with your own transport; however, some taxis do head this way from the louage stop at the south end of Tataouine on Rue 2 Mars.

KSAR OULED DEBBAB Named after the Ouled Debbab tribe that constructed it, this 15th-century *ksar* is now home to a tourist centre featuring an excellent museum (The Treasures of Islam; 10DT). On display in the vaulted galleries are a variety of antiquities, from paintings to silver jewellery to weaponry, which showcase a fascinating picture of Amazigh life under Ottoman and French rule. If you'd like to stay the night there is also a luxury hotel, also called Ksar Ouled Debbab (20 rooms, 2 suites; m 92 090 827; e ksar.debbab@gmail.com; f ksar.ouled.debbab; **$$$$$**), with air-conditioned, en-suite rooms with bath and shower, plus a café, restaurant and a massive replica *Stegosaurus*.

DOUIRET (⊕ 32.868676, 10.286663) The road to Douiret loops west from the centre of Ksar Ouled Debbab, running for 12km through land cultivated after the winter rains but barren in the summer. Perched on the hillside and dug into the rocks, 1.5km north of the modern settlement along a decent tarmac road, the old ksar has been essentially abandoned, with the majority of inhabitants moving out during the late colonial and early independence period. Now the only people you will meet up here work in the tourist facilities (accommodation and cafés), so if you come out of season you are very likely to have the place to yourself. Even with visitors, the place feels quite eerie and has a faint mystical air with its white mosque and dune-coloured, half-ruined houses merging into the hillside. Notice the inscriptionless tombstones. In the 19th century, before colonial boundaries, Douiret must have been quite a prosperous place with the trans-Saharan trade. In the early days of the French occupation, it was home to the *bureau de renseignements* (customs agency), which was subsequently moved to more accessible Tataouine (page 328).

Where to stay and eat

Gite de Douiret 'Chez Raouf' (10 rooms) ⊕ 32.867975, 10.287397; m 97 497 242, 28 497 242; w gitedouiret.com; f GiteDouiret. Troglodyte rooms, but all slightly brighter & more refined than the nearby Résidence. Also able to organise hikes & cultural tours of the area. Advanced booking essential. **$$$**

Résidence Douiret Les Troglodytiques (10 rooms) ⊕ 32.867963, 10.287803; ✆ 75 878 066/060; e latifa1509@hotmail.fr; f residencedouiretlestroglodytiques. Run by the ASNAPED (Association de Sauvegarde de la Nature et de Protection de l'Environnement de Douiret), the rooms here are traditional troglodyte cave dwellings dug into the hillside, with communal bathrooms. There is also a small museum with a beautiful historic photography exhibition. Advanced booking essential. **$$$**

Centre de Camping Douiret ⊕ 32.867647, 10.288780. Still under construction at the time of writing. Large walled compound with tiled courtyard offering camping, parking for vehicles & a few bungalow rooms. **$$**

Café Douiret ⊕ 32.867642, 10.287583. Just to the west of Résidence Douiret, offering tea, coffee & soft drinks. **$**

CHENINI Located high above the arid plain, Chenini has become the quintessential ruined hilltop Amazigh village, its distinctive silhouette, featuring a white mosque, splashed all over tourism promotional materials for the country, as well as countless Instagram posts. Though it has become part of the tourist route and gets crowded with people climbing up and down the village, it remains worth seeing for the extraordinary setting. The streets are just ledges, scarcely wide enough for two people to pass. The houses, which are built into the rock, each have a small courtyard where animals are kept. There are some *ghorfas* at the top of the village, but few are still in use. Like those of other Amazigh villages, Chenini men began to migrate to the cities in the 20th century, where they became established as newspaper sellers. In the centre, the **Nassamo-Samo Art Gallery** (⊕ 32.911378, 10.262236) is the go-to location for local art exhibitions and cultural events; details on current exhibitions are available from Association ILEF Tataouine (✆ 75 846 513; e ileftataouin@gmail.com).

It is possible to hike from Chenini Nouvelle – the modern settlement on the main road, 1.5km to the east of the old hilltop town – to Douiret, which is only 5.5km to the south. Ensure you are confident where you are going (or bring a guide), as the path is quite rocky and not signposted. As you hike south from Chenini Nouvelle, the route leads to **Jema Kedima** (Seven Sleepers Mosque; ⊕ 32.909787, 10.274950); according to local legend, the elongated underground tombs here are said to house the bodies of local Christians who were locked underground in Roman times, but then converted to Islam centuries later.

Where to stay and eat

✷ **Dar Kenza** (9 rooms) ⊕ 32.911389, 10.263880; m 97 284 086; w kenza-chenini.com. A visit to Chenini would not be complete without a night in the incomparable Dar Kenza. With 16 beds & 8 bathrooms spread across various room types, it likely has the perfect troglodyte set-up for larger groups. Assuming it is warm, you can even spend the evening relaxing in the (very small) pool, watching the sunset over the hills. **$$$$**

Restaurant Mabrouk Chenini ⊕ 32.910608, 10.260733; m 98 282 400; f hoteltataouine; ⌚ 08.00–late daily). Opposite the post office on the main road, this 3-storey building houses a restaurant that mainly caters for tour groups, serving couscous, meat dishes & good chorba. The hotel in the same building was closed at time of writing. **$$–$$$**

Des Vagues des Village ⊕ 32.911639, 10.264025; m 92 924 623; ⌚ 07.00–late daily. Near the famous mosque, with an amazing roof terrace that is great for panoramic photos of Chenini. **$**

GUERMESSA ✷ It still amazes me that this abandoned Amazigh hilltop settlement is not a UNESCO World Heritage Site, as it should be the highlight of any visit to this area. In the same mould as Chenini or Douiret, but with far fewer visitors, the village stretches almost 1.5km along a ridgeline of the Dahar Mountains, and is a labyrinth of multistorey houses, caves, religious structures, an olive press and goods storage sites. It was built in the 7th or 8th centuries AD around the Zaouia of Sidi Hamza – the son of a mythical holy man (Sidi Ibrahim) who was originally from Kairouan.

The new town, which sits at the eastern base of a hill, can be easily reached along a tarmac road from both Tataouine (which sits 20km to the southeast) or Ghomrassen (which sits 12km to the northeast). You can also hike here from Chenini, 8km to the south, although a guide is highly recommended. To access the ancient settlement, take the westward turning to the north of the new town (⊕ 32.996469, 10.266047) and then head southwards at ⊕ 32.999175, 10.233597. Both of these roads are newly paved and in excellent condition. Park at the base and walk up a series of restored, stone-paved paths to the distinctive whitewashed mosque (⊕ 32.985611, 10.251406). The panoramic views from up here, in both directions, are breath-taking, encompassing Tataouine to the east, the sands to the west towards Jebil National Park, and the summit of Chenini to your south. Continuing southwards along the hilltop, you reach a turquoise-and-white shrine featuring Arabic inscriptions and handprints on the interior. Just outside is a weathered graveyard where human remains can be seen, exposed to the elements. The whole area around the hilltop here is worth a few hours of exploration. The ruined multistorey structures, some with their original doorways still in place, are fascinating to walk around – you can really imagine what life must have been like up here just 100 years ago. Be careful entering some structures though, as many are unstable and you may be hit by falling masonry.

GHOMRASSEN AND AROUND This large market town of ancient Amazigh origins, 25km northwest of Tataouine on the C107, has a rather strange claim to fame: it is known throughout Tunisia for making good *ftayer* – a sweet, deep-fried pastry. It is known for its wealth of historic sites, including cave paintings, well-preserved ksour and dinosaur footprints, but is also a good place for outdoor excursions. Based in town, the excellent **South Tunisia Adventures** (52 Pl de l'Indépendance; m 95 637 398; w southadventures.tn; ⌚ 08.30–17.00 Mon–Fri) can organise mountain biking, camping and trekking trips in the region.

As you head into town from Tataouine along the C207 you will pass **Ksar el Ferch** (⊕ 33.006550, 10.342728), an unusual *ksar* located as it is on a flat valley floor. It was likely built in the early 20th century, which explains the lack of concern for defensibility. Some 4km northeast of here sits **Ksar Mourabtine** (⊕ 33.031939, 10.377300), located up a very rocky 1km track from the village of the same name that is really only accessible on foot. It is worth the hike, however, as it is well preserved and very isolated, with some sections rising four storeys above the desert ground.

Ghomrassen itself has a great selection of ancient historical sites. The action starts the minute you drive in from the west on the C121 (imaginatively named Avenue Habib Bourguiba), with the **Taguet Hamed cave paintings** on the south side of the road (⊕ 33.059683, 10.322030). Sadly, many of these Neolithic etchings have weathered away, but you can still make out horse, deer and human figures painted in red on the rock face. Just 200m east is the **Fountain Café** (Av Habib Bourguiba; ⌚ 09.00–18.00 daily; $), worth visiting for the massive *T. rex* in its prehistoric-looking outdoor seating area. Another set of cave paintings is found around 550m northeast of the café (⊕ 33.062917, 10.328689), though they involve a fair amount of scrambling up the hillside to reach. Despite being protected by steel bars, the

Chaabet el Maarek cave paintings have sadly been vandalised, but you can still see Neolithic painted elephants, human figures and a hunting scene involving gazelle.

Sticking to the north side, the strangely shaped ancient **Ibn Arafa Mosque** (⊕ 33.061651, 10.336596) sits on a hill overlooking the town below. It is dedicated to a 14th-century Maliki religious leader, Ibn Arafa, who was a very prominent Amazigh from southern Tunisia and one of the most senior representatives of Maliki Islam during the Hafsid period. The mosque was restored in 2017. Looking out over town from the mosque, to the south you should be able to pick out **Ksar al Rufsa**, an early-20th-century construction that is currently protected by security forces, so do not go wandering up there. Further south from the *ksar* are the best-preserved of Ghomrassen's trio of cave paintings: **Chaabet Insefri** (⊕ 33.047486, 10.338194). Set in a valley that would make a good camping spot, there are two sets of Neolithic paintings here, one on each side of the valley floor, both protected by bars. Again, only small sections of painted cave wall remain, but you can see herds of four-legged animals including cows.

Ghomrassen's most exciting attraction, a vast set of **fossilised dinosaur footprints**, lie 3km north of town on an exposed ancient riverbed perched atop a hill (⊕ 33.081550, 10.347608). Discovered in 2017, these 136 footprints constitute some of the oldest evidence of dinosaur presence in Tunisia. There are clear impressions of a herd, with at least two types of dinosaur plodding through the river during the Middle to Upper Jurassic period (about 150 million years ago). Palaeontologists have been reluctant to definitively attribute the tracks to a specific species of dinosaur, but believe that one set looks like it might be from a kayentapus. The tracks are signposted from town as 'Geosite Beni Ghedir', but you will need to do a fair amount of scrambling to reach the exposed ancient riverbed.

ALONG THE C207 Running from Tataouine in the south, through Ghomrassen and Beni Kheddache before ending in Ksar Hallouf, the C207 is a dramatic, winding desert road. Eight kilometres north of Ghomrassen is **Ksar Hadada**, whose eponymous *ksar* (⊕ 33.100165, 10.313728) is best known to Star Wars fans as the filming location of the Mos Espa slave quarters in *Episode I – The Phantom Menace*. The current owner, Saidi Fahmi, speaks English and is a huge Star Wars fan, having lovingly restored elements of the mid-19th-century structures to resemble the set that was constructed here in 1997. You can see the porch used during filming by Liam Neeson (Qui-Gon Jinn), Natalie Portman (Padmé Amidala Naberrie) and Pernilla August (Shmi Skywalker) in the *ksar*'s northwest corner. For more information about this site, check out w galaxytours.com.

As the C207 snakes northwards from Ksar Hadada towards the boundary with Medenine Governorate, note **Gattar Canyon** on your right (⊕ 33.127933, 10.296533) – the area turns into a waterfall during heavy rains. A little further north is a large and rather random replica *Diplodocus* sitting on a hilltop (⊕ 33.149155, 10.285612), possibly put there by the Tunisian sculptor Abdelaziz Krid. It is possible to hike up to the dinosaur, as well as down into the canyon. This area is incorporated into some hiking trails on Géotourisme Dahar (page 328).

Turning eastwards off the C207 just before hitting the Medenine Governorate boundary, you reach the rural settlement of **Krerachfa**, 3.5km off the main road. To the south of the modern town are the ruins of the 15th-century **Ksar Krerachfa** (⊕ 33.188602, 10.292616), with a surviving underground mosque. Continuing for another 11km east you will reach the farming community of **Oued el Khil**, home to the excellent agro-tourism project, **Domaine Oued el Khil** (⊕ 33.164878, 10.362511; m 98 668 284; e domaine.oued.el.khil@gmail.com; w domaine-elkhil.com; **$$$**).

Set on a 3ha working farm, it consists of five rooms in the main house, plus a 'super adobe' – a large, domed living space made of earth. It is fully organic, using local materials. The menu is also full of home-grown produce, featuring barley-based couscous, *tchicha* (barley semolina soup), *tbikha* (vegetable stew), moringa-based salads and a variety of herbal teas. They can organise hikes in the area and agricultural experiences on the farm. You can just stop by for lunch, but you'll need to book in advance.

SAMAR This town, 45km east of Tataouine on the C111, has a long tradition of animal husbandry and horseriding. In April, it hosts the annual **Festival National de la Tonte** (f FestivalnationaldelaTontedeSmar), a massive sheep-shearing festival where you can watch demonstrations on sheep-shearing, attend workshops on how different animals' wool is used, listen to local fables about sheep (and wolves!) and listen to local musicians.

At the time of writing, the **Equestrian Centre of Samar** was under construction in the southern end of town and there are plans to also situate an eight-chalet maison d'hôte at the same location. There is a small **museum** of local artefacts from Ottoman and colonial times, including craft items and tools (⊕ 32.993544, 10.823039; ⌚ 10.00–16.00 Sun–Thu) next door to the primary school.

If in the area, it is worth making the drive some 13km southeast of Samar (around ⊕ 32.928034, 10.926701) to witness the very strange, lunar-like landscape, where the winds have sculpted and smoothed rocks on the salt flats of Sebkhet Areg Makhizene. It is sometimes used by tour groups as a wild campsite.

The Southwest and Deep South

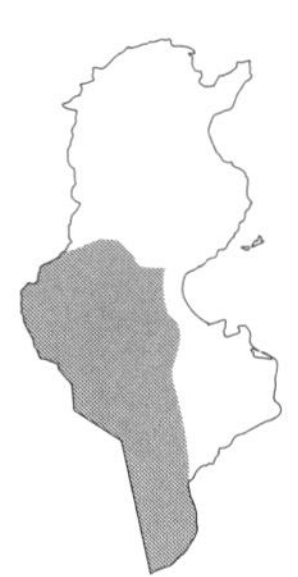

Encompassing the governorates of Gafsa, Tozeur and Kebili, the southwest is known as El Djerid ('palm leaf'). Those coming from the north will notice a shift here from arid to desert climate, characterised by rolling pink hills, oasis towns and a number of *chotts* (salt pans) that stretch across the border into neighbouring Algeria. Both Tozeur and Douz are well-established tourist hubs for those wishing to visit the desert or for Star Wars fans keen to explore some of the franchise's most iconic filming sites. Douz is also known for its annual Festival du Sahara, which celebrates traditional desert culture with camel races and horseback shows. Elsewhere, you will also find Nefta, the spiritual home of Sufism, and Gafsa, the former centre of the ancient Capsian culture which is today home to a spectacular tourist train that passes through the remarkable Selja Gorge.

THE ORIGINS OF TUNISIA'S AMAZIGH PEOPLE

A distinct Capsian civilisation has been identified by archaeologists as existing in southern Tunisia between 7000BC and 4500BC. It is debated whether these were migrant arrivals westward from the Levant, or originally from Tunisia. Either way, their complex food-gathering culture was centred around Gafsa.

The transition from Capsian to Amazigh civilisation in this region is poorly understood. The Amazigh themselves appear to be the result of a merging of Capsian and other regional cultures, which included successive waves of migration into the area at some stage after 3000BC. DNA analysis of Amazigh populations carried out in 2010, which included Amazigh from As-Sened in Gafsa Governorate (page 345), showed genetic links to West Africa, East Africa and Iberia. The Amazigh were distinct from the Capsian in that their culture saw the development of agricultural communities following the introduction of domesticated livestock (likely from the Nile Valley) and finally horses, around 1200BC.

The Phoenicians arrived in Tunisia in the 9th century BC and set up commercial outposts as far south as Gabès (then Tacapae) and Meninx (on the island of Djerba). However, the Amazigh populations in the southwest managed to retain independence. In fact, for many centuries the Amazigh were able to impose a tribute on Phoenician settlements such as Carthage, which only ended when the balance of power shifted in the 5th century BC. As such, this part of the country offers some distinctive ancient material culture, as well as the usual assortment of Punic, Roman and Byzantine remains.

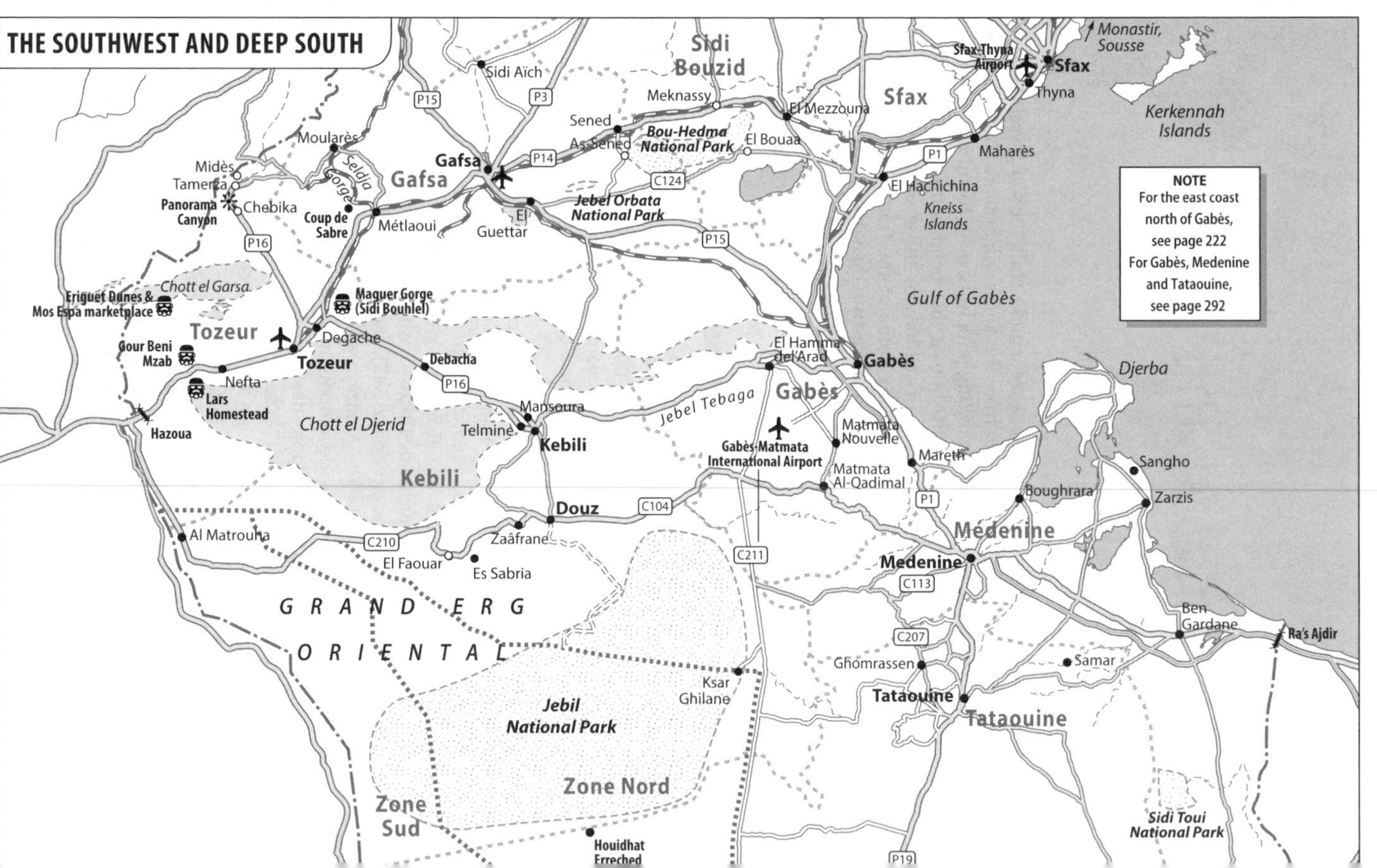
THE SOUTHWEST AND DEEP SOUTH
Sidi Aïch
Sidi Bouzid
Meknassy
El Mezzouna
Sfax
Sfax-Thyna Airport
Sfax
Monastir, Sousse
Thyna
Kerkennah Islands
Moularès
Sened
As-Sened
Bou-Hedma National Park
El Bouaa
Maharès
Midès
Tamerza
Panorama Canyon
Chebika
Seldja Gorge
Gafsa
Gafsa
Coup de Sabre
Métlaoui
El Guettar
Jebel Orbata National Park
El Hachichina
Kneiss Islands
NOTE
For the east coast north of Gabès, see page 222
For Gabès, Medenine and Tataouine, see page 292
Chott el Garsa
Eriguet Dunes & Mos Espa marketplace
Maguer Gorge (Sidi Bouhlel)
Gulf of Gabès
Tozeur
Degache
Gour Beni Mzab
Tozeur
Debacha
El Hamma del'Arad
Gabès
Nefta
Lars Homestead
Djerba
Hazoua
Chott el Djerid
Mansoura
Telmine
Kebili
Jebel Tebaga
Gabès
Gabès-Matmata International Airport
Matmata Nouvelle
Mareth
Sangho
Kebili
Matmata Al-Qadimal
Boughrara
Zarzis
Douz
Al Matrouha
Zaâfrane
El Faouar
Es Sabria
Médenine
Medenine
GRAND ERG ORIENTAL
Ben Gardane
Ra's Ajdir
Ksar Ghilane
Ghomrassen
Samar
Tataouine
Tataouine
Jebil National Park
Zone Nord
Zone Sud
Houidhat Errached
Sidi Toui National Park
P1
P3
P14
P15
P16
P19
C104
C113
C124
C207
C210
C211

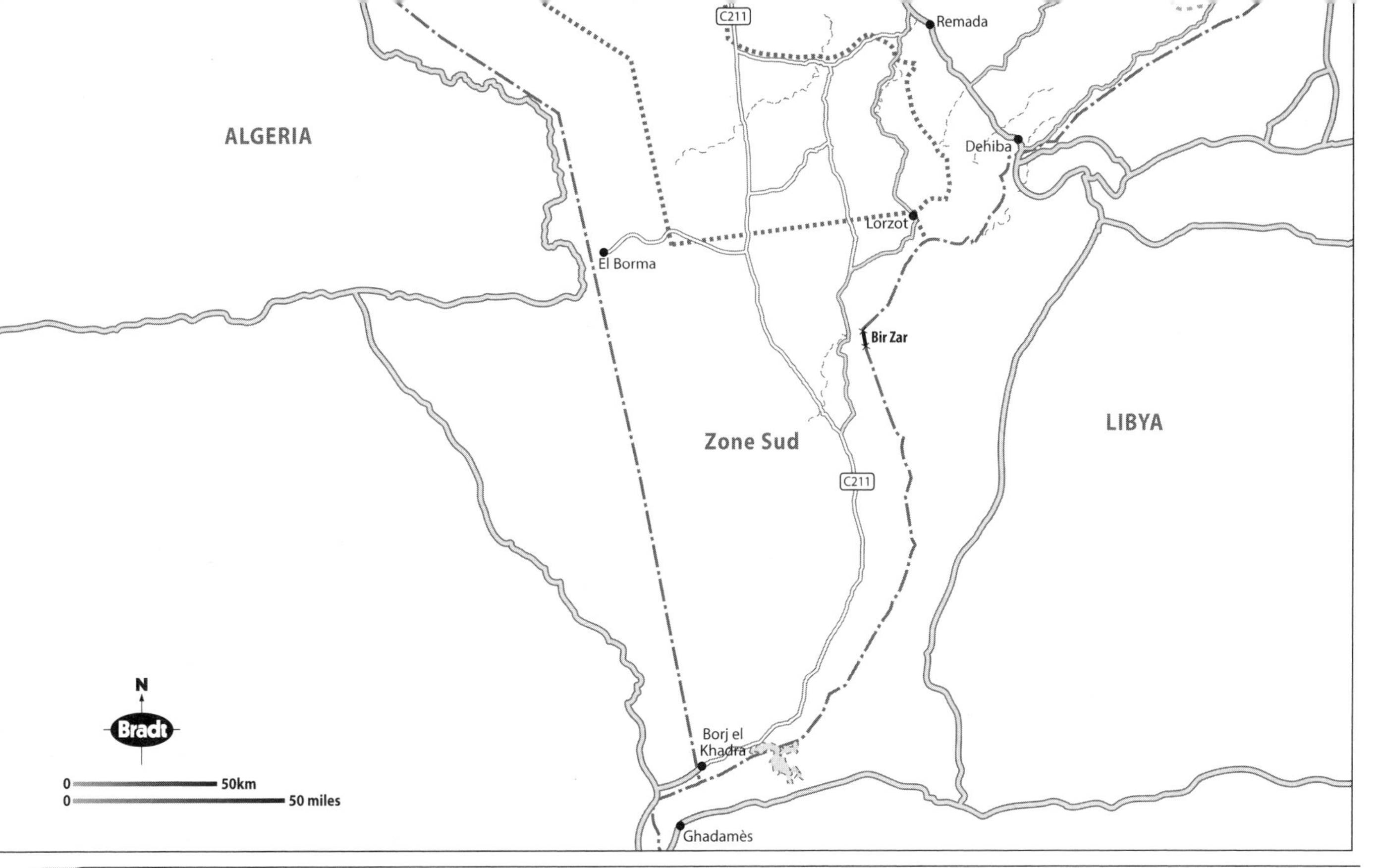
C211
Remada
ALGERIA
Dehiba
Lorzot
El Borma
Bir Zar
LIBYA
Zone Sud
C211
N
Bradt
Borj el Khadra
0
50km
0
50 miles
Ghadamès

The far south of this region sees the beginning of the Grand Erg Oriental, a vast field of sand dunes in northeastern Algeria that spills over into this area. Heading along the famous 'pipeline road' (so-called as it connects Tunisia's oil refineries in the deep south to the rest of the country), you enter the Sahara proper, surrounded by the desert in Libya to your east and Algeria to your west. The entire bottom third of the country, with its triangular shape and straight colonial-era boundaries, is off-limits without special permits, which are straightforward to obtain for those intrepid enough to venture south. It is worth noting that southwestern Tunisia was not always as arid as we see today. The Sahara did not expand northwards until around 4500BC, and before this great climatic change much of the southwest was fertile savannah, where animals such as rhino and zebra thrived. In 2016, researchers from Tunisia's National Heritage Institute (INP) and the University of Oxford discovered Stone Age flint tools near Tozeur estimated to be up to 92,000 years old.

GAFSA GOVERNORATE *Telephone code: +76*

Approaching from the north or the east, Gafsa – the northernmost significant oasis town in Tunisia – hints at the desert treasures to be found to its south. Highlights in the governorate include the well-preserved Roman pools in Gafsa town, the vintage Lézard Rouge train which travels through Seldja Gorge, and the traditional Amazigh settlement of As-Sened.

GAFSA

History Gafsa was originally a centre of Capsian culture, some 9,000 years ago. Recent archaeological finds, some of which can be seen in the town's archaeological museum (page 343), attest to thousands of years of continuous occupation of this area by Mousterian, Aterian and Capsian cultures.

In 146BC, when the Roman Republic finally conquered the Carthaginians, it then turned its attention southwards and in 106BC conquered the Numidians, who controlled Gafsa (known as Capsa to the Romans). Following the Final War of the Roman Republic, Emperor Augustus's Third Augustan Legion built a road southwards from its base at Ammaedara (modern-day Haïdra, page 287) through Thelepte to Capsa. The town served as an important Roman settlement in Africa Proconsularis, both as a base from which the Romans protected their southern frontier and also as an administrative centre, especially for tax collection. In fact, Capsa served as the easternmost point of the Fossatum Africae (African ditch), a 750km-long series of defensive structures that stretched all the way to Setifis (Sétif) in Algeria.

Over the following centuries, despite the walls, the settlement changed hands from the Romans to the Vandals, and then to the Amazigh. For a short time, the Byzantine emperor Justinian I made Capsa the capital of the province of Byzacena (taking over from Hadrumetum, modern-day Sousse), and it was during this time that the city walls were expanded. The Arab armies of Okba ibn Nafi conquered Gafsa in AD688, although it did not maintain the same military significance under Arab rule: Okba ibn Nafi preferred to use Kairouan, 200km northeast, which he had founded 18 years previously.

During French colonial times, Gafsa took on new significance after phosphate deposits were discovered in 1885 in nearby Métlaoui (page 344), turning it into a hub for exporting these minerals. Later, during World War II, Gafsa saw heavy fighting and bombardment as the Allies and Axis powers battled for control of Tunisia. In

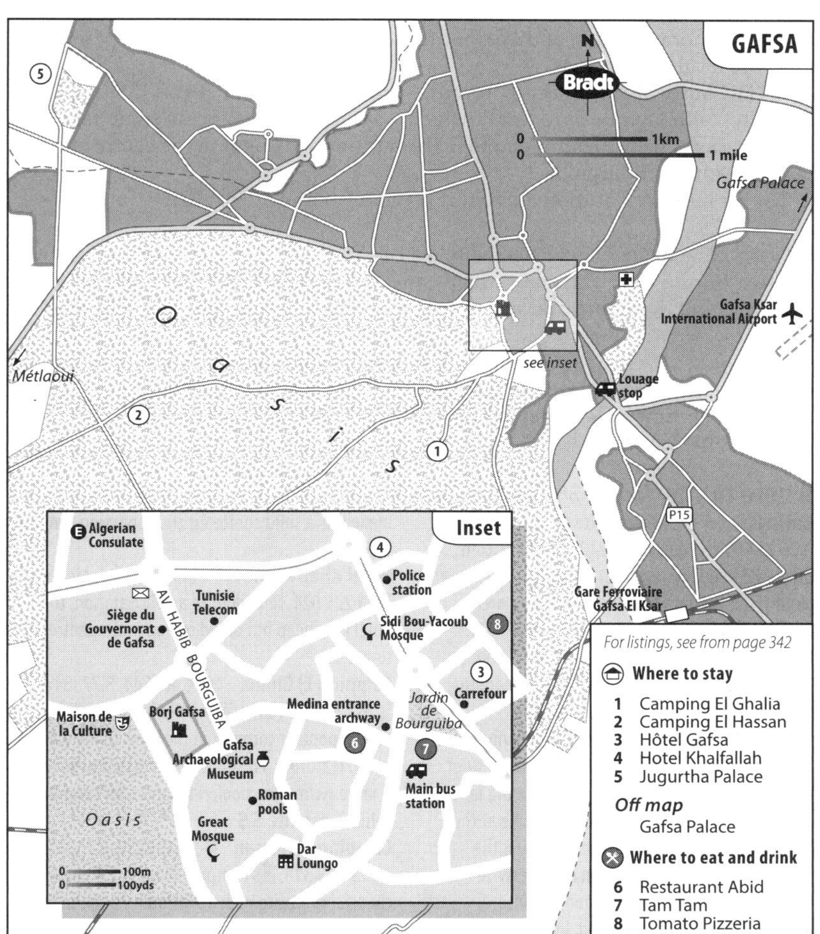

November 1942, US paratroopers fought an Italian tank brigade for control of the city's airfield. These periods of fighting destroyed sections of the city's 13th-century kasbah, which had been built by the Hafsids on Byzantine foundations.

In more recent times, Gafsa has acted as a hub for anti-government protest and even insurrection. On 27 January 1980, a group of men, armed and trained by Libya and calling themselves the Tunisian Liberation Army, attacked the city. The insurrection was eventually put down, but not before 48 people were killed. Likewise, in 2008 there were anti-government riots against the rule of President Ben Ali that were brutally suppressed by security forces. Historians point to this event as one of the catalysts for the Tunisian Revolution that took place two years later.

Getting there and around

By road Gafsa is 350km southwest of Tunis (5hrs on the P2 and P3). **Louage** services run to all neighbouring large settlements including Tozeur, Kebili, Gabès and Kasserine. There are two main louage stops: one in the southeast, by the river crossing to the train station (off Av Taïeb Mehiri), which tends to serve inter-governorate routes; and another more central one, by the MG supermarket, for more local destinations.

SNTRI **buses** also connect to Tozeur, Nefta, Kairouan and Tunis (5½hrs; 25DT one-way), although be sure to ask which way the bus is going as some take very indirect routes with 200km+ detours! The bus station is right in the centre of town, just off Jardin de Bourguiba.

For **car hire**, try Location de Voiture à Gafsa (m 58 477 351; f).

By rail The main Gare Ferroviaire Gafsa El Ksar is a few kilometres south of town on the P15. There are usually two trains per day to Tunis (8hrs) with a mid-morning departure and an overnight service. Tickets can be bought online (page 56).

By air Gafsa Ksar International Airport is 2km east of the town centre. It was closed at the time of writing, although Tunisair Express intermittently flies from here to Tunis-Carthage.

Where to stay *Map, page 341*

Gafsa Palace (159 rooms) Rte de Tunis, km3; ☎76 217 600; e gafsaplace2100@outlook.com. On the P3 heading northeast out of town near the airport, this modern business hotel has a great pool. **$$$$**

Hôtel Gafsa (38 rooms) 10 Rue Ahmed Snoussi; ☎76 224 000, 76 225 000. Good-value, modern hotel right in the centre of town. **$$$**

✷ **Jugurtha Palace** (118 rooms) Sidi Ahmed Zarroug; ☎76 211 200; e jugurtha.palace@gnet.tn; f Hôtel-Jugurtha-Palace-Gafsa. In the far northwest corner of town, this used to be at the heart of the Zone Touristique but today is the only decent hotel remaining in an otherwise abandoned area. Low prices, good service, massive old rooms & sprawling, leafy grounds make this a solid choice for those passing through. **$$$**

Hotel Khalfallah (11 rooms) Av Taïeb Mehiri; ☎76 225 624. Next door to a police station, this hotel is a cheap but dated option in the centre of town. **$$**

Camping El Ghalia ⊕ 34.405544, 8.778844; ☎76 229 135/165; e campingelghalia@gmail.com. A popular complex in the oasis to the west of town, featuring a restaurant, entertainment venue & large swimming pool. Has spaces for camping vehicles or tents. **$$**

Camping El Hassan ⊕ 34.409350, 8.750850; m 25 333 318; f Camping.Elhassan. A cheap-&-cheerful campsite with a swimming pool, situated in the oasis. **$**

Where to eat and drink *Map, page 341*

Tam Tam Rue Mongi Slim; ☎97 013 004; f Cafe.resto.TAMTAM; ⏱ 07.00–20.00 daily. Spread over 3 levels, this glass-fronted building offers views over the park & serves mainly Mediterranean fare including pasta, pizzas & seafood. **$$$**

Restaurant Abid Rue Kilani Metoui; ☎76 221 812; m 98 429 137; ⏱ 09.00–22.00 daily. A popular little restaurant serving traditional southern Tunisian cuisine. **$$**

Tomato Pizzeria Rue Abou el Kaccem Echebbi; m 23 429 319; ⏱ 09.00–22.00 daily. Excellent Neapolitan pizzas in a wooden-beamed dining hall. **$$**

Other practicalities There are branches of all Tunisia's main **banks** in Gafsa, with at least three ATMs accepting international cards centred around Jardin de Bourguiba near the bus station. The main **hospital** (Rue Ibn Sina; ☎76 100 200, 76 225 055) is in the east of town.

If you need a permit for one of the nearby national parks (page 291), head to the **government buildings** (officially Siège du Gouvernorat de Gafsa; Av Habib

Bourguiba; ☎ 76 228 060; e gov.gafsa@gmail.com; w gouvernorat-gafsa.gov.tn; f Gouvernorat.De.Gafsa; ⏰ 09.00–14.00 Mon–Fri) and visit the Direction Générale des Forêts, which is part of the Ministry of Agriculture. Ask security at the front gate which office to go to.

What to see and do

The old quarter Most of the main sights are clustered in the old quarter, west of the bus stop. Passing through the **archway** that denotes the entrance to Gafsa's **medina** you come to the souks and then, continuing southwards, the more open area containing the **Roman pools** – the last well-preserved remnants of Roman Capsa. They are popular in the summer with local children who perform acrobatic jumps into the deep water for eager spectators in the cafés nearby. Also here is the **Gafsa Archaeological Museum** (Pl des Piscines; ⏰ winter 09.30–16.30 Tue–Sun, summer 07.30–noon & 15.00–19.00; 5/4DT foreigners/Tunisians & residents), featuring an impressive collection of artefacts spanning over 8,000 years, all the way from the Neolithic era through to the Roman Empire. These include Capsian stone tools and mosaics depicting ancient Roman athletics events, including boxing and pankration (a precursor to modern mixed martial arts).

Less than 100m from the museum is **Dar Loungo** (☎ 76 223 759; e asm.gafsa@planet.tn; w asmgafsa.org.tn; ⏰ 09.00–16.00 Mon–Fri, 09.00–15.00 Sat). Built in 1818, this fully restored home gives an idea of what life was like for the wealthy landowning class during the time of the beys, and was possibly owned by a prominent local Jewish family. Inside you enter a large courtyard, with luxurious apartments upstairs and a museum of local craft items downstairs. The roof terrace also offers great views of the surrounding town.

Just west of this is one of the largest mosques in the country, Gafsa's **Great Mosque**, originally built by the Aghlabids around the 9th century and then significantly expanded during the Hafsid dynasty in the 14th century. The other major religious structure in town is the much more modern **Sidi Bou-Yacoub Mosque**, just north of the medina, with its distinctive white dome topped by a crescent moon and three spheres.

To the northwest is the **Borj Gafsa**, the town's imposing kasbah, whose main entrance is off Avenue Habib Bourguiba. It was originally built by the Byzantines around AD540 then adapted by the Hafsids; in 1663, the Ottoman beys added bastions and adapted the walls to deal with artillery fire. Unfortunately, during World War II it served as an Allied munitions dump which exploded in 1943, partially destroying the walls. Today the kasbah is a popular spot in the evenings, and often hosts a bazaar. A southern section of the structure is also set aside as **Cinema El Borj**, although this was closed at the time of writing, while nestled in the southwestern corner are the **Jewish baths** (*mikveh*), which date to Roman times. These baths were originally used by Gafsa's ancient Jewish community for purification rituals, although sadly today they have fallen into disrepair and are full of litter. Just behind the kasbah is the **Maison de la Culture** (☎ 76 225 039; ⏰ 10.00–18.30 daily), easily spotted by the rusty metal horse statue in the grounds. It has a theatre as well as an outdoor café, and hosts various cultural events throughout the year.

The oasis If you continue walking westwards from the kasbah you will enter Gafsa's oasis. Home to over 100,000 palm trees spread across 700ha, it is most famous for its pistachios and apricots, which Gafsans will proudly tell you are among the best in Tunisia. The oasis has been designated as a Globally Important Agricultural Heritage System by the Food and Agriculture Organization of the

United Nations. The Association pour la Sauvegarde de la Médina de Gafsa also works to conserve Gafsa's oasis, and can provide more information on how best to enjoy the site, as well as a map.

AROUND GAFSA

Métlaoui Almost 40km southwest of Gafsa on the P3 is the phosphate-mining town of Métlaoui (Al-Metlawi). The phosphate deposits were first discovered by French veterinarian and amateur geologist Philippe Thomas when he visited in 1885, and though Métlaoui remains a busy mining town, since the Musée National des Mines closed down a few years ago there is little reason for tourists to stop here now – that is, of course, unless you are a train enthusiast (see below).

Seldja Gorge With expansive sandstone cliffs rising to 200m in sections, this gorge 9km northwest of Métlaoui was, for centuries, a hub in a trade network stretching from the Mediterranean into the Sahara. Under the Carthaginians, and then the Romans, caravans would head southwards from the coast via Sbeïtla and Thelepte before passing through the gorge, and then continuing via Gightis (off the coast of Djerba) and then Ghadames, an oasis town in modern-day Libya. Today the gorge has a railway line through it (newly repaired following landslides), connecting the phosphate-mining towns of Métlaoui and Redeyef.

To reach the gorge, take the C122 road northwards from Métlaoui towards Moularès; after 13km there is a left turn on to another paved road (⊕ 34.405904, 8.425847), signed to Kef Edour, which you follow for 10km to Selja train station, which sits at the northern entrance to the gorge (⊕ 34.385415, 8.340136). Note that the entire area around the station is an active phosphate mine, so be sure not

THE LÉZARD ROUGE ✷ ⚑

A trip on this historic train, built in France in 1910, is a true highlight of a visit to Gafsa Governorate. Originally owned by the last beys of the Husseinite dynasty in Tunis, it was used to transport them in luxury between the royal palace in Bardo and the coastal resort areas of La Marsa and Hammam-Lif, right on the eastern coastal border between Greater Tunis and Nabeul Governorate. Featuring velvet interiors and dark wooden panelling and painted royal red, the six-carriage train was decommissioned in 1957, but then lovingly restored in 1974 and put back to work as a tourist train, plying the 35km, 1¾-hour return route between Métlaoui and Selja train station.

Sadly, economic factors – combined with a series of landslides in the gorge – mean that the train hasn't been running since 2017, instead sitting in storage in the railway sidings at Métlaoui. In July 2021, the SNCFT finally managed to repair the track in the gorge, meaning that phosphate exports could resume on the line also used by the Lézard Rouge. However, at the time of writing, it remains to be seen whether this luxury tourist train will start taking passengers again – although according to the Facebook page, this might happen in 2023. If it does resume, reservations were historically handled by a private society operating from the train station in Métlaoui (☎76 241 469; **m** 93 592 962; **e** lezardrouge@topnet.tn; **w** lezard-rouge.com; **f** le.lezard.rouge), with departures from Métlaoui at 10.30 every two or three days.

to trespass if you intend to hike into the gorge from here. There are no tourist facilities down here and no trail markings. You can also reach the gorge on foot from Métlaoui by hiking 6km northeast from town to the rock passage known as the Coup de Sabre ('sword cut'; ⊕ 34.336611, 8.334560). The gorge is subject to flash floods, so be sure to check weather reports before hiking into it. It's also worth checking the train timetable in Métlaoui before you go walking into one of the tunnels in the gorge.

As-Sened Complete with troglodyte houses built into the hillside, this Amazigh settlement is 50km east of Gafsa, just south of the modern town of Sened on the P14. The caves here are large, so the houses have standard-height doors and large chambers with relatively high ceilings. Many of the inhabitants here were recorded as still speaking Tamazight well into the 20th century. Every year, they host the Festival National des Grottes Montagneuses de Sened, a week-long celebration of Amazigh sports and culture (though this has not happened since the pandemic).

El Guettar Famed for its pistachio nuts, this agricultural town is 20km southeast of Gafsa along the P15. In the morning, the approach road is one of the most beautiful in the country, with the cloud-capped Jebel Orbata to your north across the plain. This area was also the scene of a significant tank battle during World War II (23 March 1943), during which US general George Patton's forces were, for the first time, able to defeat German tank units, following the disaster of the Battle of the Kasserine Pass (page 284) the previous month.

Just south of El Guettar is the road to **Jebel Orbata National Park**, but at the time of writing this was closed to tourists because of security issues and it is unclear if there is any tourism infrastructure currently in place in the park. Those wishing to visit should seek further information from an accredited tour agency (page 40) or visit the ministry directly in Gafsa (page 343) or Tunis (page 209). Foreigners are currently being denied entry to the area on the C124 road that runs parallel to the mountain chain (see page 49 for more details).

Sidi Aïch This town, 40km north of Gafsa, is home to a pair of well-preserved but unidentified Roman mausoleums (⊕ 34.732505, 8.774310), barely 200m north of the main road through town and with an incredible backdrop of the mountains that mark the boundary between Gafsa and Kasserine governorates to the north. The area around the two mausoleums was a production site for African red slipware, a distinctive type of ancient Roman pottery produced in Africa Proconsularis from between the 1st and 7th centuries AD.

The town's other claim to fame is that it was the birthplace of Mohammed Gammoudi, the legendary 5,000m and 10,000m runner who won four Olympic medals across three sets of games between 1964 and 1972.

TOZEUR AND AROUND

The true capital of the Djerid region, Tozeur provides visitors with all the romanticism they would expect from an oasis settlement: rolling sand dunes, thousands of palm trees, ancient desert architecture and camels aplenty. It is also a centre for Star Wars tourism, being home to some of the most iconic filming sites in the country, especially the Lars Homestead exterior out on the Chott el Djerid salt flats. Like Douz to the southeast, it also serves as a hub for desert tourism.

HISTORY Tozeur is strategically located between two seasonal *chotts* (salt lakes): the vast Chott el Djerid, to the south, and the Chott el Gharsa to the north. Human settlement here goes back at least to Roman times, no doubt because of the abundant water close to the surface. Tozeur was conquered by the Muslim Amazigh dynasties which came out of Morocco in the early Middle Ages. It was the key town in a region known as Kastiliya, perhaps because of the number of abandoned Roman forts or *castella*. Tozeur basically remained an independent statelet, until brought under Hafsid rule in the later Middle Ages. The settlement was dominated by rivalry between different groups, which often erupted into open feuding. In the 18th and 19th centuries, Tozeur was the final stop on the bey's annual tax-gathering expedition (*mahalla*).

Under the Protectorate, Tozeur remained an independent-minded sort of place. Charles Lallemand, propagandist for French rule in the late 1800s, noted that there was little interest in modern, European education, unlike the rest of Tunisia where demand was huge. Traditional forms of learning remained strong, and it is hardly surprising that the town produced Abou el Kacem Chabbi, the romantic poet who wrote of love and freedom and was adopted as Tunisia's national bard after independence.

GETTING THERE AND AROUND

By air Tozeur-Nefta International Airport is amazingly close to the town centre, less than 2.5km northwest of the train station. Tunisair Express usually runs two flights per week from Tunis (1hr 10mins; Thu & Sun).

By road Tozeur sits on the northwestern banks of the Chott el Djerid endorheic salt lake. Those coming from Tunis and the coast tend to arrive on the spectacular P16 road via Kebili, which takes you over the salt lake (inaccurately marked as an actual lake on some mapping software), while those coming from Gafsa will approach along the P3 road.

Louages run to all neighbouring large settlements including Nefta, Gafsa, Kebili and Gabès, while SNTRI **buses** connect to Tunis (7hrs; 30DT one-way), Douz, Sidi Bouzid, Gafsa, Sousse and Kairouan. The main louage stop and bus station are opposite each other, right in the centre of town on Avenue Farhat Hached.

By rail The main train station is in the northeast of town, where the P3 and C106 roads merge. Tozeur sits at the end of the line from Tunis and there are usually two trains per day (9½hrs), with a morning departure and an overnight service. Tickets can be bought online (page 56).

LOCAL TOUR OPERATORS

South Explorer Services Av Abdul El Kacem Chebbi; 76 468 200; m 54 448 511; e contact@south-explorer.com; f. Organises desert trips across the south in a fleet of white Toyota Land Cruisers.

WHERE TO STAY *Map, opposite*

Just outside town is one of the most luxurious hotels in the country: Anantara Tozeur. Those wishing to stay more centrally have an excellent selection of dars either in the medina or the Palmeraie (the cultivated palm oasis immediately southeast of town).

Luxury

✷ **Anantara Tozeur** (93 suites, villas & pool villas) Mrah Lahwar; 70 100 800; w anantara.com/en/sahara-tozeur. A Qatari-owned 5-star resort, 5km southwest of town. The levels of opulence on display seem a little

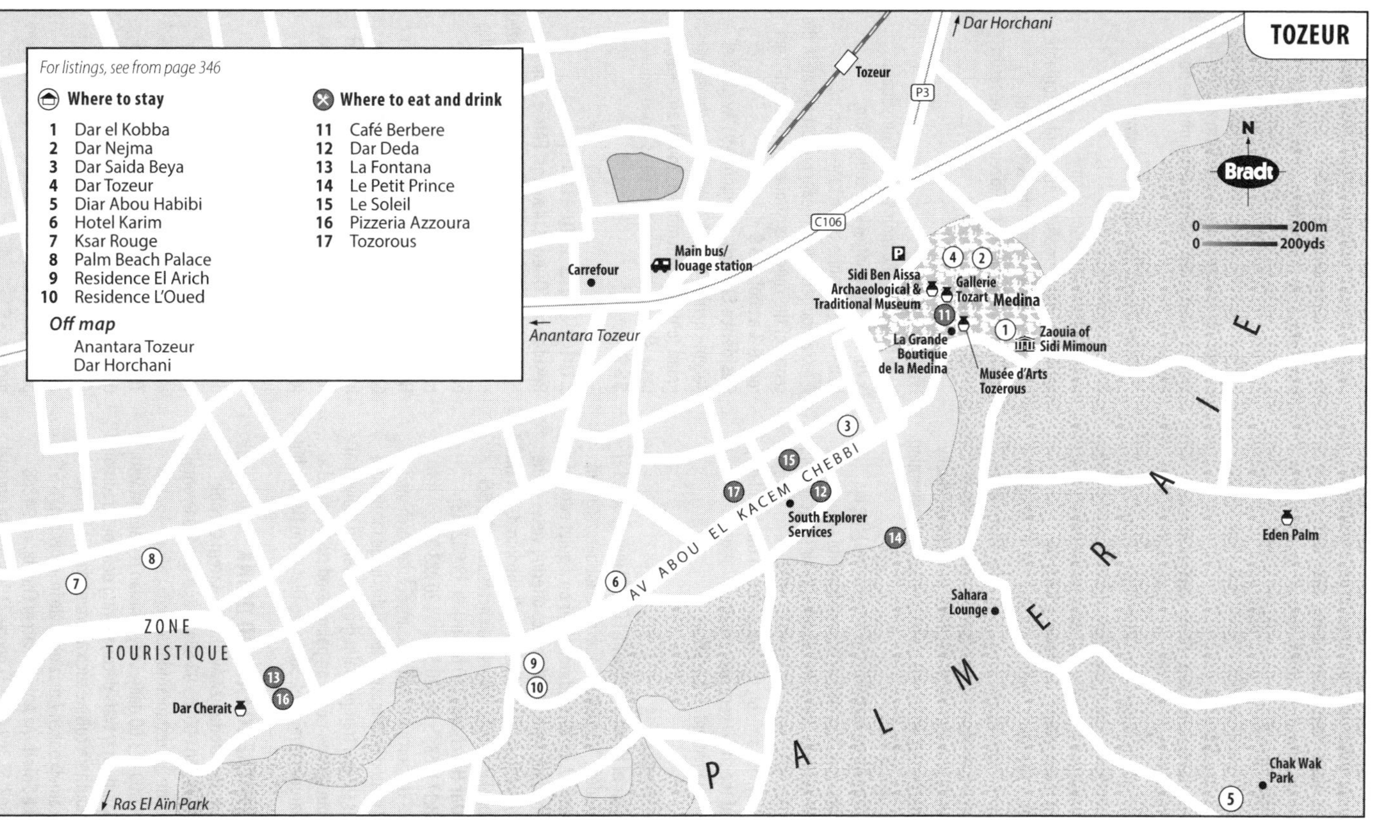
TOZEUR
For listings, see from page 346
Where to stay
1 Dar el Kobba
2 Dar Nejma
3 Dar Saida Beya
4 Dar Tozeur
5 Diar Abou Habibi
6 Hotel Karim
7 Ksar Rouge
8 Palm Beach Palace
9 Residence El Arich
10 Residence L'Oued
Off map
Anantara Tozeur
Dar Horchani
Where to eat and drink
11 Café Berbere
12 Dar Deda
13 La Fontana
14 Le Petit Prince
15 Le Soleil
16 Pizzeria Azzoura
17 Tozorous
Dar Horchani
Tozeur
P3
C106
N
Bradt
0 200m
0 200yds
Carrefour
Main bus/ louage station
Anantara Tozeur
Sidi Ben Aissa Archaeological & Traditional Museum
Gallerie Tozart
Medina
La Grande Boutique de la Medina
Zaouia of Sidi Mimoun
Musée d'Arts Tozerous
AV ABOU EL KACEM CHEBBI
South Explorer Services
Eden Palm
Sahara Lounge
PALMERAIE
ZONE TOURISTIQUE
Dar Cherait
Chak Wak Park
Ras El Aïn Park

incongruous with the Tunisian desert context: an Asian-themed restaurant, villas with private pools, a luxurious spa & even an *Arabian Nights*-themed souk & entertainment complex. The quality of accommodation here is a rare find for Tunisia. **$$$$$**

✷ **Dar Saida Beya** (9 rooms) Rue Ahmed El Ayech; 76 452 331; m 25 566 066; w darsaidabeya.com. Luxuriously decorated boutique hotel in the heart of Tozeur, with its own hammam & a great rooftop terrace offering views of the medina & the oasis. **$$$$$**

Dar Tozeur (7 rooms) Medina; m 98 318 252; w dartozeur.com. An oasis of calm on the edge of the medina, featuring a number of green & leafy interior courtyards. Each suite is individually decorated, & there is an on-site spa & 2 swimming pools. **$$$$$**

Diar Abou Habibi (16 tree-houses) Rte de Touareg; 76 460 270; w diarhabibi.com. Beautifully decorated wooden cabins perched high up in the canopy of the oasis palms. A relaxing stay, but difficult to book owing to the popularity of the site & very poor communication from management. **$$$$$**

Upmarket

Dar el Kobba (3 rooms) Oued Lihoud, Ouled el Hadeff; 53 840 774; e darelkobbatoz@gmail.com. A small, traditional dar on a quiet edge of the medina, with a roof terrace offering views of the oasis. Rooms are clean & well appointed. Advanced bookings only. Wheelchair accessible. **$$$$**

Dar Horchani (10 rooms) ⊕ 33.982348, 8.171663; 76 420 594; m 20 283 273; e darhorchani@yahoo.com; f darhorchani2017. Located northeast of town, this large farmhouse is set in a tranquil palm grove, offering individual bungalows raised on palm-wood stilts around a large central pool. Similar to Diar Abou Habibi, but cheaper & much easier to contact! Meals available by prior arrangement. **$$$$**

Dar Nejma (6 rooms) Medina; m 98 318 252; e darnejma@gmail.com; f darnejma. Owned by the same team as Dar Tozeur, this is another beautifully restored townhouse with a castle-like interior courtyard featuring an impressive pool. **$$$$**

Palm Beach Palace (128 rooms) Zone Touristique; 76 453 211; w magichotelsandresorts.com/palmbeachpalacetozeur. Surprisingly affordable, with generously sized rooms & excellent facilities, this is the best of Tozeur's large resort hotels. **$$$$**

Mid-range

Ksar Rouge (180 rooms) Zone Touristique; 76 454 933; e info@ksar-rouge.com, ksar-rouge@orange.tn; w ksar-rouge.tn; f KsarRougeHotel. A cheaper resort option in the centre of the Zone Touristique, with decent-sized rooms & a pool. **$$$**

Residence El Arich (20 rooms) 93 Av Abou el Kacem Chebbi; 76 462 644; e elarichtozeur@gmail.com; f elarichtozeur. Rooms are clean & basic, some with views over oasis. Good value. **$$$**

Budget and shoestring

Residence L'Oued (14 rooms) Entrée Sahraoui; 76 463 036; f residenceloued. Generously sized rooms in this good-value hotel with a pool on the edge of the Palmeraie. Staff are able to arrange tours & vehicle rentals. **$$**

Hotel Karim (22 rooms) 50 Av Abou El Kacem Chebbi; 76 454 574. The cheapest decent bed in town, some with shared bathrooms. The tiled rooms vary in size so check before picking. Good rooftop terrace. **$–$$**

WHERE TO EAT AND DRINK *Map, page 347*

✷ **Dar Deda** 27 Av Abou El Kacem Chebbi; 76 460 000; m 98 694 198; e dardeda@gmail.com; f restaurantdardeda; ⌚ noon–16.00 & 18.00–23.00 daily. Cosy Tunisian restaurant with subtle Star Wars décor, serving delicious traditional southern cuisine such as *dromadaire à la jarre* – camel cooked Amazigh-style in a clay pot. **$$$**

Le Soleil Av Abou El Kacem Chebbi; m 94 868 567, 53 369 448; ⌚ noon–22.30 daily. An unusual dining experience: come here to savour delicious traditional Tunisian cuisine in the shade of an artificial palm tree, with a techno soundtrack. **$$$**

Tozorous 86 Av Abou El Kacem Chebbi; m 95 603 783, 20 932 634; e tozeurous@hotmail.fr; ⌚ 10.00–23.00 Tue–Sun. Traditional Tunisian cuisine, including some delicious sharing plates, in a friendly atmosphere. Good value for money. **$$$**

La Fontana Av Abou El Kacem Chebbi; 76 462 776; m 98 296 209; LaFontanaTozeur; 10.00–23.00 daily. Popular family pizza & Mediterranean cuisine restaurant overlooking the main square, where quad bikes & horse-drawn carriages park up in the hope of luring in tourists emerging from the nearby all-inclusive hotels. $$–$$$

Le Petit Prince Palmeraie; 76 452 518; e petitprince.tozeur@gmail.com; 10.00–late daily. Once a popular restaurant, this is now a rare find: a bar on the edge of the Palmeraie. For fans of Celtia & Tunisian drum & bass! $$

Pizzeria Azzoura Av Abou El Kacem Chebbi; m 97 346 500, 52 805 805; 10.00–midnight daily. Pizza restaurant in the tourist quarter, with a pleasant green terrace. $$

Café Berbere Medina; m 50 719 277; berberecafe; 08.30–21.30 daily. Open-air café in the heart of the medina, offering panoramic views of the 14th-century surroundings. A welcome, shaded rest stop while exploring. $–$$

SHOPPING

La Grande Boutique de la Medina Ouled El Hadef; m 50 719 277; lagrandeboutiquedelamedina; 10.00–19.00 daily. On the same square as Café Berbere, this treasure trove of artisanal products is spread across 3 floors, including antiques, leather goods, jewellery, rugs & pottery. Also accepts international card payments, which is highly unusual for Tunisia.

WHAT TO SEE AND DO

The medina Dating to the 14th century, Tozeur's medina is one of the best preserved in the country. While it may not have the vast ribats and towering minarets found in Sousse or Tunis, its architecture is still remarkably striking. Look out for the three-dimensional patterns displayed on brick walls, which serve to cast small shadows and keep the outside of buildings cool in the summer heat.

The best place to start a walking tour of the medina is at the north end near Dar Tozeur, as this is the easiest spot to park or get dropped by a taxi. Your first port of call should be the **Sidi Ben Aissa Archaeological and Traditional Museum** (m 97 091 083; 08.00–noon & 15.00–18.00 Tue–Sun; 5DT), a 14th-century tomb converted into a museum covering popular traditions such as carpet weaving, all enthusiastically explained by the guides in an immersive experience. The central courtyard is also filled with displays of local arts and crafts. About 50m down the street is **Galerie Tozart** (m 98 629 676; e raoudha.bribech@yahoo.fr; w ibike.org/africaguide/Tozart/index.htm; irregular hours, contact owner), owned by artist Raoudha Bribech and featuring works by her and a variety of other local artists. The space also hosts cultural events from time to time.

From here, you can head another 50m south to stop at Café Berbere for a drink (see above) or La Grande Boutique de la Medina next door to pick up some gifts. In this same square is the **Musée d'Arts Tozeurous** (09.00–18.00 Sat–Thu; 5DT). Easily recognisable by its yellow geometric brickwork front – a traditional technique that was imported from Iraq in the 10th century – this small museum features traditionally made puppets as well as other artworks, though note it was closed at the time of writing. Your final stop is the **Zaouia of Sidi Mimoun** (closed to non-Muslims) another 180m to the southwest, right at the southern edge of the medina. Dedicated to the 16th-century historical figure, it continues to be a religiously significant site today and has an information sign outside in English, French and Arabic.

Palmeraie At the southeast of town, Tozeur's 17km^2 oasis palm orchard was developed around a 13th-century irrigation system. The best place to learn more about the Palmeraie is at the wonderfully informative **Eden Palm** ✱ (76 454 474;

m 58 085 059; e info@eden-palm.com; w eden-palm.com; ⌚ 08.30–20.00 daily; 6DT). This complex, dedicated to showcasing the treasures of its working date palm orchard, offers guided tours of the museum and the palm grove, with information panels in English, French and Arabic. I had no idea the history of date cultivation was so fascinating; for example, did you know they put dates into HP sauce? There is also a shop selling locally produced palm products and a restaurant offering delicious local specialities, which you can eat outside under the palms (this generally needs to be booked in advance).

The Palmeraie also offers a couple of family-friendly attractions, and those travelling with children could easily spend a whole day down here, splitting their time between two equally entertaining sights. At **Sahara Lounge** (☎ 71 720 800; m 29 631 411, 50 287 900; e sales@sahara-lounge.com; f SAHARA.LOUNGE.Tozeur; activities from 15/10DT adult/child), an extensive ropes course explores the Palmeraie canopy, and there's also a zip line, climbing wall and paintballing. Slightly more bizarre but no less entertaining, **Chak Wak Park** (☎ 76 460 400; e chakwak@planet.tn; f parcchakwak; ⌚ 10.00–19.00 daily; 15/5DT adult/child) is the brainchild of former Tozeur mayor, Abderrazak Cheraït. Scattered around the grounds are life-size models that tell the history of the planet, all the way from the evolution of the dinosaurs to modern times (via the Carthaginians, of course). There is also a section on icons from world religions, plus a good bar and pizza restaurant.

Zone Touristique At the far western end of town is the Zone Touristique, home to Tozeur's package-holiday hotels. There are, however, a couple of sights worth seeking out. The long-established **Dar Cherait** (☎ 76 452 188; f darcheraittozeur; ⌚ 08.00–22.00 daily; 10/5DT adults/children) is a private museum housing three different spaces: a collection of art and popular tradition; the 'Médina of 1001 Nights', which is a park featuring entertaining displays aimed at children; and Dar Zamen, a 45-minute sound and light show summarising 3,000 years of Tunisian history. It's all a little bit Disneyland, but highly entertaining for those with children in tow. A kilometre southwest is **Ras El Aïn Park** (⊕ 33.908415, 8.111352), also known as Belvedere or Tozeur Park, and perhaps Tunisia's answer to Mount Rushmore. Also spearheaded by former Tozeur mayor, Abderrazak Cheraït, in the 1990s, these rock formations have been carved into majestic figures, including an eagle and the face of Tozeur-born national poet, Abou el Kacem Chebbi, on which visitors like to climb to be photographed.

AROUND TOZEUR

Degache and around Just 13km north of Tozeur on the C106, the town of Degache may not be worth a visit in its own right but the tranquil oasis to the south certainly is, especially if you want to visit a less-developed palmeraie than the one in Tozeur. Here you will find charming **Dar Nanoo** (m 24 235 137; e yassertirellile@gmail.com; **$$–$$$**); looking like a fortress from the outside thanks to the large wooden doors, the interior hides a verdant set of gardens with small yellow-brick bungalows hidden among the foliage. The restaurant here is also very popular. Further north is the **Mosque of Awled Majed** (⊕ 33.995543, 8.242614), its imposing minaret towering over the surrounding palm forest; the mosque dates to 1330 but was renovated in 2021.

Continuing northeast from Degache, you eventually reach an unmarked turning (⊕ 34.020630, 8.288822) where a road snakes north to the well-preserved **zaouias of Sidi Bouhlel and Sidi Ben Abbes**, perched at the mouth of a canyon, overlooking the

MAGUER GORGE (SIDI BOUHLEL)

Davin Anderson, Galaxy Tours (w galaxytours.com)

Nicknamed 'Star Wars Canyon' because of its prolific use by Lucasfilm crews, Maguer Gorge (⊕ 34.036182, 8.280345) served as the rocky mesa desert canyon setting for two distinct *Episode IV* locations on Tatooine: the Jundland Wastes and a desert wasteland bluff overlooking Mos Eisley. The natural landscape of the gorge – which incidentally was the largest and visibly most diverse Star Wars film site in Tunisia – required limited set dressings, and local Tunisian (possibly Amazigh) graffiti scratched into the eastern gorge wall near the landspeeder location was incorporated into the Jundland Wastes aesthetics.

Film crews returned to the gorge in 1997 for *Episode I* to shoot sniper sequences at fictional Canyon Dune Turn, part of the Mos Espa podrace circuit on Tatooine. No set dressings or major props were needed for the one-day shoot, which involved four local extras in Tusken Raider costumes.

Despite some litter and Star Wars-inspired graffiti dotted around the area, Maguer Gorge remains one of the best-preserved Star Wars film sites in Tunisia and arguably the most exciting to explore.

surrounding desert. Much of the appeal here lies in the hike up the canyon, known locally as **Maguer Gorge** or **Sidi Bouhlel** (but also nicknamed '**Star Wars Canyon**') as the site was used by George Lucas as a filming location for *Episode IV – A New Hope* in 1976 and *Episode I – The Phantom Menace* in 1997. But it isn't just in Star Wars that this canyon has been seen on the silver screen: Steven Spielberg also used the area to film scenes from *Raiders of the Lost Ark* in 1980, while parts of *The Little Prince* (1974) and *The English Patient* (1996) were also shot here.

For true Indiana Jones aficionados, if you continue back to the main road and head further east, a dirt track turn-off (⊕ 34.023830, 8.297041) leads north to an isolated date palm orchard, which served as the Tanis Digs set for *Raiders of the Lost Ark*, including the exterior of the map room (⊕ 34.031213, 8.293410) and the entrance to the Well of Souls (⊕ 34.031212, 8.29266). Be prepared for some very confused looks from the local farmers as you wander around the palm groves with your GPS device! If you don't fancy going it alone, Tunisian outfit **WildyNess** (m 90 675 385; e hello@wildyness.com; w wildyness.com) runs organised hiking tours along this route.

NORTH OF TOZEUR Within easy day-tripping distance of Tozeur (60km north), close to the border with Algeria, are the much-touted mountain oases of Chebika, Tamerza and Midès.

Chebika This is the closest of the three mountain oases to Tozeur, 55km northwest along the P16, and at peak times is often filled with tour groups eager to see where scenes from *The English Patient* were filmed. The location has been inhabited since Roman times, when it was known as Ad Speculum, although the settlement on the mountainside was abandoned during the disastrous nationwide flooding of October 1969 which left over 300,000 Tunisians homeless. The new modern village is down by the roadside and clearly signposted. If you come in the late afternoon and hike into the gorge, past the picturesque little waterfall (which people sometimes swim in), you will be rewarded with views of an incredible sunset over Algeria. There is a café with a toilet and a series of the usual tourist gift shops.

Tamerza Also spelt Tameghza, this is another 14km north up the P16. Just before you reach it, you will wind your way up to a lookout point signposted as **Panorama Canyon** (⊕ 34.366439, 7.908001). There is small café here where you can sip tea or a cold drink while looking out across the expansive Algerian desert plains below. By this stage, the border is only 5km to the west. Of the three oases, Tamerza is the most developed in terms of tourism infrastructure. As you enter town from the south, the first thing you will see is the Station Touristique Grande Cascade, a large orange building, presumably a tourist information centre, closed at the time of writing. The **Grande Cascade** itself is signposted from here, but do not get your hopes up – even with peak water flow it is an underwhelming waterfall, often crowded with people selling trinkets. Instead, it's better to veer off the road just after the bridge (⊕ 34.379183, 7.916297) and drive through the oasis itself, still under cultivation. Scenes from *The English Patient* were also filmed here.

Where to stay and eat

Les Cascades (10 rooms) 98 543 093. Down on the river itself, this hotel & restaurant has a well-positioned terrace overlooking the waterfall. Camping also allowed. **$$**

Résidence des Oasis Montagneuses (8 rooms) 76 485 419; m 28 550 348; e haffoudhiwalid@gmail.com. A good budget option for accommodation, especially in the summer as the rooms have AC. **$$**

Restaurant La Tente m 97 762 127; ⊕ noon–22.00 daily. Within the oasis itself, this has an outdoor traditional dining area with tents providing shade. **$$$**

Restaurant de Soleil 76 485 296; m 98 283 239; ⊕ 09.00–21.30 daily. Just as you come into town, serving traditional food. **$$**

Midès The northernmost of the three oases – and the closest to the Algerian border, which is only 500m from the centre of the village – has a heavy security presence, with a Garde National base at the northern end of the settlement. The gorge itself is the main attraction, and it is possible to trek to the various cafés dotted along the northern rim, from which you can see the abandoned old village. There is a campsite at the western end of the oasis called **Camping El Hassi** (93 393 581; **$**), where scenes from *The English Patient* were also filmed.

NEFTA

During Ottoman rule, this oasis town was famed across the Sahara as a spiritual place, though arriving today your initial impression may be more of a dust-blown outpost town. From the cliffs above the Corbeille (surely the only oasis to be set in what looks like a large crater) there are sensational views of the town below, while on its clifftop is the brooding mass of the now-abandoned Sahara Palace. Opposite, across the Corbeille, is the El Bayadha quarter, where domes signalling the tombs of holy men tower above the low sand-brown buildings. Spend an afternoon exploring the alleyways, still suffused by a certain spirituality, but better still, head off into the palm groves where, at the right time of year, it will be possible to get a taste of the local 'palm wine', or the dates for which Nefta is famous. The town is also a good jumping-off point for Star Wars fans to visit various filming sites, including the iconic Lars Homestead. Once a year, it also plays host to the Ultra Mirage El Djerid, a pair of ultra-marathons through the desert to the north of town.

HISTORY The area around Nefta was settled back in ancient times, when it was known as Aggersel Nepte. In the 11th century, the town was destroyed for refusing to pay taxes to Tunis. Rebuilt, Nefta became an important sufi centre by the 16th century. The cult of saints fell into disrepute after independence, and Nefta no doubt suffered.

Similar to Iran and Turkey, North Africa was to prove fertile ground for the cult of saints. Shrines of earlier animist Amazigh or Roman deities tended to take on Islamic identities, but why Nefta in particular should have proved such a centre for mystic Islam is something of a mystery. There are said to be over 125 shrines in the area. Some, such as the Zaouia of Sidi Bou Ali, were extremely important, attracting adepts from far afield.

It may be that Sufism held a greater attraction for the peoples of the peripheral Islamic regions where there were already deep-rooted forms of religious practice. Sufism offers spiritual development through means other than the study of the Koran; only a select few adherents actually achieve the highest stages of sufi practice. Sufism was rejected by orthodox Islam but became quite popular due to the freedom it offered within the confines of mainstream Sunni Islam.

WHERE TO STAY AND EAT

✷ ⚑ **Dar Hi Life** (18 rooms & suites) Quartier Ezzaouia; ☎ 76 432 779; w darhilife.com. The creation of French industrial designer Matali Crasset, this is one of the most architecturally striking boutique ecohotels in Tunisia. Despite the strong, bold style & elements of brutalist architecture, the buildings fit perfectly with their oasis environment thanks to the colour composition, mimicking the ochres & pinks of the surrounding desert. Because of their floor-to-ceiling windows, each of the hotel's 9 raised living pods (*pilotis*), some of which are suites, has panoramic views of the Corbeille below, as well as Chott el Djerid. They also offer rooms & suites named 'troglodyte' & 'dune' that are dug into the hillside. The central pool is raised on stilts to offer better views, & is naturally heated by thermal spring water. **$$$$$**

Dar Zargouni (5 rooms) Rte Sahara Palace; ☎ 71 908 048; m 97 090 708, 98 621 920; e info@darzargouni.com; w darzargouni.com. A beautifully decorated traditional home made up of 2 separate courtyards, allowing independent access to the suites. Large open-plan living & dining area with a garden, pool & BBQ facilities, with views overlooking the Corbeille & the eerily abandoned Thermal Oasis hotel to the north. **$$$$–$$$$$**

Hotel Caravansérail (37 rooms) Zone Touristique, La Palmeraie; ☎ 76 430 399; m 92 045 908; e hotel.caravanserailnafta@planet.tn, contact@hotelcaravanserail.com; f caravanserailnefta. Large, clean rooms with bath, shower & balcony around a stone central courtyard with pool, overlooking the oasis to the south of town. **$$$**

Hotel Marhala Touring Club (50 rooms) Zone Touristique, La Palmeraie; ☎ 76 430 027; e marhala@yahoo.fr. The best budget option in town, this ageing 1-star hotel seems to survive mainly on selling Celtia to the locals. The rooms are nevertheless small but clean, & good value with AC at this price point. **$–$$**

Hotel Habib (10 rooms) Pl de la Libération; m 98 543 138, 52 011 470. Small rooms with not particularly clean shared bathrooms, but well located in the heart of Ouled ech Cherif. There is a larger suite upstairs with a fridge-freezer & terrace overlooking the square. **$**

Espace Ferdaous – Zombrita Grill m 52 563 871, 21 674 298; ⏲ 10.00–21.00 daily. With a wood-fired pizza oven & extensive outdoor seating overlooking the oasis, this is a relaxing spot for a meal (although watch out for the mosquitoes at dusk). **$$$**

WHAT TO SEE AND DO

Nefta's natural wonders Nefta's natural highlight is undoubtedly the **Corbeille** ('the basket' in French), a 1km-wide, 50m-deep basin which, hundreds of years ago, had springs flowing from its sides. Today the area is irrigated from an artificial pool in the northeastern corner. The Corbeille is best viewed from the northeastern ridgeline where Dar Hi Life and Dar Zargouni are located. From here you can also look across town and see the edge of Chott el Djerid and one of Tunisia's most famous Star Wars sites (see below).

To the south of town lies Nefta's **oasis**, home to around 400,000 palm trees, which produce some of the best dates in Tunisia. Some of the higher-end accommodation options in town (such as Dar Zargouni) can organise tours if you would like to see traditional farming methods in action.

Nefta town Nefta has two main neighbourhoods: **Ouled ech Cherif** on your right as you arrive from Tozeur, and **El Bayadha** to the west side of the Corbeille. Both neighbourhoods are well worth a stroll, particularly as not that many tourists make the effort, and together they are home to some 24 mosques.

In El Bayadha, at the head of the Corbeille, stands the **Zaouia of Sidi Ibrahim**, probably the most significant religious building in the neighbourhood for Sufi

NEFTA'S STAR WARS LOCATIONS

Davin Anderson, Galaxy Tours (w galaxytours.com)

LARS HOMESTEAD (EXTERIOR) (⊕ 33.842853, 7.779048) This was the first-ever filming location of the Star Wars franchise – first used in March 1976 for *Episode IV – A New Hope*, and then again in September 2000 for both *Episode II – Attack of the Clones* and *Episode III – Revenge of the Sith*. Chott el Djerid's epic landscape was chosen to represent the barren, salt-flat domain of moisture farmers on Tatooine. The homestead set (including a dome, garage crater with roof, hangar crater and living quarters crater) was constructed on three occasions as there was no structure on the site previously. Star Wars fans widely regard the Lars Homestead set as the cradle of the Star Wars universe. To preserve the legacy of the site, dedicated fans have restored the homestead dome on at least three occasions: Save Lars project volunteers in 2012, Discover Tatooine team members in 2018 and a Star Wars Tunisia team most recently in May 2022.

To get here, turn off the P3 at ⊕ 33.86492, 7.779603, where you will see a large walled complex with a domed hut on the south side of the road. In dry conditions a 4x4 is not required, but check if there has been rain recently – if so, you could get bogged down in the salt flat.

GOUR BENI MZAB (⊕ 33.871125, 7.759225) These sand dunes, 3.5km northwest of the Lars Homestead on the opposite side of the P3, served as the Tatooine dune-sea landscape for the life pod crash site and Krayt dragon skeleton scenes in *Episode IV*. However, the constantly shifting sands mean it is almost impossible to identify the exact set locations. An enormous fibreglass prop was used for the Krayt dragon (originally built and used for Disney's 1975 comedy *One of Our Dinosaurs is Missing*), and the bones were left behind by the crew. Although Star Wars collectors have excavated the vast majority of the skeleton, enterprising local Bedouins have claimed as many pieces as possible to sell (at relatively discounted prices) to enthusiasts who make the effort to explore this hard-to-visualise filming location.

Although only a few kilometres north of the tarmac P3, it has been known for 4x4s to get stuck in sand in this area, so be careful if venturing out alone.

adherents. It houses the tomb of a Sufi saint who was the descendant of the Prophet Muhammad, along with the tomb of his son and a number of close followers. Just southeast in the same area on the ridgeline is Sidi Salem's Mosque, also known as the **Great Mosque.** The title seems to be more related to its size than any particular significance, but the simple white structure is in a picturesque location overlooking the Corbeille. A little south of the town centre is the **Zaouia of Sidi Bou Ali**, another significant mausoleum in Nefta, dedicated to a holy man who came to Tunisia from Morocco in the 13th century. Pilgrims visit the zaouia to ask for the saint's blessing on important family occasions such as pregnancy, circumcision or marriage. The annual pilgrimage (*dakhla*) attracts pilgrims from both the Djerid and across the border in Algeria.

Star Wars Shop (Pl de la Libération, El Bayadha; 76 430 715; m 98 450 016, 25 298 986; by appointment) Nefta is famous for its Star Wars sites (see below), and local shop owner Kamel Souliah has capitalised on this success. He brokered a deal with CTV Services (Lucasfilm's Tunisian cinematographic partner for the Star

ERIGUET DUNES (33.994671, 7.848898) Meaning 'dune sea fields' in Arabic, Eriguet is the local appellation for the dynamic barchanoid dune landscape south of Chott el Gharsa. Composed of countless peripheral salt-saturated depressions that fill with minimal levels of salt water after intense rains, the dunes are spaced relatively close together, which creates a dynamic aeolian environment. Consistent winds sweep over the landscape primarily from the east, forming transverse barchanoid ridges in a fairly straight line, perpendicular to the wind.

Along with CTV Services Tunisia, Lucasfilm selected a remote clay-rich pan, approximately 14km northwest of Nefta, as the location for the Mos Espa marketplace set in *Episode I* in 1997. Heavily inspired by the hybrid Amazigh/Ibadi architectural design prevalent on Djerba, crews employed local labour and materials (wooden frames in plaster, wire mesh and sculpted foam) to construct 25 different exterior structures designed to form four north–south 'streets', leading to a wide central marketplace square. The majority of the filming on the set took place in the central square and the southeastern market street (decorated with food stalls and a café). Almost half of the set structures were intentionally left incomplete with no top portion/roof. Portable bluescreen backdrops were used on location to enable the inclusion of final architectural elements in post-production.

Lucasfilm returned to the set for *Episode II* production in September 2000, which focused on activity in front of Watto's Junkshop at the southwest end of the marketplace square. Constantly in danger of being engulfed by the surrounding dunes, ownership of the set currently rests in the hands of the Nefta Municipality. This is the only truly commercialised Star Wars site in Tunisia, and traders will be ready to sell you all sorts of trinkets as soon as you pull up. Every October, this area is also the start and finish line for the **Ultra Mirage El Djerid** (w ultramirage.com; f UltraMirageElDjerid), an incredible 50km and 100km ultra-marathon that winds its way across the salt flats and past the Star Wars film sets. The Mos Espa marketplace is near the start line, and runners on both courses snake around the Ong Jemel outcrop.

Today it is very easy to visit the Mos Espa marketplace, as there is a tarmac road leading all the way here from the northern end of Nefta. Note, however, that your phone signal might cut out part way into the desert along this road.

CROSSING INTO ALGERIA

There is a border crossing point at **Hazoua**, 37km west of Nefta on the P3, which is also home to an impressive geothermal fountain at ⊕ 33.751772, 7.592828. The P3 enters Algeria at the town of Taleb Larbi. Border opening hours are generally 07.00–19.00 daily, although restrictions can be imposed on Fridays, Sundays and national holidays (Algerian and Tunisian). See page 42 for more information.

Wars prequels) to assume exclusive rights to salvage for profit all set dressings and props left behind in the area after filming for *Episode I – The Phantom Menace* was complete. Kamel spent three weeks gathering truckloads of detachable memorabilia from the two sets, employing heavy lifting machinery and a crew of 20 labourers, in an effort to become *the* Tunisian galactic trader. Podracer engine parts and other large items forced Kamel to open a second shop in Nefta (now closed) from which to sell his Mos Espa collection to eager collectors and tourists. Though all podracer engines have now been sold on, one of them can be seen on display in the New Fly Restaurant in El Kantaoui (page 235). The largest prop piece still up for sale is a futuristic door from the set, with a price tag in the thousands of euros and members of foreign royal families rumoured to be interested.

KEBILI AND AROUND

Treated by most visitors simply as a refuelling stop en route to Douz or Tozeur, Kebili has a certain discreet charm.

Founded in 1892, modern Kebili had considerable military importance under the French given its strategic location at a meeting of the ways between Tozeur, Gabès and the desert settlements further south. A few kilometres southwest of the modern centre, old Kebili, like many of the traditional settlements in this part of the country, was abandoned following the flooding in 1969. Crumbling but still largely intact, the domed marabouts are perfectly preserved in the thick green shade of the palms, surrounded by fruit trees and vegetable patches. The area is home to the formerly nomadic Aoulad Yaghoub tribe of Kebili, who number around 3,000 today.

GETTING THERE AND AWAY Kebili is 515km southwest of Tunis (around a 5¼-hour drive on a fully tarmac road (all the way down the A1 then inland from Gabès along the P16). Louages connect to all neighbouring large settlements including Douz, Tozeur, Gafsa and Gabès. There are two main louage stops: to the north of town on the P16, and south near the Zone Touristique on the C206. The SNTRI bus station is to the north of town, near the regional hospital, with services to Tunis (7hrs; 35DT).

WHERE TO STAY Both Douz and Tozeur offer better accommodation options than Kebili. However, at the time of writing a new hotel was under construction opposite the Hotel du Autruches, which looked like it might be the best option in town once it opens.

Hotel Kitam (34 rooms) P16 Rte de Gabès; ☎ 75 491 465; m 98 320 307. Rooms are clean with 2 sgl beds, a toilet & shower, but no AC or heating. The downside is that the downstairs bar is packed with rowdy drinkers late into the night. **$$**

Residence Anis (14 rooms) Av Habib Bourguiba; ☎75 491 864; m 97 353 453; e ennajehlotfi@hotmail.fr. Despite having the feel of sterile temporary accommodation, this is probably the best bed in town at the time of writing: clean, spacious & the owner is very friendly. Rooms are available with en-suite or shared bathroom. **$$**

✷ **Les Amis du Camping** (4 bungalows, numerous pitches) Av Salah Ben Youssef; ☎75 492 710; m 98 567 663; f arafat.sghaier. This popular overlanders' campsite has some basic bungalows with plug sockets & lights or you can park up & pitch a tent. Dinners can be organised for 20DT pp, there is a palmeraie out back & the friendly, experienced & English-speaking owner, Arafat, can organise tours of the area. Expect a warm welcome! **$–$$**

Maison Des Jeunes (60 beds) Av des Martyrs; ☎75 490 635. Set in expansive grounds at the northern end of town, this youth hostel features an inviting reception area with hanging plants & coloured bars on the wall. Rooms are basic but cheap, with shared bathrooms. **$**

WHERE TO EAT AND DRINK

Café d'Art Jdoud ⊕ 33.686347, 8.967883 (marked as Café Beb Mdina on Google Maps); m 24 083 584; ⊙ 08.00–18.00 daily. The most scenic place for a drink or snack in Old Kebili, this café & cultural space also has a library upstairs & views of the old town. **$$**

International Culture Centre Kalaat Elborjain C206; m 96 554 898; e icckalaatelborjain@gmail.com; f kalaatelborjain; ⊙ 09.00–late daily. The faux castle entrance leads to a black-&-white-tiled café serving fast food, which is very popular with the youth of Kebili (possibly because they sometimes have a DJ blasting tunes in the middle of the day). There is also a theatre out back with irregular performances. **$$**

Sandwich el Mchakel Av Nalout; ⊙ 11.00–late daily. In the centre of town, this offers good Turkish fast food & is very busy at lunchtimes. **$$**

Chez Jabeur Av Nalout; ⊙ 08.30–18.00 daily. A good pastry shop opposite the MG Proxi supermarket. **$–$$**

La Cave Av Nalout; ⊙ 07.30–22.00 daily. Hard to miss with its distinctive Roman columns outside, this bar packs out for football matches. **$–$$**

WHAT TO SEE AND DO No trip to Kebili would be complete without a visit to Old Kebili, 2km to the south of the modern settlement, set in a palmeraie. El Bortal, the square just to the east of the main mosque in Old Kabili, was a regional hub for the trans-Saharan slave trade until its abolition in Tunisia in 1846. However, its legacy can still be seen today in the ethnic diversity and social stratification of the area. Most of the old buildings are decaying quietly, although the main mosque is still in use. As you wander the crumbling ruins, you may get lucky and hear the drumming from a Sufi religious ceremony taking place in one of the town's zaouias, some of which have been restored with EU funding. The palm-shaded gardens surrounding the zaouias are carefully tended, with the irrigation system apparently in good order.

The palmeraie produces a much-prized variety of date known as *deglet nour* (date of light), with translucent flesh. A festival celebrating the date is held at the large white-and-yellow **Maison des Cultures Ibn Haytham** (f Mc.Ibn.Haytham.kebili; ⊙ 10.00–18.00 daily) at the very northern end of town by the hospital, alongside a dazzling variety of other cultural events throughout the year.

The only other specific sight in Kebili proper is the **hot springs**. Originally, locals bathed in splendid open-air pools, said to date to Roman times. However, in the late 1990s the authorities decided that this was an unfitting spectacle and replaced the pool with a large fountain. There are now concrete hammam buildings a few metres back from the road for those wishing to enjoy the hot springs, with separate sections for men and women.

AROUND KEBILI

Mansoura Just 4km northwest of Kebili on the P16, this quiet agricultural town is home to a hammam (1.5DT) fed by a hot spring which was originally used by the ancient Romans for bathing. Men are permitted access in the morning and women in the afternoon. On the other side of the road is a massive public pool complex, which has been under construction since around 2016.

Telmine Formerly a Roman frontier outpost, this town, 6km northwest of Kebili on the P16, is home to the Oqba Mosque (⊕ 33.715528, 8.920504), founded by Okba ibn Nafi in the 7th century AD. Local residents claim it was the first mosque ever built in Tunisia or the wider Maghreb region by the conquering Umayyad Caliphate. As you drive out of town to the northwest, look out for the **Telmine Artisans Craft Centre** (⊕ 33.7182, 8.913532), which is currently under construction but may be open by the time you visit. Perched on the edge of the palmeraie, it will feature a viewing tower and individual stores selling local wares.

Debecha (⊕ 33.801174, 8.754583) Covering some 7,000m^2, this curious set of wind-sculpted limestone features just north of Fatnassa is a favourite stopping-off point for tour buses heading between Kebili and Tozeur. The natural limestone sculptures, some of them 4m high, have a somewhat otherworldly feel and make for some excellent photographs at sunrise or sunset.

DOUZ AND AROUND

Known as Tunisia's gateway to the Sahara, this oasis town is famed for its remarkable dunes, the kind you see in the Tunisian holiday brochures: rolling expanses of smooth sand that are searing white in the day, but turn golden-brown at sunset. Douz has a lot of charm, with plenty of palm trees, camel rides, hot springs, an interesting desert museum and even a folklore festival. It serves as an excellent base for a couple of nights in the desert, crunching across the sand in the company of the dromedaries and hard-bitten former nomads. It also hosts a number of annual 4x4 desert rallies, attracting competitors from across the globe. Far from any urban glow, the desert sky at night is unbeatable for stargazers.

HISTORY Douz was a centre for the Saharan caravan trade for thousands of years, with traders plying overland routes connecting to hubs such as Timbuktu in Mali, Zwila in Libya and Agadez in Niger. Archaeological finds in the area show that the Romans were trading with the various nomadic groups around Douz (the M'razig, Adhara and Sabria) to bring goods into Europe from far, far outside the empire. The population of Douz maintained a significant level of autonomy as various conquerors swept across the northern parts of the country: Romans replacing Carthaginians, Arabs replacing Byzantines, and French replacing Ottomans. Sidi Marzoug, the 15th-century leader of the M'razig tribe, highlighted this independent spirit when he declared:

> I will lead my sons far from the rainy lands which turn a man into a slave stifled under insults. Better to keep their honour, even if their stomachs be half-empty, rather than have full stomachs at the price of humiliation.

At the beginning of the 20th century, Douz remained an isolated oasis outpost. The main interest the French colonial authorities took in the town was as a leisure

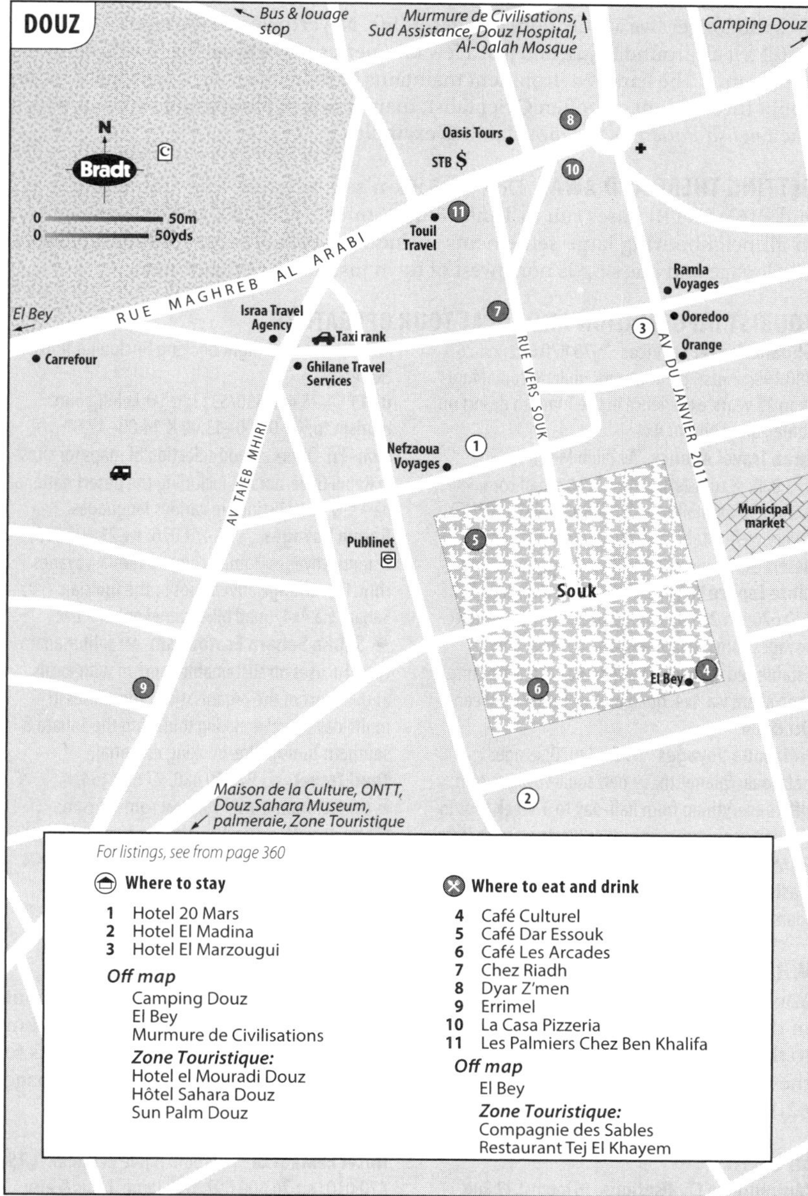

destination; the annual International Festival of the Sahara was begun in 1910. But as in oasis settlements further north, the slow encroachment of roads and influence of colonial authorities lead to significant changes in the desert way of life.

Today, true nomadism in Douz is more or less a thing of the past. In the 1920s, French observers reported encampments of up to 30 tents – something never seen today. The largest tribe in the area, the M'razig, number around 29,000 today, but most no longer live a truly nomadic desert life. Nevertheless, the presence of desert is still felt all around Douz, and just a few kilometres out of town the road is hemmed in by dunes. The harsh environment maintains its hold on visitors' imaginations, no doubt through images, often Orientalist, maintained in Hollywood myth, of which *The English Patient* is the most famous example.

GETTING THERE AND AWAY Douz is 540km southwest of Tunis (6hrs on the A1 and P16). SNTRI buses run to Tunis (8hrs 45mins; 36.50DT), and louages connect to all neighbouring large settlements including Kebili, Tozeur, Gafsa and Gabès. The louage and bus stop is northwest of town just north of the cemetery.

TOURIST INFORMATION AND LOCAL TOUR OPERATORS

Ghilane Travel Services ☎75 470 692; m 26 880 199; e gts@planet.tn; w ghilane.com. More than 25 years' experience in the Tunisian desert on camel, quad bike or 4x4.

Israa Travel Agency Av Taieb Mhiri; ☎75 473 000; e tunisieisraatravel12@gmail.com, israatravel@gmail.com; f ISRAATRAVELAGENCY. A very well-established outfit offering internal desert experiences, car hire and flight ticketing.

Libre Espace Voyages Route de Matmata; ☎75 470 620; m 28 495 690; e contact@libre-espace-voyages.com; w libre-espace-voyages.com. Established for over 20 years, they offer trips into the Sahara via 4x4, quad bike or camel between Oct & Jun.

Nefzaoua Voyages m 54 72920; e age.nefzaoua@planet.tn; w nefzaoua-voyages.com. Offers everything from half-day to 3-week trips in the desert on camel or in 4x4s. Partners with Hotel 20 Mars.

Oasis Tours ☎75 470 988, 75 472 705; e oasis.tours@planet.tn. Vehicle hire, organised excursions into the desert & flight booking (including Tunisair Express).

ONTT ☎75 492 530/5311; e crt.kebili@ontt.tourism.tn; ⌚ 08.00–13.00 & 14.00–17.00 Mon–Fri. Offers a good selection of maps for sites in Kebili Governorate, including the desert national parks, & hotel listings in various languages.

Ramla Voyages ☎75 471 076; m 21 401 595; e ramlavoyages@gmail.com; w ramla-voyages.com. Can arrange adventures in the Tunisian Sahara via 4x4, quad bike, camel or horseback.

✷ **Sahha Sahara Ecotourism** w sahhasahara.com. Focuses on sustainable tourism with locals at the heart of the organisation. Specialises in multi-day camel-trekking tours into the Sahara & southern Tunisia. Pre-booking essential.

Touil Travel m 97 780 480, 27 650 154; e contact@touiltravel.com; w sgm-ttt.com; f touiltraveltunisia. Vehicle hire & organised excursions into the desert, including quad-bike & camel tours.

WHERE TO STAY *Map, page 359*

You have two main options in Douz: in town, where the hotels tend to be older but in the heart of the action and with a lot of character, or the Zone Touristique, 2km to the south of town, where you will get better value for money and easier access to the desert, but with a package-holiday feel. If you wish to attend the festival (page 62), be sure to have booked a room well in advance.

In town

Murmure de Civilisations (6 rooms) 17 Rue des Combattants; m 22 364 896; e murmure.decivilisations@gmail.com; f maison.hotes.douz.tunisie. Originally built in 1934, this small maison d'hôtes is located down a quiet side street, offering traditional vaulted mud-brick-style rooms. Owner Salah Khalfallah offers traditional cuisine as well as other cultural activities. **$$$**

Hotel El Madina (10 rooms) Rue El Hanin; ☎75 470 010; m 26 600 692.Very large, basic & airy rooms with big bathrooms. Good for overlanders lugging loads of gear or large groups sharing. **$$**

Hotel 20 Mars (30 rooms) Rue du 20 Mars; ☎75 470 269, 75 472 920; e hotel20mars@planet.tn. Very basic but popular with backpackers. Clean bathrooms, friendly English-speaking owner & a courtyard filled with birds. 10DT extra per night to turn on the heating or AC in the room. Good value. **$**

Hotel El Marzougui (15 rooms) Av du 14 Janvier 2011; m 98 642 520. The cheapest decent bed in town if you are willing to share a bathroom. Good views from the rooftop terrace. **$**

Camping Douz ⊕ 33.460131, 9.040924; ☎ 75 470 269; m 98 967 463. This large campsite in the east of town appears to be run by the Tunisian Youth Hostel Association (Association Tunisienne des Auberges et Tourisme de Jeunes). Spacious pitches with communal toilet & shower facilities. **$**

Zone Touristique

Hôtel Sahara Douz (155 rooms) ☎ 71 785 855; w saharadouz.com. The closest hotel to the festival site in the southeast of town, this place distinguishes itself as being the easiest of all the Zone Touristique hotels to book online. Rooms feature large beds, cool stone & a desk overlooking the green space around the pool. Also has a spa & very fast Wi-Fi. **$$$$**

Hotel el Mouradi Douz (154 rooms) ☎ 75 470 303; e res.douz@elmouradi.com; w elmouradi.com; f hotelelmouradidouz. Good-value hotel. Rooms are clean & comfortable, but rather dated. **$$$**

Sun Palm Douz (129 rooms) ☎ 75 470 123; e sunpalm.douz@goldenyasmin.com; w goldenyasmin.com/fr/sun-palm; f HotelSunPalmDouz. Large resort popular with tour groups (so can get crowded in high season). Decent-sized rooms, massive pool & good service. **$$$**

Out of town

El Bey (7 tents) ⊕ 33.467647, 8.977653; m 20 081 659. This well-established traditional restaurant, 4km west of town, has now started providing accommodation in the form of beautifully well-appointed palm & canvas tents, each with its own clean bathroom. Great value for money, although you will need your own transport to get into town. **$$**

WHERE TO EAT AND DRINK *Map, page 359*

Compagnie des Sables Zone Touristique; m 97 973 597; e abdoubouali@hotmail.fr; f Pizza12; ⏲ 15.00–22.30 daily. Tented restaurant with a large garden near the festival site, mainly catering to large tour groups. Traditional grilled meats & live music. **$$$**

Dyar Z'men Pl des Martyrs; ☎ 75 469 700; m 26 702 180; f Sahara.complexe; ⏲ 09.00–late daily. Relatively new restaurant spread across 3 floors overlooking the main square. Offers traditional cuisine as well as pizza, shisha & various sweets. **$$$**

✷ **El Bey** ⊕ 33.467647, 8.977653; m 20 081 659; ⏲ noon–late daily. With a hilarious fennec fox sculpture at the entrance, this 400-seat restaurant offers the choice of lots of private tents or outdoor spaces to enjoy the traditional Douz cuisine. Also has a theatre for live music & poetry performances. **$$$**

Restaurant Tej El Khayem Zone Touristique; ☎ 75 472 446; ⏲ 18.00–late daily. Good-quality local cuisine, including mutton or camel cooked in a *gargoulette* (terracotta jar) as well as fish. Mainly caters to large tour groups. **$$$**

La Casa Pizzeria Pl des Martyrs; m 29 480 719; f LACASADOUZ; ⏲ 10.00–23.00 daily. Bright, modern, popular take-away offering pizzas, wraps & grilled meats. **$$–$$$**

✷ **Les Palmiers Chez Ben Khalifa** Av Taïeb Mhiri; m 24 232 050, 98 249 150; e tawfik.larosa@live.fr f tawfik.larosa; ⏲ 08.00–late daily. Delicious grilled meat place that is very popular with overlanders. Beautiful interior courtyard where you can eat surrounded by birds. **$$–$$$**

Errimel Av Taïeb Mhiri; m 98 249 387; ⏲ 11.30–21.30 daily. Reasonably priced local food with a small roof terrace. Good brik & couscous with grilled meats. **$$**

Café Culturel Souk; ⏲ 07.00–late daily. Good traditional spot for a coffee & people watching in the heart of the souk. **$**

Café Dar Essouk Souk; ⏲ 08.00–late daily. Very popular café for smoking shisha while looking out over the souk from the rooftop terrace. Packs out during football matches. Has Wi-Fi & good fresh juices. **$**

Café Les Arcades Souk; ⏲ 07.00–late daily. Well-established café in the heart of the souk. **$**

Chez Riadh Rue Ghara Jawal; m 22 742 368; ⏲ 10.00–late daily. Shawarma fast-food joint. **$**

ENTERTAINMENT AND NIGHTLIFE Douz is not the place for lively bars and nightclubs, although all the large hotels serve alcohol. Many of those in the Zone Touristique also host various musical and cultural events for their guests in the evenings, or you could head to one of the larger restaurants, such as El Bey (page 361), that have music and poetry readings. Ask at the Maison de la Culture (page 363) for live event listings.

SHOPPING Douz hosts a weekly market every Thursday in the main **souk** – selling everything from fruit, veg and local crafts to live animals – but it is worth visiting on any day of the week, especially if entering through the impressive main archway entrance from the west. There will always be some traders in the central area, who are generally busiest in the morning until lunchtime, although the permanent stores (mainly coffee and shisha spots) in the porticoes around the perimeter are open well into the evening. Look out for pairs of 'Douz shoes', with their coloured embroidery and high backs, or rather itchy-looking camel-hair cloaks. For souvenirs, head to **Dar El Bey** (m 22 603 062, 26 989 949; ⌚ 08.00–late daily) in the southeast corner, run by the same team as the out-of-town restaurant/accommodation (page 361). The owner, Nasser, speaks excellent Italian as well as French and offers all sorts of locally made crafts.

OTHER PRACTICALITIES The Jamal Abdennaceur Barmous **pharmacy** is the best stocked in town (Pl 7 Novembre; ☎ 75 470 376; ⌚ 08.30–17.30 Mon–Fri, 08.30–13.00 Sat). For medical emergencies head to **Douz Hospital**, 2km to the north of town on the C206 (☎ 75 476 255/7). If you plan on heading into the desert in your 4x4, it might pay to first visit **Sud Assistance** (m 98 263 159, 23 263 159; e sudassistance@hotmail.fr; f sudassistance; ⌚ 24/7), next to the Total petrol station on the C206, as these will be the guys towing you out of the sand dunes in their customised Unimog trucks if you break down!

WHAT TO SEE AND DO Douz's main selling point is its festival (see below) and as a gateway to the desert, but there are a couple of sights in town worth seeking out. Established in 1997 and renovated in late 2021, the small **Douz Sahara Museum** (Rue de Hnich; ⌚ 09.30–16.30 Tue–Sun; 5DT) has displays on local textiles and

DOUZ INTERNATIONAL FESTIVAL (FESTIVAL DU SAHARA)

Beginning under French colonial rule in 1910, this is Tunisia's oldest and most iconic festival. Generally taking place in late December, the three-day festival celebrates traditional desert culture and is centred on the large grandstand overlooking the dunes in the southeast corner of the Zone Touristique. Here they host horse and camel races, demonstrations by acrobatic riders and mock camel combat, and the ever-popular *sloughis* (desert greyhounds), bred only in the Douz region, race after unfortunate hares. There will be finely turned-out horsemen from Tunisia and Libya, and a *jahfa*, a camel topped with a bridal palanquin accompanied by musicians. In the evening, there may be poetic jousting in the nomadic tradition at the Maison de la Culture (page 363), and traders from all around come to take advantage of the crowds to do some good business for a few days. On the day after the festival, the road back to Kebili is packed with dromedaries, Arabian horses and their owners.

tents, desert plants (and their uses), domestic items, camel husbandry and even tattoos. Note that it is housed in a building opposite the military base, so be careful where you point your camera! Just east of this is the **Maison de la Culture** (Av des Martyrs; ☎ 75 474 390; e maisonculturedouz@gmail.com; f maisondeculturedouz; ⏲ 09.00–noon & 15.00–19.00 Mon–Fri, 09.00–14.00 Sat), which offers a full programme of cultural events all year round, including film screenings, theatrical performances and art exhibitions.

Douz is also home to one of largest **palmeraie** in southern Tunisia, stretching all the way from behind the museum to the Zone Touristique on the southern outskirts of town. Tours of this area can be organised via the agencies on page 360 or by most of the hotels in town.

Around 3.5km northwest of town is the **Al-Qalah Mosque** (⊕ 33.482220, 9.004042), which locals claim is one of the oldest in the region. Perched on a hilltop, it has a small park behind it which offers views of the surrounding oases.

WEST OF DOUZ Heading west from Douz, the tarmac C210 leads for 12km to Zaâfrane, and then on to the once-remote oases of Es Sabria and El Faouar. You head out through new concrete housing and small palm gardens, neatly laid out, carefully irrigated, and protected from the elements and the blowing sand by palm-frond fences. But soon the barren land appears; small salt lakes may provide birdwatchers with some interest. Lines of palm fronds stick out of the top of the dunes, the sand gleams almost white due to the high salt content. The road is a thin black line and the sky an amazing blue; young eucalyptus trees line the way.

Zaâfrane Easily reached by louage from Douz, modern Zaâfrane stretches out along the C210 with palm groves to the north. In the early years of independence, the modest housing was provided by the government to settle formerly nomadic families; each property consists of a small, square block with vaulted roofing, plus a storeroom, opening on to a courtyard. According to their resources, individuals then build on as they can. The dominant tribe here are the Adara, numbering around 17,000, who are also present in Ghlissia and Nouail region.

Tourist activity takes place on the west side of town, where there are photogenic dunes and the remains of the original village, today abandoned and slowly returning to the sands. The caravan station (⊕ 33.441472, 8.906051; ☎ 75 471 088), denoted by a big yellow sign, rents camels for day trips out into the desert. The area may be empty out of season, in which case you will need to make arrangements for camel hire in Douz or via the nearby Hotel Zaâfrane (⊕ 33.444883, 8.902426; 30 rooms; ☎ 75 450 020/33; e merdessables@gmail.com; **$$**), which is old but clean.

Es Sabria Continuing west for 25km from Zaâfrane, you will hit this small settlement which is in a constant battle to fight back the encroaching dunes. The dominant tribe here are the eponymous Sabria, today numbering around 7,000. Although there are no specific sights, there are some good accommodation options if you want to get out of Douz for the night. Run by Souad and Housem, the small **Dar Ayoub** (⊕ 33.350647, 8.747300; 2 rooms; m 24 554 763, 97 904 253; e mutuelleville6@yahoo.es, souadayoub@gmail.com; **$$**) is a simple but well-situated base from which to explore the desert to the south, and each room has an en suite with hot running water. Otherwise, **Camping Dunes Insolites** (⊕ 33.340280, 8.732170; m 27 391 501; e routeinsolite@gmail.com; f campementdunes; **$$–$$$**), 2km southwest of town, is an authentic desert camping experience.

DESERT RALLIES

The desert south and east of Douz is a popular spot for 4x4 rallies. During these events, towns such as Douz, Ksar Ghilane and Tozeur pack out with roaring off-road vehicles including motorbikes, buggies and trucks, with competitors driving in from all over the world (but with strong contingents from Tunisia, France and Italy). Two of the best-known events are the **Transfennec** (w transfennec.com), held in November, and the **Fenix Rally** (w fenix-rally.com), held in March.

El Faouar Continuing 8km west from Es Sabria you reach the surprisingly large town of El Faouar, home of the formerly nomadic Ghrib people who number around 3,000 today, and a lively Friday market. There is also a small, abandoned mosque on the outskirts of town, slowly being buried by the sands. Based in town, **Dune Voyages Esprit du Sud** (⊕ 33.356125, 8.676708; 75 460 100; ⊙ 10.00–17.00 Mon–Fri) can arrange vehicle hire and custom desert tours.

THE GRAND ERG ORIENTAL

South of Douz and stretching over the border into Algeria, the Grand Erg Oriental is what many people assume all of the Sahara looks like: a vast sea of dunes with rolling mountains of sand as far as the eye can see. (In reality, most of the Sahara is actually flat, gravelly wasteland.)

JEBIL NATIONAL PARK Accounting for a 150,000ha slice of the Grand Erg Oriental on an area of high ground is Jebil National Park, Tunisia's largest national park by a factor of nine. This is a truly unspoilt patch of wilderness, where you can camp under the stars and enjoy a night sky completely free from light pollution. The park is also home to a number of rare species, including the small dorcas gazelle and the striking white addax, an antelope endemic to the Sahara.

The park offices and entrance (⊕ 33.102601, 9.060865) are a 75km drive from Douz, much of it on sandy piste. Park infrastructure is very limited so be sure to bring everything you need with you, and come in a large enough convoy to get out of trouble if you get stuck in the sand. It is strongly advised that you do not venture here unless you are either an experienced 4x4 driver or with a reputable desert tour agency. Access to the park is usually from Douz, although it is also possible to enter from Ksar Ghilane (page 366) in the east.

Where to stay and eat There are plenty of desert campsites in this area, mainly dotted along the main piste that leads to the park entrance. The campsites will collect you from Douz and transport you safely through the desert by prior arrangement. Be sure to arrange accommodation in advance, because if you just show up you may find the site empty. Most of these sites will provide full board.

Camp Abdelmoula (50 tents) ⊕ 32.859480, 9.123336; 75 474 904; m 22 203 777, 20 532 415; w camp-abdelmoula.com. Luxurious glamping in the desert with a proper shower block with warm water. Offers dune buggy & quad rides plus camel & regular treks. **$$$$**

Camp Mars (46 tents) ⊕ 32.862653, 9.106150; m 98 347 543, 92 130 199, 58 122 122; e info@camp-mars.com; f CampementMars. Located near the flat-topped Timbaine Mountain in the middle of the Grand Erg Oriental, 100km south of Douz. Accessible only by bashing across the dunes in a 4x4, this upmarket permanent camp offers some of the best views of Tunisia's Sahara. **$$$$**

Saharansky Luxury Camp (35 tents) ⊕ 32.865990, 9.123218; **m** 24 799 997, 31 399 009; **w** saharansky.com. From the multi-award-winning Tunisian tour agency Saharansky (page 40), this is very much at the fancy end of the camping spectrum, offering luxurious beds, soft pillows, en suites & gastronomic extravaganzas. **$$$$**

Campement Bir Soltane (20 tents) ⊕ 33.284105, 9.709931; **m** 26 280 172; **e** birsoltane.camp@free.fr; **w** birsoltane.camp.free.fr; f. Located in the very east of the park, near the tri-governorate border of Gabès, Medenine and Kebili, this desert camp is only 2.4km off the tarmac C211 pipeline road. Might be convenient for those who do not have access to a 4x4 but still want a taste of the desert dune experience. **$$$**

Camping Cinderella (25 tents) ⊕ 33.404448, 9.008902; ☎ 75 477 007; **m** 98 203 719; **e** campingcinderella@gmail.com; f. This well-established site is popular with overlanders thanks to its brick shower blocks, thatch huts with rooms or pitches for tents and parking for overland vehicles. It also has good food and can organise tours. **$$–$$$**

✷ ⚑ **Camp Z'mela** ⊕ 32.858854, 9.569751; ☎ 75 470 620; **m** 94 382 034, 24 806 191; **w** campement-zmela.com. Perched on the edge of the Grand Erg Oriental, this permanent encampment is much easier to reach than Camp Mars, along a mainly gravel track that heads 15km southwest from Ksar Ghilane. It can organise transfers from Ksar Ghilane if you are not confident driving. Clean tents & bathroom/shower blocks,

THE ROMAN EMPIRE'S SOUTHERN FRONTIER

In the 2nd and 3rd centuries AD, the Roman Province of Africa Proconsularis flourished in relative peace. The pre-Saharan and Saharan regions were populated by Amazigh nomads, who no doubt moved northwards in the summer when the scarce desert pasture for their flocks ran out. To keep a check on the nomads entering their territory, the Romans, with their usual efficiency, developed a frontier defence system referred to as 'the *limes*'. Unlike massive works like Hadrian's Wall in England, it was designed more as a filter than a linear frontier. The area running through modern Libyan, Tunisian and Algerian territory was known as Limes Tripolitanus.

The northern section of the Limes Tripolitanus ran east–west from Tacapae (Gabès) via Thelepte to Haïdra. Eventually, as Romanisation advanced, it was extended to Theveste (Tébessa) and Lambaesis, both in contemporary Algeria. The southern limit of the Limes Tripolitanus, completed under the Severan emperors, ran from Leptis Magna (in Libya) across to Turris Tamalleni (Telmine), just north of modern Kebili. The frontier was designated by forts and camps, watchtowers (equipped with mirrors for signalling) and short sections of wall and ditch (*fossatum*). The whole system made good use of natural features such as the *chotts*, which became impassable in winter and spring after the rains. Scholars believe that the whole point was to regulate pastoral tribes, ensuring that their livestock did not stray into Roman farmlands when the crops were young. The Limes Tripolitanus also served a practical end, no doubt, permitting the taxing of the nomads as they passed through.

More than 140 sites forming part of the Limes Tripolitanus have been identified. Some of the most important ones – including Turris Tamalleni (Telmine) and Talalati (today Ras el Ain Tlalit, near Tataouine) – are little more than heaps of stones today. The outpost of Tisavar outside Ksar Ghilane has survived, witness to Roman tenacity.

low prices, great food, a friendly welcome & excellent opportunities to explore the dunes on your doorstep make this a great choice for a desert experience. **$$–$$$**

KSAR GHILANE A small settlement out in the desert, Ksar Ghilane (Roman Tisavar) is the most isolated of Tunisia's populated oases. Once difficult to reach, today it is accessed via an excellent tarmac road branching out from the pipeline C211, which heads south from El Hamma all the way to the southern tip of Tunisia at Borj el Khadra. Some tour agencies also offer transfers eastwards from Douz to Ksar Ghilane, but this is a wild slog through the desert and not to be undertaken lightly. The town gets very busy during peak season, home to a bounty of tamarisk trees, quad-bike rental outfits and a growing number of hotels.

Where to stay

Campement Oasis (10 rooms) ⊕ 32.989561, 9.64034; m 23 169 436; e oasiscamp12@yahoo.fr; f campementleksar. Fully renovated in 2022, it features cool, vaulted-roof rooms around a shared courtyard right on the edge of town in the dunes. Also organises desert excursions. **$$$$**

Diar Ghilane (30 rooms) ⊕ 32.989196, 9.640278; m 22 793 536; e diarghilane.com@gmail.com; f diarghilane. 2 floors of rooms with AC in a modern fort-like structure. Great top-floor restaurant overlooking the desert. **$$$**

Résidence La Source (22 rooms) ⊕ 32.98879, 9.640665; m 26 684 764, 92 927 747; e info@residencelasource.com; f ResidenceLaSource.KsarGhilane. Simple concrete rooms with large beds around a shared courtyard, with the option of private or communal bathrooms. Also organises desert excursions. **$$$**

Campement Le Paradis ⊕ 32.986531, 9.637559; m 26 257 053, 98 373 222, 20 543 071; e Campement.leparadis.ghilane@gmail.com; f moncefchetoui2017. Offers both tents & beds in concrete bungalows, with a shared shower/toilet block. Cheap & cheerful. **$$**

Campement Ghilane (11 rooms) ⊕ 32.988517, 9.639574; m 25 601 714; e campementghilane@gmail.com. Very basic vaulted rooms with no electricity & a clean communal shower block. Also has some tents at peak season. **$**

Where to eat and drink

Ghilane Restaurant Touristique ⊕ 32.988599, 9.639893; ⊙ noon–late daily. This restaurant serves set menus to tour groups & visiting families, right on the edge of the hot spring (which you can swim in). **$$$**

Ksar Ghilane Insolite ⊕ 32.989304, 9.639972; m 20 703 988, 26 076 880; e samisahara79@hotmail.fr; f ksarghilaneinsolite. Traditional restaurant. Owner Sami Arbi also offers desert tours (on camel or quad) & camping. **$$$**

✷ **Sahara Lounge** ⊕ 32.990098, 9.638427; m 98 668 835, 22 038 279; ⊙ 11.00–late daily. Offers a delicious daily set menu, usually featuring a starter of olives, bread, harissa, chorba, salad tunisienne & brik, then a main course of couscous with steamed vegetables & meat, with tea, fruit & dates for dessert. A feast on the edge of the dunes! **$$$**

What to see and do Ksar Ghilane's most significant sight is the nearby remains of the ancient Roman fort of **Tisavar** (⊕ 33.00859, 9.616181), situated on a low rise looking out over the dunes. The military objective of this fort was control of an important watering point midway between the Nefzaoua and the *castrum* (camp) at Remada (ancient Tillibari), in the far south of modern Tunisia. The fort is thought to have been built under the Emperor Commodus in the 2nd century AD; it may well have continued in use into the Middle Ages, and was excavated by the French, who discovered an altar to the spirit of Tisavar. The fort was an outpost of the main *limes* which lay further north (page 365).

> **THE BATTLE OF KSAR GHILANE**
>
> *Trevor Sheehan, Defence Photography (w defencephotography.com)*
> Ksar Ghilane was occupied by French, Moroccan, Algerian, Greek and British forces in 1943 under the command of the French General Leclerc. His French and French-colonial troops had travelled here all the way from Chad in order to fight Italian and German forces. The village was a base for British Special Forces, most notably Colonel David Stirling's Special Air Service. A major land and air attack on the village and nearby road network by German forces was defeated in March 1943, with particular support from the Royal Air Force Spitfires.

The fort itself is only 3.5km out of town, and it is very easy to rent quad bikes to head out to the fort, but do not be surprised to be initially quoted more than the cost of a hotel room for the night! No quad-bike rental outfit will allow you to head off independently with their vehicles, so you will need to convoy. Try **Ksar Ghilane Quad Rental** (⊕ 32.988384, 9.639844; m 25 115 277; e benammarwl15@gmail.com; f ksarghilane.quad). Alternatively you could hike the trail to the fort, though be sure to take a GPS device and some water.

On the way into town, note the **monument to General Leclerc** (⊕ 32.976653, 9.650723), a Free French general during World War II who, in 1943, led his men on a three-month, 2,400km march from French Equatorial Africa to Libya (via Tunisia) to fight the Axis forces.

HOUIDHAT ERRECHED (⊕ 32.593831, 9.106026) Located just south of the Kebili–Tataouine governorate boundary where Jebil National Park ends, this remote desert oasis is a popular camping spot for overland 4x4 groups as well as a destination for some camel-trekking tours. Note that this is 56km west into the desert from the C211 pipeline road, or 96km south of Douz, so for serious desert enthusiasts only!

THE DEEP SOUTH

Tunisia's deep south is a tough place to access, requiring special permits and specialist vehicles (page 368), but it is very alluring if you wish to explore the Grand Erg Oriental without any of the tourists (or infrastructure) found further north. This is the wildest of Tunisia's wild spaces, where intrepid 4x4 enthusiasts and camel trekkers set out in convoy over the sand dunes in search of ancient oases, wild camping as they go.

Remada, 80km south of Tataouine on the P19, is as far south as you can drive independently before you hit the military checkpoints that control the entire southern wedge of the country. Likewise, if coming down the C211 pipeline road from Kebili Governorate, you will not get more than 50km south before the military at Kamor start asking you for permits to continue.

REMADA This former French military outpost once formed part of the Roman *limes* (frontier controls; page 365) that stretched up to Ksar Ghilane. Today there is not much of interest for tourists, but the town is usually the starting point for journeys southwest to the military posts of Borj Bourguiba or southeast to Dehiba, the border post with Libya. Heading south, you come to Lorzot (86km down the P19) and then the border crossing of Bir Zar (135km down the P19). From here, the

PERMITS FOR TUNISIA'S EXTREME SOUTH

At the time of writing, independent travel in Tunisia's restricted southern zone is not permitted. The long, straight desert borders are very isolated, making them permeable to smugglers, jihadists and all sorts of other undesirable character. It has been this way since at least the Middle Ages, when Arab travellers would talk in hushed tones of the lawlessness of the area. Fast-forward 500 years and the Tunisian authorities remain very paranoid about the security of tourists heading into this part of the country. However, with a little organisation, it is still possible to visit the most remote parts of the Tunisian Sahara.

The south is divided into two different zones – Nord and Sud – each with varying degrees of permit requirements. Tours are offered by eight approved tour agencies (based in Tataouine, page 328), who handle the entire application process for you. Everything south of El Borma is basically the Zone Sud, with everything north up to Ksar Ghilane is designated as Zone Nord. Note that the border region with Algeria is all classified as Zone Sud. You may only enter these two zones at Al Matrouha, Jebil, Ksar Ghilane, Kamor, Combot or Lorzot, and only if your approved tour operator has obtained a permit, issued by the governor's office or the regional tourism delegate in Tataouine, Remada, Kebili or Tozeur.

For both zones, you will require a permit, accompanying guide, a GPS device and a satellite phone. For Zone Nord you require a minimum of two 4x4 vehicles; in Zone Sud you need a minimum of four 4x4 vehicles (maximum 14 passengers total), and you will also need to pay the travel agency for an additional 4x4 for your military escort to use.

The paperwork required for an application includes a written letter explaining the purpose of your trip, a copy of your route with all camping spots marked out, a signed commitment to not stray from your designated itinerary or cross international borders, and copies of passports for all participants. Your tour operator will organise all of this and have you sign the relevant documents before submission.

P19 continues for only another 20km before it merges with the C211 pipeline road, from where it is 155km south to Borj el Khadra.

EL BORMA The oilfields of El Borma, over by the Algerian border, are reached by a desert piste that takes you 55km west of the pipeline road, starting at ⊕ 31.689329, 9.755429. Most people (oil workers) heading here fly into El Borma Airport rather than driving, but there are no civilian commercial flights available! The main reason to visit El Borma is to see the extraordinary, 950m-wide oasis at ⊕ 31.714562, 9.182700.

BORJ EL KHADRA Tunisia's southernmost settlement is where Tunisia, Libya and Algeria meet (although there is no official border crossing to either neighbouring country). Formerly known as Fort Saint, it was the scene of fighting between French and Italian colonial forces during World War II and played a role during the Bizerte Crisis in July 1961 (page 179). President Bourguiba paired his two territorial disputes with France when presenting them to the UN that summer: the issue of continued French military presence in Bizerte, and disagreements with

France over the delineation of Tunisia's southern border with Algeria. Ultimately, Bourguiba managed to force the evacuation of French troops from Bizerte in 1963, but he did not get his way with regards to Tunisia's southern border, which he envisaged as stretching directly southwards from Bi'r ar Ruman (the border area near Jebil National Park in Kebili Governorate) into the Sahara. Had he gotten his way, Tunisia's southernmost tip would have been at least 250km further south, adding at least 55,000km^2 of territory – and increasing the country's size by a third.

Today Borj el Khadra is an oil town, with Italian oil major ENI operating a concession along with Anglo Tunisian Oil and Gas, OMV (Austrian) and Tunisia's national oil company, Entreprise Tunisienne d'Activités Pétrolières (ETAP). The most interesting site in the area, the ancient Amazigh oasis town of Ghadames, is unfortunately 11km over the Libyan side of the border so, even though you can see it from Tunisian territory, visiting would involve driving back up to Dehiba and coming down the Libyan side of the border (a journey of over 660km).

Appendix 1

LANGUAGE

Writing Arabic in the Latin alphabet is more of an art than a science, especially as the Arabic alphabet contains sounds not used in English. For example, the letter 'ق' (which sounds like a deep 'ka') is represented in the following list by '9', and is pronounced like the 'ch' in 'loch'. The letter 'ح' (a strong, breathy-sounding 'ha') is represented by '7', but is not a sound used in the English language. You will see a huge variety of Latin alphabet spellings on your travels, which can get confusing for place names. The following guide attempts to be as phonetic as possible, but do not be surprised to see many spelling variations for these words and phrases.

ESSENTIALS

	Arabic	**French**
Welcome	*Marhbe*	*Bienvenue*
Good morning	*Sabah el khir*	*Bonjour*
Good evening	*Msa el khir*	*Bonsoir*
Hello	*Aslema/ahl*	*Salut*
Goodbye	*Beslema*	*Au revoir*
Please	*Brabi*	*S'il vous plaît*
Thank you (very much)	*Aychek (allekhr)*	*Merci (beaucoup)*
Yes	*Ey*	*Oui*
No	*Le*	*Non*
My name is...	*Ismi...*	Je m'appelle...
What is your name?	*Chnouwa? (m)* *Ismik? (f)*	Comment appelez-vous?
I am from England	*Ena min enguiltra*	*Je viens d'Angleterre*
I am from America	*Ena min amarikiya*	*Je viens des États-Unis*
I am from Australia	*Ena min australia*	*Je viens d'Australie*
How are you?	*Chniya? (m)* *Hwelik? (f)*	*Comment allez-vous?*
Pleased to meet you	*Nitcharfou*	*Enchanté*
Don't mention it	*Ma tothkrouch (m)* *Ma tothkorhash (f)*	*De rien/Je vous en prie*
I don't understand	*Ma fhimtich*	*Je ne comprends pas*
Please would you speak more slowly?	*Brabi tnajamchi tahki b chwaya*	*Pourriez-vous parler plus lentement?*
Sorry	*Samahni*	*Pardon*
Enjoy your meal	*Sahha*	*Bon appétit*
Congratulations	*Mabrouk*	*Félicitations*

QUESTIONS

Do you understand?	*Fhimt?*	*Comprenez-vous?*
How?	*Kifech?*	*Comment?*
What?	*Chnouwa?*	*Quoi?*
Where?	*Win?*	*Où?*
What is it?	*Chnouwa? (m)* *Chniya? (f)*	*Qu'est-ce que c'est?*
When?	*Wa9tech?*	*Quand?*
Which?	*Anehou? (m)* *Anehi? (f)* *Anehom? (pl)*	*Quel? (m)* *Quelle? (f)* *Quelles? (pl)*
Why?	*Alech?*	*Pourquoi?*
Who?	*Chkoun?*	*Qui?*
How much?	*9adech?*	*Combien?*

NUMBERS

1	*wehid*	*un*	16	*sittach*	*seize*
2	*thnin*	*deux*	17	*sbaatach*	*dix-sept*
3	*tletha*	*trois*	18	*thmantach*	*dix-huit*
4	*arbaa*	*quatre*	19	*tsaatach*	*dix-neuf*
5	*khamsa*	*cinq*	20	*ichrin*	*vingt*
6	*sitta*	*six*	30	*tlethin*	*trente*
7	*sabaa*	*sept*	40	*arbiin*	*quarante*
8	*thmaniya*	*huit*	50	*khamsin*	*cinquante*
9	*tisâa*	*neuf*	60	*sittin*	*soixante*
10	*achra*	*dix*	70	*sabiin*	*soixante-dix*
11	*hdach*	*onze*	80	*thmanin*	*quatre-vingts*
12	*thnach*	*douze*	90	*tisiin*	*quatre-vingt-dix*
13	*tlatach*	*treize*	100	*mya*	*cent*
14	*arbaatach*	*quatorze*	1,000	*alf*	*mille*
15	*khmastach*	*quinze*			

TIME

What time is it?	*9adech l wa9t?*	*Quelle heure est-il?*
today	*lyoum*	*aujourd'hui*
tonight	*ellila*	*ce soir/cette nuit*
tomorrow	*ghodwa*	*demain*
yesterday	*lberah*	*hier*
morning	*sbe7*	*matin*
evening	*âachiya*	*soir*

DAYS

Monday	*Elthnin*	*lundi*
Tuesday	*Elthletha*	*mardi*
Wednesday	*Ellerbaâ*	*mercredi*
Thursday	*Elkhmis*	*jeudi*
Friday	*Eljomâa*	*vendredi*
Saturday	*Elsebt*	*samedi*
Sunday	*Elahad*	*dimanche*

MONTHS

January	*janfi*	*janvier*
February	*fivri*	*février*
March	*mares*	*mars*
April	*avril*	*avril*
May	*may*	*mai*
June	*jwa*	*juin*
July	*jwiliya*	*juillet*
August	*out*	*août*
September	*septembr*	*septembre*
October	*octobr*	*octobre*
November	*novembr*	*novembre*
December	*decembr*	*décembre*

GETTING AROUND

Public transport

I'd like…	*Nhib…*	*Je voudrais*
…a one-way ticket	*…tikey mashi*	*…un billet aller simple*
…a return ticket	*…tikey rjouaâ*	*…un billet retour/un aller retour*
I want to go to…	*Nhib nimchi l…*	*Je veux aller à…*
How much is it?	*Bkadech?*	*C'est combien?*
What time does it leave?	*Waktech tokhrej?*	*A quelle heure part-il?*
delayed	*twakhar*	*en retardé*
cancelled	*annuler*	*en annulé*
first/second class	*daraja oula/thaniya*	*première/seconde classe*
ticket office	*maktab al tathaker*	*guichet*
timetable	*calendrier*	*horaire*
map	*kharita*	*carte*
bus station	*ma7atat el car*	*gare routière*
airport	*matar*	*aéroport*
port	*bort*	*port*
bus	*car*	*autobus/autocar*
plane	*tayara*	*avion*
boat	*battou/flouka* (if it's very small)	*bateau*
ferry	*battou*	*ferry*
car	*karhba*	*voiture*
4x4	*cat fwa cat*	*quatre quatre*
taxi	*taxi*	*taxi*
shared taxi	*louage*	*servees*
minibus	*minibaas*	*minibus*
motorbike	*moubilat*	*moto*
moped	*vispa*	*cyclomoteur/vélomoteur*
Have a safe journey	*Sayes rouhek*	*Bon voyage*

Private transport

Is this the road to…?	*Hetha trik l…?*	*C'est par là la route de…?*
Where is the service station?	*Win el kiosk?*	*Où se trouve la station-service?*
Please fill it up…	*Brabi âabeha*	*Faites-le plein, s'il vous plaît*
diesel	*mazout*	*diesel*

leaded/unleaded petrol	*essence âadi/sans plomb*	*essence au plomb/sans plomb*
I have broken down	*Toht en panne*	*Je suis en panne*

Signs

give way	*afsah al tarik*	*céder le passage*
danger	*khatar*	*danger*
entry	*entrée*	*entrée*
exit	*khourouj*	*sortie*
detour	*iltifaf*	*déviation*
one-way	*itijah wahid*	*voie à sens unique*
toll	*péage*	*péage*
no entry	*mamnouâ al doukhoul*	*entrée interdit*
keep clear	*koun wathah*	*défense d'entrer*
open	*mahloul*	*ouvert*
closed	*moghlak*	*fermé*
toilets (m/f)	*twalette rjal/nsa*	*toilettes des hommes/dames*
information (desk)	*maktab maâloumat*	*accueil*

Directions

Where is…?	*Win…?*	*Où se trouve…?*
straight ahead	*toul*	*tout droit*
left	*alisar*	*à gauche*
right	*alimin*	*à droite*
at the traffic lights	*thaw la7mar*	*feux de signalisation*
at the roundabout	*rond-point*	*rond-point*
north	*chamal*	*nord*
south	*janoub*	*sud*
east	*shark*	*est*
west	*gharb*	*ouest*
behind	*wra*	*derrière*
in front of	*kodem*	*devant*
near	*krib*	*près*
opposite	*âaks*	*en face de*

ACCOMMODATION

hotel	*wtil*	*hôtel*
campsite	*moukhayam*	*camping*
Do you have any rooms available?	*Âandik byout fargha?*	*Aves-vous des chambres libres?*
I'd like…	*Nhib…*	*Je voudrais…*
…a single/double room	*…bit simple/double*	*…une chambre simple/double*
…a room with two beds	*…bit fiha zouz frouchat*	*…une chambre à deux lits*
…a room with a bathroom	*…bit fiha bitbanou*	*…une chambre avec salle de bains*
…to share a dorm	*…naksmou l bit*	*…partager un dortoir*
How much is it per night?	*Bkadech f lila?*	*C'est combien la nuit?*
How much is it per person?	*Bkadech el wahed?*	*C'est combien par personne?*
Is there hot water?	*Famma ma skhoun?*	*Y a-t-il de l'eau chaude?*

Is there electricity?	*Famma thaw/ famma électricité?*	*Y a-t-il de l'électricité?*

EATING AND DRINKING

I am a vegetarian	*Végétarien nabati*	*Je suis végétarien*
Please bring me…	*Brabi jibli…*	*Apportez-moi, s'il vous plaît…*
…a fork	*…forshita*	*…une fourchette*
…a knife	*…sekina*	*…un couteau*
…a spoon	*…mgharfa*	*…une cuillère*
Please may I have the bill?	*L fatoura yâaychek?*	*L'addition, s'il vous plaît?*

Food

bread	*khobz*	*pain*
butter	*zebda*	*beurre*
cheese	*fromage*	*fromage*
eggs	*âatham*	*oeuf*
oil	*zit*	*huile*
pepper	*filfil*	*poivre*
salt	*milh*	*sel*
sugar	*sokkor*	*sucre*
yoghurt	*yoghurt*	*yaourt*
apples	*toffah*	*pommes*
bananas	*bananes*	*bananes*
grapes	*âneb*	*raisins*
oranges	*borgdan*	*oranges*
broccoli	*brouklou*	*brocoli*
carrots	*sfenaria*	*carottes*
garlic	*thoum*	*ail*
onion	*bsal*	*oignon*
potato	*batata*	*pomme de terre*
salad	*slata*	*salade*
fish	*hout*	*poisson*
beef	*bakry*	*boeuf*
chicken	*djaj*	*poulet*
pork	*hallouf*	*porc*
lamb	*âallouch*	*agneau*
sausage	*merguez*	*saucisse*

Drink

water	*ma*	*eau*
wine	*vin*	*vin*
beer	*bira*	*bière*
coffee	*kahwa*	*café*
tea	*tèy*	*thé*
fruit juice	*âasir ghalla*	*jus de fruit*
milk	*hlib*	*lait*

SHOPPING

I'd like to buy…	*Nhib nichri…*	*Je voudrais acheter…*
I'm just looking	*Naamal fi doura*	*Je voudrais juste regarder*

It's too expensive	*Ghali barsha*	*C'est trop cher*
I'll take it	*Bech nekhouh (m)*	*Je le prends (m)*
	Bech nekhouha (f)	*Je la prends (f)*
Please may I have…?	*Aychik najam nekhou…*	*Puis-je avoir…?*
Do you accept credit cards?	*Tikblou carta?*	*Acceptez-vous des cartes de crédits?*

HEALTH *(These terms tend to be communicated in French)*

I am ill	*Ena mrith*	*Je suis malade*
Call a doctor	*Otlob tbib*	*Appelez le médecin*
diarrhoea	*jaruan jouf*	*diarrhée*
nausea	*radda*	*nausée*
doctor	*tbib*	*médecin*
prescription	*notice*	*ordonnance*
pharmacy	*sbisiriya*	*pharmacie*
paracetamol	*hrabich mtaa wjiâa*	*paracétamol*
antibiotics	*mouthad hayawi*	*antibiotiques*
antiseptic	*antiseptique*	*antiseptique*
tampon	*tampon*	*tampon hygiénique*
condom	*préservatif*	*préservatif*
contraceptive (pills)	*pilules contraceptives*	*pilules contraceptives*
suncream	*écran solaire*	*écran solaire*
asthmatic	*fadda*	*asmatique*

AMAZIGH PHRASES

With thanks to Amazigh World News and Tenast _Imazighen. See page 29 for more on the Amazigh languages in Tunisia.

hello	*azul*
goodbye	*artufat*
please	*mara taxsad* (with the '*x*' pronounced as '*kh*')
thank you	*tanmert*
yes	*ayeh*
no	*uho*
good	*yebha*
bad	*ur yahri*
toilet	*tachlaft*
police	*police/tamsulta*
hospital	*asganfo/sbitar*
help	*aweni/dhel*
Do you speak English/French?	*Is tuggidh s Tanglizt/Tanfransist?*
My name is…	*Netch ismiw da…*
Who?	*Manwan?*
What?	*Mamech?*
When?	*Melmi?*
Where?	*Mani?*
How much?	*Geddeh?*
How do I get to…?	*Mamek adggureg i…?*

epileptic	*sarââ*	*épileptique*
diabetic	*sokor*	*diabétique*
I'm allergic to...	*Âandi hassasiya...*	*Allergique...*
...penicillin	*...penicillin*	*...pénicilline*
...nuts	*...fawakeh jaffa*	*...des noisettes*
...bees	*...nahla*	*...abeilles*

EMERGENCY

Help!	*Âawenni!*	*Au secours!*
There's been an accident	*Famma hadeth*	*Il y a eu un accident*
I'm lost	*Ena thayaâ*	*Je suis perdu/perdue (m/f)*
police	*boulice*	*police*
fire	*nar*	*incendie*
ambulance	*ambulance*	*ambulance*
thief	*sarak*	*voleur*
hospital	*sbitar/clinique* (if it's private)	*hôpital*
Stop!	*Ekif!*	*Arrêt!*

ITALIAN IN TUNISIA

Given that Sicily is only 145km away from Tunisia, and the Italian island of Pantelleria is less than 72km off the coast of Cap Bon, the territories of Italy and Tunisia have had close cultural ties for thousands of years. This is reflected in the language, with Tounsi using many loan words from Italian. Thanks to the availability of Italian television and radio, Italian is often understood in the north but is also quite prevalent in Tunisia's deep south, which sees its fair share of Italian overlanders. Trying a couple of phrases in Italian is at the very least likely to elicit a smile.

hello	*buongiorno*
goodbye	*arrivederci*
please	*per favore*
thank you	*grazie*
yes	*sí*
no	*no*
good	*bene*
bad	*male*
toilet	*il bagno*
police	*la polizia*
hospital	*l'ospedale*
help	*aiuto*
Do you speak English/French?	*Parla inglese/francese?*
My name is...	*Mi chiamo...*
Who?	*Chi?*
What?	*Che cosa?*
When?	*Quando?*
Where?	*Dove?*
How much?	*Quanto?*
How do I get to...?	*Scusi, per andare a...?*

Appendix 2

FURTHER INFORMATION

BOOKS AND ARTICLES

Architecture

Binous, Jamila, *et al. Ifriqiya: Thirteen Centuries of Art and Architecture in Tunisia* Museum With No Frontiers, 2014

Bloom, Jonathan M *Architecture of the Islamic West: North Africa and the Iberian Peninsula, 700–1800* Yale University Press, 2020

Ancient history and archaeology

Aouadi-Abdeljaouad, N, and L Belhouchet *Modern Origins: A North African Perspective* Springer, 2014. Contains a good chapter on the Middle Stone Age in Tunisia.

Hoyos, Dexter, *Carthage's Other Wars: Carthaginian Warfare Outside the 'Punic Wars' Against Rome*, Pen & Sword Military, Barnsley (2019)

O'Connell, Robert L *The Ghosts of Cannae: Hannibal and the Darkest Hour of the Roman Republic* Random House, 2011

Raven, Susan *Rome in Africa* Routledge, 1993 (3rd ed)

Soren, David *et al. Carthage: Uncovering the Mysteries and Splendors of Ancient Tunisia* Simon and Schuster, 1990

Wells, Colin *The Roman Empire* Fontana, 1992 (2nd ed)

History and culture

Brown, L C *The Tunisia of Ahmad Bey, 1837–1855* Princeton University Press, 1974

Lloyd, Christopher *English Corsairs on the Barbary Coast* W M Collins & Sons, 1981

Messenger, Charles *The Tunisian Campaign* Ian Allen, 1982

Language, literature and poetry

Douagi, Ali *Sleepless Nights* Foundation Nationale, 1991. Short stories from one of the pioneers of modern Tunisian literature, with a focus on east–west encounters.

Kaddour, Hédi *The Influence Peddlers* Yale University Press, 2017. A story of French colonial rule in 1920s Tunisia, with cultural clashes between colonialists and nationalists, plus a few Hollywood film-makers thrown into the mix.

Mabkhout, Shukri *L'Italiano* Edizioni e/o, 2017. Winner of the 2015 International Prize for Arabic Fiction. Set in late 1980s and early 1990s Tunisia, it tells the story of the rebellious Abdel Nasser, a student activist and journalist, and his love affair with philosophy student, Zeina.

Moorhead, Alan *African Trilogy* Hamish Hamilton, 1944. Chronicles of the World War II campaigns in 'one of the great battlegrounds of history', as Field-Marshall Viscount Wavell puts it in his foreword.

Saïd, Amina *The Present Tense of the World: Poems 2000–2009* Black Widow Press, 2011. The first ever English translations of multi-award-winning Tunisian-French poet Saïd, covering themes of love, death, exile, home (specifically Tunisia) and belonging.

Travel guides and literature

Chesshyre, Tom *A Tourist in the Arab Spring*, Bradt Guides, 2013
Pritchard-Jones, Sian, and Bob Gibbons *Africa Overland*, Bradt Guides, 2022
Scott, Chris *Sahara Overland* Trailblazer, 2000

Politics

Hopwood, Derek *Habib Bourguiba of Tunisia – The Tragedy of Longevity* Macmillan, 1992
Masri, Safwan M *Tunisia: An Arab Anomaly* Columbia University Press, 2017
Murphy, Emma *Economic and Political Change in Tunisia: From Bourguiba to Ben Ali* Macmillan, 1999

WEBSITES

Security

w **gov.uk/foreign-travel-advice** UK Foreign, Commonwealth & Development Office travel advice and security updates.
w **diplomatie.gouv.fr** French Ministry of Europe & Foreign Affairs travel advice and security updates.
w **travel.state.gov** US State Department travel advice and security updates.
w **viaggiaresicuri.it** Italian Ministry of Foreign Affairs & International Co-operation travel advice and security updates.

Transport and travel

w **opengeodata-ageos-tunisie.hub.arcgis.com/datasets/bus-stations-lignes-transtu-tunis/explore** Visualisation of all the bus stops and routes in Greater Tunis.
w **opengeodata-ageos-tunisie.hub.arcgis.com/datasets/lignes-des-trains-sncft** Visualisation of all the SNCFT train stops and routes across Tunisia.

NGOs and humanitarian organisations

w **aswatnissa.org** Aswat Nissa is a feminist Tunisian NGO created in 2011 which promotes gender equality and fights all forms of gender discrimination.
w **britishtunisiansociety.org** The British Tunisian Society is a London-based organisation aiming to further relations and understanding between the people of Tunisia and the UK.
w **dawnmena.org** Democracy for the Arab World Now (DAWN) is a dedicated group of analysts, researchers, lawyers and activists who aim to fulfil Jamal Kashoggi's vision of helping to promote democracy and human rights in the MENA.
f **femmesdemocrates** The Tunisian Association of Democratic Women (Association tunisienne des femmes démocrates: ATFD) is a large feminist association founded on 6 August 1989, working to eliminate all forms of discrimination against women.
w **visittunisiaproject.org** USAID Visit Tunisia Project, designed to build a diverse, competitive and resilient tourism sector in Tunisia.

Newspapers and magazines

w **managers.tn** Tunisian business magazine, with tourism features (French-language).
w **tap.info.tn/en** A Tunis-based source for timely English-language news on Tunisia.

PODCASTS AND SOCIAL ACCOUNTS

@AfrikyaTN Tweeting stunning daily landscape images from across Tunisia.

@ahmedfachfouch Tweets mainly about military news, especially about the Tunisian armed forces, in English, French and Arabic.

@beki_ksri Tunisian YouTuber and painter; one of the most famous influencers in the country with a massive following across the MENA.

@BradtTunisia Official account for the Bradt Guide to Tunisia, run by author Oscar Scafidi.

@DiscoverTUN Tunisian National Tourism Office official account. Tweeting in English.

@dismalden Street photographer focusing on abandoned buildings from across the country.

w **erinclarebrown.com** Tunis-based North Africa editor at *New Lines Magazine*, who produces an excellent podcast called *Revolution 1: The Story of the Tunisian Uprising*, linked on her website.

@IgnitionUK Freelance journalist, gentleman explorer and noted raconteur Simon S Cordall: a good source of timely English-language news updates from Tunis.

@medghdiri Tataouine-based photographer and film-maker who collaborates with Galaxy Tours (page 40) to cover Tunisia's Star Wars sites.

@StayTounsi Picturesque photography from across the country.

@thedreamerwildandfree Rabii Ben Brahim is a nature and environmental documentary film-maker based in Tunisia, who posts some of the best drone footage of the country.

@WildTunis Photography from the nation's capital.

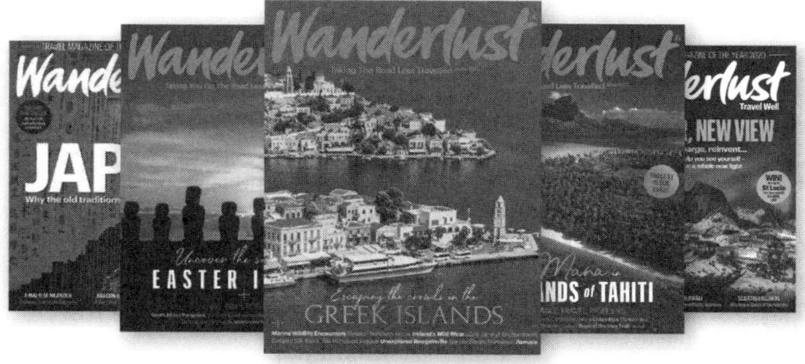

Appendix 3

YOUTUBE VIDEO QR CODES

Between August 2020 and September 2022, I travelled to all 24 governorates across Tunisia while researching this guidebook, filming my adventures as I went. Below is a selection of the videos from my YouTube channel, Scafidi Travels.

CHAPTER 2

Highlights *page 35*

Star Wars sites *page 39*

Tunisia's UNESCO World Heritage Sites *page 35*

Working in Tunisia *page 42*

CHAPTER 3

The Residence *page 80*

Borj Cedria German Military Cemetery *page 109*

Medina *page 90*

Jebel Ressas *page 109*

Kayaking from La Marsa to Tabarka *page 106*

Uthina (Oudna) *page 109*

CHAPTER 4

Béja *page 112*

Thibar *page 118*

Béja's northern coastline *page 119*

Medjez el Bab Commonwealth war cemetery *page 120*

Testour *page 121*

Aïn Tounga *page 123*

Dougga *page 124*

Hotel Thugga *page 125*

Zama Regia (aka Zama Minor) *page 132*

Gaâfour *page 133*

Mustis *page 133*

Kbor-Klib *page 134*

Ellès *page 134*

Maktar (Mactaris) *page 135*

Kesra *page 137*

Dar Sidi Abdallah *page 142*

GOVERNORATE PLAYLISTS

More videos will be added to these in future playlists. Be sure to subscribe to the Scafidi Travels YouTube channel for updates on all things tourism-related in Tunisia!

Ariana Governorate

Béja Governorate

Ben Arous Governorate

Bizerte Governorate

Gabès Governorate

Gafsa Governorate

Jendouba Governorate

Kairouan Governorate

Kasserine Governorate

Kebili Governorate

Kef Governorate

Mahdia Governorate

Jugurtha's Table *page 148*

Althiburos *page 148*

Assuras *page 149*

Bulla Regia *page 152*

Manouba Governorate

Siliana Governorate

Medenine Governorate

Sousse Governorate

Monastir Governorate

Tataouine Governorate

Nabeul Governorate

Tozeur Governorate

Sfax Governorate

Tunis Governorate

Sidi Bouzid Governorate

Zaghouan Governorate

Chemtou (Simitthus) *page 155*

Aïn Draham *page 160*

Beni M'Tir *page 159*

Hammam Bourguiba *page 164*

Tabarka *page 164*

Hotel La Cigale *page 168*

Hotel Thabraca (and ultra-marathon) *page 169*

CHAPTER 5
What to see and do in Bizerte *page 184*

Africa's northernmost point (Cap Angela) *page 185*

Bizerte's northern coastline *page 189*

Sidi Mechreg *page 190*

RafRaf Peninsula *page 191*

Les Jardins de la Mer *page 192*

Dar el Lamma *page 192*

Dar Sabri *page 195*

Les Orangers Beach Resort *page 199*

La Badira *page 201*

Villa du Zodiaque (Mussolini's Villa) *page 204*

Korbous *page 206*

Thuburbo Majus *page 218*

CHAPTER 6

Dar Antonia *page 228*

Sousse Medina *page 229*

New Fly (Star Wars Café) *page 235*

Enfidha and Takrouna *page 236*

Monastir *page 238*

Appart Hôtel Monastir *page 242*

El Djem *page 252*

Sfax medina *page 262*

Kerkennah Islands *page 264*

CHAPTER 7

Dar el Henchir *page 282*

Ksar Lemsa *page 282*

Exploring Kasserine Town *page 284*

Sbeïtla *page 284*

Thala *page 289*

Thelepte *page 289*

Bou-Hedma National Park *page 291*

CHAPTER 8

Dar el Ferdaous *page 295*

The real Lars Homestead *page 302*

L'Auberge de Tamezret *page 303*

The Mareth Line *page 303*

General Rommel's Afrika Korps command bunker *page 303*

Mareth Military Museum *page 304*

Globalkite Djerba *page 321*

Djerba's Star Wars sites *page 322*

Djerbahood *page 324*

Hotel Dakyanus *page 329*

Tataouine's *ksour* circuit *page 330*

Ksar Ouled Debbab *page 332*

Chenini *page 333*

Guermessa *page 333*

Ghomrassen and around *page 334*

Ksar Hadada *page 335*

CHAPTER 9

Lézard Rouge *page 344*

Driving from Douz to Tozeur *page 346*

Anantara Tozeur *page 346*

Palm Beach Palace *page 348*

Maguer Gorge *page 351*

Chebika *page 351*

Tamerza *page 352*

Dar Hi Life *page 353*

Lars Homestead (exterior) *page 354*

Star Wars Shop *page 355*

Eriguet Dunes *page 355*

Douz *page 358*

Hôtel Sahara Douz *page 361*

Camp Z'mela *page 365*

Fenix Rally *page 364*

Ksar Ghilane *page 366*

THEMATIC PLAYLISTS

Looking for inspiration while exploring Tunisia, or planning your visit? More videos will be added to these playlists after publication of the Bradt Guide to Tunisia in June 2023. Be sure to subscribe to the Scafidi Travels YouTube channel for updates on all things tourism-related in Tunisia!

Day Trips & Weekends from Tunis

Tunisia's Star Wars Filming Sites

Tunisia's Hotels and Dars (Maison d'Hôtes) - Tours & Reviews

Tunisia's UNESCO World Heritage Sites

Tunisia's Jewish Cultural Heritage

Life as an Immigrant (Expat) in Tunisia

Tunisia's Archaeological Sites

Military Cemeteries across Tunisia

Tunisian Urbex (Urban Exploration / Abandoned Sites)

Index

Page numbers in bold indicate major entries; those in italics indicate maps.

INDEX OF ADVERTISERS